Out of dead-ends of Poverty,
Through wildernesses of Superstition,
Across barricades of Jim Crowism . . .
We advance!

from "Dark Symphony"
by Melvin B. Tolson

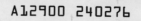

DARK SYMPHONY

DARK
SYMPHONY

NEGRO LITERATURE IN AMERICA

*edited by James A. Emanuel
and Theodore L. Gross*

THE FREE PRESS, NEW YORK   COLLIER-MACMILLAN LIMITED, LONDON

Copyright © 1968 by The Free Press

A DIVISION OF THE MACMILLAN COMPANY

Printed in the United States of America

"Black jam for dr. negro," by Mari Evans, Copyright © 1968 by Mari Evans. Printed here for the first time.

Collier-Macmillan Canada, Ltd., Toronto, Ontario

Library of Congress Catalog Card Number: 68-54984

Second printing November 1968

For Our Children,
James, Jr.,
Donna, and Jonathan

PREFACE

The literature of American Negroes has not yet been discovered by a wide audience. We have scarcely named the artists who are worthy of our attention, not to speak of estimating their individual achievements; we have insisted upon the central significance of racial issues in American culture, but we have not yet seriously consulted the Negro writers themselves. A vast and varied literature awaits our consideration, one that we need to possess imaginatively if we are to know ourselves more fully as Americans.

Until recently Americans have viewed the Negro through the eyes of white authors. This perspective has an interest of its own, but whenever we read about the Negro as conceived by our traditional writers, we sense that his dialect, his laughter, his sorrow, his life style—so often close to caricature, so often touching upon fantasy—obscure his complexity, diversity, and essential humanity. This book is a record of that humanity, as expressed by our most eloquent Negro writers.

The criterion for inclusion in this volume is the intrinsic artistic merit of the story, the poem, or the essay. Most previous collections of American Negro literature have necessarily brought together works of historical and social as well as of literary importance; scholars have occupied themselves with the primary task of gathering the written materials of Negro culture without making those aesthetic distinctions that help to create a literary tradition. But we have reached the moment in our history when it becomes possible, and indeed necessary, to designate which works by Negroes deserve to be part of the heritage of American literature.

If, as Richard Wright observed more than a generation ago, the Negro is America's metaphor, it is particularly significant to understand the meaning of that metaphor: to know it organically, from within the mind and spirit of the American Negro himself. And if one of our primary aims as readers of native works of art is to discover the complex fate of being American, to banish stereotypes of thought and character and discover the truth about our own people, then it is time we viewed the Negro through his own clear eyes, listened to the Negro in his own best voice, and felt the complexity of the Negro's humanity in the most intimate and permanent form that has been available to him—literary expression.

JAMES A. EMANUEL
THEODORE L. GROSS

CONTENTS

DARK SYMPHONY

PART I
EARLY LITERATURE

INTRODUCTION

The real beginnings of literature written by Negroes involve matter excluded by the purposes of this anthology. Detailed references to the earliest of eighteenth-century slave narratives, folk materials, and poems, as well as to nineteenth-century fiction and drama, belong in a historical study. A literature meaningfully begins, however, with its early instances of lasting achievement, with works that skillfully initiate or characterize dominant trends. The stories, poems, and essays reprinted in this volume because of their quality and significance do convey historical development, in the way that elevations mark out the contour of terrain for the traveler. And a passage through all the Negro writings that have been accumulating rapidly since 1746 needs to be made. The convenience of perspective made possible by selective anthologizing, however, need not obscure the general background which the omitted works helped to create.

Among early short story writers, the contemporaries Charles W. Chesnutt and Paul Laurence Dunbar deserve to be remembered, both for their craftsmanship and for their survival of a dilemma that has too long a history in Negro literature. Both men, but especially Chesnutt. wrote at a time—the late nineteenth century—when Southern regionalism had hardened the fictional image of the Negro acceptable to the magazine readers who alone could sustain a writer's career. Only the "tragic mulatto" (confounded by the dilemmas proceeding from mixed blood) and the genial buffoons and storytellers common in the works of Thomas Nelson Page and Joel Chandler Harris were credible to the purchasers of popular magazines. Negro journals did not yet offer suitable outlets for the more realistic presentation of Negro experience and character, for *The Crisis* (the organ of the National Association for the Advancement of Colored People) and *Opportunity: Journal of Negro Life* (the organ of the National Urban League) were to be formed more than a generation later. And even if such journals had existed then, Chesnutt and Dunbar would have faced the problem of satisfying divergent audiences, both expecting more exaggeration than truth.

While the *Atlantic Monthly* did not reveal Chesnutt's race for about a dozen years, the author explored acceptable themes with pioneering insight. In representative tales he presented interracial color bias ("A Matter of Principle"), folk Negro psychology ("The Goophered Grapevine"), subtle racist injuries ("The Bouquet"), and brutality in Southern life ("The Sheriff's Children"). Dunbar, on the other hand, yielded more steadily to the restrictions of the plantation tradition, producing stories like "Anner 'Lizer's Stumblin' Block," "Aunt Tempe's Triumph," "The Walls of Jericho," and "The Trial Sermons on Bull-Skin." He widened his themes, however, in such tales as "The Lynching of Jube Benson," "Scapegoat" (about Negro leadership), "At Shaft 11" (about a mining strike), and "The Ordeal of Mt. Hope" (about industrial education in a small town). Neither writer emphasized significant kinds of humor and realism common in Negro experience; nevertheless, their success laid a solid foundation for the building of an authentic tradition in short story writing. Their predecessors and followers, of lesser ability, who worked at the genre before the end of World War I include Frances E. W. Harper (whose "The Two Offers" [1859] Hugh M. Gloster has called "perhaps the first published short story by an American Negro"), George Marion McClellan, James E. McGirt, and Joseph S. Cotter.

As a group, the thirty-odd novels written by Negroes before 1920 represent the initial stage in an evolution of sensibility, aesthetics, and political sophistication. Novelists from the Talented Tenth (W. E. B. DuBois's term for the best-educated Negroes), trapped in the post-Reconstruction era of disfranchisement and multiform repression, and suspended by literary inexperience between the Romantic and Realistic traditions, plunged into the endless war of words with detractors of their race. Thus motivated largely by a proud but nonliterary purpose, and surrounded by unworthy models in the form of melodramatic popular fiction and inherited stereotypes, early Negro novelists inevitably turned out much aesthetically inferior work.

Among these novelists, Sutton E. Griggs was the most prolific, with his five novels; Dunbar published four, Chesnutt three, DuBois and James Weldon Johnson one apiece before 1920. Almost twenty other authors wrote early novels, the first, *Clotel, or The President's Daughter: A Narrative of Slave Life in the United States*, by William Wells Brown, appearing in 1853; the second, *The Garies and Their Friends*, by Frank J. Webb, in 1857. After a thirty-year lapse, more novels began to appear. Griggs' works, such as *Unfettered* and *Pointing the Way*, were didactic and technically weak. Chesnutt's *The House Behind the Cedars*, *The Marrow of Tradition*, and *The Colonel's Dream*, treating respectively the tragic mulatto, Negro retaliation against brutality, and the need for Southern postwar reforms, were attenuated too often by stylistic excesses and defective plotting. Dunbar's rather autobiographical *The Uncalled*, as well as *The Fanatics* and *The Love of Landry*, was inferior to *The Sport of the Gods*, his only novel presenting Negro characters. *The Sport of the Gods* showed traces of Dunbar's lingering alliance with the plantation tradition that declares "primitive" Negroes happier under the solicitous eye of the slaveholder than in the competitive environs of the big city.

In 1911, several years after the publication of most of Dunbar's and Chesnutt's novels, DuBois's *The Quest of the Silver Fleece* injected a factual political sophistication into the narration of racial struggle. Just as Frank Norris had used the production of wheat to demonstrate the forces that govern man, DuBois used cotton to expose Washington politics, Northern industrialism, and Southern caste. At the expense of weakened characterization and plot, he brought twentieth-century scholarly thought into the fictional record of interracial life.

In 1912, the most important early novel, *The Autobiography of an Ex-Colored Man*, by James Weldon Johnson, appeared anonymously. A transitional novelist forecasting the subtler tones and artistry of the Negro Awakening of the 1920's, Johnson moved his ever-fleeing hero through ideological and physical encounters in schools, factories, and churches, and through experiences with Bohemians, aristocrats, and lynchers, in such a way as to suggest man's universal self-betrayal.

This volume does not apportion any of its restricted space to examples of folk literature, drama, and certain nonfictional forms that belong in an exhaustive record of Negro writing. Some comment, however, upon accomplishments in these forms is important to the wholeness of even a brief survey.

Negro spirituals, the earliest significant contribution of displaced Africans to the culture of their new land, have a complex history that has left a trail of divergent scholarship since the publication of *Slave Songs of the United States* in 1867. Matters of folk composition and re-creation, African versus European origins, and specific musical inter-relationships are being resolved in favor of the certainty that spirituals are uniquely Negro expressions and are America's most creative music. Their words are conceded to be beautiful poetry, using allegory and ambiguity, and singing variously of freedom, hard times, and alienation with hopeful vigor as well as melancholy. Spirituals like "Sometimes I Feel Like a Motherless Child," "Go Down, Moses," "Steal Away," and "Joshua Fit De Battle of Jericho" are permanent testaments to the resiliency of man's spirit as demonstrated in the lives of Negroes.

Almost as important as the spirituals are the blues: folk songs definitely attributed to Negroes, probably originating in slavery. Usually employing repetition of line and rhyme within a simple form, blues bemoan unrequited love and varieties of bad luck, or they express a superficial joy undercut by sadness. The "Father of the Blues," W. C. Handy, had written the most famous of them, "St. Louis Blues," by 1912. Retention of blues in large numbers by the Library of Congress is recognition of their importance. The more militant and daily useful work songs and songs of protest reveal the moods of plantation and industrial laborers, and of other Negroes in prisons and on chain gangs. Additional Negro folk literature meriting study includes ballads (for example, the outlaw ballad, "Stackalee"; "John Henry," the celebration of the heroic railroad worker; and "Frankie and Johnny," which, according to legend, treats the murder of a Negro by his mistress in St. Louis in the 1840's). Pithy aphorisms, like "De quagmire don't hang out no sign," and folk sermons and folk tales of the picturesque kind found in Zora Neale Hurston's work add to the earthy wisdom and humanity in Negro folk culture.

Early Negro playwrights encountered special difficulties, more so than did Negro actors, whose entry upon the stage was frustrated, until after the Civil War, by whites in blackface mimicking the buffoonery, singing, and dancing acceptable to audiences. Before 1920, Negroes rarely could deviate from these roles, despite the efforts of such New York groups as The African Company in 1821 and the Lafayette Players after the turn of the century. Ira Aldridge was hardly an exception, since he became a British subject and made brilliant successes of opportunities to play his favorite, Othello, on European stages. Postwar Negro minstrel companies revealed the talents of dancer Billy Kersands, "Dad" Lucas, and James Bland (composer of "Carry Me Back to Old Virginny" and "In De Evenin' by De Moonlight"). Ragtime began to break the domination of whites over the supposedly Negro stage when, just before 1900, Bob Cole's musical *A Trip to Coon-Town* and Will Marion Cook and Paul Laurence Dunbar's *Clorindy—The Origin of the Cakewalk* showed symphonic possibilities in Negro syncopation and rhythm. In the meantime, however, the Negro playwright, who was disadvantaged not only by the strictures that plagued the actor, but also by his greater distance from the concerns of an entertainer, had not fared well. Negro authorship accounted for two unactable plays, the versatile William Wells Brown's pioneering *The Escape, or a Leap for Freedom* (1858) and Joseph S. Cotter, Sr.'s *Caleb, The Degenerate*, a topical drama reflecting the controversy between DuBois and Booker T. Washington that opened the twentieth century for Negro educators. Angelina Grimké's *Rachel* developed its theme of racism with better stagecraft, in 1916. But not until the 1920's, when postwar American introspection and several works by such white playwrights as Ridgely Torrence and Eugene O'Neill began to prepare audiences for more realistic racial drama, could Negroes participate meaningfully in writing for the stage.

Nonfiction written by Negroes was, in its early stages, largely polemical and autobiographical; it later included biographical and historical efforts; and before the 1920's it encompassed broadly cultural types. The polemical tradition represented by early pamphlets, newspapers, and journals was fostered, naturally, by free Negroes in the North, although a Long Island slave, Jupiter Hammon, pioneered in 1787 with his nonmilitant *Address to the Negroes in the State of New York*. Notable among the pamphleteers were David Walker, whose ringing *Appeal* of 1829 (reprinted in 1964) was labeled "totally subversive" in the South, and David Ruggles, a sharp-tongued defender of antislavery workers in New York. In the history of magazine publication, Ruggles takes precedence with his *Mirror of Liberty*, appearing in two or more numbers near the start of 1839—one month earlier, according to Vernon Loggins, than William Whipper's short-lived *National Reformer*; it was twenty years earlier than the first Negro literary magazine, the *Anglo-African* of Thomas Hamilton, a sort of "Negro *Atlantic Monthly*" that published poetry, fiction, and various essays for two or more years. Important magazines that continued the polemical tradition were *The Crisis* (established in 1910 and called by its editor, DuBois, an "organ of propaganda and defense") and the later *Opportunity*—though both were to encourage creative writing emphatically in the 1920's. Antislavery and Reconstruction oratory has historical value, of course, as does the nineteenth-century correspondence of Negroes that has been infrequently collected, or published in magazines like the *Liberator* of William Lloyd Garrison.

Autobiographical prose by Negroes appeared earliest in *A Narrative of the Uncommon Sufferings and Surprising Deliverance of Briton Hammon, a Negro Man* (1760), and in the better-written *The Interesting Narrative of the Life of Olondah Equiano, or Gustavus Vassa, the African* (1789). Half a century later, antislavery agitation fostered autobiographical slave narratives—fictional, related by slaves and edited, and written by slaves or former slaves themselves—narratives often published in Northern newspapers before dissemination as books. Sometimes sensational, and generally reflecting the sentimentalism and humanitarianism nurtured by the Romantic movement, these works are best represented by *Narrative of William Wells Brown*, Samuel Ringgold Ward's *The Autobiography of a Fugitive Slave*, and Frederick Douglass's *My Bondage and My Freedom* at midcentury, and especially by the *Life and Times of Frederick Douglass* (1881). The meaning of American culture is incomplete without reference to such works. They connect solidly, through the strain of hopefulness in them, with end-of-the-century autobiographies —Congressman John Mercer Langston's *From the Virginia Plantation to the National Capitol* and Booker T. Washington's *Up From Slavery*— as well as with Kelly Miller's *Out of the House of Bondage* (1914).

Negro biographers have developed their exacting controls and purposes rather slowly. Early biographers, led by William Wells Brown's sketches in *The Black Man: His Antecedents, His Genius, and His Achievements* (1863), responded to psychological needs of their race. Their works, ranging from William J. Simmons' *Men of Mark* in 1887 to the prolific Benjamin Brawley's *Women of Achievement* in 1919, were written to enhance the self-image and historical pride of Negroes, rather than to illuminate the personalities—weaknesses and strengths included —of their subjects. White biographers, joining the tradition so conducive to their successful publication and to their dominance within interracial cooperation, brought out books on Sojourner Truth, Harriet Tubman, and others. Solid biographies, however, were published by Negroes before the 1920's, for Archibald H. Grimké's works on William Lloyd Garrison and Charles Sumner and Chesnutt's *Frederick Douglass*—all in the 1890's —genuinely observe the criteria of the genre.

Negro historians initially had purposes like those of the biographers: to record Negroes' wartime military services and their peacetime struggles to gain their rights as citizens. Among the fledgling historians, James McCune Smith and James W. C. Pennington in 1841 published books on the Haitian revolution and on the origins of colored people, respectively. In 1855, William Wells Brown published a study maintaining Smith's concentration on the revolutionary hero, Toussaint L'Ouverture, while

William C. Nell's *The Colored Patriots of the American Revolution* enlarged his own treatment of American Negro heroism begun in 1851.
That heroism was further documented in the 1880's, and updated to include the Civil War, in two books by George Washington Williams,
himself a soldier at fourteen. By 1915, two of the best-trained historians
ever to appear in America were at work, DuBois and Carter G. Woodson.
In that year the former, already distinguished for his 1896 study of the
African slave trade, published *The Negro*; and the latter published *The
History of the Negro Church* (a subject explored in print since the
1850's) and figured prominently in the establishment of the Association
for the Study of Negro Life and History. In 1916, Woodson became the
founding editor of *The Journal of Negro History*.

Among the other kinds of early nonfiction relevant to the purpose of
this anthology are the writings influenced by the Washington-DuBois
controversy, in addition, of course, to the works of the first literary critics
and editors. That controversy dates substantially from Washington's conciliatory speech at the Cotton States Exposition in Atlanta in 1895. The
often-quoted essence of his remarks—"In all things that are purely social
we can be as separate as the fingers, yet one as the hand in all things
essential to mutual progress"—underscored his belief in racial separat-
ism, as well as in the supremacy of industrial over academic education
and of material acquisitions over political equality; and it reversed the
militant tradition of such leaders as Frederick Douglass. But the brilliant
opposition of DuBois, supported by most educated Negroes, weakened the
Tuskegee educator's tremendous power before his death in 1915. Thereafter, the emergencies and opportunities accompanying World War I—
opening new jobs to Negroes and broadening their social visions through
democratic experiences attending migrations to the North and military
travel abroad—gradually reduced Washington's name to an uncomplimentary symbol. Perhaps somewhat unfairly, it has long connoted a
truckling acceptance of America's disrespect for Negroes and of the
institutionalized discrimination fostered by that disdain.

The ramifications of the Washington-DuBois controversy invite a
study of some length. The autobiographies of both men, DuBois's appearing in 1940 and 1968, supply personal rationales for their positions; their
other works are complementary. Washington's *The Future of the American Negro* and *Education of the Negro* appeared in 1899 and 1900,
respectively, followed in 1907 by *The Negro in the South, His Economic
Progress in Relation to His Moral and Religious Development*. DuBois,
having already begun his scholarly monographs on Negro problems, in
1903 published *The Souls of Black Folk*, poetic essays which, among
other things, took issue with the central ideas of Washington. The many
lectures of Washington add substance to the dichotomy, as do DuBois's
many years of pronouncements as editor of *The Crisis*. The aims of

DuBois's Niagara Movement and those of the newly formed NAACP, with which he merged his group in 1909, revealed the aggressive concern for civil rights, able Negro leadership, and cultural improvement that have continued to stabilize the militant tradition among Negroes. The specifically literary repercussions of the controversy, before 1920, can be glimpsed in works in several genres, among them the autobiography of James D. Corrothers; the short stories of Chesnutt; the poetry of Leslie Pinckney Hill, Fenton Johnson, and DuBois himself; and the novels of at least eight Negro authors.

Among the early poems of Negro authorship, the earliest known is "Bars Fight," the slave girl Lucy Terry's relation of an Indian raid on Deerfield, Massachusetts, in 1746. The pious verses of Jupiter Hammon first appeared in 1760. Better known are the neoclassical, largely occasional and elegiac verses of Phillis Wheatley, the popular Boston slave whose earliest work was printed in 1770. After Hammon's pieces of the 1780's, little verse was published by Negroes for almost half a century, until George Moses Horton brought out his *The Hope of Liberty* in 1829. Because of his lively wit, J. Saunders Redding labels him "the forerunner of the minstrel poets"; it is likely that his love poems and other light verse written for University of North Carolina students—most of it, unfortunately, lost to us—constitute his best offering, a contribution to the strain of humor and satire that soon afterward grew stronger in American literature. It is just as likely that he deserves to be remembered as the first slave to use poetry to protest his bondage.

Between the first appearances of Horton's poems in antislavery periodicals, about 1840, and the end of the century, Negro poetry can be generally categorized according to a prewar or postwar division. Prewar poets were, on the whole, educated and conventional versifiers bent upon proving themselves, rather imitatively, to their contemporaries as American, cultured, deserving. Thus they said little about the underside of Negroes' environment, and much about the promise of liberty. But while these poetasters (James Madison Bell, James M. Whitfield, Frances E. W. Harper, and others) were writing fashionably in the 1840's and 1850's, white writers like Irwin Russell, Sidney Lanier, and Thomas Nelson Page were being born, destined to lead the Southern "local color" school in beautifying the plantation South and stocking it with a profusion of happy, clownish slaves. During the postwar decades, therefore, Negro poets (as well as novelists) had to make a choice: facing abundant, degrading stereotypes of Negro character, they could either depose them or deepen them, counter them or humanize them. The postwar poets, as different from one another then as Negro poets are now, took both forks of the trail.

Albery A. Whitman chose to advance the counter-stereotype. His long narrative poem of 1884, *The Rape of Florida* (employing the stanza of Spenser's *The Faerie Queene*), told of Negro bravery during the forced removal of the Seminole Indians and their Negro companions from Florida to the West. Paul Laurence Dunbar, exploring the other trail, earned the praise of William Dean Howells in 1896 as the first American Negro "to feel the Negro life aesthetically and express it lyrically." Working actually within the plantation tradition, and perhaps driven by his humorous affection for his rural Negro characters to use dialect, he humanized them beyond the powers and the disposition of his white forerunners.

Dunbar was not alone in his treatment of rural Negroes, their dialect, their religious and social life, and their sports. Frances E. W. Harper had earlier made versatile use of their speech patterns—emphasizing, as J. Saunders Redding has observed, those patterns instead of the dialectal words. The poets who did continue the dialect tradition, none of them well known now, are adequately represented by three born in the 1860's: James Edwin Campbell, John Wesley Holloway, and James David Corrothers. The unique vividness of the best dialect poetry, coupled with Negroes' growing recognition that artistic exposure of folk culture has nothing to do with the progress of civil rights or in-group status, guarantees its survival.

The twentieth century opened on a Negro poetic tradition, then, that had, in the main, either followed the styles and subjects of English and American masters, or, when deviating, had argued for the dignity, heroism, and rights of Negroes or sympathetically pictured their folkways. But the new century also began with repression and violence that loudened and deepened the resentment that had often been the undertone of the victims. Some of them breathed their wrath into their poetry. Stirred by the Atlanta Riot of 1906, DuBois, who possessed that combination of brilliance and passion so dire in the being of a Negro, wrote some of the earliest free verse of the race. Riding on a train, he wrote the line, "Done at Atlanta, in the Day of Death, 1906," to open his vehement "A Litany at Atlanta." The prose-poetry of the twenty-odd stanzas burns from the internal forces that finally drove this literary warrior, grown old in the narrow arenas of his native America, to spend his own "day of death" in Africa.

Some Negro poets, unlike DuBois, Fenton Johnson, and other lesser early twentieth-century men who trenchantly criticized racial oppression, chose not to be literary warriors. Like Tennyson's Lady of Shalott, who chose to sing and weave beyond the reach and the curse of Camelot, these learned poets chose to sing and weave under the tutelage of English masters from earlier centuries. In this spirit, the pacemaker William Stanley Braithwaite penned crystalline lyrics on universal themes, like "Rhapsody"; Benjamin Brawley wrote the charming tribute to Robert Gould Shaw, "My Hero"; and nature poet George Marion McClellan composed his gossamer "Dogwood Blossoms." As poets—their scholarship and editing aside—these men reflected the conventional intellectual forces that always tend to direct, and sometimes to devitalize, the main course of literature.

On the bridge of time that links such poets with their followers of the 1920's and afterward, stands James Weldon Johnson, professional in nonliterary fields before his first volume of poetry appeared in 1917. Like DuBois, he responded authentically to the Negro mood of his day. He justified its militancy, in his poem "Fifty Years," by references to history before urging: "And for our foes let this suffice—/We've bought a rightful sonship here/And we have more than paid the price." Realizing the past undervaluations of folk materials, and developing in his own poetry through overt racial defense, conventional lyricism, and Dunbar-like "Jingles and Croons," Johnson moved toward the 1920's with motives as a writer and editor that placed him in the forefront of that revolutionary decade.

To round out this brief survey of early writings by Negroes (which merit only a few selections when measured against the abundance of excellent works published within the last fifty years), some mention of literary criticism must be made. That highly necessary form of literature scarcely developed beyond the level of biographical notations before the twentieth century. Brawley and Braithwaite, already mentioned for their nonracial poetry, were the Negro pioneers in literary criticism worthy of the name. Brawley's *The Negro in Literature and Art* (1910), revised and enlarged in 1918 and later, gave to its subject the first comprehensive discussion. In this book and in his relevant periodical essays, Brawley recorded better biography than criticism; but in this regard he differed little from other American critics then disposed to favor some practices of the fading Genteel Tradition. He revealed more interest in Negro achievement than did Braithwaite, who, as reviewer for the *Boston Transcript* and as editor of the annual *Anthology of Magazine Verse* (1913 to 1929) and certain period anthologies, was only incidentally concerned with Negro authors. This fact by no means diminishes Braithwaite's contribution to American literature in his bringing to public attention the works of poets in whom he early detected much merit, including Edwin Arlington Robinson, Robert Frost, Vachel Lindsay, Edgar Lee Masters, Carl Sandburg, Amy Lowell, and others. These two critics, like the other pioneers of Negro literature, could not measure their own efforts; nor could they know that, approaching the 1920's, they faced the threshold of a marvelous decade.

FREDERICK DOUGLASS

1817-1895

Born a slave at Tuckahoe on the eastern shore of Maryland in February 1817, Frederick Douglass grew up on a plantation of Colonel Edward Lloyd until his tenth year, when he was sent to Baltimore. There he was taught to read by his master's wife, Mrs. Hugh Auld; and there, at seventeen, he taught himself a lesson in manhood by returning in kind the beatings given him by a cruel "Negro-breaker." Escaping from Maryland in 1838, Douglass went to New York, married, and legally gained his freedom in 1846, by which time he was spreading to the Continent his distinguished reputation as antislavery orator and writer. Between that time and his death on February 20, 1895, he championed emancipation and enfranchisement for Negroes, as well as their vocational training, military privileges, and rights as laborers. The breadth of his capabilities and vision was further demonstrated by his services as Recorder of Deeds in Washington and as Minister Resident and Consul General to Haiti, and by his advocacy of women's rights, temperance, and fair treatment of the working class in England, Scotland, and Ireland.

One of the greatest orators of the nineteenth century, Douglass published many speeches after 1846, addresses delivered from the platform, according to some of his contemporaries, in the manner of "an African prince," always majestic, sometimes angry, characteristically powerful and ironic. Breaking his antislavery connections with William Lloyd Garrison in 1847, Douglass began an independent career in journalism with his own weekly, *The North Star,* and continued it until 1863 through his subsequent *Frederick Douglass' Paper* and *Douglass' Monthly.* The eloquence and sincerity of his oratory were matched by the passion and sense of vivid detail in his three autobiographies: *Narrative of the Life of Frederick Douglass* (1845), *My Bondage and My Freedom* (1855), and *Life and Times of Frederick Douglass* (1881), finally enlarged in 1892.

The very substance of Douglass's life—the intimate facts about his years as a slave and about his rise to international fame—belongs to American history, just as national tragedy and national idealism belong in the record of our culture. His autobiographical writing, then, a part of our literary heritage because of its moving style, remains staple fare that nourishes us as readers who have a need for moral realism unique in the modern world. The facts in the following chapter from Douglass's last version of his autobiography speak poignantly and instructively for themselves. The letter to his former master, Thomas Auld, which appeared in the *Liberator,* September 22, 1848, significantly reveals Douglass's fortunate combination of magnanimity and moral determination—a disposition later to expand into the national vision that marked his attitude during the Civil War:

We are fighting for unity of idea, unity of sentiment, unity of object, unity of institutions, in which there shall be no North, no South, no East, no West, no black, no white, but a solidarity of the nation, making every slave free, and every free man a voter.

A Child's Reasoning

THE INCIDENTS RELATED in the foregoing chapter led me thus early to inquire into the origin and nature of slavery. Why am I a slave? Why are some people slaves and others masters? These were perplexing questions and very troublesome to my childhood. I was very early told by some one that *"God up in the sky"* had made all things, and had made black people to be slaves and white people to be masters. I was told too that God was good, and that He knew what was best for everybody. This was, however, less satisfactory than the first statement. It came point blank against all my notions of goodness. The case of Aunt Esther was in my mind. Besides, I could not tell how anybody could know that God made black people to be slaves. Then I found, too, that there were puzzling exceptions to this theory of slavery, in the fact that all black people were not slaves, and all white people were not masters.

An incident occurred about this time that made a deep impression on my mind. My Aunt Jennie and one of the men slaves of Captain Anthony ran away. A great noise was made about it. Old master was furious. He said he would follow them and catch them and bring them back, but he never did, and somebody told me that Uncle Noah and Aunt Jennie had gone to the free states and were free. Besides this occurrence, which brought much light to my mind on the subject, there were several slaves on Mr. Lloyd's place who remembered being brought from Africa. There were others who told me that their fathers and mothers were stolen from Africa.

This to me was important knowledge, but not such as to make me feel very easy in my slave condition. The success of Aunt Jennie and Uncle Noah in getting away from slavery was, I think, the first fact that made me seriously think of escape for myself. I could not have been more than seven or eight years old at the time of this occurrence, but young as I was, I was already, in spirit and purpose, a fugitive from slavery.

Up to the time of the brutal treatment of my Aunt Esther, already narrated, and the shocking plight in which I had seen my cousin from Tuckahoe, my attention had not been especially di-

Chapter 6, "A Child's Reasoning," from *Life and Times of Frederick Douglass;* reprinted from the revised edition of 1892 (New York: Collier Books of The Crowell-Collier Publishing Company, 1962).

rected to the grosser and more revolting features of slavery. I had, of course, heard of whippings and savage mutilations of slaves by brutal overseers, but happily for me I had always been out of the way of such occurrences. My play time was spent outside of the corn and tobacco fields, where the overseers and slaves were brought together and in conflict. But after the case of my Aunt Esther I saw others of the same disgusting and shocking nature. The one of these which agitated and distressed me most was the whipping of a woman, not belonging to my old master, but to Col. Lloyd. The charge against her was very common and very indefinite, namely, "impudence." This crime could be committed by a slave in a hundred different ways, and depended much upon the temper and caprice of the overseer as to whether it was committed at all. He could create the offense whenever it pleased him. A look, a word, a gesture, accidental or intentional, never failed to be taken as impudence when he was in the right mood for such an offense. In this case there were all the necessary conditions for the commission of the crime charged. The offender was nearly white, to begin with; she was the wife of a favorite hand on board of Mr. Lloyd's sloop, and was, besides, the mother of five sprightly children. Vigorous and spirited woman that she was, a wife and a mother, with a predominating share of the blood of the master running in her veins, Nellie (for that was her name) had all the qualities essential to impudence to a slave overseer. My attention was called to the scene of the castigation by the loud screams and curses that proceeded from the direction of it. When I came near the parties engaged in the struggle the overseer had hold of Nellie, endeavoring with his whole strength to drag her to a tree against her resistance. Both his and her faces were bleeding, for the woman was doing her best. Three of her children were present, and though quite small, (from seven to ten years old, I should think), they gallantly took the side of their mother against the overseer, and pelted him well with stones and epithets. Amid the screams of the children, "Let my mammy go! Let my mammy go!" the hoarse voice of the maddened overseer was heard in terrible oaths that he would teach her how to give a white man *impudence*. The blood on his face and on hers attested her skill in the use of her nails, and his dogged determination to conquer. His purpose was to tie her up to a tree and give her, in slaveholding parlance, a "genteel flogging," and he evidently had not expected the stern and protracted resistance he was meeting, or the strength and skill needed to its execution. There were times when she seemed likely to get the better of the brute, but he finally overpowered her and succeeded in getting her arms firmly tied to the tree towards which he had been dragging her. The victim was now at the mercy of his merciless lash. What followed I need not here describe. The cries of the now helpless woman, while undergoing the terrible infliction, were mingled with the hoarse curses of the overseer and the wild cries of her distracted children. When the poor woman was untied her back was covered with blood. She was whipped, terribly whipped, but she was not subdued, and continued to denounce the overseer and to pour upon him every vile epithet of which she could think.

Such floggings are seldom repeated on the same persons by overseers. They prefer to whip those who are the most easily whipped. The doctrine that submission to violence is the best cure for violence did not hold good as between slaves and overseers. He was whipped oftener who was whipped easiest. That slave who had the courage to stand up for himself against the overseer, although he might have many hard stripes at first, became while legally a slave virtually a freeman. "You can shoot me," said a slave to Rigby Hopkins, "but you can't whip me," and the result was he was neither whipped nor shot. I do not know that Mr. Sevier ever attempted to whip Nellie again. He probably never did, for he was taken sick not long after and died. It was commonly said that his deathbed was a wretched one, and that, the ruling passion being strong in death, he died flourishing the slave whip and with horrid oaths upon his lips. This deathbed scene may only be the imagining of the slaves. One thing is certain, that when he was in health his profanity was enough to chill the blood of an ordinary man. Nature, or habit, had given to his face an expression of uncommon savageness. Tobacco and rage had ground his teeth short, and nearly every sentence that he uttered was commenced or completed with an oath. Hated for his cruelty, despised for his cowardice, he went to his grave lamented by nobody on the place outside of his own house, if, indeed, he was even lamented there.

In Mr. James Hopkins, the succeeding overseer, we had a different and a better man, as good perhaps as any man could be in the position of a slave overseer. Though he sometimes wielded the lash, it was evident that he took no pleasure in it and did it with much reluctance. He stayed but a short time here, and his removal from the position was much regretted by the slaves generally. Of the successor of Mr. Hopkins I shall have something to say at another time and in another place.

For the present we will attend to a further description of the businesslike aspect of Col. Lloyd's "Great House" farm. There was always much bustle and noise here on the two days at the end of each month, for then the slaves belonging to the different branches of this great estate assembled here by their representatives to obtain their monthly allowances of cornmeal and pork. These were gala days for the slaves of the outlying farms, and there was much rivalry among them as to who should be elected to go up to the Great House farm for the "Allowances," and indeed to attend to any other business at this great place, to them the capital of a little nation. Its beauty and grandeur, its immense wealth, its numerous population, and the fact that uncles Harry, Peter, and Jake, the sailors on board the sloop, usually kept on sale trinkets which they bought in Baltimore to sell to their less fortunate fellow-servants, made a visit to the Great House farm a high privilege, and eagerly sought. It was valued, too, as a mark of distinction and confidence, but probably the chief motive among the competitors for the office was the opportunity it afforded to shake off the monotony of the field and to get beyond the overseer's eye and lash. Once on the road with an oxteam and seated on the tongue of the cart, with no overseer to look after him, one felt comparatively free.

Slaves were expected to sing as well as to work. A silent slave was not liked, either by masters or overseers. "Make a noise there! Make a noise there!" and "bear a hand," were words usually addressed to slaves when they were silent. This, and the natural disposition of the Negro to make a noise in the world, may account for the almost constant singing among them when at their work. There was generally more or less singing among the teamsters, at all times. It was a means of telling the overseer, in the distance, where they were and what they were about. But on the allowance days those commissioned to the Great House farm were peculiarly vocal. While on the way they would make the grand old woods for miles around reverberate with their wild and plaintive notes. They were indeed both merry and sad. Child as I was, these wild songs greatly depressed my spirits. Nowhere outside of dear old Ireland, in the days of want and famine, have I heard sounds so mournful.

In all these slave songs there was some expression of praise of the Great House farm—something that would please the pride of the Lloyds.

> I am going to the Great House farm,
> O, yea! O, yea! O, yea!
> My old master is a good old master,
> O, yea! O, yea! O, yea!

These words would be sung over and over again, with others, improvised as they went along—jargon, perhaps, to the reader, but full of meaning to the singers. I have sometimes thought that the mere hearing of these songs would have done more to impress the good people of the North with the soul-crushing character of slavery than whole volumes exposing the physical cruelties of the slave system, for the heart has no language like song. Many years ago, when recollecting my experience in this respect, I wrote of these slave songs in the following strain:

"I did not, when a slave, fully understand the deep meaning of those rude and apparently incoherent songs. I was, myself, within the circle, so that I could then neither hear nor see as those without might see and hear. They breathed the prayer and complaint of souls overflowing with the bitterest anguish. They depressed my spirits and filled my heart with ineffable sadness."

The remark in the olden time was not unfrequently made, that slaves were the most contented and happy laborers in the world, and their dancing and singing were referred to in proof of this alleged fact; but it was a great mistake to suppose them happy because they sometimes made those joyful noises. The songs of the slaves represented their sorrows, rather than their joys. Like tears, they were a relief to aching hearts. It is not inconsistent with the constitution of the human mind that it avails itself of one and the same method for expressing opposite emotions. Sorrow and desolation have their songs, as well as joy and peace.

It was the boast of slaveholders that their slaves enjoyed more of the physical comforts of life than the peasantry of any country in the world. My experience contradicts this. The men and the women slaves on Col. Lloyd's farm received, as their monthly allowance of food, eight pounds of pickled pork, or its equivalent in fish. The pork was often tainted, and the fish were of the poorest quality. With their pork or fish, they had given them one bushel of Indian meal, unbolted, of which quite fifteen per cent was more fit for pigs than for men. With this, one pint of salt was given, and this was the entire monthly allowance of a full-grown slave, working constantly in the open field from morning till night every day in the month except Sunday. There is no kind of work which really requires a better supply of food to prevent physical exhaustion than the field-work of a slave. The yearly allowance of clothing was not more ample than the supply of food. It consisted of two tow-linen shirts, one pair of trousers of the same coarse material, for summer, and a woolen pair of trousers and a woolen jacket for winter, with one pair of yarn stockings and a pair of shoes of the coarsest description. Children under ten years old had neither shoes, stockings, jackets, nor trousers. They had two coarse tow-linen shirts per year, and when these were worn out they went naked till the next allowance day—and this was the condition of the little girls as well as of the boys.

As to beds, they had none. One coarse blanket was given them, and this only to the men and women. The children stuck themselves in holes and corners about the quarters, often in the corners of huge chimneys, with their feet in the ashes to keep them warm. The want of beds, however, was not considered a great privation by the field hands. Time to sleep was of far greater importance. For when the day's work was done most of these had their washing, mending, and cooking to do, and having few or no facilities for doing such things, very many of their needed sleeping hours were consumed in necessary preparations for the labors of the coming day. The sleeping apartments, if they could have been properly called such, had little regard to comfort or decency. Old and young, male and female, married and single, dropped down upon the common clay floor, each covering up with his or her blanket, their only protection from cold or exposure. The night, however, was shortened at both ends. The slaves worked often as long as they could see, and were late in cooking and mending for the coming day, and at the first gray streak of the morning they were summoned to the field by the overseer's horn. They were whipped for oversleeping more than for any other fault. Neither age nor sex found any favor. The overseer stood at the quarter door, armed with stick and whip, ready to deal heavy blows upon any who might be a little behind time. When the horn was blown there was a rush for the door, for the hindermost one was sure to get a blow from the overseer. Young mothers who worked in the field were allowed an hour about ten o'clock in the morning to go home to nurse their children. This was when they were not required to take them to the field with them, and leave them upon "turning row," or in the corner of the fences.

As a general rule the slaves did not come to their quarters to take their meals, but took their ashcake (called thus because baked in the ashes) and piece of pork, or their salt herrings, where they were at work.

But let us now leave the rough usage of the field, where vulgar coarseness and brutal cruelty flourished as rank as weeds in the tropics and where a vile wretch, in the shape of a man, rides, walks, and struts about, with whip in hand, dealing heavy blows and leaving deep gashes on the flesh of men and women, and turn our attention to the less repulsive slave life as it existed in the home of my childhood. Some idea of the splendor of that place sixty years ago has already been given. The contrast between the condition of the slaves and that of their masters was marvelously sharp and striking. There were pride, pomp, and luxury on the one hand, servility, dejection, and misery on the other.

Letter to His Master

THOMAS AULD:

Sir—The long and intimate, though by no means friendly relation which unhappily subsisted between you and myself, leads me to hope that you will easily account for the great liberty which I now take in addressing you in this open and public manner. The same fact may possibly remove any disagreeable surprise which you may experience on again finding your name coupled with mine, in any other way than in an advertisement, accurately describing my person, and offering a large sum for my arrest. In thus dragging you again before the public, I am aware that I shall subject myself to no inconsiderable amount of censure. I shall probably be charged with an unwarrantable, if not a wanton and reckless disregard of the rights and proprieties of private life. There are those North as well as South who entertain a much higher respect for rights which are merely conventional, than they do for rights which are personal and essential. Not a few there are in our country, who, while they have no scruples against robbing the laborer of the hard earned results of his patient industry, will be shocked by the extremely indelicate manner of bringing your name before the public. . . .

I have selected this day on which to address you, because it is the anniversary of my emancipation; and knowing of no better way, I am led to this as the best mode of celebrating that truly important event. Just ten years ago this beautiful September morning, yon bright sun beheld me a slave—a poor, degraded chattel—trembling at the sound of your voice, lamenting that I was a man, and wishing myself a brute. The hopes which I had treasured up for weeks of a safe and successful escape from your grasp, were powerfully confronted at this last hour by dark clouds of doubt and fear, making my person shake and my bosom to heave with the heavy contest between hope and fear. I have no words to describe to you the deep agony of soul which I experienced on that never to be forgotten morning—(for I left by daylight). I was making a leap in the dark. The probabilities, so far as I could by reason determine them, were stoutly against the undertaking. The preliminaries and precautions I had adopted previously, all worked badly. I was like one going to war without weapons—ten chances of defeat to one of

Letter to Thomas Auld, which appeared in the *Liberator*, September 22, 1848; as reprinted in *The Negro Caravan*, ed. Brown, Davis, and Lee (New York: The Dryden Press, 1941), 608–612.

victory. One in whom I had confided, and one who had promised me assistance, appalled by fear at the trial hour, deserted me, thus leaving the responsibility of success or failure solely with myself. You, sir, can never know my feelings. As I look back to them, I can scarcely realize that I have passed through a scene so trying. Trying however as they were, and gloomy as was the prospect, thanks be to the Most High, who is ever the God of the oppressed, at the moment which was to determine my whole earthly career. His grace was sufficient, my mind was made up, I embraced the golden opportunity, took the morning tide at the flood, and a free man, young, active and strong, is the result. . . .

Since I left you, I have had a rich experience. I have occupied stations which I never dreamed of when a slave. Three out of the ten years since I left you, I spent as a common laborer on the wharves of New Bedford, Massachusetts. It was there I earned my first free dollar. It was mine. I could spend it as I pleased. I could buy hams or herring with it, without asking any odds of any body. That was a precious dollar to me. You remember when I used to make seven or eight, or even nine dollars a week in Baltimore, you would take every cent of it from me every Saturday night, saying that I belonged to you, and my earnings also. I never liked this conduct on your part—to say the best, I thought it a little mean. I would not have served you so. But let that pass. I was a little awkward about counting money in New England fashion when I first landed in New Bedford. I like to have betrayed myself several times. I caught myself saying phip, for fourpence; and at one time a man actually charged me with being a runaway, whereupon I was silly enough to become one by running away from him, for I was greatly afraid he might adopt measures to give me again into slavery, a condition I then dreaded more than death.

I soon, however, learned to count money, as well as to make it, and got on swimmingly. I married soon after leaving you; in fact, I was engaged to be married before I left you; and instead of finding my companion a burden, she was truly a helpmeet. She went to live at service, and I to work on the wharf, and though we toiled hard the first winter, we never lived more happily. After remaining in New Bedford for three years, I met with Wm. Lloyd Garrison, a person of whom you have *possibly* heard, as he is pretty generally known among slave-holders. He put it into my head that I might make myself serviceable to the cause of the slave by devoting a portion of my time to telling my own sorrows, and those of other slaves which had come under my observation. This was the commencement of a higher state of existence than any to which I had ever aspired. I was thrown into society the most pure, enlightened and benevolent that the country affords. Among these I have never forgotten you, but have invariably made you the topic of conversation—thus giving you all the notoriety I could do. I need not tell you that the opinion formed of you in these circles, is far from being favorable. They have little respect for your honesty, and less for your religion.

But I was going on to relate to you something of my interesting experience. I had not long enjoyed the excellent society to which I have referred, before the light of its excellence exerted a beneficial influence on my mind and heart. Much of my early dislike of white persons was removed, and their manners, habits and customs, so entirely unlike what I had been used to in the kitchen-quarters on the plantations of the South, fairly charmed me, and gave me a strong disrelish for the coarse and degrading customs of my former condition. I therefore made an effort so to improve my mind and deportment as to be somewhat fitted to the station to which I seemed almost providentially called. The transition from degradation to respectability was indeed great, and to get from one to the other without carrying some marks of one's former condition, is truly a difficult matter. I would not have you think that I am now entirely clear of all plantation peculiarities, but my friends here, while they entertain the strongest dislike to them, regard me with that charity to which my past life somewhat entitles me, so that my condition in this respect is exceedingly pleasant. So far as my domestic affairs are concerned, I can boast of as comfortable a dwelling as your own. I have an industrious and neat companion, and four dear children—the oldest a girl of nine years, and three fine boys, the oldest eight, the next six, and the youngest four years old. The three oldest are now going regularly to school—two can read and write, and the other can spell with tolerable correctness words of two syllables: Dear fellows! they are all in comfortable beds, and are sound asleep, perfectly secure under my own roof. There are no slaveholders here to rend my heart by snatching them from my arms, or blast a mother's dearest hopes by tearing them from her bosom. These dear children are ours—not to work up into rice, sugar and tobacco, but to watch over, regard, and protect, and to rear them up in the nurture and admonition of the gospel—to train them up in the paths of wisdom and virtue, and, as far as we can to make them useful to the world and to themselves. Oh! sir, a slaveholder never appears to me so completely an agent of hell, as when I think of and look upon my dear children. It is then that my feelings rise above my control. I meant to have said more with respect to my own prosperity and happiness, but thoughts and feelings which this recital has quickened unfit me to proceed further in that direction. The grim horrors of slavery rise in all their ghastly terror before me, the wails of millions pierce my heart, and chill my blood. I remember the chain, the gag, the bloody whip, the death-like gloom overshadowing the broken spirit of the fettered bondman, the appalling liability of his being torn away from wife and children, and sold like a beast in the market. Say not that this is a picture of fancy. You well know that I wear stripes on my back inflicted by your direction; and that you, while we were brothers in the same church, caused this right hand, with which I am now penning this letter, to be closely tied to my left, and my person dragged at the pistol's mouth, fifteen miles, from the Bay side to Easton to be sold like a beast in the market, for the alleged crime of intending to escape from your possession. All this and more you remember, and know to be perfectly true, not only of yourself, but of nearly all of the slaveholders around you.

At this moment, you are probably the guilty holder of at least three of my own dear sisters, and my only brother in bondage. These you regard as your property. They are recorded on your ledger, or perhaps have been sold to human flesh mongers, with a view to filling your own ever-hungry purse. Sir, I desire to know how and where these dear sisters are. Have you sold them? or are they still in your possession? What has become of them? are they living or dead? And my dear old grand-mother, whom you turned out like an old horse, to die in the woods—is she still alive? Write and let me know all about them. If my grandmother be still alive, she is of no service to you, for by this time she must be nearly eighty years old—too old to be cared for by one to whom she has ceased to be of service, send her to me at Rochester, or bring her to Philadelphia, and it shall be the crowning happiness of my life to take care of her in her old age. Oh! she was to me a mother, and a father, so far as hard toil for my comfort could make her such. Send me my grandmother! that I may watch over and take care of her in her old age. And my sisters, let me know all about them. I would write to them, and learn all I want to know of them, without disturbing you in any way, but that, through your unrighteous conduct, they have been entirely deprived of the power to read and write. You have kept them in utter ignorance, and have therefore robbed them of the sweet enjoyments of writing or receiving letters from absent friends and relatives. Your wickedness and cruelty committed in this respect on your fellow-creatures, are greater than all the stripes you have laid upon my back, or theirs. It is an outrage upon the soul—a war upon the immortal spirit, and one for which you must give account at the bar of our common Father and Creator. . . .

I will now bring this letter to a close, you shall hear from me again unless you let me hear from you. I intend to make use of you as a weapon with which to assail the system of slavery—as a means of concentrating public attention on the system, and deepening their horror of trafficking in the souls and bodies of men. I shall make use of you as a means of exposing the character of the American church and clergy—and as a means of bringing this guilty nation with yourself to repentance. In doing this I entertain no malice towards you personally. There is no roof under which you would be more safe than mine, and there is nothing in my house which you might need for your comfort, which I would not readily grant. Indeed, I should esteem it a privilege, to set you an example as to how mankind ought to treat each other.

I am your fellow man, but not your slave,

FREDERICK DOUGLASS.

CHARLES WADDELL CHESNUTT

1858-1932 Charles Waddell Chesnutt was born on June 20, 1858, in Cleveland, Ohio. With only a grade-school education, but with the determination to learn by his own efforts, he equipped himself to teach and to act as principal in the schools of North Carolina. After acquiring enough knowledge of law in Cleveland to pass bar examinations, and enough skill in stenography to work as a court reporter, Chesnutt remained in Cleveland pursuing the latter vocation almost without interruption until his death on November 15, 1932.

Chesnutt's career as a writer began with the appearance of his story, "The Goophered Grapevine," in the *Atlantic Monthly* in 1887. Using his experiences in North Carolina, he wrote stories published together as *The Conjure Woman* in 1899, so styled that his race was not apparent. In the same year he assembled his "stories of the color line" in the volume *The Wife of His Youth*. His biography of Frederick Douglass, the second of the relatively few that exist, appeared in 1899 also. Turning to the novel, he produced three—*The House Behind the Cedars* (1900), *The Marrow of Tradition* (1901), and *The Colonel's Dream* (1905)— which were the last of his books, although he lived another twenty-seven years. In 1952, Helen M. Chesnutt, his daughter, published *Charles Waddell Chesnutt*, revealing his letters and other documents that increase the number of his accessible writings.

Although Chesnutt's three novels break some new ground in

their picture of Negroes during Reconstruction years—for example, the exploration of "passing" in the first novel—the author's achievement as a short story writer upholds his reputation. His fictional technique, "nonracial" to readers, and his artistic competence, which invited the praise of William Dean Howells in the *Atlantic Monthly,* gave his publishers both the time and the occasion for a prudent decision—not to reveal his race—that slowed down the career of racism in publishing and criticism: the double standard which presumed the inferiority of Negro writing forever lost its rigidity. Thematically, although Chesnutt followed the bent of his stated preference for the problems of mixed blood, he brought to his work a clear understanding of the dramatic complexity of Negro experience. His honesty of intention, seen in his treatment of intraracial prejudice in "A Matter of Principle," as well as in his not always complimentary analysis of Negro "blue vein" society in Cleveland in the title story of the same volume, "The Wife of His Youth," was itself a forecast of the Negro artistic awakening of the 1920's.

A similar kind of integrity informed Chesnutt's special handling of the folk tale, which was still being employed to infuse the antebellum plantation South with the childlike warmth and abandon patronizingly attributed to the lounging, shuffling, and singing Negroes common in the works of Thomas Nelson Page and Joel Chandler Harris. Chesnutt, in writing of his stories as "the fruit of my own imagination," differentiated between them and Harris' Uncle Remus folk tales—excepting "The Goophered Grapevine," however, as derived from that folklore. That story, selected for reprinting here, is transitional in that it, in a sense, "broke the color line" in American fiction; further, it set the tone and form for a series of seven collected tales that as a group transformed the folktale into a genre capable of realistically merging the bestiality of slavery with the multiform humanity of those who survived it. The mulatto in "The Sheriff's Children" in *The Wife of His Youth* is admirably manly, is vengeful and proud, in contrast with the mulatto who presides over *The Conjure Woman* series: Julius is old, genial, and accommodating. The former protagonist moves violently toward tragedy; the latter moves leisurely and masterfully toward the protection of all that he owns, all that he is. Julius, resolved to live, made possible the literary being of Tom, resolved to die. Their coexistence in the mind of Chesnutt suggests the complexity that he so skillfully imparted to his short stories.

The Goophered Grapevine

WE ALIGHTED from the buggy, walked about the yard for a while, and then wandered off into the adjoining vineyard. Upon Annie's complaining of weariness I led the way back to the yard, where a pine log lying under the spreading elm afforded a shady though somewhat hard seat. One end of the log was already occupied by a venerable-looking colored man. He held on his knees a hat full of grapes, over which he was smacking his lips with great gusto; and a pile of grapeskins near him indicated that the performance was no new thing. We approached him at an angle from the rear, and were close to him before he perceived us. He respectfully rose as we drew near, and was moving away, when I begged him to keep his seat.

"Don't let us disturb you," I said. "There is plenty of room for us all."

He resumed his seat with some embarrassment. While he had been standing, I had observed that he was a tall man, and though slightly bowed by the weight of years, apparently quite vigorous. He was not entirely black, and this fact, together with the quality of his hair, which was about six inches long and very bushy, except on the top of his head, where he was quite bald, suggested a slight strain of other than Negro blood. There was a shrewdness in his eyes, too, which was not altogether African, and which, as we afterwards learned from experience, was indicative of a corresponding shrewdness in his character. He went on eating his grapes, but did not seem to enjoy himself quite so well as he had apparently done before he became aware of our presence.

"Do you live around here?" I asked, anxious to put him at his ease.

"Yas, suh, I lives des ober yander, behine de nex' san'hill, on de Lumberton plank-road."

"Do you know anything about the time when this vineyard was cultivated?"

"Lawd bless you, suh, I knows all about it. Dey ain' na'er a man in dis settlement w'at won' tell you ole Julius McAdoo 'uz bawn en raise' on dis yer same plantation. Is you de Norv'n gemman w'at's gwine ter buy de ole vimya'd?"

"The Goophered Grapevine" was first printed in the *Atlantic Monthly* in 1887; as found in *American Negro Short Stories*, ed. John Henrik Clarke (New York: Hill and Wang, American Century Series Edition, 1967), pp. 11–20.

"I am looking at it," I replied; "but I dont know that I shall care to buy unless I can be reasonably sure of making something out of it."

"Well, suh, you is a stranger ter me, en I is a stranger to you, en we is bofe strangers ter one anudder, but 'f I 'uz in yo' place, I wouldn't buy dis vimya'd."

"Why not?" I asked.

"Well, I dunno whe'r you b'lieves in conj'in' er not—some er de w'ite folks don't, er says dey don't—but de truf er de matter is dat dis yer ole vimya'd is goophered."

"Is what?" I asked, not grasping the meaning of this unfamilar word.

"Is goophered—cunju'd, bewitch'."

He imparted this information with such solemn earnestness and with such an air of confidential mystery that I felt somewhat interested, while Annie was evidently much impressed, and drew closer to me.

"How do you know it is bewitched?" I asked.

"I wouldn' spec' fer you ter b'lieve me 'less you know all 'bout de fac's. But ef you en young miss dere doan' min' lis'nin' ter a ole nigger run on a minute er two w'ile you er restin', I kin 'spain to you how it all happen'."

We assured him that we would be glad to hear how it all happened, and he began to tell us. At first the current of his memory —or imagination—seemed somewhat sluggish; but as his embarrassment wore off, his language flowed more freely, and the story acquired perspective and coherence. As he became more and more absorbed in the narrative, his eyes assumed a dreamy expression, and he seemed to lose sight of his auditors, and to be living over again in monologue his life on the old plantation.

"Ole Mars Dugul' McAdoo," he began, "bought dis place long many years befo' de wah, en I 'member well w'en he sot out all dis yer part er de plantation in scuppernon's. De vimes growed monst'us fas', en Mars Dugal' made a thousan' gallon er scuppernon' wine eve'y year.

"Now, ef dey's an'thing a nigger lub, nex' ter 'possum, en chick'n, en watermillyums, it's scuppernon's. Dey ain' nuffin dat kin stan' up side'n de scuppernon' fer sweetness; sugar aint a suckumstance ter scuppernon'. W'en de season is nigh 'bout ober, en de grapes begin ter swivel up des a little wid de wrinkles er ole age— we'n de skin git sof' en brown—den de scuppernon' make you smack yo' lip en roll yo' eye en wush fer mo'; so I reckon it ain' very 'stonishin' dat niggers lub scuppernon'.

"Dey wuz a sight er niggers in de naberhood er de vimya'd.

Dere wuz ole Mars Henry Brayboy's niggers, en ole Mars Jeems Mc-Lean's niggers, en Mars Dugal's own niggers; den dey wuz a settlement er free niggers en po' buckrahs down by de Wim'l'ton Road, en Mars Dugal' had de only vimya'd in de naberhood. I reckon it ain' so much so nowadays, but befo' de wah, in slab'ry times, a nigger didn' mine goin' fi' er ten mile in a night w'en dey wuz sump'n good ter eat at de yuther een'.

"So atter a w'ile Mars Dugal' begin ter miss his scuppernon's. Co'se he 'cuse' de niggers er it, but dey all 'nied it ter de las'. Mars Dugal' sot spring guns en steel traps, en he en de oberseah sot up nights once't or twice't, tel one night Mars Dugal'—he 'uz a monst'us keerless man—got his leg shot full er cow-peas. But somehow er nudder dey couldn' nebber ketch none er de niggers. I dunner how it happen, but it happen des like I tell you, en de grapes kep' on a-goin' des de same.

"But bimeby ole Mars Dugal' fix' up a plan ter stop it. Dey wuz a cunjuh 'oman livin' down 'mongs' de free niggers on de Wim'l'ton Road, en all de darkies fum Rockfish ter Beaver Crick wuz feared er her. She could wuk de mos' powerfulles' kin' er goopher—could make people hab fits, er rheumatiz', er mak 'em des dwinel away en die; en dey say she went out ridin' de niggers at night, fer she wuz a witch 'sides bein' a cunjuh 'oman. Mars Dugal' hearn 'bout Aun' Peggy's doin's, en begun ter 'flect whe'r er no he couldn' git her ter he'p him keep de niggers off'n de grapevimes. One day in de spring er de year, ole miss pack' up a basket er chick'n en poun'cake, en a bottle er scuppernon' wine, en Mars Dugal' tuk it in his buggy en driv over ter Aun' Peggy's cabin. He tuk de basket in, en had a long talk wid Aun' Peggy.

"De nex' day Aun' Peggy come up ter de vimya'd. De niggers seed her slippin' 'round, en dey soon foun' out what she 'uz doin' dere. Mars Dugal' had hi'ed her ter goopher de grapevimes. She sa'ntered 'roun' 'mongs' de vimes, en tuk a leaf fum dis one, en a grape-hull fum dat one, en den a little twig fum here, en a little pinch er dirt fum dere—en put it all in a big black bottle, wid a snake's toof en a speckle hen's gall en some ha's fum a black cat's tail, en den fill' de bottle wid scuppernon' wine. W'en she got de goopher all ready en fix', she tuk 'n went out in de woods en buried it under de root uv a red oak tree, en den come back en tole one er de niggers she done goopher de grapevimes, en a'er a nigger w'at eat dem grapes 'ud be sho ter die inside'n twel' mont's.

"Atter dat de niggers let de scuppernon's 'lone, en Mars Dugal' didn' hab no 'casion ter fine no mo' fault; en de season wuz mos' gone, w'en a strange gemman stop at de plantation one night ter see Mars Dugal' on some business; en his coachman, seein' de scuppernon's growing so nice en sweet, slip 'roun' behine de smoke-house en et all de scuppernon's he could hole. Nobody didn' notice it at de time, but dat night, on de way home, de gemman's hoss runned away en kill' de coachman. W'en we hearn de noos, Aun' Lucy, de cook, she up'n say she seed de strange nigger eat'n' er de scuppernon's behine de smoke-house; en den we knowed de goopher had be'en er wukkin'. Den one er de nigger chilluns runned away fum de quarters one day, en got in de scuppernon's, en died de nex' week. White folks say he die' er de fevuh, but de niggers knowed it wuz de goopher. So you k'n be sho de darkies didn' hab much ter do wid dem scuppernon' vimes.

"W'en de scuppernon' season 'uz ober fer dat year, Mars Dugal' foun' he had made fifteen hund'ed gallon er wine; en one er de niggers hearn him laffin' wid de oberseah fit ter kill, en sayin' dem fifteen hund'ed gallon er wine wuz monst'us good intrus' on de ten dollars he laid out on de vimya'd. So I 'low ez he paid Aun' Peggy ten dollars fer to goopher de grapevimes.

"De goopher didn' wuk no mo' tel de nex summer, w'en 'long to'ds de middle er de season one er de fiel' han's died; en ez dat lef' Mars Dugal' sho't er han's, he went off ter town fer ter buy anudder. He fotch de noo nigger home wid 'im. He wuz er ole nigger, er de color er a gingy-cake, en ball ez a hossaple on de top er his head. He wuz a peart ole nigger, do', en could do a big day's wuk.

"Now it happen dat one er de niggers on de nex' plantation, one er ole Mars Henry Brayboy's niggers, had runned away de day befo', en tuk ter de swamp, en ole Mars Dugal' en some er de yuther nabor w'ite folks had gone out wid dere guns en dere dogs fer ter he'p 'em hunt fer de nigger; en de han's on our own plantation wuz all so flusterated dat we fuhgot ter tell de noo han' 'bout de goopher on de scuppernon' vimes. Co'se he smell de grapes en see de vimes, an atter dahk de fus' thing he done wuz ter slip off ter de grapevimes 'doubt sayin' nuffin ter nobody. Nex' mawnin' he tole some er de niggers 'bout de fine bait er scuppernon' he et de night befo'.

"W'en dey tole 'im 'bout de goopher on de grapevines, he 'uz dat tarrified dat he turn pale, en look des like he gwine ter die right in his tracks. De oberseah come up en axed w'at 'uz de matter; en w'en dey tole 'im Henry been eatin' er de scuppernon's, en got de goopher on 'im, he gin Henry a big drink er w'iskey, en 'low dat de nex' rainy day he take 'im ober ter Aun' Peggy's, en see ef she wouldn' take de goopher off'n him, seein' ez he didnt know nuffin' erbout it tel he done et de grapes.

"Sho nuff, it rain de nex' day, en de oberseah went ober ter

Aun' Peggy's wid Henry. En Aun' Peggy say dat bein' ez Henry didn' know 'bout de goopher, en et de grapes in ign'ance er de conseq'ences, she reckon she mought be able ter take de goopher off'n him. So she fotch out er bottle wid some cunjuh medicine in it, en po'd some out in a go'd fer Henry ter drink. He manage ter git it down; he say it tas'e like w'iskey wid sump'n bitter in it. She 'lowed dat 'ud keep de goopher off'n him tel de spring; but w'en de sap begin ter rise in de grapevimes he ha' ter come en see her ag'in, en she tell him w'at he's ter do.

"Nex' spring, w'en de sap commence' ter rise in de scupper-non' vime, Henry tuk a ham one night. Whar'd he git de ham? *I* doan know; dey wa'n't no hams on de plantation 'cep'n' w'at 'uz in de smokehouse, but *I* never see Henry 'bout de smokehouse. But ez I wuz a-sayin', he tuk de ham ober ter Aun' Peggy's; en Aun' Peggy tole 'im dat w'en Mars Dugal' begin ter prune de grapevimes, he must go en take 'n scrape off de sap what it ooze out'n de cut een's er de vimes, en 'n'int his ball head wid it; en ef he do dat once't a year de goopher wouldn't wuk agin 'im long ez he done it. En bein' ez he fotch her de ham, she fix' it so he kin eat all de scuppernon' he want.

"So Henry 'n'int his head wid de sap out'n de big grapevime des ha'w way 'twix de quarters en de big house, en de goopher nebber wuk agin him dat summer. But the beatenes' thing you eber see happen ter Henry. Up ter dat time he wuz ez ball ez a sweeten' 'tater, but des ez soon ez de young leaves begun ter come out on de grapevimes, de ha'r begun ter grew out on Henry's head, en by de middle er de summer he had de bigges' head er ha'r on de plantation. Befo' dat, Henry had tol'able good ha'r 'roun' de aidges, but soon ez de young grapes begun ter come, Henry's ha'r begun to quirl all up in little balls, des like dis yer reg'lar grapy ha'r, en by de time de grapes got ripe his head look des like a bunch er grapes. Combin' it didn' do no good; he wuk at it ha'f de night wid er Jim Crow, en think he git it straighten' out, but in de mawnin' de grapes 'ud be dere des de same. So he gin it up, en tried ter keep de grapes down by havin' his ha'r cut sho't.

"But dat wa'n't de quares' thing 'bout de goopher. When Henry come ter de plantation, he wuz gittin' a little ole and stiff in de j'ints. But dat summer he got des ez spry en libely ez any young nigger on de plantation; fac', he got so biggity dat Mars Jackson, de oberseah, ha' ter th'eaten ter whip 'im ef he didn' stop cuttin' up his didos en behave hisse'f. But de mos cur'ouses' thing happen' in de fall, when de sap begin ter go down in de grapevimes. Fus, when de grapes 'uz gethered, de knots begun ter straighten out'n Henry's ha'r; en w'en de leaves begin ter fall, Henry's ha'r commence' ter drap out; en when de vimes 'uz bar, Henry's head wuz baller'n it wuz in de spring, en he begin ter git ole en stiff in de j'ints ag'in, en paid no mo' 'tention ter de gals dyoin' er de whole winter. En nex' spring, w'en he rub de sap on ag'in, he got young ag'in, en so soopl en libely dat none er de young niggers on de plantation couldn' jump, ner dance, ner hoe ez much cotton ez Henry. But in de fall er de year his grapes 'mence' ter straighten out, en his j'ints ter git stiff, en his ha'r drap off, en de rheumatiz begin ter wrastle wid 'im.

"Now, ef you'd 'a' knowed ole Mars Dugal' McAdoo, you'd 'a' knowed dat it ha' ter be a mighty rainy day when he couldn' fine sump'n fer his niggers ter do, en it ha' ter be a mighty little hole he couldn' crawl thoo, en ha'ter be a monst'us cloudy night when a dollar git by him in de dahkness; en w'en he see how Henry git young in de spring en ole in de fall, he 'lowed ter hisse'f ez how he could make mo' money out'n Henry dan by wukkin' him in de cotton-fiel'. 'Long de nex' spring, atter de sap 'mence' ter rise, en Henry 'n'int 'is head en sta'ted for ter git young en soopl, Mars Dugal' up'n tuk Henry ter down, en sole 'im fer fifteen hunder' dollars. Co'se de man w'at bought Henry didn' know nuffin' 'bout de goopher, en Mars Dugal' didn't see no 'casion fer ter tell 'im. Long to'ds de fall, w'en de sap went down, Henry begin ter git ole ag'in same ez yuzhal, en his noo marster begin ter git skeered les'n he gwine ter lose his fifteen-hunder'-dollar nigger. He sent fer a mighty fine doctor, but de med'cine didn' 'pear ter do no good; de goopher had a good holt. Henry tole de doctor 'bout de goopher, but de doctor des laff at 'im.

"One day in de winter Mars Dugal' went ter town, en wuz santerin' 'long de Main Street, w'en who should he meet but Henry's noo master. Dey said 'Hoddy,' en Mars Dugal' ax 'im ter hab a seegyar; en atter dey run on awhile 'bout de craps en de weather, Mars Dugal' ax 'im, sorter keerless, like ez ef he des thought of it—

" 'How you like de nigger I sole you las' spring?'

"Henry's marster shuck his head en knock de ashes off'n his seegyar.

" 'Spec' I made a bad bahgin when I bought dat nigger. Henry done good wuk all de summer, but sence de fall set in he 'pears ter be sorter pinin' away. Dey ain't nuffin pertickler de matter wid 'im—leastways de doctor say so—'cep'n' a tech er de rheumatiz; but his ha'r is all fell out, en ef he don't pick up his strenk mighty soon, I spec' I'm gwine ter lose 'im.'

"Dey smoked on awhile, en bimbeby ole mars say, 'Well, a bahgin's a bahgin, but you en me is good fren's, en I doan wan' ter see you lose all de money you paid fer dat nigger; en ef w'at you say is so, en I ain't 'sputin' it, he ain't wuf much now. I spec's you wukked him too ha'd dis summer, er e'se de swamps down here don't agree wid de san'-hill nigger. So you des lemme know, en ef he gits any wusser, I'll be willin' ter gib yer five hund'ed dollars for 'im, en take my chances on his livin'.'

"Sho' nuff, when Henry begun ter draw up wid de rheumatiz en it look like he gwine ter die fer sho, his noo marster sen' fer Mars Dugal', en Mars Dugal' gin him what he promus, en brung Henry home ag'in. He tuk good keer uv 'im dyoin' er de winter—give 'im w'iskey ter rub his rheumatiz, en terbacker ter smoke, en all he want ter eat—'caze a nigger w'at he could make a thousan' dollars a year off'n didn' grow on eve'y huckleberry bush.

"Nex' spring, w'en de sap rise en Henry's ha'r commence' ter sprout, Mars Dugal' sole 'im ag'in, down in Robeson County dis time; en he kep' dat sellin' business up fer five year er mo'. Henry nebber say nuffin' bout de goopher ter his noo marsters, 'caze he know he gwine ter be tuk good keer uv de nex' winter, w'en Mars Dugal' buy him back. En Mars Dugal' made 'nuff money off'n Henry ter buy anudder plantation ober on Beaver Crick.

"But 'long 'bout de een 'er dat five year dey come a stranger ter stop at de plantation. De fus' day he 'uz dere he went out wid Mars Dugal' en spent all de mawnin' lookin' ober de vimya'd, en atter dinner dey spent all de evenin' playin' kya'ds. De niggers soon 'skivver' dat he wuz a Yankee, en dat he come down ter Norf C'lina fer ter l'arn de w'ite folks how to raise grapes en make wine. He promus Mars Dugal' he c'd make de grapevimes b'ar twice't ez many grapes, en dat de noo winepress he wuz a-sellin' would make mo' d'n twice't ez many gallons er wine. En ole Mars Dugal' des drunk it all in, des 'peared ter be bewitch' wid dat Yankee. W'en de darkies see dat Yankee runnin' 'roun' de vimya'd en diggin' under de grapevimes, dey shuk dere heads, en 'lowed dat dey feared Mars Dugal' losin' his min'. Mars Dugal' had all de dirt dug away fum under de roots er all de scuppernon' vimes, en' let 'em stan' dat away fer a week er mo'. Den dat Yankee made de niggers fix up a mixtry er lime en ashes en manyo, en po' it 'roun' de roots er de grapevimes. Den he 'vise Mars Dugal' fer ter trim de vimes close't, en Mars Dugal' tuck 'n done eve'ything de Yankee tole him ter do. Dyoin' all er dis time, mine yer, dis yer Yankee wuz libbin' off'n de fat er de lan', at de big house, en playin' kya'ds wid Mars Dugal' eve'y night; en dey say Mars Dugal' los' mo'n a thousan' dollars dyoin' er de week dat Yankee wuz a-ruinin' de grapevimes.

'W'en de sap ris nex' spring, ole Henry 'n'inted his head ez yuzhal, en his ha'r mence' ter grow des de same ez it done eve'y year. De scuppernon' vimes growed monst's fas', en de leaves wuz greener en thicker dan dey eber be'n dyoin' my rememb'ance; en Henry's ha'r growed out thicker dan eber, en he 'peared ter git younger 'n younger, en soopler; en seein' ez he wuz sho't er han's dat spring, havin' tuk in consid'able noo groun', Mars Dugal' 'git de crap in en de cotton chop'. So he kep' Henry on de plantation.

"But 'long 'bout time fer de grapes ter come on de scuppernon' vimes, dey 'peared ter come a change ober 'em; de leaves witherd en swivel' up, en de young grapes turn' yaller, en bimeby eve'ybody on de plantation could see dat de whole vimya'd wuz dyin'. Mars Dugal' tuk'n water de vimes en done all he could, but 't wa'n no use; dat Yankee had done bus' de watermillyum. One time de vimes picked up a bit, en Mars Dugal' 'lowed dey wuz gwine ter come out ag'in; but dat Yankee done dug too close under de roots, en prune de branches too close ter de vime, en all dat lime en ashes done burn de life out'm de vimes, en dey des kep' a-with'in' en a-swivelin'.

"All dis time de goopher wuz a-wukkin'. When de vimes sta'ted ter wither, Henry 'mence' ter complain er his rheumatiz; en when de leaves begin ter dry up, his ha'r 'mence' ter drap out. When de vimes fresh' up a bit, Henry'd git peart ag'in, en when de vimes wither' ag'in, Henry'd git ole ag'in, en des kep' gittin' mo' fitten fer nuffin; he des pined away, en pined away, en fin'ly tuk ter his cabin; en when de big vime whar he got de sap ter 'n'int his head withered en turned yaller en died, Henry died too—des went out sorter like a cannel. Dey didn't 'pear ter be nuffin de matter wid 'im, 'cep'n de rheumatiz, but his strenk des dwinel' away 'tel he didn' hab ernuff lef' ter draw his bref. De goopher had got de under holt, en th'owed Henry dat time fer good en all.

"Mars Dugal' tuk on might'ly 'bout losin' his vimes en his nigger in de same year; en he swo' dat ef he could git holt er dat Yankee he'd wear 'im ter a frazzle, en den chaw up de frazzle; en he'd done it, too, for Mars Dugal' 'uz a monst'us brash man w'en he once git started. He sot de vimy'd out ober ag'in, but it wuz th'ee er fo' year befo' de vimes got ter b'arin' any scuppernon's.

"W'en de wah broke out, Mars Dugal' raise' a comp'ny, en went off ter fight de Yankees. He say he wuz mighty glad wah come, en he des want ter kill a Yankee fer eve'y dollar he los' 'long er dat grape-raisin' Yankee. En I 'spec' he would 'a' done it, too, ef de Yankees hadn' s'picioned sump'en en killed him fus'. Atter de s'render, ole Miss move' ter town, de niggers all scattered 'way fum de plantation, en de vimya'd ain' be'n cultervated sence."

"Is that story true?" asked Annie doubtfully, but seriously, as the old man concluded his narrative.

"It's des ez true ez I'm a-settin' here, miss. Dey's a easy way ter prove it: I kin lead de way right ter Henry's grave ober yonder in de plantation burying'-groun'. En I tell yer w'at, marster, I wouldn' 'vise you to buy dis yer ole vimya'd, 'caze de goopher's on it, en dey ain' no tellin' w'en it's gwine ter crap out."

"But I thought you said all the old vines died."

"Dey did 'pear ter die, but a few un 'em come out ag'in, en is mixed in 'mongs' de yuthers. I ain' skeered ter eat de grapes 'caze I knows de old vimes fum de noo ones, but wid strangers dey ain' no tellin' w'at mought happen. I wouldn' 'vise yer ter buy dis vimya'd."

I bought the vineyard, nevertheless, and it has been for a long time in a thriving condition, and is often referred to by the local press as a striking illustration of the opportunities open to Northern capital in the development of Southern industries. The luscious scuppernong holds first rank among our grapes, though we cultivate a great many other varieties; and our income from grapes packed and shipped to the Northern markets is quite considerable. I have not noticed any developments of the goopher in the vineyard, although I have a mild suspicion that our colored assistants do not suffer from want of grapes during the season.

I found, when I bought the vineyard, that Uncle Julius had occupied a cabin on the place for many years, and derived a respectable revenue from the product of the neglected grapevines. This, doubtless, accounted for his advice to me not to buy the vineyard, though whether it inspired the goopher story I am unable to state. I believe, however, that the wages I paid him for his services as coachman, for I gave him employment in that capacity, were more than an equivalent for anything he lost by the sale of the vineyard.

PAUL LAURENCE DUNBAR

1872-1906   Born in 1872 in Dayton, Ohio, Paul Laurence Dunbar graduated from high school there in 1891, then took a job as an elevator boy in a Dayton hotel. Responding to the literary impulse generated in school by his activities as editor-in-chief of the school paper, president of the literary society, and class poet, he continued writing until he could publish, at his own expense, fifty-six poems in *Oak and Ivy* (1893). His *Majors and Minors* (1895), also privately printed, was favorably reviewed by the influential William Dean Howells in *Harper's Weekly*. Encouraged by Howells, especially with regard to his dialect poems, Dunbar used the best pieces in his first two volumes to make up a third, *Lyrics of Lowly Life* (1896). The preface by Howells helped the poet win national fame and devote himself to literature entirely. By the turn of the century, he had married, had begun to suffer from declining health and domestic troubles, and had submerged himself in the overwhelming task of supplying the demands for his works.

Dunbar energetically turned out volumes of poetry: *Lyrics of the Hearthside* (1899), *Lyrics of Love and Laughter* (1903), and *Lyrics of Sunshine and Shadow* (1905), the titles themselves indicating his preference for the lyric mode. His reputation, however, offering him the chance to live almost exclusively from his royalties, demanded that he, like Chesnutt, give the buying public what it was accustomed to reading. Unlike Chesnutt, Dunbar as a novelist avoided the deeper problems of Negroes, either by writing mediocre novels about whites (*The Uncalled* in 1898, *The Love of Landry* in 1900, and *The Fanatics* in 1901) or by writing about Negroes, as in *The Sport of the Gods* (1902), with better skill but with only provincial insights into their metropolitan lives. In his short stories, Dunbar found a better medium, in that he could express his knowledge of the Negroes that he was particularly fond of—the folk—and at the same time observe the popular limitations of the plantation tradition. *Folks from Dixie* (1898), in all but two of its tales, followed the shallow antebellum pleasantries of Harris and Page. His later collections—*The Strength of Gideon* (1900), *In Old Plantation Days* (1903), and *The Heart of Happy Hollow* (1904)—contained a few stories of Southern racial injustice (for example, "The Tragedy at Three Corners" and "The Lynching of Jube Benson"), but they were largely affectionate re-creations of a bygone age.

Dunbar was primarily a poet, and as such he still commands our attention. Gaining the prominence no Negro poet had won since the eighteenth-century renown of Phillis Wheatley, he was pressed by Howells's emphasis on his dialect poems into a mold that he found more financially than personally rewarding. He wrote most of his poetry in standard English, preferring what he called his "deeper notes" to his "jingle in a broken tongue." But his depths, too often sentimental or conventional in diction, appeal to us now only when genuinely and rhythmically expressed—as in his many lyrics later set to music, and in some of his plaintive reflections on the unhappiness of his final years. His "jingle," on the other hand, he at least heard laughingly and lovingly in the midst of vivid folk action that came authentically to his imagination. Both types, in the selections that follow, belong in the heritage of a culture that owes much of its fiber to robust common people, a culture that also is attentive to the lyricism of its most sensitive members.

The dramatic imagination that enlivens "The Party," found in *Majors and Minors* (1895), creates a memorably vibrant scene. "A Song"—printed in the same volume and later set to music as "Who Knows?"—melodically combines romantic longing with the staple transience-of-life melancholy. "We Wear the Mask," also in *Majors and Minors*, keeps Dunbar grimly alive in the hearts of Negroes; its sentimental lapse is redeemed by its painfully aggressive, admonitory thrust.

The Party

Dey had a gread big pahty down to Tom's de othah night;
Was I dah? You bet! I nevah in my life see sich a sight;
All de folks f'om fou' plantations was invited, an' dey come,
Dey come troopin' thick ez chillun when dey hyeahs a fife an' drum.
Evahbody dressed deir fines'—Heish yo' mouf an' git away,
Ain't seen sich fancy dressin' sence las' quah'tly meetin' day;
Gals all dressed in silks an' satins, not a wrinkle ner a crease,
Eyes a -battin', teeth a-shinin', haih breshed back ez slick ez grease;
Sku'ts all tucked an' puffed an' ruffled, evah blessed seam an' stitch;
Ef you'd seen 'em wif deir mistus, couldn't swahed to which was
    which.
Men all dressed up in Prince Alberts, swallertails 'u'd tek you' bref!
I cain't tell you nothin' 'bout it, yo' ought to seen it fu' yo'se'f.
Who was dah? Now who you askin'? How you 'spect I gwine to
    know?
You mus' think I stood an' counted evahbody at de do'.
Ole man Babah's house boy Isaac, brung dat gal, Malindy Jane,
Huh a-hangin' to his elbow, him a struttin' wif a cane;
'My, but Hahvey Jones was jealous! seemed to stick him lak a tho'n;
But he laughed with Viney Cahteh, tryin' ha'd to not let on,
But a pusson would'a' noticed f'om de d'rection of his look,
Dat he was watchin' ev'ry step dat Ike an' Lindy took.
Ike he foun' a cheer an' asked huh: "Won't you set down?" wif a
    smile,
An' she answe'd up a-bowing', "Oh, I reckon 'tain't wuth while."
Dat was jes' fu' style, I reckon, 'cause she sot down jes' de same,
An' she stayed dah 'twell he fetched huh fu' to jine some so't o'
    game;
Den I hyeahd huh sayin' propah, ez she riz to go away,
"Oh, you raly mus' excuse me, fu' I hardly keers to play."
But I seen huh in a minute wif de othahs on de flo',
An' dah wasn't any one o' dem a-playin' any mo';
Comin' down de flo' a-bowin' an' a-swayin' an' a-swingin',
Puttin' on huh high-toned mannahs all de time dat she was singing':
"Oh, swing Johnny up an' down, swing him all around',
Swing Johnny up an' down, swing him all aroun',
Oh, swing Johnny up an' down, swing him all aroun',
Fa' yu well, my dahlin'."
Had to laff at ole man Johnson, he's a caution now you bet—
Hittin' clost onto a hunderd, but he's spry an' nimble yet;
He 'lowed how a-so't o' gigglin', "I ain't ole, I'll let you see,

D'ain't no use in gettin' feeble, now you youngstahs jes' watch me,"
An' he grabbed ole Aunt Marier—weighs th'ee hunderd mo'er less,
An' he spun huh 'roun' de cabin swingin' Johnny lak de res'.
Evahbody laffed an' hollahed: "Go it, swing huh, Uncle Jim!"
An' he swing huh too, I reckon, lak a youngstah, who but him.
Dat was bettah'n young Scott Thomas, tryin' to be so awful smaht.
You know when dey gits to singin' an dey comes to dat ere paht:

> "In some lady's new brick house,
> In some lady's gyahden.
> Ef you don't let me out, I will jump out,
> So fa' you well, my dahlin'."

Den dey's got a circle 'roun' you, an' you's got to break de line;
Well, dat dahky was so anxious, lak to bust hisse'f a-tryin';
Kep' on blund'rin' 'roun' an' foolin' 'twell he giv' one great big jump,
Broke de line, an' lit head-fo'most in de fiahplace right plump;
Hit 'ad fiah in it, mind you; well, I thought my soul I'd bust,
Tried my best to keep f'om laffin' but it seemed like die I must!
Y' ought to seen dat man a-scramblin' f'om de ashes an' de grime.
Did it bu'n him! Sich a question, why he didn't give it time;
Th'ow'd dem ashes and dem cindahs evah which-a-way I guess,
An' you nevah did, I reckon, clap yo' eyes on sich a mess;
Fu' he sholy made a picter an' a funny one to boot,
Wif his clothes all full o' ashes an' his face all full o' soot.
Well, hit laked to stopped de pahty, an' I reckon lak ez not
Dat it would ef Tom's wife, Mandy, hadn't happened on de spot,
To invite us out to suppah—well, we scrambled to de table,
An' I'd lak to tell you 'bout it—what we had—but I ain't able,
Mention jes' a few things, dough I know I hadn't orter,
Fu' I know 'twill staht a hank'rin' an' yo' mouf'll mence to worter.
We had wheat bread white ez cotton an' a egg pone jes' like gol',
Hog jole, bilin' hot an' steamin', roasted shoat, an' ham sliced cold—
Look out! What's de mattah wif you? Don't be fallin' on de flo';
Ef it's go'n to 'fect you dat way, I won't tell you nothin' mo'.
Dah now—well, we had hot chittlin's—now you's tryin' ag'in to
  fall,
Cain't you stan' to hyeah about it? S'pose you'd been an' seed it all;
Seed dem gread big sweet pertaters, layin' by de possum's side,
Seed dat coon in all his gravy, reckon den you'd up and died!
Mandy 'lowed "you all mus 'scuse me, d' wa'n't much upon my
  she'ves,
But I's done my bes' to suit you, so set down an' he'p yo'se'ves."
Tom, he 'lowed: "I don't b'lieve in 'pologizin' and perfessin',
Let 'em tek it lak dey ketch it. Eldah Thompson, ask de blessin'."

Wish you'd seed dat colo'ed preachah cleah his th'oat an' bow his
    head;
One eye shet an' one eye open,—dis is evah wud he said:
"Lawd, look down in tendah mussy on sich generous hea'ts ez dese;
Makes us truly thankful, amen. Pass dat possum, ef you please."
Well, we eat and drunk ouah po'tion, 'twell dah wasn't nothin' left',
An' we felt jes' like new sausage, we was mos' nigh stuffed to def!
Tom, he knowed how we'd be feelin', so he had de fiddlah 'roun',
An' he made us cleah de cabin fu' to dance dat suppah down.
Jim, de fiddlah, chuned his fiddle, put some rosum on his bow,
Set a pine box on de table, mounted it an' let huh go!
He's a fiddlah, now I tell you, an' he made dat fiddle ring,
'Twell de ol'est an' de lamest had to give deir feet a fling.
Jigs, cotillions, reels an' break-downs, cordrills an' a waltz er two;
Bless yo' soul, dat music winged 'em an' dem people lak to flew.
Cripple Joe, de ole rheumatic, danced dat flo' f'om side to middle,
Th'owed away his crutch an' hopped it, what's rheumatics 'ginst a
    fiddle?
Eldah Thompson got so tickled dat he lak to lo' his grace,
Had to tek bofe feet an' hol' dem so's to keep 'em in deir place.
An' de Christuns an' de sinnahs got so mixed up on dat flo',
Dat I don't see how dey'd pahted ef de trump had chanced to blow.
Well, we danced dat way an' capahed in de mos' redic'lous way,
'Twell de roostahs in de bahnyard cleahed deir th'oats an' crowed
    fu' day.
Y' ought to been dah, fu' I tell you evahthing was rich an' prime,
An' dey ain't no use in talkin', we jes' had one scrumptious time!

A Song

Thou art the soul of a summer's day,
Thou art the breath of the rose.
    But the summer is fled
    And the rose is dead.
Where are they gone, who knows, who knows?

Thou art the blood of my heart o' hearts,
Thou art my soul's repose,
    But my heart grows numb
    And my soul is dumb.
Where art thou, love, who knows, who knows?

Thou art the hope of my after years—
Sun for my winter snows.
    But the years go by
    'Neath a clouded sky.
Where shall we meet, who knows, who knows?

We Wear the Mask

We wear the mask that grins and lies,
It hides our cheeks and shades our eyes,—
This debt we pay to human guile;
With torn and bleeding hearts we smile,
And mouth with myriad subtleties.

Why should the world be overwise,
In counting all our tears and sighs?
Nay, let them only see us, while
    We wear the mask.

We smile, but, O great Christ, our cries
To Thee from tortured souls arise.
We sing, but oh, the clay is vile
Beneath our feet, and long the mile;
But let the world dream otherwise,
    We wear the mask.

"The Party," "A Song," and "We Wear the Mask" reprinted from *The Complete Poems of Paul Laurence Dunbar* (New York: Dodd, Mead, and Company, 1940).

W. E. B. DUBOIS

1868-1963 William E. Burghardt DuBois was born on February 23, 1868, in Great Barrington, Massachusetts. He received a B.A. from Fisk University, another B.A. and an M.A. from Harvard, then pursued graduate study at the University of Berlin, under great historians, philosophers, and economists, before returning to Harvard. There his dissertation, *The Suppression of the African Slave Trade to the United States* (1896), became volume one of the *Harvard Historical Studies*. DuBois's long career as scholar, teacher, historian, sociologist, editor, and creative writer in several genres—begun and ended with works of special distinction—can only be hinted at here.

Proud of his race, and declaring around 1900 that "The problem of the Twentieth Century is the problem of the color line," DuBois pursued activities that led to his convening the Niagara Conference in 1905, merging it with the newly formed NAACP in 1909, and becoming the founding editor of that organization's magazine, *The Crisis*, in 1910. The Niagara Manifesto demanded full equality for Negroes; the NAACP, which DuBois served for nearly thirty years, planned many battles to win that equality; DuBois brought to the struggle the clearest intelligence, the most scientific manner, and the most consistently moral purpose that have ever been applied to that end. His vision spiraled and widened, encompassing first the black man in America, then black men and their descendants everywhere, then—implicitly through his concern for world peace—the world itself. His contributions to Africa, "the Spiritual Frontier of human kind" to him, were notable, centered in his work as "Father of Pan-Africanism": he was primarily responsible for the second and third of the six Pan-African Conferences between 1900 and 1945 that culminated in the Manchester doctrines including "Africa for the Africans" and "one man one vote."

The fact that a forty-five–page DuBois bibliography exists indicates that the works to be mentioned here are only representative. In addition to a number of the earliest modern books and pamphlets on Africa, DuBois wrote historical and sociological books, novels, pageants, poems, autobiography, biography, and miscellaneous book chapters and magazine articles. His best known historical studies include *The Philadelphia Negro* (1899)—followed by a long series, the *Atlanta University Studies*, examinations of Negro life directed by the author—*The Negro* (1915), *Darkwater* (1920), *The Gift of Black Folk* (1924), *Black Reconstruction* (1935), *Black Folk, Then and Now* (1939), and *Color and Democracy* (1945). His three other works of nonfiction of standard interest are *The Souls of Black Folk* (1903), which has gone through twenty-odd editions and two reprintings, and the autobiographical *Dusk of Dawn* (1940) and posthumous *The Autobiography of W. E. B. DuBois* (1968). His last novels, published two years apart since 1957, compose the trilogy *The Black Flame*; more sociopolitical instruction than dramatic narrative, they are *The Ordeal of Mansart, Mansart Builds a School*, and *Worlds of Color*. DuBois's poems— characteristically emotional, unconventional, vigorously irregular— balance his image as a stern, dedicated freedom fighter. Their frequent combination of rigor and poignancy induce some speculation about the marvelous equilibrium of this man who probably felt much more poetry than he wrote. He died on August 27, 1963, the day before the historic civil rights march on Washington, D.C.

No brief selection from his voluminous work could do justice to this man of the world who could both establish a charming children's magazine (*The Brownies' Book*, January 1920–December 1921) and angrily write, after the Atlanta Riot of 1906, "Doth not this justice of hell stink in Thy nostrils, O God? How long shall the mounting flood of innocent blood roar in Thine ears and pound in our hearts for vengeance?" The following selections capture the driving fusion of spirit that was Dr. DuBois: the youthful, worldly lyricism of "The Song of the Smoke" (appearing in *The Horizon* in 1899) and the precisely thorough, analytical brilliance of the chapter "Of the Sons of Master and Man," from *The Souls of Black Folk*.

away. We feel and know that there are many delicate differences in race psychology, numberless changes that our crude social measurements are not yet able to follow minutely, which explain much of history and social development. At the same time, too, we know that these considerations have never adequately explained or excused the triumph of brute force and cunning over weakness and innocence.

It is, then, the strife of all honorable men of the twentieth century to see that in the future competition of races the survival of the fittest shall mean the triumph of the good, the beautiful, and the true; that we may be able to preserve for future civilization all that is really fine and noble and strong, and not continue to put a premium on greed and impudence and cruelty. To bring this hope to fruition, we are compelled daily to turn more and more to a conscientious study of the phenomena of race-contact,—to a study frank and fair, and not falsified and colored by our wishes or our fears. And we have in the South as fine a field for such a study as the world affords,—a field, to be sure, which the average American scientist deems somewhat beneath his dignity, and which the average man who is not a scientist knows all about, but nevertheless a line of study which by reason of the enormous race complications with which God seems about to punish this nation must increasingly claim our sober attention, study, and thought, we must ask, what are the actual relations of whites and blacks in the South? and we must be answered, not by apology or fault-finding, but by a plain, unvarnished tale.

In the civilized life of to-day the contact of men and their relations to each other fall in a few main lines of action and communication: there is, first, the physical proximity of homes and dwelling-places, the way in which neighborhoods group themselves, and the contiguity of neighborhoods. Secondly, and in our age chiefest, there are the economic relations,—the methods by which individuals coöperate for earning a living, for the mutual satisfaction of wants, for the production of wealth. Next, there are the political relations, the coöperation in social control, in group government, in laying and paying the burden of taxation. In the fourth place there are the less tangible but highly important forms of intellectual contact and commerce, the interchange of ideas through conversation and conference, through periodicals and libraries; and, above all, the gradual formation for each community of that curious *tertium quid* which we call public opinion. Closely allied with this come the various forms of social contact in everyday life, in travel, in theatres, in house gatherings, in marrying and giving in marriage. Finally, there are the varying forms of religious enterprise, of moral teaching and benevolent endeavor. These are the principle ways in which men living in the same communities are brought into contact with each other. It is my present task, therefore, to indicate, from my point of view, how the black race in the South meet and mingle with the whites in these matters of everyday life.

First, as to physical dwelling. It is usually possible to draw in nearly every Southern community a physical color-line on the map, on the one side of which whites dwell and on the other Negroes. The winding and intricacy of the geographical color line varies, of course, in different communities. I know some towns where a straight line drawn through the middle of the main street separates nine-tenths of the whites from nine-tenths of the blacks. In other towns the older settlement of whites has been encircled by a broad band of blacks; in still other cases little settlements or nuclei of blacks have sprung up amid surrounding whites. Usually in cities each street has its distinctive color, and only now and then do the colors meet in close proximity. Even in the country something of this segregation is manifest in the smaller areas, and of course in the larger phenomena of the Black Belt.

All this segregation by color is largely independent of that natural clustering by social grades common to all communities. A Negro slum may be in dangerous proximity to a white residence quarter, while it is quite common to find a white slum planted in the heart of a respectable Negro district. One thing, however, seldom occurs: the best of the whites and the best of the Negroes almost never live in anything like close proximity. It thus happens that in nearly every Southern town and city, both whites and blacks see commonly the worst of each other. This is a vast change from the situation in the past, when, through the close contact of master and house-servant in the patriarchal big house, one found the best of both races in close contact and sympathy, while at the same time the squalor and dull round of toil among the field-hands was removed from the sight and hearing of the family. One can easily see how a person who saw slavery thus from his father's parlors, and sees freedom on the streets of a great city, fails to grasp or comprehend the whole of the new picture. On the other hand, the settled belief of the mass of the Negroes that the Southern white people do not have the black man's best interests at heart has been intensified in later years by this continual daily contact of the better class of blacks with the worst representatives of the white race.

Coming now to the economic relations of the races, we are on ground made familiar by study, much discussion, and no little philanthropic effort. And yet with all this there are many essential elements in the coöperation of Negroes and whites for work and wealth that are too readily overlooked or not thoroughly understood. The average American can easily conceive of a rich land awaiting development and filled with black laborers. To him the Southern problem is simply that of making efficient workingmen out of this material, by giving them the requisite technical skill and the help of invested capital. The problem, however, is by no means as simple as this, from the obvious fact that these workingmen have been trained for centuries as slaves. They exhibit, therefore, all the advantages and defects of such training; they are willing and good-natured, but not self-reliant, provident, or careful. If now the economic development of the South is to be pushed to the verge of exploitation, as seems probable, then we have a mass of workingmen thrown into relentless competition with the workingmen of the world, but handicapped by a training the very opposite to that of the modern self-reliant democratic laborer. What the black laborer needs is careful personal guidance, group leadership of men with hearts in their bosoms, to train them to foresight, carefulness, and honesty. Nor does it require any fine-spun theories of racial differences to prove the necessity of such group training after the brains of the race have been knocked out by two hundred and fifty years of assiduous education in submission, carelessness, and stealing. After Emancipation, it was the plain duty of some one to assume this group leadership and training of the Negro laborer. I will not stop here to inquire whose duty it was,—whether that of the white ex-master who had profited by unpaid toil, or the Northern philanthropist whose persistence brought on the crisis, or the National Government whose edict freed the bondmen; I will not stop to ask whose duty it was, but I insist it was the duty of some one to see that these workingmen were not left alone and unguided, without capital, without land, without skill, without economic organization, without even the bald protection of law, order, and decency,—left in a great land, not to settle down to slow and careful internal development, but destined to be thrown almost immediately into relentless and sharp competition with the best of modern workingmen under an economic system where every participant is fighting for himself, and too often utterly regardless of the rights or welfare of his neighbor.

For we must never forget that the economic system of the South to-day which has succeeded the old regime is not the same system as that of the old industrial North, of England, or of France, with their trade-unions, their restrictive laws, their written and unwritten commercial customs, and their long experience. It is, rather, a copy of that England of the early nineteenth century, before the factory acts,—the England that wrung pity from thinkers and fired the wrath of Carlyle. The rod of empire that passed from the hands of Southern gentlemen in 1865, partly by force, partly by their own petulance, has never returned to them. Rather it has passed to those men who have come to take charge of the industrial exploitation of the New South,—the sons of poor whites fired with a new thirst for wealth and power, thrifty and avaricious Yankees, and unscrupulous immigrants. Into the hands of these men the Southern laborers, white and black, have fallen; and this to their sorrow. For the laborers as such, there is in these new captains of industry, neither love nor hate, neither sympathy nor romance; it is a cold question of dollars and dividends. Under such a system all labor is bound to suffer. Even the white laborers are not yet intelligent, thrifty, and well trained enough to maintain themselves against the powerful inroads of organized capital. The results among them, even, are long hours of toil, low wages, child labor, and lack of protection against usury and cheating. But among the black laborers all this is aggravated, first, by a race prejudice which varies from a doubt and distrust among the best element of whites to a frenzied hatred among the worst; and, secondly, it is aggravated, as I have said before, by the wretched economic heritage of the freedmen from slavery. With this training it is difficult for the freedman to learn to grasp the opportunities already opened to him, and the new opportunities are seldom given him, but go by favor to the whites.

Left by the best elements of the South with little protection or oversight, he has been made in law and custom the victim of the worst and most unscrupulous men in each community. The crop-lien system which is depopulating the fields of the South is not simply the result of shiftlessness on the part of Negroes, but is also the result of cunningly devised laws as to mortgages, liens, and misdemeanors, which can be made by conscienceless men to entrap and snare the unwary until escape is impossible, further toil a farce, and protest a crime. I have seen, in the Black Belt of Georgia, an ignorant, honest Negro buy and pay for a farm in installments three separate times, and then in the face of law and decency the enterprising American who sold it to him pocketed money and deed and left the black man landless, to labor on his own land at thirty cents a day. I have seen a black farmer fall in debt to a white storekeeper, and that storekeeper go to his farm and strip it of every single marketable article,—mules, ploughs, stored crops, tools, furniture, bedding, clocks, looking-glass,—and all this without a sheriff or officer, in the face of the law for homestead exemptions, and without rendering to a single responsible person any account or reckoning. And such proceedings can happen, and will happen, in any community where a class of ignorant toilers are placed by custom and race-prejudice beyond the pale of sympathy and race-brotherhood. So long as the best elements of a community do not feel in duty bound to protect and train and care for the weaker members of their group, they leave them to be preyed upon by these swindlers and rascals.

This unfortunate economic situation does not mean the hindrance of all advance in the black South, or the absence of a class of black landlords and mechanics who, in spite of disadvantages, are accumulating property and making good citizens. But it does mean that this class is not nearly so large as a fairer economic system might easily make it, that those who survive in the competition are handicapped so as to accomplish much less than they deserve to, and that, above all, the *personnel* of the successful class is left to chance and accident, and not to any intelligent culling or reasonable methods of selection. As a remedy for this, there is but one possible procedure. We must accept some of the race prejudice in the South as a fact,—deplorable in its intensity, unfortunate in results, and dangerous for the future, but nevertheless a hard fact which only time can efface. We cannot hope, then, in this generation, or for several generations, that the mass of the whites can be brought to assume that close sympathetic and self-sacrificing leadership of the blacks which their present situation so eloquently demands. Such leadership, such social teaching and example, must come from the blacks themselves. For some time men doubted as to whether the Negro could develop such leaders; but to-day no one seriously disputes the capability of individual Negroes to assimilate the culture and common sense of modern civilization, and to pass it on, to some extent at least, to their fellows. If this is true, then here is the path out of the economic situation, and here is the imperative demand for trained Negro leaders of character and intelligence,—men of skill, men of light and leading, college-bred men, black captains of industry, and missionaries of culture; men who thoroughly comprehend and know modern civilization, and can take hold of Negro communities and raise and train them by force of precept and example, deep sympathy, and the inspiration of common blood and ideals. But if such men are to be effective they must have some power,—they must be backed by the best public opinion of these communities, and able to wield for their objects and aims such weapons as the experience of the world has taught are indispensable to human progress.

Of such weapons the greatest, perhaps, in the modern world

is the power of the ballot; and this brings me to a consideration of the third form of contact between whites and blacks in the South,—political activity.

In the attitude of the American mind toward Negro suffrage can be traced with unusual accuracy the prevalent conceptions of government. In the fifties we were near enough the echoes of the French Revolution to believe pretty thoroughly in universal suffrage. We argued, as we thought then rather logically, that no social class was so good, so true, and so disinterested as to be trusted wholly with the political destiny of its neighbors; that in every state the best arbiters of their own welfare are the persons directly affected; consequently that it is only by arming every hand with a ballot,—with the right to have a voice in the policy of the state,—that the greatest good to the greatest number could be attained. To be sure, there were objections to these arguments, but we thought we had answered them tersely and convincingly; if some one complained of the ignorance of voters, we answered, "Educate them." If another complained of their venality, we replied, "Disfranchise them or put them in jail." And, finally, to the men who feared demagogues and the natural perversity of some human beings we insisted that time and bitter experience would teach the most hardheaded. It was at this time that the question of Negro suffrage in the South was raised. Here was a defenceless people suddenly made free. How were they to be protected from those who did not believe in their freedom and were determined to thwart it? Not by force, said the North; not by government guardianship, said the South; then by the ballot, the sole and legitimate defence of a free people, said the Common Sense of the Nation. No one thought, at the time, that the ex-slaves could use the ballot intelligently or very effectively; but they did think that the possession of so great power by a great class in the nation would compel their fellows to educate this class to its intelligent use.

Meantime, new thoughts came to the nation: the inevitable period of moral retrogression and political trickery that ever follows in the wake of war overtook us. So flagrant became the political scandals that reputable men began to leave politics alone, and politics consequently became disreputable. Men began to pride themselves on having nothing to do with their own government, and to agree tacitly with those who regarded public office as a private perquisite. In this state of mind it became easy to wink at the suppression of the Negro vote in the South, and to advise self-respecting Negroes to leave politics entirely alone. The decent and reputable citizens of the North who neglected their own civic duties

51

grew hilarious over the exaggerated importance with which the Negro regarded the franchise. Thus it easily happened that more and more the better class of Negroes followed the advice from abroad and the pressure from home, and took no further interest in politics, leaving to the careless and the venal of their race the exercise of their rights as voters. The black vote that still remained was not trained and educated, but further debauched by open and unblushing bribery, or force and fraud; until the Negro voter was thoroughly inoculated with the idea that politics was a method of private gain by disreputable means.

And finally, now, to-day, when we are awakening to the fact that the perpetuity of republican institutions on this continent depends on the purification of the ballot, the civic training of voters, and the raising of voting to the plane of a solemn duty which a patriotic citizen neglects to his peril and to the peril of his children's children,—in this day, when we are striving for a renaissance of civic virtue, what are we going to say to the black voter of the South? Are we going to tell him still that politics is a disreputable and useless form of human activity? Are we going to induce the best class of Negroes to take less and less interest in government, and to give up their right to take such an interest, without a protest? I am not saying a word against all legitimate efforts to purge the ballot of ignorance, pauperism, and crime. But few have pretended that the present movement for disfranchisement in the South is for such a purpose; it has been plainly and frankly declared in nearly every case that the object of the disfranchising laws is the elimination of the black man from politics.

Now, is this a minor matter which has no influence on the main question of the industrial and intellectual development of the Negro? Can we establish a mass of black laborers and artisans and landholders in the South who, by law and public opinion, have absolutely no voice in shaping the laws under which they live and work? Can the modern organization of industry, assuming as it does free democratic government and the power and ability of the laboring classes to compel respect for their welfare,—can this system be carried out in the South when half its laboring force is voiceless in the public councils and powerless in its own defence? To-day the black man of the South has almost nothing to say as to how much he shall be taxed, or how those taxes shall be expended; as to who shall execute the laws, and how they shall do it; as to who shall make the laws, and how they shall be made. It is pitiable that frantic efforts must be made at critical times to get law-makers in some States even to listen to the respectful presentation of the black man's side of a current controversy. Daily the Negro is coming more and more to look upon law and justice, not as protecting safeguards, but as sources of humiliation and oppression. The laws are made by men who have little interest in him; they are executed by men who have absolutely no motive for treating the black people with courtesy or consideration; and, finally, the accused law-breaker is tried, not by his peers, but too often by men who would rather punish ten innocent Negroes than let one guilty one escape.

I should be the last one to deny the patent weaknesses and shortcomings of the Negro people; I should be the last to withhold sympathy from the white South in its efforts to solve its intricate social problems. I freely acknowledge that it is possible, and sometimes best, that a partially undeveloped people should be ruled by the best of their stronger and better neighbors for their own good, until such time as they can start and fight the world's battles alone. I have already pointed out how sorely in need of such economic and spiritual guidance the emancipated Negro was, and I am quite willing to admit that if the representatives of the best white Southern public opinion were the ruling and guiding powers in the South to-day the conditions indicated would be fairly well fulfilled. But the point I have insisted upon, and now emphasize again, is that the best opinion of the South to-day is not the ruling opinion. That to leave the Negro helpless and without a ballot to-day is to leave him, not to the guidance of the best, but rather to the exploitation and debauchment of the worst; that this is no truer of the South than of the North,—of the North than of Europe: in any land, in any country under modern free competition, to lay any class of weak and despised people, be they white, black, or blue, at the political mercy of their stronger, richer, and more resourceful fellows, is a temptation which human nature seldom has withstood and seldom will withstand.

Moreover, the political status of the Negro in the South is closely connected with the question of Negro crime. There can be no doubt that crime among Negroes has sensibly increased in the last thirty years, and that there has appeared in the slums of great cities a distinct criminal class among the blacks. In explaining this unfortunate development, we must note two things: (1) that the inevitable result of Emancipation was to increase crime and criminals, and (2) that the police system of the South was primarily designed to control slaves. As to the first point, we must not forget that under a strict slave system there can scarcely be such a thing as crime. But when these variously constituted human particles are suddenly thrown broadcast on the sea of life, some swim, some sink, and some hang suspended, to be forced up or down by the chance currents of a busy hurrying world. So great an economic and social revolution as swept the South in '63 meant a weeding out among the Negroes of the incompetents and vicious, the beginning of a differentiation of social grades. Now a rising group of people are not lifted bodily from the ground like an inert solid mass, but rather stretch upward like a living plant with its roots still clinging in the mould. The appearance, therefore, of the Negro criminal was a phenomenon to be awaited; and while it causes anxiety, it should not occasion surprise.

Here again the hope for the future depended peculiarly on careful and delicate dealing with these criminals. Their offences at first were those of laziness, carelessness, and impulse, rather than of malignity or ungoverned viciousness. Such misdemeanors needed discriminating treatment, firm but reformatory, with no hint of injustice, and full proof of guilt. For such dealing with criminals, white or black, the South had no machinery, no adequate jails or reformatories; its police system was arranged to deal with blacks alone, and tacitly assumed that every white man was *ipso facto* a member of that police. Thus grew up a double system of justice, which erred on the white side by undue leniency, and the practical immunity of red-handed criminals, and erred on the black side by undue severity, injustice, and lack of discrimination. For, as I have said, the police system of the South was originally designed to keep track of all Negroes, not simply of criminals; and when the Negroes were freed and the whole South was convinced of the impossibility of free Negro labor, the first and almost universal device was to use the courts as a means of reënslaving the blacks. It was not then a question of crime, but rather one of color, that settled a man's conviction on almost any charge. Thus Negroes came to look upon courts as instruments of injustice and oppression, and upon those convicted in them as martyrs and victims.

When, now, the real Negro criminal appeared, and instead of petty stealing and vagrancy we began to have highway robbery, burglary, murder, and rape, there was a curious effect on both sides the color-line: the Negroes refused to believe the evidence of white witnesses or the fairness of white juries, so that the greatest deterrent to crime, the public opinion of one's own social caste, was lost, and the criminal was looked upon as crucified rather than hanged. On the other hand, the whites, used to being careless as to the guilt or innocence of accused Negroes, were swept in moments of passion beyond law, reason, and decency. Such a situation is bound to increase crime, and has increased it. To natural viciousness and vagrancy are being daily added motives of revolt and revenge which stir up all the latent savagery of both races and make peaceful attention to economic development often impossible.

But the chief problem in any community cursed with crime is not the punishment of the criminals, but the preventing of the young from being trained to crime. And here again the peculiar conditions of the South have prevented proper precautions. I have seen twelve-year-old boys working in chains on the public streets of Atlanta, directly in front of the schools, in company with old and hardened criminals; and this indiscriminate mingling of men and women and children makes the chain-gangs perfect schools of crime and debauchery. The struggle for reformatories, which has gone on in Virginia, Georgia, and other States, is the one encouraging sign of the awakening of some communities to the suicidal results of this policy.

It is the public schools, however, which can be made, outside the homes, the greatest means of training decent self-respecting citizens. We have been so hotly engaged recently in discussing trade-schools and the higher education that the pitiable plight of the public-school system in the South has almost dropped from view. Of every five dollars spent for public education in the State of Georgia, the white schools get four dollars and the Negro one dollar; and even then the white public-school system, save in the cities, is bad and cries for reform. If this is true of the whites, what of the blacks? I am becoming more and more convinced, as I look upon the system of common-school training in the South, that the national government must soon step in and aid popular education in some way. To-day it has been only by the most strenuous efforts on the part of the thinking men of the South that the Negro's share of the school fund has not been cut down to a pittance in some half-dozen States; and that movement not only is not dead, but in many communities is gaining strength. What in the name of reason does this nation expect of a people, poorly trained and hard pressed in severe economic competition, without political rights, and with ludicrously inadequate common-school facilities? What can it expect but crime and listlessness, offset here and there by the dogged struggles of the fortunate and more determined who are themselves buoyed by the hope that in due time the country will come to its senses?

I have thus far sought to make clear the physical, economic, and political relations of the Negroes and whites in the South, as I have conceived them, including, for the reasons set forth, crime and education. But after all that has been said on these more tangible matters of human contact, there still remains a part essential to a proper description of the South which it is difficult to describe or fix in terms easily understood by strangers. It is, in fine, the atmosphere of the land, the thought and feeling, the thousand and one little actions which go to make up life. In any community or nation it is these little things which are most elusive to the grasp and yet most essential to any clear conception of the group life taken as a whole. What is thus true of all communities is peculiarly true of the South, where, outside of written history and outside of printed law, there has been going on for a generation as deep a storm and stress of human souls, as intense a ferment of feeling, as intricate a writhing of spirit, as ever a people experienced. Within and without the sombre veil of color vast social forces have been at work,—efforts for human betterment, movements toward disintegration and despair, tragedies and comedies in social and economic life, and a swaying and lifting and sinking of human hearts which have made this land a land of mingled sorrow and joy, of change and excitement and unrest.

The centre of this spiritual turmoil has ever been the millions of black freedmen and their sons, whose destiny is so fatefully bound up with that of the nation. And yet the casual observer visiting the South sees at first little of this. He notes the growing frequency of dark faces as he rides along,—but otherwise the days slip lazily on, the sun shines, and this little world seems as happy and contented as other worlds he has visited. Indeed, on the question of questions—the Negro problem—he hears so little that there seldom mention it, and then usually in a far-fetched academic way, almost seems to be a conspiracy of silence; the morning papers and indeed almost every one seems to forget and ignore the darker half of the land, until the astonished visitor is inclined to ask if after all there *is* any problem here. But if he lingers long enough there comes the awakening: perhaps in a sudden whirl of passion which leaves him gasping at its bitter intensity; more likely in a gradually dawning sense of things he had not at first noticed. Slowly but surely his eyes begin to catch the shadows of the color-line: here he meets crowds of Negroes and whites; then he is suddenly aware that he cannot discover a single dark face; or again at the close of a day's wandering he may find himself in some strange assembly, where all faces are tinged brown or black, and where he has the vague, uncomfortable feeling of the stranger. He realizes at last that silently, resistlessly, the world about flows by him in two great streams: they ripple on in the same sunshine, they approach and mingle their waters in seeming carelessness,— then they divide and flow wide apart. It is done quietly; no mistakes are made, or if one occurs, the swift arm of the law and of public opinion swings down for a moment, as when the other day a black man and a white woman were arrested for talking together on Whitehall Street in Atlanta.

Now if one notices carefully one will see that between these two worlds, despite much physical contact and daily intermingling, there is almost no community of intellectual life or point of transference where the thoughts and feelings of one race can come into direct contact and sympathy with the thoughts and feelings of the other. Before and directly after the war, when all the best of the Negroes were domestic servants in the best of the white families, there were bonds of intimacy, affection, and sometimes blood relationship, between the races. They lived in the same home, shared in the family life, often attended the same church, and talked and conversed with each other. But the increasing civilization of the Negro since then has naturally meant the development of higher classes: there are increasing numbers of ministers, teachers, physicians, merchants, mechanics, and independent farmers, who by nature and training are the aristocracy and leaders of the blacks. Between them, however, and the best element of the whites, there is little or no intellectual commerce. They go to separate churches, they live in separate sections, they are strictly separated in all public gatherings, they travel separately, and they are beginning to read different papers and books. To most libraries, lectures, concerts, and museums, Negroes are either not admitted at all, or on terms peculiarly galling to the pride of the very classes who might otherwise be attracted. The daily paper chronicles the doings of the black world from afar with no great regard for accuracy; and so on, throughout the category of means for intellectual communication,—schools, conferences, efforts for social betterment, and the like,—it is usually true that the very representatives of the two races, who for mutual benefit and the welfare of the land ought to be in complete understanding and sympathy, are so far strangers that one side thinks all whites are narrow and prejudiced, and the other thinks educated Negroes dangerous and insolent. Moreover, in a land where the tyranny of public opinion and the intolerance of criticism is for obvious historical reasons so strong as in the South, such a situation is extremely difficult to correct. The white man, as well as the Negro, is bound and barred by the color-line, and many a scheme of friendliness and philanthropy, of broad-minded sympathy and generous fellowship between the two has dropped still-born because some busybody has forced the color-question to the front and brought the tremendous force of unwritten law against the innovators.

It is hardly necessary for me to add very much in regard to the social contact between the races. Nothing has come to replace that finer sympathy and love between some masters and house servants which the radical and more uncompromising drawing of the color-line in recent years has caused almost completely to disappear. In a world where it means so much to take a man by the hand and sit beside him, to look frankly into his eyes and feel his heart beating with red blood; in a world where a social cigar or a cup of tea together means more than legislative halls and magazine articles and speeches,—one can imagine the consequences of the almost utter absence of such social amenities between estranged races, whose separation extends even to parks and streetcars.

Here there can be none of that social going down to the people,—the opening of heart and hand of the best to the worst, in generous acknowledgment of a common humanity and a common destiny. On the other hand, in matters of simple almsgiving, where there can be no question of social contact, and in the succor of the aged and sick, the South, as if stirred by a feeling of its unfortunate limitations, is generous to a fault. The black beggar is never turned away without a good deal more than a crust, and a call for help for the unfortunate meets quick response. I remember, one cold winter, in Atlanta, when I refrained from contributing to a public relief fund lest Negroes should be discriminated against, I afterward inquired of a friend: "Were any black people receiving aid?" "Why," said he, "they were *all* black."

And yet this does not touch the kernel of the problem. Human advancement is not a mere question of almsgiving, but rather of sympathy and coöperation among classes who would scorn charity. And here is a land where, in the higher walks of life, in all the higher striving for the good and noble and true, the color-line comes to separate natural friends and co-workers; while at the bottom of the social group, in the saloon, the gambling-hell, and the brothel, that same line wavers and disappears.

I have sought to paint an average picture of real relations between the sons of master and man in the South. I have not glossed over matters for policy's sake, for I fear we have already gone too far in that sort of thing. On the other hand, I have sincerely sought to let no unfair exaggerations creep in. I do not doubt that in some Southern communities conditions are better than those I have indicated; while I am no less certain that in other communities they are far worse.

Nor does the paradox and danger of this situation fail to interest and perplex the best conscience of the South. Deeply religious and intensely democratic as are the mass of the whites, they feel acutely the false position in which the Negro problems place them. Such an essentially honest-hearted and generous people cannot cite the caste-levelling precepts of Christianity, or believe in equality of opportunity for all men, without coming to feel more and more with each generation that the present drawing of the color-line is a flat contradiction to their beliefs and professions. But just as often as they come to this point, the present social condition of the Negro stands as a menace and a portent before even the most open-minded: if there were nothing to charge against the Negro but his blackness or other physical peculiarities, they argue, the problem would be comparatively simple; but what can we say to his ignorance, shiftlessness, poverty, and crime? can a self-respecting group hold anything but the least possible fellow-ship with such persons and survive? and shall we let a mawkish sentiment sweep away the culture of our fathers or the hope of our children? The argument so put is of great strength, but it is not a whit stronger than the argument of thinking Negroes: granted, they reply, that the condition of our masses is bad; there is certainly on the one hand adequate historical cause for this, and unmistakable evidence that no small number have, in spite of tremendous disadvantages, risen to the level of American civilization. And when, by proscription and prejudice, these same Negroes are classed with and treated like the lowest of their people, simply *because* they are Negroes, such a policy not only discourages thrift and intelligence among black men, but puts a direct premium on the very things you complain of,—inefficiency and crime. Draw lines of crime, of incompetency, of vice, as tightly and uncompromisingly as you will, for these things must be proscribed; but a color-line not only does not accomplish this purpose, but thwarts it.

In the face of two such arguments, the future of the South depends on the ability of the representatives of these opposing views to see and appreciate and sympathize with each other's position,—for the Negro to realize more deeply than he does at present the need of uplifting the masses of his people, for the white people to realize more vividly than they have yet done the deadening and disastrous effect of a color-prejudice that classes Phillis Wheatley and Sam Hose in the same despised class.

It is not enough for the Negroes to declare that color-prejudice is the sole cause of their social condition, nor for the white South to reply that their social condition is the main cause of prejudice. They both act as reciprocal cause and effect, and a change in neither alone will bring the desired effect. Both must change, or neither can improve to any great extent. The Negro cannot stand the present reactionary tendencies and unreasoning drawing of the color-line indefinitely without discouragement and retrogression. And the condition of the Negro is ever the excuse for further discrimination. Only by a union of intelligence and sympathy across the color-line in this critical period of the Republic shall justice and right triumph,

> "That mind and soul according well,
> May make one music as before,
> But vaster."

PART II
THE NEGRO AWAKENING

INTRODUCTION

In 1925 Alain Locke, a formative and sophisticated Negro scholar, published an anthology of contemporary writing by Negroes that attempted "to register the transformations of the inner and outer life of the Negro in America that have so significantly taken place in the last few years"; he called his volume *The New Negro, An Interpretation*. The Negro was undergoing a metamorphosis, Locke maintained, in which he was shedding the old chrysalis of the Negro problem and "achieving something like a spiritual emancipation." Whereas the old Negro had always been a type in the fiction of white authors and had consequently seen himself in "the distorted perspective of a social problem," the new Negro was "shaking off the psychology of imitation and implied inferiority" and creating a literature concerned with the human behavior of individuals in their private lives. "The American mind," Locke concluded, "must reckon with a fundamentally changed Negro."

The metamorphosis to which Locke alluded has generally been identified as the Negro Renaissance, although naissance would be perhaps a more accurate term: Negro literature experienced a troublesome, suggestive, exhilarating awakening in the 1920's—a birth, as it were, and not a rebirth. There were many writers who examined the mores of Negro life in an honest and daring manner:

prose writers like Rudolph Fisher, Eric Walrond, and Jean Toomer; the poets Claude McKay, James Weldon Johnson, Countee Cullen, Langston Hughes, and Arna Bontemps; and essayists and social thinkers such as Kelly Miller, Charles S. Johnson, E. Franklin Frazier, Walter White, and W. E. B. DuBois. These are some of the more important writers of the Negro Awakening, and their contribution to American literature, often minor in its intrinsic aesthetic significance, is an interesting corollary to the other important literature of the 1920's.

The Negro Awakening can be understood by considering certain general aspects of the period: the historical forces that led to a new Negro attitude; the literary techniques and styles that the authors adopted; the themes that tend to dominate the literature; and, finally, the varying responses of Negro critics toward this first flowering of Negro writing.

The Negro Awakening would not have been so impressive or forceful a literary period without a confluence of historical and social developments which prepared the Negro artist for greater and more unrestrained self-expression. The defeat of Booker T. Washington's conciliatory attitude by W. E. B. DuBois and the more militant Negroes is of particular importance. DuBois opposed Washington's emphasis on the Negro's need for industrial skills, his desire to conform to the demands of a white society, and his presentation of himself as the spokesman for all Negroes. DuBois, a sociologist professionally trained at Harvard, "believed in the higher education of a Talented Tenth who through their knowledge of modern culture could guide the American Negro into a higher civilization." He refused "to emphasize the shortcomings of the Negro," as Washington often did, and tried to analyze the Negro's problems realistically, criticizing white society when he thought that criticism was justified.

As a political consequence of these ideological differences, DuBois helped to establish the NAACP in 1909, an organization that gave young Negroes a sense of solidarity and pride which they had not always felt before. A year later, DuBois was made director of publicity and editor of *The Crisis*, a journal of the organization which published some of the important Negro literature of the Awakening. Whereas a writer like

Charles Chesnutt, in the late nineteenth century, had shaped his stories to suit a white audience, the new Negroes felt more imaginatively free because they realized that they had a journal sympathetic to their ideas. Soon a white audience grew interested in racial subjects, and Negro authors found little trouble in publishing their work. As Arna Bontemps, a writer who began his career during the 1920's, has recently suggested: "When acceptances from Harpers; Harcourt, Brace; Viking; Boni & Liveright; Knopf; and other front-line publishers began coming through in quick succession, the excitement among those of us who were writing was almost unbearable. The walls of Jericho were toppling. . . . Of course we had all been writing since childhood, and all of us had vaguely hoped to have something published eventually, but I think I am safe in saying we were all surprised—more than surprised. We had never dreamed that it would happen so soon."

Other historical developments contributed to the independent state of mind that characterized so many Negro authors of the 1920's. World War I dramatically reminded Negroes of their paradoxical position in American life. Trained as soldiers in the South, many Negroes experienced racial prejudice in spite of their loyalty to the war effort; they rarely held combat positions and served, for the most part, as stevedores or messmen under white officers who often acted with bias. When they were assigned to overseas duty—in France, for example—they experienced less prejudice from foreign civilians than from white soldiers in their own army units. On occasion, officers even warned French civilians not to socialize with Negro soldiers for fear of possible rape. Upon returning to the United States, these same Negro soldiers experienced race riots in major cities across the country, riots that helped to inspire some of the most memorable literature of the Negro Awakening.

At the same time that Negro soldiers served in the Armed Forces, the great migration of Southern Negroes to Northern cities took place. From 1916 to 1919 rural Negroes were exposed to a variety and complexity of experience they had not yet known. Although most of the authors who wrote during this period grew up in cities, they were nevertheless sensitive to the movement of so many Negroes from an agrarian childhood to an urban adulthood; their literature reflects the adjustment, the wonder, at times the confusion and insecurity which attend the sudden exposure to cities as large as Chicago and New York. Adjustments proved particularly difficult, for many Negroes came to urban centers with the sense of possibility and soon found themselves in ghettos that frustrated their every attempt to transcend social and economic limitations.

Certain political spokesmen of the 1920's expressed the discontent and bitterness of the average Negro and proved to be still another contributing social force in the development of a new Negro literature. The most charismatic orator of the 1920's was Marcus Garvey, a Jamaican who formed the Universal Negro Improvement Association and urged American Negroes to return to Africa. Although Garvey was not practically successful, he influenced many common people and helped to develop a sense of pride in the working man which is, in turn, strongly reflected in the literature of the 1920's.

These forces—the defeat of Booker T. Washington's conciliatory position; the formation of the NAACP; the World War; the migration of the Southern Negro to Northern cities; and the Garvey movement—provided the proper social conditions for a literature of protest, of chauvinism, and of spontaneous expression. One can begin to see these forces affect literature when one reads James Weldon Johnson's novel, *The Autobiography of an Ex-Coloured Man*. Published in 1912 as a simulated autobiography, it tells the story of a mulatto from his own point of view and thus creates an organic and intimate sense of the difficulty a near-white boy experiences in trying to discover his racial identity. In its description of the "ways of white folks," of Negro music and of Negro life in New York, *The Autobiography of an Ex-Coloured Man* is a precursor of Negro literature in the 1920's.

The full flowering of the Negro Awakening begins with the publication of Claude McKay's "If We Must Die" in *The Liberator* in 1919. A protest poem, which was inspired by the race riots of 1919, "If We Must Die" expresses the new pride of the Negro author and pictures the Negro in uncompromising opposition to the white man: "Like men we'll face the murderous, cowardly pack, /Pressed to the wall, dying, but fighting back!" Other writers echoed McKay's militancy, although most of the Negro authors of the 1920's were primarily interested in the facts of their Negro existence rather than the political or social use to which those facts could be put. A surprising number of minor American classics appeared within a short period of time: McKay's *Harlem Shadows* (1922), in which "If We Must Die" was included, *Home to Harlem* (1928), *Banjo* (1929), and *Banana Bottom* (1933); Jean Toomer's *Cane* (1923); Countee Cullen's *Color* (1925), *Copper Sun* (1927), and *The Black Christ* (1929); Langston Hughes's *The Weary Blues* (1926), *Fine Clothes to the Jew* (1927), and *The Ways of White Folks* (1934); Eric Walrond's *Tropic Death* (1926); Rudolph Fisher's stories, *The Walls of Jericho* (1928), and *The Conjure Man* (1932); and Arna Bontemps' *God Sends Sunday* (1931) and *Black Thunder* (1935). One can see, from the publication dates of these volumes, that most of the writers of the Awakening produced their first and most characteristic work in the 1920's. With the collapse of the New York stock market in 1929, American writers in general turned to themes that were more consonant with the common person's economic problems; the Negro, acutely affected by the depression, sacrificed the exuberance of his literature for direct social protest. The important Negro author to emerge in the 1930's is Richard Wright, and his early work—*Uncle Tom's Children* (1938) and especially *Native Son* (1940)—is filled with an anger that one rarely finds in Negro literature of the 1920's.

Caught up in the postwar mood, the writers of the Negro Awakening were too self-conscious, as Ralph Ellison has recently noted, of the despair that informed the work of so many white authors in this period. But if the themes of Negro authors were typical of the "lost generation," their techniques resembled those of the local color writers who preceded them by fifty years, many of whom—Thomas Nelson Page, Joel Chandler Harris, George Washington Cable, and others—were responsible for the image of the Negro that dominated American literature until the 1920's. Like the local colorists, these Negro writers celebrate folkways and note the significance of place—British Guiana, Jamaica, Panama, Harlem, Chicago, Washington, or Georgia—in the lives of their characters; they make use of dialect or, more often, they create an idiomatic urban argot that becomes a kind of modern dialect, a device for speaking their own thoughts honestly; they are fond of the exotic, the bizarre, at times the surrealistic; and their work tends to be sentimental and impressionistic, avoiding the close or penetrating analysis of human character. We see a new Negro emerge in the 1920's—a fully human Negro and not a refraction of the white author's sensibility, a character rather than a caricature—but we do not yet see deeply into his mind.

The Negro of nineteenth-century literature was a comic, essentially idealistic Negro associated with the fiction of the Southern plantation; few writers conceived of a Negro who differed from the humorous or pathetic type. The new Negro, in contrast, is frenetic, pugnacious, curious, and at times violent. In a desire to reject the stereotypical images of the past, Negro writers used several literary approaches. At times— as in the poetry of Claude McKay or the essays of W. E. B. DuBois —they wrote overt protest. Often—as in the stories of Rudolph Fisher, Eric Walrond, and Langston Hughes—they achieved their criticism of white society through satire or cynicism. Finally—in the fiction of Jean Toomer, Eric Walrond, and Claude McKay, and in the poetry of Countee Cullen and Langston Hughes—they wrote of the highly emotional, Romantic life that some Negroes led in the early twentieth century and in the 1920's.

The latter approach, although it avoided a description of all those Negroes who were simply trying to survive and improve themselves economically, was the most common method of rejecting stereotypes, a method similar to that of most American writers in the 1920's who criticized what they considered to be the staid Victorian manners and the tepid realism of an earlier period. "We younger Negro artists who create now," Langston Hughes proclaimed, "intend to express our individual dark-skinned selves without fear or shame." In this mood the new Negro writers wrote works that were free of apologetics, free of the inhibiting morality of another period. The stories of Rudolph Fisher re-create the general ambience of Harlem life in the 1920's—its music, its humor, its frenetic tempo, its violence, and its affirmation of life; the potpourri of tales, poems, and sketches in Jean Toomer's *Cane*, set in Georgia and Washington, D.C., capture the quality of youthful striving and the frustrations that accompany the transition from adolescence to maturity; the stories of Eric Walrond record the violent moods of Negroes in the Caribbean; *Home to Harlem* (1928), by Claude McKay, concentrates upon the sexual mores of certain Negroes in Harlem; the early poetry of Langston Hughes, collected in *The Weary Blues* (1926), describes the exotic night life of Harlem cabarets, whereas his collection of short stories, *The Ways of White Folks* (1934), depicts the fantasies that white Americans often have of colored people.

These works—and the similar writings of such white authors as Dubose Heyward (in *Porgy*, 1925) and Carl Van Vechten (in *Nigger Heaven*, 1926), who celebrated the instinctual life of the Negro even more extremely—were censured by Negro critics—W. E. B. DuBois, James Weldon Johnson, Sterling Brown, and others—who felt, as Brown wrote, that "the drama of the workaday life, the struggles, the conflicts [were] missing in much of the Renaissance literature." But, in retrospect, this criticism seems only partially true—the same reservations, after all, may also be made of Hemingway, Fitzgerald, Anderson, and other genuine artists who, unlike the social writers of the thirties, avoided the "workaday life" of their characters. Negro authors of the 1920's were interested in demonstrating their humanity, in altering images of themselves that they knew were not accurate, and if, as Benjamin Brawley had warned in 1927, they offered "new stereotypes hardly better than the old," much of the reason lies in the absence of an intrinsic and vital literary tradition from which they could develop. It would be inaccurate, furthermore, to group these writers together as if they were united in their literary goals, as if they wrote in accordance with an understood manifesto. Each of them had his own distinctive voice, his own particular point of view. Rudolph Fisher is satirical in his treatment of people; Jean Toomer writes lyrically; Eric Walrond maintains a distance from his characters, as though he is an observer; Claude McKay tends toward overt criticism; and Langston Hughes is ironic and whimsical.

It is true that these writers felt "free within" themselves, as Langston Hughes suggested, that they shared a sense of liberation from the confining standards of the past; but in the expression of their renewed self-respect and self-dependence, they were singular artists using individual modes of expression. Negro critics like W. E. B. DuBois and Benjamin Brawley were sensitive to the fact that the writers of the

Awakening commanded a large white audience, and they wanted the life of the Negro presented in its most attractive form; but the artists would not shape their work to any sociological need, and there is a boldness of expression that is the most distinctive feature of this literature. With all of its limitations, the literature of the Negro Awakening depicted Negro life as the writers saw it and not as they were expected to see it. "This so-called Renaissance," as Arthur P. Davis has noted, "not only encouraged and inspired the black creative artist, but it served also to focus as never before the attention of America upon the Negro artist and scholar." In all its diverse forms—the essay, the short story, the poem, and the novel—the Negro Awakening is of critical importance in any history of Negro literature. Never again, in serious works of art, could the life of the American Negro be described in terms of stereotypes.

JAMES WELDON JOHNSON
1871-1938

James Weldon Johnson was born in Jacksonville, Florida, in 1871. His parents were exceptionally cultured and gave him a firm training in the arts. Johnson graduated from Atlanta University in 1894 and went on to teach at the Stanton School in Jacksonville; in a short while he became principal of the school.

Johnson was as close to a Renaissance man as the conditions of American society would permit a Negro to be. After his brief experience as a teacher, he studied law and became the first Negro since Reconstruction to be admitted to the bar in Florida through open examinations. When he lost interest in the law, Johnson began a short-lived Negro newspaper in Jacksonville; he then turned to music, which had always interested him, and in collaboration with his brother, John Rosamond, he began to write songs for Tin Pan Alley. The brothers enjoyed wide popularity and Johnson could have had a successful career as a composer; but he was soon involved in politics, supporting Theodore Roosevelt in the presidential campaign of 1904 and acting as the United States Consul at Puerto Cabello, Venezuela, in 1907 and then as the Consul at Corinto, Nicaragua, until Woodrow Wilson's election in 1913.

During the period he served as Consul, Johnson wrote *The Autobiography of an Ex-Coloured Man* (1912), an impressive novel that anticipates much of the fiction of the Negro Awakening. In the form of an autobiography, Johnson tells the story of a light-

69

skinned mulatto who has a musical talent that takes him into Negro circles in New York and, under the guidance of a white patron, into a wealthy white world in European cities. When the narrator returns to the United States, he witnesses varieties of racial prejudice—the most traumatic of which is a lynching in Tennessee—and, out of fear and despair, he abandons his dreams of improving the Negro race and accepts the easier existence of a white man. Written in a tempered prose style, *The Autobiography* is quietly effective in its description of the ambivalent nature of a mulatto who attempts to understand his racial roots, his relationship to his family and to America.

Johnson's novel did not become popular until it was reissued in 1927, with an introduction by Carl Van Vechten. By that time Johnson was a leader of the Negro Awakening: an important poet; a leader in the NAACP, serving as field secretary from 1916 to 1920 and as general secretary from 1920 to 1930; and an essayist, commenting upon political and literary matters during the 1920's. In the 1930's he became Professor of Creative Literature at Fisk University, where he taught until his death in an auto accident in 1938.

Johnson never achieved great stature as an author, but *The Autobiography of an Ex-Coloured Man* is still the finest novel of its kind before the 1920's; his poetry has a musical and moving quality which at its best—as in "O Black and Unknown Bards" and *God's Trombones* (1927)—evokes "the racial spirit" without resorting to dialect; and his essays suggest a close awareness of his literary contemporaries during the Negro Awakening.

O Black and Unknown Bards

O black and unknown bards of long ago,
How came your lips to touch the sacred fire?
How, in your darkness, did you come to know
The power and beauty of the minstrel's lyre?
Who first from midst his bonds lifted his eyes?
Who first from out the still watch, lone and long,
Feeling the ancient faith of prophets rise
Within his dark-kept soul, burst into song?

Heart of what slave poured out such melody
As "Steal away to Jesus"? On its strains
His spirit must have nightly floated free,
Though still about his hands he felt his chains.
Who heard great "Jordan roll"? Whose starward eye
Saw chariot "swing low"? And who was he
That breathed that comforting, melodic sigh,
"Nobody knows de trouble I see"?

What merely living clod, what captive thing,
Could up toward God through all its darkness grope,
And find within its deadened heart to sing
These songs of sorrow, love and faith, and hope?
How did it catch that subtle undertone,
That note in music heard not with the ears?
How sound the elusive reed so seldom blown,
Which stirs the soul or melts the heart to tears.

Not that great German master in his dream
Of harmonies that thundered amongst the stars
At the creation, ever heard a theme
Nobler than "Go down, Moses." Mark its bars
How like a mighty trumpet-call they stir
The blood. Such are the notes that men have sung
Going to valorous deeds; such tones there were
That helped make history when Time was young.

There is a wide, wide wonder in it all,
That from degraded rest and servile toil
The fiery spirit of the seer should call
These simple children of the sun and soil.

71

O black slave singers, gone, forgot, unfamed,
You—you alone, of all the long, long line
Of those who've sung untaught, unknown, unnamed,
Have stretched out upward, seeking the divine.

You sang not deeds of heroes or of kings;
No chant of bloody war, no exulting paean
Of arms-won triumphs; but your humble strings
You touched in chord with music empyrean.
You sang far better than you knew; the songs
That for your listeners' hungry hearts sufficed
Still live,—but more than this to you belongs:
You sang a race from wood and stone to Christ.

Sence You Went Away

Seems lak to me de stars don't shine so bright,
Seems lak to me de sun done loss his light,
Seems lak to me der's nothin' goin' right,
    Sence you went away.

Seems lak to me de sky ain't half so blue,
Seems lak to me dat ev'ything wants you,
Seems lak to me I don't know what to do,
    Sence you went away.

Seems lak to me dat ev'ything is wrong,
Seems lak to me de day's jes twice as long,
Seems lak to me de bird's forgot his song,
    Sence you went away.

Seems lak to me I jes can't he'p but sigh,
Seems lak to me ma th'oat keeps gittin' dry,
Seems lak to me a tear stays in my eye,
    Sence you went away.

ALAIN
LOCKE
1886-1954
Alain Locke is one of the seminal scholars in twentieth-century Negro literature in America. Born in Philadelphia on September 13, 1886, Locke grew up in Philadelphia and studied at Harvard College, Oxford University, and the University of Berlin. He received his Ph.D. from Harvard University in 1918 and taught philosophy at Howard University from 1912 until 1953, when he retired.

In the 1920's Locke became a spokesman for those new Negro writers who sought to express themselves freely. As the author of *Race Contacts and Inter-racial Relations* (1916) and various essays on literature and society, he urged American readers to recognize the Negro's contribution to their culture; as editor of *Survey Graphic* and other journals, he published the work of promising Negro writers. His volume *The New Negro, An Interpretation* (1925), from which the following essay is taken, is a collection of the most important writings by Negroes in the 1920's; his volume *The Negro in Art* (1941) expresses his attitude toward the minority groups in a democratic society. Toward the end of his life, Locke was preparing a study of the Negro's place in American culture, which would have represented his final views. Although he never lived to write the book, his friend and colleague, Margaret Just Butcher, completed the study, *The Negro in American Culture* (1956).

The New Negro

IN THE LAST DECADE something beyond the watch and guard of statistics has happened in the life of the American Negro and the three norns who have traditionally presided over the Negro problem have a changeling in their laps. The Sociologist, the Philanthropist, the Race-leader are not unaware of the New Negro, but they are at a loss to account for him. He simply cannot be swathed in their formulæ. For the younger generation is vibrant with a new psychology; the new spirit is awake in the masses, and under the very eyes of the professional observers is transforming what has been a perennial problem into the progressive phases of contemporary Negro life.

Could such a metamorphosis have taken place as suddenly as it has appeared to? The answer is no; not because the New Negro is not here, but because the Old Negro had long become more of a myth than a man. The Old Negro, we must remember, was a creature of moral debate and historical controversy. His has been a stock figure perpetuated as an historical fiction partly in innocent sentimentalism, partly in deliberate reactionism. The Negro himself has contributed his share to this through a sort of protective social mimicry forced upon him by the adverse circumstances of dependence. So for generations in the mind of America, the Negro has been more of a formula than a human being—a something to be argued about, condemned or defended, to be "kept down," or "in his place," or "helped up," to be worried with or worried over, harassed or patronized, a social bogey or a social burden. The thinking Negro even has been induced to share this same general attitude, to focus his attention on controversial issues, to see himself in the distorted perspective of a social problem. His shadow, so to speak, has been more real to him than his personality. Through having had to appeal from the unjust stereotypes of his oppressors and traducers to those of his liberators, friends and benefactors he has had to subscribe to the traditional positions from which his case has been viewed. Little true social or self-understanding has or could come from such a situation.

But while the minds of most of us, black and white, have thus burrowed in the trenches of the Civil War and Reconstruction,

Reprinted from *The New Negro, An Interpretation*, ed. Alain Locke (New York: Albert and Charles Boni, 1925), pp. 3–16.

the actual march of development has simply flanked these positions, necessitating a sudden reorientation of view. We have not been watching in the right direction; set North and South on a sectional axis, we have not noticed the East till the sun has us blinking.

Recall how suddenly the Negro spirituals revealed themselves; suppressed for generations under the stereotypes of Wesleyan hymn harmony, secretive, half-ashamed, until the courage of being natural brought them out—and behold, there was folk-music. Similarly the mind of the Negro seems suddenly to have slipped from under the tyranny of social intimidation and to be shaking off the psychology of imitation and implied inferiority. By shedding the old chrysalis of the Negro problem we are achieving something like a spiritual emancipation. Until recently, lacking self-understanding, we have been almost as much of a problem to ourselves as we still are to others. But the decade that found us with a problem has left us with only a task. The multitude perhaps feels as yet only a strange relief and a new vague urge, but the thinking few know that in the reaction the vital inner grip of prejudice has been broken.

With this renewed self-respect and self-dependence, the life of the Negro community is bound to enter a new dynamic phase, the buoyancy from within compensating for whatever pressure there may be of conditions from without. The migrant masses, shifting from countryside to city, hurdle several generations of experience at a leap, but more important, the same thing happens spiritually in the life-attitudes and self-expression of the Young Negro, in his poetry, his art, his education and his new outlook, with the additional advantage, of course, of the poise and greater certainty of knowing what it is all about. From this comes the promise and warrant of a new leadership. As one of them has discerningly put it:

> We have tomorrow
> Bright before us
> Like a flame.
>
> Yesterday, a night-gone thing
> A sun-down name.
>
> And dawn today
> Broad arch above the road we came.
> We march!

This is what, even more than any "most creditable record of fifty years of freedom," requires that the Negro of to-day be seen through other than the dusty spectacles of past controversy. The day of "aunties," "uncles" and "mammies" is equally gone. Uncle Tom and Sambo have passed on, and even the "Colonel" and "George" play barnstorm rôles from which they escape with relief when the public spotlight is off. The popular melodrama has about played itself out, and it is time to scrap the fictions, garret the bogeys and settle down to a realistic facing of facts.

First we must observe some of the changes which since the traditional lines of opinion were drawn have rendered these quite obsolete. A main change has been, of course, that shifting of the Negro population which has made the Negro problem no longer exclusively or even predominantly Southern. Why should our minds remain sectionalized, when the problem itself no longer is? Then the trend of migration has not only been toward the North and the Central Midwest, but city-ward and to the great centers of industry—the problems of adjustment are new, practical, local and not peculiarly racial. Rather they are an integral part of the large industrial and social problems of our present-day democracy. And finally, with the Negro rapidly in process of class differentiation, if it ever was warrantable to regard and treat the Negro *en masse* it is becoming with every day less possible, more unjust and more ridiculous.

In the very process of being transplanted, the Negro is becoming transformed.

The tide of Negro migration, northward and city-ward, is not to be fully explained as a blind flood started by the demands of war industry coupled with the shutting off of foreign migration, or by the pressure of poor crops coupled with increased social terrorism in certain sections of the South and Southwest. Neither labor demand, the boll-weevil nor the Ku Klux Klan is a basic factor, however contributory any or all of them may have been. The wash and rush of this human tide on the beach line of the northern city centers is to be explained primarily in terms of a new vision of opportunity, of social and economic freedom, of a spirit to seize, even in the face of an extortionate and heavy toll, a chance for the improvement of conditions. With each successive wave of it, the movement of the Negro becomes more and more a mass movement toward the larger and the more democratic chance—in the Negro's case a deliberate flight not only from countryside to city, but from medieval America to modern.

Take Harlem as an instance of this. Here in Manhattan is not merely the largest Negro community in the world, but the first concentration in history of so many diverse elements of Negro life. It has attracted the African, the West Indian, the Negro American;

has brought together the Negro of the North and the Negro of the South; the man from the city and the man from the town and village; the peasant, the student, the business man, the professional man, artist, poet, musician, adventurer and worker, preacher and criminal, exploiter and social outcast. Each group has come with its own separate motives and for its own special ends, but their greatest experience has been the finding of one another. Proscription and prejudice have thrown these dissimilar elements into a common area of contact and interaction. Within this area, race sympathy and unity have determined a further fusing of sentiment and experience. So what began in terms of segregation becomes more and more, as its elements mix and react, the laboratory of a great race-welding. Hitherto, it must be admitted that American Negroes have been a race more in name than in fact, or to be exact, more in sentiment than in experience. The chief bond between them has been that of a common condition rather than a common consciousness; a problem in common rather than a life in common. In Harlem, Negro life is seizing upon its first chances for group expression and self-determination. It is—or promises at least to be—a race capital. That is why our comparison is taken with those nascent centers of folk-expression and self-determination which are playing a creative part in the world to-day. Without pretense to their political significance, Harlem has the same rôle to play for the New Negro as Dublin has had for the New Ireland or Prague for the New Czechoslovakia.

Harlem, I grant you, isn't typical—but it is significant, it is prophetic. No sane observer, however sympathetic to the new trend, would contend that the great masses are articulate as yet, but they stir, they move, they are more than physically restless. The challenge of the new intellectuals among them is clear enough—the "race radicals" and realists who have broken with the old epoch of philanthropic guidance, sentimental appeal and protest. But are we after all only reading into the stirrings of a sleeping giant the dreams of an agitator? The answer is in the migrating peasant. It is the "man farthest down" who is most active in getting up. One of the most characteristic symptoms of this is the professional man himself migrating to recapture his constituency after a vain effort to maintain in some Southern corner what for years back seemed an established living and clientele. The clergyman following his errant flock, the physician or lawyer trailing his clients, supply the true clues. In a real sense it is the rank and file who are leading, and the leaders who are following. A transformed and transforming psychology permeates the masses.

When the racial leaders of twenty years ago spoke of developing race-pride and stimulating race-consciousness, and of the desirability of race solidarity, they could not in any accurate degree have anticipated the abrupt feeling that has surged up and now pervades the awakened centers. Some of the recognized Negro leaders and a powerful section of white opinion identified with "race work" of the older order have indeed attempted to discount this feeling as a "passing phase," an attack of "race nerves" so to speak, an "aftermath of the war," and the like. It has not abated, however, if we are to gauge by the present tone and temper of the Negro press, or by the shift in popular support from the officially recognized and orthodox spokesmen to those of the independent, popular, and often radical type who are unmistakable symptoms of a new order. It is a social disservice to blunt the fact that the Negro of the Northern centers has reached a stage where tutelage, even of the most interested and well-intentioned sort, must give place to new relationships, where positive self-direction must be reckoned with in ever increasing measure. The American mind must reckon with a fundamentally changed Negro.

The Negro too, for his part, has idols of the tribe to smash. If on the one hand the white man has erred in making the Negro appear to be that which would excuse or extenuate his treatment of him, the Negro, in turn, has too often unnecessarily excused himself because of the way he has been treated. The intelligent Negro of to-day is resolved not to make discrimination an extenuation for his shortcomings in performance, individual or collective; he is trying to hold himself at par, neither inflated by sentimental allowances nor depreciated by current social discounts. For this he must know himself and be known for precisely what he is, and for that reason he welcomes the new scientific rather than the old sentimental interest. Sentimental interest in the Negro has ebbed. We used to lament this as the falling off of our friends; now we rejoice and pray to be delivered both from self-pity and condescension. The mind of each racial group has had a bitter weaning, apathy or hatred on one side matching disillusionment or resentment on the other; but they face each other to-day with the possibility at least of entirely new mutual attitudes.

It does not follow that if the Negro were better known, he would be better liked or better treated. But mutual understanding is basic for any subsequent coöperation and adjustment. The effort toward this will at least have the effect of remedying in large part what has been the most unsatisfactory feature of our present stage of race relationships in America, namely the fact that the more intelligent and representative elements of the two race groups have at so many points got quite out of vital touch with one another.

The fiction is that the life of the races is separate, and increasingly so. The fact is that they have touched too closely at the unfavorable and too lightly at the favorable levels.

While inter-racial councils have sprung up in the South, drawing on forward elements of both races, in the Northern cities manual laborers may brush elbows in their everyday work, but the community and business leaders have experienced no such interplay or far too little of it. These segments must achieve contact or the race situation in America becomes desperate. Fortunately this is happening. There is a growing realization that in social effort the co-operative basis must supplant long-distance philanthropy, and that the only safeguard for mass relations in the future must be provided in the carefully maintained contacts of the enlightened minorities of both race groups. In the intellectual realm a renewed and keen curiosity is replacing the recent apathy; the Negro is being carefully studied, not just talked about and discussed. In art and letters, instead of being wholly caricatured, he is being seriously portrayed and painted.

To all of this the New Negro is keenly responsive as an augury of a new democracy in American culture. He is contributing his share to the new social understanding. But the desire to be understood would never in itself have been sufficient to have opened so completely the protectively closed portals of the thinking Negro's mind. There is still too much possibility of being snubbed or patronized for that. It was rather the necessity for fuller, truer self-expression, the realization of the unwisdom of allowing social discrimination to segregate him mentally, and a counter-attitude to cramp and fetter his own living—and so the "spite-wall" that the intellectuals built over the "color-line" has happily been taken down. Much of this reopening of intellectual contacts has centered in New York and has been richly fruitful not merely in the enlarging of personal experience, but in the definite enrichment of American art and letters and in the clarifying of our common vision of the social tasks ahead.

The particular significance in the re-establishment of contact between the more advanced and representative classes is that it promises to offset some of the unfavorable reactions of the past, or at least to re-surface race contacts somewhat for the future. Subtly the conditions that are molding a New Negro are molding a new American attitude.

However, this new phase of things is delicate; it will call for less charity but more justice; less help, but infinitely closer understanding. This is indeed a critical stage of race relationships because of the likelihood, if the new temper is not understood, of engendering sharp group antagonism and a second crop of more calculated prejudice. In some quarters, it has already done so. Having weaned the Negro, public opinion cannot continue to paternalize. The Negro to-day is inevitably moving forward under the control largely of his own objectives. What are these objectives? Those of his outer life are happily already well and finally formulated, for they are none other than the ideals of American institutions and democracy. Those of his inner life are yet in process of formation, for the new psychology at present is more of a consensus of feeling than of opinion, of attitude rather than of program. Still some points seem to have crystallized.

Up to the present one may adequately describe the Negro's "inner objectives" as an attempt to repair a damaged group psychology and reshape a warped social perspective. Their realization has required a new mentality for the American Negro. And as it matures we begin to see its effects; at first, negative, iconoclastic, and then positive and constructive. In this new group psychology we note the lapse of sentimental appeal, then the development of a more positive self-respect and self-reliance; the repudiation of social dependence, and then the gradual recovery from hypersensitiveness and "touchy" nerves, the repudiation of the double standard of judgment with its special philanthropic allowances and then the sturdier desire for objective and scientific appraisal; and finally the rise from social disillusionment to race pride, from the sense of social debt to the responsibilities of social contribution, and offsetting the necessary working and commonsense acceptance of restricted conditions, the belief in ultimate esteem and recognition. Therefore the Negro to-day wishes to be known for what he is, even in his faults and shortcomings, and scorns a craven and precarious survival at the price of seeming to be what he is not. He resents being spoken of as a social ward or minor, even by his own, and to be regarded a chronic patient for the sociological clinic, the sick man of American Democracy. For the same reasons, he himself is through with those social nostrums and panaceas, the so-called "solutions" of his "problem," with which he and the country have been so liberally dosed in the past. Religion, freedom, education, money—in turn, he has ardently hoped for and peculiarly trusted these things; he still believes in them, but not in blind trust that they alone will solve his life-problem.

Each generation, however, will have its creed, and that of the present is the belief in the efficacy of collective effort, in race co-operation. This deep feeling of race is at present the mainspring of Negro life. It seems to be the outcome of the reaction to proscription and prejudice; an attempt, fairly successful on the whole, to convert a defensive into an offensive position, a handicap into an incentive. It is radical in tone, but not in purpose and only the most stupid forms of opposition, misunderstanding or persecution could make it otherwise. Of course, the thinking Negro has shifted a little toward the left with the world-trend, and there is an increasing group who affiliate with radical and liberal movements. But fundamentally for the present the Negro is radical on race matters, conservative on others, in other words, a "forced radical," a social protestant rather than a genuine radical. Yet under further pressure and injustice iconoclastic thought and motives will inevitably increase. Harlem's quixotic radicalisms call for their ounce of democracy to-day lest to-morrow they be beyond cure.

The Negro mind reaches out as yet to nothing but American wants, American ideas. But this forced attempt to build his Americanism on race values is a unique social experiment, and its ultimate success is impossible except through the fullest sharing of American culture and institutions. There should be no delusion about this. American nerves in sections unstrung with race hysteria are often fed the opiate that the trend of Negro advance is wholly separatist, and that the effect of its operation will be to encyst the Negro as a benign foreign body in the body politic. This cannot be—even if it were desirable. The racialism of the Negro is no limitation or reservation with respect to American life; it is only a constructive effort to build the obstructions in the stream of his progress into an efficient dam of social energy and power. Democracy itself is obstructed and stagnated to the extent that any of its channels are closed. Indeed they cannot be selectively closed. So the choice is not between one way for the Negro and another way for the rest, but between American institutions frustrated on the one hand and American ideals progressively fulfilled and realized on the other.

There is, of course, a warrantably comfortable feeling in being on the right side of the country's professed ideals. We realize that we cannot be undone without America's undoing. It is within the gamut of this attitude that the thinking Negro faces America, but with variations of mood that are if anything more significant than the attitude itself. Sometimes we have it taken with the defiant ironic challenge of McKay:

> Mine is the future grinding down to-day
> Like a great landslip moving to the sea,
> Bearing its freight of debris far away
> Where the green hungry waters restlessly
> Heave mammoth pyramids, and break and roar
> Their eerie challenge to the crumbling shore.

81

Sometimes, perhaps more frequently as yet, it is taken in the fervent and almost filial appeal and counsel of Weldon Johnson's:

> O Southland, dear Southland!
> Then why do you still cling
> To an idle age and a musty page,
> To a dead and useless thing?

But between defiance and appeal, midway almost between cynicism and hope, the prevailing mind stands in the mood of the same author's *To America*, an attitude of sober query and stoical challenge:

> How would you have us, as we are?
>   Or sinking 'neath the load we bear,
> Our eyes fixed forward on a star,
>   Or gazing empty at despair?
>
> Rising or falling? Men or things?
>   With dragging pace or footsteps fleet?
> Strong, willing sinews in your wings,
>   Or tightening chains about your feet?

More and more, however, an intelligent realization of the great discrepancy between the American social creed and the American social practice forces upon the Negro the taking of the moral advantage that is his. Only the steadying and sobering effect of a truly characteristic gentleness of spirit prevents the rapid rise of a definite cynicism and counter-hate and a defiant superiority feeling. Human as this reaction would be, the majority still deprecate its advent, and would gladly see it forestalled by the speedy amelioration of its causes. We wish our race pride to be a healthier, more positive achievement than a feeling based upon a realization of the shortcomings of others. But all paths toward the attainment of a sound social attitude have been difficult; only a relatively few enlightened minds have been able as the phrase puts it "to rise above" prejudice. The ordinary man has had until recently only a hard choice between the alternatives of supine and humiliating submission and stimulating but hurtful counter-prejudice. Fortunately from some inner, desperate resourcefulness has recently sprung up the simple expedient of fighting prejudice by mental passive resistance, in other words by trying to ignore it. For the few, this manna may perhaps be effective, but the masses cannot thrive upon it.

Fortunately there are constructive channels opening out into

which the balked social feelings of the American Negro can flow
freely.

Without them there would be much more pressure and danger
than there is. These compensating interests are racial but in a new
and enlarged way. One is the consciousness of acting as the ad-
vance-guard of the African peoples in their contact with Twentieth
Century civilization; the other, the sense of a mission of rehabili-
tating the race in world esteem from that loss of prestige for which
the fate and conditions of slavery have so largely been responsible.
Harlem, as we shall see, is the center of both these movements;
she is the home of the Negro's "Zionism." The pulse of the Negro
world has begun to beat in Harlem. A Negro newspaper carrying
news material in English, French and Spanish, gathered from all
quarters of America, the West Indies and Africa has maintained
itself in Harlem for over five years. Two important magazines, both
edited from New York, maintain their news and circulation consistently on a cosmopolitan scale. Under American auspices and
backing, three pan-African congresses have been held abroad for
the discussion of common interests, colonial questions and the
future co-operative development of Africa. In terms of the race
question as a world problem, the Negro mind has leapt, so to speak,
upon the parapets of prejudice and extended its cramped horizons.
In so doing it has linked up with the growing group consciousness
of the dark-peoples and is gradually learning their common interests. As one of our writers has recently put it: "It is imperative
that we understand the white world in its relations to the non-
white world." As with the Jew, persecution is making the Negro
international.

As a world phenomenon this wider race consciousness is a
different thing from the much asserted rising tide of color. Its
inevitable causes are not of our making. The consequences are not
necessarily damaging to the best interests of civilization. Whether
it actually brings into being new Armadas of conflict or argosies
of cultural exchange and enlightenment can only be decided by
the attitude of the dominant races in an era of racial change. With
the American Negro, his new internationalism is primarily an effort
to recapture contact with the scattered peoples of African deriva-
tion. Garveyism may be a transient, if spectacular, phenomenon,
but the possible rôle of the American Negro in the future development of Africa is one of the most constructive and universally
helpful missions that any modern people can lay claim to.

Constructive participation in such causes cannot help giving
the Negro valuable group incentives, as well as increased prestige
at home and abroad. Our greatest rehabilitation may possibly come

through such channels, but for the present, more immediate hope rests in the revaluation by white and black alike of the Negro in terms of his artistic endowments and cultural contributions, past and prospective. It must be increasingly recognized that the Negro has already made very substantial contributions, not only in his folk-art, music especially, which has always found appreciation, but in larger, though humbler and less acknowledged ways. For generations the Negro has been the peasant matrix of that section of America which has most undervalued him, and here he has contributed not only materially in labor and in social patience, but spiritually as well. The South has unconsciously absorbed the gift of his folk-temperament. In less than half a generation it will be easier to recognize this, but the fact remains that a leaven of humor, sentiment, imagination and tropic nonchalance has gone into the making of the South from a humble, unacknowledged source. A second crop of the Negro's gifts promises still more largely. He now becomes a conscious contributor and lays aside the status of a beneficiary and ward for that of a collaborator and participant in American civilization. The great social gain in this is the releasing of our talented group from the arid fields of controversy and debate to the productive fields of creative expression. The especially cultural recognition they win should in turn prove the key to that revaluation of the Negro which must precede or accompany any considerable further betterment of race relationships. But whatever the general effect, the present generation will have added the motives of self-expression and spiritual development to the old and still unfinished task of making material headway and progress. No one who understandingly faces the situation with its substantial accomplishment or views the new scene with its still more abundant promise can be entirely without hope. And certainly, if in our lifetime the Negro should not be able to celebrate his full initiation into American democracy, he can at least, on the warrant of these things, celebrate the attainment of a significant and satisfying new phase of group development, and with it a spiritual Coming of Age.

CLAUDE MCKAY
1890-1948

Claude McKay was born in Sunny Ville, in the region of Clarendon Hills, Jamaica, on September 15, 1890. He lived with his parents until he was six years old and then stayed with his older brother, a schoolteacher and a lay preacher for the Anglican Church. The brother, a freethinker, exercised great influence on McKay's early development, persuading the boy to read writers like Huxley, Lecky, and Gibbon and espousing an agnostic religious position that the boy later adopted himself. At the age of sixteen McKay met an English squire, Walter Jekyll, also an agnostic, who widened the young writer's interests by introducing him to some of the major English and American poets. McKay's formal training helped him bring a technical authority to the writing of even his earliest verse.

Walter Jekyll was a specialist in the folklore of Jamaica, and he taught McKay how to use native dialect in his first poems. McKay began to experience the double life of so many poets: he wrote verse at the same time that he earned a living at a variety of jobs that held little attraction for him. When he was seventeen he received a Government Trade Scholarship and apprenticed himself as a cabinet-maker; two years later he joined the island constabulary. But he was never content with these routine positions and he continued to express himself in verse that was strongly characterized by the Jamaican dialect. His early poems were published under the titles of *Constab Ballads* (1912) and *Songs from Jamaica* (1912).

McKay came to the United States in 1912 and studied for a short time at Tuskegee Institute. He did not like the military discipline of the school, however, and transferred to the department of agriculture at Kansas State University. But he soon realized that he had no professional interest in agriculture, and with a legacy of several thousand dollars, he traveled to Harlem and became a free-lance writer. Unable to earn an income through his pen, he held a variety of jobs: he was a porter, a houseman, a longshoreman, a barman, and a waiter in dining cars and hotels. Slowly, however, the poetry that he had been writing during this period gained notice. In 1917 he published poems like "The Harlem Dancer" and "Invocation" under a pseudonym, Eli Edwards; by 1920 C. K. Ogden, the author of *The Meaning of Meaning* and the editor of *The Cambridge Magazine* in London, was publishing all of the poems that McKay could write, in his own name. McKay had gone to England and in that country his next volume of poems, *Spring in New Hampshire, and other poems* (1920), appeared.

McKay returned to New York in 1921 and served as an associate editor of *The Liberator* and *The Masses*. In 1922 he brought out his most important book of poems, *Harlem Shadows*. McKay was to write novels, exotic autobiography, social studies of Negro life, and religious pamphlets in his later career, but he never achieved the poignant lyricism and effective protest that one finds in the sonnets and lyrics of *Harlem Shadows*.

During the 1920's, McKay was politically attracted to Communism, and he traveled to Russia in 1922 and met Lenin and Trotsky. In a famous address before the Third Internationale, which he delivered as a representative of the American Workers' Party, McKay stressed that Negroes in the United States were often lynched, denied the right of free assembly, and driven into racial animosities because of class differences. He grew physically ill in Russia, because of poor sanitary conditions, and decided to leave the country. His subsequent travels took him throughout Western Europe and Africa—to Germany and Southern France, where he lived happily for several years, to Spain and to Morocco.

When he returned to America, McKay began to publish his prose fiction. *Home to Harlem* (1928), which received the Harmon Gold Award medal, depicts the saturnalian qualities of Harlem life; *Banjo* (1929) portrays the harbor life at Marseilles; the stories in *Gingertown* (1932) are set in Harlem and Jamaica and deal with racial prejudice and with McKay's memories of his childhood in Jamaica; *Banana Bottom* (1933) describes Jamaica in the early 1900's; *A Long Way from Home* (1937) is a rather impressionistic autobiography; and *Harlem: Negro Metropolis* (1940) is a sociological study of the Negro community in New York.

In 1938 McKay met Ellen Terry, a Roman Catholic and a writer of children's books; she, together with Bishop Skeil of Chicago, persuaded the writer to convert to Catholicism and on October 11, 1944, McKay became a Roman Catholic. Much of his later writing, in the form of essays and pamphlets, reflects his religious orientation. After a long illness McKay died in 1948, celebrated as a significant writer of the Negro Awakening.

In the introduction to *Harlem Shadows,* McKay emphasizes his training by English as opposed to American teachers. His rhymes and meters are traditional, modeled after the great English poets; and his own approach to composition, as he suggests, is quite self-conscious: "I have chosen my melodies and rhythms by instinct, and I have favored words and figures which flow smoothly and harmoniously into my compositions." Thus McKay identifies the two prominent characteristics of his poetry: in spirit his verse is Romantic, creating the impression of spontaneity and exploring the roots of common people; in technique his sonnets and lyrics are conventional. He was called "a kind of Robert Burns among his own people," and the description is apposite; one finds in his early dialect poems, published in *Songs of Jamaica,* tributes to the pastoral beauty of Jamaica that are given a poignant immediacy and power by the realistic, seemingly "unpoetic" details of everyday life.

McKay's most enduring poems are his sonnets. Although he had written of love in some of his early lyrics and continued to describe various aspects of love in his more mature verse, McKay's best sonnets resemble most closely those polemical, social sonnets of Milton and Wordsworth. He can be bitter and rebellious, musing upon his "life-long hate," as in "Baptism," "The White City," and "If We Must Die"; he can deplore economic and social evils, as in "White Houses" or "In Bondage"; he can lament the illicit and pagan love of Negro prostitutes, "the sacred brown feet of [his] fallen race," as in "Harlem Shadows," "The Harlem Dancer," or "On Broadway." The subject of his finest poems varies, but the theme of protest is consistent and the moods of anger, frustration, or lament are pervasive; in all of these poems McKay insists that Negroes acknowledge and protest their common suffering, that they assert their dignity and "like men . . . face the murderous, cowardly pack,/Pressed to the wall, dying, but fighting back!" Although McKay wrote many poems dealing with the beauties of Jamaica, the nostalgia for his home and for his mother, and the infidelity of love—subjects which are represented by a few of the poems selected—his most engaging verse expresses a militant protest that reflects the social reality of his time.

McKay's novels explore similar ideas, but they suffer from sentimental excess and a diffusion of point of view; they have the sensationalism but little of the horror of Gothic fiction. *Home to Harlem, Banjo,* and *Banana Bottom* are interesting attempts to express the frustrations of being black, of living in a surreal world whose morality and social behavior are forever shifting in response to a white society. McKay's work in other genres also suffers from his tendency to state his case *in extremis: A Long Way from Home* (1937) is too self-consciously literary and artificial to be a truly poignant autobiography; *Harlem: Negro Metropolis* (1940) is serviceable sociology, but it is highly impressionistic.

Claude McKay's significance as a poet is best represented by the slender volume, *Harlem Shadows* (1922). That collection of sonnets and lyrics, expressing the varieties of discontent felt by so many Negroes, exhibits the poet's distinctive qualities: his realism and social consciousness; his early paganism; his sensitivity to the suffering of his people. McKay is an interesting poet of the postwar period; like so many other writers of the Awakening, he reflects, from a point of view rarely expressed, the deliquescence of traditional values, the refusal to accept the stereotypes and myths of another generation. More than any of his black contemporaries, McKay converts social polemicism and protest into poems of permanent value.

America

Although she feeds me bread of bitterness,
And sinks into my throat her tiger's tooth,
Stealing my breath of life, I will confess
I love this cultured hell that tests my youth!
Her vigor flows like tides into my blood,
Giving me strength erect against her hate.
Her bigness sweeps my being like a flood.
Yet as a rebel fronts a king in state,
I stand within her walls with not a shred
Of terror, malice, not a word of jeer.
Darkly I gaze into the days ahead,
And see her might and granite wonders there,
Beneath the touch of Time's unerring hand,
Like priceless treasures sinking in the sand.

The White House*

Your door is shut against my tightened face,
And I am sharp as steel with discontent;
But I possess the courage and the grace
To bear my anger proudly and unbent.
The pavement slabs burn loose beneath my feet,
A chafing savage, down the decent street;
And passion rends my vitals as I pass,
Where boldly shines your shuttered door of glass.

* "My title was symbolic . . . it had no reference to the official residence of the President of the United States. . . . The title 'White Houses' changed the whole symbolic intent and meaning of the poem, making it appear as if the burning ambition of the black malcontent was to enter white houses in general." Claude McKay: *A Long Way from Home* (1937), pp. 313–314.

Oh, I must search for wisdom every hour,
Deep in my wrathful bosom sore and raw,
And find in it the superhuman power
To hold me to the letter of your law!
Oh, I must keep my heart inviolate
Against the potent poison of your hate.

Harlem Dancer

Applauding youths laughed with young prostitutes
And watched her perfect, half-clothed body sway;
Her voice was like the sound of blended flutes
Blown by black players on a picnic day.
She sang and danced on gracefully and calm,
The light gauze hanging loose about her form;
To me she seemed a proudly-swaying palm
Grown lovelier for passing through a storm.
Upon her swarthy neck black shiny curls
Luxuriant fell; and tossing coins in praise,
The wine-flushed, bold-eyed boys, and even the girls,
Devoured her shape with eager, passionate gaze;
But looking at her falsely-smiling face,
I knew her self was not in that strange place.

In Bondage

I would be wandering in distant fields
Where man, and bird, and beast, lives leisurely,
And the old earth is kind, and ever yields
Her goodly gifts to all her children free;
Where life is fairer, lighter, less demanding,
And boys and girls have time and space for play
Before they come to years of understanding—
Somewhere I would be singing, far away.
For life is greater than the thousand wars
Men wage for it in their insatiate lust,
And will remain like the eternal stars,
When all that shines to-day is drift and dust
But I am bound with you in your mean graves,
O black men, simple slaves of ruthless slaves.

Harlem Shadows

I hear the halting footsteps of a lass
    In Negro Harlem when the night lets fall
Its veil. I see the shapes of girls who pass
    To bend and barter at desire's call.
Ah, little dark girls who in slippered feet
Go prowling through the night from street to street!

Through the long night until the silver break
    Of day the little gray feet know no rest;
Through the lone night until the last snow-flake
    Has dropped from heaven upon the earth's white breast,
The dusky, half-clad girls of tired feet
Are trudging, thinly shod, from street to street.

Ah, stern harsh world, that in the wretched way
   Of poverty, dishonor and disgrace,
Has pushed the timid little feet of clay,
   The sacred brown feet of my fallen race!
Ah, heart of me, the weary, weary feet
In Harlem wandering from street to street.

The White City

I will not toy with it nor bend an inch.
Deep in the secret chambers of my heart
I muse my life-long hate, and without flinch
I bear it nobly as I live my part.
My being would be a skeleton, a shell,
If this dark Passion that fills my every mood,
And makes my heaven in the white world's hell,
Did not forever feed me vital blood.
I see the mighty city through a mist—
The strident trains that speed the goaded mass,
The poles and spires and towers vapor-kissed,
The fortressed port through which the great ships pass,
The tides, the wharves, the dens I contemplate,
Are sweet like wanton loves because I hate.

North and South

O sweet are tropic lands for waking dreams!
There time and life move lazily along.
There by the banks of blue-and-silver streams
    Grass-sheltered crickets chirp incessant song,
Gay-colored lizards loll all through the day,
    Their tongues outstretched for careless little flies,
And swarthy children in the fields at play,
    Look upward laughing at the smiling skies.
A breath of idleness is in the air
    That casts a subtle spell upon all things,
And love and mating-time are everywhere,
    And wonder to life's commonplaces clings.
The fluttering humming-bird darts through the trees
    And dips his long beak in the big bell-flowers,
The leisured buzzard floats upon the breeze,
    Riding a crescent cloud for endless hours,
The sea beats softly on the emerald strands—
O sweet for quiet dreams are tropic lands!

Baptism

Into the furnace let me go alone;
Stay you without in terror of the heat.
I will go naked in—for thus 'tis sweet—
Into the weird depths of the hottest zone.
I will not quiver in the frailest bone,
You will not note a flicker of defeat;
My heart shall tremble not its fate to meet,
My mouth give utterance to any moan.
The yawning oven spits forth fiery spears;
Red aspish tongues shout wordlessly my name.

Desire destroys, consumes my mortal fears,
Transforming me into a shape of flame.
I will come out, back to your world of tears,
A stronger soul within a finer frame.

If We Must Die

If we must die, let it not be like hogs
Hunted and penned in an inglorious spot,
While round us bark the mad and hungry dogs,
Making their mock at our accursèd lot.
If we must die, O let us nobly die,
So that our precious blood may not be shed
In vain; then even the monsters we defy
Shall be constrained to honor us though dead!
O kinsmen! we must meet the common foe!
Though far outnumbered let us show us brave,
And for their thousand blows deal one death-blow!
What though before us lies the open grave?
Like men we'll face the murderous, cowardly pack,
Pressed to the wall, dying, but fighting back!

"America," "The White House," "Harlem Dancer," "In Bondage," "Harlem Shadows," "The City White," "North and South," "Baptism," and "If We Must Die" reprinted from *Selected Poems of Claude McKay* (New York: Twayne Publishers, Inc., 1953).

JEAN TOOMER

1894-1967   "I am of no particular race, I am of the human race, a man at large in the human world, preparing a new race." The author of this proclamation is Jean Toomer, although he could easily be mistaken for Whitman or Emerson, whose self-assertion is also informed by a pervasive idealism. Toomer's poetic heroes were visionaries—Dante and Blake, as well as the American transcendentalists; and he believed that "we do not have states of being; we have states of dreaming." Furthermore, the expansive observation, which appears in a privately printed volume of defini- tions and aphorisms called *Essentials* (1931), suggests Toomer's persistent attempt to transcend the limitations of race and to con- centrate on what he termed his "first values: Understanding, Con- science, and Ability." The key word in this trinity of belief is conscience; for as we consider Toomer's artistic development, we are drawn inward by his increasing introspection, his attention to the mind rather than to the world of experience. Toomer's first and most enduring work of art, *Cane* (1923), focuses upon the senses and the ways in which they confront reality; his last published work, *The Flavor of Man* (1949), is a consecration to the life of the spirit, in which he attempts to convince us that "the alterna- tives of life are starkly these: transcendence or extinction."

The available facts of Jean Toomer's life only touch upon the inner pattern of his mind. Born on December 26, 1894, in Wash- ington, D.C., he was educated in the public schools of Washington, the University of Wisconsin (1914–1915), where he went to study law, and for another short period in the City College of New York. He taught in the schools of Sparta, Georgia, and much of the background to *Cane* stems from that experience.

Toomer was a restless man. In the twenties and thirties he settled at various times in New York, Chicago, and in Carmel, California. In New York he established himself as an important figure in the Negro Awakening, largely through the publication of *Cane*. His greatest, really his only, period of literary activity was in the twenties when his stories, essays, and poems appeared in *The Double Dealer, Broom, Opportunity, Crisis, The Little Review, Secession,* and other experimental and short-lived magazines. He formed friendships with many prominent writers of the 1920's, particularly with a coterie that included Hart Crane, Kenneth Burke, Gorham Munson, and Waldo Frank. Drawn to mysticism, Toomer was so affected by the Russian Gurdjieff that he spent part of the summer in 1926 at the Gurdjieff Institute in Fontainebleau, France. On August 22, 1932, he married the novelist, Margery Latimer, in Portage, Wisconsin, and the couple lived in Chicago until Toomer's wife died in childbirth. In November 1934, he married Marjorie Content, the daughter of a financial broker.

At the time of his second marriage Toomer, who was fair-skinned, was asked whether he was colored or white; his response suggests some of the tensions that inform *Cane* and his other works.

> I would consider it libelous for anyone to refer to me as a colored man, but I have not lived as one, nor do I really know whether there is any colored blood in me or not.
> My maternal grandfather, Pickney Bentor Stewart Pinchback, was the "carpet-bag" governor of Louisiana. In order to gain colored votes, he referred to himself as having colored blood.
> His two brothers never did so, however; so the fact is, I do not know whether colored blood flows through my veins.

Toomer's self-consciousness stems not only from the fact that his own color was almost white but also from his marriage to two white women. There is little question that his ancestry was predominantly Negro, however, and his best work focuses upon racial issues, although they are always seen in human rather than political or sociological terms. Each of the significant stories in *Cane* is strengthened by racial consciousness; the short novel, "York Beach," included in *The New American Caravan* in 1929, suggests the tensions that stem from racial differences; a long essay, "Race Problems and Modern Society" (1929), discusses the Negro's role in a predominantly white culture; and *Essentials,* a book of private meditations, recognizes the fact that "races are real; but, to men, races are prejudices."

Essentials defines Toomer's attempt to transcend the specific problems of race. He had come to feel that "Walt Whitman's average man has turned out to be Babbitt," that his generation had "two emblems, namely, the machine-gun and the contraceptive." Toomer sought to "reject compromises which give you nothing because they give you less than you want" and to insist upon the significance of man's conscience. In spite of his disillusionment with a country in which materialism was of paramount importance, Toomer still felt that "conscience, the heart of the human world, still beats feebly in our sense of decency."

Toomer ceased to write extensively after 1931. "The Flavor of Man," an address delivered to a group of Quakers at Philadelphia in 1949, suggests his allegiance to the Society of Friends, his concentration on man's spiritual condition, and his deep faith in God. "Evil is evil only because it separates our consciousness from God . . . Pain is pain only because we lack realization that we are related to divinity." Although Toomer discovered what he described as a "renewal of faith," he never transcribed that faith into fiction or poetry of significance; he died in 1967. His achievement as an artist is represented by that potpourri of stories, poems, and anecdotes entitled *Cane,* a classic of Negro literature, *sui generis,* which succeeds in capturing the quality of youthful striving and the frustrations that attend the transition from adolescence to maturity.

Cane is a miscellany of Toomer's early work, containing fictional portraits and poems of life in the villages of Georgia and in Washington, D.C. The language is impressionistic and richly textured. As a consequence, the poetry included in the volume is burdened by incremental repetitions and tends to blur before the eye like a loosely conceived verbal painting; but the fiction—particularly short stories such as "Becky," "Fern," "Esther," "Blood Burning Moon," and "Avey"—is a vivid depiction of young people at moments of intense and often primitive passion. Usually the conflict is racial; usually the victim has mixed blood; and frequently he or she is left disillusioned, like the figures in Sherwood Anderson's *Winesburg, Ohio,* as ideals or dreams are destroyed by the sudden awareness of reality. In "Becky," a white woman who has two Negro sons becomes a pariah to both Negroes and whites; in "Fern," the girl, whose name is Fernie May Rosen, is doubly scarred by a Jewish father and a Negro mother; in "Blood Burning

Moon," a Negro field hand kills the white lover and owner of the colored cook whom he loves himself and is burned alive by the community.

These poignant stories are, for the most part, elaborate character sketches, a gallery of portraits of life in Georgia and in Washington, D.C. The situations and events that Toomer presents are realistic in all their details, and most of them, when recounted, are filled with violence, murder, and human misery; but they are not depressing or morbid because of the author's attitude toward his characters and because of his graceful, tender style. Toomer never judges his characters; in describing their most debased behavior, he always reminds us of their humanity, and he brings a respect to them that inevitably becomes our respect. The facts are realistically and honestly rendered; but they are given the romantic coloring of Toomer's moral imagination. At his best, Toomer does not view their vague desires and failures as pathetic. The frustrated lovers of "Theater" and "Box Seat"; "Rhobert," the man with rickets; "Carma," the unfaithful wife; "Karintha," the prostitute— all these figures are fallible human beings rather than victims.

"Esther" and "Avey," the two stories included here, illustrate Toomer's special talents as a writer and his compassion for those people who do not have the strength to triumph over their limitations.

Esther

1

N I N E .

E S T H E R ' S   H A I R falls in soft curls about her high-cheek-boned chalk-white face. Esther's hair would be beautiful if there were more gloss to it. And if her face were not prematurely serious, one would call it pretty. Her cheeks are too flat and dead for a girl of nine. Esther looks like a little white child, starched, frilled, as she walks slowly from her home towards her father's grocery store. She is about to turn in Broad from Maple Street. White and black men loafing on the corner hold no interest for her. Then a strange thing happens. A clean-muscled, magnificent, black-skinned Negro, whom she had heard her father mention as King Barlo, suddenly drops to his knees on a spot called the Spittoon. White men, unaware of him, continue squirting tobacco juice in his direction. The saffron fluid splashes on his face. His smooth black face begins to glisten and to shine. Soon, people notice him, and gather round. His eyes are rapturous upon the heavens. Lips and nostrils quiver. Barlo is in a religious trance. Town folks know it. They are not startled. They are not afraid. They gather round. Some beg boxes from the grocery stores. From old McGregor's notion shop. A coffin-case is pressed into use. Folks line the curb-stones. Business men close shop. And Banker Warply parks his car close by. Silently, all await the prophet's voice. The sheriff, a great florid fellow whose leggings never meet around his bulging calves, swears in three deputies. "Wall, y cant never tell what a nigger like King Barlo might be up t." Soda bottles, five fingers full of shine, are passed to those who want them. A couple of stray dogs start a fight. Old Goodlow's cow comes flopping up the street. Barlo, still as an Indian fakir, has not moved. The town bell strikes six. The sun slips in behind a heavy mass of horizon cloud. The crowd is hushed and expectant. Barlo's under jaw relaxes, and his lips begin to move.

"Jesus has been awhisperin strange words deep down, O way down deep, deep in my ears."

Hums of awe and of excitement.

"He called me to His side an said, 'Git down on your knees beside me, son, Ise gwine t whisper in your ears.'"

An old sister cries, "Ah, Lord."

"'Ise agwine t whisper in your ears,' he said, an I replied, 'Thy will be done on earth as it is in heaven.'"

"Ah, Lord. Amen. Amen."

"An Lord Jesus whispered strange good words deep down, O way down deep, deep in my ears. An He said, 'Tell em till you feel your throat on fire.' I saw a vision. I saw a man arise, an he was big an black an powerful—"

Some one yells, "Preach it, preacher, preach it!"

"—but his head was caught up in th clouds. An while he was agazin at th heavens, heart filled up with th Lord, some little white-ant biddies came an tied his feet to chains. They led him t th coast, they led him t th sea, they led him across th ocean an they didnt set him free. The old coast didnt miss him, an th new coast wasnt free, he left the old-coast brothers, t give birth t you an me. O Lord, great God Almighty, t give birth t you an me."

Barlo pauses. Old gray mothers are in tears. Fragments of melodies are being hummed. White folks are touched and curiously awed. Off to themselves, white and black preachers confer as to how best to rid themselves of the vagrant, usurping fellow. Barlo looks as though he is struggling to continue. People are hushed. One can hear weevils work. Dusk is falling rapidly, and the customary store lights fail to throw their feeble glow across the gray dust and flagging of the Georgia town. Barlo rises to his full height. He is immense. To the people he assumes the outlines of his visioned African. In a mighty voice he bellows:

"Brothers an sisters, turn your faces t th sweet face of the Lord, an fill your hearts with glory. Open your eyes an see th dawnin of th mornin light. Open your ears—"

Years afterwards Esther was told that at that very moment a great, heavy, rumbling voice actually was heard. That hosts of angels and of demons paraded up and down the streets all night. That King Barlo rode out of town astride a pitch-black bull that had a glowing gold ring in its nose. And that old Limp Underwood, who hated niggers, woke up next morning to find that he held a black man in his arms. This much is certain: an inspired Negress, of wide reputation for being sanctified, drew a portrait of a black madonna on the court-house wall. And King Barlo left town. He left his image indelibly upon the mind of Esther. He became the starting point of the only living patterns that her mind was to know.

2

SIXTEEN.

Esther begins to dream. The low evening sun sets the windows of McGregor's notion shop aflame. Esther makes believe that they really are aflame. The town fire department rushes madly down the road. It ruthlessly shoves black and white idlers to one side. It whoops. It clangs. It rescues from the second-story window a dimpled infant which she claims for her own. How had she come by it? She thinks of it immaculately. It is a sin to think of it immaculately. She must dream no more. She must repent her sin. Another dream comes. There is no fire department. There are no heroic men. The fire starts. The loafers on the corner form a circle, chew their tobacco faster, and squirt juice just as fast as they can chew. Gallons on top of gallons they squirt upon the flames. The air reeks with the stench of scorched tobacco juice. Women, fat chunky Negro women, lean scrawny white women, pull their skirts up above their heads and display the most ludicrous underclothes. The women scoot in all directions from the danger zone. She alone is left to take the baby in her arms. But what a baby! Black, singed, woolly, tobacco-juice baby—ugly as sin. Once held to her breast, miraculous thing: its breath is sweet and its lips can nibble. She loves it frantically. Her joy in it changes the town folks' jeers to harmless jealousy, and she is left alone.

TWENTY-TWO.

Esther's schooling is over. She works behind the counter of her father's grocery store. "To keep the money in the family," so he said. She is learning to make distinctions between the business and the social worlds. "Good business comes from remembering that the white folks dont divide the niggers, Esther. Be just as black as any man who has a silver dollar." Esther listlessly forgets that she is near white, and that her father is the richest colored man in town. Black folk who drift in to buy lard and snuff and flour of her, call her a sweet-natured, accommodating girl. She learns their names. She forgets them. She thinks about men. "I dont appeal to them. I wonder why." She recalls an affair she had with a little fair boy while still in school. It had ended in her shame when he as much as told her that for sweetness he preferred a lollipop. She remembers the salesman from the North who wanted to take her to the movies that first night he was in town. She refused, of course. And he never came back, having found out who she was. She thinks of Barlo. Barlo's image gives her a slightly stale thrill. She spices it by telling herself his glories. Black. Magnetically so. Best cotton picker in the county, in the state, in the whole world for that matter. Best man with his fists, best man with dice, with a razor. Promoter of church benefits. Of colored fairs. Vagrant preacher. Lover of all the women for miles and miles around. Esther decides that she loves him. And with a vague sense of life slipping by, she resolves that she will tell him so, whatever people say, the next time he comes to town. After the making of this resolution which becomes a sort of wedding cake for her to tuck beneath her pillow and go to sleep upon, she sees nothing of Barlo for five years. Her hair thins. It looks like the dull silk on puny corn ears. Her face pales until it is the color of the gray dust that dances with dead cotton leaves.

3

ESTHER IS TWENTY-SEVEN.

Esther sells lard and snuff and flour to vague black faces that drift in her store to ask for them. Her eyes hardly see the people to whom she gives change. Her body is lean and beaten. She rests listlessly against the counter, too weary to sit down. From the street some one shouts, "King Barlo has come back to town." He passes her window, driving a large new car. Cut-out open. He veers to the curb, and steps out. Barlo has made money on cotton during the war. He is as rich as anyone. Esther suddenly is animate. She goes to her door. She sees him at a distance, the center of a group of credulous men. She hears the deep-bass rumble of his talk. The sun swings low. McGregor's windows are aflame again. Pale flame. A sharply dressed white girl passes by. For a moment Esther wishes that she might be like her. Not white; she has no need for being that. But sharp, sporty, with get-up about her. Barlo is connected with that wish. She mustnt wish. Wishes only make you restless. Emptiness is a thing that grows by being moved. "I'll not think. Not wish. Just set my mind against it." Then the thought comes to her that those purposeless, easy-going men will possess him, if she doesnt. Purpose is not dead in her, now that she comes to think of it. That loose women will have their arms around him at Nat Bowle's place to-night. As if her veins are full of fired sun-bleached southern shanties, a swift heat sweeps them. Dead dreams, and a forgotten resolution are carried upward by the flames. Pale flames. "They shant have him. Oh, they shall not. Not if it kills me they shant have him." Jerky, aflutter, she closes the store and starts home. Folks lazing on store window-sills wonder what on earth can be the matter with Jim Crane's gal, as she passes them. "Come to remember, she always was a little off, a little crazy, I reckon." Esther seeks her own room, and locks the door. Her mind is a pink mesh-bag filled with baby toes.

Using the noise of the town clock striking twelve to cover the creaks of her departure, Esther slips into the quiet road. The town, her parents, most everyone is sound asleep. This fact is a stable thing that comforts her. After sundown a chill wind came up from the west. It is still blowing, but to her it is a steady, settled thing like the cold. She wants her mind to be like that. Solid, contained, and blank as a sheet of darkened ice. She will not permit herself to notice the peculiar phosphorescent glitter of the sweet-gum leaves. Their movement would excite her. Exciting too, the recession of the dull familiar homes she knows so well. She doesnt know them at all. She closes her eyes, and holds them tightly. Wont do. Her being aware that they are closed recalls her purpose. She does not want to think of it. She opens them. She turns now into the deserted business street. The corrugated iron canopies and mule- and horse-gnawed hitching posts bring her a strange composure. Ghosts of the commonplaces of her daily life take stride with her and become her companions. And the echoes of her heels upon the flagging are rhythmically monotonous and soothing. Crossing the street at the corner of McGregor's notion shop, she thinks that the windows are a dull flame. Only a fancy. She walks faster. Then runs. A turn into a side street brings her abruptly to Nat Bowle's place. The house is squat and dark. It is always dark. Barlo is within. Quietly she opens the outside door and steps in. She passes through a small room. Pauses before a flight of stairs down which people's voices, muffled, come. The air is heavy with fresh tobacco smoke. It makes her sick. She wants to turn back. She goes up the steps. As if she were mounting to some great height, her head spins. She is violently dizzy. Blackness rushes to her eyes. And then she finds that she is in a large room. Barlo is before her.

"Well, I'm sholy damned—skuse me, but what, what brought you here, lil milk-white gal?"

"You." Her voice sounds like a frightened child's that calls homeward from some point miles away.

"Me?"

"Yes, you Barlo."

"This aint th place fer y. This aint th place fer y."

"I know. I know. But I've come for you."

"For me for what?"

She manages to look deep and straight into his eyes. He is

slow at understanding. Guffaws and giggles break out from all around the room. A coarse woman's voice remarks, "So thats how th dictie niggers does it." Laughs. "Mus give em credit fo their gall."

Esther doesnt hear. Barlo does. His faculties are jogged. She sees a smile, ugly and repulsive to her, working upward through thick licker fumes. Barlo seems hideous. The thought comes suddenly, that conception with a drunken man must be a mighty sin. She draws away, frozen. Like a somnambulist she wheels around and walks stiffly to the stairs. Down them. Jeers and hoots pelter bluntly upon her back. She steps out. There is no air, no street, and the town has completely disappeared.

Avey

FOR A LONG WHILE she was nothing more to me than one of those skirted beings whom boys at a certain age disdain to play with. Just how I came to love her, timidly, and with secret blushes, I do not know. But that I did was brought home to me one night, the first night that Ned wore his long pants. Us fellers were seated on the curb before an apartment house where she had gone in. The young trees had not outgrown their boxes then. V Street was lined with them. When our legs grew cramped and stiff from the cold of the stone, we'd stand around a box and whittle it. I like to think now that there was a hidden purpose in the way we hacked them with our knives. I like to feel that something deep in me responded to the trees, the young trees that whinnied like colts impatient to be let free. . . On the particular night I have in mind, we were waiting for the top-floor light to go out. We wanted to see Avey leave the flat. This night she stayed longer than usual and gave us a chance to complete the plans of how we were going to stone and beat that feller on the top floor out of town. Ned especially had it in for him. He was about to throw a brick up at the window when at last the room went dark. Some

From *Cane*, by Jean Toomer. Permission by Liveright, Publishers, New York, N.Y. Copyright © Renewed, 1951 by Jean Toomer.

minutes passed. Then Avey, as unconcerned as if she had been paying and old-maid aunt a visit, came out. I dont remember what she had on, and all that sort of thing. But I do know that I turned hot as bare pavements in the summertime at Ned's boast: "Hell, bet I could get her too if you little niggers weren't always spying and crabbing everything." I didnt say a word to him. It wasnt my way then. I just stood there like the others, and something like a fuse burned up inside of me. She never noticed us, but swung along lazy and easy as anything. We sauntered to the corner and watched her till her door banged to. Ned repeated what he'd said. I didnt seem to care. Sitting around old Mush-Head's bread box, the discussion began. "Hang if I can see how she gets away with it," Doc started. Ned knew, of course. There was nothing he didnt know when it came to women. He dilated on the emotional needs of girls. Said they werent much different from men in that respect. And concluded with the solemn avowal: "It does em good." None of us liked Ned much. We all talked dirt; but it was the way he said it. And then too, a couple of the fellers had sisters and had caught Ned playing with them. But there was no disputing the superiority of his smutty wisdom. Bubs Sanborn, whose mother was friendly with Avey's, had overheard the old ladies talking. "Avey's mother ont her," he said. We thought that only natural and began to guess at what would happen. Some one said she'd marry that feller on the top floor. Ned called that a lie because Avey was going to marry nobody but him. We had our doubts about that, but we did agree that she'd soon leave school and marry some one. The gang broke up, and I went home, picturing myself as married.

Nothing I did seemed able to change Avey's indifference to me. I played basket-ball, and when I'd make a long clean shot she'd clap with the others, louder than they, I thought. I'd meet her on the street, and there'd be no difference in the way she said hello. She never took the trouble to call me by my name. On the days for drill, I'd let my voice down a tone and call for a complicated maneuver when I saw her coming. She'd smile appreciation, but it was an impersonal smile, never for me. It was on a summer excursion down to Riverview that she first seemed to take me into account. The day had been spent riding merry-go-rounds, scenic-railways, and shoot-the-chutes. We had been in swimming and we had danced. I was a crack swimmer then. She didnt know how. I held her up and showed her how to kick her legs and draw her arms. Of course she didnt learn in one day, but she thanked me for bothering with her. I was also somewhat of a dancer. And I had already noticed that love can start on a dance floor. We danced.

But though I held her tightly in my arms, she was way away. That college feller who lived on the top floor was somewhere making money for the next year. I imagined that she was thinking, wishing for him. Ned was along. He treated her until his money gave out. She went with another feller. Ned got sore. One by one the boys' money gave out. She left them. And they got sore. Every one of them but me got sore. This is the reason, I guess, why I had her to myself on the top deck of the *Jane Mosely* that night as we puffed up the Potomac, coming home. The moon was brilliant. The air was sweet like clover. And every now and then, a salt tang, a stale drift of sea-weed. It was not my mind's fault if it went romancing. I should have taken her in my arms the minute we were stowed in that old lifeboat. I dallied, dreaming. She took me in hers. And I could feel by the touch of it that it wasnt a man-to-woman love. It made me restless. I felt chagrined. I didnt know what it was, but I did know that I couldnt handle it. She ran her fingers through my hair and kissed my forehead. I itched to break through her tenderness to passion. I wanted her to take me in her arms as I knew she had that college feller. I wanted her to love me passionately as she did him. I gave her one burning kiss. Then she laid me in her lap as if I were a child. Helpless. I got sore when she started to hum a lullaby. She wouldnt let me go. I talked. I knew damned well that I could beat her at that. Her eyes were soft and misty, the curves of her lips were wistful, and her smile seemed indulgent of the irrelevance of my remarks. I gave up at last and let her love me, silently, in her own way. The moon was brilliant. The air was sweet like clover, and every now and then, a salt tang, a stale drift of sea-weed. . .

The next time I came close to her was the following summer at Harpers Ferry. We were sitting on a flat projecting rock they give the name of Lover's Leap. Some one is supposed to have jumped off it. The river is about six hundred feet beneath. A railroad track runs up the valley and curves out of sight where part of the mountain rock had to be blasted away to make room for it. The engines of this valley have a whistle, the echoes of which sound like iterated gasps and sobs. I always think of them as crude music from the soul of Avey. We sat there holding hands. Our palms were soft and warm against each other. Our fingers were not tight. She would not let them be. She would not let me twist them. I wanted to talk. To explain what I meant to her. Avey was as silent as those great trees whose tops we looked down upon. She has always been like that. At least, to me. I had the notion that if I really wanted to, I could do with her just what I pleased. Like one can strip a tree. I did kiss her. I even let my hands cup her breasts. When I was through, she'd seek my hand and hold it till my pulse cooled down. Evening after evening we sat there. I tried to get her to talk about that college feller. She never would. There was no set time to go home. None of my family had come down. And as for hers, she didnt give a hang about them. The general gossips could hardly say more than they had. The boarding-house porch was always deserted when we returned. No one saw us enter, so the time was set conveniently for scandal. This worried me a little, for I thought it might keep Avey from getting an appointment in the schools. She didnt care. She had finished normal school. They could give her a job if they wanted to. As time went on, her indifference to things began to pique me; I was ambitious. I left the Ferry earlier than she did. I was going off to college. The more I thought of it, the more I resented, yes, hell, thats what it was, her downright laziness. Sloppy indolence. There was no excuse for a healthy girl taking life so easy. Hell! she was no better than a cow. I was certain that she was a cow when I felt an udder in a Wisconsin stock-judging class. Among those energetic Swedes, or whatever they are, I decided to forget her. For two years I thought I did. When I'd come home for the summer she'd be away. And before she returned, I'd be gone. We never wrote; she was too damned lazy for that. But what a bluff I put up about forgetting her. The girls up that way, at least the ones I knew, havent got the stuff: they dont know how to love. Giving themselves completely was tame beside just the holding of Avey's hand. One day I received a note from her. The writing, I decided, was slovenly. She wrote on a torn bit of note-book paper. The envelope had a faint perfume that I remembered. A single line told me she had lost her school and was going away. I comforted myself with the reflection that shame held no pain for one so indolent as she. Nevertheless, I left Wisconsin that year for good. Washington had seemingly forgotten her. I hunted Ned. Between curses, I caught his opinion of her. She was no better than a whore. I saw her mother on the street. The same old pinch-beck, jerky-gaited creature that I'd always known.

Perhaps five years passed. The business of hunting a job or something or other had bruised my vanity so that I could recognize it. I felt old. Avey and my real relation to her, I thought I came to know. I wanted to see her. I had been told that she was in New York. As I had no money, I hiked and bummed my way there. I got work in a ship-yard and walked the streets at night, hoping to meet her. Failing in this, I saved enough to pay my fare back home. One evening in early June, just at the time when dusk is most lovely on the eastern horizon, I saw Avey, indolent as ever, leaning on the arm of a man, strolling under the recently lit arc-lights of U Street. She had almost passed before she recognized me. She showed no surprise. The puff over her eyes had grown heavier. The eyes themselves were still sleepy-large, and beautiful. I had almost concluded—indifferent. "You look older," was what she said. I wanted to convince her that I was, so I asked her to walk with me. The man whom she was with, and whom she never took the trouble to introduce, at a nod from her, hailed a taxi, and drove away. That gave me a notion of what she had been used to. Her dress was of some fine, costly stuff. I suggested the park, and then added that the grass might stain her skirt. Let it get stained, she said, for where it came from there are others.

I have a spot in Soldier's Home to which I always go when I want the simple beauty of another's soul. Robins spring about the lawn all day. They leave their footprints in the grass. I imagine that the grass at night smells sweet and fresh because of them. The ground is high. Washington lies below. Its light spreads like a blush against the darkened sky. Against the soft dusk sky of Washington. And when the wind is from the South, soil of my homeland falls like a fertile shower upon the lean streets of the city. Upon my hill in Soldier's Home. I know the policeman who watches the place of nights. When I go there alone, I talk to him. I tell him I come there to find the truth that people bury in their hearts. I tell him that I do not come there with a girl to do the thing he's paid to watch out for. I look deep in his eyes when I say these things, and he believes me. He comes over to see who it is on the grass. I say hello to him. He greets me in the same way and goes off searching for other black splotches upon the lawn. Avey and I went there. A band in one of the buildings a fair distance off was playing a march. I wished they would stop. Their playing was like a tin spoon in one's mouth. I wanted the Howard Glee Club to sing "Deep River," from the road. To sing "Deep River, Deep River," from the road. . . Other than the first comments, Avey had been silent. I started to hum a folk-tune. She slipped her hand in mine. Pillowed her head as best she could upon my arm. Kissed the hand that she was holding and listened, or so I thought, to what I had to say. I traced my development from the early days up to the present time, the phase in which I could understand her. I described her own nature and temperament. Told how they needed a larger life for their expression. How incapable Washington was of understanding that need. How it could not meet it.

I pointed out that in lieu of proper channels, her emotions had overflowed into paths that dissipated them. I talked, beautifully I thought, about an art that would be born, an art that would open the way for women the likes of her. I asked her to hope, and build up an inner life against the coming of that day. I recited some of my own things to her. I sang, with a strange quiver in my voice, a promise-song. And then I began to wonder why her hand had not once returned a single pressure. My old-time feeling about her laziness came back. I spoke sharply. My policeman friend passed by. I said hello to him. As he went away, I began to visualize certain possibilities. An immediate and urgent passion swept over me. Then I looked at Avey. Her heavy eyes were closed. Her breathing was as faint and regular as a child's in slumber. My passion died. I was afraid to move lest I disturb her. Hours and hours, I guess it was, she lay there. My body grew numb. I shivered. I coughed. I wanted to get up and whittle at the boxes of young trees. I withdrew my hand. I raised her head to waken her. She did not stir. I got up and walked around. I found my policeman friend and talked to him. We both came up, and bent over her. He said it would be all right for her to stay there just so long as she got away before the workmen came at dawn. A blanket was borrowed from a neighbor house. I sat beside her through the night. I saw the dawn steal over Washington. The Capitol dome looked like a gray ghost ship drifting in from sea. Avey's face was pale, and her eyes were heavy. She did not have the gray crimson-splashed beauty of the dawn. I hated to wake her. Orphan-woman. . .

RUDOLPH FISHER

1897-1934

Rudolph Fisher was born in Washington, D.C., May 9, 1897, and was brought up in Providence, Rhode Island, where he attended school. He received his bachelor's and master's degrees from Brown University and then entered Howard Medical School, graduating in 1924 with the highest honors. In New York, Fisher specialized in biology at the College of Physicians and Surgeons of Columbia University. He began his practice of medicine in 1927 and went on to a further specialization in Roentgenology.

While Fisher was in medical school, he had begun to write short fiction. His first story, "The City of Refuge," appeared in the *Atlantic Monthly* in February, 1925, and was reprinted in *The Best Short Stories of 1925*; other stories—"Ringtail," "High Yaller," "The Promised Land," and "Miss Cynthie"—were subsequently published in such journals as *McClure's, Opportunity,* and *Story* as well as in the *Atlantic Monthly.* His two novels—*The Walls of Jericho* (1928) and *The Conjure Man Dies* (1932)—are not so successful as his shorter fiction, for Fisher largely conceived of his material in episodic form. The short stories, however, are distinctive and suggest the spirit of Harlem life in the 1920's.

In Rudolph Fisher's stories a similar situation recurs: an adult whose character has been formed in the South arrives in Harlem, discovers that "the city of refuge" is in fact a "city of Satan" where deceit, disloyalty, and avarice have come to dominate the lives of many Negroes. Fisher is particularly effective in evoking the saturnalian quality of Harlem life, but he attempts more than mere local color; he humanizes the corrupt as well as the innocent figures in his stories, and he suggests the great influence of place in the morality of his characters. The ambivalence of his point of view is suggested by the recurrent idealism that is beneath the surface of his fiction and that emerges as the conclusion to so much of his work.

"Miss Cynthie," published in *Story* magazine in 1933, represents Fisher at his most effective. Although the seventy-year-old woman finds it difficult to accept the role of this boy whom she had always thought of as a doctor, a dentist, or, as she reminds herself rather whimsically, at least an undertaker, she comes to realize that he has developed organically and honestly, on his own terms. The boy's terms are those of the old woman, too, for she had first sung to him; she had first given him her joy and her own love of music. Without imposing his ideas upon the reader, Fisher has contrasted ironically two generations of Negroes as they function in two areas of the country.

Miss Cynthie

FOR THE FIRST TIME in her life somebody had called her "madam." She had been standing, bewildered but unafraid, while innumerable Red Caps appropriated piece after piece of the baggage arrayed on the platform. Neither her brief seventy years' journey through life nor her long two days' travel northward had dimmed the live brightness of her eyes, which, for all their bewilderment, had accurately selected her own treasures out of the row of luggage and guarded them vigilantly. "These yours, madam?"

The biggest Red Cap of all was smiling at her. He looked for all the world like Doc Crinshaw's oldest son back home. Her little brown face relaxed; she smiled back at him.

"They got to be. You all done took all the others."

He laughed aloud. Then—"Carry 'em in for you?"

She contemplated his bulk. "Reckon you can manage it—puny little feller like you?"

Thereupon they were friends. Still grinning broadly, he surrounded himself with her impedimenta, the enormous brown extension-case on one shoulder, the big straw suitcase in the opposite hand, the carpet-bag under one arm. She herself held fast to the umbrella. "Always like to have sump'm in my hand when I walk. Can't never tell when you'll run across a snake."

"There aren't any snakes in the city."

"There's snakes everywhere, chile."

They began the tedious hike up the interminable platform. She was small and quick. Her carriage was surprisingly erect, her gait astonishingly spry. She said:

"You liked to took my breath back yonder, boy, callin' me 'madam.' Back home everybody call me 'Miss Cynthie.' Even their chillun. Black folks, white folks too. 'Miss Cynthie.' Well, when you come up with that 'madam' o' yourn, I say to myself, 'Now, I wonder who that chile's a-grinnin' at? 'Madam' stands for mist'ess o' the house, and I sho' ain' mist'ess o' nothin' in this hyeh New York.'"

"Well, you see, we call everybody 'madam.'"

"Everybody?—Hm." The bright eyes twinkled. "Seem like that's worry me some—if I was a man."

Reprinted from *Story* Magazine, as found in *The Negro Caravan*, by permission of Pearl M. Fisher.

He acknowledged his slip and observed, "I see this isn't your first trip to New York."

"First trip any place, son. First time I been over fifty mile from Waxhaw. Only travelin' I've done is in my head. Ain' seen many places, but I's seen a passel o' people. Reckon places is pretty much alike after people been in 'em awhile."

"Yes, ma'am. I guess that's right."

"You ain' no reg'lar bag-toter, is you?"

"Ma'am?"

"You talk too good."

"Well, I only do this in vacation-time. I'm still in school."

"You is. What you aimin' to be?"

"I'm studying medicine."

"You is?" She beamed. "Aimin' to be a doctor, huh? Thank the Lord for that. That's what I always wanted my David to be. My grandchile hyeh in New York. He's to meet me hyeh now."

"I bet you'll have a great time."

"Mussn't bet, chile. That's sinful. I tole him 'for' he left home, I say, 'Son, you the only one o' the chillun what's got a chance to amount to sump'm. Don't th'ow it away. Be a preacher or a doctor. Work yo' way up and don' stop short. If the Lord don' see fit for you to doctor the soul, then doctor the body. If you don' get to be a reg'lar doctor, be a tooth-doctor. If you jes' can't make that, be a foot-doctor. And if you don' get that fur, be a undertaker. That's the least you must be. That ain' so bad. Keep you acquainted with the house of the Lord. Always mind the house o' the Lord—whatever you do, do like a church-steeple: aim high and go straight.' "

"Did he get to be a doctor?"

"Don' b'lieve he did. Too late startin', I reckon. But he's done succeeded at sump'm. Mus' be at least a undertaker, 'cause he started sendin' the homefolks money, and he come home las' year dressed like Judge Pettiford's boy what went off to school in Virginia. Wouldn't tell none of us 'zackly what he was doin', but he said he wouldn' never be happy till I come and see for myself. So hyeh I is." Something softened her voice. "His mammy died befo' he knowed her. But he was always sech a good chile—" The something was apprehension. "Hope he *is* a undertaker."

They were mounting a flight of steep stairs leading to an exit-gate, about which clustered a few people still hoping to catch sight of arriving friends. Among these a tall young brown-skinned man in a light grey suit suddenly waved his panama and yelled, "Hey, Miss Cynthie!"

Miss Cynthie stopped, looked up, and waved back with a delighted umbrella. The Red Cap's eyes lifted too. His lower jaw sagged.

"Is that your grandson?"

"It sho' is," she said and distanced him for the rest of the climb. The grandson, with an abandonment that superbly ignored onlookers, folded the little woman in an exultant, smothering embrace. As soon as she could, she pushed him off with breathless mock impatience.

"Go 'way, you fool, you. Aimin' to squeeze my soul out my body befo' I can get a look at this place?" She shook herself into the semblance of composure. "Well. You don't look hungry, anyhow."

"Ho-ho! Miss Cynthie in New York! Can y' imagine this? Come on. I'm parked on Eighth Avenue."

The Red Cap delivered the outlandish luggage into a robin's egg blue open Packard with scarlet wheels, accepted the grandson's dollar and smile, and stood watching the car roar away up Eighth Avenue.

Another Red Cap came up. "Got a break, hey, boy?"

"Dave Tappen himself—can you beat that?"

"The old lady hasn't seen the station yet—starin' at him."

"That's not the half of it, bozo. That's Dave Tappen's grandmother. And what do you s'pose she hopes?"

"What?"

"She hopes that Dave has turned out to be a successful undertaker!"

"Undertaker? Undertaker!"

They stared at each other a gaping moment, then doubled up with laughter.

"Look—through there—that's the Chrysler Building. Oh, hellelujah! I meant to bring you up Broadway—"

"David—"

"Ma'am?"

"This hyeh wagon yourn?"

"Nobody else's. Sweet buggy, ain't it?"

"David—you ain't turned out to be one of them moonshiners, is you?"

"Moonshiners—? Moon—Ho! No indeed, Miss Cynthie. I got a better racket 'n that."

"Better which?"

"Game. Business. Pick-up."

"Tell me, David. What is yo' racket?"

"Can't spill it yet, Miss Cynthie. Rather show you. Tomorrow night you'll know the worst. Can you make out till tomorrow night?"

"David, you know I always wanted you to be a doctor, even if 'twasn' nothin' but a foot-doctor. The very leas' I wanted you to be was a undertaker."

"Undertaker! Oh, Miss Cynthie!—with my sunny disposition?"

"Then you ain' even a undertaker?"

"Listen, Miss Cynthie. Just forget 'bout what I am for awhile. Must till tomorrow night. I want you to see for yourself. Tellin' you will spoil it. Now stop askin', you hear?—because I'm not answerin' —I'm surprisin' you. And don't expect anybody you meet to tell you. It'll mess up the whole works. Understand? Now give the big city a break. There's the elevated train going up Columbus Avenue. Ain't that hot stuff?"

Miss Cynthie looked. "Humph!" she said. "Tain' half high as that trestle two mile from Waxhaw."

She thoroughly enjoyed the ride up Central Park West. The stagger lights, the extent of the park, the high, close, kingly buildings, remarkable because their stoves cooled them in summer as well as heated them in winter, all drew nods of mild interest. But what gave her special delight was not these: it was that David's car so effortlessly sped past the headlong drove of vehicles racing northward.

They stopped for a red light; when they started again their machine leaped forward with a triumphant eagerness that drew from her an unsuppressed "Hot you, David! That's it!"

He grinned appreciatively. "Why, you're a regular New Yorker already."

"New York nothin'! I done the same thing fifty years ago— befo' I knowed they was a New York."

"What!"

" 'Deed so. Didn' I use to tell you 'bout my young mare, Betty? Chile, I'd hitch Betty up to yo' grandpa's buggy and pass anything on the road. Betty never knowed what another horse's dust smelt like. No 'ndeedy. Shuh, boy, this ain' nothin' new to me. Why that broke-down Fo'd yo uncle Jake's got ain' nothin'—nothin' but a sorry mess. Done got so slow I jes' won' ride in it—I declare I'd rather walk. But this hyeh thing, now, this is right nice." She settled back in complete, complacent comfort, and they sped on, swift and silent.

Suddenly she sat erect with abrupt discovery.

"David—well—bless my soul!"

"What's the matter, Miss Cynthie?"

115

Then he saw what had caught her attention. They were travelling up Seventh Avenue now, and something was miraculously different. Not the road; that was as broad as ever, wide, white gleaming in the sun. Not the houses; they were lofty still, lordly, disdainful, supercilious. Not the cars; they continued to race impatiently onward, innumerable, precipitate, tumultuous. Something else, something at once obvious and subtle, insistent, pervasive, compelling.

"David—this mus' be Harlem!"

"Good Lord, Miss Cynthie—!"

"Don' use the name of the Lord in vain, David."

"But I mean—gee!—you're no fun at all. You get everything before a guy can tell you."

"You got plenty to tell me, David. But don' nobody need to tell me this. Look a yonder."

Not just a change of complexion. A completely dissimilar atmosphere. Sidewalks teeming with leisurely strollers, at once strangely dark and bright. Boys in white trousers, berets, and green shirts, with slickened black heads and proud swagger. Bareheaded girls in crisp organdie dresses, purple, canary, gay scarlet. And laughter, abandoned strong Negro laughter, some falling full on the ear, some not heard at all, yet sensed—the warm life-breath of the tireless carnival to which Harlem's heart quickens in summer.

"This is it," admitted David. "Get a good eyeful. Here's One Hundred and Twenty-fifth Street—regular little Broadway. And here's the Alhambra, and up ahead we'll pass the Lafayette."

"What's them?"

"Theatres."

"Theatres? Theatres. Humph! Look, David—is that a colored folks church?" They were passing a fine gray-stone edifice.

"That. Oh. Sure it is. So's this one on this side."

"No! Well, ain' that fine? Splendid big church like that for colored folks."

Taking his cue from this, her first tribute to the city he said, "You ain't seen nothing yet. Wait a minute."

They swung left through a side-street and turned right on a boulevard. "What do you think o' that?" And he pointed to the quarter-million-dollar St. Mark's.

"That a colored church, too?"

" 'Tain' no white one. And they built it themselves, you know. Nobody's hand-me-down gift."

She heaved a great happy sigh. "Oh, yes, it was a gift, David. It was a gift from on high." Then, "Look a hyeh—which a one you belong to?"

"Me? Why, I don't belong to any—that is, none o' these. Mine's over in another section. Y'see, mine's Baptist. These are all Methodist. See?"

"M-m. Uh-huh. I see."

They circled a square and slipped into a quiet narrow street overlooking a park, stopping before the tallest of the apartment-houses in the single commanding row.

Alighting, Miss Cynthie gave this imposing structure one side-wise, upward glance, and said, "Y'all live like bees in a hive, don't y'?—I boun' the women does all the work, too." A moment later, "So this is a elevator? Feel like I'm glory-bound sho' nuff."

Along a tiled corridor and into David's apartment. Rooms leading into rooms. Luxurious couches, easy-chairs, a brown-walnut grand piano, gay-shaded floor lamps, panelled walls, deep rugs, treacherous glass-wood floors—and a smiling golden-skinned girl in a gingham housedress, approaching with outstretched hands.

"This is Ruth, Miss Cynthie."

"Miss Cynthie!" said Ruth.

They clasped hands. "Been wantin' to see David's girl ever since he first wrote us 'bout her."

"Come—here's your room this way. Here's the bath. Get out of your things and get comfy. You must be worn out with the trip."

"Worn out? Worn out? Shuh. How you gon' get worn out on a train? Now if 'twas a horse, maybe, or Jake's no-count Fo'd—but a train—didn' but one thing bother me on that train."

"What?"

"When the man made them beds down, I jes' couldn' manage to undress same as at home. Why, s'posin' sump'm bus' the train open—where'd you be? Naked as a jay-bird in dew-berry time."

David took in her things and left her to get comfortable. He returned, and Ruth, despite his reassuring embrace, whispered:

"Dave, you can't fool old folks—why don't you go ahead and tell her about yourself? Think of the shock she's going to get—at her age."

David shook his head. "She'll get over the shock if she's there looking on. If we just told her, she'd never understand. We've got to railroad her into it. Then she'll be happy."

"She's nice. But she's got the same ideas as all old folks—"

"Yea—but with her you can change 'em. Specially if everything is really all right. I know her. She's for church and all, but she believes in good times too, if they're right. Why, when I was a kid—" He broke off. "Listen!"

Miss Cynthie's voice came quite distinctly to them, singing a jaunty little rhyme:

> Oh I danced with the gal with the hole in her stockin',
> And her toe kep' a-kickin' and her heel kep' a-knockin'—
>
> 'Come up, Jesse, and get a drink o' gin,
> 'Cause you near to the heaven as you'll ever get ag'in'."

"She taught me that when I wasn't knee-high to a cricket," David said.

Miss Cynthie still sang softly and merrily:

> "Then I danced with the gal with the dimple in her cheek,
> And if she'd 'a' kep' a-smilin', I'd 'a' danced for a week—"

"God forgive me," prayed Miss Cynthie as she discovered David's purpose the following night. She let him and Ruth lead her, like an early Christian martyr, into the Lafayette Theatre. The blinding glare of the lobby produced a merciful self-anaesthesia, and she entered the sudden dimness of the interior as involuntarily as in a dream. . . .

Attendants outdid each other for Mr. Dave Tappen. She heard him tell them them, "Fix us up till we go on," and found herself sitting between Ruth and David in the front row of a lower box. A miraculous device of the devil, a motion-picture that talked, was just ending. At her feet the orchestra was assembling. The motion-picture faded out amid a scattered round of applause. Lights blazed and the orchestra burst into an ungodly rumpus.

She looked out over the seated multitude, scanning row upon row of illumined faces, black faces, white faces, yellow, tan, brown; bald heads, bobbed heads, kinky and straight heads; and upon every countenance, expectancy—scowling expectancy in this case, smiling in that, complacent here, amused there, commentative elsewhere, but everywhere suspense, abeyance, anticipation.

Half a dozen people were ushered down the nearer aisle to reserved seats in the second row. Some of them caught sight of David and Ruth and waved to them. The chairs immediately behind them in the box were being shifted. "Hello, Tap!" Miss Cynthie saw David turn, rise, and shake hands with two men. One of them was large, bald and pink, emanating good cheer; the other short, thin, sallow with thick black hair and a sour mien. Ruth also acknowledged their greeting. "This is my grandmother," David said proudly. "Miss Cynthie, meet my managers, Lou and Lee Goldman." "Pleased to meet you," managed Miss Cynthie. "Great lad, this boy of yours," said Lou Goldman. "Great little partner he's got, too," added Lee. They also settled back expectantly.

"Here we go!"

The curtain rose to reveal a cotton-field at dawn. Pickers in blue denim overalls, bandanas, and wide-brimmed straws, or in gingham aprons and sun-bonnets, were singing as they worked. Their voices, from clearest soprano to richest bass, blended in low concordances, first simply humming a series of harmonies, until, gradually, came words, like figures forming in mist. As the sound grew, the mist cleared, the words came round and full, and the sun rose bringing light as if in answer to the song. The chorus swelled, the radiance grew, the two, as if emanating from a single source, fused their crescendos, till at last they achieved a joint transcendence of tonal and visual brightness.

"Swell opener," said Lee Goldman.

"Ripe," agreed Lou.

David and Ruth arose. "Stay here and enjoy the show, Miss Cynthie. You'll see us again in a minute."

"Go to it, kids," said Lou Goldman.

"Yea—burn 'em up," said Lee.

Miss Cynthie hardly noted that she had been left, so absorbed was she in the spectacle. To her, the theatre had always been the antithesis of the church. As the one was the refuge of righteousness, so the other was the stronghold of transgression. But this first scene awakened memories, captured and held her attention by offering a blend of truth and novelty. Having thus baited her interest, the show now proceeded to play it like the trout through swift-flowing waters of wickedness. Resist as it might, her mind was caught and drawn into the impious subsequences.

The very music that had just rounded out so majestically now distorted itself into ragtime. The singers came forward and turned to dancers; boys, a crazy, swaying background, threw up their arms and kicked out their legs in a rhythmic jamboree; girls, an agile, brazen foreground, caught their skirts up to their hips and displayed their copper calves, knees, thighs, in shameless, incredible steps. Miss Cynthie turned dismayed eyes upon the audience, to discover that mob of sinners devouring it all with fond satisfaction. Then the dancers separated and with final abandon flung themselves off the stage in both directions.

Lee Goldman commented through the applause, "They work easy, them babies."

"Yea," said Lou. "Savin' the hot stuff for later."

Two black-faced cotton-pickers appropriated the scene, indulging in dialogue that their hearers found uproarious.

"Ah'm tired."

"Ah'm hongry."

"Dis job jes' wears me out."

"Starves me to death."

"Ah'm so tired—you know what Ah'd like to do?"

"What?"

"Ah'd like to go to sleep and dream I was sleepin'."

"What good dat do?"

"Den I could wake up and still be 'sleep."

"Well y'know what Ah'd like to do?"

"No. What?"

"Ah'd like to swaller me a hog and a hen."

"What good dat do?"

"Den Ah'd always be full o' ham and eggs."

"Ham? Shuh. Don't you know a hog has to be smoked 'fo' he's a ham?"

"Well, if I swaller him, he'll have a smoke all around him, won' he?"

Presently Miss Cynthie was smiling like everyone else, but her smile soon fled. For the comics departed, and the dancing girls returned, this time in scant travesties on their earlier voluminous costumes—tiny sun-bonnets perched jauntily on one side of their glistening bobs, bandanas reduced to scarlet neck-ribbons, waists mere brassieres, skirts mere gingham sashes.

And now Miss Cynthie's whole body stiffened with a new and surpassing shock; her bright eyes first widened with unbelief, then slowly grew dull with misery. In the midst of a sudden great volley of applause her grandson had broken through that bevy of agile wantons and begun to sing.

He too was dressed as a cotton-picker, but a Beau Brummel among cotton pickers; his hat bore a pleated green band, his bandana was silk, his overalls blue satin, his shoes black patent leather. His eyes flashed, his teeth gleamed, his body swayed, his arms waved, his words came fast and clear. As he sang, his companions danced a concerted tap, uniformly wild, ecstatic. When he stopped singing, he himself began to dance, and without sacrificing crispness of execution, seemed to absorb into himself every measure of the energy which the girls, now merely standing off and swaying, had relinquished.

"Look at that boy go," said Lee Goldman.

"He ain't started yet," said Lou.

But surrounding comment, Dave's virtuosity, the eager enthusiasm of the audience were all alike lost on Miss Cynthie. She sat with stricken eyes watching this boy whom she'd raised from a babe, taught right from wrong, brought up in the church, and endowed with her prayers, this child whom she had dreamed of seeing a preacher, a regular doctor, a tooth-doctor, a foot-doctor, at the very least an undertaker—sat watching him disport himself for the benefit of a sinsick, flesh-hungry mob of lost souls, not one of whom knew or cared to know the loving kindness of God; sat watching a David she'd never foreseen, turned tool of the devil, disciple of lust, unholy prince among sinners.

For a long time she sat there watching with wretched eyes, saw portrayed on the stage David's arrival in Harlem, his escape from 'old friends' who tried to dupe him; saw him working as a trap-drummer in a night-club, where he fell in love with Ruth, a dancer; not the gentle Ruth Miss Cynthie knew, but a wild and shameless young savage who danced like seven devils—in only a girdle and breast-plates; saw the two of them join in a song-and-dance act that eventually made them Broadway headliners, an act presented *in toto* as the pre-finale of this show. And not any of the melodies, not any of the sketches, not all the comic philosophy of the tired-and-hungry duo, gave her figure a moment's relaxation or brightened the dull defeat in her staring eyes. She sat apart, alone in the box, the symbol, the epitome of supreme failure. Let the rest of the theatre be riotous, clamoring for more and more of Dave Tappen, "Tap," the greatest tapster of all time, idol of uptown and downtown New York. For her, they were lauding simply an exhibition of sin which centered about her David.

"This'll run a year on Broadway," said Lee Goldman.

"Then we'll take it to Paris."

Encores and curtains with Ruth, and at last David came out on the stage alone. The clamor dwindled. And now he did something quite unfamiliar to even the most consistent of his followers. Softly, delicately, he began to tap a routine designed to fit a particular song. When he had established the rhythm, he began to sing the song:

> "Oh I danced with the gal with the hole in her stockin,'
> And her toe kep' a-kickin' and her heel kep' a-knockin'—
>
> 'Come up, Jesse, and get a drink o' gin,
> 'Cause you near to the heaven as you'll ever get ag'in'—"

As he danced and sang this song, frequently smiling across at Miss Cynthie, a visible change transformed her. She leaned forward incredulously, listened intently, then settled back in limp wonder. Her bewildered eyes turned on the crowd, on those serried rows of shriftless sinners. And she found in their faces now an overwhelmingly curious thing: a grin, a universal grin, a gleeful and sinless grin such as not the nakedest chorus in the performance had produced. In a few seconds, with her own song, David had

121

dwarfed into unimportance, wiped off their faces, swept out of their minds every trace of what had seemed to be sin; had reduced it all to mere trivial detail and revealed these revelers as a crowd of children, enjoying the guileless antics of another child. And Miss Cynthie whispered:

"Bless my soul! They didn' mean nothin' . . . They jes' didn' see no harm in it—"

> "Then I danced with the gal with the dimple in her cheek,
> And if she'd 'a' kep' a-smilin', I'd 'a' danced for a week—
> 'Come up, Jesse—' "

The crowd laughed, clapped their hands, whistled. Someone threw David a bright yellow flower. "From Broadway!"

He caught the flower. A hush fell. He said:

"I'm really happy tonight, folks. Y'see this flower? Means success, don't it? Well, listen. The one who is really responsible for my success is here tonight with me. Now what do you think o' that?"

The hush deepened.

"Y'know folks, I'm sump'm like Adam—I never had no mother. But I've got a grandmother. Down home everybody calls her Miss Cynthie. And everybody loves her. Take that song I just did for you. Miss Cynthie taught me that when I wasn't knee-high to a cricket. But that wasn't all she taught me. Far back as I can remember, she used to always say one thing: Son, do like a church steeple—aim high and go straight. And for doin' it—" he grinned, contemplating the flower—"I get this."

He strode across to the edge of the stage that touched Miss Cynthie's box. He held up the flower.

"So y'see, folks, this isn't mine. It's really Miss Cynthie's." He leaned over to hand it to her. Miss Cynthie's last trace of doubt was swept away. She drew a deep breath of revelation; her bewilderment vanished, her redoubtable composure returned, her eyes lighted up; and no one but David, still holding the flower toward her, heard her sharply whispered reprimand:

"Keep it, you fool. Where's yo' manners—givin' 'way what somebody give you?"

David grinned:

"Take it, tyro. What you tryin' to do—crab my act?"

Thereupon, Miss Cynthie, smiling at him with bright, meaningful eyes, leaned over without rising from her chair, jerked a tiny twig off the stem of the flower, then sat decisively back, resolutely folding her arms, with only a leaf in her hand.

"This'll do me," she said.

The finale didn't matter. People filed out of the theatre. Miss Cynthie sat awaiting her children, her foot absently patting time to the orchestra's jazz recessional. Perhaps she was thinking, "God moves in a mysterious way," but her lips were unquestionably forming the words:

"—danced with the gal—hole in her stockin'—
—toe kep' a-kickin'—heel kep' a-knockin'."

ERIC
WALROND
1898-1966

Eric Walrond was born in Georgetown, British Guiana, in 1898. He was first educated at the St. Stephens Boys' School at Black Rock, Barbados, near a small settlement that his grandfather owned; subsequently, he studied in the Canal Zone public school, in Catholic schools, and under private tutors in Colon from 1913 to 1916. For a time he held a position as clerk with the Health Department of the Canal Commission, although his chief interest was journalism. At an early age, he was a reporter for the *Star-Herald*, the most important contemporaneous newspaper in the American tropics, and worked as a general news reporter, court reporter, and sports writer.

In 1918 Walrond came to New York and tried with little success to work on the Harlem newspapers. For a period of several years he studied at the City College of New York and at Columbia University. He held a variety of jobs: as secretary to a recruiting officer in the British Museum; as secretary to an architect; and as secretary to the superintendent of Broad Street Hospital. He left the hospital, however, to return to newspaper reporting. From 1921 to 1923 he worked as co-owner and editor of the *Brooklyn and Long Island Informer*. In 1923, he became an associate editor of *The Negro World* and then took a position as Business Manager of *Opportunity*.

In the mid-1920's Walrond's essays and stories began to be published in well-known journals. After the initial appearance of an essay entitled "On Being Black" in *The New Republic*, he published his work in *Success Magazine, Current History, Vanity Fair, The Independent, Smart Set*, and the *Argosy All-Story Weekly*. In 1926 he collected his stories in a volume called *Tropic Death*. The book is Walrond's singular achievement and is a particularly vivid description of life in the West Indies, viewed by a native who is interested not in writing propaganda but rather in recalling the effects of the tropics on a wide variety of people.

The titles of some of the stories included in *Tropic Death* suggest Walrond's picture of the Caribbean islands: "Drought," "The Wharf Rats," "Subjection," "The White Snake," "The Vampire," and "Tropic Death." These local color tales—one might perhaps be more justified in calling them arabesques—are concerned with the heat, the dissipation, the poverty, the sickness, the famine, the *obeah* (or superstition), the disease, the death that come to people of all colors under the tropic heat. Morbidity sets the tone of each story; death is often the conclusion. The implicit contrast between the human degradation of the islands and their natural scenic beauty heightens the tragic lives of the characters: so much tragedy amid the natural beauty of the West Indian islands seems highly unnatural—the "blue hills" of Jamaica, referred to at the end of "The Yellow One," become in fact "the dead blue hills of Jamaica."

There is little racial propaganda in the tales of *Tropic Death*. As a West Indian Negro, brought up on the British island of Barbados, Walrond felt little prejudice; he was thoroughly anglicized and was considered a "foreigner" by Negroes in Harlem. As Walrond observes, "so thorough [had] been our British upbringing that if, in the event we [had found] a Colour Bar, we would consider it 'bad form' openly to admit its existence."

"The Yellow One" suggests Walrond's characteristic qualities and presents an impressionistic portrait of the conflicting natives in the Caribbean islands. One reads the tale for the life and time evoked rather than for anything precisely defined; in this sense, "The Yellow One," like so much of the fiction of the Negro Awakening, stands in the broad tradition of local color fiction in American literature.

The Yellow One

I

ONCE CATCHING A GLIMPSE of her, they swooped down like a brood of starving hawks. But it was the girl's first vision of the sea, and the superstitions of a Honduras peasant heritage tightened her grip on the old rusty canister she was dragging with a frantic effort on to the *Urubamba's* gangplank.

"Le' me help yo', dahtah," said one.

"Go 'way, man, yo' too farrad—'way!"

" 'Im did got de fastiness fi' try fi' jump ahead o' me again, but mahn if yo' t'ink yo' gwine duh me outa a meal yo' is a dam pitty liar!"

"Wha' yo' ah try fi' do, leggo!" cried the girl, slapping the nearest one. But the shock of her words was enough to paralyze them.

They were a harum scarum lot, hucksters, ex-cable divers and thugs of the coast, bare-footed, brown-faced, raggedly—drifting from every cave and creek of the Spanish Main.

They withdrew, shocked, uncertain of their ears, staring at her; at her whom the peons of the lagoon idealized as *la madurita:* the yellow one.

Sensing the hostility, but unable to fathom it, she felt guilty of some untoward act, and guardedly lowered her eyes.

Flushed and hot, she seized the canister by the handle and started resuming the journey. It was heavy. More energy was required to move it than she had bargained on.

In the dilemma rescuing footsteps were heard coming down the gangplank. She was glad to admit she was stumped, and stood back, confronted by one of the crew. He was tall, some six feet and over, and a mestizo like herself. Latin blood bubbled in his veins, and it served at once to establish a ready means of communication between them.

"I'll take it," he said quietly, "you go aboard—"

"Oh, many thanks," she said, "and do be careful, I've got the baby bottle in there and I wouldn't like to break it." All this in Spanish, a tongue spontaneously springing up between them.

She struggled up the gangplank, dodging a sling drooping tipsily on to the wharf. "Where are the passengers for Kingston station?" she asked.

"Yonder!" he pointed, speeding past her. Amongst a contortion of machinery, cargo, nets and hatch panels he deposited the trunk.

Gazing at his hardy hulk, two emotions seared her. She wanted to be grateful but he wasn't the sort of person she could offer a tip to. And he would readily see through her telling him that Alfred was down the dock changing the money.

But he warmed to her rescue. "Oh, that's all right," he said, quite illogically, "stay here till they close the hatch, then if I am not around, somebody will help you put it where you want it."

Noises beat upon her. Vendors of tropical fruits cluttered the wharf, kept up sensuous cries; stir and clamor and screams rose from every corner of the ship. Men swerved about her, the dock hands, the crew, digging cargo off the pier and spinning it into the yawning hatch.

"Wha' ah lot o' dem," she observed, "an' dem so black and ugly. R—r—!" Her words had the anti-native quality of her Jamaica spouse's, Alfred St. Xavier Mendez.

The hatch swelled, the bos'n closed it, and the siege commenced. "If Ah did got any sense Ah would Ah wait till dem clean way de rope befo' me mek de sailor boy put down de trunk. Howsomevah, de Lawd will provide, an' all me got fi' do is put me trus' in Him till Halfred come."

With startling alacrity, her prayers were answered, for there suddenly appeared a thin moon-faced decker, a coal-black fellow with a red greasy scarf around his neck, his teeth giddy with an ague he had caught in Puerta Tela and which was destined never to leave him. He seized the trunk by one end and helped her hoist it on the hatch. When he had finished, he didn't wait for her trepid words of thanks but flew to the ship's rail, convulsively shaking.

She grew restive. "Wha' dat Halfred, dey, eh," she cried, "wha' a man can pacify time dough, eh?"

The stream of amassing deckers overran the *Urubamba's* decks. The din of parts being slugged to rights buzzed. An oily strip of canvas screened the hatch. Deckers clamorously crept underneath it.

The sea lay torpid, sizzling. Blue rust flaked off the ship's sides shone upon it. It dazzled you. It was difficult to divine its true color. Sometimes it was so blue it blinded you. Another time it would turn with the cannon roar of the sun, red. Nor was it the red of fire or of youth, of roses or of red tulips. But a sullen, grizzled red. The red of a North Sea rover's icicled beard; the red of a red-headed woman's hair, the red of a red-hot oven. It gave to the water engulfing the ship a dark, copper-colored hue. It left on it jeweled crusts.

A bow-legged old Maroon, with a trunk on his head, explored the deck, smoking a gawky clay pipe of some fiery Jamaica bush and wailing, "Scout bway, scout bway, wha' yo' dey? De old man ah look fa' you'." The trunk was beardy and fuzzy with the lashes of much-used rope. It was rapidly dusking, and a woman and an amazing brood of children came on. One pulled, screaming, at her skirt, one was astride a hip, another, an unclothed one, tugged enthusiastically at a full, ripened breast. A hoary old black man, in a long black coat, who had taken the Word, no doubt, to the yellow "heathen" of the fever-hot lagoon, shoeless, his hard white crash pants rolled up above his hairy, veiny calves, with a lone yellow pineapple as his sole earthly reward.

A tar-black Jamaica sister, in a gown of some noisy West Indian silk, her face entirely removed by the shadowy girth of a leghorn hat, waltzed grandly up on the deck. The edge of her skirt in one hand, after the manner of the ladies at Wimbledon, in the other a fluttering macaw, she was twittering, "Hawfissah, hawfissah, wear is de hawfissah, he?" Among the battering hordes there were less brusque folk; a native girl,—a flower, a brown flower—was alone, rejecting the opulent offer of a bunk, quietly vowing to pass two nights of sleepful concern until she got to Santiago. And two Costa Rica maidens, white, dainty, resentful and uncommunicative.

He came swaggering at last. La Madurita said, "Wha' yo' been, Halfred, all dis lang time, no?"

"Cho, it wuz de man dem down dey," he replied, "dem keep me back." He gave her the sleeping child, and slipped down to doze on the narrow hatch.

In a mood of selfless bluster he was returning to Kingston. He adored Jamaica. He would go on sprees of work and daring, to the jungles of Changuinola or the Cut at Culebra, but such flights, whether for a duration of one or ten years, were uplifted mainly by the traditional deprivations of Hindu coolies or Polish immigrants—sunless, joyless. Similarly up in Cabello; work, sleep, work; day in and day out for six forest-hewing years. And on Sabbaths a Kentucky evangelist, a red-headed hypochondriac, the murky hue of a British buckra from the beat of the tropic sun, tearfully urged the blacks to embrace the teachings of the Lord Jesus Christ before the wrath of Satan engulfed them. Then, one day, on a tramp to Salamanca, a fancy struck him. It stung, was unexpected. He was unused to the sensations it set going. It related to a vision—

something he had surreptitiously encountered. Behind a planter's hut he had seen it. He was slowly walking along the street, shaded by a row of plum trees, and there she was, gloriously unaware of him, bathing her feet in ample view of the sky. She was lovely to behold. Her skin was the ripe red gold of the Honduras half-breed. It sent the blood streaming to his head. He paused and wiped the sweat from his face. He looked at her, calculating. Five—six— seven-fifty. Yes, that'd do. With seven hundred and fifty pounds, he'd dazzle the foxy folk of Kingston with the mellow *Spanish* beauty of her.

In due time, and by ample means, he had been able to bring round the girl's hitherto *chumbo*-hating folk.

"Him mus' be hungry," she said, gazing intently at the baby's face.

"Cho'," replied Alfred, "leave de picknee alone, le' de gal picknee sleep." He rolled over, face downwards, and folded his arms under his chin. He wore a dirty khaki shirt, made in the States, dark green corduroy pants and big yellow shoes which he seldom took off.

Upright on the trunk, the woman rocked the baby and nursed it. By this time the hatch was overcrowded with deckers.

Down on the dock, oxen were yoked behind wagons of crated bananas. Gnawing on plugs of hard black tobacco and firing reels of spit to every side of them, New Orleans "crackers" swearingly cursed the leisurely lack of native labor. Scaly ragamuffins darted after boxes of stale cheese and crates of sun-sopped iced apples that were dumped in the sea.

II

The dawning sunlight pricked the tarpaulin and fell upon the woman's tired, sleep-sapped face. Enamel clanged and crashed. A sickly, sour-sweet odor pervaded the hatch. The sea was calm, gulls scuttled low, seizing and ecstatically devouring some reckless, sky-drunk sprat.

"Go, no, Halfred," cried the woman, the baby in her arms, "an' beg de backra man fi' giv' yo' a can o' hot water fi' mek de baby tea. Go no?"

He rolled over lazily; his loggish yellow bulk, solid, dispirited. "Cho', de man dem no ha' no hot water, giv' she a lemon, no, she na'h cry." He tossed back again, his chin on his arms, gazing at the glorious procession of the sun.

"Even de man dem, ovah yondah," she cried, gesticulating,

"a hold a kangfarance fi' get some hot water. Why yo' don't get up an' go, no man? Me can't handastan' yo', sah."

A conspiration, a pandemonium threatened—the deckers.

"How de bleedy hell dem heckspeck a man fi' trabble tree days an' tree whole a nights beout giv' him any hot watah fi' mek even a can o' tea is somet'ing de hagent at Kingston gwine hav' fi' pint out to me w'en de boat dey lan'—"

"Hey, mistah hawfissah, yo' got any hot watah?"

"Hot watah, mistah?"

"Me will giv' yo' a half pint o' red rum if yo' giv' me a quatty wut' o' hot watah."

"Come, no, man, go get de watah, no?"

"Ripe apples mek me t'row up!"

"Green tamarin' mek me tummack sick!"

"Sahft banana mek me fainty!"

"Fish sweetie giv' me de dysentery."

Craving luscious Havana nights the ship's scullions hid in refuse cans or in grub for the Chinks hot water which they peddled to the miserable deckers.

"Get up, no Halfred, an' go buy some o' de watah," the girl cried, "de baby a cry."

Of late he didn't answer her any more. And it was useless to depend upon him. Frantic at the baby's pawing of the clotted air, at the cold dribbling from its twisted mouth, which turned down a trifle at the ends like Alfred's, she began conjecturing on the use to which a decker could put a cup of the precious liquid. Into it one might pour a gill of goat's milk—a Cuban *señora*, a decker of several voyages, had fortified herself with a bucket of it—or melt a sprig of peppermint or a lump of clove or a root of ginger. So many tropical things one could do with a cup of hot water.

The child took on the color of its sweltering environs. It refused to be pacified by sugared words. It was hungry and it wished to eat, to feel coursing down its throat something warm and delicious. It kicked out of its mother's hand the toy engine she locomotioned before it. It cried, it ripped with its naked toes a hole in her blouse. It kept up an irrepressible racket.

The child's agony drove her to reckless alternatives. "If you don't go, then I'll go, yo' lazy t'ing," she said, depositing the baby beside him and disappearing down the galley corridor.

Her bare earth-red feet slid on the hot, sizzling deck. The heat came roaring at her. It swirled, enveloping her. It was a dingy corridor and there were pigmy paneled doors every inch along it. It wasn't clear to her whither she was bound; the vaporing heat dizzied things. But the scent of stewing meat and vegetables lured her on. It sent her scudding in and out of barrels of cold storage, mounds of ash debris of an exotic kind. It shot her into dark twining circles of men, talking. They either paused or grew lecherous at her approach. Some of the doors to the crew's quarters were open and as she passed white men'd stick out their heads and call, pull, tug at her. Grimy, ash-stained faces; leprous, flesh-crazed hands. Onward she fled, into the roaring, fuming galley.

Heat. Hearths aglow. Stoves aglow. Dishes clattering. Engines, donkey-engines, wheezing. Bright-faced and flame-haired Swedes and Bristol cockneys cursing. Half-nude figures of bronze and crimson shouting, spearing, mending the noisy fire. The wet, clean, brick-colored deck danced to the rhythm of the ship. Darky waiters—white shirt bosoms—black bow ties—black, braided uniforms—spat entire menus at the blond cooks.

"Slap it on dey, Dutch, don't starve de man."

"Hey, Hubigon, tightenin' up on any mo' hoss flesh to-day?"

"Come on fellahs, let's go—"

"There's my boy Porto Rico again Hubigon, Ah tell you' he is a sheik, tryin' to git nex' to dat hot yallah mama."

On entering she had turned, agonized and confused, to a lone yellow figure by the port hole.

"Oh, it's you," she exclaimed, and smiled wanly.

He was sourly sweeping dishes, forks, egg-stained things into a mossy wooden basket which he hoisted and dropped into a cesspool of puttering water.

He paused, blinking uncomprehendingly.

"You," she was catching at mementoes, "you remember—you helped me—my trunk—"

"Oh, yes, I remember," he said slowly. He was a Cuban, mixblooded, soft-haired, and to him, as she stood there, a bare, primitive soul, her beauty and her sex seemed to be in utmost contrast to his mechanical surroundings.

"Can you," she said, in that half-hesitant way of hers, "can you give me some hot watah fo' my baby?"

He was briefly attired; overalls, a dirty, pink singlet. His reddish yellow face, chest and neck shone with the grease and sweat. His face was buttered with it.

"Sure," he replied, seizing an empty date can on the ledge of the port hole and filling it. "Be careful," he cautioned, handing it back to her.

She took it and their eyes meeting, fell.

She started to go, but a burning touch of his hand possessed her.

"Wait," he said, "I almost forgot something." From beneath

the machine he exhumed an old moist gold dust box. Inside it he had pummeled, by some ornate instinct, odds and ends—echoes of the breakfast table. He gave the box to her, saying, "If any one should ask you where you got it, just say Jota Arosemena gave it to you."

"Hey, Porto Rico, wha' the hell yo' git dat stuff at, hotting stuff fo' decks?"

Both of them turned, and the Cuban paled at the jaunty mug of the cook's Negro mate.

"You speak to me?" he said, ice cool.

Hate shown on the black boy's face. "Yo' heard me!" he growled. "Yo' ain't cock-eyed." Ugly, grim, black, his face wore an uneasy leer. He was squat and bleary-eyed.

A son of the Florida Gulf, he hated "Porto Rico" for reasons planted deep in the Latin's past. He envied him the gentle texture of his hair. On mornings in the galley where they both did their toilet he would poke fun at the Cuban's meticulous care in parting it. "Yo' ain't gwine sho," Hubigon'd growl. "Yo' don't have to dress up like no lady's man." And Jota, failing to comprehend the point of view, would question, "What's the matter with you, mang, you mek too much noise, mang." Hubigon despised him because he was yellow-skinned; one night in Havana he had spied him and the chef cook, a nifty, freckle-faced Carolina "cracker" for whom the cook's mate had no earthly use, and the baker's assistant, a New Orleans creole,—although the Negro waiters aboard were sure he was a "yallah" nigger—drinking *anee* in a high-hat café on the prado which barred jet-black American Negroes. He loathed the Latin for his good looks and once at a port on the Buenaventura River they had gone ashore and met two native girls. One was white, her lips pure as the petals of a water lily; the other was a flaming mulatto. That night, on the steps of an adobe hut, a great, low moon in the sky, both forgot the presence of the cook's mate and pledged tear-stained love to Jota. "An' me standin' right by him, doin' a fadeaway." He envied Jota his Cuban nationality for over and over again he had observed that the Latin was the nearest thing to a white man the *ofay* men aboard had yet met. They'd play cards with him—something they never did with the Negro crew—they'd gang with him in foreign ports, they'd listen in a "natural" sort of way to all the bosh he had to say.

Now all the mate's pent-up wrath came foaming to the front.

He came up, the girl having tarried, a cocky, chesty air about him. He made deft, telling jabs at the vapors enmeshing him. "Yo' can't do that," he said, indicating the victuals, "like hell yo' kin! Who de hell yo' t'ink yo' is anyhow? Yo' ain't bettah'n nobody else.

Put it back, big boy, befo' Ah starts whisperin' to de man. Wha' yo' t'ink yo' is at, anyhow, in Porto Rico, where yo' come fum at? Com' handin' out poke chops an' cawn muffins, like yo' is any steward. Yo' cain't do dat, ole man."

It slowly entered the other's brain—all this edgy, snappy, darky talk. But the essence of it was aggressively reflected in the mate's behavior. Hubigon made slow measured steps forward, and the men came flocking to the corner.

"Go to it, Silver King, step on his corns."

"Stick him with a ice pick!"

"Easy fellahs, the steward's comin'."

All of them suddenly fell away. The steward, initiating some fruit baron into the mysteries of the galley, came through, giving them time to speed back to their posts unobserved. The tension subsided, and Jota once more fed the hardware to the dish machine.

As she flew through the corridor all sorts of faces, white ones, black ones, brown ones, leered sensually at her. Like tongues of flame, hands sped after her. Her steps quickened, her heart beat faster and faster till she left behind her the droning of the galley, and safely ascending the hatch, felt on her face the soft, cool breezes of the Caribbean ocean.

Alfred was sitting up, the unpacified baby in his arms.

" 'Im cry all de time yo' went 'way," he said, "wha' yo' t'ink is de mattah wit' 'im, he? Yo' t'ink him tummack a hut 'im?"

"Him is hungry, dat is wha' is de mattah wit' 'im! Move, man! 'Fo Ah knock yo', yah! Giv' me 'im, an' get outa me way! Yo' is only a dyam noosant!"

"Well, what is de mattah, now?" he cried in unfeigned surprise.

"Stid o' gwine fo' de watah yo'self yo' tan' back yah an' giv' hawdahs an' worryin' wha' is de mattah wit' de picknee."

"Cho, keep quiet, woman, an le' me lie down." Satisfied, he rolled back on the hatch, fatuously staring at the sun sweeping the tropic blue sea.

•   •   •   •   •   •   •

"T'un ovah, Halfred, an' lif' yo' big able self awf de baby, yo' Ah crush 'im to debt," she said, awake at last. The baby was awake and ravenous before dawn and refused to be quieted by the witty protestations of the Jamaica laborers scrubbing down the deck. But it was only after the sun, stealing a passage through a crack in the canvas, had warmed a spot on the girl's mouth, that she was constrained to respond to his zestful rantings. "Hey, yo' heah de picknee ah bawl all de time an' yo' won't even tek heed—move yah man!" She thrust the sleeping leg aside and drawing the child to her, stuck a breast in his mouth.

The boat had encountered a sultry sea, and was dipping badly. Water flooded her decks. Getting wet, dozing deckers crawled higher on top of each other. The sea was blue as indigo and white reels of foam swirled past as the ship dove ahead.

It was a disgusting spectacle. There was the sea, drumming on the tinsel sides of the ship, and on top of the terror thus resulting rose a wretched wail from the hatch, "Watah! Hot Watah!"

The galley was the Bastille. Questioning none, the Yellow One, giving the baby to Alfred rushed to the door, and flung herself through it. Once in the corridor, the energy of a dynamo possessed her. Heated mist drenched her. She slid on grimy, sticky deck.

He was hanging up the rag on a brace of iron over the port hole. His jaws were firm, grim, together.

The rest of the galley was a foetic blur to her.

He swung around, and his restless eyes met her. He was for the moment paralyzed. His eyes bore into hers. He itched to toss at her words, words, words! He wanted to say, "Oh, why couldn't you stay away—ashore—down there—at the end of the world—anywhere but on this ship."

"Some water," she said with that gentle half-hesitant smile of hers, "can I get some hot water for my little baby?" And she extended the skillet.

He took it to the sink, his eyes still on hers. The water rained into it like bullets and he brought it to her.

But a sound polluted the lovely quiet.

"Hey, Porto Rico, snap into it! Dis ain't no time to git foolin' wit' no monkey jane. Get a move on dey, fellah, an' fill dis pail full o' water."

He was sober, afar, as he swept a pale, tortured face at Hubigon. As if it were the song of a lark, he swung back to the girl, murmuring, "Ah, but you didn't tell me," he said, "you didn't tell me what the baby is, a boy or girl?" For answer, the girl's eyes widening in terror at something slowly forming behind him.

But it was not without a shadow, and Jota swiftly ducked. The mallet went galloping under the machine. He rose and faced the cook's mate. But Hubigon was not near enough to objectify the jab, sent as fast as the fangs of a striking snake, and Jota fell, cursing, to the hushed cries of the woman. For secretly easing over to the fireplace Hubigon had taken advantage of the opening to grasp a spear and as the other was about to rise brought it thundering down on the tip of his left shoulder. It sent him thudding to the deck in a pool of claret. The cook's mate, his red, red tongue licking his mouth after the manner of a collie in from a strenuous run, pounced on the emaciated figure in the corner, and kicked and kicked it murderously. He kicked him in the head, in the mouth, in the ribs. When he struggled to rise, he sent him back to the floor, dizzy from short, telling jabs with the tip of his boot.

Pale, impassive, the men were prone to take sides. Unconsciously forming a ring, the line was kept taut. Sometimes it surged; once an Atlanta mulatto had to wrest a fiery spear from Foot Works, Hubigon's side kick, and thrust it back in its place. "Keep outa this, if you don't want to get your goddam head mashed in," he said. A woman, a crystal panel in the gray, ugly pattern, tore, fought, had to be kept sane by raw, meaty hands.

Gasping, Hubigon stood by, his eyes shining at the other's languid effort to rise. "Stan' back, fellahs, an' don't interfere. Let 'im come!" With one shoulder jaunty and a jaw risen, claret-drenched, redolent of the stench and grime of Hubigon's boot, parts of it clinging to him, the Cuban rose. A cruel scowl was on his face.

The crowd stood back, and there was sufficient room for them. Hubigon was ripping off his shirt, and licking his red, bleeding lips. He circled the ring like a snarling jungle beast. "Hol' at fuh me, Foot Works, I'm gwine sho' dis monkey wheh he get off at." He was dancing round, jabbing, tapping at ghosts, awaiting the other's beastly pleasure.

As one cowed he came, his jaw swollen. Then with the vigor of a maniac he straightened, facing the mate. He shot out his left. It had the wings of a dart and juggled the mate on the chin. Hubigon's ears tingled distantly. For the particle of a second he was groggy, and the Cuban moored in with the right, flush on the chin. Down the cook's mate went. Leaping like a tiger cat, Jota was upon him, burying his claws in the other's bared, palpitating throat. His eyes gleamed like a tiger cat's. He held him by the throat and squeezed him till his tongue came out. He racked him till the blood seeped through his ears. Then, in a frenzy of frustration, he lifted him up, and pounded with his head on the bared deck. He pounded till the shirt on his back split into ribbons.

"Jesus, take him awf o' him—he's white orready."

"Now, boys, this won't do," cried the baker, a family man. "Come."

And some half dozen of them, running counter to the traditions of the coast, ventured to slug them apart. It was a gruesome job, and Hubigon, once freed, his head and chest smeared with blood, black, was ready to peg at a lancing La Barrie snake.

In the scuffle the woman collapsed, fell under the feet of the milling crew.

"Here," some one cried, "take hold o' her, Butch, she's your kind—she's a decker—hatch four—call the doctor somebody, will ya?"

They took her on a stretcher to the surgeon's room.

· · · · · · ·

The sun had leaped ahead. A sizzling luminosity drenched the sea. Aft the deckers were singing hosannas to Jesus and preparing to walk the gorgeous earth.

Only Alfred St. Xavier Mendez was standing with the baby in his arms, now on its third hunger-nap, gazing with a bewildered look at the deserted door to the galley. "Me wondah wha' mek she 'tan' so lang," he whispered anxiously.

Imperceptibly shedding their drapery of mist, there rose above the prow of the *Urubamba* the dead blue hills of Jamaica.

STERLING A. BROWN [1901–   ]

STERLING A. BROWN

1901-

Sterling A. Brown has been an influential critic and scholar of American Negro writing. Born in Washington, D.C., in 1901, he was educated in the public schools of that city and later attended Williams College and Harvard University. He has taught at a number of major universities, but his most significant association has been with Howard University, where he has conducted courses in American civilization for more than three decades.

Brown's career has been varied: he has been a key figure in American Negro culture, serving as Editor of Negro Affairs for the Federal Writers' Project from 1936 to 1939 and as a staff member of the Carnegie-Myrdal Study of the Negro in 1939. His literary achievements are best represented by his poetry and his critical essays. As a poet, Brown has published *Southern Road* (1932) as well as many poems in literary journals; his most distinctive characteristic—in poems like "Long Gone," "Southern Road," and "Break of Day"—is his use of folklore material. As an essayist, Brown has examined the sociological roots of Negro stereotypes that have been traditionally conceived by white authors and has explored the diversity of Negro life in America.

"Negro Character as Seen by White Authors" is a fine example of Brown's scholarship. The subject, which preoccupied Brown in the 1930's, is given fuller scope in *The Negro in American Fiction* (1938), *Negro Poetry and Drama* (1938), and *The Negro*

137

Caravan (1941). The last volume is a classic of its kind—an impressive anthology, indeed almost a source book—of nineteenth- and twentieth-century American Negro literature, which Brown edited with Arthur P. Davis and Ulysses Lee.

Sterling Brown's importance as a scholar of Negro writing in America rests upon those essays and books, published in the 1930's, which attempt to measure the literary image of the Negro against the actuality of the Negro's life, which seek "to lay the ghosts of the plantation tradition." Brown's criticism was not only directed against the white authors who had fixed the stereotype of the Negro in the American mind; he also censured authors of the Negro Awakening who pictured Negro life in only its extreme and distorted aspects. Brown argued that the Negro author should record the full complexity of Negro experience and thus testify to his full humanity. As a scholar of Negro culture, Brown himself has been greatly responsible for the knowledge that most Americans have of the Negro past.

Negro Character as Seen by White Authors

INTRODUCTION

THERE ARE THREE TYPES of Negroes, says Roark Bradford, in his sprightly manner: "the nigger, the 'colored person,' and the Negro—upper case N." In his foreword to *Ol' Man Adam an' His Chillun,* the source from which Marc Connelly drew the *Green Pastures,* and a book causing the author to be considered, in some circles, a valid interpreter of *the* Negro, Roark Bradford defines *the* Negro's character and potentialities. The Negro, he says, is the race leader, not too militant, concerned more with economic independence than with civil equality. The colored person, "frequently of mixed blood, loathes the blacks and despises the whites. . . . Generally he inherits the weaknesses of both races and seldom inherits the strength of either. He has the black man's emotions and the white man's inhibitions."[1] Together with the "poor white trash" it is the "colored persons" who perpetuate racial hatreds and incite race riots and lynchings. "The nigger" interests Mr. Bradford more than the rest. He is indolent, entirely irresponsible, shiftless, the bugaboo of Anglo-Saxon ideals, a poor fighter and a poor hater, primitively emotional and uproariously funny.

Such are the "original" contributions of Mr. Bradford, who states modestly that, in spite of the Negro's penchant to lying:

> I believe I know them pretty well. I was born on a plantation that was worked by them; I was nursed by one as an infant and I played with one when I was growing up. I have watched them at work in the fields, in the levee camps, and on the river. I have watched them at home, in church, at their picnics and their funerals.[2]

All of this, he believes, gives him license to step forth as their interpreter and repeat stereotypes time-hallowed in the South. It doesn't. Mr. Bradford's stories remain highly amusing; his generalizations about *the* Negro remain a far better analysis of a white man than of *the* Negro. We see that, even in pontifical moments,

Reprinted from *Journal of Negro Education*, II (January, 1933), 180–201. Reprinted by permission of the editors.
[1] Roark Bradford, *Ol' Man Adam an' His Chillun*, New York: Harper and Bros., 1928, p. xi.
[2] *Ibid.*, p. ix.

one white Southerner cannot escape being influenced by current folk-beliefs.

Mr. Bradford's views have been restated at some length to show how obviously dangerous it is to rely upon literary artists when they advance themselves as sociologists and ethnologists. Mr. Bradford's easy pigeonholing of an entire race into three small compartments is a familiar phenomenon in American literature, ·where the Indian, the Mexican, the Irishman, and the Jew have been similarly treated. Authors are too anxious to have it said, "Here is *the* Negro," rather than here are a few Negroes whom I have seen. If one wishes to learn of Negro individuals observed from very specialized points of view, American literature can help him out. Some books will shed a great deal of light upon Negro experience. But if one wishes to learn of *the* Negro, it would be best to study *the* Negro himself; a study that might result in the discovery that *the* Negro is more difficult to find than the countless human beings called Negroes.

The Negro has met with as great injustice in American literature as he has in American life. The majority of books about Negroes merely stereotype Negro character. It is the purpose of this paper to point out the prevalence and history of these stereotypes. Those considered important enough for separate classification, although overlappings *do* occur, are seven in number: (1) The Contented Slave, (2) The Wretched Freeman, (3) The Comic Negro, (4) The Brute Negro, (5) The Tragic Mulatto, (6) The Local Color Negro, and (7) The Exotic Primitive.

A detailed evaluation of each of these is impracticable because of limitations of space. It can be said, however, that all of these stereotypes are marked either by exaggeration or omissions; that they all agree in stressing the Negro's divergence from an Anglo-Saxon norm to the flattery of the latter; they could all be used, as they probably are, as justification of racial proscription; they all illustrate dangerous specious generalizing from a few particulars recorded by a single observer from a restricted point of view— which is itself generally dictated by the desire to perpetuate a stereotype. All of these stereotypes are abundantly to be found in American literature, and are generally accepted as contributions to true racial understanding. Thus one critic, setting out imposingly to discuss "the Negro character" in American literature, can still say, unabashedly, that *"The whole range of the Negro character is revealed thoroughly,"*[3] in one twenty-six-line sketch by Joel Chandler Harris of Br'er Fox and Br'er Mud Turtle.

[3] John Herbert Nelson, *The Negro Character in American Literature*, Lawrence, Kansas: The Department of Journalism Press, 1926, p. 118.

The writer of this essay does not consider everything a stereotype that shows up the weaknesses of Negro character; sometimes the stereotype makes the Negro appear too virtuous. Nor does he believe the stereotypes of contented slaves and buffoons are to be successfully balanced by pictures of Negroes who are unbelievably intellectual, noble, self-sacrificial, and faultless. Any stereotyping is fatal to great, or even to convincing literature. Furthermore, he believes that he has considered to be stereotypes only those patterns whose frequent and tedious recurrence can be demonstrably proved by even a cursory acquaintance with the literature of the subject.

THE CONTENTED SLAVE

> "Massa make de darkies lub him
> 'Case he was so kind. . . ."
> (Stephen Foster)

The first lukewarm stirrings of abolitionary sentiment in the South were chilled with Eli Whitney's invention of the cotton gin at the close of the 18th Century. Up until this time the *raison d'être* of slavery had not been so powerful. But now there was a way open to quick wealth; Cotton was crowned King, and a huge army of black servitors was necessary to keep him upon the throne; considerations of abstract justice had to give way before economic expediency. A complete rationale of slavery was evolved.

One of the most influential of the authorities defending slavery was President Dew of William and Mary College, who stated, in 1832,

. . . slavery had been the condition of all ancient culture, that Christianity approved servitude, and that the law of Moses had both assumed and positively established slavery. . . . It is the order of nature and of God that the being of superior faculties and knowledge, and therefore of superior power, should control and dispose of those who are inferior. It is as much in the order of nature that men should enslave each other as that other animals should prey upon each other.[1]

The pamphlet of this young teacher was extensively circulated, and was substantiated by Chancellor Harper of the University of South Carolina in 1838:

Man is born to subjection. . . . The proclivity of the natural man is to domineer or to be subservient. . . . If there are sordid, servile, and

[1] William E. Dodd, *The Cotton Kingdom*, Chapter III, Philosophy of the Cotton Planter, p. 53.

laborious offices to be performed, is it not better that there should be sordid, servile, and laborious beings to perform them?[5]

The economic argument had frequent proponents; an ex-governor of Virginia showed that, although Virginia was denied the tremendous prosperity accruing from cotton raising, it was still granted the opportunity to profit from selling Negroes to the far South. Sociologists and anthropologists hastened forward with proof of the Negro's three-fold inferiority: physically (except for his adaptability to cotton fields and rice swamps), mentally, and morally. Theologists advanced the invulnerable arguments from the Bible; in one of the "Bible Defences of Slavery" we read: "The curse of Noah upon *Ham,* had a *general* and *interminable* application to the whole Hamite race, in placing them under a *peculiar* liability of being enslaved by the races of the two other brothers."[6]

The expressions of these dominant ideas in the fiction and poetry of the period did not lag far behind. In fact, one influential novel was among the leaders of the van, for in 1832, the year in which Professor Dew stated the argument that was to elevate him to the presidency of William and Mary College, John P. Kennedy published a work that was to make him one of the most widely read and praised authors of the Southland. His ideas of the character of the Negro and of slavery are in fundamental agreement with those of Dew and Harper. According to F. P. Gaines, in *The Southern Plantation,* Kennedy's *Swallow Barn* has the historical significance of starting the plantation tradition, a tradition hoary and mildewed in our own day, but by no means moribund.

Swallow Barn is an idyllic picture of slavery on a tidewater plantation. The narrator, imagined to be from the North (Kennedy himself was from Tidewater, Maryland), comes to Virginia, expecting to see a drastic state of affairs. Instead, he finds a kindly patriarchy and grateful, happy slaves. After vignettes of the Negro's laziness, mirth, vanity, improvidence, done with some charm and, for a Southern audience, considerable persuasiveness, the "Northern" narrator concludes:

I am quite sure they never could become a happier people than I find them here. . . . No tribe of people has ever passed from barbarism to civilization whose . . . progress has been more secure from harm, more genial to their character, or better supplied with mild and beneficent guardianship, adapted to the actual state of their intellectual feebleness, than the Negroes of *Swallow Barn.* And, from what I can gather, it is pretty much the same on the other estates in this region.[7]

[5] *Ibid.,* p. 57.
[6] Josiah Priest, *Bible Defence of Slavery,* Glasgow, Ky.: W. S. Brown, 1851, p. 52.
[7] John P. Kennedy, *Swallow Barn,* p. 453.

Shortly after the publication of *Swallow Barn*, Edgar Allan Poe wrote:

> . . . . we must take into consideration the peculiar character (I may say the peculiar nature) of the Negro. . . . [Some believe that Negroes] are, like ourselves, the sons of Adam and must, therefore, have like passions and wants and feelings and tempers in all respects. This we deny and appeal to the knowledge of all who know. . . . We shall take leave to speak as of things *in esse*, in a degree of loyal devotion on the part of the slave to which the white man's heart is a stranger, and of the master's reciprocal feeling of parental attachment to his humble dependent. . . . That these sentiments in the breast of the Negro and his master are stronger than they would be under like circumstances between individuals of the white race, we believe.[8]

In *The Gold-Bug*, Poe shows this reciprocal relationship between Jupiter, a slave, and his master. Southern fiction of the thirties and forties supported the thesis of Kennedy and Poe without being so explicit. The mutual affection of the races, the slave's happiness with his status, and his refusal to accept freedom appear here and there, but the books were dedicated less to the defense of the peculiar institution than to entertainment. William Gilmore Simms, for instance, includes in *The Yemassee*, a novel published in the same year as *Swallow Barn*, the typical pro-slavery situation of a slave's refusing freedom: " 'I d—n to h—ll, maussa, ef I guine to be free!' roared the *adhesive* black, in a tone of unrestrainable determination."[9] But the burden of this book is not pro-slavery; Hector earns his freedom by the unslavish qualities of physical prowess, foresight, and courage in battle.

In 1853, Simms, in joining forces with Dew and Harper in the *Pro-Slavery Argument*, writes: "Slavery has elevated the Negro from savagery. The black man's finer traits of fidelity and docility were encouraged in his servile position. . . ."[10] Simms turned from cursory references to slavery to ardent pro-slavery defense, in company with other novelists of the South, for a perfectly definite reason. The abolitionary attacks made by men like Garrison had taken the form of pamphlets, and these had been answered in kind. The publication of *Uncle Tom's Cabin* in 1851, however, showed that the abolitionists had converted the novel into a powerful weapon. Pro-slavery authors were quick to take up this weapon,

---

[8] Edgar Allan Poe, *Literary Criticism*, Vol. 1, "Slavery in the United States," p. 271.
[9] William Gilmore Simms, *The Yemassee*, Richmond: B. F. Johnson Publishing Co., 1911, p. 423. The italics are mine but not the omissions.
[10] Jeanette Reid Tandy, "Pro-Slavery Propaganda in American Fiction of the Fifties," *South Atlantic Quarterly*, Vol. XXI, No. 1, p. 41.

although their wielding of it was without the power of Harriet Beecher Stowe. *Swallow Barn* was reissued in 1851, and "besides the numerous controversial pamphlets and articles in periodicals there were no fewer than fourteen pro-slavery novels and one long poem published in the three years (1852–54) following the appearance of *Uncle Tom's Cabin*."[11]

These novels are all cut out of the same cloth. Like *Swallow Barn*, they omit the economic basis of slavery, and minimize "the sordid, servile and laborious offices" which Chancellor Harper had considered the due of "sordid, servile, and laborious beings." The pro-slavery authors use the first adjective only in considering free Negroes, or those who, by some quirk of nature, are disobedient; admit the second completely; and deny the third. Slavery to all of them is a beneficent guardianship, the natural and inevitable state for a childish people.

There is very little reference to Negroes working in the fields; even then they are assigned to easy tasks which they lazily perform to the tune of slave melodies. They are generally described as "leaving the fields." They are allowed to have, for additional provisions and huckstering, their own garden-plots, which they attend in their abundant leisure. Their holidays are described at full length: the corn huskings, barbecuing, Yuletide parties, and hunting the possum by the light of a kindly moon.

In *Life at the South, or Uncle Tom's Cabin As It is* (1852), Uncle Tom, out of hurt vanity, but not for any more grievous cause, runs away. His wife, Aunt Dinah, although loving Tom, realizes that her greater loyalty is due to her master, and not to her errant spouse, and refuses to escape with him. Tom, after experiencing the harshness of the unfeeling North, begs to return to slavery. In *The Planter's Northern Bride*, the bride, having come to the slave South with misgivings, is quickly converted to an enthusiast for slavery, since it presents "an aspect so tender and affectionate." One fears that the bride is not unpartisan, however, since her appearance on the plantation elicited wild cries of worship, and her beloved husband is a great ethnologist, proving that the Negro's peculiar skull and skin were decreed by the divine fiat so that he could pick cotton. In *The Yankee Slave Dealer*, the meddling abolitionist cannot persuade any slaves to run off with him except a half-witted rogue. One slave recited to him *verbatim* a miniature *Bible Defence of Slavery*, citing the book of the Bible, the chapter, and the verse. In *The Hireling and The Slave*, William J. Grayson, "poet laureate" of South Carolina, contrasts the lot of

[11] *Ibid.*, p. 41.

the industrial worker of the North with that of the slave. Gems of this widely read poetical disquisition follow:

> And yet the life, so unassailed by care,
> So blessed with moderate work, with ample fare,
> With all the good the starving pauper needs,
> The happier slave on each plantation leads . . . . (p. 50)
> And Christian slaves may challenge as their own,
> The blessings claimed in fabled states alone . . . . (p. 50)

This pattern of the joyous contentment of the slave in a paradisaical bondage persisted and was strongly reenforced in Reconstruction days. If it was no longer needed for the defense of a tottering institution, it was needed for reasons nearly as exigent. Ancestor worshippers, the sons of a fighting generation, remembering bitterly the deaths or sufferings of their fathers, became elegists of a lost cause and cast a golden glow over the plantation past; unreconstructed "fire-eaters," determined to resurrect slavery as far as they were able, needed as a cardinal principle the belief that Negroes were happy as slaves, and hopelessly unequipped for freedom. Both types were persuasive, the first because the romantic idealizing of the past will always be seductive to a certain large group of readers, and the second because the sincere unremitting harping upon one argument will finally make it seem plausible. We find, therefore, that whereas *Uncle Tom's Cabin* had triumphed in the antebellum controversy, the pro-slavery works of Page, Russell, and Harris swept the field in Reconstruction days. It is from these last skillful authors, undeniably acquainted with Negro folklife, and affectionate toward certain aspects of it, that the American reading public as a whole has accepted the delusion of the Negro as contented slave, entertaining child, and docile ward.

Mutual affection between the races is a dominant theme. Thus, Irwin Russell, the first American poet to treat Negro life in folk speech, has his ex-slave rhapsodizing about his "Mahsr John." "Washintum an' Franklum . . . wuzn't nar a one . . . come up to Mahsr John":

> Well times is changed. De war it come an' sot de niggers free
> An' now ol' Mahsr John ain't hardly wuf as much as me:
> He had to pay his debts, an' so his lan' is mos'ly gone—
> An' I declar' I's sorry for my pore ol' Mahsr John.[12]

---

[12] Irwin Russell, *Christmas Night in the Quarters*, New York: The Century Co., 1917, pp. 63 ff.

The volume has many other references to the slave's docility toward and worship of his master.

Irwin Russell implies throughout that the Southern white best understands how to treat the Negro. Perhaps this is one reason for Joel Chandler Harris' praise:

> But the most wonderful thing about the dialect poetry of Irwin Russell is his accurate conception of the negro character. . . . I do not know where could be found today a happier or a more perfect representation of negro character.

On reading Russell's few poems, one is struck by the limited gamut of characteristics allowed to Negroes. Inclined to the peccadilloes of cheating, lying easily; a good teller of comic stories, a child of mirth, his greatest hardship that of being kicked about by refractory mules, and his deepest emotion, compassion for his master's lost estate—surely this is hardly a "perfect" representation of even Negro folk character?

Thomas Nelson Page followed Russell's lead in poetry. In the poems of *Befo' De War,* Page puts into the mouths of his Negroes yearnings for the old days and expressions of the greatest love for old marster. One old slave welcomes death if it will replace him in old "Marster's service." Old Jack entrusts his life-earnings to his son to give to young "Marster," since the latter can't work and needs them more.[13]

In most of Page's widely influential stories, there is the stock situation of the lifelong devotion of master and body-servant. In *Marse Chan,* old "Marse" is blinded in rescuing a slave from a burning barn. Sam accompanies his young Marse Chan to the war, his devotion overcoming "racial cowardice" to such a degree that he rides to the very cannon's mouth with him, and brings back his master's body. Of slavery, Sam speaks thus:

> Dem wuz good old times, marster—de bes' Sam ever see! Dey wuz, in fac'! Niggers didn't hed nothin 't all to do—jes' hed to 'ten to de feedin' an' cleanin' de hosses, an' doin' what de marster tell 'em to do; an' when dey wuz sick, dey had things sont 'em out de house, an' de same doctor come to see 'em whar ten' do de white folks when dey wuz po'ly. D'yar warn' no trouble nor nothin.[14]

Over all his fiction there is the reminiscent melancholy of an exiled Adam, banished by a flaming sword—wielded not by

[13] Thomas Nelson Page, *Befo' De War*. New York: Chas. Scribner's Sons, 1906, "Little Jack."

[14] Thomas Nelson Page, *In Ole Virginia*. New York: Chas. Scribner's Sons, 1889.

Michael but by a Yankee devil, from what was truly an Eden. In *The Negro: The Southerner's Problem,* we read:

In fact, the ties of pride were such that it was often remarked that the affection of the slaves was stronger toward the whites than toward their own offspring.[15]

And in the same book there is an apostrophe to the "mammy" that is a worthy forerunner of the bids so many orators make for inter-racial good-will, and of the many remunerative songs that emerge from Tin Pan Alley.

Joel Chandler Harris is better known for his valuable contribution to literature and folk-lore in recording the Uncle Remus stories than for his aid in perpetuation of the "plantation Negro" stereotype. Nevertheless, a merely cursory study of Uncle Remus' character would reveal his close relationship to the "Caesars," "Hectors," "Pompeys," *et al.* of the pro-slavery novel, and to Page's "Uncle Jack" and "Uncle Billy." In Uncle Remus' philosophizing about the old days of slavery there is still the wistful nostalgia. Harris comments, "In Middle Georgia the relations between master and slave were as perfect as they could be under the circumstances." This might mean a great deal, or nothing, but it is obvious from other words of Harris that, fundamentally, slavery was to him a kindly institution, and the Negro was contented. Slavery was:

. . . in some of its aspects far more beautiful and inspiring than *any* of the relations between employers and the employed in this day.[16]

George Washington Cable, although more liberal in his views upon the Negro than his Southern contemporaries, gives an example of the self-abnegating servant in *Posson Jone'*. This slave uses his wits to safeguard his master. A goodly proportion of the Negro servants are used to solve the complications of their "white folks." They are in a long literary tradition—that of the faithful, clever servant—and they probably are just as true to Latin prototypes as to real Negroes. In the works of F. Hopkinson Smith, Harry Stilwell Edwards, and in Maurice Thompson's *Balance of Power,* we have this appearance of a black *deus ex machina.*

To deal adequately with the numerous books of elegiac reminiscence of days "befo' de war" would be beyond the scope and

[15] Thomas Nelson Page, *The Negro: The Southerner's Problem.* New York: Chas. Scribner's Sons, 1904, p. 174.
[16] Julia Collier Harris, *Joel Chandler Harris, Editor and Essayist.* Chapel Hill: University of North Carolina Press, 1931, "The Old-Time Darky," p. 129.

purpose of this essay. The tone of them all is to be found in such sad sentences as these:

Aunt Phebe, Uncle Tom, Black Mammy, Uncle Gus, Aunt Jonas, Uncle Isom, and all the rest—who shall speak all your virtues or enshrine your simple faith and fidelity? It is as impossible as it is to describe the affection showered upon you by those whom you called "Marster" and "Mistis."[17]

Ambrose Gonzales grieves that "the old black folk are going fast" with the passing of the "strict but kindly discipline of slavery," yearning, in Tennysonian accents, "for the tender grace of a day that is dead."[18]

Although the realism of today is successfully discounting the sentimentalizing of the Old South, there are still many contemporary manifestations of the tradition. Hergesheimer, arch-romanticist that he is, writes that he would be happy to pay with everything the wasted presence holds for the return of the pastoral civilization based on slavery.[19]

Donald Davidson, a Tennessee poet, has written this:

Black man, when you and I were young together,
We knew each other's hearts. Though I am no longer
A child, and you perhaps unfortunately
Are no longer a child, we still understand
Better maybe than others. There is the wall
Between us, anciently erected. Once
It might have been crossed, men say. But now I cannot
Forget that I was master, and you can hardly
Forget that you were slave. We did not build
The ancient wall, but there it painfully is.
Let us not bruise our foreheads on the wall.[20]

Ol' Massa's People, by Orlando Kay Armstrong, is one of the most recent of the books in which ex-slaves speak—as in Page apparently with their master's voice—their praise of slavery. The theme seems inexhaustible; in the February issue of the *Atlantic Monthly* it is restated in nearly the words that have already been quoted. Designed originally to defend slavery, it is now a convenient argument for those wishing to keep "the Negro in his place"

[17] Essie Collins Matthews, *Aunt Phebe, Uncle Tom and Others*. Columbus, Ohio: The Champlin Press, 1915, p. 13.

[18] Ambrose Gonzales, *With Aesop Along the Black Border*. Columbia, S.C.: The State Co., 1924, p. xiv.

[19] Joseph Hergesheimer, *Quiet Cities*. New York: Alfred A. Knopf, 1928, pp. 14 ff.

[20] Donald Davidson, *The Tall Men*. New York: Houghton Mifflin Co., 1927, p. 39.

—out of great love for him, naturally—believing that he will be happier so.

THE WRETCHED FREEMAN

"Go tell Marse Linkum, to tek his freedom back."

As a foil to the contented slave, pro-slavery authors set up another puppet—the wretched free Negro. He was necessary for the argument. Most of the pro-slavery novels paid a good deal of attention to his degradation. Either the novelist interpolated a long disquisition on the disadvantages of his state both to the country and to himself, or had his happy slaves fear contact with him as with a plague.

In *Life at The South, or Uncle Tom's Cabin as It Is*, Uncle Tom experiences harsh treatment from unfeeling Northern employers, sees Negroes frozen to death in snow storms, and all in all learns that the North and freedom is no stopping place for him. In *The Yankee Slave Dealer*, the slaves are insistent upon the poor lot of free Negroes. In *The Planter's Northern Bride*, Crissy runs away from freedom in order to be happy again in servitude. Grayson in *The Hireling and Slave* prophesies thus:

> Such, too, the fate the Negro must deplore
> If slavery guards his subject race no more,
> If by weak friends or vicious counsels led
> To change his blessings for the hireling's bread. . . .
> There in the North in suburban dens and human sties,
> In foul excesses sung, the Negro lies;
> A moral pestilence to taint and stain.
> His life a curse, his death a social gain,
> Debased, despised, the Northern pariah knows
> He shares no good that liberty bestows;
> Spurned from her gifts, with each successive year,
> In drunken want his numbers disappear.[21]

There was a carry-over of these ideas in the Reconstruction. Harris, in one of his most moving stories, *Free Joe*, showed the tragedy of a free Negro in a slave-holding South, where he was considered a bad model by slave-owners, an economic rival by poor whites, and something to be avoided by the slaves. The story might be considered as a condemnation of a system, but in all probability

---

[21] William J. Grayson, *The Hireling and the Slave*. Charleston, S.C., McCarter and Co., 1856, pp. 68 ff.

was taken to be another proof of the Negro's incapacity for freedom. Although Harris wrote generously of Negro advancement since emancipation, there is little doubt that the implications of many passages furthered the stereotype under consideration.

Page, a bourbon "fire-eater," for all of his yearnings for his old mammy, saw nothing of good for Negroes in emancipation:

> Universally, they [Southerners] will tell you that while the old-time Negroes were industrious, saving, and, when not misled, well-behaved, kindly, respectful, and self-respecting, and while the remnant of them who remain still retain generally these characteristics, the "new issue," for the most part, are lazy, thriftless, intemperate, insolent, dishonest, and without the most rudimentary elements of morality . . . . Universally, they report a general depravity and retrogression of the Negroes at large in sections in which they are left to themselves, closely resembling a reversion to barbarism.[22]

The notion of the Negro's being doomed to extinction was sounded by a chorus of pseudo-scientists, bringing forth a formidable (?) array of proofs. Lafcadio Hearn yielded to the lure of posing as a prophet:

> As for the black man, he must disappear with the years. Dependent like the ivy, he needs some strong oak-like friend to cling to. His support has been cut from him, and his life must wither in its prostrate helplessness. Will he leave no trace of his past? . . . . Ah, yes! . . . the weird and beautiful melodies born in the hearts of the poor, child-like people to whom freedom was destruction.[23]

Many were the stories ringing changes on the theme: "Go tell Marse Linkum, to tek his freedom back." Thus, in *The Carolina Low Country,* Mr. Sass writes of Old Aleck, who, on being freed, spoke his little piece: "Miss, I don't want no wagis." "God bless you, old Aleck," sighs Mr. Sass.

Modern neo-confederates repeat the stereotype. Allen Tate, co-member with Donald Davidson of the Nashville saviors of the South, implies in *Jefferson Davis, His Rise and Fall,* that to educate a Negro beyond his station brings him unhappiness. One of the chief points of agreement in the Neo-Confederate *I'll Take My Stand* by Davidson, Tate and ten others is that freedom has proved to be a perilous state for the Negro. Joseph Hergesheimer agrees: "A free Negro is more often wretched than not."[24] "Slavery was

---

[22] Thomas Nelson Page, *The Negro: The Southerner's Problem, op. cit.,* p. 80.
[23] Lafcadio Hearn, *Letters from the Raven.* New York: A. & C. Boni, 1930, p. 168.
[24] Joseph Hergesheimer, *op. cit.,* p. 137.

gone, the old serene days were gone. Negroes were bad because they were neither slave nor free."[25] And finally, a modern illustration must suffice. Eleanor Mercein Kelly in an elegy for the vanishing South, called *Monkey Motions,* pities "the helplessness of a simple jungle folk, a bandar-log, set down in the life of cities and expected to be men."[26]

It is, all in all, a sad picture that these savants give. What concerns us here, however, is its persistence, a thing inexpressibly more sad.

THE COMIC NEGRO

"That Reminds Me of a Story. There Were Once Two Ethiopians, Sambo and Rastus . . . ." (1,001 After-Dinner Speakers.)

The stereotype of the "comic Negro" is about as ancient as the "contented slave." Indeed, they might be considered complementary, since, if the Negro could be shown as perpetually mirthful, his state could not be so wretched. This is, of course, the familiar procedure when conquerors depict a subject people. English authors at the time of Ireland's greatest persecution built up the stereotype of the comic Irishman, who fascinated English audiences, and unfortunately, in a manner known to literary historians, influenced even Irish authors.[27] Thus, we find, in a melodrama about Irish life, an English officer soliloquizing:

I swear, the Irish nature is beyond my comprehension. A strange people!—merry 'mid their misery—laughing through their tears, like the sun shining through the rain. Yet what simple philosophers they! They tread life's path as if 'twere strewn with roses devoid of thorns, and make the most of life with natures of sunshine and song.[28]

Any American not reading the words "Irish nature" could be forgiven for taking the characterization to refer to American Negroes. Natures of sunshine and song, whose wretchedness becomes nothing since theirs is a simple philosophy of mirth! So runs the pattern.

[25] *Ibid.,* p. 293.

[26] Blanche Colton Williams, *O. Henry Memorial Award Prize Stories of 1927.* Garden City Doubleday, Doran & Co., p. 207.

[27] *Vide:* George Bernard Shaw's *John Bull's Other Island,* Daniel Corkery's *Synge and Anglo-Irish Literature,* Yeat's *Plays and Controversies,* Lady Gregory's *Our Irish Theatre,* for attacks upon the "comic" Irishman stereotype.

[28] John Fitzgerald Murphy, *The Shamrock and The Rose.* Boston: Walter H. Baker Co., n. d., p. 25.

In her excellent book, *American Humor,* Constance Rourke points out the Negro as one of the chief ingredients of the potpourri of American humor. She traces him as far back as the early '20's when Edwin Forrest made up as a Southern plantation Negro to excite the risibilities of Cincinnati. In *The Spy,* Cooper belabors the grotesqueness of Caesar's appearance, although Caesar is not purely and simply the buffoon:

. . . . But it was in his legs that nature had indulged her most capricious humor. There was an abundance of material injudiciously used. The calves were neither before nor behind, but rather on the outer side of the limb, inclining forward . . . . The leg was placed so near the center (of the foot) as to make it sometimes a matter of dispute whether he was not walking backward.[29]

Kennedy in his *Swallow Barn* not only reveals the Negro as delighted by the master's benevolence, but also as delighting the master by his ludicrous departure from the Anglo-Saxon norm. Kennedy revels in such descriptions as the following:

His face . . . . was principally composed of a pair of protuberant lips, whose luxuriance seemed intended as an indemnity for a pair of crushed nostrils. . . . Two bony feet occupied shoes, each of the superfices and figure of a hoe. . . . Wrinkled, decrepit old men, with faces shortened as if with drawing strings, noses that seemed to have run all to nostril, and with feet of the configuration of a mattock. . . .[30]

It was in the early '30's, however, that T. D. Rice first jumped "Jim Crow" in the theaters along the Ohio River and set upon the stage the "minstrel Negro." Apparently immortal, this stereotype was to involve in its perpetuation such famous actors as Joseph Jefferson and David Belasco, to make Amos 'n' Andy as essential to American domesticity as a car in every garage, and to mean affluence for a Jewish comedian of whom only one gesture was asked: that he sink upon one knee, extend his white-gloved hands, and cry out "Mammy."

In pro-slavery fiction the authors seemed to agree on the two aspects of the comic Negro—that he was ludicrous to others, and forever laughing himself. Grayson writes in *The Hireling and The Slave:*

> The long, loud laugh, that freemen seldom share,
> Heaven's boon to bosoms unapproached by care;
> And boisterous jest and humor unrefined . . . [31]

[29] James Fenimore Cooper, *The Spy.* New York: Scott, Foresman Co., 1927, p. 45.
[30] Kennedy, *op. cit., passim.*
[31] Grayson, *op. cit.,* p. 51.

To introduce comic relief, perhaps, in stories that might defeat their own purposes if confined only to the harrowing details of slavery, anti-slavery authors had their comic characters. Topsy is the classic example; it is noteworthy that in contemporary acting versions of "Uncle Tom's Cabin," Topsy and the minstrel show note, if not dominant, are at least of equal importance to the melodrama of Eliza and the bloodhounds.

Reconstruction literature developed the stereotype. Russell's Negroes give side-splitting versions of the Biblical story (foreshadowing Bradford's *Ol' Man Adam An' His Chillun*), or have a fatal fondness for propinquity to a mule's rear end. Page's Negroes punctuate their worship of "ole Marse" with "Kyah-kyahs," generally directed at themselves. The humor of Uncle Remus is nearer to genuine folk-humor, which—it might be said in passing—is *not* the same as the "comic Negro" humor. Negroes in general, in the Reconstruction stories, are seen as creatures of mirth—who wouldn't suffer from hardship, even if they had to undergo it. Thus a Negro, sentenced to the chain-gang for stealing a pair of breeches, is made the theme of a comic poem.[32] This is illustrative. There may be random jokes in Southern court rooms, but joking about the Negroes' experiences with Southern "justice" and with the chain-gang is rather ghastly—like laughter at the mouth of hell. Creatures of sunshine and of song!

The "comic Negro" came into his own in the present century, and brought his creators into theirs. Octavius Cohen, who looks upon the idea of Negro doctors and lawyers and society belles as the height of the ridiculous, served such clienteles as that of *The Saturday Evening Post* for a long time with the antics of Florian Slappey. His work is amusing at its best, but is pseudo-Negro. Instead of being a handicap, however, that seems a recommendation to his audience. Trusting to most moth-eaten devices of farce, and interlarding a Negro dialect never heard on land or sea—compounded more of Dogberry and Mrs. Malaprop than of Birmingham Negroes,[33] he has proved to the whites that all along they have known the real Negro—"Isn't he funny, now!"—and has shown to Negroes what whites wanted them to resemble. Mrs. Octavius Roy Cohen follows in the wake of her illustrious husband in *Our Darktown Press*, a gleaning of "boners" from Aframerican newspapers. Editorial carelessness is sadly enough familiar in race

[32] Belle Richardson Harrison, *Poetry of the Southern States*, edited by Clement Wood, Girard, Kansas: Haldeman-Julius Co., 1924, p. 36.

[33] "Yeh, an' was he to git one good bite at a cullud man like me, he'd exterminate me so quick I wouldn't even have a chance to notrify my heirs," "I ain't hahdly sawn her right recent," are examples of his inimitable (fortunately so, although Amos an' Andy try it in "I'se regusted," etc.) dialect; "Drastic" "Unit" "Quinine" "Midnight," and "Sons and Daughters of I Will Arise" are examples of his nomenclature.

journals; every item in the book is vouched for, but the total effect is the reenforcing of a stereotype that America loves to believe in.

Arthur E. Akers, with a following in another widely read magazine, is another farceur. He uses the situation of the domestic difficulty, as old as medieval fabliaux and farces—and places it in a Southern Negro community, and has his characters speak an approximation to Negro dialect—but too slick and "literary" for conviction. Irate shrews and "Milquetoast" husbands, with razors wielded at departing parts of the anatomy, are Akers' stock-in-trade. Hugh Wiley with his Wildcat, inseparable from his goat, Lady Luck, unsavory but a talisman, is another creator of the farce that Negro life is too generally believed to be. E. K. Means, with obvious knowledge of Southern Negro life, is concerned to show in the main its ludicrous side, and Irvin Cobb, with a reputation of after-dinner wit to uphold, is similarly confined.

The case of Roark Bradford is different. An undoubted humorist, in the great line of Twain and the tall tales of the Southwest, he gleans from a rich store of Negro speech and folkways undeniably amusing tales. But as his belief about the Negro (cf. Introduction) might attest, he has a definite attitude to the Negro to uphold. His stories of the easy loves of the levee (frequently found in *Collier's*) concentrate upon the comic aspect of Negro life, although another observer might well see the tragic. In *Ol' Man Adam an' His Chillun* we have farce manufactured out of the Negro's religious beliefs. It seems to the writer that the weakest sections of *Green Pastures* stick closest to Bradford's stories, and that the majesty and reverence that can be found in the play must come from Marc Connelly. In *John Henry*, Bradford has definitely weakened his material by making over a folk-hero into a clown.

Although the situations in which the comic Negro finds himself range from the fantastic as in Cohen, to the possible as in "The Two Black Crows" and in "Amos 'n' Andy," his characteristics are fairly stable. The "comic Negro" is created for the delectation of a white audience, condescending and convinced that any departure from the Anglo-Saxon norm is amusing, and that any attempt to enter the special provinces of whites, such as wearing a dress suit, is doubly so. The "comic Negro" with certain physical attributes exaggerated—with his razor (generally harmless), his love for watermelon and gin, for craps, his haunting of chicken roosts, use of big words he doesn't understand, grandiloquent names and titles, "loud" clothes, bluster, hysterical cowardice, and manufactured word-play—has pranced his way by means of books, vaudeville skits, shows, radio programs, advertisements, and after-dinner speeches, into the folklore of the nation. As Guy B. Johnson urges there is a sort of—

. . . folk attitude of the white man toward the Negro. . . . One cannot help noticing that the white man must have his fun out of the Negro, even when writing serious novels about him. This is partly conscious, indeed a necessity, if one is to portray Negro life as it is, for Negroes are human and behave like other human beings. Sometimes it is unconscious, rising out of our old habit of associating the Negro with the comical.[34]

In pointing out the stereotype, one does not deny the rich comedy to be found in Negro life. One is insisting, however, that any picture concentrating upon this to the exclusion of all else is entirely inadequate, that many of the most popular creators of the "comic Negro," "doctor" their material, and are far from accurate in depicting even the small area of Negro experience they select, and that too often they exceed the prerogative of comedy by making copy out of persecution and injustice.

THE BRUTE NEGRO

"All Scientific Investigation of the Subject Proves the Negro to Be An Ape." (Chas. Carroll, The Negro a Beast.)

Because the pro-slavery authors were anxious to prove that slavery had been a benefit to the Negro in removing him from savagery to Christianity, the stereotype of the "brute Negro" was relatively insignificant in antebellum days. There were references to vicious criminal Negroes in fiction (vicious and criminal being synonymous to discontented and refractory), but these were considered as exceptional cases of half-wits led astray by abolitionists. The Bible Defence of Slavery, however, in which the Rev. Priest in a most unclerical manner waxes wrathful at abolitionists, sets forth with a great array of theological argument and as much ridiculousness, proofs of the Negro's extreme lewdness. Sodom and Gomorrah were destroyed because these were strongholds of Negro vice. The book of Leviticus proved that Negroes

outraged all order and decency of human society. Lewdness of the most hideous description was the crime of which they were guilty, blended with idolatry in their adoration of the gods, who were carved out of

---

[34] Guy B. Johnson, "Folk Values in Recent Literature on the Negro" in Folk-Say, edited by B. A. Botkin, Norman, Oklahoma, 1930, p. 371.

wood, painted and otherwise made, so as to represent the wild passions of lascivious desires. . . . The baleful fire of unchaste amour rages through the negro's blood more fiercely than in the blood of any other people . . . on which account they are a people who are suspected of being but little acquainted with the virtue of chastity, and of regarding very little the marriage oath. . . .[35]

H. R. Helper, foe of slavery, was no friend of the Negro, writing, in 1867, *Nojoque,* a lurid condemnation of the Negro, setting up black and beastly as exact synonyms. Van Evrie's *White Supremacy and Negro Subordination, or Negroes A Subordinate Race, and (so-called) Slavery Its Normal Condition* gave "anthropological" support to the figment of the "beastly Negro," and *The Negro A Beast* (1900) gave theological support. The title page of this book runs:

The Reasoner of the Age, the Revelator of the Century! The Bible As It Is! The Negro and his Relation to the Human Family! The Negro a beast, but created with articulate speech, and hands, that he may be of service to his master—the White Man. . . . by Chas. Carroll, who has spent 15 years of his life and $20,000.00 in its compilation. . . .

Who could ask for anything more?

Authors stressing the mutual affection between the races looked upon the Negro as a docile mastiff. In the Reconstruction this mastiff turned into a mad dog. "Damyanks," carpetbaggers, scalawags, and New England schoolmarms affected him with the rabies. The works of Thomas Nelson Page are good examples of this metamorphosis. When his Negro characters are in their place, loyally serving and worshipping ole Marse, they are admirable creatures, but in freedom they are beasts, as his novel *Red Rock* attests. *The Negro: The Southerner's Problem* says that the state of the Negro since emancipation is one of minimum progress and maximum regress.

[This] is borne out by the increase of crime among them, by the increase of superstition, with its black trail of unnamable immorality and vice; by the homicides and murders, and by the outbreak and growth of that brutal crime which has chiefly brought about the frightful crime of lynching which stains the *good name of the South* and has spread northward with the spread of the ravisher. . . . The crime of rape . . . . is the fatal product of new conditions. . . . The Negro's passion, always his controlling force, is now, since the new teaching, for the white woman. [Lynching is justifiable] for it has its root deep in the basic passions of humanity; the determination to put an end to the *ravishing*

---

[35] Josiah Priest, *op. cit.,* Eighth Section, *passim.*

of their women by an inferior race, or by any race, no matter what the consequence. . . . A crusade has been preached against lynching, even as far as England; but none has been attempted against the ravishing and tearing to pieces of white women and children.[36]

The best known author of Ku Klux Klan fiction after Page is Thomas Dixon. Such works as *The Clansman*, and *The Leopard's Spots*, because of their sensationalism and chapter titles (e.g., "The Black Peril," "The Unspoken Terror," "A Thousand Legged Beast," "The Hunt for the Animal"), seemed just made for the mentality of Hollywood, where D. W. Griffiths in *The Birth of a Nation* made for Thomas Dixon a dubious sort of immortality, and finally fixed the stereotype in the mass-mind. The stock Negro in Dixon's books, unless the shuffling hat-in-hand servitor, is a gorilla-like imbecile, who "springs like a tiger" and has the "black claws of a beast." In both books there is a terrible rape, and a glorious ride of the Knights on a Holy Crusade to avenge Southern civilization. Dixon enables his white geniuses to discover the identity of the rapist by using "a microscope of sufficient power [to] reveal on the retina of the dead eyes the image of this devil as if etched there by fire." . . . The doctor sees "The bestial figure of a negro—his huge black hand plainly defined. . . . It was Gus." Will the wonders of science never cease? But, perhaps, after all, Negroes have been convicted on even flimsier evidence. Fortunately for the self-respect of American authors, this kind of writing is in abeyance today. Perhaps it fell because of the weight of its own absurdity. But it would be unwise to underestimate this stereotype. It is probably of great potency in certain benighted sections where Dixon, if he could be read, would be applauded—and it certainly serves as a convenient self-justification for a mob about to uphold white supremacy by a lynching.

THE TRAGIC MULATTO

> "The gods bestow on me
> A life of hate,
> The white man's gift to see
> A nigger's fate."

> ("The Mulatto Addresses his Savior on Christmas Morning," Seymour Gordden Link.)

Stereotyping was by no means the monopoly of pro-slavery authors defending their type of commerce, or justifying their ances-

[36] Page, *The Negro: The Southerner's Problem*, *passim* (Italics mine).

tors. Anti-slavery authors, too, fell into the easy habit, but with a striking difference. Where pro-slavery authors had predicated a different set of characteristics for the Negroes, a distinctive sub-human nature, and had stereotyped in accordance with such a comforting hypothesis, anti-slavery authors insisted that the Negro had a common humanity with the whites, that in given circumstances a typically human type of response was to be expected, unless certain other powerful influences were present. The stereotyping in abolitionary literature, therefore, is not stereotyping of *character,* but of *situation.* Since the novels were propagandistic, they concentrated upon abuses: floggings, the slave mart, the domestic slave trade, forced concubinage, runaways, slave hunts, and persecuted freemen—all of these were frequently repeated. Stereotyped or not, heightened if you will, the anti-slavery novel has been supported by the verdict of history—whether recorded by Southern or Northern historians. Facts, after all, are abolitionist. Especially the fact that the Colonel's lady and old Aunt Dinah are sisters under the skin.

Anti-slavery authors did at times help to perpetuate certain pro-slavery stereotypes. Probably the novelists knew that harping upon the gruesome, to the exclusion of all else, would repel readers, who—like their present-day descendants—yearn for happy endings and do not wish their quick consciences to be harrowed. At any rate, comic relief, kindly masters (in contrast to the many brutes), loyal and submissive slaves (to accentuate the wrongs inflicted upon them) were scattered throughout the books. Such tempering of the attacks was turned to pro-slavery uses. Thus, Harris writes:

> It seems to me to be impossible for any unprejudiced person to read Mrs. Stowe's book and fail to see in it a defence of American slavery as she found it in Kentucky. . . . The real moral that Mrs. Stowe's book teaches is that the possibilities of slavery . . . . are shocking to the imagination, while the realities, under the best and happiest conditions, possess a romantic beauty and a tenderness all their own. . . .[37]

Anti-slavery fiction did proffer one stereotype, doomed to unfortunate longevity. This is the tragic mulatto. Pro-slavery apologists had almost entirely omitted (with so many other omissions) mention of concubinage. If anti-slavery authors, in accordance with Victorian gentility, were wary of illustrating the practice, they made great use nevertheless of the offspring of illicit unions. Generally the heroes and heroines of their books are near-whites. These are the intransigent, the resentful, the mentally alert, the

---

[37] Julia Collier Harris, *op. cit.,* p. 117.

proofs of the Negro's possibilities. John Herbert Nelson says with some point:

> Abolitionists tried, by making many of their characters almost white, to work on racial feeling as well. This was a curious piece of inconsistency on their part, an indirect admission that a white man in chains was more pitiful to behold than the African similarly placed. Their most impassioned plea was in behalf of a person little resembling their swarthy protégés, the quadroon or octoroon.[38]

Nelson himself, however, shows similar inconsistency, as he infers that the "true African—essentially gay, happy-go-lucky, rarely ambitious or idealistic, the eternal child of the present moment, able to leave trouble behind—is unsuited for such portrayal. . . . Only the mulattoes and others of mixed blood have, so far, furnished us with material for convincing tragedy."[39]

The tragic mulatto appears in both of Mrs. Stowe's abolitionary novels. In *Uncle Tom's Cabin*, the fugitives Liza and George Harris and the rebellious Cassy are mulattoes. Uncle Tom, the pure black, remains the paragon of Christian submissiveness. In *Dred*, Harry Gordon and his wife are nearly white. Harry is an excellent manager, and a proud, unsubmissive type:

> Mr. Jekyl, that humbug don't go down with me! I'm no more of the race of Ham than you are! I'm Colonel Gordon's oldest son—as white as my brother, who you say owns me! Look at my eyes, and my hair, and say if any of the rules about Ham pertain to me.[40]

The implication that there are "rules about Ham" that do pertain to blacks is to be found in other works. Richard Hildreth's *Archy Moore, or The White Slave,* has as its leading character a fearless, educated mulatto, indistinguishable from whites; Boucicault's *The Octoroon* sentimentalizes the hardships of a slave girl; both make the mixed blood the chief victim of slavery.

Cable, in the *Grandissimes*, shows a Creole mulatto educated beyond his means, and suffering ignominy, but he likewise shows in the character of Bras-Coupé that he does not consider intrepidity and vindictiveness the monopoly of mixed-bloods. In *Old Creole Days*, however, he discusses the beautiful octoroons, whose best fortune in life was to become the mistress of some New Orleans dandy. He shows the tragedy of their lives, but undoubtedly con-

[38] John Herbert Nelson, *op. cit.*, p. 84.
[39] *Ibid.*, p. 136.
[40] Harriet Beecher Stowe, *Nina Gordon, or Dred.* Boston: Houghton Mifflin and Co., 1881, p. 142.

tributed to the modern stereotype that the greatest yearning of the girl of mixed life is for a white lover. Harriet Martineau, giving a contemporary portrait of old New Orleans, wrote:

> The quadroon girls . . . . are brought up by their mothers to be what they have been; the mistresses of white gentlemen. The boys are some of them sent to France; some placed on land in the back of the State. . . . The women of their own color object to them, *"ils sont si degoutants!"*[41]

Lyle Saxon says that "the free men of color are always in the background; to use the Southern phrase, 'they know their place.' "

The novelists have kept them in the background. Many recent novels show this: *White Girl, The No-Nation Girl, A Study in Bronze, Gulf Stream, Dark Lustre*—all of these show luridly the melodrama of the lovely octoroon girl. Indeed "octoroon" has come to be a feminine noun in popular usage.

The stereotype that demands attention, however, is the notion of mulatto character, whether shown in male or female. This character works itself out with mathematical symmetry. The older theses ran: First, the mulatto inherits the vices of both races and none of the virtues; second, any achievement of a Negro is to be attributed to the white blood in his veins. The logic runs that even inheriting the worst from whites is sufficent for achieving among Negroes. The present theses are based upon these: The mulatto is a victim of a divided inheritance; from his white blood come his intellectual strivings, his unwillingness to be a slave; from his Negro blood come his baser emotional urges, his indolence, his savagery.

Thus, in *The No-Nation Girl*, Evans Wall writes of his tragic heroine, Précieuse:

> Her dual nature had not developed its points of difference. The warring qualities, her double inheritance of Caucasian and black mingled in her blood, had not yet begun to disturb, and torture, and set her apart from either race. . . .
> [As a child,] Précieuse had learned to dance as soon as she could toddle about on her shapely little legs; half-savage little steps with strange movements of her body, exotic gestures and movements that had originated among the remote ancestors of her mother's people in some hot African jungle.
> . . . the wailing cry of the guitar was as primitive and disturbing as the beat of a tom-tom to dusky savages gathered for an orgy of danc-

[41] Quoted in Lyle Saxon, *Fabulous New Orleans*. New York: The Century Co., 1928, p. 182.

ing and passion in some moon-flooded jungle. . . . Self-control reached its limit. The girl's half-heritage of savagery rose in a flood that washed away all trace of her father's people except the supersensitiveness imparted to her taut nerves. She must dance or scream to relieve the rising torrent of response to the wild, monotonous rhythm.

It is not long before the girl is unable to repress, what Wall calls, the lust inherited from her mother's people; the environment of debauchery, violence, and rapine is exchanged for concubinage with a white paragon, which ends, of course, in the inevitable tragedy. The girl "had no right to be born."

Dark Lustre, by Geoffrey Barnes, transfers the main essentials of the foregoing plot to Harlem. Aline, of the darkly lustrous body, thus analyzes herself in accordance with the old clichés: "The black half of me is ashamed of itself for being there, and every now and then crawls back into itself and tries to let the white go ahead and pass. . . ." Says the author: "There was too much of the nigger in her to let her follow a line of reasoning when the black cloud of her emotions settled over it." Half-white equals reason; half-black equals emotion. She too finds her ideal knight in a white man, and death comes again to the tragic octoroon who should never have been born. *White Girl, Gulf Stream, A Study in Bronze* are in substance very similar to these.

Roark Bradford in *This Side of Jordan* gives an unconscious *reductio ad absurdum* of this stereotype.

The blade of a razor flashed through the air. Scrap has concealed it in the folds of her dress. Her Negro blood sent it unerringly between two ribs. Her Indian blood sent it back for an unnecessary second and third slash.

It might be advanced that Esquimaux blood probably would have kept her from being chilled with horror. The strangest items are attributed to different racial strains: In *No-Nation Girl* a woman cries out in childbirth because of her Negro expressiveness; from the back of Précieuse's "ankles down to her heels, the flesh was slightly thicker"—due to her Negro blood; Lessie in Welbourn Kelley's *Inchin' Along* "strongly felt the urge to see people, to talk to people. . . . That was the white in her maybe. Or maybe it was the mixture of white and black."

This kind of writing should be discredited by its patent absurdity. It is generalizing of the wildest sort, without support from scientific authorities. And yet it has set these *idées fixes* in the mob mind: The Negro of unmixed blood is no theme for tragedy; rebellion and vindictiveness are to be expected only from the mulatto; the mulatto is victim of a divided inheritance and therefore miserable; he is a "man without a race" worshipping the whites and despised by them, despising and despised by Negroes, perplexed by his struggle to unite a white intellect with black sensuousness. The fate of the octoroon girl is intensified—the whole desire of her life is to find a white lover, and then go down, accompanied by slow music, to a tragic end. Her fate is so severe that in some works disclosure of "the single drop of midnight" in her veins makes her commit suicide.

The stereotype is very flattering to a race which, for all its self-assurance, seems to stand in great need of flattery. But merely looking at one of its particulars—that white blood means asceticism and Negro blood means unbridled lust—will reveal how flimsy the whole structure is. It is ingenious that mathematical computation of the amount of white blood in a mulatto's veins will explain his character. And it is a widely held belief. But it is nonsense, all the same.

THE LOCAL COLOR NEGRO

"The defects of local color inhere in the constitution of the cult itself, which, as its name suggests, thought . . . . first of the piquant surfaces and then—if at all—of the stubborn deeps of human life." (Carl Van Doren: *Contemporary American Novelists.*)

Local color stresses the quaint, the odd, the picturesque, the different. It is an attempt to convey the peculiar quality of a locality. Good realistic practice would insist upon the localizing of speech, garb, and customs; great art upon the revelation of the universal beneath these local characteristics. Local color is now in disrepute because of its being contented with merely the peculiarity of dialect and manners. As B. A. Botkin, editor of *Folk-Say,* has stated: "In the past [local consciousness] has been narrowly sectional rather than broadly human, superficially picturesque rather than deeply interpretative, provincial without being indigenous."[42]

The "local color Negro" is important in any study of the Negro character in American literature. But, since the local colorists of the Negro were more concerned with fidelity to speech and custom, with revelation of his difference in song and dance and story, than with revelation of Negro character, they accepted at face valuation the current moulds into which Negro character had been forced.

[42] B. A. Botkin, *Folk-Say, A Regional Miscellany.* Norman: The Oklahoma Folk-Lore Society, 1929, p. 12.

Therefore, local colorists have been and will be considered under other heads. Page and Russell were local colorists in that they paid close attention to Negro speech, but the Negro they portrayed was the same old contented slave. Their study of Negro speech, however, was fruitful and needed—for pro-slavery authors had been as false in recording Negro speech as they were in picturing Negro experience. Kennedy, for instance, forces a confessedly wretched dialect into the mouths of poor Negroes, and W. L. G. Smith has his Shenandoah Negroes speak Gullah, because his master, Simms, had written of South Carolina Negroes.

Cable, one of the best of the local colorists, in *The Grandissimes*, goes a step beyond the mere local color formula; *Old Creole Days* is local color, but has been considered under the "Tragic Mulatto." The Negroes in Lyle Saxon's old and new New Orleans, E. Larocque Tinker's old New Orleans, R. Emmett Kennedy's Gretna Green, are in the main kinsfolk to the contented slave; in Evans Wall's Mississippi canebrakes are exotic primitives, or tragic mulattoes; on Roark Bradford's levees are primitives; and those on Julia Peterkin's Blue Brook plantation, in Heyward's Catfish Row, and in John Vandercook's Surinam, Liberia, and Haiti, usually surmount, in the writer's opinion, the deficiencies of local color. Stereotyped, or genuinely interpreted, however, they all agree in one respect: they show the peculiar differences of certain Negroes in well-defined localities.

John B. Sale in *The Tree Named John* records with sympathy the dialect, superstitions, folk-ways of Mississippi Negroes. He is meticulous, perhaps to a fault, in his dialectal accuracy; the milieu is correspondingly convincing. His Negroes do carry on the pattern of mutual affection between the races—and yet they are far nearer flesh and blood than those of Page. Samuel Stoney and Gertrude Shelby, in *Black Genesis*, give the peculiarities of the Gullah Negro's cosmogony. Care is paid to fidelity in recording the dialect, but the authors' comments reveal a certain condescension toward quaintness which is the usual bane of local colorists. In *Po' Buckra* the authors reveal the localized tragedy of the "brass-ankle"—the Croatan-Negro-near-white caste. Much of the "tragic mulatto" theme is in this book, as well as the purely local color interest. Ambrose Gonzales in his Gullah renditions of Aesop, and in his tales of the "black border," reveals for the curious the intricacies of a little known Negro dialect, following the lead of Harris, and C. C. Jones, who recorded the Br'er Rabbit tales in the dialect of the Georgia coast.

Although most of these authors who dwell upon quaint and picturesque divergencies are discussed under other headings, it will not do to underestimate this local color Negro. The showing of Negro peculiarities in speech, superstitions, and customs has been popular for many years, and is likely to be for a long while yet. It undoubtedly has its artistic uses; but being an end in itself is surely not the chief of them.

THE EXOTIC PRIMITIVE

> *"Then I saw the Congo, cutting through the black. . . ."*—(Vachel Lindsay)

This stereotype grew up with America's post-war revolt against Puritanism and Babbittry. Literary critics urged a return to spontaneity, to unrestrained emotions; American literature had been too long conventional, drab, without music and color. Human nature had been viewed with too great a reticence. Sex, which the Victorians had considered unmentionable, was pronounced by the school of Freud to have an overwhelming importance in motivating our conduct. So the pendulum swung from the extreme of Victorian prudishness to that of modern expressiveness.

To authors searching "for life in the raw," Negro life and character seemed to beg for exploitation. There was the Negro's savage inheritance, as they conceived it: hot jungle nights, the tom-tom calling to esoteric orgies. There were the frankness and violence to be found in any underprivileged group, or on any frontier. There were the traditional beliefs of the Negro being a creature of his appetites, and although pro-slavery fiction had usually (because of Victorianism) limited these to his yearnings for hog meat and greens, 'possum and yams, and for whiskey on holidays, Reconstruction fiction had stressed his lustfulness. He seemed to be cut out for the hands of certain authors. They promptly rushed to Harlem for color. In Harlem dives and cabarets they found what they believed to be *the* Negro, *au naturel*.

The figure who emerges from their pages is a Negro synchronized to a savage rhythm, living a life of ecstasy, superinduced by jazz (repetition of the tom-tom, awakening vestigial memories of Africa) and gin, that lifted him over antebellum slavery, and contemporary economic slavery, and placed him in the comforting fastnesses of their "mother-land." A kinship exists between this stereotype and that of the contented slave; one is merely a "jazzed-up" version of the other, with cabarets supplanting cabins, and Harlemized "blues," instead of the spirituals and slave reels. Few were the observers who saw in the Negroes' abandon a release from the troubles of this world similar to that afforded in slavery by their singing. Many there were, however, who urged that the Harlem Negro's state was that of an inexhaustible *joie de vivre.*

Carl Van Vechten was one of the pioneers of the hegira from downtown to Harlem; he was one of the early discoverers of the cabaret; and his novel, *Nigger Heaven,* is to the exotic pattern what *Swallow Barn* was to the contented slave. All of the possibilities of the development of the type are inherent in the book. In the prologue, we have the portrait of the "creeper," Don Juan of Seventh Avenue, whose amatory prowess causes him to be sought by women unknown to him. We feel that this prologue sets the tone of the work: we are going to see the Harlem of gin mills and cabarets, of kept men and loose ladies, of all-day sleepers and all-night roisterers. Van Vechten, who was already famed as a sophisticated romantic novelist, writes graphically of this Harlem. His style invited emulation from young men desiring to be men-about-town first and then novelists, just as Kennedy invited emulation from young Southerners desiring to defend slavery first. Van Vechten's novel does more than present the local color of Harlem; there is as well the character study of a young Negro intellectual who cannot withstand the dissipations of the "greatest Negro city." But the Bohemian life in Harlem is the main thing, even in this youngster's life. According to the publisher's blurb, "Herein is caught the fascination and tortured ecstasies of Harlem. . . . The author tells the story of modern Negro life." The blurb claims too much. There is another, there are many other Harlems. And *the* story of modern Negro life will never be found in one volume, or in a thousand.

Lasca Sartoris, exquisite, gorgeous, golden-brown Messalina of Seventh Avenue, is one of the chief characters of the book. On seeing her one of the characters comments: "Whew! She'll make a dent in Harlem." She does. She causes the young hero, Byron, in a drunken rage, to empty his gun in the body of one of her lovers, although the man was already dead, and a policeman was approaching.

Van Vechten has a noted magazine editor comment pontifically on the possibilities of Negro literature:

Nobody has yet written a good gambling story; nobody has gone into the curious subject of the divers tribes of the region . . . . There's the servant-girl for instance. Nobody has ever done the Negro servant-girl, who refuses to 'live in.' Washing dishes in the day-time, she returns at night to her home in Harlem where she smacks her daddy in the jaw or else dances and makes love. On the whole I should say she has the best time of any domestic servant in the world . . . . The Negro fast set does everything the Long Island fast set does, plays bridge, keeps the bootlegger busy, drives around in Rolls-Royces and commits adultery, but it is vastly more amusing than the Long Island set for the simple reason that it is *amused* . . . Why, Roy McKain visited Harlem just once and then brought me in a cabaret yarn about a Negro pimp. I don't suppose he even saw the fellow. Probably just made him up, imagined him, but his imagination was based on a background of observation. The milieu is correct. . . .[43]

Although these are merely the offhand comments of an editor, and not to be taken too seriously as final critical pronouncements on *the* Negro, still certain implications are obvious. The best Negro characters for literary purposes are suggested: gamblers, fast set, servant-girl-sweet-mamma, etc. All are similar in their great capacity for enjoyment—and it is that side that must be shown. The eternal playboys of the Western hemisphere! Why even one trip to Harlem will reveal the secret of their mystery. The connection of all of this to the contented slave, comic, local color Negro is patent. Another thing to be noticed is the statement issued by the literary market: Stereotypes wanted.

In *Black Sadie*, T. Bowyer Campbell, whose preference is for the stereotype of the contented slave of the South, ironically accounts for the Harlem fad by the desire of jaded sophisticates for a new thrill. But Campbell does agree in some degree with the Harlem stereotype: "Colored people demand nothing but easy happiness, good nature." Black Sadie, child of a man hanged for raping an old white woman, having become the toast of artistic New York, remaining a kleptomaniac—"it was in her blood"—even in affluence, causing a murder, returns—in the best tradition of minstrel songs—to happy Virginia. "Easy come, easy go, niggers," Campbell closes his book, philosophically.

Sherwood Anderson, in *Dark Laughter,* expresses a genuine Rousseauism. Hostile toward the routine of industrialism and Puritanism, Anderson sets up as a foil the happy-go-lucky sensuality of river-front Negroes, who laugh, with genial cynicism, at the self-lacerations of hypersensitive Nordics. His "dark laughter" lacks the sinister undertone of Llewellyn Powys' "black laughter" heard in Africa. Anderson's Negroes are too formalized a chorus, however, for conviction, and are more the dream-children of a romanticist than actual flesh-and-blood creations. Anderson has drawn some excellent Negro characters; in *Dark Laughter*, however, he characterizes the Negroes too straitly. That the chief response of the Negro to his experience is a series of deep rounds of laughter at white sex-tangles is difficult of credence.

[43] Carl Van Vechten, *Nigger Heaven.* New York: Grosset and Dunlap, 1928, pp. 225 ff.

William Seabrook in *Magic Island* and *Jungle Ways* writes sensational travel tales—according to some, in the tradition of Munchausen and Marco Polo. He exploits the exotic and primitive, recording voodoo rites, black magic, strange sexual practices, weird superstitions, and cannibalism. His work brings a sort of vicarious satisfaction to Main Street, and advances the stereotype. He traces back to original sources what downtown playboys come up to Harlem to see.

The stereotype of the exotic-primitive would require more than a dogmatic refutation. Not so patently a "wish-fulfillment," as the "contented slave" stereotype was, nor an expression of unreasoning hatred, as the "brute Negro," it is advanced by novelists realistic in technique and rather convincing, although demonstrably "romantic" in their choice of the sensational. But it would be pertinent to question the three basic assumptions—either insinuated or expressed—underlying the stereotype: that the "natural" Negro is to be found in Harlem cabarets; that the life and character depicted there are representative of Negro life in general; and that the Negro is "himself," and startlingly different in the sensational aspects of his life.

It is strange that the "natural" Negro should be looked for in the most sophisticated of environment. Even the names "Cotton Club," "Plantation Revue," the lavish, though inaccurate, cotton bolls decorating the walls, the choruses in silken overalls and bandanas do not disguise but rather enforce the fact that Negro entertainers, like entertainers everywhere, give the public what clever managers, generally Caucasian, believe the public wants. Unwise as it is to generalize about America, or New York State, or even Queens from the Great White Way, it is no less unwise to generalize about Negro life and character from Harlem. It is even unwise to generalize about Harlem, from *the* Harlem shown in books. Strange to say, there is a Harlem that can be observed by the cold glare of daylight.

The exotic primitives of Mississippi levees and cane-brakes, of Catfish Row and Blue Brook Plantation are more convincing, as examples of frontier communities, and of underprivileged groups who are known to live violent lives. It is surely not impossible, however, to believe that observers with an eye for environmental factors might see an entirely different picture from the one presented by searchers for exotic-primitive innate tendencies.

Harvey Wickham in *The Impuritans* writes:

On Pacific Street, San Francisco, there used to be, and probably still is, a Negro dance hall called the So-Different Cafe. The name was deceptive. It was not so different from any other slum-hole. [A slum hole] is tediously the same, whether it be in Harlem, lower Manhattan, London, Paris, Berlin, Rome, Athens, Pekin, or Timbuctoo. There is no possible variety in degradation. . . .[44]

Such a comment surely deserves as careful attention as the stereotype of the exotic-primitive.

ATTEMPTS AT REALIZATION

"John Henry said to his captain,
A man ain't nothin' but a man . . . ."
(Ballad of John Henry.)

It would be a mistake to believe that the works of all white authors bear out these stereotypes. Some of the best attacks upon stereotyping have come from white authors, and from Southerners, just as some of the strongest upholding of the stereotypes has come from Negroes. Moreover, the writer of this essay hopes that he will not be accused of calling everything a stereotype that does not flatter Negro character, or of insisting that the stereotypes have no basis in reality. Few of the most apologistic of "race" orators could deny the presence of contented slaves, of wretched freemen, in our past; nor of comic Negroes (even in the joke-book tradition), of self-pitying mulattoes, of brutes, of exotic primitives in our present. Negro life does have its local color, and a rich, glowing color it can be at times. What this essay has aimed to point out is the obvious unfairness of hardening racial character into fixed moulds. True in some particulars, each of these popular generalizations is dangerous when applied to the entire group. Furthermore, most of these generalizations spring from a desire to support what is considered social expediency rather than from a sincere attempt at interpretation, and are therefore bad art.

Attempts at sincere "realization" rather than imitation of set patterns can be found in the early works of Eugene O'Neill, whose plays first brought a tragic Negro to Broadway. Ridgeley Torrence saw another side to the familiar guitar playing clown—showing him to be a dreamer of dreams like the other Playboy of the Western World—and saw dignity in his long suffering, hard-working wife. *The Rider of Dreams,* in its quiet way, did much to demolish the old stereotypes.

[44] Harvey Wickham, *The Impuritans.* New York: The Dial Press, 1929, p. 284.

Julia Peterkin, for all of her tendency to local color (*Bright April* is a storehouse of Negro superstitions and folk customs) and her emphasis on sex and violence,[45] is still of importance in her departure from the stereotypes.

In a simple, effective manner, she reveals the winning humanity of the Gullah people, whom she obviously loves and respects. If critics would refuse to call her the interpreter of *the* Negro, and realize that she writes of a very limited segment of life from a very personal point of view, they would do a service to her and to their own reputations. She has well-nigh surmounted the difficulty of being a plantation owner.

Du Bose Heyward has given us some of the best Negro characterizations in *Porgy* and *Mamba's Daughters*. Though the first is naturalistic with a flair for the exotic-primitive, Heyward does show in it essential humanity: Porgy reveals himself as capable of essential fineness, and even Bess is not completely past reclaiming. *Mamba's Daughters* reveals that Negroes, too, can be provident as Mamba was, or heroic as Hagar was, for the sake of the young. The travesty of Southern justice toward the Negro, the difficulties of the aspiring Negro, the artistic potentialities and actualities of Negroes, receive ample attention. Except for certain forgivable slips into the "comic," the book is an excellent illustration of the dignity and beauty that can be found in some aspects of lowly Negro life.

E. C. L. Adams, because he seems to let Negro characters speak for themselves, in their own idiom, and as if no white man was overhearing, has been very successful in his interpretation of Negro folk-life. Here the humor expressed by the Negro is miles away from Cohen's buffoonery. There is a sharp, acid flavor to it; in the Negroes' condemnation of the Ben Bess case there is the bitterness that has been stored up for so very long. These folk are not happy-go-lucky, nor contented; they are shrewd, realistic philosophers, viewing white pretense and injustice with cynicism— though not with Sherwood Anderson's "Dark Laughter." Illiterate they may be, but they are not being fooled.

Howard Odum, by letting the Negro speak for himself, presents a similarly convincing folk-Negro, in this case, the rambling man, who has been everywhere, and seen everybody. Many of the stereotypes are overthrown in *Rainbow Round My Shoulder,* although comic, and brutal, and submissive Negroes may be seen there. These are viewed, however, "in the round," not as walking general-

[45] *Vide: Black April, Scarlet Sister Mary* for examples of extreme promiscuity, and *Bright Skin* for violent deaths.

izations about *the* Negro, and Odum is intent on making us understand how they got to be what they are.

Evelyn Scott and T. S. Stribling, historical novelists of the Civil War, as different as may be in technique, agree in giving us rounded pictures of antebellum Negroes. Slavery is not a perpetual Mardi Gras in their novels, nor are Negroes cast in the old, rigid moulds. They are characterized as human beings, not as representatives of a peculiar species. Paul Green's *In Abraham's Bosom* shows the Negro's handicapped struggles for education during the Reconstruction; Green has brought great dramatic power to bear upon revealing that the Negro is a figure worthy of tragic dignity. In *The House of Connelly* he has disclosed aspects of the so-called "contented slave" that antebellum authors were either ignorant of, or afraid to show.

Erskine Caldwell, George Milburn, William Faulkner, and Thomas Wolfe, while their métier is the portraiture of poor whites, help in undermining the stereotypes by showing that what have been considered Negro characteristics, such as dialect, illiteracy, superstitions, sexual looseness, violence, etc., are to be found as frequently among poor whites. When they do show Negro characters, they frequently show them to be burdened by economic pressure, the playthings of Southern justice, and the catspaws for sadistic "superiors."

A recent novel, *Amber Satyr,* shows a lynching that follows a white woman's relentless and frenzied pursuit of her hired man, a good-looking Negro. Welbourne Kelley's *Inchin' Along,* although influenced by some stereotypes (his mulatto wife, true to type, is the easy prey of the first white man who rides along), does show the hard-working, provident, stoical Negro. James Knox Millen wrote a powerful attack upon lynching in *Never No More,* showing the precarious hold the Southern Negro has upon peace and happiness. Scott Nearing, with a proletarian emphasis, has presented graphically the new slavery, peonage, in the South, with its horrible concomitant lynchings, and the bitter prejudice of organized labor in the North. And finally, John L. Spivak, in *Georgia Nigger,* has written a second *Uncle Tom's Cabin,* an indictment of peonage, and convict-labor in Georgia, powerful enough to put to shame all the rhapsodists of the folk Negro's happy state.

To trace the frequency with which the Negro author has stepped out of his conventional picture frame, from the spirituals and satiric folk-rhymes down to Langston Hughes, would exceed the bounds of this paper, and for present purposes is not needed. A reading of only a few of the white authors just mentioned (many of whom are from the South) would effectively illustrate the inadequacy of the familiar stereotypes.

It is likely that, in spite of the willingness of some Negro authors to accept at face value some of these stereotypes, the exploration of Negro life and character rather than its exploitation must come from Negro authors themselves. This, of course, runs counter to the American conviction that the Southern white man knows the Negro best, and can best interpret him. Nan Bagby Stephens states what other Southern authors have insinuated:

Maybe it was because my slave-owning ancestors were fond of their darkies and treated them as individuals that I see them like that. It seems to me that no one, not even the negroes themselves, can get the perspective reached through generations of understanding such as we inherited.[46]

The writer of this essay holds to the contrary opinion, agreeing with another Southerner, F. P. Gaines,[47] that when a white man says that he knows the Negro he generally means that he knows the Negro of the joke-book tradition. Stephen Vincent Benet has written:

Oh, blackskinned epic, epic with the black spear,
I cannot sing you, having too white a heart,
And yet, some day a poet will rise to sing you
And sing you with such truth and mellowness. . . .
That you will be a match for any song . . .[48]

But whether Negro life and character are to be best interpreted from without or within is an interesting by-path that we had better not enter here. One manifest truth, however, is this: the sincere, sensitive artist, willing to go beneath the clichés of popular belief to get at an underlying reality, will be wary of confining a race's entire character to a half-dozen narrow grooves. He will hardly have the temerity to say that his necessarily limited observation of a few Negroes in a restricted environment can be taken as the last word about some mythical *the* Negro. He will hesitate to do this, even though he had a Negro mammy, or spent a night in Harlem, or has been a Negro all his life. The writer submits that such an artist is the only one worth listening to, although the rest are legion.

[46] *Contempo*, Volume II, No. 2, p. 3.
[47] F. P. Gaines, *op. cit.*, p. 17.
[48] Stephen Vincent Benet, *John Brown's Body*. Garden City, New York: Doubleday Doran and Co., 1928, p. 347.

COUNTEE CULLEN

1903-1946

Countee Cullen was born in May 1903. Little is known of his father and mother or of his early years in New York. The boy lived with his maternal grandmother until he was thirteen and was then adopted by the Reverend Frederick A. Cullen, minister of the Salem African Methodist Episcopal Church in Harlem. Countee Cullen's childhood was sheltered, although the Reverend Cullen was a political activist who made his adopted son aware of racial as well as religious issues.

Countee Cullen attended De Witt Clinton High School and New York University. He developed early as a poet, writing some of his most impressive verse while he was still a student in college. "I Have a Rendezvous with Life," "The Ballad of the Brown Girl," and "The Shroud of Color" are poems that Cullen included in *Color* (1925), his first book of verse, published the same year that he graduated from New York University. In 1926 he took his Master's degree from Harvard, then went on a short trip to Europe with his stepfather, and returned to serve as Assistant Editor of *Opportunity, Journal of Negro Life,* edited by Charles S. Johnson, the well-known Negro sociologist. Through his position on *Opportunity,* Cullen came to know the important writers of the Negro Awakening: Langston Hughes, Zora N. Hurston, Eric Walrond, E. Franklin Frazier, Claude McKay, Jean Toomer, Arna Bontemps, and Sterling Brown.

Color established Countee Cullen as an important poet of the

Negro Awakening and received the first award in literature from the William Harmon Foundation in 1927; in the same year the poet published two other volumes of verse—*Copper Sun* and *The Ballad of the Brown Girl*—and edited an anthology of Negro poetry, *Caroling Dusk*. Cullen won a Guggenheim Fellowship in 1928 and decided to study in Paris; before leaving, however, he became engaged to Nina Yolande DuBois, daughter of W. E. B. DuBois, who was then teaching art and English at Douglass High School in Baltimore. The young couple was married in 1928 but divorced a year later while Cullen lived in France. Cullen stayed in Paris for two years, and like Richard Wright and James Baldwin he experienced relatively little racial discrimination there; he was able to finish a long narrative poem, "The Black Christ," which he published together with other poems in 1929.

From 1929 until his death in 1946 Countee Cullen taught in the New York Public Schools. He remarried in 1940 and lived in Tuckahoe, New York. Although he served for a time as an editor of *Opportunity* and supported the Communist ticket in the 1932 presidential elections, Cullen did not respond intensely to social and political problems in the thirties and forties. He continued to publish volumes of verse—*The Medea and Other Poems* (1935); *The Lost Zoo* (1940), a children's book; and *My Nine Lives and How I Lost Them* (1942)—a novel, *One Way to Heaven* (1932), which is a satire on elite Negroes in Harlem; and a musical play, *St. Louis Woman*, which he wrote in collaboration with Arna Bontemps. But Cullen never developed beyond the impressive lyricism of his early poetry. Before his death, he selected his best poems, which were published posthumously under the title *On These I Stand* (1947). Those poems taken from *Color* are at least as memorable as those he selected from his later books; there is no essential progress in technique or intellectual complexity. The volume, which reveals Cullen's awareness of his own accomplishment, is testament to a gifted poet whose verse is lucid and poignant, if not always penetrating.

"If you ask any Negro what he found in Cullen's poetry," Owen Dodson once observed, "he would say: all my dilemmas are written here; the hurt pride, the indignation, the satirical thrusts, the agony of being black in America." Few critics would deny the essential truth of Dodson's comment, but when one considers the impassioned writing of Claude McKay, Richard Wright, James Baldwin, Ralph Ellison and other Negroes, one would have to add that Countee Cullen suggests the "agony of being black in America" without quite making the reader experience it. He was not by nature a protest poet, although his protest poems, so far as they go, are effective; he was not temperamentally a political writer, and for a Negro poet he responded very little to the specific social scene; he was not especially interested in the literary movements, the radical changes in versification of his day, and he used, for the most part, traditional techniques. With reluctance he yielded to racial subjects: "In spite of myself," he wrote in 1926, "I find that I am actuated by a strong sense of race consciousness. This grows upon me, I find, as I grow older, and although I struggle against it, it colors my writing, I fear, in spite of everything I can do. There have been many things in my life that have hurt me, and I find that the surest relief from these hurts is in writing."

Some of Countee Cullen's finest verse reflects generally upon the dilemma of the American Negro. The title of his first and most important volume, *Color*, suggests his self-consciousness, the existential fact of his external appearance. "Heritage" considers the Negro's unique roots in primitive Africa, and his sense that a black God would better understand his anomalous position in the Western world. "Shroud of Color" demands an equal place for the Negro in the face of God as well as in society. "Yet Do I Marvel," Cullen's most famous and perhaps most representative poem, expresses a reluctant belief in a God who has created evil and suffering; but the paradox which still bewilders him, in 1925, is that of a Negro creating poetry: "Yet do I marvel at this curious thing:/To make a poet black, and bid him sing!" Cullen included other poems that consider racial problems in his second book of poems, *Copper Sun* (1927), and in his long poetic narrative, *The Black Christ* (1929), in which he yearns for a belief in God but finds God only deaf to his pleas.

Countee Cullen could not escape his racial identification; but fundamentally he wanted to be a lyric poet like John Keats. He felt that "good poetry is a lofty thought beautifully expressed. Poetry should not be too intellectual. It should deal more, I think, with the emotions." He recognized that he had "a very romantic strain" which was not always compatible with racial protest, and, as he wrote in the introduction to *Caroling Dusk*, he wanted Negro poets to ally themselves with the English and American literary traditions rather than with the African. Some of his finest poems—like the two sonnets, "Magnets" and "Counter Mood"—reflect his concern with universal subjects. Cullen's deepest response as a poet was to the lyric beauty of John Keats and Edna St. Vincent Millay and to the more pessimistic view of A. E. Housman. Like Keats, Cullen matured early. He lived longer than his literary idol, however, and he never really developed beyond his original achievement in *Color*. It is largely true, as one critic points out, that Cullen's talent was never more "than a skill at echoing, at assuming the poetic attitudes of the late Victorian and Georgian past"; it is also true that he had too little regard for the poetry of his own time, characterizing it as "strange" and "bizarre." He was a derivative poet, whose technique was traditional and whose view was rarely subtle or intellectually engaging. At his best, in the poems he selected for *On These I Stand* and in the poems reprinted below, he is a skillful, poignant lyric poet who achieves his self-defined goal of "saying things beautifully and musically."

Yet Do I Marvel

I doubt not God is good, well-meaning, kind,
And did He stoop to quibble could tell why
The little buried mole continues blind,
Why flesh that mirrors Him must some day die,
Make plain the reason tortured Tantalus
Is baited by the fickle fruit, declare
If merely brute caprice dooms Sisyphus
To struggle up a never-ending stair.
Inscrutable His ways are, and immune
To catechism by a mind too strewn
With petty cares to slightly understand
What awful brain compels His awful hand.
Yet do I marvel at this curious thing:
To make a poet black, and bid him sing!

Heritage

(FOR HAROLD JACKMAN)

What is Africa to me:
Copper sun or scarlet sea,
Jungle star or jungle track,
Strong bronzed men, or regal black
Women from whose loins I sprang
When the birds of Eden sang?
One three centuries removed
From the scenes his fathers loved,
Spicy grove, cinnamon tree,
What is Africa to me?

So I lie, who all day long
Want no sound except the song
Sung by wild barbaric birds
Goading massive jungle herds,

Juggernauts of flesh that pass
Trampling tall defiant grass
Where young forest lovers lie,
Plighting troth beneath the sky.
So I lie, who always hear,
Though I cram against my ear
Both my thumbs, and keep them there,
Great drums throbbing through the air.
So I lie, whose fount of pride,
Dear distress, and joy allied,
Is my somber flesh and skin,
With the dark blood dammed within
Like great pulsing tides of wine
That, I fear, must burst the fine
Channels of the chafing net
Where they surge and foam and fret.

Africa? A book one thumbs
Listlessly, till slumber comes.
Unremembered are her bats
Circling through the night, her cats
Crouching in the river reeds,
Stalking gentle flesh that feeds
By the river brink; no more
Does the bugle-throated roar
Cry that monarch claws have leapt
From the scabbards where they slept.
Silver snakes that once a year
Doff the lovely coats you wear,
Seek no covert in your fear
Lest a mortal eye should see;
What's your nakedness to me?
Here no leprous flowers rear
Fierce corollas in the air;
Here no bodies sleek and wet,
Dripping mingled rain and sweat,
Tread the savage measures of
Jungle boys and girls in love.
What is last year's snow to me,
Last year's anything? The tree
Budding yearly must forget
How its past arose or set—
Bough and blossom, flower, fruit,
Even what shy bird with mute

Wonder at her travail there,
Meekly labored in its hair.
One three centuries removed
From the scenes his fathers loved,
Spicy grove, cinnamon tree,
What is Africa to me?

So I lie, who find no peace
Night or day, no slight release
From the unremittant beat
Made by cruel padded feet
Walking through my body's street.
Up and down they go, and back,
Treading out a jungle track.
So I lie, who never quite
Safely sleep from rain at night—
I can never rest at all
When the rain begins to fall;
Like a soul gone mad with pain
I must match its weird refrain;
Ever must I twist and squirm,
Writhing like a baited worm,
While its primal measures drip
Through my body, crying, "Strip!
Doff this new exuberance.
Come and dance the Lover's Dance!"
In an old remembered way
Rain works on me night and day.

Quaint, outlandish heathen gods
Black men fashion out of rods,
Clay, and brittle bits of stone,
In a likeness like their own,
My conversion came high-priced;
I belong to Jesus Christ,
Preacher of humility;
Heathen gods are naught to me.

Father, Son, and Holy Ghost,
So I make an idle boast;
Jesus of the twice-turned cheek,
Lamb of God, although I speak
With my mouth thus, in my heart
Do I play a double part.

Ever at Thy glowing altar
Must my heart grow sick and falter,
Wishing He I served were black,
Thinking then it would not lack
Precedent of pain to guide it,
Let who would or might deride it;
Surely then this flesh would know
Yours had borne a kindred woe.
Lord, I fashion dark gods, too,
Daring even to give You
Dark despairing features where,
Crowned with dark rebellious hair,
Patience wavers just so much as
Mortal grief compels, while touches
Quick and hot, of anger, rise
To smitten cheek and weary eyes.
Lord, forgive me if my need
Sometimes shapes a human creed.
All day long and all night through,
One thing only must I do:
Quench my pride and cool my blood,
Lest I perish in the flood.
Lest a hidden ember set
Timber that I thought was wet
Burning like the dryest flax,
Melting like the merest wax,
Lest the grave restore its dead.
Not yet has my heart or head
In the least way realized
They and I are civilized.

For a Poet

I have wrapped my dreams in a silken cloth,
And laid them away in a box of gold;
Where long will cling the lips of the moth,
I have wrapped my dreams in a silken cloth;
I hide no hate; I am not even wroth
Who found earth's breath so keen and cold;
I have wrapped my dreams in a silken cloth,
And laid them away in a box of gold.

For a Pessimist

He wore his coffin for a hat,
Calamity his cape,
While on his face a death's-head sat
And waved a bit of crape.

For John Keats,

APOSTLE OF BEAUTY

Not writ in water, nor in mist,
Sweet lyric throat, thy name;
Thy singing lips that cold death kissed
Have seared his own with flame.

180

For Paul Laurence Dunbar

Born of the sorrowful of heart,
    Mirth was a crown upon his head;
Pride kept his twisted lips apart
    In jest, to hide a heart that bled.

She of the Dancing Feet Sings

(TO OTTIE GRAHAM)

And what would I do in heaven, pray,
    Me with my dancing feet,
And limbs like apple boughs that sway
    When the gusty rain winds beat?

And how would I thrive in a perfect place
    Where dancing would be sin,
With not a man to love my face,
    Nor an arm to hold me in?

The seraphs and the cherubim
    Would be too proud to bend
To sing the faery tunes that brim
    My heart from end to end.

The wistful angels down in hell
    Will smile to see my face,
And understand, because they fell
    From that all-perfect place.

Counter Mood

Let this be scattered far and wide, laid low
Upon the waters as they fall and rise,
Be caught and carried by the winds that blow,
Nor let it be arrested by the skies:
I who am mortal say I shall not die;
I who am dust of this am positive,
That though my nights tend toward the grave, yet I
Shall on some brighter day arise, and live.

Ask me not how I am oracular,
Nor whence this arrogant assurance springs.
Ask rather Faith, the canny conjurer,
(Who while your reason mocks him mystifies
Winning the grudging plaudits of your eyes)—
How suddenly the supine egg has wings.

Song in Spite of Myself

Never love with all your heart,
    It only ends in aching;
And bit by bit to the smallest part
    That organ will be breaking.

Never love with all your mind,
    It only ends in fretting;
In musing on sweet joys behind,
    Too poignant for forgetting.

Never love with all your soul,
    For such there is no ending,
Though a mind that frets may find control,
    And a shattered heart find mending.

Give but a grain of the heart's rich seed,
    Confine some under cover,
And when love goes, bid him God-speed.
    And find another lover.

Nothing Endures

Nothing endures,
Not even love,
Though the warm heart purrs
Of the length thereof.

Though beauty wax,
Yet shall it wane;
Time lays a tax
On the subtlest brain.

Let the blood riot,
Give it its will;
It shall grow quiet,
It shall grow still.

Nirvana gapes
For all things given;
Nothing escapes,
Love not even.

Magnets

The straight, the swift, the debonair,
Are targets on the thoroughfare
For every kind appraising eye;
Sweet words are said as they pass by.
But such a strange contrary thing
My heart is, it will never cling
To any bright unblemished thing.
Such have their own security,
And little need to lean on me.
The limb that falters in its course,
And cries, "Not yet!" to waning force;
The orb that may not brave the sun;
The bitter mouth, its kissing done;
The loving heart that must deny
The very love it travels by;
What most has need to bend and pray,
These magnets draw my heart their way.

Sonnet

What I am saying now was said before,
And countless centuries from now again,
Some poet warped with bitterness and pain,
Will brew like words hoping to salve his sore.
And seeing written he will think the core
Of anguish from that throbbing wound, his brain,
Squeezed out; and these ill humours gone, disdain,
Or think he does, the face he loved of yore.

And then he too, as I, will turn to look
Upon his instrument of discontent,
Thinking himself a Perseus, and fit to brook
Her columned throat and every blandishment;
And looking know what brittle arms we wield,
Whose pencil is our sword, whose page our shield.

Sonnet

These are no wind-blown rumors, soft say-sos,
No garden-whispered hearsays, lightly heard.
I know that summer never spares the rose,
That spring is faithless to the brightest bird.
I know that nothing lovely shall prevail
To win from Time and Death a moment's grace;
At Beauty's birth the scythe was honed, the nail
Dipped for her hands, the cowl clipped for her face.

And yet I cannot think that this my faith,
My wingèd joy, my pride, my utmost mirth,
Centered in you, shall ever taste of death,
Or perish from the false, forgetting earth.
You are with time, as wind and weather are,
As is the sun, and every nailèd star.

To France

I have a dream of where (when I grow old,
Having no further joy to take in lip
Or limb, a graybeard caching from the cold
The frail indignity of age) some ship
Might bear my creaking, unhinged bones
Trailing remembrance as a tattered cloak,
And beach me glad, though on their sharpest stones,
Among a fair and kindly foreign folk.

There might I only breathe my latest days,
With those rich accents falling on my ear
That most have made me feel that freedom's rays
Still have a shrine where they may leap and sear,—
Though I were palsied there, or halt, or blind,
So I were there, I think I should not mind.

Scottsboro, Too, Is Worth Its Song

(A POEM TO AMERICAN POETS)

I said:
Now will the poets sing,—
Their cries go thundering
Like blood and tears
Into the nation's ears,
Like lightning dart
Into the nation's heart.
Against disease and death and all things fell,
And war,
Their strophes rise and swell
To jar
The foe smug in his citadel.

Remembering their sharp and pretty
Tunes for Sacco and Vanzetti,
I said:
Here too's a cause divinely spun
For those whose eyes are on the sun,
Here in epitome
Is all disgrace
And epic wrong,
Like wine to brace
The minstrel heart, and blare it into song.

Surely, I said,
Now will the poets sing.
    But they have raised no cry.
    I wonder why.

PART III
MAJOR AUTHORS

LANGSTON HUGHES

1902-1967
For over forty-five years, America's senior Negro professional literary man, Langston Hughes, wrote with one central purpose: "to explain and illuminate," in his words, "the Negro condition in America." Deprived early of the companionship of parents whose abomination of racial prejudice and whose struggles to overcome or escape it helped to chill their affections and collapse their marriage, Hughes took to himself a whole race in their stead. The ethnic passion that nerves his early poems and short stories is transformed later only in response to new sophistications and changing emphases among the Negro communities that inspired him. His early plays are part of his almost single-handed effort, in the 1930's especially, to establish in Harlem, Chicago, Los Angeles and elsewhere an authentic Negro national theater. Announcing in 1926, in "The Negro Artist and the Racial Mountain," his credo that he and his fellow craftsmen must explore their own racial "soul-world" without regard to the bias of the marketplace, he articulated the concept of American Negritude and defined the course of his lifelong artistic integrity. Working in every major fictional and nonfictional form, ever experimenting and ever remaining close to his racial sources without narrowing his sympathies, Hughes solidly earned his unofficial title as "the Poet Laureate of the Negro People."

James Langston Hughes was born February 1, 1902, in Joplin, Missouri, to James Nathaniel and Carrie Mercer Langston Hughes.

By the age of twelve, because of the separation of his parents, he had lived in Buffalo; Cleveland; Lawrence and Topeka, Kansas; Colorado Springs; and Mexico City. He completed grammar school in Lincoln, Illinois, reading his first poem, written as class poet, at graduation. In Cleveland's Central High School, which he attended from 1916 to 1920, he wrote his first short story, "Mary Winosky," in 1918, wrote poems imitative of Paul Laurence Dunbar and Carl Sandburg, and contributed to the school's *The Monthly* and *Belfry Owl*. His poem "When Sue Wears Red," written in his junior year, was not imitative; rather, the rhythm and fervor of its middle stanza and refrain ("When Susanna Jones wears red/ A queen from some time-dead Egyptian night/Walks once again./ Blow trumpets, Jesus!") were early expressions of the gospel and jazz cadences that he would weave into a new kind of poetry. His social experiences, too, were imbuing his teens with contrasting racial insights that would be harmonized in his later writings. "My best pal in high school," *The Big Sea* records, "was a Polish boy named Sartur Andrzejewski." But while immigrant students from Poland, Hungary, Italy, and Russia were initiating Hughes into the joys of symphony music, white rent-gougers were initiating him into the economics of racial exploitation on Cleveland's east side, where his mother, stepfather, half-brother, and other Negro families paid triple rent for makeshift quarters in sheds, garages, and stores. And white ruffians in southwest Chicago gave the Cleveland sophomore two black eyes and a swollen jaw in 1918— tokens of violence to come.

Between 1920 and 1925, by which time Hughes was deep in the currents of the Harlem Awakening, he had similarly diverse experiences. In Mexico, where his discovery of his hatred for his father had actually hospitalized the youth in August of 1919, Hughes began his publishing career in 1921. In that year, *The Crisis* published his famous poem "The Negro Speaks of Rivers" in June; *Brownie's Book* published his children's play *The Gold Piece* in July; and *The Crisis* printed his article "The Virgin of Guadalupe" in December. Shifting in 1921 from teacher to student (Hughes taught English at a finishing school in Mexico), he spent a rather uncongenial year at Columbia University, brightened only by the excitement of Harlem and of his repeated visits to Broadway, where the revue *Shuffle Along* was introducing the Negro glitter and verve that would quickly become the fashion of the decade. After quitting Columbia, whose *Spectator* used some of his poems, Hughes worked on a Staten Island truck-garden farm, made deliveries for a Manhattan florist, and gave his first public poetry reading before becoming mess boy on the *S.S. Malone,* which in six months visited thirty-odd West African ports. After the whole crew was fired in December of 1923, Hughes shipped on a Holland-bound freighter, and two months later began a series of memorable European experiences. Two jobs in Paris nightclubs, the second as dishwasher at the famous Grand Duc on the Rue Pigalle, brought him nightly familiarity with blues and jazz played by top Negro musicians. In Italy during his final four months abroad, Hughes almost starved as a beachcomber in Genoa, his wallet having been stolen during a train ride from Venice. Literary pieces evolved from these experiences include the article "Ships, Sea, and Africa," the short story "African Morning" and four little-known tales, the poetic sketch "Burutu Moon," and the charming poem "The Breath of a Rose"—a lyrical salute to his romantic interlude with a brown-skinned girl with whom he almost eloped to Florence.

The neon years of the Harlem Awakening in which Hughes personally figured with strongest effect, 1925 to 1929, have been often described in print. They date the publicity given Hughes as the Wardman Park Hotel's "bus-boy poet" by Vachel Lindsay in 1925 in Washington; the poetry prizes he won in contests sponsored by *The Crisis* and *Opportunity*; his acclaimed first volumes of poetry, *The Weary Blues* (1926) and *Fine Clothes to the Jew* (1927); the quick spread of his poetry readings, including his original use of background music; and his four years at Lincoln University in Pennsylvania—the last year being devoted to much work on his first novel, *Not Without Laughter* (1930).

The 1930's, beginning with Hughes's alienation from his patroness in December of 1930 and with the publication of two more small volumes of poetry (*Dear Lovely Death* in 1931 and *The Dream Keeper* in 1932), were primarily dedicated to short fiction and to theatrical work. The first two years of the decade were spent on travel to Cuba and Haiti, and on his first cross-country poetry-reading tour, made possible financially by a Harmon Gold Award for Literature (the novel) and by a Rosenwald Fund Fellowship, respectively. Hughes joined a Harlem group of twenty-two Negroes, mostly writers and students, in a fifteen-month movie-making trip to Russia in 1932 and 1933, extending his own travels within the Soviet Union and in Korea, Tokyo, Shanghai, and Honolulu. Articles sold to *Izvestia, International Literature,* and other Moscow publications enabled Hughes to afford the extra journeys; and association with Arthur Koestler and Boris Pasternak were literary benefits of another kind. Hughes's burst of short story writing, begun in the New Moscow Hotel early in 1933, was continued through 1934 in California, largely in the comfort of a cottage at Carmel-by-the-Sea offered him by Noel Sullivan. Fourteen stories written in these circumstances comprised *The Ways of White Folks* (1934). His shift of interest to the theater occurred in 1935, after the death of his father in Mexico (in November 1934), a springtime of translating Mexican stories and poems while stranded south of the border, and a summer of collaboration on a Haitian children's book with Arna Bontemps in Los Angeles.

It was in New York in September of 1935 that Hughes was surprised to find his play, *Mulatto*, written five years earlier at Jasper Deeter's Hedgerow Theater, scheduled to open October 24. The success of the play on Broadway and on tour established an apparently unconscious pull on Hughes, for after an unproductive year spent mostly in Cleveland with his fatally ill mother, and after several months in Spain covering the activities of Negroes in the International Brigades fighting in the Spanish Civil War, he returned vigorously to theatrical work in New York, in January of 1938. The stage was by no means new to him. Several of his plays had been produced in 1936: *Troubled Island, Little Ham,* and one written with Bontemps, *When the Jack Hollers.* The Gilpin Players of Cleveland's Karamu House had performed them, and in 1937 had added *Joy to My Soul, Soul Gone Home,* and *Drums of Haiti* (a variant title of *Troubled Island*)—staged by Elsie Roxborough, "the girl I was in love with then," Hughes wrote, the girl who had disappeared, passing for white, by the time he returned from wartime Spain. Taking up the challenge of founding a Negro theater with unpaid community actors, Hughes started the Harlem Suitcase Theater in a second-story loft, using his own historical play *Don't You Want to Be Free?* and two other dramas for the first performance, April 21, 1938. Moving to California, he founded The New Negro Theater in Los Angeles in March of 1939; *Don't You Want to Be Free?*, which had offered New York possibly its first instance of arena staging, again bolstered the first season. To it Hughes added his satirical skits, *Em-Fuehrer Jones* and *Limitations of Life*, while checking on the progress of his recent Harlem associates in trying out some of his other little-known dramas. Later in the year he and Clarence Muse, the Negro actor, completed the precedent-breaking job of writing the scenario and some of the songs for *Way Down South*, a movie starring Bobby Breen.

The 1940's brought old and new challenges to Hughes. By the autumn of 1940, Noel Sullivan's generosity again provided him with a cottage for writing, this one at the edge of his farm in Carmel Valley near Monterey, California. In that year *The Big Sea* was published. A successful autobiography behind him, Hughes left Hollow Hills Farm for Chicago, where he founded, in 1941, for the third time, a Negro theatrical group: the Skyloft Players at the Good Shepherd Community House. After the group produced in the spring of 1942 Hughes's full-length musical drama, *The Sun Do Move*, he returned to Harlem, sharing a three-room apartment at 634 St. Nicholas Avenue with his "adopted uncle and aunt," Emerson and Toy Harper, friends of his family since Kansas days. In February of the following year, the Writers War Board wrote Hughes that it was depending upon him for a flow of material useful in fighting the war. He responded with jingles, slogans, and his fifty-eight-line "Defense Bond Blues" to help the Treasury Department's bond drives; with articles on Negro soldiers and installations; with musical lyrics like *Go and Get the Enemy Blues*; and with *Freedom Road* (jointly created with Emerson and Toy Harper), which became the official troop song for several Negro army units. Dutch Underground forces, without Hughes's knowledge, in 1944 produced three hundred copies of a forty-six-page anonymous collection of his poems for use in fighting the Nazis, *Lament for Dark Peoples and Other Poems*.

More peaceful uses were made of Hughes's other works of the 1940's: his prose, drama, and poetry. He collaborated with Mercer Cook and Ben Frederick Carruthers, respectively, in translating Jacques Roumain's novel *Masters of the Dew* and poet Nicolás Guillén's *Cuba Libre*; and he placed at least two dozen of his prose essays in periodicals like *Saturday Review of Literature, Town and Country, The New Republic, Phylon, Journal of Educational Psychology, Negro Digest*, and five or six others. The metropolitan stage began to make use of his talents, for he wrote the lyrics for *Street Scene* (1947), and he collaborated with William Grant Still in turning *Troubled Island* into the first high-quality presentation of a full-length opera by Negroes. Hughes's poetry of the 1940's, more voluminous than that of any other decade, was printed mainly in *Shakespeare in Harlem* (1942), *Fields of Wonder* (1947), and *One-Way Ticket* (1949). Long a standard anthology, *The Poetry of the Negro, 1746–1949*, including fourteen poems by Hughes, and edited with Bontemps, was produced in this decade.

None of these books of the 1940's, and none of the awards or positions that came to Hughes then—the thousand-dollar grant from the American Academy of Arts and Letters in 1946, the posts as poet-in-residence at Atlanta University in 1947 and as "resource teacher" at the Laboratory School of the University of Chicago in 1949—distinguish the decade so much as the one night that the author spent at a Harlem bar near his St. Nicholas Avenue address. That night in 1942, the one great fictional character that Hughes was to conceive, Harlemite Jesse B. Semple, was born when the poet heard "Simple's" prototype tell a girl friend about his job making cranks in a New Jersey war plant. In reply to a question from Hughes, he shrugged, "I don't know what them cranks cranks. You know white folks don't tell Negroes what cranks cranks." During many later barstool conversations, Hughes observed his acquaintance's compellingly fresh diction in revealing his notion of a separate white world, and afterwards took Boswellian notes, argued with the emerging folk hero present at his typewriter while the worker himself was miles away, and merged his words with others actually heard in street-corner and barroom talk. Soon his vividness on paper had a wholeness and a reality that would rank him with Huck Finn, Mr. Dooley, and Uncle Remus. By the end of the decade, Hughes had written countless Simple columns for the weekly *Chicago Defender,* and had placed articles on him in several magazines.

By 1950, Hughes had spent three years in the three-story brownstone house on East 127th Street in Harlem where he was to remain with the Harpers for the last twenty years of his life. The 1950's excelled other decades in his career in the number and variety of books produced. *Simple Speaks His Mind* (1950), *Simple Takes a Wife* (1953), *Simple Stakes a Claim* (1957), and the Broadway presentation of his musical folk comedy, *Simply Heavenly,* established a comic mode indicative of a deepening emphasis in Hughes's works. His second collection of short stories, *Laughing to Keep from Crying* (1952), evidenced further this humorous trend. Both comedy and tragedy were in his dramatic works produced in the 1950's: *The Barrier* (based on "Father and Son," an early short story, and on *Mulatto,* conceived of as a "poetic tragedy" by Hughes) was presented by the Columbia University Opera Workshop in 1950; and *Esther,* another opera, was staged by the University of Illinois in 1957 and by Boston's New England Conservatory in 1958. And while *Simply Heavenly* was opening on Broadway, *Mulatto* was nearing the end of a two-year run in Italy and preparing to open in Buenos Aires.

The 1950's revealed Hughes's increasing interest in Negro history. This interest, evident in 1921, led in the 1950's to the publication of seven books historical or mainly historical in treatment. Two collaborative works augmented this total: *The Sweet Flypaper of Life* (1955), done with Roy De Carava, and *A Pictorial History of the Negro in America* (1956), done with Milton Meltzer —as did his Folkways phonodisc, "The Glory of Negro History." Three of the seven books represent most of Hughes's contribution to the First Book Series of Franklin Watts, Inc., the so-called "horizon-pushers" for the young: *The First Book of Negroes* (1952), *The First Book of Jazz* (1955), and *The First Book of the West*

Indies (1956). The other four books, more strictly historical except for the volume on folklore, were *Famous American Negroes* (1954), *Famous Negro Music Makers* (1955), *Famous Negro Heroes of America* (1958), and *The Book of Negro Folklore* (1958), done with Bontemps. Historical in a different sense—more intimate, literary, and contemporary—was his autobiography, *I Wonder As I Wander* (1956), covering the years 1931–1937.

Hughes's poetic activities of the 1950's, in his role as writer and reader, led to a variety of publications. He wrote relatively few new poems that appeared in volumes—somewhat like his work in the 1930's—although *Selected Poems* (1959) contained some. On the other hand, his popular *The Negro Mother,* an illustrated paperback of 1958; and his thirteen poems in *Lincoln University Poets* (1954) were not new. And his introduction to *Montage of a Dream Deferred* (1951) called it a single "poem on contemporary Harlem" made up of pieces reprinted from nine periodicals. He worked industriously, however, as a reader of his own poetry, making sixteen appearances in ten weeks, for example, in early 1951. Piano accompaniment and jazz orchestration continued as occasional support of his readings, before live audiences and before the microphones. His adapted *Shakespeare in Harlem,* with music by Margaret Bonds, played at the White Barn Theater in Westport, Connecticut, August 30, 1959.

Hughes's translating, editing, and other poetic efforts of the 1950's heralded the widening of his endeavors that was to mark the last several years of his life. His translation of Federico García Lorca's *Romancero Gitano* ("Gypsy Ballads"), begun in Spain in 1937 after the Spaniard's murder by the Fascist Falange and reworked for the *Beloit Poetry Journal,* appeared in 1951. *Selected Poems of Gabriela Mistral* (1957), another translation, brought to the English-reading public for the first time the representative works of this Nobel Prize-winning Latin-American poet. Expanding his labors in another area, Hughes explained, edited, and otherwise commented on poetry. He edited the "Negro Poets Issue" of *Voices* in 1950 and wrote the introduction to *Japanese Anthology of Negro Poetry* (Tokyo, 1952). Briefly turning to pedagogy, he published "Ten Ways to Use Poetry in Teaching" in the *CLA Bulletin* in 1951. His profound little book, *The First Book of Rhythms* (1954), originated in his talks to youngsters at the University of Chicago and in the children's rooms of various libraries. More than poetry, of course, appeared in *The Langston Hughes Reader* (1958), one of his last books of the decade; a comprehensive, selective anthology, it represented his works in several genres through the middle fifties.

Between 1960 and 1967, Hughes remained what he always

had been: poet, humorist, innovator, fictionist, writer of vital prose, and literary promoter of his race. His final volumes of poetry were *Ask Your Mama* (1961) and *The Panther and the Lash* (1967). In the former still undervalued long poem, the author updated the tradition that he originated in the 1920's; subtitled "12 Moods for Jazz" and bearing marginal notes for musical accompaniment, the poem blended folklore, topical allusions, counterpoint, juxtapositions, and symbolism in a style restlessly suitable to the jangling racialism of the day. The other volume, containing more old poems than new, both stridently and quietly expressed the turbulent years climaxed by the Black Panther Party and the "white backlash." In the span between those volumes, Hughes used poetry to honor old friends ("And So the Seed," on the Jelliffes of Karamu House), to comment on current events ("Harlem Call," on the riot of 1964), and to express the calm lyricism of himself as poet ("Silent One" and "The Innocent"). Reading tours, television shows, records, and radio appearances—the large media often including some of his earliest poems—continued the expansion of Hughes's audience; and composers and publishers of music maintained their long interest in adapting his poetry.

His reputation as a humorist already having been established, by his Simple columns and mainly by American and European editions of his three Simple books, Hughes solidified his fame with *The Best of Simple* (1961), with new material in *Simple's Uncle Sam* (1965), and with his editing of *The Book of Negro Humor* (1966). His Simple columns in the *New York Post* (1962–1965) and those continuing in the *Chicago Defender* pleased the vast audience reached by these metropolitan newspapers.

Two kinds of musical productions, one impressively innovative, occupied Hughes in the 1960's. The first kind was represented by his one-act opera, *Port Town*, performed in 1960 in Lenox, Massachusetts. More typical of his final theatrical inspiration was *Ballad of the Brown King*, a Christmas cantata about the titular king among the Three Wise Men, presented December 11, 1960, at the Clark Auditorium of the New York YMCA. Exactly one year later, Hughes's most successful elaboration of the same story appeared at New York's 41st Street Theater, *Black Nativity*. Using an all-Negro cast that dramatized the Christmas story in dialogue, narrative, pantomime, gospel song, folk spirituals, and dance, Hughes established the dimensions of the new "gospel song-play"; and he gave it an international reputation through *Black Nativity's* triumphs at the Festival of Two Worlds at Spoleto, Italy, the following summer and during its European tour. Other gospel song-plays by Hughes were produced: *Gospel Glow* (1962); *Tambourines to*

Glory (1963), based largely on his humorous novel of the same name, published in 1958; *Jerico-Jim Crow* (1964); and *The Prodigal Son* (1965). But none achieved the success of *Black Nativity,* despite their lively entertainment. The text of the play, *Tambourines to Glory* (together with the texts of *Simply Heavenly, Mulatto, Soul Gone Home,* and *Little Ham*), was offered to the public in *Five Plays of Langston Hughes* (1963), edited by Webster Smalley.

As a writer of both fiction and nonfiction, Hughes kept busy in the 1960's, especially in the latter genre. His final volume of fiction, *Something in Common and Other Stories* (1963), using most of the pieces found in *Laughing to Keep from Crying,* added eight previously uncollected and two previously unpublished stories ("Blessed Assurance," however, had been printed in German, as "Du, Meine Zuversicht," in a 1962 number of *Konkret* in Hamburg —and contained the second of Hughes's two experiments with stream-of-consciousness writing in all of his fiction). His final volumes of nonfiction were *The First Book of Africa* (1960), *Fight for Freedom: The Story of the NAACP* (1962), and *Black Magic: A Pictorial History of the Negro in American Entertainment* (1967), done with Milton Meltzer. Some of the author's primary aims were carried forward in these three books: the instruction of young people, the perpetuation of the image of Negroes as men who have long struggled and died for their human rights, and the combination of pleasant artistry and fitting substance so appropriate to the needs of a professional writer.

The year 1960 marked the beginning of Hughes's rather steady involvement with large editorial tasks, a trend that accorded with his disposition to popularize the works of African and Afro-American writers. *An African Treasury* (1960), containing essays, speeches, folk tales, stories, and poems by black Africans, was the first truly indigenous group expression of its kind. A minor emphasis in that collection became the complete focus of Hughes's next such book, *Poems from Black Africa* (1963), again the first major collection of its type; it represented thirty-eight poets from eleven countries. With *New Negro Poets: U.S.A.* (1964), averaging two poems by each of thirty-seven postwar poets, Hughes turned to his younger American contemporaries, a number of whom he again publicized in his bilingual anthology, *La Poésie Negro-Américaine* (1966). Inevitably Hughes sought manuscripts also from young writers of fiction. Combining them with dependable works by older authors like Chesnutt, Dunbar, Toomer, Wright, Ellison, Yerby, and others, he produced *The Best Short Stories by Negro Writers* (1967).

Writing more and longer than any other Negro author, Hughes has made contributions to American literature by which we can estimate the special achievements of Negro writers as a whole. His accomplishments, as established by his main publications (thirty-nine volumes of his own, five collaborative adult books, four full-length translated works, hundreds of uncollected productions in several genres) and by innumerable readings and lectures at home and abroad, can be divided into five kinds: those in poetry, fiction, humor, drama, and nonfiction.

In his ten volumes of poetry and countless separate pieces, Hughes is distinguished by his innovative genius—acknowledged in his election to the National Institute of Arts and Letters in 1961. His best poems, which include much of his early work, are vivid transcriptions of Negro urban folk life; they remain historically alive through their authentic use of the changing talk, moods, and habits in Negro communities. Racially sound in his stylistic responses to blues, jazz, bebop and boogie-woogie, and alert to national and international trends in his use of newspaper headlines, nightclub names, and varieties of ultramodern techniques, Hughes repays study as a truly American poet who genuinely reflects racial inspiration. His universality as a lyric poet, on the other hand, is demonstrable in every decade of his career.

In his sixty-six published short stories, generally conceded when they were collected in his volumes to be natural, humorous, restrained and yet powerful, Hughes is as impressively racial, universal, and technically interesting as he is in his poetry. Three-fifths of his stories attack racial prejudice, but such themes as delinquent fathers, affection-seeking women, and the plight of the artist are also emphasized. The didacticism and slight characterization in some of his stories are overbalanced by his chief virtues, mainly stylistic: dialogue unerringly shaped to the cadences, accents, and phrases familiar to most Negroes; incident, personality, and racial history woven into recurrent patterns; interspersed songs; realistically Chekhovian endings. Hughes's stories, often symbolically rich and often autobiographically meaningful, are further distinguished by their revelation of his sympathy for human foibles. The bitterness in some of his powerful early stories is to be weighed against the author's own declaration in a 1961 letter to James A. Emanuel: "I feel as sorry for [whites] as I do for the Negroes usually involved in hurtful . . . situations. Through at least one (maybe *only* one) white character in each story, I try to indicate that 'they are human, too.' "

As a humorist, Hughes fares most triumphantly in his books, columns, and articles on Jesse B. Semple, his one fully developed character—although some brief pieces in *Shakespeare in Harlem* and the "Madam to You" series of poems in *One-Way Ticket* surely prefigure and support his comic vein in the 1940's. Hughes's Negro Everyman, as Simple has been called, displays in his talk a psychologically important fusion of serious content and humorous style. While speaking of matters as crucial to American Negritude as psychic oppression and the African heritage, and while expounding on such other topics as national delusions, white liberals, and Negro leaders, Simple is almost always funny. The humor of his style usually derives from verbal play, long lists, tall-tale exuberance, confused etymologies, turnabouts, and startingly odd notions. Only Simple would call a judge "Your Honery," list thirteen kinds of greens to prove his knowledge of "greenology," tell of bedbugs that drank kerosene greedily and parachuted off the ceiling; nobody but Simple would call a historian a "hysterian," satirize Negro magazine covers by devising an imaginary caption like "Sex Seized in Passing," or elaborately conceive of himself as a black general leading his Mississippi "mens" into action. Jesse B. Semple, whose talk harmonizes a tragedy and a levity peculiarly American, and whose very name reveals the strategy used by folk Negroes to surmount that tragedy, enlivens the truth of the book jacket phrases that call him "a major figure in American literature."

As a playwright, Hughes is credited with twenty-odd dramas, operas, musicals, and gospel song-plays. They add substance to his early wish for a Negro national theater. His founding of Negro theatrical groups in Harlem, Chicago, and Los Angeles—an effort necessitated by a commercial theater seldom interested in authentic Negro drama—secures his place in the struggle for a balanced American tradition. Among Hughes's tragedies, fantasies, and comedies, his plays about urban folk Negroes, such as *Simply Heavenly*, contribute to American folk drama the musical pulse and everyday realities of a people not elsewhere accurately drawn by our playwrights. His gospel song-plays (best represented by *Black Nativity*), which are his liveliest fusion of music and drama, innovatively bring to the stage a zestful art capable of further development.

In his nonfiction, translations, and editorial work, Hughes displays the full variety of his interests and purposes. Several titles from his well over one hundred separately published essays indicate their range: "Cowards from the Colleges" (1934), "Devils in Dixie and Naziland" (1942), "Fooling Our White Folks" (1950), "Jokes Negroes Tell on Themselves" (1951), "Walt Whitman and the Negro" (1955), "Jolly Genius of Jazz" (1958), and "Problems of the Negro Writer" (1963).

In *The Big Sea* and *I Wonder As I Wander*, Hughes writes

frankly and vividly of his experiences through 1937; his death ended his active plans to continue his autobiographical series. His biographical and historical nonfiction, written mostly for the young, shows his sensitivity to their pressing need for the largely suppressed facts of Negro history. This same end stands as a motivation for his collaborative pictorial books, as well as for his translations of prose and poetry by dark-skinned Latin Americans.

It is the young, too, among American Negro authors, who figure prominently in Hughes's final edited volumes. Although his African anthologies of 1960 and 1963 vitally serve the cultural images of emerging nations, his *New Negro Poets: U.S.A.* and *The Best Short Stories by Negro Writers* have heartened and stimulated the best young Negro authors in America today. His personal influence upon them, partially recorded in several dedicatory numbers of Negro journals in 1967 and 1968, testifies to his inspirational force in a self-liberating American literature. His humanizing bequest to that literature is prophetically acknowledged by Julia Fields in closing her tribute to him in *Negro Digest* (September 1967):

Near his door at 127th Street, he grew ivy. . . . It was the only flowering on the whole street. And now I think, who will grow ivy or see that it is there?

. . . He was a fine man, a beautiful, brilliant and loving man was Langston Hughes.

We younger poets are in turn the budding new green of his IVY.

A few of Hughes's best poems show his typical substance and style. In "The Negro Speaks of Rivers," first in *The Crisis* in 1921, the young poet reconciles his estrangement from his parents in his riverlike fusion with his ancestors in majestic natural surroundings. Expressing the helplessness and damaged pride of a whole race, rather than the loneliness of a single teen-ager, "Mulatto," published in 1927 in *Saturday Review of Literature*, is a dramatic dialogue: a father-and-son conflict becomes the white father's pleasurably nagging recollection of sexual exploitation in the Negro quarter. His taunt, "What's the body of your mother?" is profoundly answered in "The Negro Mother," the 1931 broadside that has moved many a listener to tears.

Published in *Common Ground* in 1941, "Evenin' Air Blues," with its generic simplicity, humor, melancholy, and spurts of vital imagery, is almost flawless blues poetry. Hughes's kindred innovation, jazz poetry, is perfectly represented by "Dream Boogie," in *Montage of a Dream Deferred* (1951); wasting no word and varying its moods (ease, irony, sarcasm, and rough joviality), it joins the old dramatic monologue to Harlem's new boogie-woogie beat.

"On the Road" is artistically among the top five or six of Hughes's many stories. Published by *Esquire* in 1935, it is a richly symbolic fusion of dream and reality, using well over two hundred precisely patterned images. "Dear Dr. Butts," from *Simple Takes a Wife* (1953), and "Jazz, Jive, and Jam," from *Simple Stakes a Claim* (1957), characteristically using linguistic play and antic rhymes, represent Hughes's best comic prose style. The former satirizes Negro leaders too closely identified with the "white power structure" that announces them. The latter, merging instruction in Negro history with Simple's exuberant street corner sociology, also produces the serious reflections and guffaws anticipated by followers of Hughes's most famous character.

The Negro Speaks of Rivers

I've known rivers:
I've known rivers ancient as the world and older than the flow of
   human blood in human veins.

My soul has grown deep like the rivers.

I bathed in the Euphrates when dawns were young.
I built my hut near the Congo and it lulled me to sleep.
I looked upon the Nile and raised the pyramids above it.
I heard the singing of the Mississippi when Abe Lincoln went down
   to New Orleans, and I've seen its muddy bosom turn all golden
   in the sunset.

I've known rivers:
Ancient, dusky rivers.

My soul has grown deep like the rivers.

Mulatto

I am your son, white man!

Georgia dusk
And the turpentine woods.
One of the pillars of the temple fell.

You are my son!
Like hell!

"The Negro Speaks of Rivers" reprinted from *American Negro Poetry*, ed. Arna Bontemps (New York: Hill and Wang American Century Series paperback, 1963), pp. 63–64. Poem first appeared in *The Crisis*, June, 1921. Copyright 1926 by Langston Hughes. Reprinted by permission of Harold Ober Associates, Inc.

"Mulatto" reprinted from *Selected Poems of Langston Hughes* (New York: Alfred A. Knopf, 1959). Poem first appeared in *Saturday Review of Literature*, January 29, 1927. Copyright 1927 by Langston Hughes. Reprinted by permission of Harold Ober Associates, Inc.

The moon over the turpentine woods.
The Southern night
Full of stars,
Great big yellow stars.
   What's a body but a toy?
     Juicy bodies
     Of nigger wenches
     Blue black
     Against back fences.
     O, you little bastard boy,
     What's a body but a toy?
The scent of pine woods stings the soft night air.
    What's the body of your mother?
Silver moonlight everywhere.
    What's the body of your mother?
Sharp pine scent in the evening air.
      A nigger night,
      A nigger joy,
      A little yellow
      Bastard boy.

   Naw, you ain't my brother.
   Niggers ain't my brother.
   Not ever.
   Niggers ain't my brother.

The Southern night is full of stars,
Great big yellow stars.
     O, sweet as earth,
     Dusk dark bodies
     Give sweet birth
To little yellow bastard boys.

   Git on back there in the night,
   You ain't white.

The bright stars scatter everywhere.
Pine wood scent in the evening air.
     A nigger night,
     A nigger joy.

I am your son, white man!

A little yellow
Bastard boy.

The Negro Mother

Children, I come back today
To tell you a story of the long dark way
That I had to climb, that I had to know
In order that the race might live and grow.
Look at my face—dark as the night—
Yet shining like the sun with love's true light.
I am the child they stole from the sand
Three hundred years ago in Africa's land.
I am the dark girl who crossed the wide sea
Carrying in my body the seed of the free.
I am the woman who worked in the field
Bringing the cotton and the corn to yield.
I am the one who labored as a slave,
Beaten and mistreated for the work that I gave—
Children sold away from me, husband sold, too.
No safety, no love, no respect was I due.
Three hundred years in the deepest South:
But God put a song and a prayer in my mouth.
God put a dream like steel in my soul.
Now, through my children, I'm reaching the goal.
Now, through my children, young and free,
I realize the blessings denied to me.
I couldn't read then. I couldn't write.
I had nothing, back there in the night.
Sometimes, the valley was filled with tears,
But I kept trudging on through the lonely years.
Sometimes, the road was hot with sun,
But I had to keep on till my work was done:
I *had* to keep on! No stopping for me—
I was the seed of the coming Free.

Reprinted from *Selected Poems of Langston Hughes* (New York: Alfred A. Knopf, 1959). Poem first appeared in Golden Stair Press Broadsides group, 1931. Copyright 1959 by Langston Hughes. Reprinted by permission of Harold Ober Associates, Inc.

I nourished the dream that nothing could smother
Deep in my breast—the Negro mother.
I had only hope then, but now through you,
Dark ones of today, my dreams must come true:
All you dark children in the world out there,
Remember my sweat, my pain, my despair.
Remember my years, heavy with sorrow—
And make of those years a torch for tomorrow.
Make of my past a road to the light
Out of the darkness, the ignorance, the night.
Lift high my banner out of the dust.
Stand like free men supporting my trust.
Believe in the right, let none push you back.
Remember the whip and the slaver's track.
Remember how the strong in struggle and strife
Still bar you the way, and deny you life—
But march ever forward, breaking down bars.
Look ever upward at the sun and the stars.
Oh, my dark children, may my dreams and my prayers
Impel you forever up the great stairs—
For I will be with you till no white brother
Dares keep down the children of the Negro mother.

Evenin' Air Blues

Folks, I come up North
Cause they told me de North was fine.
I come up North
Cause they told me de North was fine.
Been up here six months—
I'm about to lose my mind.

This mornin' for breakfast
I chawed de mornin' air.
This mornin' for breakfast
Chawed de mornin' air.

Reprinted from *Shakespeare in Harlem* (New York: Alfred A. Knopf, 1942). Poem first appeared in *Common Ground* in Spring 1941 issue. Copyright 1941 by Langston Hughes. Reprinted by permission of Harold Ober Associates, Inc.

But this evenin' for supper,
I got evenin' air to spare.

Believe I'll do a little dancin'
Just to drive my blues away—
A little dancin'
To drive my blues away,
Cause when I'm dancin'
De blues forgets to stay.

But if you was to ask me
How de blues they come to be,
Says if you was to ask me
How de blues they come to be—
You wouldn't need to ask me:
Just look at me and see!

Dream Boogie

Good morning, daddy!
Ain't you heard
The boogie-woogie rumble
Of a dream deferred?

Listen closely:
You'll hear their feet
Beating out and beating out a—

You think
It's a happy beat?

Reprinted from *Selected Poems of Langston Hughes* (New York: Alfred A. Knopf, 1959). Poem first appeared in *Montage of a Dream Deferred* (New York: Henry Holt & Co., Inc., 1951). Copyright 1951 by Langston Hughes. Reprinted by permission of Harold Ober Associates, Inc.

Listen to it closely:
Ain't you heard
something underneath
like a—

What did I say?

Sure,
I'm happy!
Take it away!

Hey, pop!
Re-bop!
Mop!

Y-e-a-h!

On the Road

HE WAS NOT INTERESTED in the snow. When he got off the freight, one early evening during the depression, Sargeant never even noticed the snow. But he must have felt it seeping down his neck, cold, wet, sopping in his shoes. But if you had asked him, he wouldn't have known it was snowing. Sargeant didn't see the snow, not even under the bright lights of the main street, falling white and flaky against the night. He was too hungry, too sleepy, too tired.

The Reverend Mr. Dorset, however, saw the snow when he switched on his porch light, opened the front door of his parsonage,

Reprinted from *Something in Common and Other Stories* (New York: Hill and Wang American Century Series paperback, 1963). Story first appeared in *Esquire*, January 1935 issue. Copyright 1952 by Langston Hughes. Reprinted by permission of Harold Ober Associates, Inc.

and found standing there before him a big black man with snow on his face, a human piece of night with snow on his face—obviously unemployed.

Said the Reverend Mr. Dorset before Sargeant even realized he'd opened his mouth: "I'm sorry. No! Go right on down this street four blocks and turn to your left, walk up seven and you'll see the Relief Shelter. I'm sorry. No!" He shut the door.

Sargeant wanted to tell the holy man that he had already been to the Relief Shelter, been to hundreds of relief shelters during the depression years, the beds were always gone and supper was over, the place was full, and they drew the color line anyhow. But the minister said, "No," and shut the door. Evidently he didn't want to hear about it. And he *had* a door to shut.

The big black man turned away. And even yet he didn't see the snow, walking right into it. Maybe he sensed it, cold, wet, sticking to his jaws, wet on his black hands, sopping in his shoes. He stopped and stood on the sidewalk hunched over—hungry, sleepy, cold—looking up and down. Then he looked right where he was—in front of a church. Of course! A church! Sure, right next to a parsonage, certainly a church.

It had *two* doors.

Broad white steps in the night all snowy white. Two high arched doors with slender stone pillars on either side. And way up, a round lacy window with a stone crucifix in the middle and Christ on the crucifix in stone. All this was pale in the street lights, solid and stony pale in the snow.

Sargeant blinked. When he looked up, the snow fell into his eyes. For the first time that night he *saw* the snow. He shook his head. He shook the snow from his coat sleeves, felt hungry, felt lost, felt not lost, felt cold. He walked up the steps of the church. He knocked at the door. No answer. He tried the handle. Locked. He put his shoulder against the door and his long black body slanted like a ramrod. He pushed. With loud rhythmic grunts, like the grunts in a chain-gang song, he pushed against the door.

"I'm tired . . . Huh! . . . Hongry . . . Uh! . . . I'm sleepy . . . Huh! I'm cold . . . I got to sleep somewheres," Sargeant said. "This here is a church, ain't it? Well, uh!"

He pushed against the door.

Suddenly, with an undue cracking and screaking, the door began to give way to the tall black Negro who pushed ferociously against it.

By now two or three white people had stopped in the street, and Sargeant was vaguely aware of some of them yelling at him concerning the door. Three or four more came running, yelling at him.

"Hey!" they said. "Hey!"

"Uh-huh," answered the big tall Negro, "I know it's a white folks' church, but I got to sleep somewhere." He gave another lunge at the door. "Huh!"

And the door broke open.

But just when the door gave way, two white cops arrived in a car, ran up the steps with their clubs, and grabbed Sargeant. But Sargeant for once had no intention of being pulled or pushed away from the door.

Sargeant grabbed, but not for anything so weak as a broken door. He grabbed for one of the tall stone pillars beside the door, grabbed at it and caught it. And held it. The cops pulled and Sargeant pulled. Most of the people in the street got behind the cops and helped them pull.

"A big black unemployed Negro holding onto our church!" thought the people. "The idea!"

The cops began to beat Sargeant over the head, and nobody protested. But he held on.

And then the church fell down.

Gradually, the big stone front of the church fell down, the walls and the rafters, the crucifix and the Christ. Then the whole thing fell down, covering the cops and the people with bricks and stones and debris. The whole church fell down in the snow.

Sargeant got out from under the church and went walking on up the street with the stone pillar on his shoulder. He was under the impression that he had buried the parsonage and the Reverend Mr. Dorset who said, "No!" So he laughed, and threw the pillar six blocks up the street and went on.

Sargeant thought he was alone, but listening to the *crunch, crunch, crunch* on the snow of his own footsteps, he heard other footsteps, too, doubling his own. He looked around, and there was Christ walking along beside him, the same Christ that had been on the cross on the church—still stone with a rough stone surface, walking along beside him just like he was broken off the cross when the church fell down.

"Well, I'll be dogged," said Sargeant. "This here's the first time I ever seed you off the cross."

"Yes," said Christ, crunching his feet in the snow. "You had to pull the church down to get me off the cross."

"You glad?" said Sargeant.

"I sure am," said Christ.

They both laughed.

"I'm a hell of a fellow, ain't I?" said Sargeant. "Done pulled the church down!"

"You did a good job," said Christ. "They have kept me nailed on a cross for nearly two thousand years."

"Whee-ee-e!" said Sargeant. "I know you are glad to get off."

"I sure am," said Christ.

They walked on in the snow. Sargeant looked at the man of stone.

"And you have been up there two thousand years?"

"I sure have," Christ said.

"Well, if I had a little cash," said Sargeant, "I'd show you around a bit."

"I been around," said Christ.

"Yeah, but that was a long time ago."

"All the same," said Christ, "I've been around."

They walked on in the snow until they came to the railroad yards. Sargeant was tired, sweating and tired.

"Where you goin'?" Sargeant said, stopping by the tracks. He looked at Christ. Sargeant said, "I'm just a bum on the road. How about you? Where you goin'?"

"God knows," Christ said, "but I'm leavin' here."

They saw the red and green lights of the railroad yard half veiled by the snow that fell out of the night. Away down the track they saw a fire in a hobo jungle.

"I can go there and sleep," Sargeant said.

"You can?"

"Sure," said Sargeant. "That place ain't got no doors."

Outside the town, along the tracks, there were barren trees and bushes below the embankment, snow-gray in the dark. And down among the trees and bushes there were makeshift houses made out of boxes and tin and old pieces of wood and canvas. You couldn't see them in the dark, but you knew they were there if you'd ever been on the road, if you had ever lived with the homeless and hungry in a depression.

"I'm side-tracking," Sargeant said. "I'm tired."

"I'm gonna make it on to Kansas City," said Christ.

"O.K.," Sargeant said. "So long!"

He went down into the hobo jungle and found himself a place to sleep. He never did see Christ no more. About 6:00 A.M. a freight came by. Sargeant scrambled out of the jungle with a dozen or so more hobos and ran along the track, grabbing at the freight. It was dawn, early dawn, cold and gray.

"Wonder where Christ is by now?" Sargeant thought. "He

musta gone on way on down the road. He didn't sleep in this jungle."

Sargeant grabbed the train and started to pull himself up into a moving coal car, over the edge of a wheeling coal car. But strangely enough, the car was full of cops. The nearest cop rapped Sargeant soundly across the knuckles with his night stick. Wham! Rapped his big black hands for clinging to the top of the car. Wham! But Sargeant did not turn loose. He clung on and tried to pull himself into the car. He hollered at the top of his voice, "Damn it, lemme in this car!"

"Shut up," barked the cop. "You crazy coon!" He rapped Sargeant across the knuckles and punched him in the stomach. "You ain't out in no jungle now. This ain't no train. You in jail."

Wham! across his bare black fingers clinging to the bars of his cell. Wham! between the steel bars low down against his shins.

Suddenly Sargeant realized that he really was in jail. He wasn't on no train. The blood of the night before had dried on his face, his head hurt terribly, and a cop outside in the corridor was hitting him across the knuckles for holding onto the door, yelling and shaking the cell door.

"They musta took me to jail for breaking down the door last night," Sargeant thought, "that church door."

Sargeant went over and sat on a wooden bench against the cold stone wall. He was emptier than ever. His clothes were wet, clammy cold wet, and shoes sloppy with snow water. It was just about dawn. There he was, locked up behind a cell door, nursing his bruised fingers.

The bruised fingers were his, but not the *door*.

Not the *club*, but the fingers.

"You wait," mumbled Sargeant, black against the jail wall. "I'm gonna break down this door, too."

"Shut up—or I'll paste you one," said the cop.

"I'm gonna break down this door," yelled Sargeant as he stood up in his cell.

Then he must have been talking to himself because he said, "I wonder where Christ's gone? I wonder if he's gone to Kansas City?"

Dear Dr. Butts

"DO YOU KNOW what has happened to me?" said Simple.

"No."

"I'm out of a job."

"That's tough. How did that come about?"

"Laid off—they're converting again. And right now, just when I am planning to get married this spring, they have to go changing from civilian production to war contracts, installing new machinery. Manager says it might take two months, might take three or four. They'll send us mens notices. If it takes four months, that's up to June, which is no good for my plans. To get married a man needs money. To stay married he needs more money. And where am I? As usual, behind the eight-ball."

"You can find another job meanwhile, no doubt."

"That ain't easy. And if I do, they liable not to pay much. Jobs that pay good money nowadays are scarce as hen's teeth. But Joyce says she do not care. She is going to marry me, come June, anyhow—even if she has to pay for it herself. Joyce says since I paid for the divorce, she can pay for the wedding. But I do not want her to do that."

"Naturally not, but maybe you can curtail your plans somewhat and not have so big a wedding. Wedlock does not require an elaborate ceremony."

"I do not care if we don't have none, just so we get locked. But you know how womens is. Joyce has waited an extra year for her great day. Now here I am broke as a busted bank."

"How're you keeping up with your expenses?"

"I ain't. And I don't drop by Joyce's every night like I did when I was working. I'm embarrassed. Then she didn't have to ask me to eat. Now she does. In fact, she insists. She says, 'You got to eat somewheres. I enjoy your company. Eat with me.' I do, if I'm there when she extends the invitation. But I don't go looking for it. I just sets home and broods, man, and looks at my four walls, which gives me plenty of time to think. And do you know what I been thinking about lately?"

"Finding work, I presume."

Reprinted from *Simple Takes a Wife* (New York: Simon and Schuster, 1953). Copyright 1953 by Langston Hughes. Reprinted by permission of Harold Ober Associates, Inc.

"Besides that?"

"No. I don't know what you've been thinking about."

"Negro leaders, and how they're talking about how great democracy is—and me out of a job. Also how there is so many leaders I don't know that white folks know about, because they are always in the white papers. Yet *I'm* the one they are supposed to be leading. Now, you take that little short leader named Dr. Butts, I do not know him, except in name only. If he ever made a speech in Harlem it were not well advertised. From what I reads, he teaches at a white college in Massachusetts, stays at the Commodore when he's in New York, and ain't lived in Harlem for ten years. Yet he's leading me. He's an article writer, but he does not write in colored papers. But lately the colored papers taken to reprinting parts of what he writes—otherwise I would have never seen it. Anyhow, with all this time on my hands these days, I writ him a letter last night. Here, read it."

Harlem, U.S.A.
One Cold February Day

Dear Dr. Butts,

I seen last week in the colored papers where you have writ an article for The New York Times *in which you say America is the greatest country in the world for the Negro race and Democracy the greatest kind of government for all, but it would be better if there was equal education for colored folks in the South, and if everybody could vote, and if there were not Jim Crow in the army, also if the churches was not divided up into white churches and colored churches, and if Negroes did not have to ride on the back seats of busses South of Washington.*

Now, all this later part of your article is hanging onto your but. *You start off talking about how great American democracy is, then you* but *it all over the place. In fact, the* but *end of your see-saw is so far down on the ground I do not believe the other end can ever pull it up. So me myself, I would not write no article for no* New York Times *if I had to put in so many* buts. *I reckon maybe you come by it naturally, though, that being your name, dear Dr. Butts.*

I hear tell that you are a race leader, but I do not know who you lead because I have not heard tell of you before and I have not laid eyes on you. But if you are leading me, make me know it, *because I do not read the* New York Times *very often, less I happen to pick up a copy blowing around in the subway, so I did not know you were my leader. But since you are my leader, lead on, and see*

215

if I will follow behind your but—*because there is more behind that* but *than there is in front of it.*

Dr. Butts, *I am glad to read that you writ an article in* The New York Times, *but also* sometime *I wish you would write one in the colored papers and let me know how to get out from behind all these* buts *that are staring me in the face. I know America is a great country* but—*and it is that* but *that has been keeping me where I is all these years. I can't get over it, I can't get under it, and I can't get around it, so what am I supposed to do? If you are leading me, lemme see. Because we have too many colored leaders now that nobody knows until they get from the white papers to the colored papers and from the colored papers to me who has never seen hair nor hide of you. Dear Dr. Butts, are you hiding from me —and* leading *me, too?*

From the way you write, a man would think my race problem was made out of nothing but buts. *But* this, *but* that, *and, yes, there is Jim Crow in Georgia* but—. *America admits they bomb folks in Florida—but Hitler gassed the Jews. Mississippi is bad— but Russia is worse. Detroit slums are awful—but compared to the slums in India, Detroit's Paradise Valley is Paradise.*

Dear Dr. Butts, *Hitler is dead. I don't live in Russia. India is across the Pacific Ocean. And I do not hope to see Paradise no time soon. I am nowhere near some of them foreign countries you are talking about being so bad.* I am here! *And you know as well as I do, Mississippi is hell. There ain't no* but *in the world can make it out different. They tell me when Nazis gas you, you die slow. But when they put a bomb under you like in Florida, you don't have time to say your prayers. As for Detroit, there is as much difference between Paradise Valley and Paradise as there is between heaven and Harlem. I don't know nothing about India, but I been in Washington, D.C. If you think there ain't slums there, just take your* but *up Seventh Street late some night, and see if you still got it by the time you get to Howard University.*

I should not have to be telling you these things. You are colored just like me. To put a but *after all this Jim Crow fly-papering around our feet is just like telling a hungry man, "But Mr. Rockefeller has got plenty to eat." It's just like telling a joker with no overcoat in the winter time, "But you will be hot next summer." The fellow is liable to haul off and say, "I am hot now!" And bop you over your head.*

Are you in your right mind, dear Dr. Butts? Or are you just writing? Do you really think a new day is dawning? *Do you really think Christians are having a change of heart? I can see you now taking your pen in hand to write, "But just last year the Southern*

Denominations of Hell-Fired Salvation resolved to work toward Brotherhood." In fact, that is what you already writ. Do you think Brotherhood means colored *to them Southerners?*

Do you reckon they will recognize you *for a brother, Dr. Butts, since you done had your picture taken in the Grand Ballroom of the Waldorf-Astoria shaking hands at some kind of meeting with five hundred white big-shots and* five *Negroes, all five of them Negro leaders, so it said underneath the picture? I did not know any of them Negro leaders by sight, neither by name, but since it says in the white papers that they are leaders, I reckon they are. Anyhow, I take my pen in hand to write you this letter to ask you to make yourself clear to me. When you answer me, do not write no "so-and-so-and-so but—." I will not take* but *for an answer. Negroes have been looking at Democracy's* but *too long. What we want to know is how to get rid of that* but.

Do you dig me, dear Dr. Butts?

Sincerely very truly,
JESSE B. SEMPLE

Jazz, Jive, and Jam

"IT BEING Negro History Week," said Simple, "Joyce took me to a pay lecture to hear some Negro hysterian——"

"Historian," I corrected.

"—hysterian speak," continued Simple, "and he laid our Negro race low. He said we was misbred, misread, and misled, also losing our time good-timing. Instead of time-taking and money-making, we are jazz-shaking. Oh, he enjoyed his self at the expense of the colored race—and him black as me. He really delivered a lecture—in which, no doubt, there is some truth."

"Constructive criticism, I gather—a sort of tearing down in order to build up."

"He tore us down good," said Simple. "Joyce come out saying to me, her husband, that he had really got my number. I said,

Reprinted from *The Best of Simple* (New York: Hill and Wang American Century Series paperback, 1961). Piece first appeared in *Simple Stakes a Claim* (New York: Holt, Rinehart & Winston, Inc., 1957). Copyright 1957 by Langston Hughes. Reprinted by permission of Harold Ober Associates, Inc.

'Baby, he did not miss you, neither.' But Joyce did not consider herself included in the bad things he said.

"She come telling me on the way home by subway, 'Jess Semple, I have been pursuing culture since my childhood. But you, when I first met you, all you did was drape yourself over some beer bar and argue with the barflies. The higher things of life do not come out of a licker trough.'

"I replied, 'But, Joyce, how come culture has got to be so dry?'

"She answers me back, 'How come your gullet has got to be so wet? You are sitting in this subway right now looking like you would like to have a beer.'

" 'Solid!' I said. 'I would. How did you guess it?'

" 'Married to you for three years, I can read your mind,' said Joyce. 'We'll buy a couple of cans to take home. I might even drink one myself.'

" 'Joyce, baby,' I said, 'in that case, let's buy three cans.'

"Joyce says, 'Remember the budget, Jess.'

"I says, 'Honey, you done busted the budget going to that lecture program which cost One Dollar a head, also we put some small change in the collection to help Negroes get ahead.'

" 'Small change?' says Joyce, 'I put a dollar.'

" 'Then our budget is busted real good,' I said, 'so we might as well dent it some more. Let's get six cans of beer.'

" 'All right,' says Joyce, 'go ahead, drink yourself to the dogs —instead of saving for that house we want to buy!'

" 'Six cans of beer would not pay for even the bottom front step,' I said. 'But they would lift my spirits this evening. That Negro high-speaking doctor done tore my spirits down. I did not know before that the colored race was so misled, misread, and misbred. According to him there is hardly a pure black man left. But I was setting in the back, so I guess he did not see me.'

" 'Had you not had to go to sleep in the big chair after dinner,' says Joyce, 'we would have been there on time and had seats up front.'

" 'I were near enough to that joker,' I said. 'Loud as he could holler, we did not need to set no closer. And he certainly were nothing to look at!'

" 'Very few educated men look like Harry Belafonte,' said Joyce.

" 'I am glad I am handsome instead of wise,' I said. But Joyce did not crack a smile. She had that lecture on her mind.

" 'Dr. Conboy is smart,' says Joyce. 'Did you hear him quoting Aristotle?'

" 'Who were Harry Stottle?' I asked.

" 'Some people are not even misread,' said Joyce. 'Aristotle was a Greek philosopher like Socrates, a great man of ancient times.'

" 'He must of been before Booker T. Washington then,' I said, 'because, to tell the truth, I has not heard of him at all. But tonight being *Negro* History Week, how come Dr. Conboy has to quote some Greek?'

" 'There were black Greeks,' said Joyce. 'Did you not hear him say that Negroes have played a part in all history, throughout all time, from Eden to now?'

" 'Do you reckon Eve was brownskin?' I requested.

" 'I do not know about Eve,' said Joyce, 'but Cleopatra was of the colored race, and the Bible says Sheba, beloved of Solomon, was black but comely.'

" 'I wonder would she come to me?' I says.

" 'Solomon also found Cleopatra comely. He was a king,' says Joyce.

" 'And I am Jesse B. Semple,' I said.

"But by that time the subway had got to our stop. At the store Joyce broke the budget again, opened up her pocket purse, and bought us six cans of beer. So it were a good evening. It ended well—except that I ain't for going to any more meetings—especially interracial meetings."

"Come now! Don't you want to improve race relations?"

"Sure," said Simple, "but in my opinion, jazz, jive, and jam would be better for race relations than all this high-flown gab, gaff, and gas the orators put out. All this talking that white folks do at meetings, and big Negroes, too, about how to get along together—just a little jam session would have everybody getting along fine without having to listen to so many speeches. Why, last month Joyce took me to a Race Relations Seminar which her club and twenty other clubs gave, and man, it lasted three days! It started on a Friday night and it were not over until Sunday afternoon. They had sessions' mammy! Joyce is a fiend for culture."

"And you sat through all that?"

"I did not set," said Simple. "I stood. I walked in and walked out. I smoked on the corner and snuck two drinks at the bar. But I had to wait for Joyce, and I thought them speeches would never get over! My wife were a delegate from her club, so she had to stay, although I think Joyce got tired her own self. But she would not admit it. Joyce said, 'Dr. Hillary Thingabod was certainly brilliant, were he not?'

"I said, 'He were not.'

"Joyce said, 'What did you want the man to say?'

"I said, 'I wish he had sung, instead of *said*. That program needed some music to keep folks awake.'

"Joyce said, 'Our forum was not intended for a musical. It was intended to see how we can work out integration.'

"I said, 'With a jazz band, they could work out integration in ten minutes. Everybody would have been dancing together like they all did at the Savoy—colored and white—or down on the East Side at them Casinos on a Friday night where jam holds forth—and we would have been integrated.'

"Joyce said, 'This was a serious seminar, aiming at facts, not fun.'

"'Baby,' I said, 'what is more facts than acts? Jazz makes people get into action, move! Didn't nobody move in that hall where you were—except to jerk their head up when they went to sleep, to keep anybody from seeing that they was nodding. Why, that chairman, Mrs. Maxwell-Reeves, almost lost her glasses off her nose, she jerked her head up so quick one time when that man you say was so brilliant were speaking!'

"'Jess Semple, that is not so!' yelled Joyce. 'Mrs. Maxwell-Reeves were just lost in thought. And if you think you saw *me* sleeping——'

"'You was too busy trying to look around and see where I was,' I said. 'Thank God, I did not have to set up there like you with the delegation. I would not be a delegate to no such gab-fest for nothing on earth.'

"'I thought you was so interested in saving the race!' said Joyce. 'Next time I will not ask you to accompany me to no cultural events, Jesse B., because I can see you do not appreciate them. That were a discussion of ways and means. And you are talking about jazz bands!'

"'There's more ways than one to skin a cat,' I said. 'A jazz band like Duke's or Hamp's or Basie's sure would of helped that meeting. At least on Saturday afternoon, they could have used a little music to put some pep into the proceedings. Now, just say for instant, baby, they was to open with jazz and close with jam—and do the talking in between. Start out, for example, with "The St. Louis Blues," which is a kind of colored national anthem. That would put every human in a good humor. Then play "Why Don't You Do Right?" which could be addressed to white folks. They could pat their feet to that. Then for a third number before introducing the speaker, let some guest star like Pearl Bailey sing "There'll Be Some Changes Made"—which, as I understand it, were the theme of the meeting, anyhow—and all the Negroes could say *Amen!*

"'Joyce, I wish you would let me plan them interracial seminaries next time. After the music, let the speechmaking roll for a while—with maybe a calypso between speeches. Then, along about five o'clock, bring on the jam session, extra-special. Start serving tea to "Tea For Two," played real cool. Whilst drinking tea and dancing, the race relationers could relate, the integraters could integrate, and desegregators desegregate. Joyce, you would not have to beg for a crowd to come out and support your efforts then. Jam—and the hall would be jammed! Even I would stick around, and not be outside sneaking a smoke, or trying to figure how I can get to the bar before the resolutions are voted on. *Resolved: that we solve* the race problem! Strike up the band! Hit it, men! Aw, play that thing! "How High the Moon!" How high! Wheee-ee-e!'"

"What did Joyce say to that?" I demanded.

"Joyce just thought I was high," said Simple.

RICHARD WRIGHT

1908-1960

Richard Wright was the first twentieth-century writer to deal extensively with the economic and moral problems of the Negro as they existed in the ghetto. His concentration upon subjugation, alienation, violence, and frustration is similar to that of subsequent authors who have used Wright's achievement as a literary touchstone and a point of departure. Moreover, Wright's evolution from an intellectually barren childhood in Mississippi to a sophisticated maturity in Chicago, New York, and Paris encouraged later Negro writers, for it was a cultural journey accomplished through Wright's tenacious will and ambition, through his determination not to be defeated by his environment.

An understanding of Wright's human as well as artistic accomplishment begins with an examination of the peculiar difficulties that confronted him in his youth. Born on a farm near Natchez, Mississippi, in 1908, he was taken in his early youth to Memphis, Tennessee. His father deserted the family, reducing the boy, his brother, and his mother to penury. Wright's mother soon became partially paralyzed and was compelled to put Wright and his younger brother into an orphanage; but Wright's distrust of all people, his loneliness, his discontent with the poverty of his family, and his impatience—that impatience which was to be the most notable characteristic of his entire career—were only exacerbated. His mother withdrew the boy and sent him to various relatives and ultimately to his grandmother and his aunt. These ladies were

Seventh-Day Adventists and imposed their religious attitudes on young Wright; he rebelled, renouncing formal religion then and for the rest of his life, certain that "the naked will to power seems always to walk in the wake of a hymn."

As Wright matured, he became increasingly concerned with the sources of power in America, manifested particularly by the individual employers whom he served. Unwilling to humble himself before his white employers, unwilling to acknowledge a condition of inferiority which he did not feel, he reacted unpredictably and violently. Violence became the dominant characteristic of his life and work. *Black Boy*, an autobiography which traces the first seventeen years of his life, suggests how Wright attempted to suppress his tendency toward extreme behavior, how he had to dissemble before those white Southerners who expected him to be submissive. When he discovered the imaginative possibilities of literature, his own discontent found itself mirrored in the violence of fictional characters in the contemporary American literature of his time. "I vowed that as soon as I was old enough I would buy all the novels there were and read them to feed that thirst for violence that was in me, for intrigue, for plotting, for secrecy, for bloody murders."

Soon he was able to borrow if not buy fiction from the library by pretending that the note he presented to the librarian had been written by a white man: "Dear Madam: Will you please let this nigger boy have some books by H. L. Mencken?" Mencken, the editor of *The American Mercury* and the iconoclastic figure many young writers admired for his repeated criticism of parochial values in America, impressed Wright because of his courage in attacking prejudice. "He was using words as a weapon," Wright recalls in *Black Boy*, "using them as one would a club." Inspired by Mencken's candor, Wright turned to Sinclair Lewis, Theodore Dreiser, and other social novelists and found their indictments of American materialism corroborated by his own experiences; soon he felt that he must live in the North, where he imagined that "life could be lived with dignity."

Wright came to Chicago in 1927, but he found little dignity in the way Negroes were treated. Because of his disillusionment with American democracy, he was attracted to the Communist Party, and in one of his earliest essays, "Blueprint for Negro Writing," he urged the Negro writer to adopt the Marxist point of view. Wright began publishing poems and essays in various radical journals: *Left Front, New Masses, Midland, The Daily Worker,* and *International.* He joined the John Reed Club, but when he refused to abandon his writing for a more political role in Communist activities, he decided to resign from the club. In the following years, Wright was director of the Federal Negro Theater and a member of the Federal Writers Project, a subdivision of the WPA which sought work for unemployed authors. Throughout this period he found himself resisting the authority of the Communist Party, although he remained in sympathy with its principles. "I knew in my heart," he wrote later, "that I should never be able to write that way again, should never be able to feel with that simple sharpness about life, should never again make so total a commitment of faith."

Wright's first important work was *Uncle Tom's Children* (1938), a collection of stories that emphasize the alienation and frustration of Negro sharecroppers in the rural South and the violence that occurs when these individuals contend with the restrictions of the white world—none of them accepts the legacy bequeathed by Uncle Tom, the emasculated Negro slave in Harriet Beecher Stowe's novel. Wright was dissatisfied with his work, however, for he felt that he "had written a book which even bankers' daughters could read and weep over and feel good about." He was determined to create a novel which "would be so hard and deep that they [the white readers] would have to face it without the consolation of tears."

Native Son (1940) was the result; and the novel, which is Wright's most significant work of fiction, marks the first flowering of contemporary Negro literature, for it concentrates upon the economic and social conditions of the Negro in the city and expresses those conditions in the form of the protest novel. *Native Son* is an awkward book in terms of style, structure, and characterization, and it suffers from a tendentious quality that one finds in many naturalistic novels; but its very clumsiness gives its subject —the victimization and crucifixion of the Negro by a white society—a strength that is absent from more carefully written, more subtly conceived works of art. The book has the haunting quality of revelation, for never had the Negro's suppressed feelings been so ruthlessly exposed, and it succeeds in inducing guilt on the part of the American reader as he realizes that Bigger Thomas, the protagonist of the novel, is a part of America too, that he is also one of its native sons.

Native Son established Wright's reputation as a forceful writer of naturalistic fiction. *Black Boy,* the famous autobiography published in 1945, was immediately recognized as a significant social document as well as a moving personal history; it traces Wright's life until the age of seventeen and documents his loneliness, fear, and suffering, his distrust of the world he wanted so much to enter. That world became available to him in the 1940's. Having rejected the ideologies of Christianity and communism, Wright was attracted to existentialism and influenced by the philosophic attitudes of Heidegger, Jaspers, Kierkegaard, Nietzsche, Jean Paul Sartre, and especially Albert Camus. His next novel, *The Outsider* (1953), expressed Wright's criticism of Western society, and though the protagonist is Negro, his hostility is significantly different from that of Bigger Thomas in *Native Son*. Whereas Bigger resents his exclusion from the middle-class of the white man, Cross Damon— the central figure of *The Outsider*—rejects completely all middle-class values in America.

Wright became an expatriate because of his estrangement from American racism and materialism; and, except for a short period in England, he lived in France from 1947 until his death in 1960, in Paris and in Ailly, Normandy. During this period he composed, in addition to *The Outsider, The Long Dream* (1958) and *Lawd Today* (1963), novels which are concerned with racial issues; *Eight Men* (1961), stories that had been written at various times during his life; *Black Power* (1954) and *White Man, Listen!* (1957), sociological studies; and innumerable essays and reviews. Toward the end of his life he was drawn to African nationalism, but he found his "westernness" a barrier between himself and the Africans. He remained a "rootless man," as he characterized himself, a wanderer who cherished "the state of abandonment, of aloneness."

When we consider Richard Wright's special contribution to American literature, we remember several of the stories in *Uncle Tom's Children* and *Eight Men*; the novel, *Native Son*; the autobiography, *Black Boy*; and some of the writing of his later period— *The Long Dream, Lawd Today,* and *Black Power*. This work reflects Wright's position in an alien society, his attempt to possess and contribute to the culture of the Western world. With relentless honesty, Wright depicts areas of experience that had not been thoroughly explored before his time; he is the kind of writer who awakens readers to unknown lives, who culminates a tradition— the protest tradition in Negro literature—and establishes a new direction—the persistent attempt to explore the actual psychological attitudes of American Negroes. The history of his struggle, as reflected in his major works, is part of our cultural history; for if the Negro is America's metaphor, as Wright himself has maintained, that metaphor is for the first time fully articulated by Wright's own novels, stories, essays, and poems. His was a haunted tower, as one critic suggests, but it was nevertheless a tower in the landscape of American writing.

"The Man Who Killed a Shadow" is a short story included in

Eight Men and bears some of the typical characteristics of Wright's fiction: the unwillingness of the Negro to accept his condition of inferiority; the frustration and ultimate violence that develop as a consequence of his attitude; and the sense of alienation that the Negro feels because of the white world in which he must learn self-adjustment. Although it is not as carefully wrought as later short fiction by Negro writers, it has the sense of life, the verisimilitude often absent from more artful tales; and it concentrates knowingly upon the subject of sex—and the fantasies of some white people about sex—that is central to a discussion of racial issues in America.

"The Ethics of Living Jim Crow" is one of the classic statements of racial prejudice in America. In the title one senses Wright's ironic point of view; in the essay one feels the tension between innocence and outrage, between idealism and cynicism, that characterizes Wright's best work. One merely has to recall the names of Wright's first three books—*Uncle Tom's Children, Native Son,* and *Black Boy*—to remember that their central issues are focused on youth. One need only consider *The Outsider, The Long Dream,* and *Lawd Today* to sense the estrangement from a dominant culture which serves as a pervasive theme in Wright's fiction. More than a decade has passed since most of Wright's significant work was published; it is clear now that his vision was indeed prophetic, his understanding of racial issues perceptive and at times profound. His most important nonfiction—*Black Power* (1954), *The Color Curtain* (1956), and *White Man, Listen!* (1957)—was written in the mid 1950's; yet it speaks of all the unresolved problems that still trouble black and white Americans.

Black Boy (1945), in which the ideas of "The Ethics of Living Jim Crow" are given fuller treatment, marks the end of Wright's best-known period. But Wright's entire career is undergoing revaluation, and the judgment of Irving Howe in a farewell tribute to the author may well be the critical estimate of our time: "men whose lives have been torn by suffering must live with their past so that it too becomes part of the present reality. And by remembering, Wright kept faith with the experience of the boy who had fought his way out of the depths to speak for those who remained behind."

The Man Who Killed a Shadow

IT ALL BEGAN long ago when he was a tiny boy who was already used, in a fearful sort of way, to living with shadows. But what were the shadows that made him afraid? Surely they were not those beautiful silhouettes of objects cast upon the earth by the sun. Shadows of that kind are innocent and he loved trying to catch them as he ran along sunlit paths in summer. But there were subtler shadows which he saw and which others could not see: the shadows of his fears. And this boy had such shadows and he lived to kill one of them.

Saul Saunders was born black in a little Southern town, not many miles from Washington, the nation's capital, which means that he came into a world that was split in two, a white world and a black one, the white one being separated from the black by a million psychological miles. So, from the very beginning, Saul looking timidly out from his black world, saw the shadowy outlines of a white world that was unreal to him and not his own.

It so happened that even Saul's mother was but a vague, shadowy thing to him, for she died long before his memory could form an image of her. And the same thing happened to Saul's father, who died before the boy could retain a clear picture of him in his mind.

People really never became personalities to Saul, for hardly had he ever got to know them before they vanished. So people became for Saul symbols of uneasiness, of a deprivation that evoked in him a sense of the transitory quality of life, which always made him feel that some invisible, unexplainable event was about to descend upon him.

He had five brothers and two sisters who remained strangers to him. There was, of course, no adult in his family with enough money to support them all, and the children were rationed out to various cousins, uncles, aunts, and grandparents.

It fell to Saul to live with his grandmother who moved constantly from one small Southern town to another, and even physical landscapes grew to have but little emotional meaning for the boy. Towns were places you lived in for a while, and then you moved on. When he had reached the age of twelve, all reality seemed to him to be akin to his mother and father, like the white world that surrounded the black island of his life, like the parade of dirty little towns that passed forever before his eyes, things that had names but not substance, things that happened and then retreated into an incomprehensible nothingness.

Saul was not dumb or lazy, but it took him seven years to reach the third grade in school. None of the people who came and went in Saul's life had ever prized learning and Saul did likewise. It was quite normal in his environment to reach the age of fourteen and still be in the third grade, and Saul liked being normal, liked being like other people.

Then the one person—his grandmother—who Saul had thought would endure forever, passed suddenly from his life, and from that moment on Saul did not ever quite know what to do. He went to work for the white people of the South and the shadow-like quality of his world became terribly manifest, continuously present. He understood nothing of this white world into which he had been thrown; it was just there, a faint and fearful shadow cast by some object that stood between him and a hidden and powerful sun.

He quickly learned that the strange white people for whom he worked considered him inferior; he did not feel inferior and he did not think that he was. But when he looked about him he saw other black people accepting this definition of themselves, and who was he to challenge it? Outwardly he grew to accept it as part of that vast shadow-world that came and went, pulled by forces which he nor nobody he knew understood.

Soon all of Saul's anxieties, fears, and irritations became focused upon this white shadow-world which gave him his daily bread in exchange for his labor. Feeling unhappy and not knowing why, he projected his misery out from himself and upon the one thing that made him most constantly anxious. If this had not happened, if Saul had not found a way of putting his burden upon others, he would have early thought of suicide. He finally did, in the end, think of killing himself, but then it was too late . . .

At the age of fifteen Saul knew that the life he was then living was to be his lot, that there was no way to rid himself of his plaguing sense of unreality, no way to relax and forget. He was most self-forgetful when he was with black people, and that made things a little easier for him. But as he grew older, he became more afraid, yet none of his friends noticed it. Indeed, many of Saul's friends liked him very much. Saul was always kind, attentive; but no one suspected that his kindness, his quiet, waiting loyalty came from his being afraid.

Then Saul changed. Maybe it was luck or misfortune; it is hard to tell. When he took a drink of whisky, he found that it helped to banish the shadows, lessened his tensions, made the world more reasonably three-dimensional, and he grew to like drinking. When he was paid off on a Saturday night, he would drink with his friends and he would feel better. He felt that whisky made life complete, that it stimulated him. But, of course, it did not. Whisky really depressed him, numbed him somewhat, reduced the force and number of the shadows that made him tight inside.

When Saul was sober, he almost never laughed in the presence of the white shadow-world, but when he had a drink or two he found that he could. Even when he was told about the hard lives that all Negroes lived, it did not worry him, for he would take a drink and not feel too badly. It did not even bother him when he heard that if you were alone with a white woman and she screamed, it was as good as hearing your death sentence, for, though you had done nothing, you would be killed. Saul got used to hearing the siren of the police car screaming in the Black Belt, got used to seeing white cops dragging Negroes off to jail. Once he grew wildly angry about it, felt that the shadows would some day claim him as he had seen them claim others, but his friends warned him that it was dangerous to feel that way, that always the black man lost, and the best thing to do was to take a drink. He did, and in a little while they were all laughing.

One night when he was mildly drunk—he was thirty years old and living in Washington at the time—he got married. The girl was good for Saul, for she too liked to drink and she was pretty and they got along together. Saul now felt that things were not so bad; as long as he could stifle the feeling of being hemmed in, as long as he could conquer the anxiety about the unexpected happening, life was bearable.

Saul's jobs had been many and simple. First he had worked on a farm. When he was fourteen he had gone to Washington, after his grandmother had died, where he did all kinds of odd jobs. Finally he was hired by an old white army colonel as chauffeur and butler and he averaged about twenty dollars every two weeks. He lived in and got his meals and uniform and remained with the colonel for five years. The colonel too liked to drink, and sometimes they would both get drunk. But Saul never forgot that the colonel, though drunk and feeling fine, was still a shadow, unreal, and might suddenly change toward him.

One day, when whisky was making him feel good, Saul asked the colonel for a raise in salary, told him that he did not have enough to live on, and that prices were rising. But the colonel was sober and hard that day and said no. Saul was so stunned that he quit the job that instant. While under the spell of whisky he had for a quick moment felt that the world of shadows was over, but when he had asked for more money and had been refused, he knew that he had been wrong. He should not have asked for money; he should have known that the colonel was a no-good guy, a shadow.

Saul was next hired as an exterminator by a big chemical company and he found that there was something in his nature that made him like going from house to house and putting down poison for rats and mice and roaches. He liked seeing concrete evidence of his work and the dead bodies of rats were no shadows. They were real. He never felt better in his life than when he was killing with the sanction of society. And his boss even increased his salary when he asked for it. And he drank as much as he liked and no one cared.

But one morning, after a hard night of drinking which had made him irritable and high-strung, his boss said something that he did not like and he spoke up, defending himself against what he thought was a slighting remark. There was an argument and Saul left.

Two weeks of job hunting got him the position of janitor in the National Cathedral, a church and religious institution. It was the solitary kind of work he liked; he reported for duty each morning at seven o'clock and at eleven he was through. He first cleaned the Christmas card shop, next he cleaned the library; and his final chore was to clean the choir room.

But cleaning the library, with its rows and rows of books, was what caught Saul's attention, for there was a strange little shadow woman there who stared at him all the time in a most peculiar way. The library was housed in a separate building and, whenever he came to clean it, he and the white woman would be there alone. She was tiny, blonde, blue-eyed, weighing about 110 pounds, and standing about five feet three inches. Saul's boss had warned him never to quarrel with the lady in charge of the library. "She's a crackpot," he had told Saul. And naturally Saul never wanted any trouble, in fact, he did not even know the woman's name. Many times, however, he would pause in his work, feeling that his eyes were being drawn to her and he would turn around and find her staring at him. Then she would look away quickly, as though ashamed. "What in hell does she want from me?" he wondered uneasily. The woman never spoke to him except to say good morning and she even said that as though she did not want to say it. Saul thought that maybe she was afraid of him; but how could that be? He could not recall when anybody had ever been afraid of him, and he had never been in any trouble in his life.

One morning while sweeping the floor he felt his eyes being drawn toward her and he paused and turned and saw her staring at him. He did not move, neither did she. They stared at each other for about ten seconds, then she went out of the room, walking with quick steps, as though angry or afraid. He was frightened, but forgot it quickly. "What the hell's wrong with that woman?" he asked himself.

Next morning Saul's boss called him and told him, in a nice quiet tone—but it made him scared and mad just the same—that the woman in the library had complained about him, had said that he never cleaned under her desk.

"Under her desk?" Saul asked, amazed.

"Yes," his boss said, amused at Saul's astonishment.

"But I clean under her desk every morning," Saul said.

"Well, Saul, remember, I told you she was a crackpot," his boss said soothingly. "Don't argue with her. Just do your work."

"Yes, sir," Saul said.

He wanted to tell his boss how the woman always stared at him, but he could not find courage enough to do so. If he had been talking with his black friends, he would have done so quite naturally. But why talk to one shadow about another queer shadow?

That day being payday, he got his weekly wages and that night he had a hell of a good time. He drank until he was drunk, until he blotted out almost everything from his consciousness. He was getting regularly drunk now whenever he had the money. He liked it and he bothered nobody and he was happy while doing it. But dawn found him broke, exhausted, and terribly depressed, full of shadows and uneasiness, a way he never liked it. The thought of going to his job made him angry. He longed for deep, heavy sleep. But, no, he had a good job and he had to keep it. Yes, he would go.

After cleaning the Christmas card shop—he was weak and he sweated a lot—he went to the library. No one was there. He swept the floor and was about to dust the books when he heard the footsteps of the woman coming into the room. He was tired, nervous, half asleep; his hands trembled and his reflexes were overquick. "So you're the bitch who snitched on me, hunh?" he said irritably to himself. He continued dusting and all at once he had the queer feeling that she was staring at him. He fought against the impulse to look at her, but he could not resist it. He turned slowly and saw that she was sitting in her chair at her desk, staring at him with unblinking eyes. He had the impression that she was about to speak. He could not help staring back at her, waiting.

"Why don't you clean under my desk?" she asked him in a tense but controlled voice.

"Why, ma'am," he said slowly, "I just did."

"Come here and look," she said, pointing downward.

He replaced the book on the shelf. She had never spoken so many words to him before. He went and stood before her and his mind protested against what his eyes saw, and then his senses leaped in wonder. She was sitting with her knees sprawled apart and her dress was drawn halfway up her legs. He looked from her round blue eyes to her white legs whose thighs thickened as they went to a V clothed in tight, sheer, pink panties; then he looked quickly again into her eyes. Her face was a beet red, but she sat very still, rigid, as though she was being impelled into an act which she did not want to perform but was being driven to perform. Saul was so startled that he could not move.

"I just cleaned under your desk this morning," he mumbled, sensing that he was not talking about what she meant.

"There's dust there now," she said sternly, her legs still so wide apart that he felt that she was naked.

He did not know what to do; he was so baffled, humiliated, and frightened that he grew angry. But he was afraid to express his anger openly.

"Look, ma'am," he said in a tone of suppressed rage and hate, "you're making trouble for me!"

"Why don't you do your work?" she blazed at him. "That's what you're being paid to do, you black nigger!" Her legs were still spread wide and she was sitting as though about to spring upon him and throw her naked thighs about his body.

For a moment he was still and silent. Never before in his life had he been called a "black nigger." He had heard that white people used that phrase as their supreme humiliation of black people, but he had never been treated so. As the insult sank in, as he stared at her gaping thighs, he felt overwhelmed by a sense of wild danger.

"I don't like that," he said and before he knew it he had slapped her flat across her face.

She sucked in her breath, sprang up, and stepped away from him. Then she screamed sharply, and her voice was like a lash cutting into his chest. She screamed again and he backed away from her. He felt helpless, strange; he knew what he had done, knew its meaning for him; but he knew that he could not have helped it. It seemed that some part of him was there in that room watching him do things that he should not do. He drew in his breath and for a moment he felt that he could not stand upon his legs. His world was now full of all the shadows he had ever feared. He was in the worst trouble that a black man could imagine.

The woman was screaming continuously now and he was running toward the stairs. Just as he put his foot on the bottom step, he paused and looked over his shoulder. She was backing away from him, toward an open window at the far end of the room, still screaming. Oh God! In her scream he heard the sirens of the police cars that hunted down black men in the Black Belts and he heard the shrill whistles of white cops running after black men and he felt again in one rush of emotion all the wild and bitter tales he had heard of how whites always got the black who did a crime and this woman was screaming as though he had raped her.

He ran on up the steps, but her screams were coming so loud that when he neared the top of the steps he slowed. Those screams would not let him run any more, they weakened him, tugged and pulled him. His chest felt as though it would burst. He reached the top landing and looked round aimlessly. He saw a fireplace and before it was a neat pile of wood and while he was looking at that pile of wood the screams tore at him, unnerved him. With a shaking hand he reached down and seized in his left hand—for he was lefthanded—a heavy piece of oaken firewood that had jagged, sharp edges where it had been cut with an ax. He turned and ran back down the steps to where the woman stood screaming. He lifted the stick of wood as he confronted her, then paused. He wanted her to stop screaming. If she had stopped, he would have fled, but while she screamed all he could feel was a hotness bubbling in him and urging him to do something. She would fill her lungs quickly and deeply and her breath would come out at full blast. He swung down his left arm and hit her a swinging blow on the side of her head, not to hurt her, not to kill her, but to stop that awful noise, to stop that shadow from screaming a scream that meant death . . . He felt her skull crack and give as she sank to the floor, but she still screamed. He trembled from head to feet. Goddamn that woman . . . Why didn't she stop that yelling? He lifted his arm and gave her another blow, feeling the oaken stick driving its way into her skull. But still she screamed. He was about to hit her again when he became aware that the stick he held was light. He looked at it and found that half of it had broken off, was lying on the floor. But she screamed on, with blood running down her dress, her legs sprawled nakedly out from under her. He dropped the remainder of the stick and grabbed her throat and choked her to stop her screams. That seemed to quiet her; she looked as though she had fainted. He choked her for a long time, not trying to kill her, but just to make sure that she would not

scream again and make him wild and hot inside. He was not react-
ing to the woman, but to the feelings that her screams evoked in
him.

The woman was limp and silent now and slowly he took his
hands from her throat. She was quiet. He waited. He was not certain. Yes, take her downstairs into the bathroom and if she
screamed again no one would hear her . . . He took her hands in
his and started dragging her away from the window. His hands
were wet with sweat and her hands were so tiny and soft that time
and again her little fingers slipped out of his palms. He tried holding her hands tighter and only succeeded in scratching her. Her
ring slid off into his hand while he was dragging her and he stood
still for a moment, staring in a daze at the thin band of shimmering gold, then mechanically he put it into his pocket. Finally he
dragged her down the steps to the bathroom door.

He was about to take her in when he saw that the floor was
spotted with drippings of blood. That was bad . . . He had been
trained to keep floors clean, just as he had been trained to fear
shadows. He propped her clumsily against a wall and went into the
bathroom and took wads of toilet paper and mopped up the red
splashes. He even went back upstairs where he had first struck her
and found blood spots and wiped them up carefully. He stiffened;
she was hollering again. He ran downstairs and this time he recalled that he had a knife in his pocket. He took it out, opened it,
and plunged it deep into her throat; he was frantic to stop her
from hollering . . . He pulled the knife from her throat and she was
quiet.

He stood, his eyes roving. He noticed a door leading down
to a recess in a wall through which steam pipes ran. Yes, it would
be better to put her there; then if she started yelling no one would
hear her. He was not trying to hide her; he merely wanted to make
sure that she would not be heard. He dragged her again and her
dress came up over her knees to her chest and again he saw her
pink panties. It was too hard dragging her and he lifted her in his
arms and while carrying her down the short flight of steps he
thought that the pink panties, if he would wet them, would make
a good mop to clean up the blood. Once more he sat her against
the wall, stripped her of her pink panties—and not once did he
so much as glance at her groin—wetted them and swabbed up the
spots, then pushed her into the recess under the pipes. She was in
full view, easily seen. He tossed the wet ball of panties in after her.

He sighed and looked around. The floor seemed clean. He
went back upstairs. That stick of broken wood . . . He picked up
the two shattered ends of wood and several splinters; he carefully

joined the ends together and then fitted the splinters into place. He laid the mended stick back upon the pile before the fireplace. He stood listening, wondering if she would yell again, but there was no sound. It never occurred to him that he could help her, that she might be in pain; he never wondered even if she were dead. He got his coat and hat and went home.

He was nervously tired. It seemed that he had just finished doing an old and familiar job of dodging the shadows that were forever around him, shadows that he could not understand. He undressed, but paid no attention to the blood on his trousers and shirt; he was alone in the room; his wife was at work. When he pulled out his billfold, he saw the ring. He put it in the drawer of his night table, more to keep his wife from seeing it than to hide it. He climbed wearily into bed and at once fell into a deep, sound sleep from which he did not awaken until late afternoon. He lay blinking bloodshot eyes and he could not remember what he had done. Then the vague, shadowlike picture of it came before his eyes. He was puzzled, and for a moment he wondered if it had happened or had someone told him a story of it. He could not be sure. There was no fear or regret in him.

When at last the conviction of what he had done was real in him, it came only in terms of flat memory, devoid of all emotion, as though he were looking when very tired and sleepy at a scene being flashed upon the screen of a movie house. Not knowing what to do, he remained in bed. He had drifted off to sleep again when his wife came home late that night from her cooking job.

Next morning he ate the breakfast his wife prepared, rose from the table and kissed her, and started off toward the Cathedral as though nothing had happened. It was not until he actually got to the Cathedral steps that he became shaky and nervous. He stood before the door for two or three minutes, and then he realized that he could not go back in there this morning. Yet it was not danger that made him feel this way, but a queer kind of repugnance. Whether the woman was alive or not did not enter his mind. He still did not know what to do. Then he remembered that his wife, before she had left for her job, had asked him to buy some groceries. Yes, he would do that. He wanted to do that because he did not know what else on earth to do.

He bought the groceries and took them home, then spent the rest of the day wandering from bar to bar. Not once did he think of fleeing. He would go home, sit, turn on the radio, then go out into the streets and walk. Finally he would end up at a bar, drinking.

On one of his many trips into the house, he changed his clothes, rolled up his bloody shirt and trousers, put the blood-stained knife inside the bundle, and pushed it into a far corner of a closet. He got his gun and put it into his pocket, for he was nervously depressed.

But he still did not know what to do. Suddenly he recalled that some months ago he had bought a cheap car which was now in a garage for repairs. He went to the garage and persuaded the owner to take it back for twenty-five dollars; the thought that he could use the car for escape never came to his mind. During that afternoon and early evening he sat in bars and drank. What he felt now was no different from what he had felt all his life.

Toward eight o'clock that night he met two friends of his and invited them for a drink. He was quite drunk now. Before him on the table was a sandwich and a small glass of whisky. He leaned forward, listening sleepily to one of his friends tell a story about a girl, and then he heard:

"Aren't you Saul Saunders?"

He looked up into the faces of two white shadows.

"Yes," he admitted readily. "What do you want?"

"You'd better come along with us. We want to ask you some questions," one of the shadows said.

"What's this all about?" Saul asked.

They grabbed his shoulders and he stood up. Then he reached down and picked up the glass of whisky and drank it. He walked steadily out of the bar to a waiting auto, a policeman to each side of him, his mind a benign blank. It was not until they were about to put him into the car that something happened and whipped his numbed senses to an apprehension of danger. The policeman patted his waist for arms; they found nothing because his gun was strapped to his chest. Yes, he ought to kill himself . . . The thought leaped into his mind with such gladness that he shivered. It was the answer to everything. Why had he not thought of it before?

Slowly he took off his hat and held it over his chest to hide the movement of his left hand, then he reached inside of his shirt and pulled out the gun. One of the policemen pounced on him and snatched the gun.

"So, you're trying to kill us too, hunh?" one asked.

"Naw. I was trying to kill myself," he answered simply.

"Like hell you were!"

A fist came onto his jaw and he sank back limp.

Two hours later, at the police station, he told them everything, speaking in a low, listless voice without a trace of emotion, vividly describing every detail, yet feeling that it was utterly hopeless for him to try to make them understand how horrible it was for him to hear that woman screaming. His narrative sounded so brutal that the policemen's faces were chalky.

Weeks later a voice droned in a court room and he sat staring dully.

". . . The Grand Jurors of the United States of America, in and for the District of Columbia aforesaid, upon their oath, do present:

"That one Saul Saunders, on, to wit, the first day of March, 19——, and at and within the District of Columbia aforesaid, contriving and intending to kill one Maybelle Eva Houseman . . ."

"So *that's* her name," he said to himself in amazement.

". . . Feloniously, wilfully, purposefully, and of his deliberate and premeditated malice did strike, beat, and wound the said Maybelle Eva Houseman, in and upon the front of the head and in and upon the right side of the head of her, the said Maybelle Eva Houseman, two certain mortal wounds and fractures; and did fix and fasten about the neck and throat of her, the said Maybelle Eva Houseman, his hand or hands—but whether it was one of his hands or both of his hands is to the Grand Jury aforesaid unknown —and that he, the said Saul Saunders, with his hand or hands as aforesaid fixed and fastened about the throat of her, did choke and strangle the said Maybelle Eva Houseman, of which said choking and strangling the said Maybelle Eva Houseman, on, to wit, the said first day of March, 19——, and at and within the said District of Columbia, did die."

He longed for a drink, but that was impossible now. Then he took a deep breath and surrendered to the world of shadows about him, the world he had feared so long; and at once the tension went from him and he felt better than he had felt in a long time. He was amazed at how relaxed and peaceful it was when he stopped fighting the world of shadows.

". . . By force and violence and against resistance and by putting in fear, did steal, take, and carry away, from and off the person and from the immediate, actual possession of one Maybelle Eva Houseman, then and there being, a certain finger ring, of the value of, to wit, ten dollars."

He listened now with more attention but no anxiety:

"And in and while perpetrating robbery aforesaid did kill and murder the said Maybelle Eva Houseman; against the form of the statute in such case made and provided, and against the peace and government of the said United States of America."

P.S. Thereupon Dr. Herman Stein was called as a witness and being first duly sworn testified as follows:

". . . On examination of the genital organs there was no evidence of contusion, abrasion, or trauma, and the decedent's hymen ring was intact. This decedent had not been criminally assaulted or attempted to be entered. It has been ascertained that the decedent's age was 40."

The Ethics of Living Jim Crow

AN AUTOBIOGRAPHICAL SKETCH

I

MY FIRST LESSON in how to live as a Negro came when I was quite small. We were living in Arkansas. Our house stood behind the railroad tracks. Its skimpy yard was paved with black cinders. Nothing green ever grew in that yard. The only touch of green we could see was far away, beyond the tracks, over where the white folks lived. But cinders were good enough for me and I never missed the green growing things. And anyhow cinders were fine weapons. You could always have a nice hot war with huge black cinders. All you had to do was crouch behind the brick pillars of a house with your hands full of gritty ammunition. And the first woolly black head you saw pop out from behind another row of pillars was your target. You tried your very best to knock it off. It was great fun.

I never fully realized the appalling disadvantages of a cinder environment till one day the gang to which I belonged found itself engaged in a war with the white boys who lived beyond the tracks. As usual we laid down our cinder barrage, thinking that this would wipe the white boys out. But they replied with a steady bombardment of broken bottles. We doubled our cinder barrage, but they hid behind trees, hedges, and the sloping embankments of their lawns. Having no such fortifications, we retreated to the brick pillars of our homes. During the retreat a broken milk bottle caught me behind the ear, opening a deep gash which bled profusely. The sight of blood pouring over my face completely demoralized our ranks. My fellow-combatants left me standing paralyzed in the center of the yard, and scurried for their homes. A kind neighbor saw me, and rushed me to a doctor, who took three stitches in my neck.

I sat brooding on my front steps, nursing my wound and waiting for my mother to come from work. I felt that a grave injustice had been done me. It was all right to throw cinders. The greatest harm a cinder could do was leave a bruise. But broken bottles were dangerous; they left you cut, bleeding, and helpless.

When night fell, my mother came from the white folks' kitchen. I raced down the street to meet her. I could just feel in my bones that she would understand. I knew she would tell me exactly what to do next time. I grabbed her hand and babbled out the whole story. She examined my wound, then slapped me.

"How come yuh didn't hide?" she asked me. "How come yuh awways fightin'?"

I was outraged, and bawled. Between sobs I told her that I didn't have any trees or hedges to hide behind. There wasn't a thing I could have used as a trench. And you couldn't throw very far when you were hiding behind the brick pillars of a house. She grabbed a barrel stave, dragged me home, stripped me naked, and beat me till I had a fever of one hundred and two. She would smack my rump with the stave, and, while the skin was still smarting impart to me gems of Jim Crow wisdom. I was never to throw cinders any more. I was never to fight any more wars. I was never, never, under any conditions, to fight *white* folks again. And they were absolutely right in clouting me with the broken milk bottle. Didn't I know she was working hard every day in the hot kitchens of the white folks to make money to take care of me? When was I ever going to learn to be a good boy? She couldn't be bothered with my fights. She finished by telling me that I ought to be thankful to God as long as I lived that they didn't kill me.

All that night I was delirious and could not sleep. Each time I closed my eyes I saw monstrous white faces suspended from the ceiling, leering at me.

From that time on, the charm of my cinder yard was gone. The green trees, the trimmed hedges, the cropped lawns grew very meaningful, became a symbol. Even today when I think of white folks, the hard, sharp outlines of white houses surrounded by trees, lawns, and hedges are present somewhere in the background of my mind. Through the years they grew into an overreaching symbol of fear.

It was a long time before I came in close contact with white folks again. We moved from Arkansas to Mississippi. Here we had the good fortune not to live behind the railroad tracks, or close to white neighborhoods. We lived in the very heart of the local Black Belt. There were black churches and black preachers; there were black schools and black teachers; black groceries and black clerks. In fact, everything was so solidly black that for a long time I did not even think of white folks, save in remote and vague terms. But this could not last forever. As one grows older one eats more. One's clothing costs more. When I finished grammar school I had to go to work. My mother could no longer feed and clothe me on her cooking job.

There is but one place where a black boy who knows no trade can get a job, and that's where the houses and faces are white, where the trees, lawns, and hedges are green. My first job was with an optical company in Jackson, Mississippi. The morning I applied I stood straight and neat before the boss, answering all his questions with sharp yessirs and nosirs. I was very careful to pronounce my *sirs* distinctly, in order that he might know that I was polite, that I knew where I was, and that I knew he was a *white* man. I wanted that job badly.

He looked me over as though he were examining a prize poodle. He questioned me closely about my schooling, being particularly insistent about how much mathematics I had had. He seemed very pleased when I told him I had had two years of algebra.

"Boy, how would you like to try to learn something around here?" he asked me.

"I'd like it fine, sir," I said, happy. I had visions of "working my way up." Even Negroes have those visions.

"All right," he said. "Come on."

I followed him to the small factory.

"Pease," he said to a white man of about thirty-five, "this is Richard. He's going to work for us."

Pease looked at me and nodded.

I was then taken to a white boy of about seventeen.

"Morrie, this is Richard, who's going to work for us."

"Whut yuh sayin' there, boy!" Morrie boomed at me.

"Fine!" I answered.

The boss instructed these two to help me, teach me, give me jobs to do, and let me learn what I could in my spare time.

My wages were five dollars a week.

I worked hard, trying to please. For the first month I got along O.K. Both Pease and Morrie seemed to like me. But one thing was missing. And I kept thinking about it. I was not learning anything

and nobody was volunteering to help me. Thinking they had forgotten that I was to learn something about the mechanics of grinding lenses, I asked Morrie one day to tell me about the work. He
grew red.

"Whut yuh tryin' t' do, nigger, get smart?" he asked.

"Naw; I ain' tryin' t' git smart," I said.

"Well, don't, if yuh know whut's good for yuh!"

I was puzzled. Maybe he just doesn't want to help me, I
thought. I went to Pease.

"Say, are yuh crazy, you black bastard?" Pease asked me, his
gray eyes growing hard.

I spoke out, reminding him that the boss had said I was to be
given a chance to learn something.

"Nigger, you think you're *white*, don't you?"

"Naw, sir!"

"Well, you're acting mighty like it!"

"But, Mr. Pease, the boss said . . ."

Pease shook his fist in my face.

"This is a *white* man's work around here, and you better watch
yourself!"

From then on they changed toward me. They said good-
morning no more. When I was just a bit slow in performing some
duty, I was called a lazy black son-of-a-bitch.

Once I thought of reporting all this to the boss. But the mere
idea of what would happen to me if Pease and Morrie should learn
that I had "snitched" stopped me. And after all the boss was a
white man, too. What was the use?

The climax came at noon one summer day. Pease called me
to his work-bench. To get to him I had to go between two narrow
benches and stand with my back against a wall.

"Yes, sir," I said.

"Richard, I want to ask you something," Pease began pleas-
antly, not looking up from his work.

"Yes, sir," I said again.

Morrie came over, blocking the narrow passage between the
benches. He folded his arms, staring at me solemnly.

I looked from one to the other, sensing that something was
coming.

"Yes, sir," I said for the third time.

Pease looked up and spoke very slowly.

"Richard, *Mr.* Morrie here tells me you called me *Pease.*"

I stiffened. A void seemed to open up in me. I knew this was
the show-down.

He meant that I had failed to call him Mr. Pease. I looked at

Morrie. He was gripping a steel bar in his hands. I opened my mouth to speak, to protest, to assure Pease that I had never called him simply *Pease,* and that I had never had any intentions of doing so, when Morrie grabbed me by the collar, ramming my head against the wall.

"Now, be careful, nigger!" snarled Morrie, baring his teeth. "*I* heard yuh call 'im *Pease!* 'N' if yuh say yuh didn't, yuh're callin' me a *lie,* see?" He waved the steel bar threateningly.

If I had said: No, sir, Mr. Pease, I never called you *Pease,* I would have been automatically calling Morrie a liar. And if I had said: Yes, sir, Mr. Pease, I called you *Pease,* I would have been pleading guilty to having uttered the worst insult that a Negro can utter to a southern white man. I stood hesitating, trying to frame a neutral reply.

"Richard, I asked you a question!" said Pease. Anger was creeping into his voice.

"I don't remember calling you *Pease,* Mr. Pease," I said cautiously. "And if I did, I sure didn't mean . . ."

"You black son-of-a-bitch! You called me *Pease,* then!" he spat, slapping me till I bent sideways over a bench. Morrie was on top of me, demanding:

"Didn't yuh call 'im *Pease?* If yuh say yuh didn't, I'll rip yo' gut string loose with this bar, yuh black granny dodger! Yuh can't call a white man a lie 'n' git erway with it, you black son-of-a-bitch!"

I wilted. I begged them not to bother me. I knew what they wanted. They wanted me to leave.

"I'll leave," I promised. "I'll leave right *now.*"

They gave me a minute to get out of the factory. I was warned not to show up again, or tell the boss.

I went.

When I told the folks at home what had happened, they called me a fool. They told me that I must never again attempt to exceed my boundaries. When you are working for white folks, they said, you got to "stay in your place" if you want to keep working.

II

My Jim Crow education continued on my next job, which was portering in a clothing store. One morning, while polishing brass out front, the boss and his twenty-year-old son got out of their car and half dragged and half kicked a Negro woman into the store. A policeman standing at the corner looked on, twirling his nightstick. I watched out of the corner of my eye, never slackening the strokes of my chamois upon the brass. After a few minutes, I heard shrill screams coming from the rear of the store. Later the woman stumbled out, bleeding, crying, and holding her stomach. When she reached the end of the block, the policeman grabbed her and accused her of being drunk. Silently, I watched him throw her into a patrol wagon.

When I went to the rear of the store, the boss and his son were washing their hands at the sink. They were chuckling. The floor was bloody and strewn with wisps of hair and clothing. No doubt I must have appeared pretty shocked, for the boss slapped me reassuringly on the back.

"Boy, that's what we do to niggers when they don't want to pay their bills," he said, laughing.

His son looked at me and grinned.

"Here, hava cigarette," he said.

Not knowing what to do, I took it. He lit his and held the match for me. This was a gesture of kindness, indicating that even if they had beaten the poor old woman, they would not beat me if I knew enough to keep my mouth shut.

"Yes, sir," I said, and asked no questions.

After they had gone, I sat on the edge of a packing box and stared at the bloody floor till the cigarette went out.

That day at noon, while eating in a hamburger joint, I told my fellow Negro porters what had happened. No one seemed surprised. One fellow, after swallowing a huge bite, turned to me and asked:

"Huh! Is tha' all they did t' her?"

"Yeah. Wasn't tha' enough?" I asked.

"Shucks! Man, she's a lucky bitch!" he said, burying his lips deep into a juicy hamburger. "Hell, it's a wonder they didn't lay her when they got through."

III

I was learning fast, but not quite fast enough. One day, while I was delivering packages in the suburbs, my bicycle tire was punctured. I walked along the hot, dusty road, sweating and leading my bicycle by the handle-bars.

A car slowed at my side.

"What's the matter, boy?" a white man called.

I told him my bicycle was broken and I was walking back to town.

"That's too bad," he said. "Hop on the running board."

He stopped the car. I clutched hard at my bicycle with one hand and clung to the side of the car with the other.

"All set?"

"Yes, sir," I answered. The car started.

It was full of young white men. They were drinking. I watched the flask pass from mouth to mouth.

"Wanna drink, boy?" one asked.

I laughed as the wind whipped my face. Instinctively obeying the freshly planted precepts of my mother, I said:

"Oh, no!"

The words were hardly out of my mouth before I felt something hard and cold smash me between the eyes. It was an empty whisky bottle. I saw stars, and fell backwards from the speeding car into the dust of the road, my feet becoming entangled in the steel spokes of my bicycle. The white men piled out and stood over me.

"Nigger, ain' yuh learned no better sense'n tha' yet?" asked the man who hit me. "Ain' yuh learned t' say *sir* t' a white man yet?"

Dazed, I pulled to my feet. My elbows and legs were bleeding. Fists doubled, the white man advanced, kicking my bicycle out of the way.

"Aw, leave the bastard alone. He's got enough," said one.

They stood looking at me. I rubbed my shins, trying to stop the flow of blood. No doubt they felt a sort of contemptuous pity, for one asked:

"Yuh wanna ride t' town now, nigger? Yuh reckon yuh know enough t' ride now?"

"I wanna walk," I said, simply.

Maybe it sounded funny. They laughed.

"Well, walk, yuh black son-of-a-bitch!"

When they left they comforted me with:

"Nigger, yuh sho better be damn glad it wuz us yuh talked t' tha' way. Yuh're a lucky bastard, 'cause if yuh'd said tha' t' somebody else, yuh might've been a dead nigger now."

IV

Negroes who have lived South know the dread of being caught alone upon the streets in white neighborhoods after the sun has set. In such a simple situation as this the plight of the Negro in America is graphically symbolized. While white strangers may be in these neighborhoods trying to get home, they can pass unmolested. But the color of a Negro's skin makes him easily recognizable, makes him suspect, converts him into a defenseless target.

Late one Saturday night I made some deliveries in a white neighborhood. I was pedaling my bicycle back to the store as fast as I could, when a police car, swerving toward me, jammed me into the curbing.

"Get down and put up your hands!" the policemen ordered.

I did. They climbed out of the car, guns drawn, faces set, and advanced slowly.

"Keep still!" they ordered.

I reached my hands higher. They searched my pockets and packages. They seemed dissatisfied when they could find nothing incriminating. Finally, one of them said:

"Boy, tell your boss not to send you out in white neighborhoods after sundown."

As usual, I said:

"Yes, sir."

V

My next job was as hall-boy in a hotel. Here my Jim Crow education broadened and deepened. When the bell-boys were busy, I was often called to assist them. As many of the rooms in the hotel were occupied by prostitutes, I was constantly called to carry them liquor and cigarettes. These women were nude most of the time. They did not bother about clothing, even for bell-boys. When you went into their rooms, you were supposed to take their nakedness for granted, as though it startled you no more than a blue vase or a red rug. Your presence awoke in them no sense of shame, for you were not regarded as human. If they were alone, you could steal sidelong glimpses at them. But if they were receiving men, not a flicker of your eyelids could show. I remember one incident vividly. A new woman, a huge, snowy-skinned blonde, took a room on my floor. I was sent to wait upon her. She was in bed with a thick-set man; both were nude and uncovered. She said she wanted some liquor and slid out of bed and waddled across the floor to get her money from a dresser drawer. I watched her.

"Nigger, what in hell you looking at?" the white man asked me, raising himself upon his elbows.

"Nothing," I answered, looking miles deep into the blank wall of the room.

"Keep your eyes where they belong, if you want to be healthy!" he said.

"Yes, sir."

VI

One of the bell-boys I knew in this hotel was keeping steady company with one of the Negro maids. Out of a clear sky the police descended upon his home and arrested him, accusing him of bastardy. The poor boy swore he had had no intimate relations with the girl. Nevertheless, they forced him to marry her. When the child arrived, it was found to be much lighter in complexion than either of the two supposedly legal parents. The white men around the hotel made a great joke of it. They spread the rumor that some white cow must have scared the poor girl while she was carrying the baby. If you were in their presence when this explanation was offered, you were supposed to laugh.

VII

One of the bell-boys was caught in bed with a white prostitute. He was castrated and run out of town. Immediately after this all the bell-boys and hall-boys were called together and warned. We were given to understand that the boy who had been castrated was a "mighty, mighty lucky bastard." We were impressed with the fact that next time the management of the hotel would not be responsible for the lives of "trouble-makin' niggers." We were silent.

VIII

One night, just as I was about to go home, I met one of the Negro maids. She lived in my direction, and we fell in to walk part of the way home together. As we passed the white night-watchman, he slapped the maid on her buttock. I turned around, amazed. The watchman looked at me with a long, hard, fixed-under stare. Suddenly he pulled his gun and asked:

"Nigger, don't yuh like it?"

I hesitated.

"I asked yuh don't yuh like it?" he asked again, stepping forward.

"Yes, sir," I mumbled.

"Talk like it, then!"

"Oh, yes, sir!" I said with as much heartiness as I could muster.

Outside, I walked ahead of the girl, ashamed to face her. She caught up with me and said:

"Don't be a fool! Yuh couldn't help it!"

This watchman boasted of having killed two Negroes in self-defense.

Yet, in spite of all this, the life of the hotel ran with an amazing smoothness. It would have been impossible for a stranger to detect anything. The maids, the hall-boys, and the bell-boys were all smiles. They had to be.

IX

I had learned my Jim Crow lessons so thoroughly that I kept the hotel job till I left Jackson for Memphis. It so happened that while in Memphis I applied for a job at a branch of the optical company. I was hired. And for some reason, as long as I worked there, they never brought my past against me.

Here my Jim Crow education assumed quite a different form. It was no longer brutally cruel, but subtly cruel. Here I learned to lie, to steal, to dissemble. I learned to play that dual role which every Negro must play if he wants to eat and live.

For example, it was almost impossible to get a book to read. It was assumed that after a Negro had imbibed what scanty schooling the state furnished he had no further need for books. I was always borrowing books from men on the job. One day I mustered enough courage to ask one of the men to let me get books from the library in his name. Surprisingly, he consented. I cannot help but think that he consented because he was a Roman Catholic and felt a vague sympathy for Negroes, being himself an object of hatred. Armed with a library card, I obtained books in the following manner: I would write a note to the librarian, saying: "Please let this nigger boy have the following books." I would then sign it with the white man's name.

When I went to the library, I would stand at the desk, hat in hand, looking as unbookish as possible. When I received the books desired I would take them home. If the books listed in the note happened to be out, I would sneak into the lobby and forge a new one. I never took any chances guessing with the white librarian about what the fictitious white man would want to read. No doubt if any of the white patrons had suspected that some of the volumes they enjoyed had been in the home of a Negro, they would not have tolerated it for an instant.

The factory force of the optical company in Memphis was much larger than that in Jackson, and more urbanized. At least they liked to talk, and would engage the Negro help in conversation whenever possible. By this means I found that many subjects were taboo from the white man's point of view. Among the topics they did not like to discuss with Negroes were the following: American white women; the Ku Klux Klan; France, and how Negro soldiers fared while there; French women; Jack Johnson; the entire northern part of the United States; the Civil War; Abraham Lincoln; U. S. Grant; General Sherman; Catholics; the Pope; Jews; the Republican Party; slavery; social equality; Communism; Socialism;

the 13th and 14th Amendments to the Constitution; or any topic calling for positive knowledge or manly self-assertion on the part of the Negro. The most accepted topics were sex and religion.

There were many times when I had to exercise a great deal of ingenuity to keep out of trouble. It is a southern custom that all men must take off their hats when they enter an elevator. And especially did this apply to us blacks with rigid force. One day I stepped into an elevator with my arms full of packages. I was forced to ride with my hat on. Two white men stared at me coldly. Then one of them very kindly lifted my hat and placed it upon my armful of packages. Now the most accepted response for a Negro to make under such circumstances is to look at the white man out of the corner of his eye and grin. To have said: "Thank you!" would have made the white man *think* that you *thought* you were receiving from him a personal service. For such an act I have seen Negroes take a blow in the mouth. Finding the first alternative distasteful, and the second dangerous, I hit upon an acceptable course of action which fell safely between these two poles. I immediately—no sooner than my hat was lifted—pretended that my packages were about to spill, and appeared deeply distressed with keeping them in my arms. In this fashion I evaded having to acknowledge his service, and, in spite of adverse circumstances, salvaged a slender shred of personal pride.

How do Negroes feel about the way they have to live? How do they discuss it when alone among themselves? I think this question can be answered in a single sentence. A friend of mine who ran an elevator once told me:

"Lawd, man! Ef it wuzn't fer them polices 'n' them ol' lynch-mobs, there wouldn't be nothin' but uproar down here!"

RALPH ELLISON
1914-

In 1965 a *Book Week* poll of critics, authors, and editors judged Ralph Ellison's *Invisible Man* (1952) to be "the most distinguished single work" published in America since 1945. Ellison had previously written stories and essays which anticipated the central concerns of *Invisible Man*, but not until the publication of the novel was he recognized as a major American author.

Ellison's youth was significantly different from that of many twentieth-century Negro writers. Although he recognized the limitations inflicted upon him in Oklahoma City, Oklahoma, where he was born in 1914 and where he grew up, Ellison "thought those limitations were unjust." As he notes in *Shadow and Act* (1964), a collection of his critical essays, "I felt no innate sense of inferiority which would keep me from getting those things I desired out of life." At the time of his birth, Oklahoma had been a state for only seven years; "thus it had no tradition of slavery, and while it was segregated, relationships between the races were more fluid and thus more human than in the old slave states." Ellison was compelled to attend the usual segregated schools, but he was able to develop his interest in jazz and then in classical music because of the excellent programs that his teachers offered. "Interestingly enough," he has remarked, "by early adolescence the idea of Renaissance Man had drifted down to about six of us [students], and we discussed mastering ourselves and everything in sight as though no such thing as racial discrimination existed."

Ellison wanted to be a composer of symphonic music, and from 1933 to 1936 he attended Tuskegee Institute. During his junior year he went to New York to study sculpture; but he lost professional interest in the art form and resumed his study of musical composition. In New York he met Richard Wright, who had just published his first collection of stories, *Uncle Tom's Children,* and in 1937 Ellison wrote a review for *New Challenge,* a magazine which Wright was editing. Soon Ellison was publishing regularly in *New Masses* and *The Negro Quarterly,* clarifying many of his ideas in regard to race, politics, and literature. Like Richard Wright and many intellectuals of the 1930's, Ellison was attracted to political radicalism, and some of his early work—"The Birthmark" (*New Masses,* 1940); "Recent Negro Fiction" (*New Masses,* 1941); and "The Way It Is" (*New Masses,* 1942)—expresses his interest in left-wing politics. Unlike Wright, with whom he formed a close friendship, Ellison never joined the Communist Party or formally aligned himself with any organization; this strong sense of individuality characterizes his work, too, and is one of the central themes of *Invisible Man.*

Ellison thought of himself primarily as an artist, and after 1943 he ceased to concern himself actively with politics. In his fiction of the early 1940's he dramatizes the idea that recurs in all of his later work and public statements: the need for white Americans to recognize Negro identity in all of its complexity. "Mister Toussan" (1941), a short story published in *New Masses,* had already explored that idea, and later stories approached it from various points of view. Within a few years Ellison had published several short stories: "That I Had the Wings" (reprinted as "Mr. Toussaint"), "Slick Gonna Learn" (1939), "Afternoon" (1940), "In a Strange Country" (1944), "Flying Home" (1944), and "King of the Bingo Game" (1944). These stories, together with "Did You Ever Dream Lucky?" (1954), "A Coupla Scalped Indians" (1956), and "And Hickman Arrives" (1956), have not yet been collected, but they indicate that Ellison is an impressive short story writer as well as a novelist and an essayist.

The theme of racial identity and the literary techniques of irony, symbolism, and fantasy—all reflected in the stories—reach artistic fruition in *Invisible Man.* The novel received the National Book Award for Fiction in 1953 and has enjoyed high critical acclaim. It is not only the finest novel in the history of Negro writing but an important work in modern American literature as well, for it dramatizes the surreal world that confronts a Southern Negro who tries to make his way in the North, the frenetic and tyrannical qualities of American life that encourage the perverse response, the Gothic vision of a black man who is forced to live in the underground; and this vision is controlled by Ellison's earthy, strongly wrought prose style.

Like so much American Negro writing, *Invisible Man* is cast in the form of an autobiographical odyssey. A Southern Negro boy inherits the legacy of Uncle Tom, rejects it, and struggles toward defining his own character and his consequent relationship to a white society. Ellison sets the beginning of his novel in a Negro college which is similar to that of Booker T. Washington's Tuskegee Institute; and he traces the ways in which Negro officials pander, and teach the young narrator to pander, to the white philanthropist who helps support the school. The philanthropist urges the narrator to learn about Ralph Waldo Emerson, "for he was important to [his] people. . . . Self-reliance is a most worthy virtue." The Negro boy agrees "to read Emerson" and in fact attempts to embody Emersonian idealism; but his experiences in the North as well as in the South, his attempt to find work, to be of service to a Negro Brotherhood, and to achieve leadership within the Negro community of New York only convince him that he is invisible in the eyes of white Americans. He becomes "ill of affirmation, of saying 'Yes' against the nay-saying of [his] stomach—not to mention [his] brain"; and he hibernates beneath the ground.

But despite the satirical commentary upon American self-reliance, the Negro himself decides, by the end of the novel, to "affirm the principle on which the country was built and not the men, or at least not the men who did the violence." Having dealt with the realities of his racial existence in America, the invisible man knows that "in spite of all I find that I love. In order to get some of it down I *have* to love. I sell you no phony forgiveness, I'm a desperate man—but too much of your life will be lost, its meaning lost, unless you approach it as much through love as through hate." Self-reliance has developed from his personal suffering, and he has a mature awareness of society; now he realizes that "even an invisible man has a socially responsible role to play."

"Flying Home" and "King of the Bingo Game" are Ellison's finest stories, and they reflect his thinking about racial issues in the period that immediately precedes the writing of *Invisible Man*. In "Flying Home," which was published in *Cross Section* in 1944, Ellison underscores the difficulty that a young Negro has in knowing his place in contemporary white society and his own complex relationship to his racial heritage. "Son, how come you want to fly way up there in the air?" the old, officious Negro asks the hero,

who has been on a training mission and has crashed into a plantation in Alabama; and the flyer thinks, "Because it's the most
meaningful act in the world . . . because it makes me less like
you." Feeling cut off from this Negro field hand "by age, by understanding, by sensibility, by technology, and by his need to measure
himself against the mirror of other men's appreciation," the flyer,
who is waiting for a plane from the nearby airbase, seeks admiration in the eyes of his white superiors; but assimilation is impossible, whether he wants it or not—too much of the white world,
as represented by the plantation owner who tries to have the flyer
put in a straitjacket, will not permit it. Ellison is particularly successful in suggesting the hero's unwilling realization that part of
him is represented by the old, unattractive Negro—the field hand
is the one who saves him finally from the white man—and in suggesting his pathetic attempt to be as white as the white world will
permit him to be. In a recent interview, published in *Harper's*
(March 1967), Ellison sums up the feeling that runs through this
story and all of his subsequent work: "If I cannot look at the most
brutalized Negro on the street, even when he irritates me and
makes me want to bash his head in because he's goofing off, I must
still say within myself, 'Well, that's you too, Ellison.' And I'm not
talking about guilt, but of an identification which goes beyond
race."

"King of the Bingo Game," published in *Tomorrow* (November
1944), was the last story that Ellison wrote before he began
Invisible Man. It is an excellent introduction to the novel, for it
employs the techniques of gothicism and macabre humor that one
finds in the larger work; and like *Invisible Man* it develops the
themes of protest, identity, pride, and freedom. The setting for
these techniques and themes is particularly appropriate, for the
modern movie house invites fantasies, even the desperate fantasies
of the Southern Negro in the story, a man close to psychological
breakdown. For this man the bingo game is life, and he is inevitably a loser. When he is finally taken away and his hand is released from the wheel, it stops at double-zero; but he senses that
"his luck [has] run out on the stage" and that he has been stricken
by men who represent a society that will never permit him to win,
no matter how many cards he holds, no matter how carefully he
studies the rules of the game, no matter how willful or obstinate
he is. For him the wheel is God, as he cries, but God is part of the
illusion in the movie house that has nothing to do with the man's
actual life.

"King of the Bingo Game" is a hard gem of a story, written
at that point in an author's career when he has come to realize his

full creative powers, poised delicately between the grotesque and the realistic, between the illusory and the actual, between madness and seeming sanity. The bingo game, as America's particular wheel of fortune, is compelling—and frightening when Ellison reminds us of who in fact operates the game.

The distinguishing quality of Ralph Ellison's work—particularly of the essays he has published since *Invisible Man*—is a pervasive idealism. In his various essays, interviews, and public statements, Ellison assumes a confident and optimistic attitude and urges the writer "to explore the full range of American Negro humanity and to affirm those qualities which are of value beyond any question of segregation, economics or previous condition of servitude. The obligation was always there and there is much to affirm. In fact, all Negroes affirm certain feelings of identity, certain foods, certain types of dancing, music, religious experiences, certain tragic attitudes toward experience and toward our situation as Americans. . . . Our strength is that with the total society saying to us, 'No, No, No, No.' we continue to move toward our goal." Fully aware of the limitations placed upon the Negro in America, Ellison has nevertheless chosen to emphasize those positive elements of Negro life that have helped to keep American culture rich and varied. "Hidden Name and Complex Fate," reprinted from *Shadow and Act*, clearly illustrates Ellison's central ideas: his affinity to Emersonian idealism and his insistence that we cherish those human differences that make being American a complex fate.

In the past fifteen years, Ralph Ellison has combined his career as an author with that of lecturer. After living in Rome for two years, he taught at Bard College and Bennington, and was a writer in residence at Rutgers University, a visiting fellow at Yale, and a lecturer at the State University of New York at Stony Brook, Long Island. In 1964 he brought out the group of essays and interviews, *Shadow and Act*, which trace his political, social, and aesthetic views during the previous two decades. At present he lives in New York and is completing a second novel.

Flying Home

WHEN TODD CAME TO, he saw two faces suspended above him in a sun so hot and blinding that he could not tell if they were black or white. He stirred, feeling a pain that burned as though his whole body had been laid open to the sun which glared into his eyes. For a moment an old fear of being touched by white hands seized him. Then the very sharpness of the pain began slowly to clear his head. Sounds came to him dimly. He done come to. Who are they? he thought. Naw he ain't, I coulda sworn he was white. Then he heard clearly:

"You hurt bad?"

Something within him uncoiled. It was a Negro sound.

"He's still out," he heard.

"Give 'im time. . . . Say, son, you hurt bad?"

Was he? There was that awful pain. He lay rigid, hearing their breathing and trying to weave a meaning between them and his being stretched painfully upon the ground. He watched them warily, his mind traveling back over a painful distance. Jagged scenes, swiftly unfolding as in a movie trailer, reeled through his mind, and he saw himself piloting a tailspinning plane and landing and landing and falling from the cockpit and trying to stand. Then, as in a great silence, he remembered the sound of crunching bone, and now, looking up into the anxious faces of an old Negro man and a boy from where he lay in the same field, the memory sickened him and he wanted to remember no more.

"How you feel, son?"

Todd hesitated, as though to answer would be to admit an inacceptable weakness. Then, "It's my ankle," he said.

"Which one?"

"The left."

With a sense of remoteness he watched the old man bend and remove his boot, feeling the pressure ease.

"That any better?"

"A lot. Thank you."

He had the sensation of discussing someone else, that his concern was with some far more important thing, which for some reason escaped him.

"You done broke it bad," the old man said. "We have to get you to a doctor."

He felt that he had been thrown into a tailspin. He looked at his watch; how long had he been here? He knew there was but one important thing in the world, to get the plane back to the field before his officers were displeased.

"Help me up," he said. "Into the ship."

"But it's broke too bad. . . ."

"Give me your arm!"

"But, son . . ."

Clutching the old man's arm he pulled himself up, keeping his left leg clear, thinking, "I'd never make him understand," as the leather-smooth face came parallel with his own.

"Now, let's see."

He pushed the old man back, hearing a bird's insistent shrill. He swayed giddily. Blackness washed over him, like infinity.

"You best sit down."

"No, I'm O.K."

"But, son. You jus' gonna make it worse. . . ."

It was a fact that everything in him cried out to deny, even against the flaming pain in his ankle. He would have to try again.

"You mess with that ankle they have to cut your foot off," he heard.

Holding his breath, he started up again. It pained so badly that he had to bite his lips to keep from crying out and he allowed them to help him down with a pang of despair.

"It's best you take it easy. We gon' git you a doctor."

Of all the luck, he thought. Of all the rotten luck, now I have done it. The fumes of high-octane gasoline clung in the heat, taunting him.

"We kin ride him into town on old Ned," the boy said.

Ned? He turned, seeing the boy point toward an ox team browsing where the buried blade of a plow marked the end of a furrow. Thoughts of himself riding an ox through the town, past streets full of white faces, down the concrete runways of the airfield made swift images of humiliation in his mind. With a pang he remembered his girl's last letter. "Todd," she had written, "I don't need the papers to tell me you had the intelligence to fly. And I have always known you to be as brave as anyone else. The papers annoy me. Don't you be contented to prove over and over again that you're brave or skillful just because you're black, Todd. I think they keep beating that dead horse because they don't want to say why you boys are not yet fighting. I'm really disappointed, Todd. Anyone with brains can learn to fly, but then what? What about using it, and who will you use it for? I wish, dear, you'd write about this. I sometimes think they're playing a trick on us. It's very humiliating. . . ." He wiped cold sweat from his face, thinking, What does she know of humiliation? She's never been down South. Now the humiliation would come. When you must have them judge you, knowing that they never accept your mistakes as your own, but hold it against your whole race—that was humiliation. Yes, and humiliation was when you could never be simply yourself, when you were always a part of this old black ignorant man. Sure, he's all right. Nice and kind and helpful. But he's not you. Well, there's one humiliation I can spare myself.

"No," he said, "I have orders not to leave the ship. . . ."

"Aw," the old man said. Then turning to the boy, "Teddy, then you better hustle down to Mister Graves and get him to come. . . ."

"No, wait!" he protested before he was fully aware. Graves might be white. "Just have him get word to the field, please. They'll take care of the rest."

He saw the boy leave, running.

"How far does he have to go?"

"Might' nigh a mile."

He rested back, looking at the dusty face of his watch. But now they know something has happened, he thought. In the ship there was a perfectly good radio, but it was useless. The old fellow would never operate it. That buzzard knocked me back a hundred years, he thought. Irony danced within him like the gnats circling the old man's head. With all I've learned I'm dependent upon this "peasant's" sense of time and space. His leg throbbed. In the plane, instead of time being measured by the rhythms of pain and a kid's legs, the instruments would have told him at a glance. Twisting upon his elbows he saw where dust had powdered the plane's fuselage, feeling the lump form in his throat that was always there when he thought of flight. It's crouched there, he thought, like the abandoned shell of a locust. I'm naked without it. Not a machine, a suit of clothes you wear. And with a sudden embarrassment and wonder he whispered, "It's the only dignity I have. . . ."

He saw the old man watching, his torn overalls clinging limply to him in the heat. He felt a sharp need to tell the old man what he felt. But that would be meaningless. If I tried to explain why I need to fly back, he'd think I was simply afraid of white officers. But it's more than fear . . . a sense of anguish clung to him like the veil of sweat that hugged his face. He watched the old man, hearing him humming snatches of a tune as he admired the plane. He felt a furtive sense of resentment. Such old men often came to the field to watch the pilots with childish eyes. At first it had made him proud; they had been a meaningful part of a new experience. But soon he realized they did not understand his accomplishments and they came to shame and embarrass him, like the distasteful praise of an idiot. A part of the meaning of flying had gone then, and he had not been able to regain it. If I were a prizefighter I would be more human, he thought. Not a monkey doing tricks, but a man. They were pleased simply that he was a Negro who could fly, and that was not enough. He felt cut off from them by age, by understanding, by sensibility, by technology and by his need to measure himself against the mirror of other men's appreciation. Somehow he felt betrayed, as he had when as a child he grew to discover that his father was dead. Now for him any real appreciation lay with his white officers; and with them he could never be sure. Between ignorant black men and condescending whites, his course of flight seemed mapped by the nature of things away from all needed and natural landmarks. Under some sealed orders, couched in ever more technical and mysterious terms, his path curved swiftly away from both the shame the old man symbolized and the cloudy terrain of white men's regard. Flying blind, he knew but one point of landing and there he would receive his wings. After that the enemy would appreciate his skill and he would assume his deepest meaning, he thought sadly, neither from those who condescended nor from those who praised without understanding, but from the enemy who would recognize his manhood and skill in terms of hate. . . .

He sighed, seeing the oxen making queer, prehistoric shadows against the dry brown earth.

"You just take it easy, son," the old man soothed. "That boy won't take long. Crazy as he is about airplanes."

"I can wait," he said.

"What kinda airplane you call this here'n?"

"An Advanced Trainer," he said, seeing the old man smile. His fingers were like gnarled dark wood against the metal as he touched the low-slung wing.

" 'Bout how fast can she fly?"

"Over two hundred an hour."

"Lawd! That's so fast I bet it don't seem like you moving!"

Holding himself rigid, Todd opened his flying suit. The shade had gone and he lay in a ball of fire.

"You mind if I take a look inside? I was always curious to see. . . ."

"Help yourself. Just don't touch anything."

257

He heard him climb upon the metal wing, grunting. Now the questions would start. Well, so you don't have to think to answer. . . .

He saw the old man looking over into the cockpit, his eyes bright as a child's.

"You must have to know a lot to work all these here things."

He was silent, seeing him step down and kneel beside him.

"Son, how come you want to fly way up there in the air?"

Because it's the most meaningful act in the world . . . because it makes me less like you, he thought.

But he said: "Because I like it, I guess. It's as good a way to fight and die as I know."

"Yeah? I guess you right," the old man said. "But how long you think before they gonna let you all fight?"

He tensed. This was the question all Negroes asked, put with the same timid hopefulness and longing that always opened a greater void within him than that he had felt beneath the plane the first time he had flown. He felt light-headed. It came to him suddenly that there was something sinister about the conversation, that he was flying unwillingly into unsafe and uncharted regions. If he could only be insulting and tell this old man who was trying to help him to shut up!

"I bet you one thing . . ."

"Yes?"

"That you was plenty scared coming down."

He did not answer. Like a dog on a trail the old man seemed to smell out his fears and he felt anger bubble within him.

"You sho' scared me. When I seen you coming down in that thing with it a-rollin' and a-jumpin' like a pitchin' hoss, I thought sho' you was a goner. I almost had me a stroke!"

He saw the old man grinning, "Ever'thin's been happening round here this morning, come to think of it."

"Like what?" he asked.

"Well, first thing I know, here come two white fellers looking for Mister Rudolph, that's Mister Graves's cousin. That got me worked up right away. . . ."

"Why?"

"Why? 'Cause he done broke outta the crazy house, that's why. He liable to kill somebody," he said. "They oughta have him by now though. Then here you come. First I think it's one of them white boys. Then doggone if you don't fall outta there. Lawd, I'd done heard about you boys but I haven't never seen one o' you-all. Cain't tell you how it felt to see somebody what look like me in a airplane!"

The old man talked on, the sound streaming around Todd's thoughts like air flowing over the fuselage of a flying plane. You were a fool, he thought, remembering how before the spin the sun had blazed bright against the billboard signs beyond the town, and how a boy's blue kite had bloomed beneath him, tugging gently in the wind like a strange, odd-shaped flower. He had once flown such kites himself and tried to find the boy at the end of the invisible cord. But he had been flying too high and too fast. He had climbed steeply away in exultation. Too steeply, he thought. And one of the first rules you learn is that if the angle of thrust is too steep the plane goes into a spin. And then, instead of pulling out of it and going into a dive you let a buzzard panic you. A lousy buzzard!

"Son, what made all that blood on the glass?"

"A buzzard," he said, remembering how the blood and feathers had sprayed back against the hatch. It had been as though he had flown into a storm of blood and blackness.

"Well, I declare! They's lots of 'em around here. They after dead things. Don't eat nothing what's alive."

"A little bit more and he would have made a meal out of me," Todd said grimly.

"They bad luck all right. Teddy's got a name for 'em, calls 'em jimcrows," the old man laughed.

"It's a damned good name."

"They the damnedest birds. Once I seen a hoss all stretched out like he was sick, you know. So I hollers, 'Gid up from there, suh!' Just to make sho! An' doggone, son, if I don't see two ole jimcrows come flying right up outa that hoss's insides! Yessuh! The sun was shinin' on 'em and they couldn't a been no greasier if they'd been eating barbecue."

Todd thought he would vomit, his stomach quivered.

"You made that up," he said.

"Nawsuh! Saw him just like I see you."

"Well, I'm glad it was you."

"You see lots a funny things down here, son."

"No, I'll let you see them," he said.

"By the way, the white folks round here don't like to see you boys up there in the sky. They ever bother you?"

"No."

"Well, they'd like to."

"Someone always wants to bother someone else," Todd said. "How do you know?"

"I just know."

"Well," he said defensively, "no one has bothered us."

Blood pounded in his ears as he looked away into space. He tensed, seeing a black spot in the sky, and strained to confirm what he could not clearly see.

"What does that look like to you?" he asked excitedly.

"Just another bad luck, son."

Then he saw the movement of wings with disappointment. It was gliding smoothly down, wings outspread, tail feathers gripping the air, down swiftly—gone behind the green screen of trees. It was like a bird he had imagined there, only the sloping branches of the pines remained, sharp against the pale stretch of sky. He lay barely breathing and stared at the point where it had disappeared, caught in a spell of loathing and admiration. Why did they make them so disgusting and yet teach them to fly so well? It's like when I was up in heaven, he heard, starting.

The old man was chuckling, rubbing his stubbled chin.

"What did you say?"

"Sho', I died and went to heaven . . . maybe by time I tell you about it they be done come after you."

"I hope so," he said wearily.

"You boys ever sit around and swap lies?"

"Not often. Is this going to be one?"

"Well, I ain't so sho', on account of it took place when I was dead."

The old man paused, "That wasn't no lie 'bout the buzzards, though."

"All right," he said.

"Sho' you want to hear 'bout heaven?"

"Please," he answered, resting his head upon his arm.

"Well, I went to heaven and right away started to sproutin' me some wings. Six good ones, they was. Just like them the white angels had. I couldn't hardly believe it. I was so glad that I went off on some clouds by myself and tried 'em out. You know, 'cause I didn't want to make a fool outta myself the first thing. . . ."

It's an old tale, Todd thought. Told me years ago. Had forgotten. But at least it will keep him from talking about buzzards.

He closed his eyes, listening.

". . . First thing I done was to git up on a low cloud and jump off. And doggone, boy, if them wings didn't work! First I tried the right; then I tried the left; then I tried 'em both together. Then Lawd, I started to move on out among the folks. I let 'em see me. . . ."

He saw the old man gesturing flight with his arms, his face full of mock pride as he indicated an imaginary crowd, thinking, It'll be in the newspapers, as he heard, ". . . so I went and found me some colored angels—somehow I didn't believe I was an angel till I seen a real black one, ha, yes! Then I was sho'—but they tole me I better come down 'cause us colored folks had to wear a special kin' a harness when we flew. That was how come they wasn't flyin'. Oh yes, an' you had to be extra strong for a black man even, to fly with one of them harnesses. . . ."

This is a new turn, Todd thought, what's he driving at?

"So I said to myself, I ain't gonna be bothered with no harness! Oh naw! 'Cause if God let you sprout wings you oughta have sense enough not to let nobody make you wear something what gits in the way of flyin'. So I starts to flyin'. Heck, son," he chuckled, his eyes twinkling, "you know I had to let eve'ybody know that old Jefferson could fly good as anybody else. And I could too, fly smooth as a bird! I could even loop-the-loop—only I had to make sho' to keep my long white robe down roun' my ankles. . . ."

Todd felt uneasy. He wanted to laugh at the joke, but his body refused, as of an independent will. He felt as he had as a child when after he had chewed a sugar-coated pill which his mother had given him, she had laughted at his efforts to remove the terrible taste.

". . . Well," he heard, "I was doing all right 'til I got to speeding. Found out I could fan up a right strong breeze, I could fly so fast. I could do all kin'sa stunts too. I started flying up to the stars and divin' down and zooming roun' the moon. Man, I like to scare the devil outa some ole white angels. I was raisin' hell. Not that I meant any harm, son. But I was just feeling good. It was so good to know I was free at last. I accidentally knocked the tips offa some stars and they tell me I caused a storm and a coupla lynchings down here in Macon County—though I swear I believe them boys what said that was making up lies on me. . . ."

He's mocking me, Todd thought angrily. He thinks it's a joke. Grinning down at me . . . His throat was dry. He looked at his watch; why the hell didn't they come? Since they had to, why? One day I was flying down one of them heavenly streets. You got yourself into it, Todd thought. Like Jonah in the whale.

"Justa throwin' feathers in everybody's face. An' ole Saint Peter called me in. Said, 'Jefferson, tell me two things, what you doin' flyin' without a harness; an' how come you flyin' so fast?' So I tole him I was flyin' without a harness 'cause it got in my way, but I couldn'ta been flyin' so fast, 'cause I wasn't usin' but one wing. Saint Peter said, 'You wasn't flyin' with but one wing?' 'Yessuh,' I says, scared-like. So he says, 'Well, since you got sucha extra fine pair of wings you can leave off yo' harness awhile. But from now on none of that there one-wing flyin', 'cause you gittin' up too damn much speed!' "

And with one mouth full of bad teeth you're making too

damned much talk, thought Todd. Why don't I send him after the boy? His body ached from the hard ground and seeking to shift his position he twisted his ankle and hated himself for crying out.

"It gittin' worse?"

"I . . . I twisted it," he groaned.

"Try not to think about it, son. That's what I do."

He bit his lip, fighting pain with counter-pain as the voice resumed its rhythmical droning. Jefferson seemed caught in his own creation.

". . . After all that trouble I just floated roun' heaven in slow motion. But I forgot, like colored folks will do, and got to flyin' with one wing again. This time I was restin' my old broken arm and got to flyin' fast enough to shame the devil. I was comin' so fast, Lawd, I got myself called befo' ole Saint Peter again. He said, 'Jeff, didn't I warn you 'bout that speedin'?' 'Yessuh,' I says, 'but it was an accident.' He looked at me sad-like and shook his head and I knowed I was gone. He said, 'Jeff, you and that speedin' is a danger to the heavenly community. If I was to let you keep on flyin', heaven wouldn't be nothin' but uproar. Jeff, you got to go!' Son, I argued and pleaded with that old white man, but it didn't do a bit of good. They rushed me straight to them pearly gates and gimme a parachute and a map of the state of Alabama . . ."

Todd heard him laughing so that he could hardly speak, making a screen between them upon which his humiliation glowed like fire.

"Maybe you'd better stop awhile," he said, his voice unreal.

"Ain't much more," Jefferson laughed. "When they gimme the parachute ole Saint Peter ask me if I wanted to say a few words before I went. I felt so bad I couldn't hardly look at him, specially with all them white angels standin' around. Then somebody laughed and made me mad. So I tole him, 'Well, you done took my wings. And you puttin' me out. You got charge of things so's I can't do nothin' about it. But you got to admit just this: While I was up here I was the flyinest sonofabitch what ever hit heaven!'"

At the burst of laughter Todd felt such an intense humiliation that only great violence would wash it away. The laughter which shook the old man like a boiling purge set up vibrations of guilt within him which not even the intricate machinery of the plane would have been adequate to transform and he heard himself screaming, "Why do you laugh at me this way?"

He hated himself at that moment, but he had lost control. He saw Jefferson's mouth fall open, "What—?"

"Answer me!"

His blood pounded as though it would surely burst his temples and he tried to reach the old man and fell, screaming, "Can I help it because they won't let us actually fly? Maybe we are a bunch of buzzards feeding on a dead horse, but we can hope to be eagles, can't we? Can't we?"

He fell back, exhausted, his ankle pounding. The saliva was like straw in his mouth. If he had the strength he would strangle this old man. This grinning, gray-headed clown who made him feel as he felt when watched by the white officers at the field. And yet this old man had neither power, prestige, rank nor technique. Nothing that could rid him of this terrible feeling. He watched him, seeing his face struggle to express a turmoil of feeling.

"What you mean, son? What you talking 'bout . . . ?"

"Go away. Go tell your tales to the white folks."

"But I didn't mean nothing like that. . . . I . . . I wasn't tryin' to hurt your feelings. . . ."

"Please. Get the hell away from me!"

"But I didn't, son. I didn't mean all them things a-tall."

Todd shook as with a chill, searching Jefferson's face for a trace of the mockery he had seen there. But now the face was somber and tired and old. He was confused. He could not be sure that there had ever been laughter there, that Jefferson had ever really laughed in his whole life. He saw Jefferson reach out to touch him and shrank away, wondering if anything except the pain, now causing his vision to waver, was real. Perhaps he had imagined it all.

"Don't let it get you down, son," the voice said pensively.

He heard Jefferson sigh wearily, as though he felt more than he could say. His anger ebbed, leaving only the pain.

"I'm sorry," he mumbled.

"You just wore out with pain, was all. . . ."

He saw him through a blur, smiling. And for a second he felt the embarrassed silence of understanding flutter between them.

"What you was doin' flyin' over this section, son? Wasn't you scared they might shoot you for a cow?"

Todd tensed. Was he being laughed at again? But before he could decide, the pain shook him and a part of him was lying calmly behind the screen of pain that had fallen between them, recalling the first time he had ever seen a plane. It was as though an endless series of hangars had been shaken ajar in the air base of his memory and from each, like a young wasp emerging from its cell, arose the memory of a plane.

The first time I ever saw a plane I was very small and planes were new in the world. I was four-and-a-half and the only plane that I had ever seen was a model suspended from the ceiling of the automobile exhibit at the State Fair. But I did not know that it was only a model. I did not know how large a real plane was, nor how expensive. To me it was a fascinating toy, complete in itself, which my mother said could only be owned by rich little white boys. I stood rigid with admiration, my head straining backwards as I watched the gray little plane describing arcs above the gleaming tops of the automobiles. And I vowed that, rich or poor, someday I would own such a toy. My mother had to drag me out of the exhibit and not even the merry-go-round, the Ferris wheel, or the racing horses could hold my attention for the rest of the Fair. I was too busy imitating the tiny drone of the plane with my lips, and imitating with my hands the motion, swift and circling, that it made in flight.

After that I no longer used the pieces of lumber that lay about our back yard to construct wagons and autos . . . now it was used for airplanes. I built biplanes, using pieces of board for wings, a small box for the fuselage, another piece of wood for the rudder. The trip to the Fair had brought something new into my small world. I asked my mother repeatedly when the Fair would come back again. I'd lie in the grass and watch the sky, and each fighting bird became a soaring plane. I would have been good a year just to have seen a plane again. I became a nuisance to everyone with my questions about airplanes. But planes were new to the old folks, too, and there was little that they could tell me. Only my uncle knew some of the answers. And better still, he could carve propellers from pieces of wood that would whirl rapidly in the wind, wobbling noisily upon oiled nails.

I wanted a plane more than I'd wanted anything; more than I wanted the red wagon with rubber tires, more than the train that ran on a track with its train of cars. I asked my mother over and over again:

"Mamma?"

"What do you want, boy?" she'd say.

"Mamma, will you get mad if I ask you?" I'd say.

"What do you want now? I ain't got time to be answering a lot of fool questions. What you want?"

"Mamma, when you gonna get me one . . . ?" I'd ask.

"Get you one what?" she'd say.

"You know, Mamma; what I been asking you. . . ."

"Boy," she'd say, "if you don't want a spanking you better come on an' tell me what you talking about so I can get on with my work."

"Aw, Mamma, you know. . . ."

"What I just tell you?" she'd say.

"I mean when you gonna buy me a airplane."

"AIRPLANE! Boy, is you crazy? How many times I have to tell you to stop that foolishness. I done told you them things cost too much. I bet I'm gon' wham the living daylight out of you if you don't quit worrying me 'bout them things!"

But this did not stop me, and a few days later I'd try all over again.

Then one day a strange thing happened. It was spring and for some reason I had been hot and irritable all morning. It was a beautiful spring. I could feel it as I played barefoot in the backyard. Blossoms hung from the thorny black locust trees like clusters of fragrant white grapes. Butterflies flickered in the sunlight above the short new dew-wet grass. I had gone in the house for bread and butter and coming out I heard a steady unfamiliar drone. It was unlike anything I had ever heard before. I tried to place the sound. It was no use. It was a sensation like that I had when searching for my father's watch, heard ticking unseen in a room. It made me feel as though I had forgotten to perform some task that my mother had ordered . . . then I located it, overhead. In the sky, flying quite low and about a hundred yards off was a plane! It came so slowly that it seemed barely to move. My mouth hung wide; my bread and butter fell into the dirt. I wanted to jump up and down and cheer. And when the idea struck I trembled with excitement: "Some little white boy's plane's done flew away and all I got to do is stretch out my hands and it'll be mine!" It was a little plane like that at the Fair, flying no higher than the eaves of our roof. Seeing it come steadily forward I felt the world grow warm with promise. I opened the screen and climbed over it and clung there, waiting. I would catch the plane as it came over and swing down fast and run into the house before anyone could see me. Then no one could come to claim the plane. It droned nearer. Then when it hung like a silver cross in the blue directly above me I stretched out my hand and grabbed. It was like sticking my finger through a soap bubble. The plane flew on, as though I had simply blown my breath after it. I grabbed again, frantically, trying to catch the tail. My fingers clutched the air and disappointment surged tight and hard in my throat. Giving one last desperate grasp, I strained forward. My fingers ripped against the screen. I was falling. The ground burst hard against me. I drummed the earth with my heels and when my breath returned, I lay there bawling.

My mother rushed through the door.

"What's the matter, chile! What on earth is wrong with you?"

"It's gone! It's gone!"

"What gone?"

"The airplane . . ."

"Airplane?"

"Yessum, jus' like the one at the Fair. . . . I . . . I tried to stop it an' it kep' right on going. . . ."

"When, boy?"

"Just now," I cried, through my tears.

"Where it go, boy, what way?"

"Yonder, there . . ."

She scanned the sky, her arms akimbo and her checkered apron flapping in the wind as I pointed to the fading plane. Finally she looked down at me, slowly shaking her head.

"It's gone! It's gone!" I cried.

"Boy, is you a fool?" she said. "Don't you see that there's a real airplane 'stead of one of them toy ones?"

"Real . . . ?" I forgot to cry. "Real?"

"Yass, real. Don't you know that thing you reaching for is bigger'n a auto? You here trying to reach for it and I bet it's flying 'bout two hundred miles higher'n this roof." She was disgusted with me. "You come on in this house before somebody else sees what a fool you done turned out to be. You must think these here lil ole arms of you'n is mighty long. . . ."

I was carried into the house and undressed for bed and the doctor was called. I cried bitterly, as much from the disappointment of finding the plane so far beyond my reach as from the pain.

When the doctor came I heard my mother telling him about the plane and asking if anything was wrong with my mind. He explained that I had had a fever for several hours. But I was kept in bed for a week and I constantly saw the plane in my sleep, flying just beyond my fingertips, sailing so slowly that it seemed barely to move. And each time I'd reach out to grab it I'd miss and through each dream I'd hear my grandma warning:

> *Young man, young man,*
> *Yo' arms too short*
> *To box with God. . . .*

"Hey, son!"

At first he did not know where he was and looked at the old man pointing, with blurred eyes.

"Ain't that one of you-all's airplanes coming after you?"

As his vision cleared he saw a small black shape above a distant field, soaring through waves of heat. But he could not be sure and with the pain he feared that somehow a horrible recurring fantasy of being split in twain by the whirling blades of a propeller had come true.

"You think he sees us?" he heard.

"See? I hope so."

"He's coming like a bat outa hell!"

Straining, he heard the faint sound of a motor and hoped it would soon be over.

"How you feeling?"

"Like a nightmare," he said.

"Hey, he's done curved back the other way!"

"Maybe he saw us," he said. "Maybe he's gone to send out the ambulance and ground crew." And, he thought with despair, maybe he didn't even see us.

"Where did you send the boy?"

"Down to Mister Graves," Jefferson said. "Man what owns this land."

"Do you think he phoned?"

Jefferson looked at him quickly.

"Aw sho'. Dabney Graves is got a bad name on accounta them killings but he'll call though. . . ."

"What killings?"

"Them five fellers . . . ain't you heard?" he asked with surprise.

"No."

"Everybody knows 'bout Dabney Graves, especially the colored. He done killed enough of us."

Todd had the sensation of being caught in a white neighborhood after dark.

"What did they do?" he asked.

"Thought they was men," Jefferson said. "An' some he owed money, like he do me. . . ."

"But why do you stay here?"

"You black, son."

"I know, but . . ."

"You have to come by the white folks, too."

He turned away from Jefferson's eyes, at once consoled and accused. And I'll have to come by them soon, he thought with despair. Closing his eyes, he heard Jefferson's voice as the sun burned blood-red upon his lips.

"I got nowhere to go," Jefferson said, "an' they'd come after me if I did. But Dabney Graves is a funny fellow. He's all the time making jokes. He can be mean as hell, then he's liable to turn right around and back the colored against the white folks. I seen him do it. But me, I hates him for that more'n anything else. 'Cause just as soon as he gits tired helping a man he don't care what happens to him. He just leaves him stone cold. And then the other white folks is double hard on anybody he done helped. For him it's just a joke. He don't give a hilla beans for nobody—but hisself. . . ."

Todd listened to the thread of detachment in the old man's voice. It was as though he held his words arm's length before him to avoid their destructive meaning.

"He'd just as soon do you a favor and then turn right around and have you strung up. Me, I stays outa his way 'cause down here that's what you gotta do."

If my ankle would only ease for a while, he thought. The closer I spin toward the earth the blacker I become, flashed through his mind. Sweat ran into his eyes and he was sure that he would never see the plane if his head continued whirling. He tried to see Jefferson, what it was that Jefferson held in his hand? It was a little black man, another Jefferson! A little black Jefferson that shook with fits of belly-laughter while the other Jefferson looked on with detachment. Then Jefferson looked up from the thing in his hand and turned to speak, but Todd was far away, searching the sky for a plane in a hot dry land on a day and age he had long forgotten. He was going mysteriously with his mother through empty streets where black faces peered from behind drawn shades and someone was rapping at a window and he was looking back to see a hand and a frightened face frantically beckoning from a cracked door and his mother was looking down the empty perspective of the street and shaking her head and hurrying him along and at first it was only a flash he saw and a motor was droning as through the sun-glare he saw it gleaming silver as it circled and he was seeing a burst like a puff of white smoke and hearing his mother yell, Come along, boy, I got no time for them fool airplanes, I got no time, and he saw it a second time, the plane flying high, and the burst appeared suddenly and fell slowly, billowing out and sparkling like fireworks and he was watching and being hurried along as the air filled with a flurry of white pinwheeling cards that caught in the wind and scattered over the rooftops and into the gutters and a woman was running and snatching a card and reading it and screaming and he darted into the shower, grabbing as in winter he grabbed for snowflakes and bounding away at his mother's, Come on here, boy! Come on, I say! and he was watching as she took the card away, seeing her face grow puzzled and turning taut as her voice quavered, "Niggers Stay From the Polls," and died to a moan of terror as he saw the eyeless sockets of a white hood staring at him from the card and above he saw the plane spiraling gracefully, agleam in the sun like a fiery sword. And seeing it soar he was caught, transfixed between a terrible horror and a horrible fascination.

The sun was not so high now, and Jefferson was calling and gradually he saw three figures moving across the curving roll of the field.

"Look like some doctors, all dressed in white," said Jefferson.

They're coming at last, Todd thought. And he felt such a release of tension within him that he thought he would faint. But no sooner did he close his eyes than he was seized and he was struggling with three white men who were forcing his arms into some kind of coat. It was too much for him, his arms were pinned to his sides and as the pain blazed in his eyes, he realized that it was a straitjacket. What filthy joke was this?

"That oughta hold him, Mister Graves," he heard.

His total energies seemed focused in his eyes as he searched their faces. That was Graves; the other two wore hospital uniforms. He was poised between two poles of fear and hate as he heard the one called Graves saying, "He looks kinda purty in that there suit, boys. I'm glad you dropped by."

"This boy ain't crazy, Mister Graves," one of the others said. "He needs a doctor, not us. Don't see how you led us way out here anyway. It might be a joke to you, but your cousin Rudolph liable to kill somebody. White folks or niggers, don't make no difference. . . ."

Todd saw the man turn red with anger. Graves looked down upon him, chuckling.

"This nigguh belongs in a straitjacket, too, boys. I knowed that the minit Jeff's kid said something 'bout a nigguh flyer. You all know you cain't let the nigguh git up that high without his going crazy. The nigguh brain ain't built right for high altitudes. . . ."

Todd watched the drawling red face, feeling that all the unnamed horror and obscenities that he had ever imagined stood materialized before him.

"Let's git outta here," one of the attendants said.

Todd saw the other reach toward him, realizing for the first time that he lay upon a stretcher as he yelled.

"Don't put your hands on me!"

They drew back, surprised.

"What's that you say, nigguh?" asked Graves.

He did not answer and thought that Graves's foot was aimed at his head. It landed on his chest and he could hardly breathe. He coughed helplessly, seeing Graves's lips stretch taut over his yellow teeth, and tried to shift his head. It was as though a half-dead fly was dragging slowly across his face and a bomb seemed to burst within him. Blasts of hot, hysterical laughter tore from his chest, causing his eyes to pop and he felt that the veins in his neck would surely burst. And then a part of him stood behind it all, watching the surprise in Graves's red face and his own hysteria. He thought he would never stop, he would laugh himself to death. It rang in his ears like Jefferson's laughter and he looked for him, centering his eyes desperately upon his face, as though somehow he had become his sole salvation in an insane world of outrage and humiliation. It brought a certain relief. He was suddenly aware that although his body was still contorted it was an echo that no longer rang in his ears. He heard Jefferson's voice with gratitude.

"Mister Graves, the Army done tole him not to leave his airplane."

"Nigguh, Army or no, you gittin' off my land! That airplane can stay 'cause it was paid for by taxpayers' money. But you gittin' off. An' dead or alive, it don't make no difference to me."

Todd was beyond it now, lost in a world of anguish.

"Jeff," Graves said, "you and Teddy come and grab holt. I want you to take this here black eagle over to that nigguh airfield and leave him."

Jefferson and the boy approached him silently. He looked away, realizing and doubting at once that only they could release him from his overpowering sense of isolation.

They bent for the stretcher. One of the attendants moved toward Teddy.

"Think you can manage it, boy?"

"I think I can, suh," Teddy said.

"Well, you better go behind then, and let yo' pa go ahead so's to keep that leg elevated."

He saw the white men walking ahead of Jefferson and the boy carried him along in silence. Then they were pausing and he felt a hand wiping his face; then he was moving again. And it was as though he had been lifted out of his isolation, back into the world of men. A new current of communication flowed between the man and boy and himself. They moved him gently. Far away he heard a mockingbird liquidly calling. He raised his eyes, seeing a buzzard poised unmoving in space. For a moment the whole afternoon seemed suspended and he waited for the horror to seize him again. Then like a song within his head he heard the boy's soft humming and saw the dark bird glide into the sun and glow like a bird of flaming gold.

King of the Bingo Game

THE WOMAN IN FRONT of him was eating roasted peanuts that smelled so good that he could barely contain his hunger. He could not even sleep and wished they'd hurry and begin the bingo game. There, on his right, two fellows were drinking wine out of a bottle wrapped in a paper bag, and he could hear soft gurgling in the dark. His stomach gave a low, gnawing growl. "If this was down South," he thought, "all I'd have to do is lean over and say, 'Lady, gimme a few of those peanuts, please ma'am,' and she'd pass me the bag and never think nothing of it." Or he could ask the fellows for a drink in the same way. Folks down South stuck together that way; they didn't even have to know you. But up here it was different. Ask somebody for something, and they'd think you were crazy. Well, I ain't crazy. I'm just broke, 'cause I got no birth certificate to get a job, and Laura 'bout to die 'cause we got no money for a doctor. But I ain't crazy. And yet a pinpoint of doubt was focused in his mind as he glanced toward the screen and saw the hero stealthily entering a dark room and sending the beam of a flashlight along a wall of bookcases. This is where he finds the trapdoor, he remembered. The man would pass abruptly through the wall and find the girl tied to a bed, her legs and arms spread wide, and her clothing torn to rags. He laughed softly to himself. He had seen the picture three times, and this was one of the best scenes.

On his right the fellow whispered wide-eyed to his companion, "Man, look a-yonder!"

"Damn!"

"Wouldn't I like to have her tied up like that . . ."

"Hey! That fool's letting her loose!"

"Aw, man, he loves her."

"Love or no love!"

The man moved impatiently beside him, and he tried to involve himself in the scene. But Laura was on his mind. Tiring quickly of watching the picture he looked back to where the white beam filtered from the projection room above the balcony. It started small and grew large, specks of dust dancing in its whiteness as it reached the screen. It was strange how the beam always landed

Reprinted from *Tomorrow*, IV (November 1944), 29–33. Copyright © 1944 by Ralph Ellison. Reprinted by permission of the author.

right on the screen and didn't mess up and fall somewhere else. But they had it all fixed. Everything was fixed. Now suppose when they showed that girl with her dress torn the girl started taking off the rest of her clothes, and when the guy came in he didn't untie her but kept her there and went to taking off his own clothes? *That* would be something to see. If a picture got out of hand like that those guys up there would go nuts. Yeah, and there'd be so many folks in here you couldn't find a seat for nine months! A strange sensation played over his skin. He shuddered. Yesterday he'd seen a bedbug on a woman's neck as they walked out into the bright street. But exploring his thigh through a hole in his pocket he found only goose pimples and old scars.

The bottle gurgled again. He closed his eyes. Now a dreamy music was accompanying the film and train whistles were sounding in the distance, and he was a boy again walking along a railroad trestle down South, and seeing the train coming, and running back as fast as he could go, and hearing the whistle blowing, and getting off the trestle to solid ground just in time, with the earth trembling beneath his feet, and feeling relieved as he ran down the cinder-strewn embankment onto the highway, and looking back and seeing with terror that the train had left the track and was following him right down the middle of the street, and all the white people laughing as he ran screaming . . .

"Wake up there, buddy! What the hell do you mean hollering like that? Can't you see we trying to enjoy this here picture?"

He stared at the man with gratitude.

"I'm sorry, old man," he said. "I musta been dreaming."

"Well, here, have a drink. And don't be making no noise like that, damn!"

His hands trembled as he tilted his head. It was not wine, but whiskey. Cold rye whiskey. He took a deep swoller, decided it was better not to take another, and handed the bottle back to its owner.

"Thanks, old man," he said.

Now he felt the cold whiskey breaking a warm path straight through the middle of him, growing hotter and sharper as it moved. He had not eaten all day, and it made him light-headed. The smell of the peanuts stabbed him like a knife, and he got up and found a seat in the middle aisle. But no sooner did he sit than he saw a row of intense-faced young girls, and got up again, thinking, "You chicks musta been Lindy-hopping somewhere." He found a seat several rows ahead as the lights came on, and he saw the screen disappear behind a heavy red and gold curtain; then the curtain rising, and the man with the microphone and a uniformed attendant coming on the stage.

He felt for his bingo cards, smiling. The guy at the door wouldn't like it if he knew about his having *five* cards. Well, not everyone played the bingo game; and even with five cards he didn't have much of a chance. For Laura, though, he had to have faith. He studied the cards, each with its different numerals, punching the free center hole in each and spreading them neatly across his lap; and when the lights faded he sat slouched in his seat so that he could look from his cards to the bingo wheel with but a quick shifting of his eyes.

Ahead, at the end of the darkness, the man with the microphone was pressing a button attached to a long cord and spinning the bingo wheel and calling out the number each time the wheel came to rest. And each time the voice rang out his finger raced over the cards for the number. With five cards he had to move fast. He became nervous; there were too many cards, and the man went too fast with his grating voice. Perhaps he should just select one and throw the others away. But he was afraid. He became warm. Wonder how much Laura's doctor would cost? Damn that, watch the cards! And with despair he heard the man call three in a row which he missed on all five cards. This way he'd never win . . .

When he saw the row of holes punched across the third card, he sat paralyzed and heard the man call three more numbers before he stumbled forward, screaming,

"Bingo! Bingo!"

"Let that fool up there," someone called.

"Get up there, man!"

He stumbled down the aisle and up the steps to the stage into a light so sharp and bright that for a moment it blinded him, and he felt that he had moved into the spell of some strange, mysterious power. Yet it was as familiar as the sun, and he knew it was the perfectly familiar bingo.

The man with the microphone was saying something to the audience as he held out his card. A cold light flashed from the man's finger as the card left his hand. His knees trembled. The man stepped closer, checking the card against the numbers chalked on the board. Suppose he had made a mistake? The pomade on the man's hair made him feel faint, and he backed away. But the man was checking the card over the microphone now, and he had to stay. He stood tense, listening.

"Under the O, forty-four," the man chanted. "Under the I, seven. Under the G, three. Under the B, ninety-six. Under the N, thirteen!"

His breath came easier as the man smiled at the audience.

"Yessir, ladies and gentlemen, he's one of the chosen people!"

The audience rippled with laughter and applause.

"Step right up to the front of the stage."

He moved slowly forward, wishing that the light was not so bright.

"To win tonight's jackpot of $36.90 the wheel must stop between the double zero, understand?"

He nodded, knowing the ritual from the many days and nights he had watched the winners march across the stage to press the button that controlled the spinning wheel and receive the prizes. And now he followed the instructions as though he'd crossed the slippery stage a million prize-winning times.

The man was making some kind of a joke, and he nodded vacantly. So tense had he become that he felt a sudden desire to cry and shook it away. He felt vaguely that his whole life was determined by the bingo wheel; not only that which would happen now that he was at last before it, but all that had gone before, since his birth, and his mother's birth and the birth of his father. It had always been there, even though he had not been aware of it, handing out the unlucky cards and numbers of his days. The feeling persisted, and he started quickly away. I better get down from here before I make a fool of myself, he thought.

"Here, boy," the man called. "You haven't started yet."

Someone laughed as he went hesitantly back.

"Are you all reet?"

He grinned at the man's jive talk, but no words would come, and he knew it was not a convincing grin. For suddenly he knew that he stood on the slippery brink of some terrible embarrassment.

"Where are you from, boy?" the man asked.

"Down South."

"He's from down South, ladies and gentlemen," the man said. "Where from? Speak right into the mike."

"Rocky Mont," he said. "Rock' Mont, North Car'lina."

"So you decided to come down off that mountain to the U. S.," the man laughed. He felt that the man was making a fool of him, but then something cold was placed in his hand, and the lights were no longer behind him.

Standing before the wheel he felt alone, but that was somehow right, and he remembered his plan. He would give the wheel a short quick twirl. Just a touch of the button. He had watched it many times, and always it came close to double zero when it was short and quick. He steeled himself; the fear had left, and he felt a profound sense of promise, as though he were about to be repaid for all the things he'd suffered all his life. Trembling, he pressed the button. There was a whirl of lights, and in a second he realized with finality that though he wanted to, he could not stop. It was as though he held a high-powered line in his naked hand. His nerves tightened. As the wheel increased its speed it seemed to draw him more and more into his power, as though it held his fate; and with it came a deep need to submit, to whirl, to lose himself in its swirl of color. He could not stop it now, he knew. So let it be.

The button rested snugly in his palm where the man had placed it. And now he became aware of the man beside him, advising him through the microphone, while behind the shadowy audience hummed with noisy voices. He shifted his feet. There was still that feeling of helplessness within him, making part of him desire to turn back, even now that the jackpot was right in his hand. He squeezed the button until his fist ached. Then, like the sudden shriek of a subway whistle, a doubt tore through his head. Suppose he did not spin the wheel long enough? What could he do, and how could he tell? And then he knew, even as he wondered, that as long as he pressed the button, he could control the jackpot. He and only he could determine whether or not it was to be his. Not even the man with the microphone could do anything about it now. He felt drunk. Then, as though he had come down from a high hill into a valley of people, he heard the audience yelling.

"Come down from there, you jerk!"

"Let somebody else have a chance . . ."

"Ole Jack thinks he done found the end of the rainbow . . ."

The last voice was not unfriendly, and he turned and smiled dreamily into the yelling mouths. Then he turned his back squarely on them.

"Don't take too long, boy," a voice said.

He nodded. They were yelling behind him. Those folks did not understand what had happened to him. They had been playing the bingo game day in and night out for years, trying to win rent money or hamburger change. But not one of those wise guys had discovered this wonderful thing. He watched the wheel whirling past the numbers and experienced a burst of exaltation: This is God! This is the really truly God! He said it aloud, "This is God!"

He said it with such absolute conviction that he feared he would fall fainting into the footlights. But the crowd yelled so loud that they could not hear. Those fools, he thought. I'm here trying to tell them the most wonderful secret in the world, and they're yelling like they gone crazy. A hand fell upon his shoulder.

"You'll have to make a choice now, boy. You've taken too long."

He brushed the hand violently away.

"Leave me alone, man. I know what I'm doing!"

The man looked surprised and held on to the microphone for support. And because he did not wish to hurt the man's feelings he smiled, realizing with a sudden pang that there was no way of explaining to the man just why he had to stand there pressing the button forever.

"Come here," he called tiredly.

The man approached, rolling the heavy microphone across the stage.

"Anybody can play this bingo game, right?" he said.

"Sure, but . . ."

He smiled, feeling inclined to be patient with this slick looking white man with his blue sport shirt and his sharp gabardine suit.

"That's what I thought," he said. "Anybody can win the jackpot as long as they get the lucky number, right?"

"That's the rule, but after all . . ."

"That's what I thought," he said. "And the big prize goes to the man who knows how to win it?"

The man nodded speechlessly.

"Well then, go on over there and watch me win like I want to. I ain't going to hurt nobody," he said, "and I'll show you how to win. I mean to show the whole world how it's got to be done."

And because he understood, he smiled again to let the man know that he held nothing against him for being white and impatient. Then he refused to see the man any longer and stood pressing the button, the voices of the crowd reaching him like sounds in distant streets. Let them yell. All the Negroes down there were just ashamed because he was black like them. He smiled inwardly, knowing how it was. Most of the time he was ashamed of what Negroes did himself. Well, let them be ashamed for something this time. Like him. He was like a long thin black wire that was being stretched and wound upon the bingo wheel; wound until he wanted to scream; wound, but this time himself controlling the winding and the sadness and the shame, and because he did, Laura would be all right. Suddenly the lights flickered. He staggered backwards. Had something gone wrong? All this noise. Didn't they know that although he controlled the wheel, it also controlled him, and unless he pressed the button forever and forever and ever it would stop, leaving him high and dry, dry and high on this hard high slippery hill and Laura dead? There was only one chance; he had to do whatever the wheel demanded. And gripping the button in despair, he discovered with surprise that it imparted a nervous energy. His spine tingled. He felt a certain power.

Now he faced the raging crowd with defiance, its screams penetrating his eardrums like trumpets shrieking from a juke-box. The vague faces glowing in the bingo lights gave him a sense of himself that he had never known before. He was running the show, by God! They had to react to him, for he was their luck. This is *me,* he thought. Let the bastards yell. Then someone was laughing inside him, and he realized that somehow he had forgotten his own name. It was a sad, lost feeling to lose your name, and a crazy thing to do. That name had been given him by the white man who had owned his grandfather a long lost time ago down South. But maybe those wise guys knew his name.

"Who am I?" he screamed.

"Hurry up and bingo, you jerk!"

They didn't know either, he thought sadly. They didn't even know their own names, they were all poor nameless bastards. Well, he didn't need that old name; he was reborn. For as long as he pressed the button he was The-man-who-pressed-the-button-who-held-the-prize-who-was-the-King-of-Bingo. That was the way it was, and he'd have to press the button even if nobody understood, even though Laura did not understand.

"Live!" he shouted.

The audience quieted like the dying of a huge fan.

"Live, Laura, baby. I got holt of it now, sugar. Live!"

He screamed it, tears streaming down his face. "I got nobody but YOU!"

The screams tore from his very guts. He felt as though the rush of blood to his head would burst out in baseball seams of small red droplets, like a head beaten by police clubs. Bending over he saw a trickle of blood splashing the toe of his shoe. With his free hand he searched his head. It was his nose. God, suppose something has gone wrong? He felt that the whole audience had somehow entered him and was stamping its feet in his stomach and he was unable to throw them out. They wanted the prize, that was it. They wanted the secret for themselves. But they'd never get it; he would keep the bingo wheel whirling forever, and Laura would be safe in the wheel. But would she? It had to be, because if she were not safe the wheel would cease to turn; it could not go on. He had to get away, *vomit* all, and his mind formed an image of himself running with Laura in his arms down the tracks of the subway just ahead of an A train, running desperately *vomit* with people screaming for him to come out but knowing no way of leaving the tracks because to stop would bring the train crushing down upon him and to attempt to leave across the other tracks would mean to run into a hot third rail as high as his waist which threw blue sparks that blinded his eyes until he could hardly see.

He heard singing and the audience was clapping its hands.

> *Shoot the liquor to him, Jim, boy!*
> *Clap-clap-clap*
> *Well a-calla the cop*
> *He's blowing his top!*
> *Shoot the liquor to him, Jim, boy!*

Bitter anger grew within him at the singing. They think I'm crazy. Well let 'em laugh. I'll do what I got to do.

He was standing in an attitude of intense listening when he saw that they were watching something on the stage behind him. He felt weak. But when he turned he saw no one. If only his thumb did not ache so. Now they were applauding. And for a moment he thought that the wheel had stopped. But that was impossible, his thumb still pressed the button. Then he saw them. Two men in uniform beckoned from the end of the stage. They were coming toward him, walking in step, slowly, like a tap-dance team returning for a third encore. But their shoulders shot forward, and he backed away, looking wildly about. There was nothing to fight them with. He had only the long black cord which led to a plug somewhere back stage, and he couldn't use that because it operated the bingo wheel. He backed slowly, fixing the men with his eyes as his lips stretched over his teeth in a tight, fixed grin; moved toward the end of the stage and realizing that he couldn't go much further, for suddenly the cord became taut and he couldn't afford to break the cord. But he had to do something. The audience was howling. Suddenly he stopped dead, seeing the men halt, their legs lifted as in an interrupted step of a slow-motion dance. There was nothing to do but run in the other direction and he dashed forward, slipping and sliding. The men fell back, surprised. He struck out violently going past.

"Grab him!"

He ran, but all too quickly the cord tightened, resistingly, and he turned and ran back again. This time he slipped them, and discovered by running in a circle before the wheel he could keep the cord from tightening. But this way he had to flail his arms to keep the men away. Why couldn't they leave a man alone? He ran, circling.

"Ring down the curtain," someone yelled. But they couldn't do that. If they did the wheel flashing from the projection room would be cut off. But they had him before he could tell them so, trying to pry open his fist, and he was wrestling and trying to bring

the button, for it was his
t coming down, crushing
wheel whirling serenely

hen quietly, in a confiden-

And in the blank moment
how. He fought them trying
tched the wheel spin slowly
rest at double-zero.

of the men said smiling.
ead to someone he could not
d receive what all the winners

ce of the man's tight smile he
see the bow-legged man behind
ending curtain and set himself
n exploding in his skull, and he
n that his luck had run out on

Hidden Name and Complex Fate

A WRITER'S EXPERIENCE IN THE UNITED STATES

IN *Green Hills of Africa* Ernest Hemingway reminds us that both Tolstoy and Stendhal had seen war, that Flaubert had seen a revolution and the Commune, that Dostoievsky had been sent to Siberia and that such experiences were important in shaping the art of these great masters. And he goes on to observe that "writers are forged in injustice as a sword is forged." He declined to describe the many personal forms which injustice may take in

From *Shadow and Act*, by Ralph Ellison. © Copyright 1964 by Ralph Ellison. Reprinted by permission of Random House, Inc. This was originally an address sponsored by the Gertrude Clarke Whittall Foundation, Library of Congress, January 6, 1964.

this chaotic world—who would be so mad as to try?—nor does he go into the personal wounds which each of these writers sustained. Now, however, thanks to his brother and sister, we do know something of the injustice in which he himself was forged, and this knowledge has been added to what we have long known of Hemingway's artistic temper.

In the end, however, it is the quality of his art which is primary. It is the art which allows the wars and revolutions which he knew, and the personal and social injustice which he suffered, to lay claims upon our attention; for it was through his art that they achieved their most enduring meaning. It is a matter of outrageous irony, perhaps, but in literature the great social clashes of history no less than the painful experience of the individual are secondary to the meaning which they take on through the skill, the talent, the imagination and personal vision of the writer who transforms them into art. Here they are reduced to more manageable proportions; here they are imbued with humane values; here, injustice and catastrophe become less important in themselves than what the writer makes of them. This is *not* true, however, of the writer's struggle with that recalcitrant angel called Art; and it was through *this* specific struggle that Ernest Hemingway became *Hemingway* (now refined to a total body of transcendent work, after forty years of being endlessly dismembered and resurrected, as it continues to be, in the styles, the themes, the sense of life and literature of countless other writers). And it was through this struggle with form that he became the master, the culture hero, whom we have come to know and admire.

It was suggested that it might be of interest if I discussed here this evening some of my notions of the writer's experience in the United States, hence I have evoked the name of Hemingway, not by way of inviting far-fetched comparisons but in order to establish a perspective, a set of assumptions from which I may speak, and in an attempt to avoid boring you by emphasizing those details of racial hardship which for some forty years now have been evoked whenever writers of my own cultural background have essayed their experience in public.

I do this *not* by way of denying totally the validity of these by now stylized recitals, for I have shared and still share many of their detailed injustices—what Negro can escape them?—but by way of suggesting that they are, at least in a discussion of a writer's experience, as *writer*, as artist, somewhat beside the point.

For we select neither our parents, our race nor our nation; these occur to us out of the love, the hate, the circumstances, the fate, of others. But we *do* become writers out of an act of will, out of an act of choice; a dim, confused and ofttimes regrettable choice, perhaps, but choice nevertheless. And what happens thereafter causes all those experiences which occurred before we began to function as writers to take on a special quality of uniqueness. If this does not happen then as far as writing goes, the experiences have been misused. If we do not make of them a value, if we do not transform them into forms and images of meaning which they did not possess before, then we have failed as artists.

Thus for a writer to insist that his personal suffering is of special interest in itself, or simply because he belongs to a particular racial or religious group, is to advance a claim for special privileges which members of his group who are not writers would be ashamed to demand. The kindest judgment one can make of this point of view is that it reveals a sad misunderstanding of the relationship between suffering and art. Thomas Mann and André Gide have told us much of this and there are critics, like Edmund Wilson, who have told of the connection between the wound and the bow.

As I see it, it is through the process of making artistic forms —plays, poems, novels—out of one's experience that one becomes a writer, and it is through this process, this struggle, that the writer helps give meaning to the experience of the group. And it is the process of mastering the discipline, the techniques, the fortitude, the culture, through which this is made possible that constitutes the writer's real experience as *writer*, as artist. If this sounds like an argument for the artist's withdrawal from social struggles, I would recall to you W. H. Auden's comment to the effect that:

> In our age, the mere making of a work of art is itself a political act. So long as artists exist, making what they please, and think they ought to make, even if it is not terribly good, even if it appeals to only a handful of people, they remind the Management of something managers need to be reminded of, namely, that the managed are people with faces, not anonymous members, that *Homo Laborans* is also *Homo Ludens. . . .*

Without doubt, even the most *engagé* writer—and I refer to true artists, not to artists *manqués*—begin their careers in play and puzzlement, in dreaming over the details of the world in which they become conscious of themselves.

Let Tar Baby, that enigmatic figure from Negro folklore, stand for the world. He leans, black and gleaming, against the wall of life utterly noncommittal under our scrutiny, our questioning, starkly unmoving before our naïve attempts at intimidation. Then we touch him playfully and before we can say *Sonny Liston!* we find ourselves stuck. Our playful investigations become a labor, a fearful struggle, an *agon*. Slowly we perceive that our task is to learn the proper way of freeing ourselves to develop, in other words, technique.

Sensing this, we give him our sharpest attention, we question him carefully, we struggle with more subtlety; while he, in his silent way, holds on, demanding that we perceive the necessity of calling him by his true name as the price of our freedom. It is unfortunate that he has so many, many "true names"—all spelling chaos; and in order to discover even one of these we must first come into the possession of our own names. For it is through our names that we first place ourselves in the world. Our names, being the gift of others, must be made our own.

Once while listening to the play of a two-year-old girl who did not know she was under observation, I heard her saying over and over again, at first with questioning and then with sounds of growing satisfaction, "I am Mimi Livisay? . . . *I* am Mimi Livisay. I *am* Mimi Livisay . . . I am *Mimi* Li-vi-say! I am Mimi . . ."

And in deed and in fact she was—or became so soon thereafter, by working playfully to establish the unit between herself and her name.

For many of us this is far from easy. We must learn to wear our names within all the noise and confusion of the environment in which we find ourselves; make them the center of all of our associations with the world, with man and with nature. We must charge them with all our emotions, our hopes, hates, loves, aspirations. They must become our masks and our shields and the containers of all those values and traditions which we learn and/or imagine as being the meaning of our familial past.

And when we are reminded so constantly that we bear, as Negroes, names originally possessed by those who owned our enslaved grandparents, we are apt, especially if we are potential writers, to be more than ordinarily concerned with the veiled and mysterious events, the fusions of blood, the furtive couplings, the business transactions, the violations of faith and loyalty, the assaults; yes, and the unrecognized and unrecognizable loves through which our names were handed down unto us.

So charged with emotion does this concern become for some of us, that we have, earlier, the example of the followers of Father Divine and, now, the Black Muslims, discarding their original names in rejection of the bloodstained, the brutal, the sinful images of the past. Thus they would declare new identities, would clarify a new program of intention and destroy the verbal evidence of a willed and ritualized discontinuity of blood and human intercourse.

Not all of us, actually only a few, seek to deal with our names in this manner. We take what we have and make of them what we can. And there are even those who know where the old broken connections lie, who recognize their relatives across the chasm of historical denial and the artificial barriers of society, and who see themselves as bearers of many of the qualities which were admirable in the original sources of their common line (Faulkner has made much of this); and I speak here not of mere forgiveness, nor of obsequious insensitivity to the outrages symbolized by the denial and the division, but of the conscious acceptance of the harsh realities of the human condition, of the ambiguities and hypocrisies of human history as they have played themselves out in the United States.

Perhaps, taken in aggregate, these European names which (sometimes with irony, sometimes with pride, but always with personal investment) represent a certain triumph of the spirit, speaking to us of those who rallied, reassembled and transformed themselves and who under dismembering pressures refused to die. "Brothers and sisters," I once heard a Negro preacher exhort, "let us make up our faces before the world, and our names shall sound throughout the land with honor! For we ourselves are our *true* names, not their epithets! So let us, I say, Make Up Our Faces and Our Minds!"

Perhaps my preacher had read T. S. Eliot, although I doubt it. And in actuality, it was unnecessary that he do so, for a concern with names and naming was very much part of that special area of American culture from which I come, and it is precisely for this reason that this example should come to mind in a discussion of my own experience as a writer.

Undoubtedly, writers begin their *conditioning* as manipulators of words long before they become aware of literature—certain Freudians would say at the breast. Perhaps. But if so, that is far too early to be of use at this moment. Of this, though, I am certain: that despite the misconceptions of those educators who trace the reading difficulties experienced by large numbers of Negro children in Northern schools to their Southern background, these children are, in *their* familiar South, facile manipulators of words. I know, too, that the Negro community is deadly in its ability to create nicknames and to spot all that is ludicrous in an unlikely name or that which is incongruous in conduct. Names are not qualities; nor are words, in this particular sense, actions. To assume that they are could cost one his life many times a day. Language skills depend to a large extent upon a knowledge of the details, the manners, the objects, the folkways, the psychological patterns, of a given environment. Humor and wit depend upon much the same awareness, and so does the suggestive power of names.

"A small brown bowlegged Negro with the name 'Franklin D. Roosevelt Jones' might sound like a clown to someone who looks at him from the outside," said my friend Albert Murray, "but on the other hand he just might turn out to be a hell of a fireside operator. He might just lie back in all of that comic juxtaposition of names and manipulate you deaf, dumb and blind—and you not even suspecting it, because you're thrown out of stance by his name! There you are, so dazzled by the F.D.R. image—which you *know* you can't see—and so delighted with your own superior position that you don't realize that it's *Jones* who must be confronted."

Well, as you must suspect, all of this speculation on the matter of names has a purpose, and now, because it is tied up so ironically with my own experience as a writer, I must turn to my own name.

For in the dim beginnings, before I ever thought consciously of writing, there was my own name, and there was, doubtless, a certain magic in it. From the start I was uncomfortable with it, and in my earliest years it caused me much puzzlement. Neither could I understand what a poet was, nor why, exactly, my father had chosen to name me after one. Perhaps I could have understood it perfectly well had he named me after his own father, but that name had been given to an older brother who died and thus was out of the question. But why hadn't he named me after a hero, such as Jack Johnson, or a soldier like Colonel Charles Young, or a great seaman like Admiral Dewey, or an educator like Booker T. Washington, or a great orator and abolitionist like Frederick Douglass? Or again, why hadn't he named me (as so many Negro parents had done) after President Teddy Roosevelt?

Instead, he named me after someone called Ralph Waldo Emerson, and then, when I was three, he died. It was too early for me to have understood his choice, although I'm sure he must have explained it many times, and it was also too soon for me to have made the connection between my name and my father's love for reading. Much later, after I began to write and work with words, I came to suspect that he was aware of the suggestive powers of names and of the magic involved in naming.

I recall an odd conversation with my mother during my early teens in which she mentioned their interest in, of all things, prenatal culture! But for a long time I actually knew only that my father read a lot, and that he admired this remote Mr. Emerson, who was something called a "poet and philosopher"—so much so that he named his second son after him.

I knew, also, that whatever his motives, the combination of names he'd given me caused me no end of trouble from the moment when I could talk well enough to respond to the ritualized question which grownups put to very young children. Emerson's name was quite familiar to Negroes in Oklahoma during those days when World War I was brewing, and adults, eager to show off their knowledge of literary figures, and obviously amused by the joke implicit in such a small brown nubbin of a boy carrying around such a heavy moniker, would invariably repeat my first two names and then to my great annoyance, they'd add "Emerson."

And I, in my confusion, would reply, "No, *no, I'm* not Emerson, he's the little boy who lives next door." Which only made them laugh all the louder. "Oh no," they'd say, *"you're* Ralph Waldo Emerson," while I had fantasies of blue murder.

For a while the presence next door of my little friend, Emerson, made it unnecessary for me to puzzle too often over this peculiar adult confusion. And since there were other Negro boys named Ralph in the city, I came to suspect that there was something about the combination of names which produced their laughter. Even today I know of only one other Ralph who had as much comedy made out of his name, a campus politician and deep-voiced orator whom I knew at Tuskegee, who was called in friendly ribbing, *Ralph Waldo Emerson Edgar Allan Poe*, spelled Powe. This must have been quite a trial for him, but I had been initiated much earlier.

During my early school years the name continued to puzzle me, for it constantly evoked in the faces of others some secret. It was as though I possessed some treasure or some defect, which was invisible to my own eyes and ears; something which I had but did not *possess*, like a piece of property in South Carolina, which was mine but which I could not have until some future time. I recall finding, about this time, while seeking adventure in back alleys—which possess for boys a superiority over playgrounds like that which kitchen utensils possess over toys designed for infants—a large photographic lens. I remember nothing of its optical qualities, of its speed or color correction, but it gleamed with crystal mystery and it was beautiful.

Mounted handsomely in a tube of shiny brass, it spoke to me of distant worlds of possibility. I played with it, looking through it with squinted eyes, holding it in shafts of sunlight, and tried to use it for a magic lantern. But most of this was as unrewarding as my attempts to make the music come from a phonograph record by holding the needle in my fingers.

I could burn holes through newspapers with it, or I could pretend that it was a telescope, the barrel of a cannon, or the third eye of a monster—*I* being the monster—but I could do nothing at all about its proper function of making images, nothing to make it yield its secret. But I could not discard it.

Older boys sought to get it away from me by offering knives or tops, agate marbles or whole zoos of grass snakes and horned toads in trade, but I held on to it. No one, not even the white boys I knew, had such a lens, and it was my own good luck to have found it. Thus I would hold on to it until such time as I could acquire the parts needed to make it function. Finally I put it aside and it remained buried in my box of treasures, dusty and dull, to be lost and forgotten as I grew older and became interested in music.

I had reached by now the grades where it was necessary to learn something about Mr. Emerson and what he had written, such as the "Concord Hymn" and the essay "Self-Reliance," and in following his advice, I reduced the "Waldo" to a simple and, I hoped, mysterious "W," and in my own reading I avoided his works like the plague. I could no more deal with my name—I shall never really master it—than I could find a creative use for my lens. Fortunately there were other problems to occupy my mind. Not that I forgot my fascination with names, but more about that later.

Negro Oklahoma City was starkly lacking in writers. In fact, there was only Roscoe Dungee, the editor of the local Negro newspaper and a very fine editorialist in that valuable tradition of personal journalism which is now rapidly disappearing; a writer who in his emphasis upon the possibilities for justice offered by the Constitution anticipated the anti-segregation struggle by decades. There were also a few reporters who drifted in and out, but these were about all. On the level of *conscious* culture the Negro community was biased in the direction of music.

These were the middle and late twenties, remember, and the state was still a new frontier state. The capital city was one of the great centers for southwestern jazz, along with Dallas and Kansas City. Orchestras which were to become famous within a few years were constantly coming and going. As were the blues singers—Ma Rainey and Ida Cox, and the old bands like that of King Oliver. But best of all, thanks to Mrs. Zelia N. Breaux, there was an active and enthusiastic school music program through which any child who had the interest and the talent could learn to play an instrument and take part in the band, the orchestra, the brass quartet.

And there was a yearly operetta and a chorus and a glee club. Harmony was taught for four years and the music appreciation program was imperative. European folk dances were taught throughout the Negro school system, and we were also taught complicated patterns of military drill.

I tell you this to point out that although there were no incentives to write, there was ample opportunity to receive an artistic discipline. Indeed, once one picked up an instrument it was difficult to escape. If you chafed at the many rehearsals of the school band or orchestra and were drawn to the many small jazz groups, you were likely to discover that the jazzmen were apt to rehearse far more than the school band, it was only that they seemed to enjoy themselves better and to possess a freedom of imagination which we were denied at school. And one soon learned that the wild, transcendent moments which occurred at dances or "battles of music," moments in which memorable improvisations were ignited, depended upon a dedication to a discipline which was observed even when rehearsals had to take place in the crowded quarters of Halley Richardson's shoeshine parlor. It was not the place which counted, although a large hall with good acoustics was preferred, but what one did to perfect one's performance.

If this talk of musical discipline gives the impression that there were no forces working to nourish one who would one day blunder, after many a twist and turn, into writing, I am misleading you. And here I might give you a longish lecture on the Ironies and Uses of Segregation. When I was a small child there was no library for Negroes in our city, and not until a Negro minister invaded the main library did we get one. For it was discovered that there was no law, only custom, which held that we could not use these public facilities. The results were the quick renting of two large rooms in a Negro office building (the recent site of a pool hall), the hiring of a young Negro librarian, the installation of shelves and a hurried stocking of the walls with any and every book possible. It was, in those first days, something of a literary chaos.

But how fortunate for a boy who loved to read! I started with the fairy tales and quickly went through the junior fiction; then through the Westerns and the detective novels, and very soon I was reading the classics—only I didn't know it. There were also the Haldeman Julius Blue Books, which seem to have floated on the air down from Girard, Kansas; the syndicated columns of O. O. McIntyre, and the copies of *Vanity Fair* and the *Literary Digest* which my mother brought home from work—how could I ever join uncritically in the heavy-handed attacks on the so-called Big Media which have become so common today?

There were also the pulp magazines and, more important, that other library which I visited when I went to help my adopted grandfather, J. D. Randolph (my parents had been living in his rooming house when I was born), at his work as custodian of the law library of the Oklahoma State Capitol. Mr. Randolph had been one of the first teachers in what became Oklahoma City, and he'd also been one of the leaders of a group who walked from Gallatin, Tennessee, to the Oklahoma Territory. He was a tall man, as brown as smoked leather, who looked like the Indians with whom he'd herded horses in the early days.

And while his status was merely the custodian of the law library, I was to see the white legislators come down on many occasions to question him on points of law, and often I was to hear him answer without recourse to the uniform rows of books on the shelves. This was a thing to marvel at in itself, and the white lawmakers did so, but even more marvelous, ironic, intriguing, haunting—call it what you will—is the fact that the Negro who knew the answers was named after Jefferson Davis. What Tennessee lost, Oklahoma was to gain, and after gaining it (a gift of courage, intelligence, fortitude and grace), used it only in concealment and, one hopes, with embarrassment.

So, let us, I say, make up our faces and our minds!

In the loosely structured community of that time, knowledge, news of other ways of living, ancient wisdom, the latest literary fads, hate literature—for years I kept a card warning Negroes away from the polls, which had been dropped by the thousands from a plane which circled over the Negro community—information of all kinds, found its level, catch-as-catch can, in the minds of those who were receptive to it. Not that there was no conscious structuring—I read my first Shaw and Maupassant, my first Harvard Classics in the home of a friend whose parents were products of that stream of New England education which had been brought to Negroes by the young and enthusiastic white teachers who staffed the schools set up for the freedmen after the Civil War. These parents were both teachers and there were others like them in our town.

But the places where a rich oral literature was truly functional were the churches, the schoolyards, the barbershops, the cotton-picking camps; places where folklore and gossip thrived. The drug store where I worked was such a place, where on days of bad weather the older men would sit with their pipes and tell tall tales, hunting yarns and homely versions of the classics. It was here that I heard stories of searching for buried treasure and of headless horsemen, which I was told were my own father's versions told long before. There were even recitals of popular verse, "The Shooting of Dan McGrew," and, along with these, stories of Jesse James, of Negro outlaws and black United States marshals, of slaves who became the chiefs of Indian tribes and of the exploits of Negro cowboys. There was both truth and fantasy in this, intermingled in the mysterious fashion of literature.

Writers, in their formative period, absorb into their consciousness much that has no special value until much later, and often much which is of no special value even then—perhaps, beyond the fact that it throbs with affect and mystery and in it "time and pain and royalty in the blood" are suspended in imagery. So, long before I thought of writing, I was claimed by weather, by speech rhythms, by Negro voices and their different idioms, by husky male voices and by the high shrill singing voices of certain Negro women, by music, by tight spaces and by wide spaces in which the eyes could wander, by death, by newly born babies, by manners of various kinds, company manners and street manners, the manners of white society and those of our own high society, and by interracial manners; by street fights, circuses and minstrel shows, by vaudeville and moving pictures, by prize fights and foot races, baseball games and football matches. By spring floods and blizzards, catalpa worms and jack rabbits, honeysuckle and snapdragons (which smelled like old cigar butts); by sunflowers and hollyhocks, raw sugar cane and baked yams; pigs' feet, chili and blue haw ice cream. By parades, public dances and jam sessions, Easter sunrise ceremonies and large funerals. By contests between fire-and-brimstone preachers and by presiding elders who got "laughing-happy" when moved by the spirit of God.

I was impressed by expert players of the "dozens" and certain notorious bootleggers of corn whiskey. By jazz musicians and fortunetellers and by men who did anything well; by strange sicknesses and by interesting brick or razor scars; by expert cursing vocabularies as well as by exalted praying and terrifying shouting, and by transcendent playing or singing of the blues. I was fascinated by old ladies, those who had seen slavery and those who were defiant of white folk and black alike; by the enticing walks of prostitutes and by the limping walks affected by Negro hustlers, especially those who wore Stetson hats, expensive shoes with well-starched overalls, usually with a diamond stickpin (when not in hock) in their tieless collars as their gambling uniforms.

And there were the blind men who preached on corners, and

the blind men who sang the blues to the accompaniment of washboard and guitar; and the white junkmen who sang mountain music and the famous hucksters of fruit and vegetables.

And there was the Indian-Negro confusion. There were Negroes who were part Indian and who lived on reservations, and Indians who had children who lived in towns as Negroes, and Negroes who were Indians and traveled back and forth between the groups with no trouble. And Indians who were wild as wild Negroes and others who were as solid and steady as bankers. There were the teachers, too, inspiring teachers and villainous teachers who chased after the girl students, and certain female teachers who one wished would chase after young male students. And a handsome old principal of military bearing who had been blemished by his classmates at West Point when they discovered on the eve of the graduation that he was a Negro. There were certain Jews, Mexicans, Chinese cooks, a German orchestra conductor and an English grocer who owned a Franklin touring car. And certain Negro mechanics—"Cadillac Slim," "Sticks" Walker, Buddy Bunn and Oscar Pitman—who had so assimilated the automobile that they seemed to be behind a steering wheel even as they walked the streets or danced with girls. And there were the whites who despised us and the others who shared our hardships and joys.

There is much more, but this is sufficient to indicate some of what was present even in a segregated community to form the background of my work, my sense of life.

And now comes the next step. I went to Tuskegee to study music, hoping to become a composer of symphonies and there, during my second year, I read *The Waste Land* and that, although I was then unaware of it, was the real transition to writing.

Mrs. L. C. McFarland had taught us much of Negro history in grade school and from her I'd learned of the New Negro Movement of the twenties, of Langston Hughes, Countee Cullen, Claude McKay, James Weldon Johnson and the others. They had inspired pride and had given me a closer identification with poetry (by now, oddly enough, I seldom thought of my hidden name), but with music so much on my mind it never occurred to me to try to imitate them. Still I read their work and was excited by the glamour of the Harlem which emerged from their poems and it was good to know that there were Negro writers.—Then came *The Waste Land.*

I was much more under the spell of literature than I realized at the time. *Wuthering Heights* had caused me an agony of unexpressible emotion and the same was true of *Jude the Obscure*, but *The Waste Land* seized my mind. I was intrigued by its power to move me while eluding my understanding. Somehow its rhythms were often closer to those of jazz than were those of the Negro poets, and even though I could not understand then, its range of allusion was as mixed and as varied as that of Louis Armstrong. Yet there were its discontinuities, its changes of pace and its hidden system of organization which escaped me.

There was nothing to do but look up the references in the footnotes to the poem, and thus began my conscious education in literature.

For this, the library at Tuskegee was quite adequate and I used it. Soon I was reading a whole range of subjects drawn upon by the poet, and this led, in turn, to criticism and to Pound and Ford Maddox Ford, Sherwood Anderson and Gertrude Stein, Hemingway and Fitzgerald and "round about 'til I was come" back to Melville and Twain—the writers who are taught and doubtlessly overtaught today. Perhaps it was my good luck that they were not taught at Tuskegee, I wouldn't know. But at the time I was playing, having an intellectually interesting good time.

Having given so much attention to the techniques of music, the process of learning something of the craft and intention of modern poetry and fiction seemed quite familiar. Besides, it was absolutely painless because it involved no deadlines or credits. Even then, however, a process which I described earlier had begun to operate. The more I learned of literature in this conscious way, the more the details of my background became transformed. I heard undertones in remembered conversations which had escaped me before, local customs took on a more universal meaning, values which I hadn't understood were revealed; some of the people whom I had known were diminished while others were elevated in stature. More important, I began to see my own possibilities with more objective, and in some ways, more hopeful eyes.

The following summer I went to New York seeking work, which I did not find, and remained there, but the personal transformation continued. Reading had become a conscious process of growth and discovery, a method of reordering the world. And that world had widened considerably.

At Tuskegee I had handled manuscripts which Prokofiev had given to Hazel Harrison, a Negro concert pianist who taught there and who had known him in Europe, and through Miss Harrison I had become aware of Prokofiev's symphonies. I had also become aware of the radical movements in politics and art, and in New York had begun reading the work of André Malraux, not only the fiction but chapters published from his *Psychology of Art*. And in my search for an expression of modern sensibility in the works of Negro writers I discovered Richard Wright. Shortly thereafter I was to meet Wright, and it was at his suggestion that I wrote both my first book review and my first short story. These were fatal suggestions.

For although I had tried my hand at poetry while at Tuskegee, it hadn't occurred to me that I might write fiction, but once he suggested it, it seemed the most natural thing to try. Fortunately for me, Wright, then on the verge of his first success, was eager to talk with a beginner and I was able to save valuable time in searching out those works in which writing was discussed as a craft. He guided me to Henry James' prefaces, to Conrad, to Joseph Warren Beach and to the letters of Dostoievsky. There were other advisers and other books involved, of course, but what is important here is that I was consciously concerned with the art of fiction, that almost from the beginning I was grappling quite consciously with the art through which I wished to realize myself. And this was not done in isolation; the Spanish Civil War was now in progress and the Depression was still on. The world was being shaken up, and through one of those odd instances which occur to young provincials in New York, I was to hear Malraux make an appeal for the Spanish Loyalists at the same party where I first heard the folk singer Leadbelly perform. Wright and I were there seeking money for the magazine which he had come to New York to edit.

Art and politics; a great French novelist and a Negro folk singer; a young writer who was soon to publish *Uncle Tom's Children*; and I who had barely begun to study his craft. It is such accidents, such fortuitous meetings, which count for so much in our lives. I had never dreamed that I would be in the presence of Malraux, of whose work I became aware on my second day in Harlem when Langston Hughes suggested that I read *Man's Fate* and *Days of Wrath* before returning them to a friend of his. And it is this fortuitous circumstance which led to my selecting Malraux as a literary "ancestor," whom, unlike a relative, the artist is permitted to choose. There was in progress at the time all the agitation over the Scottsboro boys and the Herndon Case, and I was aware of both. I had to be; I myself had been taken off a freight train at Decatur, Alabama, only three years before while on my way to Tuskegee. But while I joined in the agitation for their release, my main energies went into learning to write.

I began to publish enough, and not too slowly, to justify my hopes for success, and as I continued, I made a most perplexing discovery; namely, that for all his conscious concern with technique, a writer did not so much create the novel as he was created *by* the novel. That is, one did not make an arbitrary gesture when one sought to write. And when I say that the novelist is created by the novel, I mean to remind you that fictional techniques are not a mere set of objective tools, but something much more intimate: a way of feeling, of seeing and of expressing one's sense of life. And the process of *acquiring* technique is a process of modifying one's responses, of learning to see and feel, to hear and observe, to evoke and evaluate the images of memory and of summoning up and directing the imagination; of learning to conceive of human values in the ways which have been established by the great writers who have developed and extended the art. And perhaps the writer's greatest freedom, as artist, lies precisely in his possession of technique; for it is through technique that he comes to possess and express the meaning of his life.

Perhaps at this point it would be useful to recapitulate the route—perhaps as mazelike as those of *Finnegan's Wake*—which I have been trying to describe, that which leads from the writer's discovery of a sense of purpose, which is that of becoming a writer, and then the involvement in the passionate struggle required to master a bit of technique, and then, as this begins to take shape, the disconcerting discovery that it is *technique* which transforms the individual before he is able in turn to transform it. And in that personal transformation he discovers something else: he discovers that he has taken on certain obligations, that he must not embarrass his chosen form, and that in order to avoid this he must develop taste. He learns—and this is most discouraging—that he is involved with values which turn in their *own* way, and not in the ways of politics, upon the central issues affecting his nation and his time. He learns that the American novel, from its first consciousness of itself as a literary form, has grappled with the meaning of the American experience, that it has been aware and has sought to define the nature of that experience by addressing itself to the specific details, the moods, the landscapes, the city-scapes, the tempo of American change. And that it has borne, at its best, the full weight of that burden of conscience and con-sciousness which Americans inherit as one of the results of the revolutionary circumstances of our national beginnings.

We began as a nation not through the accidents of race or religion or geography (Robert Penn Warren has dwelled on these circumstances) but when a group of men, *some* of them political philosophers, put down, upon what we now recognize as being quite sacred papers, their conception of the nation which they intended to establish on these shores. They described, as we know, the obligations of the state to the citizen, of the citizen to the state;

they committed themselves to certain ideas of justice, just as they committed us to a system which would guarantee all of its citizens equality of opportunity.

I need not describe the problems which have arisen from these beginnings. I need only remind you that the contradiction between these noble ideals and the actualities of our conduct generated a guilt, an unease of spirit, from the very beginning, and that the American novel at its best has always been concerned with this basic moral predicament. During Melville's time and Twain's, it was an implicit aspect of their major themes, by the twentieth century and after the discouraging and traumatic effect of the Civil War and the Reconstruction it had gone underground, had become *understated*. Nevertheless it did not disappear completely and it is to be found operating in the work of Henry James as well as in that of Hemingway and Fitzgerald. And then (and as one who believes in the impelling moral function of the novel and who believes in the moral seriousness of the form) it pleases me no end that it comes into explicit statement again in the works of Richard Wright and William Faulkner, writers who lived close to moral and political problems which would not stay put underground.

I go into these details not to recapitulate the history of the American novel but to indicate the trend of thought which was set into motion when I began to discover the nature of that process with which I was actually involved. Whatever the opinions and decisions of critics, a novelist must arrive at his own conclusions as to the meaning and function of the form with which he is engaged, and these are, in all modesty, some of mine.

In order to orient myself I also began to learn that the American novel had long concerned itself with the puzzle of the one-and-the-many; the mystery of how each of us, despite his origin in diverse regions, with our diverse racial, cultural, religious backgrounds, speaking his own diverse idiom of the American in his own accent, is, nevertheless, American. And with this concern with the implicit pluralism of the country and with the composite nature of the ideal character called "the American," there goes a concern with gauging the health of the American promise, with depicting the extent to which it was being achieved, being made manifest in our daily conduct.

And with all of this there still remained the specific concerns of literature. Among these is the need to keep literary standards high, the necessity of exploring new possibilities of language which would allow it to retain that flexibility and fidelity to the common speech which has been its glory since Mark Twain. For me this meant learning to add to it the wonderful resources of Negro American speech and idiom and to bring into range as fully and eloquently as possible the complex reality of the American experience as it shaped and was shaped by the lives of my own people.

Notice that I stress as "fully" as possible, because I would no more strive to write great novels by leaving out the complexity of circumstances which go to make up the Negro experience and which alone go to make the obvious injustice bearable, than I would think of preparing myself to become President of the United States simply by studying Negro American history or confining myself to studying those laws affecting civil rights.

For it seems to me that one of the obligations I took on when I committed myself to the art and form of the novel was that of striving for the broadest range, the discovery and articulation of the most exalted values. And I must squeeze these from the life which I know best. (A highly truncated impression of that life I attempted to convey to you earlier.)

If all this sounds a bit heady, remember that I did not destroy that troublesome middle name of mine, I only suppressed it. Sometimes it reminds me of my obligations to the man who named me.

It is our fate as human beings always to give up some good things for other good things, to throw off certain bad circumstances only to create others. Thus there is a value for the writer in trying to give as thorough a report of social reality as possible. Only by doing so may we grasp and convey the cost of change. Only by considering the broadest accumulation of data may we make choices that are based upon our own hard-earned sense of reality. Speaking from my own special area of American culture, I feel that to embrace uncritically values which are extended to us by others is to reject the validity, even the sacredness, of our own experience. It is also to forget that the small share of reality which each of our diverse groups is able to snatch from the whirling chaos of history belongs not to the group alone, but to all of us. It is a property and a witness which can be ignored only to the danger of the entire nation.

I could suppress the name of my namesake out of respect for the achievements of its original bearer but I cannot escape the obligation of attempting to achieve some of the things which he asked of the American writer. As Henry James suggested, being an American is an arduous task, and for most of us, I suspect, the difficulty begins with the name.

JAMES BALDWIN

1924-

James Baldwin has created a vivid and lasting portrait of urban Negro life in mid-twentieth century America. His fiction explores the personal lives of Negroes in an authoritative way; his essays are among the finest polemics of our generation, part of the permanent record of racial relations in this country. Baldwin's work describes a search for identity—the word is one of the author's favorites—that is really the quest for an ideality in which love, public and personal, has triumphed over hatred, bigotry, and oppression. As an idealist who has known the realities of life in a city ghetto, Baldwin has formulated a cogent criticism of American culture in our time.

Born in New York on August 2, 1924, Baldwin was the first of nine children. His early life was dominated by an authoritarian father who, as a minister in the church, insisted upon strict religious behavior in his family. Baldwin himself became a minister at the age of fourteen, but by the time of his graduation from high school in 1942, he had decided to leave the church, the community of Harlem, and his family. Encouraged in his writing by Richard Wright, whose "work was an immense liberation and revelation" for him, Baldwin won the Eugene F. Saxton Memorial Trust Award for an early draft of *Go Tell It on the Mountain*; and during the next few years he struggled with his first novel and with his early essays.

Baldwin felt that he could not develop as an artist in America.

He wanted greater aesthetic distance from the racial problems that formed the substance of his formative work, and he went to Paris in 1948. His expatriation, which lasted for almost ten years, permitted him to view his youth with an objectivity that characterizes his early writing and makes it a thoughtful record as well as a protest of the Negro's place in American society. In 1953 he published *Go Tell It on the Mountain*, a lyrical, poignant novel dealing with his early religious experiences in Harlem and the former lives of his family in the South; in 1956 he brought out *Notes of a Native Son*, and, as the title suggests, the essays describe the lives of Negroes in the generation following that of Richard Wright; in the same year Baldwin published *Giovanni's Room*, a novel which avoids racial problems altogether—the characters are white, the setting is France, and the theme concerns a young American's discovery that he is a homosexual.

When Baldwin returned to America in 1958, he became a literary spokesman on Negro problems. His writing grew more militant and pugnacious, more directly tendentious. The essays of *Nobody Knows My Name* (1961) had been written over a five-year period and recall in mood and theme the earlier pieces in *Notes of a Native Son* (1956); but in the 1960's Baldwin's point of view, tone, and style changed sharply. In 1962 he published his third novel, *Another Country*; in 1963, the long essay, *The Fire Next Time*; in 1964, the sociological drama, *Blues for Mr. Charlie*; and in 1968, his last novel, *Tell Me How Long the Train's Been Gone*. These works are more threatening, hortatory, and evangelical than anything Baldwin had previously written; they are protests as violent as those of his predecessor, Richard Wright, whom Baldwin had once found artistically limited because of Wright's tendency to use the characters of fiction as types. In *Going to Meet the Man* (1965), a collection of short stories that span Baldwin's entire career, one can trace his movement away from those early impressionistic sketches that ultimately became the novel, *Go Tell It on the Mountain*, to his hostile and thinly disguised political satire, "Going to Meet the Man."

Baldwin's career is marked by his persistent attempt to cast aside inherited superstitions, inherited religious attitudes which have never convinced him that he could achieve the freedom and the love he sought in life. From a youth governed by the strict Protestant orthodoxy of his father, Baldwin has now turned to the more sensual aspects of the life immediately around him. "It now seems," as he writes in *The Fire Next Time*, that "if the concept of God has any validity or any use, it can only be to make us larger, freer, and more loving. If God cannot do this, then it is time we got rid of Him." His early essays—"Notes of a Native Son," "Stranger in the Village," "Fifth Avenue, Uptown," "The Harlem Ghetto"—are an attempt to search beneath those abstractions—freedom, equality, moral and social improvement—that the white man champions and that determine what is actually the American reality. One of Baldwin's most compelling qualities is this persistent attempt to remove all the masks that Americans wear, to strip the country of its self-created illusions, and to speak the simple, often painful truth.

Notes of a Native Son, Nobody Knows My Name, and The Fire Next Time achieve their distinction through their point of view, style, and moral urgency. In writing his early essays, Baldwin assumes the white man's angle of vision and thus implicates the reader in his indictment of American society. He speaks for America rather than to America and demonstrates implicitly as well as explicitly that color itself is not a reality but only a symbol of some inward reality, that our reaction to the Negro is one way of measuring our own moral condition: "It is a terrible, an inexorable, law," he concludes in "Fifth Avenue, Uptown," "that one cannot deny the humanity of another without diminishing one's own: in the face of one's victim, one sees oneself. Walk through the streets of Harlem and see what we, this nation, have become." This point of view, which helps to control a natural tendency toward sentimentality and bombast, is not so firm in The Fire Next Time as it is in the earlier essays, for Baldwin's posture assumes prophetic, priest-like proportions; the essayist points his accusatory finger at his readers and sacrifices his artistic distance, his practical effectiveness, for a role that is more immediate and intense, more socially rooted.

Baldwin's eloquent, forceful style has given his work its wide recognition. The intricate, convoluted sentences; the musical, sinuous rhythms of the prose; the dramatic stance, poised between a straightforward rendition of the facts and a lyrical interpretation of them; the oratorical cadences of clauses within clauses—all these characteristics contribute to a style that is immediately recognizable, the inimitable signature of an absolutely lucid vision. But Baldwin's style is more than a fit instrument for his ideas. It is the living illustration of what can be achieved by a Negro who has existed in a culturally constricting environment; and in its discussion of oppression, racial segregation, inadequate social and cultural opportunities, its sophisticated grace serves as ironic commentary on the problems it considers.

The last significant quality of Baldwin's work that we might note is its sense of moral urgency. In The Fire Next Time, Baldwin suggests that "to be born, in a white country, an Anglo-Teutonic, anti-sexual country, black is to realize the great necessity for some, for any gimmick—even if it is the religion of one's ancestors, borrowed from the white world." At an early age, Baldwin knew that he had to discover "a gimmick, to lift him out, to start him on his way"; and the gimmick he used "was his career in the church." The religion of this church has been enormously influential on Baldwin's writing, but it is the music of the religion, the fire and excitement that have lingered, and not the essence. Still, in terms of form and technique, theological overtones can be felt everywhere in his work. *The Fire Next Time* is, in many ways, a sermon; *Blues for Mr. Charlie* is, in its more effective moments, a morality play. Indeed one of the central problems in Baldwin's novels, most obviously illustrated in *Another Country*, is the conflict between naturalistic and transcendental elements. When these elements are in a moral tension, as in *Go Tell It on the Mountain*, Baldwin's achievement is impressive, but when the naturalistic elements become dominant, his fiction can become harsh, grating, or embarrassingly sentimental, as in *Giovanni's Room* and *Another Country*. The idea commands our respect, but it tends to be more important than the characters who represent the idea; conception and form have not yet coalesced.

Whatever limitations we may attribute to Baldwin's work, his considerable achievement is already clear. He is one of the finest essayists of twentieth-century literature, an artist who has broadened the scope of racial issues on the political and social levels and deepened these issues in human, personal terms. His most successful essays—"Everybody's Protest Novel," "Notes of a Native Son," "Stranger in the Village," "The Harlem Ghetto," "Fifth Avenue, Uptown," "Nobody Knows My Name," and "The Fire Next Time"—are a permanent and unique contribution to American literature.

At its best, Baldwin's cultural criticism suggests the public significance of his personal dilemmas. In "Notes of a Native Son," for example, the private relationship of Baldwin and his father is viewed in the public context of the 1943 race riot in Harlem: the father's deep commitment to religion does not relate to external reality, and the boy's absolute rejection of his inherited moral view is dramatically meaningful and justified. The essay is particularly significant to an understanding of Baldwin's development, for it concentrates upon that moment when the artist becomes aware of his father's legacy. "Nothing is ever escaped," he realizes; but the religious context of his father's statement becomes, in Baldwin's terms, the existentialist's axiom of life.

One of the commonplaces of literary criticism is that Baldwin's essays are more successful than his novels and stories, even though he has considered himself primarily a novelist. But this observation is only accurate because of Baldwin's high achievement as an essayist: *Go Tell It on the Mountain* is a compelling lyric novel which recounts the author's early Harlem days without sentimentality; parts of *Another Country* express the bitterness of urban Negroes in a direct and forceful manner; and short stories like "Sonny's Blues" dramatize the various ways in which people choose to survive in a world that always threatens, in Baldwin's words, "to smash" them.

In "Sonny's Blues" Baldwin has focused upon the significant conflict between a Negro who has accepted the moral and social terms of a white society and his younger brother who challenges those terms. It is a particularly powerful story, for it suggests the frailty of Sonny without making him seem pathetic.

Notes of a Native Son

ON THE 29TH OF JULY, in 1943, my father died. On the same day, a few hours later, his last child was born. Over a month before this, while all our energies were concentrated in waiting for these events, there had been, in Detroit, one of the bloodiest race riots of the century. A few hours after my father's funeral, while he lay in state in the undertaker's chapel, a race riot broke out in Harlem. On the morning of the 3rd of August, we drove my father to the graveyard through a wilderness of smashed plate glass.

The day of my father's funeral had also been my nineteenth birthday. As we drove him to the graveyard, the spoils of injustice, anarchy, discontent, and hatred were all around us. It seemed to me that God himself had devised, to mark my father's end, the most sustained and brutally dissonant of codas. And it seemed to me, too, that the violence which rose all about us as my father left the world had been devised as a corrective for the pride of his eldest son. I had declined to believe in that apocalypse which had been central to my father's vision; very well, life seemed to be saying, here is something that will certainly pass for an apocalypse until the real thing comes along. I had inclined to be contemptuous of my father for the conditions of his life, for the conditions of our lives. When his life had ended I began to wonder about that life and also, in a new way, to be apprehensive about my own.

I had not known my father very well. We had got on badly, partly because we shared, in our different fashions, the vice of stubborn pride. When he was dead I realized that I had hardly ever spoken to him. When he had been dead a long time I began to wish I had. It seems to be typical of life in America, where opportunities, real and fancied, are thicker than anywhere else on the globe, that the second generation has no time to talk to the first. No one, including my father, seems to have known exactly how old he was, but his mother had been born during slavery. He was of the first generation of free men. He, along with thousands of other Negroes, came North after 1919 and I was part of that generation which had never seen the landscape of what Negroes sometimes call the Old Country.

He had been born in New Orleans and had been a quite young

Reprinted from *Notes of a Native Son*, by James Baldwin (Boston: Beacon Press, 1955). Reprinted by permission of the Beacon Press, © 1955 by James Baldwin.

man there during the time that Louis Armstrong, a boy, was running errands for the dives and honky-tonks of what was always presented to me as one of the most wicked of cities—to this day, whenever I think of New Orleans, I also helplessly think of Sodom and Gomorrah. My father never mentioned Louis Armstrong, except to forbid us to play his records; but there was a picture of him on our wall for a long time. One of my father's strong-willed female relatives had placed it there and forbade my father to take it down. He never did, but he eventually maneuvered her out of the house and when, some years later, she was in trouble and near death, he refused to do anything to help her.

He was, I think, very handsome. I gather this from photographs and from my own memories of him, dressed in his Sunday best and on his way to preach a sermon somewhere, when I was little. Handsome, proud, and ingrown, "like a toe-nail," somebody said. But he looked to me, as I grew older, like pictures I had seen of African tribal chieftains: he really should have been naked, with war-paint on and barbaric mementos, standing among spears. He could be chilling in the pulpit and indescribably cruel in his personal life and he was certainly the most bitter man I have ever met; yet it must be said that there was something else in him, buried in him, which lent him his tremendous power and, even, a rather crushing charm. It had something to do with his blackness, I think—he was very black—with his blackness and his beauty, and with the fact that he knew that he was black but did not know that he was beautiful. He claimed to be proud of his blackness but it had also been the cause of much humiliation and it had fixed bleak boundaries to his life. He was not a young man when we were growing up and he had already suffered many kinds of ruin; in his outrageously demanding and protective way he loved his children, who were black like him and menaced, like him; and all these things sometimes showed in his face when he tried, never to my knowledge with any success, to establish contact with any of us. When he took one of his children on his knee to play, the child always became fretful and began to cry; when he tried to help one of us with our homework the absolutely unabating tension which emanated from him caused our minds and our tongues to become paralyzed, so that he, scarcely knowing why, flew into a rage and the child, not knowing why, was punished. If it ever entered his head to bring a surprise home for his children, it was, almost unfailingly, the wrong surprise and even the big watermelons he often brought home on his back in the summertime led to the most appalling scenes. I do not remember, in all those years, that one of his children was ever glad to see him come home. From what I was able to gather of his early life, it seemed that this inability to establish contact with other people had always marked him and had been one of the things which had driven him out of New Orleans. There was something in him, therefore, groping and tentative, which was never expressed and which was buried with him. One saw it most clearly when he was facing new people and hoping to impress them. But he never did, not for long. We went from church to smaller and more improbable church, he found himself in less and less demand as a minister, and by the time he died none of his friends had come to see him for a long time. He had lived and died in an intolerable bitterness of spirit and it frightened me, as we drove him to the graveyard through those unquiet, ruined streets, to see how powerful and overflowing this bitterness could be and to realize that this bitterness now was mine.

When he died I had been away from home for a little over a year. In that year I had had time to become aware of the meaning of all my father's bitter warnings, had discovered the secret of his proudly pursed lips and rigid carriage: I had discovered the weight of white people in the world. I saw that this had been for my ancestors and now would be for me an awful thing to live with and that the bitterness which had helped to kill my father could also kill me.

He had been ill a long time—in the mind, as we now realize, reliving instances of his fantastic intransigence in the new light of his affliction and endeavoring to feel a sorrow for him which never, quite, came true. We had not known that he was being eaten up by paranoia, and the discovery that his cruelty, to our bodies and our minds, had been one of the symptoms of his illness was not, then, enough to enable us to forgive him. The younger children felt, quite simply, relief that he would not be coming home anymore. My mother's observation that it was he, after all, who had kept them alive all these years meant nothing because the problems of keeping children alive are not real for children. The older children felt, with my father gone, that they could invite their friends to the house without fear that their friends would be insulted or, as had sometimes happened with me, being told that their friends were in league with the devil and intended to rob our family of everything we owned. (I didn't fail to wonder, and it made me hate him, what on earth we owned that anybody else would want.)

His illness was beyond all hope of healing before anyone realized that he was ill. He had always been so strange and had lived, like a prophet, in such unimaginably close communion with the Lord that his long silences which were punctuated by moans and hallelujahs and snatches of old songs while he sat at the living-room window never seemed odd to us. It was not until he refused to eat because, he said, his family was trying to poison him that my mother was forced to accept as a fact what had, until then, been only an unwilling suspicion. When he was committed, it was discovered that he had tuberculosis and, as it turned out, the disease of his mind allowed the disease of his body to destroy him. For the doctors could not force him to eat, either, and, though he was fed intravenously, it was clear from the beginning that there was no hope for him.

In my mind's eye I could see him, sitting at the window, locked up in his terrors; hating and fearing every living soul including his children who had betrayed him, too, by reaching towards the world which had despised him. There were nine of us. I began to wonder what it could have felt like for such a man to have had nine children whom he could barely feed. He used to make little jokes about our poverty, which never, of course, seemed very funny to us; they could not have seemed very funny to him, either, or else our all too feeble response to them would never have caused such rages. He spent great energy and achieved, to our chagrin, no small amount of success in keeping us away from the people who surrounded us, people who had all-night rent parties to which we listened when we should have been sleeping, people who cursed and drank and flashed razor blades on Lenox Avenue. He could not understand why, if they had so much energy to spare, they could not use it to make their lives better. He treated almost everybody on our block with a most uncharitable asperity and neither they, nor, of course, their children were slow to reciprocate.

The only white people who came to our house were welfare workers and bill collectors. It was almost always my mother who dealt with them, for my father's temper, which was at the mercy of his pride, was never to be trusted. It was clear that he felt their very presence in his home to be a violation: this was conveyed by his carriage, almost ludicrously stiff, and by his voice, harsh and vindictively polite. When I was around nine or ten I wrote a play which was directed by a young, white schoolteacher, a woman, who then took an interest in me, and gave me books to read and, in order to corroborate my theatrical bent, decided to take me to see what she somewhat tactlessly referred to as "real" plays. Theater-going was forbidden in our house, but, with the really cruel intuitiveness of a child, I suspected that the color of this woman's skin would carry the day for me. When, at school, she suggested taking me to the theater, I did not, as I might have done if she had been a Negro, find a way of discouraging her, but agreed that she should pick me up at my house one evening. I then, very cleverly, left all the rest to my mother, who suggested to my father, as I knew she would, that it would not be very nice to let such a kind woman make the trip for nothing. Also, since it was a schoolteacher, I imagine that my mother countered the idea of sin with the idea of "education," which word, even with my father, carried a kind of bitter weight.

Before the teacher came my father took me aside to ask *why* she was coming, what *interest* she could possibly have in our house, in a boy like me. I said I didn't know but I, too, suggested that it had something to do with education. And I understood that my father was waiting for me to say something—I didn't quite know what; perhaps that I wanted his protection against this teacher and her "education." I said none of these things and the teacher came and we went out. It was clear, during the brief interview in our living room, that my father was agreeing very much against his will and that he would have refused permission if he had dared. The fact that he did not dare caused me to despise him: I had no way of knowing that he was facing in that living room a wholly unprecedented and frightening situation.

Later, when my father had been laid off from his job, this woman became very important to us. She was really a very sweet and generous woman and went to a great deal of trouble to be of help to us, particularly during one awful winter. My mother called her by the highest name she knew: she said she was a "christian." My father could scarcely disagree but during the four or five years of our relatively close association he never trusted her and was always trying to surprise in her open, Midwestern face the genuine, cunningly hidden, and hideous motivation. In later years, particularly when it began to be clear that this "education" of mine was going to lead me to perdition, he became more explicit and warned me that my white friends in high school were not really my friends and that I would see, when I was older, how white people would do anything to keep a Negro down. Some of them could be nice, he admitted, but none of them were to be trusted and most of them were not even nice. The best thing was to have as little to do with them as possible. I did not feel this way and I was certain, in my innocence, that I never would.

But the year which preceded my father's death had made a great change in my life. I had been living in New Jersey, working in defense plants, working and living among southerners, white and black. I knew about the south, of course, and about how southerners treated Negroes and how they expected them to behave, but it had never entered my mind that anyone would look at me and expect *me* to behave that way. I learned in New Jersey that to be a Negro meant, precisely, that one was never looked at but was simply at the mercy of the reflexes the color of one's skin caused in other people. I acted in New Jersey as I had always acted, that is as though I thought a great deal of myself—I had to *act* that way—with results that were, simply, unbelievable. I had scarcely arrived before I had earned the enmity, which was extraordinarily ingenious, of all my superiors and nearly all my co-workers. In the beginning, to make matters worse, I simply did not know what was happening. I did not know what I had done, and I shortly began to wonder what *anyone* could possibly do, to bring about such unanimous, active, and unbearably vocal hostility. I knew about jim-crow but I had never experienced it. I went to the same self-service restaurant three times and stood with all the Princeton boys before the counter, waiting for a hamburger and coffee; it was always an extraordinarily long time before anything was set before me; but it was not until the fourth visit that I learned that, in fact, nothing had ever been set before me: I had simply picked something up. Negroes were not served there, I was told, and they had been waiting for me to realize that I was always the only Negro present. Once I was told this, I determined to go there all the time. But now they were ready for me and, though some dreadful scenes were subsequently enacted in that restaurant, I never ate there again.

It was the same story all over New Jersey, in bars, bowling alleys, diners, place to live. I was always being forced to leave, silently, or with mutual imprecations. I very shortly became notorious and children giggled behind me when I passed and their elders whispered or shouted—they really believed that I was mad. And it did begin to work on my mind, of course; I began to be afraid to go anywhere and to compensate for this I went places to which I really should not have gone and where, God knows, I had no desire to be. My reputation in town naturally enhanced my reputation at work and my working day became one long series of acrobatics designed to keep me out of trouble. I cannot say that these acrobatics succeeded. It began to seem that the machinery of the organization I worked for was turning over, day and night, with but one aim: to eject me. I was fired once, and contrived, with the aid of a friend from New York, to get back on the payroll; was fired again, and bounced back again. It took a while to fire me for the third time, but the third time took. There were no loopholes anywhere. There was not even any way of getting back inside the gates.

That year in New Jersey lives in my mind as though it were the year during which, having an unsuspected predilection for it,

I first contracted some dread, chronic disease, the unfailing symptom of which is a kind of blind fever, a pounding in the skull and fire in the bowels. Once this disease is contracted, one can never be really carefree again, for the fever, without an instant's warning, can recur at any moment. It can wreck more important things than race relations. There is not a Negro alive who does not have this rage in the blood—one has the choice, merely, of living with it consciously or surrendering to it. As for me, this fever has recurred in me, and does, and will until the day I die.

My last night in New Jersey, a white friend from New York took me to the nearest big town, Trenton, to go to the movies and have a few drinks. As it turned out, he also saved me from, at the very least, a violent whipping. Almost every detail of that night stands out very clearly in my memory. I even remember the name of the movie we saw because its title impressed me as being so patly ironical. It was a movie about the German occupation of France, starring Maureen O'Hara and Charles Laughton and called *This Land Is Mine*. I remember the name of the diner we walked into when the movie ended: it was the "American Diner." When we walked in the counterman asked what we wanted and I remember answering with the casual sharpness which had become my habit: "We want a hamburger and a cup of coffee, what do you think we want?" I do not know why, after a year of such rebuffs, I so completely failed to anticipate his answer, which was, of course, "We don't serve Negroes here." This reply failed to discompose me, at least for the moment. I made some sardonic comment about the name of the diner and we walked out into the streets.

This was the time of what was called the "brownout," when the lights in all American cities were very dim. When we re-entered the streets something happened to me which had the force of an optical illusion, or a nightmare. The streets were very crowded and I was facing north. People were moving in every direction but it seemed to me, in that instant, that all of the people I could see, and many more than that, were moving toward me, against me, and that everyone was white. I remember how their faces gleamed. And I felt, like a physical sensation, a *click* at the nape of my neck as though some interior string connecting my head to my body had been cut. I began to walk. I heard my friend call after me, but I ignored him. Heaven only knows what was going on in his mind, but he had the good sense not to touch me—I don't know what would have happened if he had—and to keep me in sight. I don't know what was going on in my mind, either; I certainly had no conscious plan. I wanted to do something to crush these white faces, which were crushing me. I walked for perhaps a block or two until I came to an enormous, glittering, and fashionable restaurant in which I knew not even the intercession of the Virgin would cause me to be served. I pushed through the doors and took the first vacant seat I saw, at a table for two, and waited.

I do not know how long I waited and I rather wonder, until today, what I could possibly have looked like. Whatever I looked like, I frightened the waitress who shortly appeared, and the moment she appeared all of my fury flowed towards her. I hated her for her white face, and for her great, astounded, frightened eyes. I felt that if she found a black man so frightening I would make her fright worth-while.

She did not ask me what I wanted, but repeated, as though she had learned it somewhere, "We don't serve Negroes here." She did not say it with the blunt, derisive hostility to which I had grown so accustomed, but, rather, with a note of apology in her voice, and fear. This made me colder and more murderous than ever. I felt I had to do something with my hands. I wanted her to come close enough for me to get her neck between my hands.

So I pretended not to have understood her, hoping to draw her closer. And she did step a very short step closer, with her pencil poised incongruously over her pad, and repeated the formula: ". . . don't serve Negroes here."

Somehow, with the repetition of that phrase, which was already ringing in my head like a thousand bells of a nightmare, I realized that she would never come any closer and that I would have to strike from a distance. There was nothing on the table but an ordinary water-mug half full of water, and I picked this up and hurled it with all my strength at her. She ducked and it missed her and shattered against the mirror behind the bar. And, with that sound, my frozen blood abruptly thawed, I returned from wherever I had been, I *saw*, for the first time, the restaurant, the people with their mouths open, already, as it seemed to me, rising as one man, and I realized what I had done, and where I was, and I was frightened. I rose and began running for the door. A round, potbellied man grabbed me by the nape of the neck just as I reached the doors and began to beat me about the face. I kicked him and got loose and ran into the streets. My friend whispered, *"Run!"* and I ran.

My friend stayed outside the restaurant long enough to misdirect my pursuers and the police, who arrived, he told me, at once. I do not know what I said to him when he came to my room that night. I could not have said much. I felt, in the oddest, most awful way, that I had somehow betrayed him. I lived it over and over and over again, the way one relives an automobile accident after it has happened and one finds oneself alone and safe. I could not get over two facts, both equally difficult for the imagination to grasp, and one was that I could have been murdered. But the other was that I had been ready to commit murder. I saw nothing very clearly but I did see this: that my life, my *real* life, was in danger, and not from anything other people might do but from the hatred I carried in my own heart.

II

I had returned home around the second week in June—in great haste because it seemed that my father's death and my mother's confinement were both but a matter of hours. In the case of my mother, it soon became clear that she had simply made a miscalculation. This had always been her tendency and I don't believe that a single one of us arrived in the world, or has since arrived anywhere else, on time. But none of us dawdled so intolerably about the business of being born as did my baby sister. We sometimes amused ourselves, during those endless, stifling weeks, by picturing the baby sitting within in the safe, warm dark, bitterly regretting the necessity of becoming a part of our chaos and stubbornly putting it off as long as possible. I understood her perfectly and congratulated her on showing such good sense so soon. Death, however, sat as purposefully at my father's bedside as life stirred within my mother's womb and it was harder to understand why he so lingered in that long shadow. It seemed that he had bent, and for a long time, too, all of his energies toward dying. Now death was ready for him but my father held back.

All of Harlem, indeed, seemed to be infected by waiting. I had never before known it to be so violently still. Racial tensions throughout this country were exacerbated during the early years of the war, partly because the labor market brought together hundreds of thousands of ill-prepared people and partly because Negro soldiers, regardless of where they were born, received their military training in the south. What happened in defense plants and army camps had repercussions, naturally, in every Negro ghetto. The situation in Harlem had grown bad enough for clergymen, policemen, educators, politicians, and social workers to assert in one breath that there was no "crime wave" and to offer, in the very next breath, suggestions as to how to combat it. These suggestions always seemed to involve playgrounds, despite the fact that racial skirmishes were occurring in the playgrounds, too. Playground or not, crime wave or not, the Harlem police force had been augmented in March, and the unrest grew—perhaps, in fact, partly as a result of the ghetto's instinctive hatred of policemen. Perhaps the most revealing news item, out of the steady parade of reports of muggings, stabbings, shootings, assaults, gang wars, and accusations of police brutality, is the item concerning six Negro girls who set upon a white girl in the subway because, as they all too accurately put it, she was stepping on their toes. Indeed she was, all over the nation.

I had never before been so aware of policemen, on foot, on horseback, on corners, everywhere, always two by two. Nor had I ever been so aware of small knots of people. They were on stoops and on corners and in doorways, and what was striking about them, I think, was that they did not seem to be talking. Never, when I passed these groups, did the usual sound of a curse or a laugh ring out and neither did there seem to be any hum of gossip. There was certainly, on the other hand, occurring between them communication extraordinarily intense. Another thing that was striking was the unexpected diversity of the people who made up these groups. Usually, for example, one would see a group of sharpies standing on the street corner, jiving the passing chicks; or a group of older men, usually, for some reason, in the vicinity of a barber shop, discussing baseball scores, or the numbers, or making rather chilling observations about women they had known. Women, in a general way, tended to be seen less often together—unless they were church women, or very young girls, or prostitutes met together for an unprofessional instant. But that summer I saw the strangest combinations: large, respectable, churchly matrons standing on the stoops or the corners with their hair tied up, together with a girl in sleazy satin whose face bore the marks of gin and the razor, or heavy-set, abrupt, no-nonsense older men, in company with the most disreputable and fanatical "race" men, or these same "race" men with the sharpies, or these sharpies with the churchly women. Seventh Day Adventists and Methodists and Spiritualists seemed to be hobnobbing with Holyrollers and they were all, alike, entangled with the most flagrant disbelievers; something heavy in their stance seemed to indicate that they had all, incredibly, seen a common vision, and on each face there seemed to be the same strange, bitter shadow.

The churchly women and the matter-of-fact, no-nonsense men had children in the Army. The sleazy girls they talked to had lovers there, the sharpies and the "race" men had friends and brothers there. It would have demanded an unquestioning patriotism, happily as uncommon in this country as it is undesirable, for these people not to have been disturbed by the bitter letters they received, by the newspaper stories they read, not to have been enraged by the posters, then to be found all over New York, which described the Japanese as "yellow-bellied Japs." It was only the "race" men, to be sure, who spoke ceaselessly of being revenged—how this vengeance was to be exacted was not clear—for the indignities and dangers suffered by Negro boys in uniform; but everybody felt a directionless, hopeless bitterness, as well as that panic which can scarcely be suppressed when one knows that a human being one loves is beyond one's reach, and in danger. This helplessness and this gnawing uneasiness does something, at length, to even the toughest mind. Perhaps the best way to sum all this up is to say that the people I knew felt, mainly, a peculiar kind of relief when they knew that their boys were being shipped out of the south, to do battle overseas. It was, perhaps, like feeling that the most dangerous part of a dangerous journey had been passed and that now, even if death should come, it would come with honor and without the complicity of their countrymen. Such a death would be, in short, a fact with which one could hope to live.

It was on the 28th of July, which I believe was a Wednesday, that I visited my father for the first time during his illness and for the last time in his life. The moment I saw him I knew why I had put off this visit so long. I had told my mother that I did not want to see him because I hated him. But this was not true. It was only that I *had* hated him and I wanted to hold on to this hatred. I did not want to look on him as a ruin: it was not a ruin I had hated. I imagine that one of the reasons people cling to their hates so stubbornly is because they sense, once hate is gone, that they will be forced to deal with pain.

We traveled out to him, his older sister and myself, to what seemed to be the very end of a very Long Island. It was hot and dusty and we wrangled, my aunt and I, all the way out, over the fact that I had recently begun to smoke and, as she said, to give myself airs. But I knew that she wrangled with me because she could not bear to face the fact of her brother's dying. Neither could I endure the reality of her despair, her unstated bafflement as to what had happened to her brother's life, and her own. So we wrangled and I smoked and from time to time she fell into a heavy reverie. Covertly, I watched her face, which was the face of an old woman; it had fallen in, the eyes were sunken and lightless; soon she would be dying, too.

In my childhood—it had not been so long ago—I had thought her beautiful. She had been quick-witted and quick-moving and very generous with all the children and each of her visits had been an event. At one time one of my brothers and myself had thought of running away to live with her. Now she could no longer produce out of her handbag some unexpected and yet familiar delight. She made me feel pity and revulsion and fear. It was awful to realize that she no longer caused me to feel affection. The closer we came to the hospital the more querulous she became and at the same time, naturally, grew more dependent on me. Between pity and guilt and fear I began to feel that there was another me trapped in my skull like a jack-in-the-box who might escape my control at any moment and fill the air with screaming.

She began to cry the moment we entered the room and she saw him lying there, all shriveled and still, like a little black monkey. The great, gleaming apparatus which fed him and would have compelled him to be still even if he had been able to move brought to mind, not beneficence, but torture; the tubes entering his arm made me think of pictures I had seen when a child, of Gulliver, tied down by the pygmies on that island. My aunt wept and wept, there was a whistling sound in my father's throat; nothing was said; he could not speak. I wanted to take his hand, to say something. But I do not know what I could have said, even if he could have heard me. He was not really in that room with us, he had at last really embarked on his journey; and though my aunt told me that he said he was going to meet Jesus, I did not hear anything except that whistling in his throat. The doctor came back and we left, into that unbearable train again, and home. In the morning came the telegram saying that he was dead. Then the house was suddenly full of relatives, friends, hysteria, and confusion and I quickly left my mother and the children to the care of those impressive women, who, in Negro communities at least, automatically appear at times of bereavement armed with lotions, proverbs, and patience, and an ability to cook. I went downtown. By the time I returned, later the same day, my mother had been carried to the hospital and the baby had been born.

III

For my father's funeral I had nothing black to wear and this posed a nagging problem all day long. It was one of those problems, simple, or impossible of solution, to which the mind insanely clings in order to avoid the mind's real trouble. I spent most of that day at the downtown apartment of a girl I knew, celebrating my birthday with whiskey and wondering what to wear that night. When planning a birthday celebration one naturally does not expect that it will be up against competition from a funeral and this girl had anticipated taking me out that night, for a big dinner and a night club afterwards. Sometime during the course of that long day we decided that we would go out anyway, when my father's funeral service was over. I imagine *I* decided it, since, as the funeral hour approached, it became clearer and clearer to me that I would not know what to do with myself when it was over. The girl, stifling her very lively concern as to the possible effects of the whiskey on one of my father's chief mourners, concentrated on being conciliatory and practically helpful. She found a black shirt for me somewhere and ironed it and, dressed in the darkest pants and jacket I owned, and slightly drunk, I made my way to my father's funeral.

The chapel was full, but not packed, and very quiet. There were, mainly, my father's relatives, and his children, and here and there I saw faces I had not seen since childhood, the faces of my father's one-time friends. They were very dark and solemn now, seeming somehow to suggest that they had known all along that something like this would happen. Chief among the mourners was my aunt, who had quarreled with my father all his life; by which I do not mean to suggest that her mourning was insincere or that she had not loved him. I suppose that she was one of the few people in the world who had, and their incessant quarreling proved precisely the strength of the tie that bound them. The only other person in the world, as far as I knew, whose relationship to my father rivaled my aunt's in depth was my mother, who was not there.

It seemed to me, of course, that it was a very long funeral. But it was, if anything, a rather shorter funeral than most, nor, since there were no overwhelming, uncontrollable expressions of grief, could it be called—if I dare to use the word—successful. The minister who preached my father's funeral sermon was one of the few my father had still been seeing as he neared the end. He presented to us in his sermon a man whom none of us had ever seen—a man thoughtful, patient, and forbearing, a Christian inspiration to all who knew him, and a model for his children. And no doubt the children, in their disturbed and guilty state, were almost ready to believe this; he had been remote enough to be anything and, anyway, the shock of the incontrovertible, that it was really our father lying up there in that casket, prepared the mind for anything. His sister moaned and this grief-stricken moaning was taken as corroboration. The other faces held a dark, noncommittal thoughtfulness. This was not the man they had known, but they had scarcely expected to be confronted with *him;* this was, in a sense deeper than questions of fact, the man they had not known, and the man they had not known may have been the real one. The real man, whoever he had been, had suffered and now he was dead: this was all that was sure and all that mattered now. Every man in the chapel hoped that when his hour came he, too, would be eulogized, which is to say forgiven, and that all of his lapses, greeds, errors, and strayings from the truth would be invested with coherence and looked upon with charity. This was perhaps the last thing human beings could give each other and it was what they demanded, after all, of the Lord. Only the Lord saw the midnight tears, only He was present when one of His children, moaning and wringing hands, paced up and down the room. When one slapped one's child in anger the recoil in the heart reverberated through heaven and became part of the pain of the universe. And when the children were hungry and sullen and distrustful and one watched them, daily, growing wilder, and further away, and running headlong into danger, it was the Lord who knew what the charged heart endured as the strap was laid to the backside; the Lord alone who knew what one *would* have said if one had had, like the Lord, the gift of the living word. It was the Lord who knew of the impossibility every parent in that room faced: how to prepare the child for the day when the child would be despised and how to *create* in the child—by what means?— a stronger antidote to this poison than one had found for oneself. The avenues, side streets, bars, billiard halls, hospitals, police stations, and even the playgrounds of Harlem—not to mention the houses of correction, the jails, and the morgue—testified to the potency of the poison while remaining silent as to the efficacy of whatever antidote, irresistibly raising the question of whether or not such an antidote existed; raising, which was worse, the question of whether or not an antidote was desirable; perhaps poison should be fought with poison. With these several schisms in the mind and with more terrors in the heart than could be named, it was better not to judge the man who had gone down under an impossible burden. It was better to remember: *Thou knowest this man's fall; but thou knowest not his wrassling.*

While the preacher talked and I watched the children—years of changing their diapers, scrubbing them, slapping them, taking them to school, and scolding them had had the perhaps inevitable result of making me love them, though I am not sure I knew this then—my mind was busily breaking out with a rash of disconnected impressions. Snatches of popular songs, indecent jokes, bits of books I had read, movie sequences, faces, voices, political issues—I thought I was going mad; all these impressions suspended, as it were, in the solution of the faint nausea produced in me by the heat and liquor. For a moment I had the impression that my alcoholic breath, inefficiently disguised with chewing gum, filled the entire chapel. Then someone began singing one of my father's favorite songs and, abruptly, I was with him, sitting on his knee, in the hot, enormous, crowded church which was the first church we attended. It was the Abyssinia Baptist Church on 138th Street. We had not gone there long. With this image, a host of others came. I had forgotten, in the rage of my growing up, how proud my father had been of me when I was little. Apparently, I had had a voice and my father had liked to show me off before the members of the church. I had forgotten what he had looked like when he was pleased but now I remembered that he had always been grinning with pleasure when my solos ended. I even remembered certain expressions on his face when he teased my mother—had he loved her? I would never know. And when had it all begun to change? For now it seemed that he had not always been cruel. I remembered being taken for a haircut and scraping my knee on the footrest of the barber's chair and I remembered my father's face as he soothed my crying and applied the stinging iodine. Then I remembered our fights, fights which had been of the worst possible kind because my technique had been silence.

I remembered the one time in all our life together when we had really spoken to each other.

It was on a Sunday and it must have been shortly before I left home. We were walking, just the two of us, in our usual silence, to or from church. I was in high school and had been doing a lot of writing and I was, at about this time, the editor of the high school magazine. But I had also been a Young Minister and had been preaching from the pulpit. Lately, I had been taking fewer engagements and preached as rarely as possible. It was said in the church, quite truthfully, that I was "cooling off."

My father asked me abruptly, "You'd rather write than preach, wouldn't you?"

I was astonished at his question—because it was a real question. I answered, "Yes."

That was all we said. It was awful to remember that that was all we had *ever* said.

The casket now was opened and the mourners were being led up the aisle to look for the last time on the deceased. The assumption was that the family was too overcome with grief to be allowed to make this journey alone and I watched while my aunt was led to the casket and, muffled in black, and shaking, led back to her seat. I disapproved of forcing the children to look on their dead father, considering that the shock of his death, or, more truthfully,

315

the shock of death as a reality, was already a little more than a child could bear, but my judgment in this matter had been overruled and there they were, bewildered and frightened and very small, being led, one by one, to the casket. But there is also something very gallant about children at such moments. It has something to do with their silence and gravity and with the fact that one cannot help them. Their legs, somehow, seem *exposed,* so that it is at once incredible and terribly clear that their legs are all they have to hold them up.

I had not wanted to go to the casket myself and I certainly had not wished to be led there, but there was no way of avoiding either of these forms. One of the deacons led me up and I looked on my father's face. I cannot say that it looked like him at all. His blackness had been equivocated by powder and there was no suggestion in that casket of what his power had or could have been. He was simply an old man dead, and it was hard to believe that he had ever given anyone either joy or pain. Yet, his life filled that room. Further up the avenue his wife was holding his newborn child. Life and death so close together, and love and hatred, and right and wrong, said something to me which I did not want to hear concerning man, concerning the life of man.

After the funeral, while I was downtown desperately celebrating my birthday, a Negro soldier, in the lobby of the Hotel Braddock, got into a fight with a white policeman over a Negro girl. Negro girls, white policemen, in or out of uniform, and Negro males—in or out of uniform—were part of the furniture of the lobby of the Hotel Braddock and this was certainly not the first time such an incident had occurred. It was destined, however, to receive an unprecedented publicity, for the fight between the policeman and the soldier ended with the shooting of the soldier. Rumor, flowing immediately to the streets outside, stated that the soldier had been shot in the back, an instantaneous and revealing invention, and that the soldier had died protecting a Negro woman. The facts were somewhat different—for example, the soldier had not been shot in the back, and was not dead, and the girl seems to have been as dubious a symbol of womanhood as her white counterpart in Georgia usually is, but no one was interested in the facts. They preferred the invention because this invention expressed and corroborated their hates and fears so perfectly. It is just as well to remember that people are always doing this. Perhaps many of those legends, including Christianity, to which the world clings began their conquest of the world with just some such concerted surrender to distortion. The effect, in Harlem, of this particular legend was like the effect of a lit match in a tin of gasoline. The mob gathered before the doors of the Hotel Braddock simply began to swell and to spread in every direction, and Harlem exploded.

The mob did not cross the ghetto lines. It would have been easy, for example, to have gone over Morningside Park on the west side or to have crossed the Grand Central railroad tracks at 125th Street on the east side, to wreak havoc in white neighborhoods. The mob seems to have been mainly interested in something more potent and real than the white face, that is, in white power, and the principal damage done during the riot of the summer of 1943 was to white business establishments in Harlem. It might have been a far bloodier story, of course, if, at the hour the riot began, these establishments had still been open. From the Hotel Braddock the mob fanned out, east and west along 125th Street, and for the entire length of Lenox, Seventh, and Eighth avenues. Along each of these avenues, and along each major side street— 116th, 125th, 135th, and so on—bars, stores, pawnshops, restaurants, even little luncheonettes had been smashed open and entered and looted—looted, it might be added, with more haste than efficiency. The shelves really looked as though a bomb had struck them. Cans of beans and soup and dog food, along with toilet paper, corn flakes, sardines and milk tumbled every which way, and abandoned cash registers and cases of beer leaned crazily out of the splintered windows and were strewn along the avenues. Sheets, blankets, and clothing of every description formed a kind of path, as though people had dropped them while running. I truly had not realized that Harlem *had* so many stores until I saw them all smashed open; the first time the word *wealth* ever entered my mind in relation to Harlem was when I saw it scattered in the streets. But one's first, incongruous impression of plenty was countered immediately by an impression of waste. None of this was doing anybody any good. It would have been better to have left the plate glass as it had been and the goods lying in the stores.

It would have been better, but it would also have been intolerable, for Harlem had needed something to smash. To smash something is the ghetto's chronic need. Most of the time it is the members of the ghetto who smash each other, and themselves. But as long as the ghetto walls are standing there will always come a moment when these outlets do not work. That summer, for example, it was not enough to get into a fight on Lenox Avenue, or curse out one's cronies in the barber shops. If ever, indeed, the violence which fills Harlem's churches, pool halls, and bars erupts outward in a more direct fashion, Harlem and its citizens are likely to vanish in an apocalyptic flood. That this is not likely to happen is due to a great many reasons, most hidden and powerful among them the Negro's real relation to the white American. This relation prohibits, simply, anything as uncomplicated and satisfactory as pure hatred. In order really to hate white people, one has to blot so much out of the mind—and the heart—that this hatred itself becomes an exhausting and self-destructive pose. But this does not mean, on the other hand, that love comes easily: the white world is too powerful, too complacent, too ready with gratuitous humiliation, and, above all, too ignorant and too innocent for that. One is absolutely forced to make perpetual qualifications and one's own reactions are always canceling each other out. It is this, really, which has driven so many people mad, both white and black. One is always in the position of having to decide between amputation and gangrene. Amputation is swift but time may prove that the amputation was not necessary—or one may delay the amputation too long. Gangrene is slow, but it is impossible to be sure that one is reading one's symptoms right. The idea of going through life as a cripple is more than one can bear, and equally unbearable is the risk of swelling up slowly, in agony, with poison. And the trouble, finally, is that the risks are real even if the choices do not exist.

"But as for me and my house," my father had said, "we will serve the Lord." I wondered, as we drove him to his resting place, what this line had meant for him. I had heard him preach it many times. I had preached it once myself, proudly giving it an interpretation different from my father's. Now the whole thing came back to me, as though my father and I were on our way to Sunday school and I were memorizing the golden text: *And if it seem evil unto you to serve the Lord, choose you this day whom you will serve; whether the gods which your fathers served that were on the other side of the flood, or the gods of the Amorites, in whose land ye dwell: but as for me and my house, we will serve the Lord.* I suspected in these familiar lines a meaning which had never been there for me before. All of my father's texts and songs, which I had decided were meaningless, were arranged before me at his death like empty bottles, waiting to hold the meaning which life would give them for me. This was his legacy: nothing is ever escaped. That bleakly memorable morning I hated the unbelievable streets and the Negroes and whites who had, equally, made them that way. But I knew that it was folly, as my father would have said, this bitterness was folly. It was necessary to hold on to the things that mattered. The dead man mattered, the new life mattered; blackness and whiteness did not matter; to believe that they did was to acquiesce in one's own destruction. Hatred, which could destroy so much, never failed to destroy the man who hated and this was an immutable law.

It began to seem that one would have to hold in the mind forever two ideas which seemed to be in opposition. The first idea was acceptance, the acceptance, totally without rancor, of life as it is, and men as they are: in the light of this idea, it goes without saying that injustice is a commonplace. But this did not mean that one could be complacent, for the second idea was of equal power: that one must never, in one's own life, accept these injustices as commonplace but must fight them with all one's strength. This fight begins, however, in the heart and it now had been laid to my charge to keep my own heart free of hatred and despair. This intimation made my heart heavy and, now that my father was irrecoverable, I wished that he had been beside me so that I could have searched his face for the answers which only the future would give me now.

Sonny's Blues

I READ ABOUT IT in the paper, in the subway, on my way to work. I read it, and I couldn't believe it, and I read it again. Then perhaps I just stared at it, at the newsprint spelling out his name, spelling out the story. I stared at it in the swinging lights of the subway car, and in the faces and bodies of the people, and in my own face, trapped in the darkness which roared outside.

It was not to be believed, and I kept telling myself that as I walked from the subway station to the high school. And at the same time I couldn't doubt it. I was scared, scared for Sonny. He became real to me again. A great block of ice got settled in my belly and kept melting there slowly all day long, while I taught my classes algebra. It was a special kind of ice. It kept melting, sending trickles of ice water all up and down my veins, but it never got less. Sometimes it hardened and seemed to expand until I felt my guts were going to come spilling out or that I was going to choke or scream. This would always be at a moment when I was remembering some specific thing Sonny had once said or done.

When he was about as old as the boys in my classes, his face

First published in *Partisan Review* (1957): reprinted from *Going to Meet the Man* (New York: The Dial Press, 1965). Copyright © 1948, 1951, 1957, 1958, 1960, 1965 by James Baldwin and used with permission of the publishers, The Dial Press, Inc.

had been bright and open, there was a lot of copper in it; and he'd had wonderfully direct brown eyes, and great gentleness and privacy. I wondered what he looked like now. He had been picked up, the evening before, in a raid on an apartment downtown, for peddling and using heroin.

I couldn't believe it: but what I mean by that is that I couldn't find any room for it anywhere inside me. I had kept it outside me for a long time. I hadn't wanted to know. I had had suspicions, but I didn't name them, I kept putting them away. I told myself that Sonny was wild, but he wasn't crazy. And he'd always been a good boy, he hadn't ever turned hard or evil or disrespectful, the way kids can, so quick, so quick, especially in Harlem. I didn't want to believe that I'd ever see my brother going down, coming to nothing, all that light in his face gone out, in the condition I'd already seen so many others. Yet it had happened and here I was, talking about algebra to a lot of boys who might, every one of them for all I knew, be popping off needles every time they went to the head. Maybe it did more for them than algebra could.

I was sure that the first time Sonny had ever had horse, he couldn't have been much older than these boys were now. These boys, now, were living as we'd been living then, they were growing up with a rush and their heads bumped abruptly against the low ceiling of their actual possibilities. They were filled with rage. All they really knew were two darknesses, the darkness of their lives, which was now closing in on them, and the darkness of the movies, which had blinded them to that other darkness, and in which they now, vindictively, dreamed, at once more together than they were at any other time, and more alone.

When the last bell rang, the last class ended, I let out my breath. It seemed I'd been holding it for all that time. My clothes were set—I may have looked as though I'd been sitting in a steam bath, all dressed up, all afternoon. I sat alone in the classroom a long time. I listened to the boys outside, downstairs, shouting and cursing and laughing. Their laughter struck me for perhaps the first time. It was not the joyous laughter which—God knows why—one associates with children. It was mocking and insular, its intent was to denigrate. It was disenchanted, and in this, also, lay the authority of their curses. Perhaps I was listening to them because I was thinking about my brother and in them I heard my brother. And myself.

One boy was whistling a tune, at once very complicated and very simple, it seemed to be pouring out of him as though he were a bird, and it sounded very cool and moving through all that harsh, bright air, only just holding its own through all those other sounds.

I stood and walked over to the window and looked down into the courtyard. It was the beginning of the spring, and the sap was rising in the boys. A teacher passed through them every now and again, quickly, as though he or she couldn't wait to get out of that courtyard, to get those boys out of their sight and off their minds. I started collecting my stuff. I thought I'd better get home and talk to Isabel.

The courtyard was almost deserted by the time I got downstairs. I saw this boy standing in the shadow of a doorway, looking just like Sonny. I almost called his name. Then I saw that it wasn't Sonny, but somebody we used to know, a boy from around our block. He'd been Sonny's friend. He'd never been mine, having been too young for me, and, anyway, I'd never liked him. And now, even though he was a grown-up man, he still hung around that block, still spent hours on the street corner, was always high and raggy. I used to run into him from time to time, and he'd often work around to asking me for a quarter or fifty cents. He always had some real good excuse, too, and I always gave it to him, I don't know why.

But now, abruptly, I hated him. I couldn't stand the way he looked at me, partly like a dog, partly like a cunning child. I wanted to ask him what the hell he was doing in the school courtyard.

He sort of shuffled over to me, and he said, "I see you got the papers. So you already know about it."

"You mean about Sonny? Yes, I already know about it. How come they didn't get you?"

He grinned. It made him repulsive and it also brought to mind what he'd looked like as a kid. "I wasn't there. I stay away from them people."

"Good for you." I offered him a cigarette and I watched him through the smoke. "You come all the way down here just to tell me about Sonny?"

"That's right." He was sort of shaking his head and his eyes looked strange, as though they were about to cross. The bright sun deadened his damp dark brown skin and it made his eyes look yellow and showed up the dirt in his conked hair. He smelled funky. I moved a little away from him and I said, "Well, thanks. But I already know about it and I got to get home."

"I'll walk you a little ways," he said. We started walking. There were a couple of kids still loitering in the courtyard and one of them said good night to me and looked strangely at the boy beside me.

"What're you going to do?" he asked me. "I mean, about Sonny?"

"Look. I haven't seen Sonny for over a year, I'm not sure I'm going to do anything. Anyway, what the hell *can* I do?"

"That's right," he said quickly, "ain't nothing you can do. Can't much help old Sonny no more, I guess."

It was what I was thinking and so it seemed to me he had no right to say it.

"I'm surprised at Sonny, though," he went on—he had a funny way of talking, he looked straight ahead as though he were talking to himself—"I thought Sonny was a smart boy, I thought he was too smart to get hung."

"I guess he thought so, too," I said sharply, "and that's how he got hung. And how about you? You're pretty goddamn smart, I bet."

Then he looked directly at me, just for a minute. "I ain't smart," he said. "If I was smart, I'd have reached for a pistol a long time ago."

"Look. Don't tell *me* your sad story, if it was up to me, I'd give you one." Then I felt guilty—guilty probably, for never having supposed that the poor bastard *had* a story of his own, much less a sad one, and I asked, quickly, "What's going to happen to him now?"

He didn't answer this. He was off by himself someplace. "Funny thing," he said, and from his tone we might have been discussing the quickest way to get to Brooklyn, "when I saw the papers this morning, the first thing I asked myself was if I had anything to do with it. I felt sort of responsible."

I began to listen more carefully. The subway station was on the corner, just before us, and I stopped. He stopped, too. We were in front of a bar and he ducked slightly, peering in, but whoever he was looking for didn't seem to be there. The juke box was blasting away with something black and bouncy, and I half watched the barmaid as she danced her way from the juke box to her place behind the bar. And I watched her face as she laughingly responded to something someone said to her, still keeping time to the music. When she smiled one saw the little girl, one sensed the doomed, still-struggling woman beneath the battered face of the semi-whore.

"I never *give* Sonny nothing," the boy said finally, "but a long time ago I come to school high and Sonny asked me how it felt." He paused, I couldn't bear to watch him, I watched the barmaid, and I listened to the music which seemed to be causing the pavement to shake. "I told him it felt great." The music stopped, the barmaid paused and watched the juke box until the music began again. "It did."

All this was carrying me someplace I didn't want to go. I certainly didn't want to know how it felt. It filled everything, the people, the houses, the music, the dark, quicksilver barmaid, with menace; and this menace was their reality.

"What's going to happen to him now?" I asked again.

"They'll send him away someplace and they'll try to cure him." He shook his head. "Maybe he'll even think he's kicked the habit. Then they'll turn him loose"—He gestured, throwing his cigarette into the gutter. "That's all."

"What do you mean, that's *all*?"

But I knew what he meant.

"I *mean*, that's *all*." He turned his head and looked at me, pulling down the corners of his mouth. "Don't you know what I mean?" he asked softly.

"How the hell *would* I know what you mean?" I almost whispered it, I don't know why.

"That's right," he said to the air, "how would *he* know what I mean?" He turned toward me again, patient and calm, and yet I somehow felt him shaking, shaking as though he were going to fall apart. I felt that ice in my guts again, the dread I'd felt all afternoon; and again I watched the barmaid, moving about the bar, washing glasses, and singing. "Listen. They'll let him out and then it'll just start over again. That's what I mean."

"You mean—they'll let him out. And then he'll just start working his way back in again. You mean he'll never kick the habit. Is that what you mean?"

"That's right," he said, cheerfully. "*You* see what I mean."

"Tell me," I said at last, "why does he want to die? He must want to die, he's killing himself, why does he want to die?"

He looked at me in surprise. He licked his lips. "He don't want to die. He wants to live. Don't nobody want to die, ever."

Then I wanted to ask him—too many things. He could not have answered, or if he had, I could not have borne the answers. I started walking. "Well, I guess it's none of my business."

"It's going to be rough on old Sonny," he said. We reached the subway station. "This is your station?" he asked. I nodded. I took one step down. "Damn!" he said, suddenly. I looked up at him. He grinned again. "Damn if I didn't leave all my money home. You ain't got a dollar on you, have you? Just for a couple of days, is all."

All at once something inside gave and threatened to come pouring out of me. I didn't hate him any more. I felt that in another moment I'd start crying like a child.

"Sure," I said. "Don't sweat." I looked in my wallet and didn't have a dollar, I only had a five. "Here," I said. "That hold you?"

He didn't look at it—he didn't want to look at it. A terrible, closed look came over his face, as though he were keeping the number on the bill a secret from him and me. "Thanks," he said, and now he was dying to see me go. "Don't worry about Sonny. Maybe I'll write him or something."

"Sure," I said. "You do that. So long."

"Be seeing you," he said. I went on down the steps.

And I didn't write Sonny or send him anything for a long time. When I finally did, it was just after my little girl died, he wrote me back a letter which made me feel like a bastard.

Here's what he said:

Dear brother,

You don't know how much I needed to hear from you. I wanted to write you many a time but I dug how much I must have hurt you and so I didn't write. But now I feel like a man who's been trying to climb up out of some deep, real deep and funky hole and just saw the sun up there, outside. I got to get outside.

I can't tell you much about how I got here. I mean I don't know how to tell you. I guess I was afraid of something or I was trying to escape from something and you know I have never been very strong in the head (smile). I'm glad Mama and Daddy are dead and can't see what's happened to their son and I swear if I'd known what I was doing I would never have hurt you so, you and a lot of other fine people who were nice to me and who believed in me.

I don't want you to think it had anything to do with me being a musician. It's more than that. Or maybe less than that. I can't get anything straight in my head down here and I try not to think about what's going to happen to me when I get outside again. Sometime I think I'm going to flip and *never* get outside and sometime I think I'll come straight back. I tell you one thing, though, I'd rather blow my brains out than go through this again. But that's what they all say, so they tell me. If I tell you when I'm coming to New York and if you could meet me, I sure would appreciate it. Give my love to Isabel and the kids and I was sure sorry to hear about little Gracie. I wish I could be like Mama and say the Lord's will be done, but I don't know it seems to me that trouble is the one thing that never does get stopped and I don't know what good it does to blame it on the Lord. But maybe it does some good if you believe it.

Your brother,
SONNY

Then I kept in constant touch with him and I sent him whatever I could and I went to meet him when he came back to New York. When I saw him, many things I thought I had forgotten came flooding back to me. This was because I had begun, finally, to wonder about Sonny, about the life that Sonny lived inside. This life, whatever it was, had made him older and thinner and it had deepened the distant stillness in which he had always moved. He looked very unlike my baby brother. Yet, when he smiled, when we shook hands, the baby brother I'd never known looked out from the depths of his private life, like an animal waiting to be coaxed into the light.

"How you been keeping?" he asked me.

"All right. And you?"

"Just fine." He was smiling all over his face. "It's good to see you again."

"It's good to see you."

The seven years' difference in our ages lay between us like a chasm: I wondered if these years would ever operate between us as a bridge. I was remembering, and it made it hard to catch my breath, that I had been there when he was born; and I had heard the first words he had ever spoken. When he started to walk, he walked from our mother straight to me. I caught him just before he fell when he took the first steps he ever took in this world.

"How's Isabel?"

"Just fine. She's dying to see you."

"And the boys?"

"They're fine, too. They're anxious to see their uncle."

"Oh, come on. You know they don't remember me."

"Are you kidding? Of course they remember you."

He grinned again. We got into a taxi. We had a lot to say to each other, far too much to know how to begin.

As the taxi began to move, I asked, "You still want to go to India?"

He laughed. "You still remember that. Hell, no. This place is Indian enough for me."

"It used to belong to them," I said.

And he laughed again. "They damn sure knew what they were doing when they got rid of it."

Years ago, when he was around fourteen, he'd been all hipped on the idea of going to India. He read books about people sitting on rocks, naked, in all kinds of weather, but mostly bad, naturally, and walking barefoot through hot coals and arriving at wisdom. I used to say that it sounded to me as though they were getting away from wisdom as fast as they could. I think he sort of looked down on me for that.

"Do you mind," he asked, "if we have the driver drive alongside the park? On the west side—I haven't seen the city in so long."

"Of course not," I said. I was afraid that I might sound as though I were humoring him, but I hoped he wouldn't take it that way.

So we drove along, between the green of the park and the stony, lifeless elegance of hotels and apartment buildings, toward the vivid, killing streets of our childhood. These streets hadn't changed, though housing projects jutted up out of them now like rocks in the middle of a boiling sea. Most of the houses in which we had grown up had vanished, as had the stores from which we had stolen, the basements in which we had first tried sex, the rooftops from which we had hurled tin cans and bricks. But houses exactly like the houses of our past yet dominated the landscape, boys exactly like the boys we once had been found themselves smothering in these houses, came down into the streets for light and air and found themselves encircled by disaster. Some escaped the trap, most didn't. Those who got out always left something of themselves behind, as some animals amputate a leg and leave it in the trap. It might be said, perhaps, that I had escaped, after all, I was a schoolteacher; or that Sonny had, he hadn't lived in Harlem for years. Yet, as the cab moved uptown through streets which seemed, with a rush, to darken with dark people, and as I covertly studied Sonny's face, it came to me that what we both were seeking through our separate cab windows was that part of ourselves which had been left behind. It's always at the hour of trouble and confrontation that the missing member aches.

We hit 110th Street and started rolling up Lenox Avenue. And I'd known this avenue all my life, but it seemed to me again, as it had seemed on the day I'd first heard about Sonny's trouble, filled with a hidden menace which was its very breath of life.

"We almost there," said Sonny.

"Almost." We were both too nervous to say anything more.

We live in a housing project. It hasn't been up long. A few days after it was up it seemed uninhabitably new, now, of course, it's already rundown. It looked like a parody of the good, clean, faceless life—God knows the people who live in it do their best to make it a parody. The beat-looking grass lying around isn't enough to make their lives green, the hedges will never hold out the streets, and they know it. The big windows fool no one, they aren't big enough to make space out of no space. They don't bother with the windows, they watch the TV screen instead. The playground is most popular with the children who don't play at jacks, or skip rope, or roller skate, or swing, and they can be found in it after dark. We moved in partly because it's not too far from where I teach, and partly for the kids; but it's really just like the houses in which Sonny and I grew up. The same things happen, they'll have the same things to remember. The moment Sonny and I started into the house I had the feeling that I was simply bringing him back into the danger he had almost died trying to escape.

Sonny has never been talkative. So I don't know why I was sure he'd be dying to talk to me when supper was over the first night. Everything went fine, the oldest boy remembered him, and the youngest boy liked him, and Sonny had remembered to bring something for each of them; and Isabel, who is really much nicer than I am, more open and giving, had gone to a lot of trouble about dinner and was genuinely glad to see him. And she'd always been able to tease Sonny in a way that I haven't. It was nice to see her face so vivid again and to hear her laugh and watch her make Sonny laugh. She wasn't, or, anyway, she didn't seem to be, at all uneasy or embarrassed. She chatted as though there were no subject which had to be avoided and she got Sonny past his first, faint stiffness. And thank God she was there, for I was filled with that icy dread again. Everything I did seemed awkward to me, and everything I said sounded freighted with hidden meaning. I was trying to remember everything I'd heard about dope addiction and I couldn't help watching Sonny for signs. I wasn't doing it out of malice. I was trying to find out something about my brother. I was dying to hear him tell me he was safe.

"Safe!" my father grunted, whenever Mama suggested trying to move to a neighborhood which might be safer for children. "Safe, hell! Ain't no place safe for kids, nor nobody."

He always went on like this, but he wasn't, ever, really as bad as he sounded, not even on weekends, when he got drunk. As a matter of fact, he was always on the lookout for "something a little better," but he died before he found it. He died suddenly, during a drunken weekend in the middle of the war, when Sonny was fifteen. He and Sonny hadn't ever got on too well. And this was partly because Sonny was the apple of his father's eye. It was because he loved Sonny so much and was frightened for him, that he was always fighting with him. It doesn't do any good to fight with Sonny. Sonny just moves back, inside himself, where he can't be reached. But the principal reason that they never hit it off is that they were so much alike. Daddy was big and rough and loud-talking, just the opposite of Sonny, but they both had—that same privacy.

Mama tried to tell me something about this, just after Daddy died. I was home on leave from the army.

This was the last time I ever saw my mother alive. Just the same, this picture gets all mixed up in my mind with pictures I had of her when she was younger. The way I always see her is the way she used to be on a Sunday afternoon, say, when the old folks were talking after the big Sunday dinner. I always see her wearing pale blue. She'd be sitting on the sofa. And my father would be sitting in the easy chair, not far from her. And the living room would be full of church folks and relatives. There they sit, in chairs all around the living room, and if the night is creeping up outside, but nobody knows it yet. You can see the darkness growing against the windowpanes and you hear the street noises every now and again, or maybe the jangling beat of a tambourine from one of the churches close by, but it's real quiet in the room. For a moment nobody's talking, but every face looks darkening, like the sky outside. And my mother rocks a little from the waist, and my father's eyes are closed. Everyone is looking at something a child can't see. For a minute they've forgotten the children. Maybe a kid is lying on the rug, half asleep. Maybe somebody's got a kid in his lap and is absent-mindedly stroking the kid's head. Maybe there's a kid, quiet and big-eyed, curled up in a big chair in the corner. The silence, the darkness coming, and the darkness in the faces frighten the child obscurely. He hopes that the hand which strokes his forehead will never stop—will never die. He hopes that there will never come a time when the old folks won't be sitting around the living room, talking about where they've come from, and what they've seen, and what's happened to them and their kinfolk.

But something deep and watchful in the child knows that this is bound to end, is already ending. In a moment someone will get up and turn on the light. Then the old folks will remember the children and they won't talk any more that day. And when light fills the room, the child is filled with darkness. He knows that every time this happens he's moved just a little closer to that darkness outside. The darkness outside is what the old folks have been talking about. It's what they've come from. It's what they endure. The child knows that they won't talk any more because if he knows too much about what's happened to *them*, he'll know too much too soon, about what's going to happen to *him*.

The last time I talked to my mother, I remember I was restless. I wanted to get out and see Isabel. We weren't married then and we had a lot to straighten out between us.

There Mama sat, in black, by the window. She was humming an old church song, *Lord, you brought me from a long ways off*. Sonny was out somewhere. Mama kept watching the streets.

"I don't know," she said, "if I'll ever see you again, after you go off from here. But I hope you'll remember the things I tried to teach you."

"Don't talk like that," I said, and smiled. "You'll be here a long time yet."

She smiled, too, but she said nothing. She was quiet for a long time. And I said, "Mama, don't you worry about nothing. I'll be writing all the time, and you be getting the checks. . . ."

"I want to talk to you about your brother," she said, suddenly. "If anything happens to me, he ain't going to have nobody to look out for him."

"Mama," I said, "ain't nothing going to happen to you or Sonny. Sonny's all right. He's a good boy and he's got good sense."

"It ain't a question of his being a good boy," Mama said, "nor of his having good sense. It ain't only the bad ones, nor yet the dumb ones that gets sucked under." She stopped, looking at me. "Your Daddy once had a brother," she said, and smiled in a way that made me feel she was in pain. "You didn't never know that, did you?"

"No," I said. "I never knew that," and I watched her face.

"Oh, yes," she said, "your Daddy had a brother." She looked out of the window again. "I know you never saw your Daddy cry. But I did—many a time, through all these years."

I asked her, "What happened to his brother? How come nobody's ever talked about him?"

This was the first time I ever saw my mother look old.

"His brother got killed," she said, "when he was just a little younger than you are now. I knew him. He was a fine boy. He was maybe a little full of the devil, but he didn't mean nobody no harm."

Then she stopped, and the room was silent, exactly as it had sometimes been on those Sunday afternoons. Mama kept looking out into the streets.

"He used to have a job in the mill," she said, "and, like all young folks, he just liked to perform on Saturday nights. Saturday nights, him and your father would drift around to different places, go to dances and things like that, or just sit around with people they knew, and your father's brother would sing, he had a fine voice, and play along with himself on his guitar. Well, this particular Saturday night, him and your father was coming home from some place, and they were both a little drunk and there was a moon that night, it was bright like day. Your father's brother was feeling kind of good, and he was whistling to himself, and he had his guitar slung over his shoulder. They was coming down a hill, and beneath them was a road that turned off from the highway. Well, your father's brother, being always kind of frisky, decided to run down this hill, and he did, with that guitar banging and clanging behind him, and he ran across the road, and he was making water behind a tree. And your father was sort of amused at him and he was still coming down the hill, kind of slow. Then he heard a car motor and that same minute his brother stepped from behind the tree, into the road, in the moonlight. And he started to cross the road. And your father started to run down the hill, he says he don't know why. This car was full of white men. They was all drunk, and when they seen your father's brother they let out a great whoop and holler and they aimed the car straight at him. They was having fun, they just wanted to scare him, the way they do sometimes, you know. But they was drunk. And I guess the boy, being drunk, too, and scared, kind of lost his head. By the time he jumped it was too late. Your father says he heard his brother scream when the car rolled over him, and he heard the wood of that guitar when it give, and he heard them strings go flying, and he heard them white men shouting, and the car kept on a-going and it ain't stopped till this day. And, time your father got down the hill, his brother weren't nothing but blood and pulp."

Tears were gleaming on my mother's face. There wasn't anything I could say.

"He never mentioned it," she said, "because I never let him mention it before you children. Your Daddy was like a crazy man that night and for many a night thereafter. He says he never in his life seen anything as dark as that road after the lights of that car had gone away. Weren't nothing, weren't nobody on that road, just your Daddy and his brother and that busted guitar. Oh, yes. Your Daddy never did really get right again. Till the day he died he weren't sure but that every white man he saw was the man that killed his brother."

She stopped and took out her handkerchief and dried her eyes and looked at me.

"I ain't telling you all this," she said, "to make you scared or bitter or to make you hate nobody. I'm telling you this because you got a brother. And the world ain't changed."

I guess I didn't want to believe this. I guess she saw this in my face. She turned away from me, toward the window again, searching those streets.

"But I praise my Redeemer," she said at last, "that he called your Daddy home before me. I ain't saying it to throw no flowers at myself, but, I declare, it keeps me from feeling too cast down to know I helped your father get safely through this world. Your father always acted like he was the roughest, strongest man on earth. And everybody took him to be like that. But if he hadn't had *me* there—to see his tears!"

She was crying again. Still, I couldn't move. I said, "Lord, Lord, Mama, I didn't know it was like that."

"Oh, honey," she said, "there's a lot that you don't know. But you are going to find it out." She stood up from the window and came over to me. "You got to hold on to your brother," she said, "and don't let him fall, no matter what it looks like is happening to him and no matter how evil you gets with him. You going to be evil with him many a time. But don't you forget what I told you, you hear?"

"I won't forget," I said. "Don't you worry, I won't forget. I won't let nothing happen to Sonny."

My mother smiled as though she were amused at something she saw in my face. Then, "You may not be able to stop nothing from happening. But you got to let him know you's *there*."

Two days later I was married, and then I was gone. And I had a lot of things on my mind and I pretty well forgot my promise to Mama until I got shipped home on a special furlough for her funeral.

And, after the funeral, with just Sonny and me alone in the empty kitchen, I tried to find out something about him.

"What do you want to do?" I asked him.

"I'm going to be a musician," he said.

For he had graduated, in the time I had been away, from dancing to the juke box to finding out who was playing what, and what they were doing with it, and he had bought himself a set of drums.

"You mean, you want to be a drummer?" I somehow had the feeling that being a drummer might be all right for other people but not for my brother Sonny.

"I don't think," he said, looking at me very gravely, "that I'll ever be a good drummer. But I think I can play a piano."

I frowned. I'd never played the role of the older brother quite so seriously before, had scarcely ever, in fact, *asked* Sonny a damn thing. I sensed myself in the presence of something I didn't really know how to handle, didn't understand. So I made my frown a little deeper as I asked: "What kind of musician do you want to be?"

He grinned. "How many kinds do you think there are?"

"Be *serious*," I said.

He laughed, throwing his head back, and then looked at me. "I *am* serious."

"Well, then, for Christ's sake, stop kidding around and answer a serious question. I mean, do you want to be a concert pianist, you want to play classical music and all that, or—or, what?"

Long before I finished he was laughing again. "For Christ's *sake*, Sonny!"

He sobered, but with difficulty. "I'm sorry. But you sound so— *scared!*" And he was off again.

"Well, you may think it's funny now, baby, but it's not going to be so funny when you have to make your living at it, let me tell you *that*." I was furious because I knew he was laughing at me and I didn't know why.

"No," he said, very sober now, and afraid, perhaps, that he'd hurt me, "I don't want to be a classical pianist. That isn't what interests me. I mean"—he paused, looking hard at me, as though his eyes would help me to understand, and then gestured help- lessly, as though perhaps his hand would help—"I mean, I'll have a lot of studying to do, and I'll have to study *everything*, but, I mean, I want to play *with*—jazz musicians." He stopped. "I want to play jazz," he said.

Well, the word had never before sounded as heavy, as real, as it sounded that afternoon in Sonny's mouth. I just looked at him and I was probably frowning a real frown by this time. I simply couldn't see why on earth he'd want to spend his time hanging around night clubs, clowning around on bandstands, while people pushed each other around a dance floor. It seemed—beneath him, somehow. I had never thought about it before, had never been forced to, but I suppose I had always put jazz musicians in a class with what Daddy called "good-time people."

"Are you *serious*?"

"Hell, *yes*, I'm serious."

He looked more helpless than ever, and annoyed, and deeply hurt.

I suggested, helpfully: "You mean—like Louis Armstrong?"

His face closed as though I'd struck him. "No. I'm not talking about none of that old-time, down home crap."

"Well, look, Sonny, I'm sorry, don't get mad. I just don't alto- gether get it, that's all. Name somebody—you know, a jazz musician you admire."

"Bird."

"Who?"

"Bird! Charlie Parker! Don't they teach you nothing in the goddamn army?"

I lit a cigarette. I was surprised and then a little amused to discover that I was trembling. "I've been out of touch," I said. "You'll have to be patient with me. Now. Who's this Parker character?"

"He's just one of the greatest jazz musicians alive," said Sonny, sullenly, his hands in his pockets, his back to me. "Maybe *the* greatest," he added bitterly, "that's probably why *you* never heard of him."

"All right," I said, "I'm ignorant. I'm sorry. I'll go out and buy all the cat's records right away, all right?"

"It don't," said Sonny, with dignity, "make any difference to me. I don't care what you listen to. Don't do me no favors."

I was beginning to realize that I'd never seen him so upset before. With another part of my mind I was thinking that this would probably turn out to be one of those things kids go through and that I shouldn't make it seem important by pushing it too hard. Still, I didn't think it would do any harm to ask: "Doesn't all this take a lot of time? Can you make a living at it?"

He turned back to me and half leaned, half sat, on the kitchen table. "Everything takes time," he said, "and—well, yes, sure, I can make a living at it. But what I don't seem to be able to make you understand is that it's the only thing I want to do."

"Well, Sonny," I said gently, "you know people can't always do exactly what they want to do—"

"*No,* I don't know that," said Sonny, surprising me. "I think people *ought* to do what they want to do, what else are they alive for?"

"You getting to be a big boy," I said desperately, "it's time you started thinking about your future."

"I'm thinking about my future," said Sonny, grimly. "I think about it all the time."

I gave up. I decided, if he didn't change his mind, that we could always talk about it later. "In the meantime," I said, "you got to finish school." We had already decided that he'd have to move in with Isabel and her folks. I knew this wasn't the ideal arrangement because Isabel's folks are inclined to be dicty and they hadn't especially wanted Isabel to marry me. But I didn't know what else to do. "And we have to get you fixed up at Isabel's."

There was a long silence. He moved from the kitchen table to the window. "That's a terrible idea. You know it yourself."

"Do you have a *better* idea?"

He just walked up and down the kitchen for a minute. He was as tall as I was. He had started to shave. I suddenly had the feeling that I didn't know him at all.

He stopped at the kitchen table and picked up my cigarettes. Looking at me with a kind of mocking, amused defiance, he put one between his lips. "You mind?"

"You smoking already?"

He lit the cigarette and nodded, watching me through the

smoke. "I just wanted to see if I'd have the courage to smoke in front of you." He grinned and blew a great cloud of smoke to the ceiling. "It was easy." He looked at my face. "Come on, now. I bet you was smoking at my age, tell the truth."

I didn't say anything but the truth was on my face, and he laughed. But now there was something very strained in his laugh. "Sure. And I bet that ain't all you was doing."

He was frightening me a little. "Cut the crap," I said. "We already decided that you was going to go and live at Isabel's. Now what's got into you all of a sudden?"

"*You* decided it," he pointed out. "*I* didn't decide nothing." He stopped in front of me, leaning against the stove, arms loosely folded. "Look, brother. I don't want to stay in Harlem no more, I really don't." He was very earnest. He looked at me, then over toward the kitchen window. There was something in his eyes I'd never seen before, some thoughtfulness, some worry all his own. He rubbed the muscle of one arm. "It's time I was getting out of here."

"Where do you want to *go*, Sonny?"

"I want to join the army. Or the navy, I don't care. If I say I'm old enough, they'll believe me."

Then I got mad. It was because I was so scared. "You must be crazy. You goddamn fool, what the hell do you want to go and join the *army* for?"

"I just told you. To get out of Harlem."

"Sonny, you haven't even finished *school*. And if you really want to be a musician, how do you expect to study if you're in the *army*?"

He looked at me, trapped, and in anguish. "There's ways. I might be able to work out some kind of deal. Anyway, I'll have the G.I. Bill when I come out."

"*If* you come out." We stared at each other. "Sonny, please. Be reasonable. I know the setup is far from perfect. But we got to do the best we can."

"I ain't learning nothing in school," he said. "Even when I go." He turned away from me and opened the window and threw his cigarette out into the narrow alley. I watched his back. "At least, I ain't learning nothing you'd want me to learn." He slammed the window so hard I thought the glass would fly out, and turned back to me. "And I'm sick of the stink of these garbage cans!"

"Sonny," I said, "I know how you feel. But if you don't finish school now, you're going to be sorry later that you didn't." I grabbed him by the shoulders. "And you only got another year. It ain't so bad. And I'll come back and I swear I'll help you do *whatever* you want to do. Just try to put up with it till I come back. Will you please do that? For me?"

He didn't answer and he wouldn't look at me.

"Sonny. You hear me?"

He pulled away. "I hear you. But you never hear anything *I* say."

I didn't know what to say to that. He looked out of the window and then back at me. "OK," he said, and sighed. "I'll try."

Then I said, trying to cheer him up a little, "They got a piano at Isabel's. You can practice on it."

And as a matter of fact, it did cheer him up for a minute. "That's right," he said to himself. "I forgot that." His face relaxed a little. But the worry, the thoughtfulness, played on it still, the way shadows play on a face which is staring into the fire.

But I thought I'd never hear the end of that piano. At first, Isabel would write me, saying how nice it was that Sonny was so serious about his music and how, as soon as he came in from school, or wherever he had been when he was supposed to be at school, he went straight to that piano and stayed there until supper-time. And, after supper, he went back to that piano and stayed there until everybody went to bed. He was at that piano all day Saturday and all day Sunday. Then he bought a record player and started playing records. He'd play one record over and over again, all day long sometimes, and he'd improvise along with it on the piano. Or he'd play one section of the record, one chord, one change, one progression, then he'd do it on the piano. Then back to the record. Then back to the piano.

Well, I really don't know how they stood it. Isabel finally confessed that it wasn't like living with a person at all, it was like living with sound. And the sound didn't make any sense to her, didn't make any sense to any of them—naturally. They began, in a way, to be afflicted by this presence that was living in their home. It was as though Sonny were some sort of god, or monster. He moved in an atmosphere which wasn't like theirs at all. They fed him and he ate, he washed himself, he walked in and out of their door; he certainly wasn't nasty or unpleasant or rude, Sonny isn't any of those things; but it was as though he were all wrapped up in some cloud, some fire, some vision all his own; and there wasn't any way to reach him.

At the same time, he wasn't really a man yet, he was still a child, and they had to watch out for him in all kinds of ways. They certainly couldn't throw him out. Neither did they dare to make a great scene about that piano because even they dimly sensed, as I sensed, from so many thousands of miles away, that Sonny was at that piano playing for his life.

But he hadn't been going to school. One day a letter came from the school board, and Isabel's mother got it—there had, apparently, been other letters but Sonny had torn them up. This day, when Sonny came in, Isabel's mother showed him the letter and asked where he'd been spending his time. And she finally got it out of him that he'd been down in Greenwich Village, with musicians and other characters, in a white girl's apartment. And this scared her and she started to scream at him, and what came up, once she began—though she denies it to this day—was what sacrifices they were making to give Sonny a decent home and how little he appreciated it.

Sonny didn't play the piano that day. By evening, Isabel's mother had calmed down but then there was the old man to deal with, and Isabel herself. Isabel says she did her best to be calm but she broke down and started crying. She says she just watched Sonny's face. She could tell, by watching him, what was happening with him. And what was happening was that they penetrated his cloud, they had reached him. Even if their fingers had been a thousand times more gentle than human fingers ever are, he could hardly help feeling that they had stripped him naked and were spitting on that nakedness. For he also had to see that his presence, that music, which was life or death to him, had been torture for them and that they had endured it, not at all for his sake, but only for mine. And Sonny couldn't take that. He can take it a little better today than he could then but he's still not very good at it and, frankly, I don't know anybody who is.

The silence of the next few days must have been louder than the sound of all the music ever played since time began. One morning, before she went to work, Isabel was in his room for something and she suddenly realized that all of his records were gone. And she knew for certain that he was gone. And he was. He went as far as the navy would carry him. He finally sent me a postcard from someplace in Greece, and that was the first I knew that Sonny was still alive. I didn't see him any more until we were both back in New York and the war had long been over.

He was a man by then, of course, but I wasn't willing to see it. He came by the house from time to time, but we fought almost every time we met. I didn't like the way he carried himself, loose and dreamlike all the time, and I didn't like his friends, and his music seemed to be merely an excuse for the life he led. It sounded just that weird and disordered.

Then we had a fight, a pretty awful fight, and I didn't see him for months. By and by I looked him up, where he was living, in a furnished room in the Village, and I tried to make it up. But there were lots of other people in the room, and Sonny just lay on his bed, and he wouldn't come downstairs with me, and he treated these other people as though they were his family and I weren't. So I got mad and then he got mad, and then I told him that he might just as well be dead as live the way he was living. Then he stood up and he told me not to worry about him any more in life, that he *was* dead as far as I was concerned. Then he pushed me to the door, and the other people looked on as though nothing were happening, and he slammed the door behind me. I stood in the hallway, staring at the door. I heard somebody laugh in the room and then the tears came to my eyes. I started down the steps, whistling to keep from crying, I kept whistling to myself, *You going to need me, baby, one of these cold, rainy days.*

I read about Sonny's trouble in the spring. Little Grace died in the fall. She was a beautiful little girl. But she only lived a little over two years. She died of polio and she suffered. She had a slight fever for a couple of days, but it didn't seem like anything and we just kept her in bed. And we would certainly have called the doctor, but the fever dropped, she seemed to be all right. So we thought it had just been a cold. Then, one day, she was up, playing, Isabel was in the kitchen fixing lunch for the two boys when they'd come in from school, and she heard Grace fall down in the living room. When you have a lot of children you don't always start running when one of them falls, unless they start screaming or something. And, this time, Grace was quiet. Yet, Isabel says that when she heard that *thump* and then that silence, something happened in her to make her afraid. And she ran to the living room and there was little Grace on the floor, all twisted up, and the reason she hadn't screamed was that she couldn't get her breath. And when she did scream, it was the worst sound, Isabel says, that she'd ever heard in all her life, and she still hears it sometimes in her dreams. Isabel will sometimes wake me up with a low, moaning, strangled sound, and I have to be quick to awaken her and hold her to me and where Isabel is weeping against me seems a mortal wound.

I think I may have written Sonny the very day that little Grace was buried. I was sitting in the living room in the dark, by myself, and I suddenly thought of Sonny. My trouble made his real.

One Saturday afternoon, when Sonny had been living with us, or, anyway, been in our house, for nearly two weeks, I found myself wandering aimlessly about the living room, drinking from a can of beer, and trying to work up the courage to search Sonny's room. He was out, he was usually out whenever I was home, and Isabel had taken the children to see their grandparents. Suddenly I was standing still in front of the living-room window, watching Seventh Avenue. The idea of searching Sonny's room made me still. I scarcely dared to admit to myself what I'd be searching for. I didn't know what I'd do if I found it. Or if I didn't.

On the sidewalk across from me, near the entrance to a barbecue joint, some people were holding an old-fashioned revival meeting. The barbecue cook, wearing a dirty white apron, his conked hair reddish and metallic in the pale sun, and a cigarette between his lips, stood in the doorway, watching them. Kids and older people paused in their errands and stood there, along with some older men and a couple of very tough-looking women who watched everything that happened on the avenue, as though they owned it, or were maybe owned by it. Well, they were watching this, too. The revival was being carried on by three sisters in black, and a brother. All they had were their voices and their Bibles and a tambourine. The brother was testifying and while he testified two of the sisters stood together, seeming to say, Amen, and the third sister walked around with the tambourine outstretched and a couple of people dropped coins into it. Then the brother's testimony ended, and the sister who had been taking up the collection dumped the coins into her palm and transferred them to the pocket of her long black robe. Then she raised both hands, striking the tambourine against the air, and then against one hand, and she started to sing. And the two other sisters and the brother joined in.

It was strange, suddenly, to watch, though I had been seeing these street meetings all my life. So, of course, had everybody else down there. Yet, they paused and watched and listened and I stood still at the window. " *'Tis the old ship of Zion*," they sang, and the sister with the tambourine kept a steady, jangling beat, "*it has rescued many a thousand!*" Not a soul under the sound of their voices was hearing this song for the first time, not one of them had been rescued. Nor had they seen much in the way of rescue work being done around them. Neither did they especially believe in the holiness of the three sisters and the brother, they knew too much about them, knew where they lived, and how. The woman with the tambourine, whose voice dominated the air, whose face was bright with joy, was divided by very little from the woman who stood watching her, a cigarette between her heavy, chapped lips, her hair a cuckoo's nest, her face scarred and swollen from many beatings, and her black eyes glittering like coal. Perhaps they both knew this, which was why, when, as rarely, they addressed each other, they addressed each other as Sister. As the singing filled the air, the watching, listening faces underwent a change, the eyes focusing on something within; the music seemed to soothe a poison out of them; and time seemed, nearly, to fall away from the sullen, belligerent, battered faces, as though they were fleeing back to their first condition, while dreaming of their last. The barbecue cook half shook his head and smiled, and dropped his cigarette and disappeared into his joint. A man fumbled in his pockets for change and stood holding it in his hand impatiently, as though he had just remembered a pressing appointment further up the avenue. He looked furious. Then I saw Sonny, standing on the edge of the crowd. He was carrying a wide, flat notebook with a green cover, and it made him look, from where I was standing, almost like a schoolboy. The coppery sun brought out the copper in his skin, he was very faintly smiling, standing very still. Then the singing stopped, the tambourine turned into a collection plate again. The furious man dropped in his coins and vanished, so did a couple of the women, and Sonny dropped some change in the plate, looking directly at the woman with a little smile. He started across the avenue, toward the house. He has a slow, loping walk, something like the way Harlem hipsters walk, only he's imposed on this his own half-beat. I had never really noticed it before.

I stayed at the window, both relieved and apprehensive. As Sonny disappeared from my sight, they began singing again. And they were still singing when his key turned in the lock.

"Hey," he said.

"Hey, yourself. You want some beer?"

"No. Well, maybe." But he came up to the window and stood beside me, looking out. "What a warm voice," he said.

They were singing *If I could only hear my mother pray again!*

"Yes," I said, "and she can sure beat that tambourine."

"But what a terrible song," he said, and laughed. He dropped his notebook on the sofa and disappeared into the kitchen. "Where's Isabel and the kids?"

"I think they went to see their grandparents. You hungry?"

"No." He came back into the living room with his can of beer. "You want to come someplace with me tonight?"

I sensed, I don't know how, that I couldn't possibly say no. "Sure. Where?"

He sat down on the sofa and picked up his notebook and started leafing through it. "I'm going to sit in with some fellows in a joint in the Village."

"You mean, you're going to play, tonight?"

"That's right." He took a swallow of his beer and moved back to the window. He gave me a sidelong look. "If you can stand it."

"I'll try," I said.

He smiled to himself, and we both watched as the meeting across the way broke up. The three sisters and the brother, heads bowed, were singing *God be with you till we meet again*. The faces around them were very quiet. Then the song ended. The small crowd dispersed. We watched the three women and the lone man walk slowly up the avenue.

"When she was singing before," said Sonny, abruptly, "her voice reminded me for a minute of what heroin feels like sometimes—when it's in your veins. It makes you feel sort of warm and cool at the same time. And distant. And—and sure." He sipped his beer, very deliberately not looking at me. I watched his face. "It makes you feel—in control. Sometimes you've got to have that feeling."

"Do you?" I sat down slowly in the easy chair.

"Sometimes." He went to the sofa and picked up his notebook again. "Some people do."

"In order," I asked, "to play?" And my voice was very ugly, full of contempt and anger.

"Well"—he looked at me with great, troubled eyes, as though, in fact, he hoped his eyes would tell me things he could never otherwise say—"they *think* so. And *if* they think so—!"

"And what do *you* think?" I asked.

He sat on the sofa and put his can of beer on the floor. "I don't know," he said, and I couldn't be sure if he were answering my question or pursuing his thoughts. His face didn't tell me. "It's not so much to *play*. It's to *stand* it, to be able to make it at all. On any level." He frowned and smiled: "In order to keep from shaking to pieces."

"But these friends of yours," I said, "they seem to shake themselves to pieces pretty goddamn fast."

"Maybe." He played with the notebook. And something told me that I should curb my tongue, that Sonny was doing his best to talk, that I should listen. "But of course you only know the ones that've gone to pieces. Some don't—or at least they haven't *yet* and that's just about all *any* of us can say." He paused. "And then there are some who just live, really, in hell, and they know it and they see what's happening and they go right on. I don't know." He sighed, dropped the notebook, folded his arms. "Some guys, you can tell from the way they play, they on something *all* the time. And you can see that, well, it makes something real for them. But of course," he picked up his beer from the floor and sipped it and put the can down again, "they *want* to, too, you've got to see that. Even some of them that say they don't—*some*, not all."

"And what about you?" I asked—I couldn't help it. "What about you? Do *you* want to?"

He stood up and walked to the window and remained silent for a long time. Then he sighed. "Me," he said. Then: "While I was downstairs before, on my way here, listening to that woman sing, it struck me all of a sudden how much suffering she must have had to go through—to sing like that. It's *repulsive* to think you have to suffer that much."

I said: "But there's no way not to suffer—is there, Sonny?"

"I believe not," he said, and smiled, "but that's never stopped anyone from trying." He looked at me. "Has it?" I realized, with this mocking look, that there stood between us, forever, beyond the power of time or forgiveness, the fact that I had held silence— so long!—when he had needed human speech to help him. He turned back to the window. "No, there's no way not to suffer. But you try all kinds of ways to keep from drowning in it, to keep on top of it, and to make it seem—well, like *you*. Like you did something, all right, and now you're suffering for it. You know?" I said nothing. "Well you know," he said, impatiently, "why *do* people suffer? Maybe it's better to do something to give it a reason, *any* reason."

"But we just agreed," I said, "that there's no way not to suffer. Isn't it better, then, just to—take it?"

"But nobody just takes it," Sonny cried, "that's what I'm telling you! *Everybody* tries not to. You're just hung up on the *way* some people try—it's not *your* way!"

The hair on my face began to itch, my face felt wet. "That's not true," I said, "that's not true. I don't give a damn what other people do, I don't even care how they suffer. I just care how *you* suffer." And he looked at me. "Please believe me," I said, "I don't want to see you—die—trying not to suffer."

"I won't," he said, flatly, "die trying not to suffer. At least, not any faster than anybody else."

"But there's no need," I said, trying to laugh, "is there, in killing yourself?"

I wanted to say more, but I couldn't. I wanted to talk about will power and how life could be—well, beautiful. I wanted to say that it was all within; but was it? Or, rather, wasn't that exactly the trouble? And I wanted to promise that I would never fail him again. But it would all have sounded—empty words and lies.

So I made the promise to myself and prayed that I would keep it.

"It's terrible sometimes, inside," he said, "that's what's the trouble. You walk these streets, black and funky and cold, and there's not really a living ass to talk to, and there's nothing shaking, and there's no way of getting it out—that storm inside. You can't talk it and you can't make love with it, and when you finally try to get with it and play it, you realize *nobody's* listening. So *you've* got to listen. You got to find a way to listen."

And then he walked away from the window and sat on the sofa again, as though all the wind had suddenly been knocked out of him. "Sometimes you'll do *anything* to play, even cut your mother's throat." He laughed and looked at me. "Or your brother's." Then he sobered. "Or your own." Then: "Don't worry. I'm all right now and I think I'll *be* all right. But I can't forget—where I've been. I don't mean just the physical place I've been, I mean where I've *been*. And *what* I've been."

"What have you been, Sonny?" I asked.

He smiled—but sat sideways on the sofa, his elbow resting on the back, his fingers playing with his mouth and chin, not looking at me. "I've been something I didn't recognize, didn't know I could be. Didn't know anybody could be." He stopped, looking inward, looking helplessly young, looking old. "I'm not talking about it now because I feel *guilty* or anything like that—maybe it would be better if I did, I don't know. Anyway, I can't really talk about it. Not to you, not to anybody." And now he turned and faced me. "Sometimes, you know, and it was actually when I was most out of the world, I felt that I was in it, that I was *with* it, really, and I could play or I didn't really have to *play,* it just came out of me, it was there. And I don't know how I played, thinking about it now, but I know I did awful things, those times, sometimes, to people. Or it wasn't that I *did* anything to them—it was that they weren't real." He picked up the beer can; it was empty; he rolled it between his palms: "And other times—well, I needed a fix, I needed to find a place to lean, I needed to clear a space to *listen*—and I couldn't find it, and I—went crazy, I did terrible things to *me,* I was terrible *for* me." He began pressing the beer can between his hands, I watched the metal begin to give. It glittered, as he played with it, like a knife, and I was afraid he would cut himself, but I said nothing. "Oh well. I can never tell you. I was all by myself at the bottom of something, stinking and sweating and crying and shaking, and I smelled it, you know? *My* stink, and I thought I'd die if I couldn't get away from it and yet, all the same, I knew that everything I was doing was just locking me in with it. And I didn't know," he paused, still flattening the beer can, "I didn't know, I still *don't* know, something kept telling me that maybe it was good to smell your own stink, but I didn't think that *that* was what I'd been trying to do—and—who can stand it?" And he abruptly dropped the ruined beer can, looking at me with a small, still smile, and then rose, walking to the window as though it were the lodestone rock. I watched his face, he watched the avenue. "I couldn't tell you when Mama died—but the reason I wanted to leave Harlem so bad was to get away from drugs. And then, when I ran away, that's what I was running from—really. When I came back, nothing had changed, *I* hadn't changed, I was just—older." And he stopped, drumming with his fingers on the windowpane. The sun had vanished, soon darkness would fall. I watched his face. "It can come again," he said, almost as though speaking to himself. Then he turned to me. "It can come again," he repeated. "I just want you to know that."

"All right," I said at last. "So it can come again. All right."

He smiled, but the smile was sorrowful. "I had to try to tell you," he said.

"Yes," I said. "I understand that."

"You're my brother," he said, looking straight at me, and not smiling at all.

"Yes," I repeated, "yes. I understand that."

He turned back to the window, looking out. "All that hatred down there," he said, "all that hatred and misery and love. It's a wonder it doesn't blow the avenue apart."

We went to the only night club on a short, dark street, downtown. We squeezed through the narrow, chattering, jam-packed bar to the entrance of the big room, where the bandstand was. And we stood there for a moment, for the lights were very dim in this room and we couldn't see. Then, "Hello, boy," said a voice, and an enormous black man, much older than Sonny or myself, erupted out of all that atmospheric lighting and put an arm around Sonny's shoulder. "I been sitting right here," he said, "waiting for you."

He had a big voice, too, and heads in the darkness turned toward us.

Sonny grinned and pulled a little away, and said, "Creole, this is my brother. I told you about him."

Creole shook my hand. "I'm glad to meet you, son," he said, and it was clear that he was glad to meet me *there*, for Sonny's sake. And he smiled. "You got a real musician in *your* family," and he took his arm from Sonny's shoulder and slapped him, lightly, affectionately, with the back of his hand.

"Well. Now I've heard it all," said a voice behind us. This was another musician, and a friend of Sonny's, a coal-black, cheerful-looking man, built close to the ground. He immediately began confiding to me, at the top of his lungs, the most terrible things about Sonny, his teeth gleaming like a lighthouse and his laugh coming up out of him like the beginning of an earthquake. And it turned out that everyone at the bar knew Sonny, or almost everyone; some were musicians, working there, or nearby, or not working, some were simply hangers-on, and some were there to hear Sonny play. I was introduced to all of them and they were all very polite to me. Yet, it was clear that, for them, I was only Sonny's brother. Here, I was in Sonny's world. Or, rather: his kingdom. Here, it was not even a question that his veins bore royal blood.

They were going to play soon, and Creole installed me, by myself, at a table in a dark corner. Then I watched them, Creole, and the little black man, and Sonny, and the others, while they horsed around, standing just below the bandstand. The light from the bandstand spilled just a little short of them and, watching them laughing and gesturing and moving about, I had the feeling that they, nevertheless, were being most careful not to step into that circle of light too suddenly: that if they moved into the light too suddenly, without thinking, they would perish in flame. Then, while I watched, one of them, the small, black man, moved into the light and crossed the bandstand and started fooling around with his drums. Then—being funny and being, also, extremely ceremonious—Creole took Sonny by the arm and led him to the piano. A woman's voice called Sonny's name, and a few hands started clapping. And Sonny, also being funny and being ceremonious, and so touched, I think, that he could have cried, but neither hiding it nor showing it, riding it like a man, grinned, and put both hands to his heart and bowed from the waist.

Creole then went to the bass fiddle and a lean, very bright-skinned brown man jumped up on the bandstand and picked up his horn. So there they were, and the atmosphere on the bandstand and in the room began to change and tighten. Someone stepped up to the microphone and announced them. Then there were all kinds of murmurs. Some people at the bar shushed others. The waitress ran around, frantically getting in the last orders, guys and chicks got closer to each other, and the lights on the bandstand, on the quartet, turned to a kind of indigo. Then they all looked different there. Creole looked about him for the last time, as though he were making certain that all his chickens were in the coop, and then he—jumped and struck the fiddle. And there they were.

All I know about music is that not many people ever really hear it. And even then, on the rare occasions when something opens within, and the music enters, what we mainly hear, or hear corroborated, are personal, private, vanishing evocations. But the man who creates the music is hearing something else, is dealing with the roar rising from the void and imposing order on it as it hits the air. What is evoked in him, then, is of another order, more terrible because it has no words, and triumphant, too, for that same reason. And his triumph, when he triumphs, is ours. I just watched Sonny's face. His face was troubled, he was working hard, but he wasn't with it. And I had the feeling that, in a way, everyone on the bandstand was waiting for him, both waiting for him and pushing him along. But as I began to watch Creole, I realized that it was Creole who held them all back. He had them on a short rein. Up there, keeping the beat with his whole body, wailing on the fiddle, with his eyes half closed, he was listening to everything, but he was listening to Sonny. He was having a dialogue with Sonny. He wanted Sonny to leave the shore line and strike out for the deep water. He was Sonny's witness that deep water and drowning were not the same thing—he had been there, and he knew. And he wanted Sonny to know. He was waiting for Sonny to do the things on the keys which would let Creole know that Sonny was in the water.

And, while Creole listened, Sonny moved, deep within, exactly like someone in torment. I had never before thought of how awful the relationship must be between the musician and his instrument. He has to fill it, this instrument, with the breath of life, his own. He has to make it do what he wants it to do. And a piano is just a piano. It's made out of so much wood and wires and little hammers and big ones, and ivory. While there's only so much you can do with it, the only way to find this out is to try to try and make it do everything.

And Sonny hadn't been near a piano for over a year. And he wasn't on much better terms with his life, not the life that stretched before him now. He and the piano stammered, started one way, got scared, stopped; started another way, panicked, marked time, started again; then seemed to have found a direction, panicked again, got stuck. And the face I saw on Sonny I'd never seen before. Everything had been burned out of it, and, at the same time, things usually hidden were being burned in, by the fire and fury of the battle which was occurring in him up there.

Yet, watching Creole's face as they neared the end of the first set, I had the feeling that something had happened, something I hadn't heard. Then they finished, there was scattered applause, and then, without an instant's warning, Creole started into something else, it was almost sardonic, it was *Am I Blue*. And, as though he commanded, Sonny began to play. Something began to happen. And Creole let out the reins. The dry, low, black man said something awful on the drums, Creole answered, and the drums talked back. Then the horn insisted, sweet and high, slightly detached perhaps, and Creole listened, commenting now and then, dry, and driving, beautiful and calm and old. Then they all came together again, and Sonny was part of the family again. I could tell this from his face. He seemed to have found, right there beneath his fingers, a damn brand-new piano. It seemed that he couldn't get over it. Then, for a while, just being happy with Sonny, they seemed to be agreeing with him that brand-new pianos certainly were a gas.

Then Creole stepped forward to remind them that what they were playing was the blues. He hit something in all of them, he hit something in me, myself, and the music tightened and deepened, apprehension began to beat the air. Creole began to tell us what the blues were all about. They were not about anything very new. He and his boys up there were keeping it new, at the risk of ruin, destruction, madness, and death, in order to find new ways to make us listen. For, while the tale of how we suffer, and how we are delighted, and how we may triumph is never new, it always must be heard. There isn't any other tale to tell, it's the only light we've got in all this darkness.

And this tale, according to that face, that body, those strong hands on those strings, has another aspect in every country, and a new depth in every generation. Listen, Creole seemed to be saying, listen. Now these are Sonny's blues. He made the little black man on the drums know it, and the bright, brown man on the horn. Creole wasn't trying any longer to get Sonny in the water. He was wishing him Godspeed. Then he stepped back, very slowly, filling the air with the immense suggestion that Sonny speak for himself.

Then they all gathered around Sonny, and Sonny played. Every now and again one of them seemed to say, Amen. Sonny's fingers filled the air with life, his life. But that life contained so many others. And Sonny went all the way back, he really began with the spare, flat statement of the opening phrase of the song. Then he began to make it his. It was very beautiful because it wasn't hurried and it was no longer a lament. I seemed to hear with what burning he had made it his, with what burning we had yet to make it ours, how we could cease lamenting. Freedom lurked around us and I understood, at last, that he could help us to be free if we would listen, that he would never be free until we did. Yet, there was no battle in his face now. I heard what he had gone through, and would continue to go through until he came to rest in earth. He had made it his: that long line, of which we knew only Mama and Daddy. And he was giving it back, as everything must be given back, so that, passing through death, it can live forever. I saw my mother's face again, and felt, for the first time, how the stones of the road she had walked on must have bruised her feet. I saw the moonlit road where my father's brother died. And it brought something else back to me, and carried me past it. I saw my little girl again and felt Isabel's tears again, and I felt my own tears begin to rise. And I was yet aware that this was only a moment, that the world waited outside, as hungry as a tiger, and that trouble stretched above us, longer than the sky.

Then it was over. Creole and Sonny let out their breath, both soaking wet, and grinning. There was a lot of applause and some of it was real. In the dark, the girl came by and I asked her to take drinks to the bandstand. There was a long pause, while they talked up there in the indigo light and after a while I saw the girl put a Scotch and milk on top of the piano for Sonny. He didn't seem to notice it, but just before they started playing again, he sipped from it and looked toward me, and nodded. Then he put it back on top of the piano. For me, then, as they began to play again, it glowed and shook above my brother's head like the very cup of trembling.

PART IV
CONTEMPORARY
LITERATURE

INTRODUCTION

During the Negro Awakening, wrote Alain Locke in *Opportunity*, Negro writers "got jazz-mad and cabaret-crazy instead of getting folk-wise and sociologically sober." Many succumbed to the fever of good times and open-door hospitality that linked nighttime Harlem and daytime Publishers Row. But the stock market crash of 1929 sobered them—patrons and publishers vanishing —in the same way that getting fired and standing in relief lines sobered their working-class acquaintances. The convergence of certain economic and ideological forces, such as poverty and racial prejudice on the one hand and Marxist opportunism on the other, caused both concentration and expansion of Negro thought. While the national tendency, especially among liberal white thinkers, was to explore possibilities of more equitable government, Negro workers, politicians, and organizational leaders accepted interracial cooperation wherever it was feasible. The literary counterpart was an increased effort by some white authors, such as Erskine Caldwell and William Faulkner, to depict Negro working-class characters more realistically and to connect their lot with the fate of the larger society. At the same time, a concentration of Negro selfappraisal, mediating between the diminished Garveyite enthusiasm and the newer emphasis upon systematic study, was indicated by the establishment of *The Journal of Negro Education* in 1931 and *The Negro History Bulletin* in 1933, and by specific historical interests that increasingly worked their way into Negro writings.

In the short story, two authors largely held sway in the 1930's: Langston Hughes and Richard Wright (see the detailed introductions which precede the selections from their work). In *The Ways of White Folks* (1934), Hughes's fourteen stories comprehensively revealed hitherto unexplored depths of Negro experience, with an easy and natural style elastic enough to convey his restraint, humor, and satire as well as his bitterness. In *Uncle Tom's Children* (1938), four novellas by Wright forcefully and vividly dramatized ways in which Southern Negroes, young and old, were brutalized at work, at play, and even at times of community disaster. The themes of working-class interracial cooperation, intensified by the additional "Bright and Morning Star" in the second edition, and sexual exploitation of Negro women at the cruel expense of Negro manhood, expanded the ideological and cultural significance of the volume. The word *proletarian* is superficially valuable in categorizing these collections, but it has little to do with their artistic importance. These two books opened new realms to the literary imagination, Hughes deftly sounding all the chords in the average Negro's life, Wright looking through his characters' "knot-hole in the fence" and wanting to communicate their agony in a new language so authentic that readers would be left "without the consolation of tears." The matter thus raised in its full dimensions was Negro "soul"—to use Hughes's language of the 1920's and the general racial idiom of today—and the attendant literary problem was the question of style, the linguistic means by which to convey that matter substantively, emotionally, and intellectually.

Other Negro short story writers who published works during the 1930's were John F. Matheus, Marita Bonner, Rudolph Fisher, Dorothy West, and the now better-known Ralph Ellison, Claude McKay, Arna Bontemps, Ted Poston, and Zora Neale Hurston. Matheus, Bonner, and Fisher had earlier won contests sponsored by *The Crisis* and *Opportunity*; West and Poston had been trained as journalists, and Hurston as a folklorist. McKay's volume, *Gingertown* (1932), with half of the twelve stories about the tropics and half about Harlem, concentrated its realism on the narrow world of sexual intrigue and its related color bias among Negroes. Bontemps and Ellison, by means of individually published stories, were mounting careers that would encompass other genres.

The 1940's brought additional names into the field: Ann Petry, Chester B. Himes, Frank Yerby, and John Henrik Clarke. Ann Petry's work appeared in *The Crisis* and *Phylon*, and in Foley's *Best American Short Stories of 1946*, before she turned to writing novels. While working in California shipyards, Himes also produced competent short stories, by 1946 (the year his first novel appeared) increasing to ten the number published in *Esquire* alone—a sequence that had begun with the prison-life narrative "Crazy in the Stir" in 1934. Clarke, whose poems, articles, and book reviews began to appear increasingly in the 1940's, and whose editorial associations with Negro journals were continual, published stories portraying miscellaneous injustices endured by Negroes; "Santa Claus Is a White Man," with which he opened this decade of his career in the pages of *Opportunity*, is an example. Yerby, with his first-published story, "Health Card," which appeared in *Harper's* in 1944, won an O. Henry Memorial Award; he soon, however, turned from short fiction, while teaching English in various Southern colleges, to devote himself to a lucrative career as a novelist. Stories published by these writers in first-class magazines belied the double standard of judgment (presuming inferior capabilities in Negro writers) which Wright, and Chesnutt before him, had shaken. They found special hospitality, nevertheless, in such magazines as *Negro Story*, which in the spring of 1945 alone published two stories by Ellison, two by Himes, three by Hughes, and a number by minor authors.

Out of the approximately fifty Negro writers who have published short stories since 1950, and whose names have appeared in critical or historical commentary, about fifteen have attracted distinctly favorable notice. Of that fifteen, three had already made names for themselves (Hughes, Wright, and the poet and playwright Owen Dodson); eight began their literary careers in or near the 1950's without decisive dedication to the short story form (James Baldwin, Albert Murray, Mary Elizabeth Vroman, William Melvin Kelley, Paule Marshall, LeRoi Jones, Alston Anderson, and Ernest J. Gaines); the others have published little —most were born after 1935—either within or beyond the genre (Cyrus Colter, Clifford V. Johnson, Lindsay Patterson, Alice Walker, and Martin Hamer). The only existing comprehensive collections of short stories by Negroes, edited in 1966 by John Henrik Clarke (*American Negro Short Stories*) and in 1967 by Langston Hughes (*The Best Short Stories by Negro Writers*), disclose the names of other young writers who, through continued practice, are capable of becoming good craftsmen.

These short stories have often been so different from one another that variety might best describe the contemporary trend. Langston

Hughes's stories in *Laughing to Keep from Crying* (1952), for example, range from Harlem to Hong Kong in setting, from jealousy to crucifixion in plot, and from revival-tent jubilation to dining-table sophistication in atmosphere. In Alston Anderson's *Lover Man* (1959), rural and urban Negroes' slang and humor, as well as customs like "signifying" and characters like Mutton Head, enliven the generally simple narratives. Two collections appearing in 1961, Richard Wright's posthumous *Eight Men* and Paule Marshall's *Soul Clap Hands and Sing*, exhibit contrasts that mark the work of some of their contemporaries. The harsh passion with which Wright fired his stories of the 1930's, undiminished in *Eight Men* when it surfaces, even in the all-dialogue tales, makes his collection a final testament to the resentful disillusion that drove him from America. In the other collection, Paule Marshall's words, rather than straightforward expressions of alienation from brutal racist surroundings, are more indirect guides to her sense of the universal complexities faced by aging men, in settings as different as Brooklyn and British Guiana. Like Anderson, William Melvin Kelley shows a good ear for dialogue in his sixteen narratives in *Dancers on the Shore* (1964), interlaced with the four-letter words that feed a sometimes specious realism into modern writing. Another sixteen stories, in LeRoi Jones's *Tales* (1967)—their heroes moving through ghetto and campus and through sexy fun, bravado, and despair —are prologue to the retreat of the black underground man, restlessly unfit either for the ghetto or for escape from it.

No analytical criticism has yet defensibly identified the best short stories written by Negroes. Between Chesnutt's "The Goophered Grapevine" (1887) and Lindsay Patterson's "Red Bonnet"—to choose a competent story by one of the youngest authors now working at the genre —there is much to read and to ponder in ways not characteristic of established arbiters of taste. Certain stories have been praised enough to suggest undeniably high quality: Toomer's "Fern," Hughes's "On the Road," Ellison's "Flying Home," Wright's "The Man Who Lived Underground," and Yerby's "Health Card," among others. Now critics have the task of further assessing the merits attributed to such recent pieces as Albert Murray's "Train Whistle Guitar" (in Clarke's collection) and Ernest J. Gaines's "A Long Day in November" (in Hughes's). Using those collections and others sure to appear, as well as additional places of publication they reveal, scholars can add vitality and comprehensiveness to the body of American fiction.

Since 1930, an undetermined number of novels by Negroes have been published. More than eighty can be counted by reference to bibliographies patently incomplete, and other notices in Negro periodicals alone justify the conclusion that well over a hundred worthy of examination have appeared. Relatively little can be said of these novels in a few pages, but fundamental trends can be identified. Many of the authors—

developing their talents during the depression only with the help of the Federal Writers' Project—endured the hardships which made Negroes feel the need for a new self-image and social consciousness. These hardships, and the enforced new perceptions of the racial past, present, and future, form the subject matter of the best novels produced in the 1930's.

George Wylie Henderson's novel that deserves mention—he was working on his third when he died in 1965—is *Ollie Miss* (1935), the first to treat sharecropping. Almost exclusively about Negroes in rural Alabama, it throws some light on the relatively unexplored tradition of romantic love in Negro writings. In 1936, Arna Bontemps published *Black Thunder*, representing a departure from the exotic strain of the 1920's: the historical novel inspired by literary regionalism and by Negro organizations, magazines, and universities then increasing their emphasis on Negro history. Written with restraint, the novel used the unsuccessful but daring slave rebellion led by Gabriel Prosser in Virginia in 1800 to advance the theme of black men's love of freedom. In 1937, Zora Neale Hurston's steady historical interest in folkways and her immediate personal drive to plumb the mysteries of feminine love successfully merged in *Their Eyes Were Watching God*; set in the Florida past, the novel examined intraracial color prejudice and miscegenation, at the same time carrying forward the Washington-DuBois controversy. It is historically just that 1940 be associated primarily with one great novel, *Native Son*. With all of its unforgettable indications—literal, allusive, metaphorical, and symbolical—of how a sensitive author and his doomed protagonist struggle toward human self-identity, Richard Wright's work stands quite alone, above the timberline, in American fiction. It closed and rose above a decade in which other achievements, however, merit notice; among them were the first contemporary war novel by a Negro, Victor Daly's *Not Only War* (1932); the first novel of Negro college life, O'Wendell Shaw's *Greater Need Below* (1936); and the first novels to chronicle Negro family life, Waters Edward Turpin's *These Low Grounds* (1937) and *O Canaan!* (1939), respectively concerned with Maryland lowlanders and Mississippi migrants in Chicago.

The 1940's, which opened so promisingly with *Native Son*, saw the expansion of some themes and matter characteristic of the 1920's and 1930's, as well as the evolution of new substance. William Attaway's *Blood on the Forge* (1941) ably widened Turpin's earlier picture of migrants by his variously symbolic and realistic depiction of the troubles faced by three Kentucky sharecropping brothers who had to migrate and pit their whole beings against the steel mills. In the middle 1940's, a few novels falteringly but significantly mounted an aggressive tradition. Chester Himes's *If He Hollers Let Him Go* (1945), following in the wake of Wright, battered the protagonist with the full arsenal of racial discrimination before allowing him a dubious release through military service. Similar to Wright's work in a different way, Willard Motley's *Knock on Any Door* (1947) used narrative action like that of *Native Son* for a naturalistic account of external pressures that overwhelm his young Italian hero. The two novels by Himes and Motley show the emotional and thematic magnetism of Wright's work; they also disclose the pitfalls that lay before those of his followers whose psychological rapport with the protagonists was incomplete or whose personalities did not invite intestinal concern with race. (Frank Yerby, whose string of popular novels —Robert Bone calls him "the prince of pulpsters"—began in 1946, might have become another follower of Wright, as his short stories of the 1940's indicate; but his series of best-sellers altered his destiny.)

Two women, born about a year apart, and both starting their careers as journalists and short story writers, did some of the best novel-writing of the 1940's. Ann Petry's *Country Place* (1947) scarified small-town life, deepening her incisions by using white characters nurtured in the parochialism and delusion that cannot survive change, as well as metaphors and symbols reminiscent of Hawthorne. In *The Living Is Easy* (1948), Dorothy West, one-time editor of *Challenge* and *New Challenge* (magazines of the 1930's dedicated to revitalizing Negro writing and art), satirically exposed the shallow, wasteful creeds that deteriorate many middle-class Negroes. The racial consciousness which, for Negro authors as a whole, concentrated in the 1920's and expanded in the 1930's appeared, showing both tendencies, in *The Living Is Easy*. The two novels, published close together by authors of undeniable ability, demonstrate the inherent viability of Negro writing, which constantly responds to divergent tendencies in the colored populace and yet so mirrors the individuality of each author as to include in its tradition works almost completely nonracial.

Between 1950 and the present, the pendulum has swung as widely as ever. In 1951 Owen Dodson published *Boy at the Window*, one of a series of novels by Negroes substantially about youth painfully maturing. Dodson's nine-year-old protagonist, protected by his mother until she dies, draws the reader into his thoughts and talk as he struggles through problems of sex, religion, and race in Brooklyn and Washington, in a narrative that combines stream-of-consciousness style with childlike language. In James Baldwin's *Go Tell It on the Mountain* (1953), written with vivid autobiographical recall, his fifteen-year-old Harlem hero gropes turbulently through violence and doubt toward salvation. A boy of about the same age figures prominently in William Demby's *Beetlecreek* (1950), a novel employing him and his Negro identity symbolically, along with an eccentric old white man, to dramatize themes of alienation and existentialist choice of good and evil against the background of a stagnant town. Two novels more affirmatively resolving the dilemmas of teenagers are Julian Mayfield's *The Long Night* (1958) and Paule Marshall's

Brown Girl, Brownstones (1959); the former moves a Harlem boy courageously through the bewilderments of a broken home, and the latter depicts a warm-hearted, second-generation Barbadian girl who manages to save her heritage: her strong-willed mother's ambition and her genial father's island-rooted love of life. Plying the same general theme, Gordon Parks's *The Learning Tree* (1963) recalls the author's native Kansas of the 1920's as the environment of his farm boy protagonist. Two later novels, Henry Van Dyke's *Ladies of the Rachmaninoff Eyes* (1965) and Ronald Fair's *Hog Butcher* (1966), offer further variations of young people's troubles. The former, a first-novel winner of a Hopwood Award at the University of Michigan, traces the comfortable eccentricities of a seventeen-year-old narrator who reads Baudelaire, attends a seance, and refuses a female bedroom interloper with almost equal equanimity. Fair's novel pictures Chicago as "butcher" of ghetto-enclosed Negroes, particularly the two ten-year-old protagonists who see two policemen accidentally shoot their adult friend; yet one of the boys holds on to his integrity as a witness, despite the hostilities and corruptions that press upon them.

Family history, rather than a struggling youngster—portrayed first by Turpin in the 1930's and later in novels like C. R. Offord's *The White Face* (1943)—was developed in 1954 in two novels descriptive of Southern Negro family life. Chester Himes's *The Third Generation* follows such a family from slavery times to the present, detailing rather naturalistically the disasters, marital strife, and racial biases that drag family members down. The two generations of the Georgia family pictured by John O. Killens in his first novel, *Youngblood*, encounter sadistic violence in their attempts to endure with dignity. Less violence erupts in Julian Mayfield's *The Hit* (1957), but small tragedy stalks a Harlem family almost daily as the father's dream of escape from despair flowers and then vanishes with the numbers runner who does not pay up after the big hit. Tension of a different, often deeper kind pervades the movement of *Sissie* (1963), by John A. Williams, in which matriarchal dominance and seemingly unrewarded parental sacrifices collide with youthful drives toward success in the competitive, sophisticated world of culture and art. The 1964 movie "The Cool World" was based on the novel of the same name published in 1959 by Warren Miller, which emphasizes, not family allegiances, but a juvenile gang member's shifting ties and troubles among the "Royal Crocodiles" of East Harlem. Kristin Hunter's protagonist, in *God Bless the Child* (1965), uselessly expends her money-making ambitions trying to escape allegiances to family members who represent three generations of unprofitable attitudes toward whites.

Semiautobiographical novels, not radically unlike family chronicles, have been recently published by at least three writers. The best-known, LeRoi Jones, in his *The System of Dante's Hell* (1965) sets forth an expressionistic, lyrical, sometimes fragmented account of a child taking in sense impressions in Newark slums, of a teen-ager growing cynical and tough there, and of a man enduring a Southern small town by means of a memory and consciousness able to adjust imaginatively to what the author would call Dantean "holes of hell." In its way just as unusual is the expatriate William Demby's *The Catacombs*, published the same year, making complex use of the discontinuities of film-makers, the geometrical and spatial particulars of the Roman catacombs, and the relevances of sex, social status, and world news to the human psyche—thus sometimes illuminating and sometimes darkening the protagonist's awkward search for meaningful personal attachments. Although the third author, Carlene Hatcher Polite, took notes for ten years before writing *The Flagellants* (1967), her love story, complicated by racial conflict, is less demanding on the reader.

Racial conflict as expressed through the crucial drive of sex, rather than love, has been dramatized in novels of the last decade or so. Baldwin's *Giovanni's Room* (1956) unfolds the exultations and terrors of homosexual allurements without special reference to race. His *Another Country* (1962), on the other hand, repeatedly mixes race into a violent amalgam of characters so variously seized by either racial or erotic passions as to portend a country to be laid waste by its inability to foster human love. A different kind of novel, Charles Wright's *The Messenger* (1963) lacks the anguished vituperation of Baldwin's work, but the mixture of tender reflections, lonesomeness, and evanescent hopes in the Manhattan messenger boy turned prostitute is the bygone sadness that has turned so sour in the older novelist's vocal characters. Still more different is Chester Himes's *Pinktoes* (1965), a satirical novel of the erotic rambling and self-deceiving verbal integration of middle-class Negroes and whites deftly misguided at gatherings arranged by a Harlem woman.

A jazz background, in contrast, largely orders the substance of two novels in which sexual adventures are employed: John A. Williams' *Night Song* (1961) and William Melvin Kelley's *A Drop of Patience* (1965). The former, using much bebop language and revealing the special troubles and achievements of jazz musicians like the saxophonist hero, adds an interracial amour. Kelley's novel is a grim account of the rise to fame and the mental and spiritual deterioration of a jazz musician born blind—a rise through an outcast's necessary pluck and cunning, a fall through betrayal by his neurotic white mistress, one of the four women with whom he suffers misunderstanding and humiliation. In young Jane Philips' *Mojo Hand* (1966), the humiliation and deterioration endured by a possessed teen-aged white girl at the hands of a guitar-plucking Negro blues singer whom she trails across the country are morally neutralized by the author's apparent acceptance of society as a cold, dull wasteland. But the protagonist of Charles Wright's *The Wig* (1966), spruced up with Silky Smooth Hair Relaxer, schemes hopefully and humorously among pretenders whom tenement life in Harlem has left vulnerable to his craft.

Negro novelists' use of sex and sensationalism has not dulled their alertness to literary possibilities in such matters as housing and education. Frank London Brown's *Trumbull Park* (1959), based on facts, recounts the terrifying ordeals of Negro families who move into a Chicago housing development occupied by whites. Julian Mayfield's *The Grand Parade* (1961), shifting to racial hatreds that have flamed during desegregation crises, exposes the shameless politics and personal corruption that make discrimination in education official, then naturalistically adds rape, bombing, and murder—without forsaking the humorous touches also found in *The Hit*. Negro college life, necessitated by racism in education, is scathingly depicted in J. Saunders Redding's *Stranger and Alone* (1950), the satire gathering around the degraded character of a kowtowing Negro educator. The timeserver, whose characterization continues the Washington-DuBois controversy, is comparable to Ralph Ellison's Southern Negro educator in *Invisible Man* (1952). In that remarkable novel, which merges the substance, style, and meaning of much Negro experience with eminent traditions in world literature, the author moves his twice-born protagonist through signally representative places and ideological crises in American life, allowing him selfhood only through pain and love. Kristin Hunter's rather witty *The Landlord* (1966), in which Negro tenants variously deploy know-me-if-you-can engagements with their sympathetic white playboy landlord, treats more superficial kinds of cultural adjustment.

The special meaning of racial crises to Negro soldiers and veterans, first explored by a Negro novelist in 1932, was examined about thirty years later by three authors. John O. Killens, in *And Then We Heard the Thunder* (1963), focuses on World War II itself as the arena in which the crudities of army life accumulate with the nuances and overt tyrannies of racism to launch wars within war. In the same year, *If We Must Die*, a first novel by Junius Edwards, shifts the battleground to a small Southern town where a veteran comes home determined to vote —only to be fired, beaten, and almost castrated for his civic ambition. The soldier whose chaotic two days in an army hospital in France are shown in young Robert Boles's *The People One Knows* (1964) undergoes more psychic violence: his cultured Cape Cod background having been reduced to disordered memories by his late exposure to racial bigotry, he attempts suicide and suffers a Kafka-like alienation, accompanied by physical and mental agitations mirroring his torturous redefinitions of his past and present. The same year, Ernest J. Gaines, in his first novel, *Catherine Carmier*, uses Louisiana backwater people and an isolated, passioned-ruined Creole family to explore another young man's redefinition of his past, a Southern boy whose college education in the North has destroyed his affinities for strife-ridden farmlands and for towns uplifted by no more than intraracial status based on skin color.

The historical sense beneath the novelists' turn to war and regional life—a sense first expressed abundantly in the journals, organizations, and books of the 1930's—has in the last dozen years been found in novels variously approaching the past. The intense scholarship of DuBois is evident in his *The Black Flame*, a trilogy composed of *The Ordeal of Mansart* (1957), *Mansart Builds a School* (1959), and *Worlds of Color* (1961), designed to reveal neglected historical truths about Negroes, beginning with Reconstruction. An earlier period is covered in Alston Anderson's *All God's Children* (1965), in which a heroic Negro slave lives through a number of cruelties before the Civil War. A Rosenthal Foundation Award went to William Melvin Kelley for his *A Different Drummer* (1962), which vividly dramatizes the imagined consequences of Negroes' total departure from a Southern state. (William Gardner Smith's *Stone Face*, a novel appearing the next year, suggested that, should some of them move as far away as Paris, they would find a comparable racial prejudice in French attitudes toward Africans.) In 1965, Ronald Fair's *Many Thousands Gone* fancies a Southern county in which Negroes have been held in slavery, illiteracy, and ignorance of the outside world since 1836; and it humorously narrates how an old Negro woman—aided by militant youngsters—precipitates in 1963 the downfall of the murderous officialdom. Slavery and racist violence necessarily figure in *Jubilee* (1966), poet Margaret Walker's long re-creation of the life and times of her great-grandmother, one of "Marse Dutton's" fifteen slave children, who suffers beatings, floods, and fires in this first Civil War novel by a Negro. *Of Love and Dust*, published by Ernest J. Gaines the following year, shows antebellum varieties of murder and degeneracy still virulent in rural Louisiana, where in 1958 Gaines's young, city-bred Negro rashly careers to his doom, inspiring in the plantation hand who narrates his tragedy a manly determination.

Negro novelists' endless concern with the endless enormities of racial discrimination is to be compared with their flow of novels outside that tradition. The bitterness and horror that Richard Wright eloquently brought to the fictional expression of Negro thought continues in his *The Outsider* (1953), the chronicle of a Chicago postal worker accidentally freed from nagging human ties for a violent pursuit of life's meaning-within-absurdity in New York. Ann Petry, on the other hand, in *The Narrows*, published the same year, modifies the basically sociological approach she took to a Negro family's environment in *The Street* (1946) to a concern with New England villagers responding to an interracial love affair. A further modification of the racial theme is found in Dale Wright's *They Harvest Despair* (1965). Based on the journalist-author's own travels in 1961 with seasonal workers migrating from Florida to New York, this novel exposes the cycle of exploitation and debt that impoverishes and isolates them. The final novel of a Negro who steadily worked outside the racial tradition, Willard Motley's posthumous *Let Noon Be Fair* (1966), objectively and panoramically sweeps through generations of whites whose drunkenness and crudity, as well as their idealism and progressiveness, are reflected in the transformed natives of a small town in Mexico.

The diversity in recent novels by Negroes—even in novels by a single author—is evidenced by Negro participation in an internationally popular genre: the detective novel. First tried by Rudolph Fisher in *The Conjure Man Dies* (1932), the genre has been congenial to the talents of Chester Himes, who entertains Continental readers especially with quick-trigger, action-packed novels in which his two Harlem detectives roughly make their way among the addicts, drunkards, stool pigeons, and plentiful decent people of the ghetto. Such a novel is *Cotton Comes to Harlem* (1965), in which the humor, realistic dialogue, and everpresent sex are characteristic; named after one of the detectives, Cotton Ed Johnson, it describes a fake Garveyite and eighty-seven-thousand-dollar swindle of Harlem residents bilked into a back-to-Africa scheme. A different sort of detective appears in Himes's *Run Man Run* (1967), a maniacal New Yorker whose black victims and white brother-in-law afford human interest, while lifelike pictures of Manhattan and of Harlem's inhabitants add genuine background.

A sampling of novels published in 1966 and 1967 by Negroes reveals the continued rise of new authors and the pattern of concerns likely to engage some of their prolific contemporaries. First-time novelists George "Hal" Bennett (*A Wilderness of Vines*), Nathan Barrett (*Bars of Adamant*), and John Edgar Wideman (*A Glance Away*) have yet to prove themselves. Two novels about Harlem—a humorous but undistinguished work by Himes, *The Heat's On*, and a psychologically perceptive first novel by Rosa Guy, *Bird at My Window*—forecast undiminished probes of that challenging community. Three others, all published in 1967 by productive authors, show a particular circle of influences working on Negro creative thought today. John O. Killens' *Sippi* represents the nightmarish imprint of the South upon his consciousness, rather than his best literary imagination or style. William Melvin Kelley's *Dem*, conceived in angry reaction to a similar nightmare, transfers a historical sense of it to a white husband confounded by his wife's delivery of twins, one colored, then surrealistically stretches the theme of twin American responsibilities by a counterthrust of episodes in which a psychopathic Marine veteran murders his family. John A. Williams ends his quickly popular *The Man Who Cried I Am* with his dying protagonist's discovery of Washington's nightmarish "final solution" to the Negro problem, a tragic intention forecast by the racist rejections suffered and observed by the writer-hero.

Although no novels have been excerpted for this anthology, a glimpse of their representative contents is vital background for understanding other works. Negro short story writers are often novelists too, and those who are not have often been influenced by the novelists personally or vicariously. Their combined fiction offers the voluminous realities of Negro experience, physical and psychological. In their diversity—itself a constant illumination—these works amass a complex picture of the jobs, dwellings, diversions, and schools; the talk, folkways, and character types; and the shared hopes and cynicisms of Negroes. The future of fiction by Negroes—which J. Saunders Redding believes is in the hands of Paule Marshall, Killens, Ellison, and one or two others—is imponderable. Filled with the possibilities yearly raised by new writers with their new visions of American reality, and steadied by a racial tradition deepening and widening through superior individual works, this fiction promises to add moral toughness and maturity to our imaginative prose.

Between 1930 and the present time, scores of plays written by Negroes have been produced, and Negro theatrical groups have struggled to bring realistic dramas to their communities. The 1930's remain distinguished by the Federal Theater Project, which encouraged Negro playwrights and gave superior productions to many of their works, among them Frank Wilson's *Walk Together, Children* and Theodore Browne's *Natural Man*, both based on folk material; Arna Bontemps and Countee Cullen's dramatization of Rudolph Fisher's *The Conjure-Man Dies*; and Theodore Ward's *Big White Fog*, one of the best. Broadway's ablest presentations included Hall Johnson's *Run, Little Children* and Langston Hughes's *Mulatto*. Little theater groups like the Harlem Suitcase Theater and the Rose McClendon Workshop Theater, founded respectively by Langston Hughes and Dick Campbell, staged Negro-authored plays in Harlem libraries, lofts, and basements. Campbell's group presented such successful works as Abram Hill's *On Strivers' Row* and George Norford's *Joy Exceeding Glory*. In the 1930's, Negro colleges strengthened their efforts, partly through the Negro Intercollegiate Drama Association, to create a Negro theater. Faculty members wrote plays (for example, Thomas D. Pawley's *Jedgement Day* and Owen Dodson's *Divine Comedy*); and the folk drama of the decade, such as that of Willis Richardson and Randolph Edmonds, both of whom pioneered in anthologizing Negro plays, added historical substance to the tradition.

Plays enthusiastically received by Negro community audiences were at times critical of society—a characteristic which, in the early 1940's, harmonized less and less with wartime public attitudes. New little theater groups, the American Negro Theater (the "Ants") and the

Negro Playwrights Company, for example, encouraged racial group expression with such efforts as the former's production of Abram Hill's *Walk Hard*; this adaptation of Len Zinberg's novel about prejudices endured by a Negro boxer pleased colored audiences but not the critics. Other plays by Negroes were weakened by Broadway alterations, such as Theodore Ward's *Our Lan'* and Oliver Pitcher's *Spring Beginning*. Crosscurrents in literary and national affairs were evinced near the end of this decade that had opened with a dramatization of Wright's *Native Son*, for new Negro names like Harold Holifield and Gertrude Jeanette were appearing on little theater handbills, new groups of Negro actors were diminishing their emphasis upon specifically Negro drama, and, while whites were throwing rocks at Paul Robeson's home-going audience at Peekskill, New York, the American Negro Theater was collapsing.

In the early 1950's, however, the Council on the Harlem Theater formed; it supported more works by Holifield, Jeanette, and others. Since 1950, when Alice Childress's *Just a Little Simple* (also supported by that Council) appeared as an adaptation of Langston Hughes's *Simple Speaks His Mind*, at least seventy of the numerous plays by Negroes have been produced. Many have reached the public only on little theater and university stages, a fact reflected in a paper read by playwright William Branch in 1965 at the New School for Social Research; he noted that only sixteen Negro playwrights had ever had work presented on Broadway.

Some knowledge of this recent Negro drama can be gained from observations on themes and content most often found. Among these plays, the largest category can be described as tragicomic dramatizations of domestic life. Chief among them is Lorraine Hansberry's Circle Award-winning *A Raisin in the Sun* (1959), about the troubles of the Youngers when they move into Chicago's white Clybourne Park area. Louis Peterson's *Take a Giant Step* (1953) engrossingly explores the problems (complicated by racism in housing) of a Negro teen-ager. In a play written about 1953 but not produced in New York until 1965, Baldwin's *The Amen Corner*, another youngster has problems, exacerbated in this case by his mother's and father's unequal love of life. Other plays in this category were produced in the 1950's: Sidney Easton's *Miss Trudie Fair*, about an exploited boardinghouse operator, and Charles Sebree and Greer Johnston's *Mrs. Patterson*, about the frustrations of a teen-age Southern Negro girl. More appeared in the 1960's, such as Roger Furman and Doris Brunson's *Three Shades of Harlem*, which surveys that community's many deferred hopes, and young Ronald Milner's *Who's Got His Own*, a grim portrayal of a youngster's comfortless realizations upon the death of his father.

Negro history and the less tragic areas of urban life account for the next two largest groups of plays. Critics have generally liked the historical plays, William Branch's *In Splendid Error*, for example, and Alice Childress's *Gold Through the Trees*, the former treating Frederick Douglass and John Brown, the latter covering hundreds of years. A well-produced later work, from the 1960's, John O. Killens and Loften Mitchell's *Ballad of the Winter Soldiers*, offers a panorama of freedom fighters. The urban comedy set forth in 1955 in Alice Childress's *Trouble in Mind* is sharply underscored by the use of racial stupidities in theatrical circles. Douglas Turner Ward's *Happy Ending*, a 1965 play about two domestics and their snappy nephew, captures both the ardor of modern Negro militancy and the ageless truth of human limitations. The historical and comic dimensions of these two groups have been included in a new theatrical genre, the gospel song-play, introduced in the 1960's by Langston Hughes; of his four lively presentations, the first and best was *Black Nativity*.

The companion piece to Ward's *Happy Ending*, his *Day of Absence*, belongs to one of two groups of plays that take almost opposite approaches to that staple, racial prejudice, which provides the bulk of so much writing by Negroes. Substantially comparable numbers of plays launch either frontal or lateral attacks on prejudice. The latter technique deepens such well-received folk comedies as Alice Childress's *Just a Little Simple* and Ossie Davis's *Purlie Victorious* (from the 1950's) and *Day of Absence*, the humor in each case often attaching to ordinary Negroes' realistic appraisals of the hypocrisies and weaknesses of whites. On the other hand, the assault is frontal in Loften Mitchell's *A Land Beyond the River* (1957) and in LeRoi Jones's companion-pieces, *The Toilet* and *The Slave* (1965). Mitchell's play is based on the severe economic reprisals and other punishments inflicted upon petitioning Clarendon County, South Carolina, Negroes around the time of the famous Supreme Court decision of 1954; the thematic assault is in the narrative material itself. But Jones's thrust is his symbolism, not his sensational or obscene matter: the toilet is his sense of the current national environment, and the slave is the creature into whose being that environment would crush him.

Smaller groups of plays with strong racial themes have been sometimes trenchant, sometimes lighthearted. Those few that have emphasized sex in racial relations have often been trenchant, Jones's *Dutchman* and Baldwin's *Blues for Mr. Charlie*, for example. Jones is again symbolic in his vision, for the white girl who lures and then kills the Negro man on the subway is America taunting and then destroying the manhood of its Negro citizens. Baldwin, writing a longer play and remembering the Emmett Till and Medgar Evers murders, uses no less symbolism but records Southern-style homicide and sexual pathology so forcefully that some whites have been unable or unwilling to sit through the play. Writing about a decade apart, and pondering the unique disabilities of

Negro soldiers under the strain of prejudice, William Branch and William Hairston produced *A Medal for Willie* and *Walk in Darkness*, respectively. In the earlier (1951) and better play, Branch has a Negro mother fling her son's posthumous war medal into the faces of Southern townspeople who have come to honor him. Other dramas of the 1950's focus on Negroes' attitudes toward themselves and their racial loyalties. Loften Mitchell's *The Cellar*, for example, melodramatically shows a Negro blues singer helping a fugitive from the South. A more subtly vicious, historical theme pervades Ossie Davis's *Alice in Wonder*, in which marital strife breaks out when the husband weakens under a television network's bribe to persuade him to denounce a militant Negro singer.

Miscellaneous other themes, sometimes emphatic in only one play, or a very few plays, are important in the Negro theatrical tradition. The "tragedy" of being a Negro—a long-standing fictional phenomenon both absurd and compelling—harrows the introspection of Edward Albee's student, Adrienne Kennedy, in her fifty-minute play, *The Funnyhouse of a Negro* (1964); her later *A Rat's Mass* and *The Owl Answers* are so allusive and abstruse that their appeal seems limited to Renaissance and other specialists. A comparable air of desolation and withdrawal from human comforts hovers about Arthur Roberson's *Don't Leave Go My Hand* (1965). A physically, more so than psychologically, depressing environment adds texture to the urban realism of Julian Mayfield's *A World Full of Men* (1952); that realism contrasts with the fantasy in Harold Holifield's *J. Toth*, which also appeared in the early 1950's. The underside of drug addiction and the miscellaneous intrigues, despairs, and small victories in Negro urban life are realistically—and often profanely—expressed in the 1965–1968 productions of energetic Ed Bullins: *The Rally, How Do You Do, Clara's Old Man, Goin'a Buffalo, In the Wine Time,* and *The Electronic Nigger*. A complex of themes and attitudes invests Lorraine Hansberry's *The Sign in Sidney Brustein's Window* (1964) with a fullness rendered urgent and compassionate by her death at thirty-four shortly after its opening. Negro playwrights have been both serious and gay in other efforts. William Branch's *Light in the Southern Sky* (1957), written about Mary McLeod Bethune for the National Broadcasting Company, won the Robert E. Sherwood Award (but thereafter, Branch said at the 1965 writers' conference at the New School for Social Research, neither NBC nor CBS gave him any more assignments—although the former offered him a job as a janitor.) Lightheartedness is understandably expressed in musicals, examples from the 1960's being Oscar Brown, Jr.'s *Kicks and Company* and Loften Mitchell's more successful *Ballad for Bimshire*. All the foregoing moods and materials cohere in *A Hand Is on the Gate*, the dramatized presentation in 1966 of Negro poetry and folk music.

The old and the new moods of Negro dramatists are now fermenting. After a twenty-year silence, Theodore Ward has organized theatrical activity in Chicago, revised his Broadway-thinned *Our Lan'*, and announced production plans for his *Candle in the Wind* and *Of Human Grandeur*. New names like George Houston Bass and William Wellington Mackey, on the other hand, continually appear. Bass, winner of a Rosenthal Award for a film script in 1964, has opened his career as playwright with experimental rhythms and associative repetitions in *Games*. Mackey, writing and staging his socially meaningful productions between 1965 and 1968 in Denver, Chicago, and New York, has to his credit *Behold! Cometh the Vanderkellans, Requiem for Brother X, Family Meeting*, and *Death of Charlie Blackman*. Lonnie Elder, whose *Ceremonies in Dark Old Men* (1965) is strongly perceptive, especially near the end, has already won two impressive awards. Loften Mitchell, author of the literary history, *Black Drama*, who is chronologically on middle ground, represents the steady drive and purpose of Negro playwrights in his *Tell Pharaoh*, a historical play appropriately termed "theatrical 'soul food' " in a newspaper account of its presentation in Brooklyn in October 1967.

The future of Negro dramatists is as broad as that of their fellow artists working in fiction. Stronger bridges to potential audiences are being built by determined theatrical groups such as those arising in 1967: in New York, the Ford Foundation-supported Negro Ensemble Company (founded by Douglas Turner Ward, Robert Hooks, and Gerald Krone) and the New Heritage Repertory Theater; in Chicago, the Afro-Arts Theater. The cultural demands and opportunities to which new public and managerial vision must respond in support of Negro playwrights and actors are well explored from the Negro point of view in a series of essays in the April 1966 and April 1967 annual theater numbers of *Negro Digest*. After the awakening argued for persuasively in those essays (among them pieces by James Baldwin, LeRoi Jones, Alice Childress, Ed Bullins, Ronald Milner, and others) and in articles by Douglas Turner Ward on August 14, 1966, and Ossie Davis on August 23, 1964, in *The New York Times*, Negro drama will vitalize the American stage.

In nonfiction, the earliest forms used by Negroes have contemporary equivalents in works far too numerous to identify in this essay. The mild protest in Jupiter Hammon's *Address* of 1787 has given way, in the pamphleteering tradition, to the militant commemoration of sit-in demonstrations found in the NAACP's booklet of 1962, *The Day They Changed Their Minds*. Briton Hammon's autobiographical *Uncommon Sufferings* of 1760 has its modern analogue in Claude Brown's shocking record of slum life in Harlem, *Manchild in the Promised Land* (1965). In 1863, William Wells Brown's biographical sketches of men and women of marked achievement in *The Black Man* was a pacemaker; exactly one century later, the collective biography of the year and one of the two individual biographies of the year were written on Negroes in sports. While the 1850's were distinguished by William C. Nell's histories of Negro military heroism, by William T. Catto's church history, and by William Wells Brown's writing on revolutionary patriots, the 1950's have been similarly notable for books by such Negro writers of history as Arna Bontemps, John Hope Franklin, Benjamin Quarles, J. Saunders Redding, and J. A. Rogers. Some of the titles reveal both continuing and shifting emphases: Franklin's *The Militant South* and *From Slavery to Freedom*, Quarles's *The Negro in the Civil War*, and Redding's *They Came in Chains*. Objective history also continues to merge with personal memoirs, for Elizabeth Keckley's White House experiences as a dress-maker, published in 1868 in her *Behind the Scenes*, can be compared with the recollections of a maid printed in 1961, Lillian Rogers Parks's *My Thirty Years Backstairs at the White House*, and with the executive insights afforded by E. Frederic Morrow in 1963 in *Black Man in the White House*. History and autobiography combine in Ely Green's *Ely* (1967), in which the social history of a Tennessee community at the turn of the century illuminates the author's memories of his boyhood.

The nonfictional books produced by Negroes since 1950 are well represented by the approximately two hundred thirty titles traceable in standard books, periodicals, pamphlets, and newspapers. The frequency with which these prose writers employ different subject matter, when categories are ranked, reveals their primary involvements. Autobiographies rank highest in number, constituting roughly twenty percent of the titles. Over half of these autobiographies have been written—often with a collaborator—by individuals popular in sports or entertainment, although others have been composed by teachers, civic workers, and adventurers. About fifteen percent of the books are histories, and the third largest category is the treatise on civil rights. The histories, including significant works by scholars already named, as well as by Rayford Logan, Lerone Bennett, Charles H. Wesley, and others, have documented the long-neglected truths of Negro participation in the intellectual and moral, in addition to the physical, building of America. The subject of civil rights has been only slightly less popular than history. The warnings of Richard Wright in 1957 in *White Man, Listen!* echo in another key in 1967 in Harold Cruse's *The Crisis of the Negro Intellectual*; and whereas John Hope, writing *Equality of Opportunity*, centers his attention upon a single trade union in 1956, the editorial staff of *Ebony*, assembling *The White Problem in America* in 1967, launch the critical arguments of several famous contributors against the complexities of racism.

The publication rate of such argumentative and expository coverage of the battle for civil rights has been almost double that of books more broadly sociological and psychological. Nevertheless, controversial and classic volumes have been written in the latter mode. E. Franklin Frazier's

Black Bourgeoisie (1957) is not always congenially secretive—or scientifically valid—in its picture of the uneasy mobility of middle-class Negroes. Nathan Hare in 1965 handles sociological tools and middle-class egos with some abandon, perhaps with satirical intent, placing in eleven uncomplimentary categories the "Black Anglo-Saxons" who give the book its title. The poet Calvin C. Hernton in the same year, and with a more aggressive disregard for sociological formalities, brings a wayward candor to his *Sex and Racism in America*. A third book in 1965, Kenneth B. Clark's Sidney Hillman Award-winning *Dark Ghetto*, strikes the balance in methodology, cogency, and timeliness with its analytical inquiry into thoughts and possibilities of power in the ghetto. Martin Luther King, whose very name was both sociology and psychology to Negroes; C. Eric Lincoln, whose book on the Black Muslims first played expansive light over a rumor-laden enterprise; and Malcolm X, whose bold, quick manliness and boyish mediation between hate and love became legendary—these and others have been the authors and the substance of important sociological books since 1950.

Slightly less common are three other kinds of books, each of which comprises about five percent of the nonfictional volumes recently printed: reportorial narratives focusing upon national and international events; collective biographies; and literary works with historical, critical, and biographical emphases. Two books published in 1956 by Richard Wright and Carl T. Rowan, the former's *The Color Curtain* about the Bandung Conference, the latter's report on his Far Eastern trip in *The Pitiful and the Proud*, represent the first kind. In the same category are chronicles of upheavals and explosive attitudes in the American South, such as Rowan's *Go South to Sorrow* (1957); King's *Stride Toward Freedom* (1958)—on the memorable Montgomery, Alabama, bus boycott; and Daisy Bates's *The Long Shadow of Little Rock* (1962). Among the recent collective biographies, Langston Hughes has written three (largely for young readers), Arna Bontemps and Andrew S. Young two apiece, and J. Saunders Redding one.

The third category—volumes that offer various combinations of literary history, criticism, and biography—is of special interest to students of literature written by Negroes. Such volumes, exclusive of microfilmed dissertations otherwise available only for restricted use in university libraries, are the only means of public access to Negroes' large-scale judgments of the literary accomplishments of the race. To secure professional assessments of any productive Negro author's total achievement or of the full meaning of any tradition, movement, or period in Negro writing, one must turn to comprehensive studies. Unfortunately, thorough examinations of the works of Negro authors have rarely been made since the critical analyses by Benjamin Brawley, Sterling Brown, J. Saunders Redding, and Nick Aaron Ford in the 1930's, and the work of Hugh M. Gloster in the 1940's, although excellent critical essays have appeared in journals and their infrequent publication in anthologies will probably increase. Brown's able criticism appears again in his thirty-year survey contributed to *The New Negro Thirty Years Afterward*, Howard University's record of its symposium of 1955. His colleague, Margaret Just Butcher (using materials left upon his death by Alain Locke), the following year published her broadly informative *The Negro in American Culture*. In 1960, the American Society of African Culture printed *The American Negro Writer and His Roots*, a collection of papers read at the previous year's First Conference of Negro Writers. The book-length studies of Negro writing published by Negroes during the last twenty years are Gloster's *Negro Voices in American Fiction* (1948) and two volumes appearing in 1967, Loften Mitchell's *Black Drama* and James A. Emanuel's *Langston Hughes*.

A peculiar social, but not scholarly, injustice inheres in the racial anonymity of some literary scholarship. The academic community at large does not realize its debt to some Negro scholars. In 1953, the authors of *Go Tell It on the Mountain, Maud Martha,* and *The Outsider* were known to be Negroes, but few realized the racial identity of Nathan A. Scott, Jr., author of *Rehearsals of Discomposure*, a scholarly study of Kafka, Lawrence, Silone, and Eliot. In 1962, books published by Langston Hughes, Daisy Bates, and William Melvin Kelley were credited to the Negro race; but the titles *George W. Cable* (by Philip Butcher) and *Faulkner and the Negro* (by Charles H. Nilon) seemed related to Negroes only through the semistereotypes of Cable and Faulkner, rather than through the race of Professors Butcher and Nilon. Similarly, few students among the many who profit conveniently from the use of *Digests of Great American Plays*, published also in 1962, by John Lovell, Jr., give credit to another Negro professor.

Briefer scholarly nonfiction by Negroes, assessing works by both Negroes and whites, is available in a few anthologies and in many journals. Almost one hundred pages of the Winter 1950 number of *Phylon* are devoted to a group of literary essays by Negroes; that journal is still a main Negro publisher of such essays, along with *Negro Digest*, *CLA Journal* (a good source of essays by Negroes on literature by whites), *Freedomways*, and *Negro History Bulletin*. Newsletters, like the *Negro American Literature Forum*, established at Indiana State University late in 1967, might become additional sources. The physical permanence and accessibility of anthologies enhance them as repositories of essays. *The Negro Caravan* (1941) of Sterling A. Brown, Arthur P. Davis, and Ulysses Lee, unexcelled in its comprehensiveness and informative introductory essays, contains few literary essays. They are supplemented, however, by several in Sylvestre C. Watkins' *Anthology of American Negro Literature* (1944) and by several more contemporary pieces in *Soon, One Morning* (1963) and *Anger, and Beyond* (1966), both assembled by a white editor, Herbert Hill. The few essays by Negroes found in a 1967 anthology, John A. Williams' *Beyond the Angry Black*, bring to a total of less than thirty the pieces of literary commentary printed in collections of Negro writing in the past quarter of a century. Besides these books and the Negro journals already mentioned as abundant sources, scholarly essays can be located in recent issues of *Massachusetts Review, Saturday Review, Southwest Review, Mainstream,* and *The New Leader,* as well as in earlier issues of *Partisan Review, Midwest Journal, Antioch Review, University of Kansas City Review,* and other periodicals.

This unassembled prose, representing much of the best literary reflection of some of the best-trained minds of the race, carries on the tradition recorded in the 1930's and 1940's in *The Crisis, Opportunity, Challenge, New Challenge, The Negro Quarterly,* and other journals born of early twentieth-century desperation and cultural ferment. An even dozen names taken from the list of authors whose deliberations lie uncollected in these journals, some of whose essays are sampled in this anthology, suggest the richness of their offerings. They include Ralph Ellison, Sterling A. Brown, Arna Bontemps, Langston Hughes, J. Saunders Redding, Nathan A. Scott, Jr., Arthur P. Davis, Nick Aaron Ford, LeRoi Jones, Hoyt W. Fuller, Thomas D. Jarrett, and John A. Williams. When these Negro critics and their deserving colleagues are discovered to be a crucial group in the national scholarly tradition, themselves expressive of both stimulating dissent and viable orthodoxy, an overdue readjustment of literary history, and possibly of aesthetic principles, will occur.

Poetry is fittingly the genre with which to round out developments since 1930. Negro poets have been uniquely molded by American experience to act as dissenters and prophets. The record left by them after that decade in which America first seriously questioned its democratic assumptions and possibilities—and after that racial awakening which stirred them to honest introspection and historical consciousness—is remarkable as both heritage and prologue.

The concentration and expansion which diversified Negro thought in the 1930's found poetic expression in regionalism and in deepened social criticism. The intensive regional and slavery-time studies fostered by the Federal Writers' Project, which nurtured some poets during the depression (Arna Bontemps, Claude McKay, and Margaret Walker, for example), combined with lingering Garveyism and the fact-finding zeal of new Negro journals and organizations to entrench and historically justify the poets' continuing racial pride. Sterling A. Brown's *Southern Road* (1932), faithfully capturing the idioms and attitudes of Southern Negroes in natural settings, expressed the new regionalism; at the same time, his individual poems like "To Nat Turner" and "Strong Men" bitingly conveyed social criticism. Frank Marshall Davis's volumes, *Black Man's Verse* (1935) and *I Am the American Negro* (1937), aggressively revealed his historical awareness and pride. Another title, *Black Labor Chant* (1939), by David Wadsworth Cannon, Jr., who died while a doctoral student at Columbia, was born of new economic perceptions. By the end of the decade, names better known today were being heard —Melvin B. Tolson, Robert Hayden, Owen Dodson, Margaret Walker— sometimes linked with socially realistic poems that would long merit esteem, such as "For My People" (Margaret Walker's, in *Poetry* in 1937) and "Dark Symphony" (Tolson's, a national first-prize winner at the American Negro Exposition in Chicago—and the inspiration for the title of this volume).

In the 1940's more Negro poets accepted the stylistic freedoms which had been used by Walt Whitman and Emily Dickinson, by French Symbolists and Parnassians, and by Spanish Modernists, and which had revived American poetry between 1912 and 1925 with the liberating techniques of free verse, imagism, vorticism, polyphonic prose, and other modes. This delayed aesthetic response on the part of many Negro poets —to be ultimately balanced, perhaps, by their tougher resistance to those disillusions about national and global immoralities that have brought cycles of intellectual sterility and cynicism to many white poets—increased the technical innovations in their volumes of the 1940's. The experiments and metrical freedoms of the new poetics appeared variously in Bruce McWright's *From the Shaken Tower* (1944), in Owen Dodson's *Powerful Long Ladder* (1946), and in Robert Hayden and Myron O'Higgins's *The Lion and the Archer* (1948). Other collections of the decade, like Hayden's *Heart-Shape in the Dust* (1940), Naomi Long Madgett's *Songs to a Phantom Nightingale* (1941), Melvin B. Tolson's *Rendezvous with America* (1944), and William Stanley Braithwaite's *Selected Poems* (1948), continued an essentially lyric tradition. Emphasis on Negro experience, on the other hand, evident in Frank Marshall Davis's *47th Street* (1948), was marked by fresh imagery in Gwendolyn Brooks's *A Street in Bronzeville* (1945) and by experimental syntax and deepening symbolism in her Pulitzer Prize-winning *Annie Allen* (1949). Langston Hughes, with his various satirical poems in *Shakespeare in Harlem* (1942), and with his "Madam to You" series in *One-Way Ticket* (1949), mixed humor with a social criticism hard-hitting enough to balance the mildness of the latter volume. *One-Way Ticket*, however, in addition to topographical experiments, carried forward his blues and jazz poetry—the blues tradition having been joined by Waring Cuney in the 1940's. Two Negro-edited anthologies of the decade, *The Negro Caravan* (1941), and the less selective *Ebony Rhythm* (1948), compiled by Beatrice M. Murphy, sampled this divergent poetry.

A consolidation of known forces and a gathering of new ones marked the 1950's for Negro poets. Prewar economic and social gains dating back to the New Deal and the "Black Cabinet" in Washington, combined with postwar ideological and educational advances implicit in the Declaration of Human Rights and the Supreme Court Decision of 1954, seemed to assure a period more congenial than the wartime 1940's to an art requiring some detachment and calm perspective. But in the new decade only about a dozen volumes easily traceable today were printed. Thus a few firm reputations became more solid, and a few slender ones waxed; a few unknown poets, too, published collections. In 1951, Hughes, updating his poetry of Negro urban life and talk, shifted to the use of boogie-woogie and bebop cadences in *Montage of a Dream Deferred*. In the same year, *Poetry* carried Tolson's specially commissioned *Libretto for the Republic of Liberia*, ultramodern enough in the style of Eliot and Pound to require later sixteen pages of explanatory notes from the author. A posthumous *Selected Poems* by McKay appeared in 1953, and a similar title by Hughes closed the decade in 1959. Although Myron O'Higgins, Frank Marshall Davis, and Sterling A. Brown stopped contributing poetry, Robert Hayden continued his symbolic work in *Figure of Time* (1955), and Naomi Long Madgett kept her lyrical sequence in *One and the Many* (1956). Other poets made first appearances. Two were in their twenties: Gloria Oden, beginning lyrically and rather intellectually with *The Naked Frame* (1952); and Conrad Kent Rivers, showing in the title and content of his first slender book, *Perchance to Dream, Othello* (1959), the prowling introspection that would continue. Oliver Pitcher at thirty-five published *Dust of Silence* (1958), containing free-verse pieces often made more dramatic by the actor-poet's sense of timing.

The 1960's, with their pernicious invasions of individual freedom and privacy, their havoc of civil rights demonstrations and retaliatory violence, their assassinations, and their menacing international depredations, are testing the value and function of literature. In this welter of forces, Negro poets have demonstrated both individuality and cohesiveness in a stream of published volumes that promises to total close to fifty before the end of the decade. For the most part sophisticated and formally conversant with literary traditions, they knowingly select forms that seem able to transmit their personal light through the present chaos. No reduction here of their aims or content or style to a maneuverable unity is possible. Yet certain names and substance command notice, representing either dependable, steady performance or earnest of vital work ahead.

Gwendolyn Brooks's *The Bean Eaters* (1960) leads the thirty-odd volumes already printed, and her *Selected Poems* (1963) contains most of her best work. Hughes's *Ask Your Mama* and LeRoi Jones's *Preface to a Twenty Volume Suicide Note* present, in 1961, the double feature of a familiar poet muddling the critics with new techniques, and a new poet stirring them with gleams of unsuspected originality to come. *Sixes and Sevens* (a brief anthology of works by thirteen new Negro poets), Hayden's *A Ballad of Remembrance*, and Frank Horne's *Haverstraw*, all printed by Paul Breman in London in 1962, represent for the most part the initial, middle, and closing decades in the publishing careers involved. The moving poems of Horne, long known as an optometrist and public official rather than as a poet, are a welcome anomaly not without parallel. Conrad Kent Rivers' *These Black Bodies and This Sun-burnt Face* and Georgia Douglas Johnson's *Share my World* (both 1962) contrast a young poet continuing his racial self-interrogation with an old one devoting her final book to the feminine song which defines her main contribution.

The anthologies edited in 1963 and 1964 by Arna Bontemps (*American Negro Poetry*) and Langston Hughes (*New Negro Poets: U.S.A.*) make accessible early works once available in collections now out of print, as well as recent poems by new writers. Bontemps' own twenty-three poems in *Personals* (1963) are prefaced with nostalgic and prophetic reflections on the beauty and near-suicide of Harlem. Of the two first volumes appearing in 1964, Alfred B. Spellman's *The Beautiful Day and Others* gains body and modernity from his knowledge of jazz; on the other hand, Calvin C. Hernton's *The Coming of Chronos to the House of Nightsong* reveals the racial passion of a young poet admittedly writing "out of a deep, human, psychopathic need for salvation or murder." Such a need—apparently as much American as personal—moves also through *The Dead Lecturer* (1964) of LeRoi Jones, to whom poetry writing is "the most beautiful resolution of energies," and who declares, "I have to write poetry. I'd last about maybe a day if I didn't. I'd go crazy."

Bob Kaufman's *Solitudes Crowded with Loneliness*, his first volume, and Tolson's *Harlem Gallery*, his final one, both appearing in 1965, show the accumulation of modernist influences. Surrealism and cryptic historical allusions are mixed with parental sentimentality in young Kaufman, whereas Tolson's highly praised book is a sometimes humorous and sometimes obscure fusion of rich erudition and closely packed details from Negro city life. The variety and craftsmanship in Hayden's *Selected Poems* of 1966 overshadow the achievement, but not the promise, of twenty-two-year-old D. L. Graham's well-titled pamphlet, *Black Song*. A burst of volumes in 1967, including the quite selective *Kaleidoscope: Poems by American Negro Poets*, edited by Hayden, reflects the excitement and maturing self-appraisal of the times. Another anthology, *For Malcolm: Poems on the Life and Death of Malcolm X*, edited by Dudley Randall and Margaret Burroughs, ministers to Negroes' need for a sensitive collective eulogy for the martyred man whom Ossie Davis called their "shining black prince." Randall's own poetry complements Margaret Danner's with sonorous power in their slender *Poem Counterpoem*. In his posthumous *The Panther and the Lash*, Langston Hughes speaks with Negroes' latest accents, voicing their demands, closing with a hopeful poem from his mid-career. Three poems in the book, stylistic departures for Hughes in their lines consisting only of punctuation marks or dollar signs, update him in the manner of LeRoi Jones, whose lines in *Black Art*, a mimeographed collection, sometimes make units of scarcely related words and sometimes make halting sense of scrambled letters taken from a beginning typist's manual.

Other volumes of 1967, such as David Henderson's *Felix of the Silent Forest*, roughly but feelingly alive with memories of New York City street life, as well as Nanina Alba's very different *The Parchments II*, are part of the growing tradition. Other poets with recent books (Evelyn Tooley Hunt, Lou LaTour, Roy L. Hill, Sam Cornish, and Don L. Lee, for example), in addition to poets whose volumes date back to the 1940's (like Beatrice M. Murphy) and the 1930's (like Lucy Foster Gulliford)—to indicate some not noted in current anthologies—can merely be named here. Series of small volumes being prepared by Paul Breman in London and by Dudley Randall of Broadside Press in Detroit promise to augment the available works of Negro poets.

For these writers, a Negro audience is slowly being established. Journals and their coteries have formed and are still forming, although some are transient: *Yugen* in Greenwich Village, *Dasein* at Howard University, the new *Journal of Black Poetry* in San Francisco, with additional names like *Soulbook*, *Black Dialogue*, and *Black People* expressive of their focus. Chicago's Organization of Black American Culture, founded in 1967 by Hoyt W. Fuller, Conrad Kent Rivers, Val Gray Ward, David Moore, and other writers to foster "black experientialism in the arts," typifies related organizational support. Negroes are writing and publishing amid the rumor-tossed "black power" and "white backlash" impasse; many are stoically accepting white authors' demoralizing revelations in *Spy Government* and *Privacy and Freedom* as well as black authors' fateful analyses in *Black Skin, White Masks*; *The Crisis of the Negro Intellectual*; and *Ready to Riot*. Among all these beleaguered writers, it is the poets, if they are true to themselves and to their history, who will lift our inward selves from behind what DuBois would call the Veil of Color, for preservation by wiser men.

ALBERT MURRAY
1916-

Albert Murray was born in Nokomis, Alabama, and spent his early youth in Mobile. After attending Tuskegee Institute, he took courses at the University of Michigan, the University of Chicago, the University of Paris, Northwestern, and New York University. A retired United States Air Force major, he has taught literature at Tuskegee, has been an associate professor of air science in the Air Force ROTC, and has served as a consultant to National Educational Television and to the United States Information Agency. Murray's short stories, criticism, and miscellaneous essays have been published in the anthologies *Anger, and Beyond* and *New World Writing*, as well as in magazines (*The New Leader, Book Week, Time, Life*, and others). Sociologically sound as they are, they reveal his primarily aesthetic and historical approach to the craft of writing—an attitude based not on a hope that Negroes will imitate the masters, but on his recorded faith that, once they "really dig the literary scene, black writers will begin playing the same highly imaginative improvisations on the works of James Joyce, Thomas Mann, Proust . . . and Robert Lowell that the Harlem Globetrotters play with 'the white man's' baseball,* and Sugar Ray used to play with 'the white man's' boxing gloves and Jim Brown with 'the white man's' pigskin." Murray

* The Harlem Globetrotters have been known to play a game of "baseball" with a basketball on the basketball court during a game. —*Eds.*

has detailed his literary theories in a book-length manuscript, the very existence of which heralds the birth and growth of that "Black Aesthetic" lately the subject of much speculation.

In "Train Whistle Guitar," a tale of Negro manhood conceived by two boys as both liberation and heroic style, Murray writes at his best. He artfully fuses poetry, jazz, Southern Negro folklore, and the nostalgic sensory feel of the generation that was enthusiastic about the Hudson Super-Six as well as the "box-back coat with hickory-striped peg-top pants."

Train Whistle Guitar

LITTLE BUDDY'S color was that sky blue in which hens cackled; it was that smoke blue in which dogs barked and mosquito hawks lit on barbed-wire fences. It was the color above meadows. It was my color too because it was a boy's color. It was whistling blue and hunting blue, and it went with baseball, and that was old Little Buddy again, and that blue beyond outfields was exactly what we were singing about when we used to sing that old song about it ain't gonna rain no more no more.

Steel blue was a man's color. That was the clean, oil-smelling color of rifle barrels and railroad iron. That was the color that went with Louisiana Charley, and he had a steel-blue 32-20 on a 44 frame. His complexion was not steel blue but leather brown like dark rawhide, but steel blue was the color that went with what he was. His hands were just like rawhide, and when he was not dressed up he smelled like green oak steam. He had on slick starched blue denim overalls then, and when he was dressed up he wore a black broadcloth box-back coat with hickory-striped peg-top pants, and he smelled like the barber shop and new money.

Louisiana Charley was there in that time and place as far back as I can remember, even before Little Buddy was. Because I can remember when I didn't know Little Buddy at all. I can remember when that house they moved to was built (Little Buddy's papa and mama were still living together when they came to Gasoline Point from Choctaw County, which was near the Mississippi State line), and I can also remember when that street (which was called Chattanooga Lookout Street) was pushed all the way through to the AT&N cut. That was before I had ever even heard of Little Buddy, and my buddy then was old Willie Marlowe. Little Buddy didn't come until after Willie Marlowe had gone to Detroit, Michigan, and that was not until after Mister One-Arm Will had been dead and buried for about nine months.

I can remember him there in that wee time when I couldn't even follow the stories I knew later they were telling about him, when it was only just grown folks talking, and all I could make of it was *Luzana, they are talking something about old Luzana*

Reprinted from *American Negro Short Stories*, ed. John Henrik Clarke (New York: Hill and Wang, 1966); originally published in *New World Writing IV* as "The Luzana Cholly Kick." The story has been revised by Mr. Murray especially for this volume.

again, and I didn't know what, to say nothing of where Louisiana was. But old Luze was there even then and I could see him very clearly when they said his name because I had already seen him coming up that road that came by that house with the chinaberry yard, coming from around the bend and down in the railroad bottom; and I had already heard whatever that was he was picking on his guitar and heard that holler too. That was always far away and long coming. It started low like it was going to be a song, and then it jumped all the way to the very top of his voice and broke off, and then it started again, and this time was already at the top, and then it gave some quick jerking squalls and died away in the woods, the water, and the darkness (you always heard it at night), and Mama always said he was whooping and hollering like somebody back in the rosin-woods country, and Papa said it was one of them old Luzana swamp hollers. I myself always thought it was like a train, like a bad train saying look out this is me, and here I come, and I'm coming through.

That was even before I was big enough to climb the chinaberry tree. That was when they used to talk about the war and the Kaiser, and I can remember that there was a war book with Germans in it, and I used to see sure-enough soldiers marching in the Mardi Gras parades. Soldier Boy Crawford was still wearing his Army coat then, and he was the one who used to tell about how Luze used to play his guitar in France, telling about how they would be going through some French town like the ones called Nancy and Saint Die and old Luze would drop out of the company and go and play around in the underground wine shops until he got as much cognac and as many French Frogs as he wanted and then he would turn up in the company again and Capt'n would put him out by himself on the worst outpost he could find in No Man's Land and old Luze would stay out there sometimes for three or four days and nights knocking off patrol after patrol, and one time in another place, which was the Hindenburg Line, old Luze was out there again and there were a few shots late in the afternoon and then it was quiet until about three o'clock the next morning and then all hell broke loose, and the Capt'n thought that a whole German battalion was about to move in, and he sent five patrols out to find out what was happening, but when they got there all they found was old Luze all dug in and bristling with enough ammunition to blow up Kingdom Come. He had crawled around all during the afternoon collecting hand grenades and a mortar and two machine guns and even a light two-wheel cannon, and when they asked him what was going on he told them that he had fallen off to sleep in spite of himself and when he woke up he didn't know whether or not any Germans had snuck up so he thought he'd better lay himself down a little light barrage. The next morning they found out that old Luze had wiped out a whole German platoon but when the Capt'n sent for him to tell him he was going to give him a medal, old Luze had cut out and was off somewhere picking the guitar and drinking cognac and chasing the mademoiselles again. He went through the whole war like that and he came out of the Army without a single scratch, didn't even get flat feet.

I heard a lot of stories about the war and I used to draw pictures of them fighting with bayonets in the Argonne Forest, and Soldier Boy Crawford used to look at them and shake his head and give me a nickel and say that some day I was going to be a soldier too.

I used to draw automobiles too, especially the Hudson Super-Six, like old Long George Nisby had. He said it would do sixty on a straightaway, and he had a heavy blasting cut-out on it that jarred the ground. Old Man Perc Stranahan had a Studebaker but he was a white man and he didn't have a cut-out, and he drove as slow as a hearse. Old Gander said Old Man Perc always drove like he was trying to sneak up on something but he never was going to catch it like that. The cars I didn't like then were the flat-engine Buick and the old humpbacked Hupmobile. I liked the Maxwell and the Willys Knight and the Pierce Arrow.

I was always playing train then too, and the trains were there before the automobiles were (there were many more horses and buggies in that part of town than there were automobiles then). I couldn't sit up in my nest in the chinaberry tree and see the trains yet, because I could not climb it yet, but I saw them when Papa used to take me to the L&N bottom to see them come by and I knew them all, and the Pan American was the fastest and Number Four was the fastest that ran in the daytime. Old Luzana could tell you all about the Southern Pacific and the Santa Fe, but that was later. But I already knew something about the Southern Pacific because Cousin Roberta had already gone all the way to Los Angeles, California, on the Sunset Limited.

I used to be in bed and hear the night trains coming by. The Crescent came by at nine-thirty and if you woke up way in the middle of the night you could hear Number Two. I was in my warm bed in that house, and I could hear the whistle coming even before it got to Chickasabogue Bridge and it had a bayou sound then, and then I could hear the engine batting it hell-for-leather on down the line bound for Mobile and New Orleans, and the next time the whistle came it was for Three Mile Creek. It was getting on into the beel then. I played train by myself in the daytime then, looking out the window along the side of the house like an engineer looking down along the drivers.

I used to hear old Stagolee playing the piano over in Hot Water Shorty's jook at night too, even then, especially on Saturday night. They rocked all night long, and I was lying in my warm quilted bed by the window. Uncle Jimmy's bed was by the window on the other side of the fireplace. When it was cold, you could wake up way in the night and still see the red embers in the ashes, and hear the wind whining outside, and sometimes you could hear the boat whistles too, and I could lie listening from where I was and tell you when it was a launch pulling a log raft or a tugboat pulling a barge or a riverboat like the *Nettie Queen*, and sometimes it was a big ship like the *Luchenback* calling the Looking Back, which was all the way down at the city wharf at the foot of Government Street.

I knew a lot about the big ships because Uncle Jerome worked on the wharf. That was before the state docks were built and the big Gulf-going and ocean-going ships didn't come on past Mobile then unless they were going up to Chickasaw to be overhauled, but I had already seen them and had been on ships from England and France and Holland and naturally there were always ships from the Caribbean and South America because that was where the fruit boats came from.

All I could do was see old Luzana Cholly and hear him coming. I didn't really know him then, but I knew that he was blue steel and that he was always going and coming and that he had the best walk in the world, because I had learned how to do that walk and was already doing the stew out of it long before Little Buddy ever saw it. They were calling me Mister Man during that time, and that was when some knuckleheads started calling me The Little Blister, because they said I was calling myself blister trying to say Mister. Aun Tee called me My Mister and Mama called me My Little Man, but she had to drop the little part off when Little Buddy came, and that was how everybody started calling me The Man, although I was still nothing but a boy, and I said to myself old Luzana is the man, old Luzana is the one I want to be like.

Then I was getting to be big enough to go everywhere by myself and I was going to school. That was when I knew about Dunkin's Hill and going up through Egerton Lane. That was the short way to school, because that was the way the bell sound came. Buddy Babe and Sister Babe and old double-jointed, ox-jawed Jack Johnson all went that way too, but when it rained you couldn't get across the bottom, and that was when everybody went the Shelton way, going through behind Stranahan's store and Good Hope Baptist to the old car line and then along that red clay road by the Hillside store.

Then Little Buddy was there and it was sky blue and we were blue hunters and every day was for whistling and going somewhere to do something you had to be rawhide to do, and some day we were going to live in times and places that were blue steel too. We found out a lot about old Luzana then, and then we not only knew him we knew how to talk to him.

The best time (except when he was just sitting somewhere strumming on his guitar) was when he was on his way to the Gambling Woods. (So far as anybody knew, gambling and guitar picking and grabbing freight trains were the only steady jobs he ever had or ever would have, except during the time he was in the Army and the times he was in jail—and he not only had been in jail, he had been in the penitentiary!) We were his good luck when he was headed for a skin game, and we always used to catch him late Saturday afternoon right out there where Gins Alley came into the oil-tank road, because he would be coming from Miss Pauline's cookshop then. The Gambling Woods trail started right out across from Sargin' Jeff's. Sometimes old Luze would have the guitar slung across his back even then, and naturally he had his famous 32-20 in the holster under his right arm.

"Say now hey Mister Luzana," I would holler at him.

"Mister Luzana Cholly one-time," Little Buddy always said, and he said that was what old Luze's swamp holler said too.

"Mister Luzana Cholly all night long," I would say then.

"Nobody else!" he would holler back at us then, "nobody else but."

"The one and only Mister Luzana Cholly from Booze Ana Bolly."

"Talk to me, little ziggy, talk to me."

"Got the world in a jug," I might say then.

"And the stopper in your hand," old Little Buddy would say.

"You tell 'em, little crust busters, 'cause I ain't got the heart."

"He's a man among men."

"And Lord God among women!"

"Well tell the dy ya," old Luz would say then, standing wide-legged, laughing, holding a wad of Brown's Mule chewing tobacco in with his tongue at the same time. Then he would skeet a stream of amber juice to one side like a batter does when he steps up to the plate and then he would wipe the back of his leathery hand across his mouth and squint his eyes.

"Tell the dy-damn-ya!"

"Can't tell no more," Little Buddy would say then, and old Luze would frown and wink at me.

"How come, little sooner, how goddam come?"

"Cause money talks."

"Well shut my mouth and call me suitcase."

"Ain't nobody can do that."

"I knowed you could tell 'em little ziggabo, I knowed good and damn well you could tell 'em."

"But we ain't gonna tell 'em no more."

"We sure ain't."

"Talk ain't no good if you ain't got nothing to back it up with."

Old Luze would laugh again and we would stand waiting and then he would run his hands deep down into his pockets and come out with two quarters between his fingers. He would throw them into the air and catch them again, one in each hand, and then he would cross his hands and flip one to me and one to Little Buddy.

"Now talk," he would say then. "Now talk, but don't say too much and don't talk too loud, and handle your money like the white folks does."

We were going to be like him even before we were going to be like cowboys. And we knew that blue steel was also root hog or die poor, which was what we were going to have to do whether we liked it or not. Little Buddy said it was not just how rough-and-ready old hard-cutting Luze was and how nobody, black or white, was going to do him any dirt and get away with it, and all that. It was that too, but it was also something else. It was also the way he could do whatever he was doing and make it look so easy that he didn't even seem to have to think about it, and once he did it, that seemed to be just about the only real way to do it.

Old Luze did everything his own way just like old Satch played baseball his way. But we knew that we wanted to be like him for more reasons than that too. Somehow or other just as he always seemed to be thirty-five years old and blue steel because he had already been so many places and done so many things you'd never heard of before, he also always seemed to be absolutely alone and not needing anybody else, self-sufficient, independent, dead sure, and at the same time so unconcerned.

Mama said he was don't-carified, and that was it too (if you know the full meaning of the Negro meaning of that expression). He was living in blue steel and his way was don't-carified, because he was blue steel too. Little Buddy said hellfied, and he didn't mean hell-defying either, you couldn't say he was hell-defying all the time, and you couldn't say he went for bad either, not even when he was doing that holler he was so notorious for. That *was* hell-defying in a way, but it was really I don't give a damn if I *am* hell-defying, and he was not going for bad because he didn't need to, since everybody, black and white, who knew anything about him at all already knew that when he made a promise it meant if it's the last thing I do, if it's the last thing I do on this earth—and they knew that could mean I'll kill you and pay for you as much as it meant anything else. Because the idea of going to jail didn't scare him at all, and the idea of getting shot at didn't seem to scare him either. *Because all he ever said about that was if they shoot at me they sure better not miss me, they sure better get me the first time.*

He was a Negro who was an out and out Nigger in the very best meaning of the word as Negroes use it among themselves (who are the only ones who can), and nobody in that time and that place seemed to know what to make of him. White folks said he was crazy, but what they really meant or should have meant was that he was confusing to them, because if they knew him well enough to say he was crazy they also had to know enough about him to know that he wasn't even foolhardy, not even careless, not even what they wanted to mean by biggity. The funny thing, as I remember it now, was how their confusion made them respect him in spite of themselves. Somehow or other it was as if they respected him precisely because he didn't care anything about them one way or the other. They certainly respected the fact that he wasn't going to take any foolishness off of them.

Negroes said he was crazy too, but they meant their own meaning. They did not know what to make of him either, but when they said he was crazy they almost did, because when they said it they really meant something else. They were not talking so much about what he did, as about how he was doing it. They were talking about something like poetic madness, and that was the way they had of saying that he was doing something unheard of, doing the hell out of it, and getting away with whatever it was. You could tell that was what they meant by the very way they said it, by the sound of it, and by the way they were shaking their heads and laughing when they said it.

The way he always operated as a lone wolf and the uncon-cernedness, not the Negro-ness as such, were the main things then. (Naturally Little Buddy and I knew about Negroes and white folks, and we knew that there was something generally wrong with white folks, but it didn't seem so very important then. We knew that if you hit a white boy he would turn red and call you nigger that did not sound like the Nigger the Negroes said and he would run and get as many other white boys as he could and come back at you, and we knew that a full-grown white man had to get somebody to back him up too, but we didn't really think about it much, because there were so many other things we were doing then.)

Nobody ever said anything about old Luzana's papa and mama, and when you suddenly wondered about them you realized that he didn't seem to have or need any family at all, it really was as if he had come full-grown out of the swamp somewhere. And he didn't seem to need a wife either. But that was because he was not going to settle down yet. Because he had lived with more women from time to time and place to place than the average man could even shake a stick at.

We knew somehow or other that the Negro-ness had something to do with the way we felt about him too, but except for cowboys like Tom Mix and Buck Jones, and the New York Yankees and one or two other things, almost everything was Negro then; that is, everything that mattered was. So the Negro part was only natural, although I can see something special about it too now.

When you boil it all down, I guess the main thing was how when you no more than just said his name, *Louisiana Charlie*, old *Luzana Cholly*, old *Luze*, that was enough to make you know not only him and how he looked and talked and walked that sporty limp walk, but his whole way of being, and how you knew right off the bat that he all alone and unconcerned in his sharp-edged and rough-backed steel had made it what it was himself.

Because that was what old Little Buddy and I were going to do too, make a name for ourselves. Because we knew even then (and I already knew it before he came) that doing that was exactly what made you the kind of man we wanted to be. Mama said I was her little man, and Aun Tee always called me her little mister, but I wasn't anybody's man and mister yet and I knew it, and when I heard the sound of the name that Mama taught me how to write I always felt funny, and I always jumped even when I didn't move. That was in school, and I wanted to hide, and I always said *they are looking for me, they are trying to see who I am*, and I had to answer because it would be the teacher calling the roll, and I said Present, and it sounded like somebody else.

And when I found out what I found out about me and Aun Tee and knew that she was my flesh and blood mama, I also found out that I didn't know my real name at all, because I didn't know who my true father was. So I said *My name is Reynard the Fox*, and Little Buddy said *My name is Jack the Rabbit and my home is in the briar patch*. That was old Luzana too, and when you heard that holler coming suddenly out of nowhere just as old Luze himself always seemed to come, it was just like it was coming from the briar patch.

So when Mama said what she said about me and Aun Tee at that wake that time and I heard it and had to believe it, I wished that old Luzana had been my real papa, but I didn't tell anybody that, not even Little Buddy although Little Buddy was almost in the same fix because he didn't have a mama any more and he didn't really love his papa because it was his papa that ran his mama away.

But we were buddies and we both did old Luzana's famous walk and we were going to be like him, and the big thing that you had to do to really get like him was to grab yourself a fast armful of fast freight train and get long gone from here. That was the real way to learn about the world, and we wanted to learn everything about it that we could. That was when we started practicing on the switch engine. That was down in the oilyards. You had to be slick to do even that because naturally your folks didn't want you doing stuff like that, because there was old Peg Leg Nat. Old Peg Leg butt-headed Nat could hop a freight almost as good as old Luzana could. He called himself mister-some-big-shit-on-a-stick. He spent most of his time fishing and sometimes he would come around pushing a wheelbarrow selling fresh fish, shrimps, and crabs, but every now and then he would strike out for somewhere on a freight just like old Luze did. Mama used to try to scare us with old Nat, telling us that a peg leg was just what messing around with freight trains would get you, and for a while she did scare us, but not for long, because then we found out that it never would have happened to old Nat if he hadn't been drunk and showing off. And anybody could see that getting his leg cut off hadn't stopped old Nat himself anyway since he could still beat any two-legged man we knew doing it except old Luze himself. Naturally we had to think about it, naturally it did slow us up for a while, but it didn't really stop us. Because there was still old Luze, and that was who we were anyway, not old Peg Leg Nat.

Then that time when I found out all about me and Aun Tee, I was going to run away, and Little Buddy was ready too. Then old Little Buddy found out that old Luze was getting ready to get moving again and we were all set and just waiting and then it was the day itself.

I will always remember that one.

I had on my brogan shoes and I had on my corduroy pants under my overalls with my jumper tucked in. I had on my blue baseball cap too and my rawhide wristband and I had my pitching glove folded in my hip pocket. Little Buddy had on just about the same thing except that he was carrying his first-base pad instead of his catcher's mitt. We had our other things and something to eat rolled up in our blanket rolls so that we could sling them over our shoulders and have our arms free.

Little Buddy had gotten his papa's pearl-handled .38 Smith & Wesson, and we both had good jackknives. We had some hooks and twine to fish with too, just in case, and of course we had our trusty old slingshots for birds.

It was May and school was not out yet, and so not only were we running away, we were playing hooky too. It was hot, and with that many clothes on we were sweating, but you had to have them, and that was the best way to carry them.

There was a thin breeze that came across the railroad from the river, the marsh, and Pole Cat Bay, but the sun was hot and bright, and you could see the rails downright shimmering under the high and wide open sky. We had always said that we were going to wait until school was out, but this was our chance now, and we didn't care about school much any more anyhow. This was going to be school now anyway, except it was going to be much better.

We were waiting in the thicket under the hill. That was between where the Dodge mill road came down and where the oil spur started, and from where we were, we could see up and down the clearing as far as we needed to, to the south all the way across Three Mile Creek bridge to the roundhouse, and where Mobile was, and to the north all the way up past that mill to the Chickasabogue bridge. We knew just about from where old Luzana was going to come running, because we had been watching him do it for a long time now. We had that part down pat.

I don't know how long we had been waiting because we didn't have a watch but it had been a long time, and there was nothing to do but wait then.

"I wish it would hurry up and come on," Little Buddy said.

"Me too," I said.

"Got to get to splitting."

We were squatting on the blanket rolls, and Little Buddy was smoking another Lucky Strike, smoking the way we both used to smoke them in those old days, letting it hang dangling in the corner of your mouth, and tilting your head to one side with one eye squinted up like a gambler.

"Goddam it, watch me nail that sapsucker," he said.

"Man, you watch me."

You could smell the May woods there then, the dogwood, the

honeysuckle, and the warm smell of the undergrowth; and you could hear the birds too, the jays, the thrushes, and even a woodpecker somewhere on a dead tree. I felt how moist and cool the soft dark ground was there in the shade, and you could smell that smell too, and smell the river and the marsh too.

Little Buddy finished the cigarette and flipped it out into the sunshine, and then sat with his back against a sapling and sucked his teeth. I looked out across the railroad to where the gulls were circling over the marsh and the river.

"Goddam it, when I come back here to this burg, I'm going to be a goddam man and a half," Little Buddy said all of a sudden.

"And don't care who knows it," I said.

"Boy, Chicago."

"Man, Detroit."

"Man, Philadelphia."

"Man, New York."

"Boy, I kinda wish old Gander was going too."

"I kinda wish so too."

"Old cat-eyed Gander."

"Old big-toed Gander."

"Old Gander is all right."

"Man, who you telling."

"That son of a bitch know his natural stuff."

"That bastard can steal lightning if he have to."

"Boy, how about that time."

"Man, hell yeah."

"Boy, but old Luze though."

"That Luze takes the cake for everything."

"Hot damn, boy we going!"

"It won't be long now."

"Boy, Los Angeles."

"Boy, St. Louis."

"Man, you know we going."

"Boy, you just watch me swing the sapsucker."

"Boy, snag it."

"Goddam."

"I'm going to natural-born kick that son of a bitch."

"Kick the living hocky out of it."

"Boy and when we get back!" I said that and I could see it, coming back on the Pan American I would be carrying two suitcases and have a money belt and an underarm holster, and I would be dressed fit to kill.

"How long you think it will take us to get fixed to come back?" I said.

"Man, I don't know and don't care."

"You coming back when old Luze come back?"

"I don't know."

I didn't say anything else then. Because I was trying to think about how it was really going to be then. Because what I had been thinking about before was how I wanted it to be. I didn't say anything because I was thinking about myself then, thinking: *I always said I was going but I don't really know whether I want to go or not now. I want to go and I don't want to go.* I tried to see what was really going to happen and I couldn't, and I tried to forget it and think about something else, but I couldn't do that either.

I looked over at Little Buddy again. Who was lying back against the tree with his hands behind his head and his eyes closed. Whose legs were crossed, and who was resting easy like a ball-player rests before time for the game to start. I wondered what he was really thinking. Did he really mean it when he said he did not know and didn't care? You couldn't tell what he was thinking, but you could tell that he wasn't going to back out now, no matter how he was feeling about it.

So I said to myself goddam it if Little Buddy can make it I can too, and I had more reason to be going away than he did anyway. *I had forgotten about that. I had forgotten all about it. And then I knew that I still loved Papa and they had always loved me and they had always known about me and Aun Tee.*

But I couldn't back out then, because what I had found out wasn't the real reason for going anyway. Old Luze was really the reason, old Luze and blue steel, old Luze and rawhide, old Luze and ever-stretching India Rubber.

"Hey Lebud."

"Hey."

"Going to the big league."

"You said it."

"Skipping city."

"You tell 'em."

"Getting further."

"Ain't no lie."

"Long gone."

"No dooky."

That was when Little Buddy said my home is in the briar patch. My name is Jack the Rabbit and my natural home is in the briar patch. And I said it too, and I said that was where I was bred and born.

"Goddam it to hell," Little Buddy said then, "why don't it come on?"

"Son of a bitch," I said.

Then I was leaning back against my tree looking out across the sandy clearing at the sky and there were clean white pieces of clouds that looked like balled-up sheets in a washtub, and the sky was blue like rinse water with bluing in it, and I was thinking about Mama again, and hoping that it was all a dream.

But then the train was really coming and it wasn't a dream at all, and Little Buddy jumped up.

"Come on."

"I'm here."

The engine went by, and we were running across the clearing. My ears were ringing and I was sweating, and my collar was hot and my pants felt as if the seat had been ripped away. There was nothing but the noise and we were running into it, and then we were climbing up the hill and running along the slag and cinders. We were trotting along in reach of it then. We remembered to let an empty boxcar go by, and when the next gondola came, Little Buddy grabbed the front end and I got the back. I hit the hotbox with my right foot and stepped onto the step and pulled up. The wind was in my ears then, but I knew about that from practicing. I climbed on up the ladder and got down on the inside, and there was Little Buddy coming back toward me.

"Man, what did I tell you!"

"Did you see me lam into that sucker?"

"Boy, we low more nailed it."

"I bet old Luze will be kicking it any minute now."

"Cool hanging it."

"Boy, yair," I said, but I was thinking I hope old Luze didn't change his mind. I hope we don't miss him. I hope we don't have to start out all by ourselves.

"Going boy."

"Yeah."

"*Going,*
don't know where I'm going
but I'm going
Say now I'm going
don't know where I'm going
but I'm going."

We crawled up into the left front corner out of the wind, and there was nothing to do but wait then. We knew that she was going to have to pull into the hole for Number Four when she got twelve miles out, and that was when we were going to get to the open boxcar.

We got the cigarettes out and lit up, and there was nothing

but the rumbling noise that the wide-open car made then, and the faraway sound of the engine and the low-rolling smoke coming back. That was just sitting there, and after we got a little more used to the vibration, nothing at all was happening except being there. You couldn't even see the scenery going by.

It was just being there and being in that time, and you never really remember anything about things like that except the sameness and the way you felt, and all I can remember now about that part is the nothingness of doing nothing and the feeling not of going but of being taken.

All I could see after we went through the bridge was the sky and the bare floor and the sides of the gondola, and all I can remember about myself is how I wished that something would happen, because I definitely did not want to be going then, and I was lost even though I knew good and well that I was not even twelve miles from home yet. Because although we certainly had been many times farther away and stayed longer, this already seemed to be farther and longer than all the other times put together.

Then we could tell that it was beginning to slow down, and we stood up and started getting ready. And then it was stopping, and we were ready, and we climbed over and got down and started running for it. That was still in the bayou country and beyond the train smell there was the sour-sweet smell of the swamp. We were running on hard pounded slag then, and with the train quiet and waiting for Number Four, you could hear the double running of our feet echoing through the cypresses and the marshland.

The wide roadbed was almost half as high as the telegraph wires, and along the low right-of-way where the black creosote poles went along, you could see the blue and white lilies floating on the slimy green water. We came hustling hot to get to where we knew the empty car was, and then there we were.

And there old Luzana himself was.

He stood looking down at us from the door with an unlighted cigarette in his hand. We stopped dead in our tracks. I knew exactly what was going to happen then. It was suddenly so quiet that you could hear your heart pounding inside your head, and I was so embarrassed I didn't know what to do and I thought *now he's going to call us a name. Now he's never going to have anything to do with us any more.*

We were just standing there waiting and he just let us stand there and feel like two puppies with their tails tucked between their legs, and then he started talking.

"It ain't like that. It ain't like that. It just ain't like that, it just ain't."

And he was shaking his head not only as if we couldn't understand him but also as if we couldn't even hear him.

"It ain't. Oh, but it ain't."

We didn't move. Little Buddy didn't even dig his toe into the ground.

"So this is what y'all up to. Don't say a word, not a word. Don't open your mouth."

I could have sunk right on down into the ground.

"What the hell y'all think y'all doing? Tell me that. Tell me. Don't say a word. Don't say a goddam mumbling word to me."

We weren't even about to say anything.

"I got a good mind to whale the sawdust out of you both. That's just what I oughta do."

But he didn't move. He just stood looking down.

"Well, I'll be a son of a bitch."

That was all he said then, and then he jumped down, walked us back to where the switch frog was, and then there was nothing but just shamefaced waiting. Then Number Four came by and then finally we heard the next freight coming south and when it got there and slowed down for the switch he was standing waiting for a gondola and when it came he picked me up and put me on and then he picked Little Buddy up and put him on and then he caught the next car and came to where we were.

So we came slowpoking it right on back and got back in Gasoline Point before the whistles even started blowing for one o'clock. Imagine that. All of that had happened and it wasn't really afternoon yet. I could hardly believe it.

We came on until the train all but stopped for Three Mile Creek bridge and then he hopped down and took us off. He led us down the hill and went to a place the hobos used under the bridge. He sat down and lit another cigarette and flipped the match into the water and watched it float away and then he was looking at us and then he motioned for us to sit down too.

That was when he really told us what hitting the road was, and what blue steel was. He was talking evenly then, not scolding, just telling us man to boys, saying he was talking for our own good because doing what we were trying to do was more than a notion. He was talking quietly and evenly but you still couldn't face him, I know I couldn't and Little Buddy naturally couldn't because he never looked anybody straight in the eye anyway.

We were back and sitting under Three Mile Creek bridge and he was not really angry and then we were all eating our something-to-eat and then we could talk too, but we didn't have much to say that day. He was doing the talking and all we wanted to do was ask questions and listen.

That was when he told us all about the chain gang and the penitentiary and the white folks, and you could see everything he said and you were there too, but you were not really in it this time because it was happening to him, not you, and it was him and you were not him, you were you. You could be rawhide and you could be blue steel but you couldn't really be Luzana Cholly, because he himself was not going to let you.

Then he was talking about going to school and learning to use your head like the smart white folks. You had to be rawhide but you had to be patent leather too, then you would really be nimble, then you would really be not only a man but a big man. He said we had a lot of spunk and that was good but it wasn't good enough, it wasn't nearly enough.

And then he was talking about Negroes and white folks again, and he said the young generation of Negroes were supposed to be like Negroes and be like white folks too and still be Negroes. He sat looking out across the water then, and then we heard another freight coming and he got up and got ready and he said we could watch him but we'd better not try to follow him.

Then we were back up on the hill again and the train was coming and he stood looking at us with the guitar slung over his shoulder and then he put his hands on our shoulders and looked straight at us, and we had to look at him then, and we knew that we were not to be ashamed in front of him any more.

"Make old Luze proud of you," he said then, and he was almost pleading. "Make old Luze glad to take his hat off to you some of these days. You going further than old Luze ever even dreamed of. Old Luze ain't been nowhere. Old Luze don't know from nothing."

And then the train was there and we watched him snag it and then he was waving good-by.

JOHN
A.
WILLIAMS
1925-

Born in Jackson, Mississippi, and reared in Syracuse, New York, John A. Williams delayed his higher education until after his World War II service. He left Syracuse University six semester hours short of the requirements for a baccalaureate degree and began a series of jobs as foundry worker, vegetable clerk, and welfare investigator. Returning to New York from California, he worked intermittently—in addition to his own writing—as a book promoter, a business newsletter publisher, an advertising agency representative, and as Information Director for the American Committee on Africa.

Williams first commanded large public attention in the winter of 1961 as the victim of the American Academy in Rome's racist rejection of the literary fellowship awarded him by the American Academy of Arts and Letters at home. In 1963, he took an eight-month trip throughout the United States; in 1964, he visited ten countries in Africa, staying longest in Nigeria, where he became acquainted with Malcolm X. The following year, he went to France and Spain with his wife to complete his fourth novel. After his return to New York in 1967 and the publication that year of *The Man Who Cried I Am*, Williams found himself attended by the urgent curiosity of new readers, some eager for rumored scandal, and some studious about the novel's revelation of Washington's plan for the extermination of Negroes—only semifictional in the author's eyes. At the start of 1968, his literary career thus favorably balanced, Williams accepted a position as lecturer at the City College of New York.

Although the author's first novel, *The Angry Ones* (1960), is little known, *Night Song* (1961) and *Sissie* (1963) credit Williams as a lively conveyor—sometimes in bebop jargon—of the jazz world and, in the case of *Sissie*, as a sensitive chronicler of the matriarchal Negro mother. He has also written poetry, short stories, historical and semiautobiographical nonfiction, and edited anthologies; some of his titles in nonfiction are *Africa, Her History, Lands and People* (1962), *This Is My Country Too* (1965), and *Beyond the Angry Black* (1966). A writer of television scripts and often a book reviewer, Williams has published essays in many magazines, among them *Saturday Review, The New Leader, Ebony,* and *Holiday.*

"Angry" even in his early titles, alert to ironies in politics and history and black African biases, and yet interracial in his editorial and personal activities, Williams is classically black American in his equilibrium. His easily underestimated story, "Son in the Afternoon," found in his *The Angry Black* (1962), explains that balance. The Los Angeles writer-protagonist, steadily forced by the racial stupidities of his white peers, and by the misplaced tenderness of his maidservant mother, into resentful memories of his own childhood, turns the half-drunken sexual immorality of a white child's mother into an opportunity to scar the boy's image of her. The simple prose style, often laconic and restless, befits the thematic perversion of sensibilities inseparable from racism, as well as the writer's shame, "hating the long drive back to Watts."

Son in the Afternoon

IT WAS HOT. I tend to be a bitch when it's hot. I goosed the little Ford over Sepulveda Boulevard toward Santa Monica until I got stuck in the traffic that pours from L.A. into the surrounding towns. I'd had a very lousy day at the studio.

I was—still am—a writer and this studio had hired me to check scripts and films with Negroes in them to make sure the Negro moviegoer wouldn't be offended. The signs were already clear one day the whole of American industry would be racing pell-mell to get a Negro, showcase a spade. I was kind of a pioneer. I'm a *Negro* writer, you see. The day had been tough because of a couple of verbs—slink and walk. One of those Hollywood hippies had done a script calling for a Negro waiter to slink away from the table where a dinner party was glaring at him. I said the waiter should walk, not slink, because later on he becomes a hero. The Hollywood hippie, who understood it all because he had some colored friends, said that it was essential to the plot that the waiter slink. I said you don't slink one minute and become a hero the next; there has to be some consistency. The Negro actor I was standing up for said nothing either way. He had played Uncle Tom roles so long that he had become Uncle Tom. But the director agreed with me.

Anyway . . . hear me out now. I was on my way to Santa Monica to pick up my mother, Nora. It was a long haul for such a hot day. I had planned a quiet evening: a nice shower, fresh clothes, and then I would have dinner at the Watkins and talk with some of the musicians on the scene for a quick taste before they cut to their gigs. After, I was going to the Pigalle down on Figueroa and catch Earl Grant at the organ, and still later, if nothing exciting happened, I'd pick up Scottie and make it to the Lighthouse on the Beach or to the Strollers and listen to some of the white boys play. I liked the long drive, especially while listening to Sleepy Stein's show on the radio. Later, much later of course, it would be home, back to Watts.

So you see, this picking up Nora was a little inconvenient. My mother was a maid for the Couchmans. Ronald Couchman was an architect, a good one I understood from Nora who has a fine

Reprinted from *The Angry Black* (New York: Lancer Books, 1962). Reprinted by permission of the author.

sense for this sort of thing; you don't work in some hundred-odd houses during your life without getting some idea of the way a house should be laid out. Couchman's wife, Kay, was a playgirl who drove a white Jaguar from one party to another. My mother didn't like her too much; she didn't seem to care much for her son, Ronald, junior. There's something wrong with a parent who can't really love her own child, Nora thought. The Couchmans lived in a real fine residential section, of course. A number of actors lived nearby, character actors, not really big stars.

Somehow it is very funny. I mean that the maids and butlers knew everything about these people, and these people knew nothing at all about the help. Through Nora and her friends I knew who was laying whose wife; who had money and who *really* had money; I knew about the wild parties hours before the police, and who smoked marijuana, when, and where they got it.

To get to Couchman's driveway I had to go three blocks up one side of a palm-planted center strip and back down the other. The driveway bent gently, then swept back out of sight of the main road. The house, sheltered by slim palms, looked like a transplanted New England Colonial. I parked and walked to the kitchen door, skirting the growling Great Dane who was tied to a tree. That was the route to the kitchen door.

I don't like kitchen doors. Entering people's houses by them, I mean. I'd done this thing most of my life when I called at places where Nora worked to pick up the patched or worn sheets or the half-eaten roasts, the battered, tarnished silver—the fringe benefits of a housemaid. As a teen-ager I'd told Nora I was through with that crap; I was not going through anyone's kitchen door. She only laughed and said I'd learn. One day soon after, I called for her and without knocking walked right through the front door of this house and right on through the living room. I was almost out of the room when I saw feet behind the couch. I leaned over and there was Mr. Jorgensen and his wife making out like crazy. I guess they thought Nora had gone and it must have hit them sort of suddenly and they went at it like the hell-bomb was due to drop any minute. I've been that way too, mostly in the spring. Of course, when Mr. Jorgensen looked over his shoulder and saw me, you know what happened. I was thrown out and Nora right behind me. It was the middle of winter, the old man was sick and the coal bill three months overdue. Nora was right about those kitchen doors: I learned.

My mother saw me before I could ring the bell. She opened the door. "Hello," she said. She was breathing hard, like she'd been running or something. "Come in and sit down. I don't know *where* that Kay is. Little Ronald is sick and she's probably out gettin' drunk again." She left me then and trotted back through the house, I guess to be with Ronnie. I hated the combination of her white nylon uniform, her dark brown face and the wide streaks of gray in her hair. Nora had married this guy from Texas a few years after the old man had died. He was all right. He made out okay. Nora didn't have to work, but she just couldn't be still; she always had to be doing something. I suggested she quit work, but I had as much luck as her husband. I used to tease her about liking to be around those white folks. It would have been good for her to take an extended trip around the country visiting my brothers and sisters. Once she got to Philadelphia, she could go right out to the cemetery and sit awhile with the old man.

I walked through the Couchman home. I liked the library. I thought if I knew Couchman I'd like him. The room made me feel like that. I left it and went into the big living room. You could tell that Couchman had let his wife do that. Everything in it was fast, dart-like, with no sense of ease. But on the walls were several of Couchman's conceptions of buildings and homes. I guess he was a disciple of Wright. My mother walked rapidly through the room without looking at me and said, "Just be patient, Wendell. She should be here real soon."

"Yeah," I said, "with a snootful." I had turned back to the drawings when Ronnie scampered into the room, his face twisted with rage.

"Nora!" he tried to roar, perhaps the way he'd seen the parents of some of his friends roar at their maids. I'm quite sure Kay didn't shout at Nora, and I don't think Couchman would. But then no one shouts at Nora. "Nora, you come right back here this minute!" the little bastard shouted and stamped and pointed to a spot on the floor where Nora was supposed to come to roost. I have a nasty temper. Sometimes it lies dormant for ages and at other times, like when the weather is hot and nothing seems to be going right, it's bubbling and ready to explode. "Don't talk to *my* mother like that, you little—!" I said sharply, breaking off just before I cursed. I wanted him to be large enough for me to strike. "How'd you like for me to talk to *your* mother like that?"

The nine-year-old looked up at me in surprise and confusion. He hadn't expected me to say anything. I was just another piece of furniture. Tears rose in his eyes and spilled out onto his pale cheeks. He put his hands behind him, twisted them. He moved backwards, away from me. He looked at my mother with a "Nora, come help me" look. And sure enough, there was Nora, speeding back across the room, gathering the kid in her arms, tucking his robe together. I was too angry to feel hatred for myself.

Ronnie was the Couchman's only kid. Nora loved him. I suppose that was the trouble. Couchman was gone ten, twelve hours a day. Kay didn't stay around the house any longer than she had to. So Ronnie had only my mother. I think kids should have someone to love, and Nora wasn't a bad sort. But somehow when the six of us, her own children, were growing up we never had her. She was gone, out scuffling to get those crumbs to put into our mouths and shoes for our feet and praying for something to happen so that all the space in between would be taken care of. Nora's affection for us took the form of rushing out into the morning's five o'clock blackness to wake some silly bitch and get her coffee; took form in her trudging five miles home every night instead of taking the streetcar to save money to buy tablets for us, to use at school, we said. But the truth was that all of us liked to draw and we went through a writing tablet in a couple of hours every day. Can you imagine? There's not a goddamn artist among us. We never had the physical affection, the pat on the head, the quick, smiling kiss, the "gimmee a hug" routine. All of this Ronnie was getting.

Now he buried his little blond head in Nora's breast and sobbed. "There, there now," Nora said. "Don't you cry, Ronnie. Ol' Wendell is just jealous, and he hasn't much sense either. He didn't mean nuthin'."

I left the room. Nora had hit it of course, hit it and passed on. I looked back. It didn't look so incongruous, the white and black together, I mean. Ronnie was still sobbing. His head bobbed gently on Nora's shoulder. The only time I ever got that close to her was when she trapped me with a bearhug so she could whale the daylights out of me after I put a snowball through Mrs. Grant's window. I walked outside and lit a cigarette. When Ronnie was in the hospital the month before, Nora got me to run her way over to Hollywood every night to see him. I didn't like that worth a damn. All right, I'll admit it: it did upset me. All that affection I didn't get nor my brothers and sisters going to that little white boy who, without a doubt, when away from her called her the names he'd learned from adults. Can you imagine a nine-year-old kid calling Nora a "girl," "our girl?" I spat at the Great Dane. He snarled and then I bounced a rock off his fanny. "Lay down, you bastard," I muttered. It was a good thing he was tied up.

I heard the low cough of the Jaguar slapping against the road. The car was throttled down, and with a muted roar it swung into the driveway. The woman aimed it for me. I was evil enough not to move. I was tired of playing with these people. At the last moment, grinning, she swung the wheel over and braked. She bounded out of the car like a tennis player vaulting over a net.

"Hi," she said, tugging at her shorts.

"Hello."

"You're Nora's boy?"

"I'm Nora's son." Hell, I was as old as she was; besides, I can't stand "boy."

"Nora tells us you're working in Hollywood. Like it?"

"It's all right."

"You must be pretty talented."

We stood looking at each other while the dog whined for her attention. Kay had a nice body and it was well tanned. She was high, boy, was she high. Looking at her, I could feel myself going into my sexy bastard routine; sometimes I can swing it great. Maybe it all had to do with the business inside. Kay took off her sunglasses and took a good look at me. "Do you have a cigarette?"

I gave her one and lit it. "Nice tan," I said. Most white people I know think it's a great big deal if a Negro compliments them on their tans. It's a large laugh. You have all this volleyball about color and come summer you can't hold the white folks back from the beaches, anyplace where they can get some sun. And of course the blacker they get, the more pleased they are. Crazy. If there is ever a Negro revolt, it will come during the summer and Negroes will descend upon the beaches around the nation and paralyze the country. You can't conceal cattle prods and bombs and pistols and police dogs when you're showing your birthday suit to the sun.

"You like it?" she asked. She was pleased. She placed her arm next to mine. "Almost the same color," she said.

"Ronnie isn't feeling well," I said.

"Oh, the poor kid. I'm so glad we have Nora. She's such a charm. I'll run right in and look at him. Do have a drink in the bar. Fix me one too, will you?" Kay skipped inside and I went to the bar and poured out two strong drinks. I made hers stronger than mine. She was back soon. "Nora was trying to put him to sleep and she made me stay out." She giggled. She quickly tossed off her drink. "Another, please?" While I was fixing her drink she was saying how amazing it was for Nora to have such a talented son. What she was really saying was that it was amazing for a servant to have a son who was not also a servant. "Anything can happen in a democracy," I said. "Servants' sons drink with madames and so on."

"Oh, Nora isn't a servant," Kay said. "She's part of the family."

Yeah, I thought. Where and how many times had I heard *that* before?

In the ensuing silence, she started to admire her tan again. "You think it's pretty good, do you? You don't know how hard I worked to get it." I moved close to her and held her arm. I placed my other arm around her. She pretended not to see or feel it, but she wasn't trying to get away either. In fact she was pressing closer and the register in my brain that tells me at the precise moment when I'm in, went off. Kay was very high. I put both arms around her and she put both hers around me. When I kissed her, she responded completely.

"Mom!"

"Ronnie, come back to bed," I heard Nora shout from the other room. We could hear Ronnie running over the rug in the outer room. Kay tried to get away from me, push me to one side, because we could tell that Ronnie knew where to look for his Mom: he was running right for the bar, where we were. "Oh, please," she said, "don't let him see us." I wouldn't let her push me away. "Stop!" she hissed. "He'll *see* us!" We stopped struggling just for an instant, and we listened to the echoes of the word *see*. She gritted her teeth and renewed her efforts to get away.

Me? I had the scene laid right out. The kid breaks into the room, see, and sees his mother in this real wriggly clinch with this colored guy who's just shouted at him, see, and no matter how his mother explains it away, the kid has the image—the colored guy and his mother—for the rest of his life, see?

That's the way it happened. The kid's mother hissed under her breath, *"You're crazy!"* and she looked at me as though she were seeing me or something about me for the very first time. I'd released her as soon as Ronnie, romping into the bar, saw us and came to a full, open-mouthed halt. Kay went to him. He looked first at me, then at his mother. Kay turned to me, but she couldn't speak.

Outside in the living room my mother called, "Wendell, where are you? We can go now."

I started to move past Kay and Ronnie. I felt many things, but I made myself think mostly, *There you little bastard, there.*

My mother thrust her face inside the door and said, "Good-bye, Mrs. Couchman. See you tomorrow. 'Bye, Ronnie."

"Yes," Kay said, sort of stunned. "Tomorrow." She was reaching for Ronnie's hand as we left, but the kid was slapping her hand away. I hurried quickly after Nora, hating the long drive back to Watts.

PAULE
MARSHALL
1929-

Paule Marshall was born in Brooklyn of Barbadian parents who had immigrated to America, along with many other West Indians, soon after World War I. The beauty of Barbados, first revealed to her at the age of nine when she visited her parents' homeland, inspired her only juvenilia: a notebook full of poems. Her voluminous reading was followed by formal studies at Brooklyn College, from which she graduated a member of Phi Beta Kappa. Thereafter she married, worked in various New York City libraries, and wrote features for the magazine *Our World,* sometimes traveling on assignments to Brazil and the West Indies.

Encouraged by the publication of a short story in a little magazine, Paule Marshall spent a few years (much of the time in Barbados) writing her first novel, *Brown Girl, Brownstones* (1959), which emphasizes the emotional life of the Boyce family after its move from Barbados to a brownstone house in Brooklyn. The maturing of the ten-year-old heroine, Selina, amid clashes between her parents—centered in irreconcilable differences between their old world and their new—adds tension to the fully evoked locale and picturesque dialogue. *Soul Clap Hands and Sing* (1961) contains four stories titled according to their geographic settings (Barbados, Brooklyn, British Guiana, and Brazil), each of which shows an aging, dying man challenged by the decline of his virility. Using old men whose dynamism induces a final encounter between their solitary and their social proclivities, made urgent by a womanly presence, the author artistically expands her racial insights to a compassionate view of a universal dilemma.

Paule Marshall, a writer whose reputation among critics augurs well for her future, and whose sense of ambitious responsibility to her sex and to her race has added genuineness to her high aesthetic aims, demonstrates her gifts in "Brazil," the final story in *Soul Clap Hands and Sing*. O Grande Caliban, shriveled and rheumy-eyed after thirty-five years of fame for a song-and-dance act with a female partner whom he has bullied with menacing fists and "visually lethal" stances, aggressively personalizes the author's theme of impending death. His vile profanity, his "patent-leather shoes with built-up heels and diamond cuff links glinting in turn with the many rings he wore," his reckless driving down mountain roads, his amazingly violent final destruction of Miranda's apartment— all are modes of response to imminent decay. But the author does not depend entirely upon dramatic action and exposition of emotional crises. The "vaporous gray" of Miranda's eyes, the "gray swirl" of her mind, and the "mushrooming cloud of pink dust" that envelops her shattered bed are images meant to enhance the atmosphere of deterioration. And old Caliban's search for his lost identity along the Rua Gloria subtly dramatizes the universal dilemma motivating the desperate activity that toughens the story.

Brazil

THREE TRUMPETS, two saxophones, a single trombone; a piano, drums and a bass fiddle. Together in the dimness of the night club they shaped an edifice of sound glittering with notes and swaying to the buffeting of the drums the way a tall building sways imperceptibly to the wind when, suddenly, one of the trumpets sent the edifice toppling with a high, whinnying chord that seemed to reach beyond sound into silence. It was a signal and the other instruments quickly followed, the drums exploding into the erotic beat of a samba, the bass becoming a loud pulse beneath the shrieking horns—and in the midst of the hysteria, a voice announced, first in Portuguese and then in English, "Ladies and gentlemen, the Casa Samba presents *O Grande Caliban e a Pequena Miranda*—The Great Caliban and the Tiny Miranda!"

The music ended in a taut, expectant silence and in the darkness a spotlight poured a solid cone of light onto the stage with such force smoke seemed to rise from its wide edge and drift out across the audience. Miranda stood within the cone of light, alone but for the shadowy forms of the musicians behind her, as rigid and stiff-faced as a statue. She was a startlingly tall, long-limbed woman with white skin that appeared luminous in the spotlight and blond hair piled like whipped cream above a face that was just beginning to slacken with age and was all the more handsome and arresting because of this. Her brief costume of sequins and tulle gave off what seemed an iridescent dust each time she breathed, and a smile was affixed like a stamp to her mouth, disguising an expression that was, at once, calculating and grasping —but innocently so, like a child who has no sense of ownership and claims everything to be his. Blue eye shadow sprinkled with gold dust and a pair of dramatic, blue-tinged eyelashes hid her sullen, bored stare.

She filled the night club with a powerful animal presence, with a decisive, passionless air that was somehow Germanic. And she was part German, one of those Brazilians from Rio Grande do Sul who are mixed German, Portuguese, native Indian and sometimes African. With her the German had triumphed. She was a Brunhild without her helmet and girdle of mail, without her spear.

There was a rap on the drums and Miranda clutched one of her buttocks as if she had been struck there; another rap, louder this time, and she clutched the other, feigning shock and outrage.

"Hey, lemme in, stupid!" a rough male voice called in Portuguese behind her, and she whirled like a door that had been kicked open as a dark, diminutive figure burst around her thigh, wearing a scarlet shirt with billowing sleeves and a huge C embroidered on the breast like the device of a royal house, a pair of oversized fighter's trunks of the same scarlet which fell past his knees and a prize fighter's high laced shoes.

He was an old man. His hair beneath the matted wig he wore had been gray for years now and his eyes under crumpled lids were almost opaque with rheum and innocent with age. Yet, as he turned to Miranda with a motion of kicking the door shut, his movements were deft and fluid—his body was still young, it seemed —and as he turned to the audience his face, despite the wrinkles which like fine incisions had drawn his features into an indistinct knot, was still mobile, eloquent, subtle, each muscle beneath the black skin under his absolute control.

Applause greeted him and he assumed the stance of a prize fighter, his body dropping to a wary, menacing crouch, his head ducking and weaving and his tiny fists cocked as he did a dazzling swift dance on his toes. . . . Suddenly he unleashed a flurry of savage jabs, first in the direction of Miranda, who quailed, then at the audience. He pommeled the air and when the knockout blow finally came, it was an uppercut so brilliantly timed, so visually lethal, that those in the audience who had never seen him before jerked their heads out of the way of that fist. "Joe Louis, the champion," he cried, and held up a triumphant right hand.

He always opened his act this way and the caricature had made him famous and become his trademark. But he had burlesqued at other times in his long career, and just as effectively, a rustic gazing up at Rio's high buildings of tinted glass and steel for the first time (this was his favorite since fifty years ago he had himself come to Rio from a small jewel-mining town in Minas Gerais), an American who had just missed his plane (and it had never mattered that his skin was black or that he spoke Portuguese, the illusion had held), a matron from the Brazilian upper class whose costume had begun unraveling during the carnival ball at Copacabana palace . . . and others.

He had been Everyman, so much so that it had become difficult over his thirty-five years in show business to separate out of the welter of faces he could assume his face, to tell where O Grande Caliban ended and he, Heitor Baptista Guimares, began. He had begun to think about this dimly ever since the night he had decided to retire—and to be vaguely disturbed.

Their act was mostly slapstick, with Caliban using the cowed Miranda as a butt for his bullying and abuse. And it was this incongruous and contradictory relationship—Caliban's strength, his bossiness despite his age and shriveled body and Miranda's weakness, which belied her imposing height and massive limbs—that was the heart of their act. It shaped everything they did. When they sang, as they were doing now, his voice was an ominous bass rumble beneath her timid soprano. They broke into a dance routine and Miranda took little mincing steps while Caliban spurred his body in a series of impressive leaps and spins, and forced his legs wide in a split.

It looked effortless, but he felt his outraged muscles rebel as he repeated the split, his joints stiffen angrily. He smiled to disguise both his pain and the disgust he felt for his aging body. He was suddenly overwhelmed by rage and, as usual when his anger became unbearable and he felt helpless, he blamed Miranda. She caught his angry scowl and paused for an instant that was no longer than the natural pause between her dance steps, bewildered, thinking that she had done something wrong and then understanding (she knew him far better now that they openly hated each other), and her own anger streaked across her eyes even as her smile remained intact.

Halfway through their act Miranda left the stage and, alone with the spotlight narrowed to just his face, Caliban spun off a ream of old off-color jokes and imitations. Everything he did was flawlessly timed and full of the subtlety and slyness he had perfected over the years, but he was no longer funny. The audience laughed, but for reasons other than his jokes: the Brazilians out of affection and loyalty, and the tourists, mostly Americans from a Moore-McCormack ship in the harbor, out of a sense of their own well-being and in relief—relief because in the beginning when Caliban's dark face had appeared around Miranda's white thigh they had tensed, momentarily outraged and alarmed until, with smiles that kept slipping out of place, they had reminded each other that this was Brazil after all, where white was never wholly white, no matter how pure it looked. They had begun laughing then in loud, self-conscious gusts, turning to each other for cues and reassurance, whispering, "I don't know why I'm laughing. I don't understand a word of Spanish. Or is this the place where they speak Portuguese?"

Miranda returned for a brief, noisy finale and at the very end she reversed the roles by scooping Caliban up with one hand and marching triumphantly off stage with him kicking, his small arms flailing, high above her head.

"*Senhor* and *Senhoras*, *O Grande Caliban e a Pequena Miranda!*"

Usually, they took two curtain calls, the first with Miranda still holding the protesting Caliban aloft and the other with Caliban on the ground and in command again, chasing the frightened Miranda across the stage. But, tonight, as soon as they were behind the wing, he ordered her to set him down and when she did, he turned and walked toward his dressing room without a word, his legs stiff with irritability and his set shoulders warning her off.

"Hey, are you crazy, where are you going? The curtain call . . ."

"You take it," he said, without turning. "You think it's your show, so you take it."

She stared after him, helpless and enraged, her eyes a vaporous gray which somehow suggested that her mind was the same gray swirl, and her hair shining like floss in the dimness and dust backstage. Then she bounded after him, an animal about to attack. "Now what did I do wrong?" she shouted against the dwindling sound of the applause.

He turned abruptly and she stopped. "Everything," he said quietly. "You did everything wrong. You were lousy."

"So were you."

"Yes, but only because of you."

"Bastard, whenever something's worrying you or you feel sick, you take it out on me. I swear you're like a woman changing life. Nobody told you to try doing the split out there tonight, straining yourself. You're too old. You should retire. You're finished."

"Shut up."

"Why don't you take out your worries on the little mamita you have home, your holiest of virgins . . . ?" He walked rapidly away and she cried after him, gesturing furiously, her voice at a scathing pitch, "Yes, go home to mamita, your child bride. And has the holiest of virgins given birth to your little Jesus yet?"

"Pig," he said, and opened the door to his dressing room.

"Children of old men come out crooked." She began to cry, the false eyelashes staining her cheeks blue.

"Barren bitch."

"Runt! Despoiler of little girls."

He slammed the door on her, jarring the mirror on his dressing table so that his reflection wavered out of shape within its somber, mottled depth. He remained near the door, waiting for the mirror to settle and his own anger to subside, aware, as always, of a critical silence in the room. It was a pleasant silence, welcoming him when his performance was good, but mocking and cold—as it was now—when he failed. And he was aware of something else in the room, a subtle disturbance he had sensed there ever since the night, two months ago, when he had decided to retire. He had thought, at first, that the disturbance was due to something out of place within the familiar disorder or to some new object which had been placed there without his knowing it. But after searching and finding nothing, he had come to believe that what he felt was really a disturbance within himself, some worry he could not define which had become dislodged and escaped along with his breath and taken a vague, elusive form outside of him. Each night it awaited him in the cubicle of a dressing room and watched him while he took off his make-up and dressed, mute yet somehow plaintive, like the memory of someone he had known at another time, but whose face he could no longer remember.

Taking off the scarlet shirt, he tossed it among the other costumes littering the room and, sitting at the dressing table, began taking off the make-up, pausing each time the bulb over the mirror flickered out as the music, playing now for the patrons' dancing, jarred the walls. As his face emerged it was clear that it had once been appealing—the way a child's face is—with an abrupt little nose flattened at the tip, a wry mouth and softly molded contours which held dark shadows within their hollows—a face done in miniature over which the black skin had been drawn tight and eyes which held like a banked fire the intensity of the Latin.

He avoided looking at his face now that he was old. Without the make-up it reminded him of a piece of old fruit so shriveled and spotted with decay that there was no certainty as to what it had been originally. Above all, once he removed the make-up, his face was without expression, bland, as though only on stage made up as Caliban in the scarlet shirt and baggy trunks was he at all certain of who he was. Caliban might have become his reality.

So that now, while his hands did the work of his eyes, he gazed absently at his body, imposing on his slack shoulders and on the sunken chest which barely stirred with his breathing the dimmed memory of his body at the height of his fame (he could not remember what it had looked like before becoming Caliban). He had held himself like a military man then, very erect, his small shoulders squared, all of him stretching it seemed toward the height which had been denied him—and this martial stance, so incongruous somehow, had won him the almost hysterical admiration of the crowds. Yet in the midst of this admiration, he had always felt vaguely like a small animal who had been fitted out in an absurd costume and trained to amuse, some Lilliputian in a kingdom of giants who had to play the jester in order to survive. The world had been scaled without him in mind—and his rage and contempt for it and for those who belonged was always just behind his smile, in the vain, superior lift of his head, in his every gesture.

He pulled on a robe of the same red satin, with a large C embroidered on the breast, hiding himself. He flung aside the towel he was using and the light flickered and then flickered again as the door opened and the porter, Henriques, who also served as Caliban's valet, entered with the cup of *café Sinho* he always brought him after the last show.

Caliban watched the reflection take shape behind his in the mirror: the bloated form dressed in a discarded evening jacket with a cummerbund spanning his vast middle, the face a white globule until the beaked nose which absorbed it appeared, and then the fringe of black hair which Henriques kept waved and pomaded. Caliban felt comforted and younger suddenly, so that as Henriques placed the coffee beside him he motioned him to a chair and, turning, said, his voice loud and casual but strained:

"Henriques, we are in business, old man. Or better out of business. The signs are finished. I saw them today. And they are good. Very bold. They used my red and it hits the eye like one of Caliban's uppercuts"—his fist cut through the air and, although Henriques laughed and nodded, no smile stirred within his old eyes.

"And, thank God, they got the C in Caliban right. I was worried about that because they got it all wrong on the posters they made for my tour last year. But it pleased me the way they did the C this time. Very large and sweeping. Up at the top it says, 'O Grande Caliban retiring,' in big print to catch the eye, with the C coming at you like a fist, then below that 'Brazil's greatest and most beloved comedian leaving the stage after thirty-five years,' and at the bottom, 'See him perform for the last times this month at the Casa Samba.' That's all. And enough, I think. It is more dramatic that way. . ."

"And when will they be put on display, Senhor Caliban?" Henriques asked with elaborate courtesy.

"The day after tomorrow. The posters will go up all over the city, but the big signs only downtown and in Copacabana. There'll be announcements in all the papers of course—a full-page ad which will run for a week, and on radio and television."

"I have a confession, senhor," Henriques said, his voice edging in beside Caliban's, which had grown louder, filling the room. "I personally did not believe it. You know, senhor, how you sometimes talk about retiring but . . . well, you know. But now with the signs and the announcements . . ."

"The talk has ended, Henriques. Two more weeks. The signs are ready, old man!" He shouted as though informing someone beyond the room and held up two fingers the color and shape of dried figs. "Two weeks from tonight Caliban does his last boxing match. That night will mark my anniversary. Thirty-five years ago that same night I won the amateur contest at the Teatro Municipal. Do you remember the old Teatro Municipal? There's a clinic there now for the children of the poor. The night I won, the producer, Julio Baretos, right away booked me in his regular show and christened me O Grande Caliban. After that . . ." His gesture summed up the success which had followed that night.

"And what is your real name, Senhor Caliban?" Henriques said.

Caliban paused, surprised for the moment, and then quickly said, "Guimares. Heitor Guimares. Heitor Baptista Guimares." He gave an embarrassed laugh. "I haven't used it for so long I had to stop and think."

"Perhaps you will begin using it now that you are retiring."

"Of course," he said, and sat back, his smile and gesture dying, his eyes becoming troubled again under their crumpled lids. He quickly drank the *café Sinho* and, as his glance met Henriques' over the cup, he gave a shapeless smile. "Of course," he repeated loudly, even as his gaze wandered over the costumes hung like the bright skins of imaginary animals on the walls, over the trunks containing his juggling and magician equipment. His eyes lingered on each object, possessing it. He tied the scarlet robe more securely around him.

"You are wise to retire," Henriques said quietly. "After all, you are not that old yet and you have a new life ahead what with a young wife and a child soon."

"Of course," Caliban murmured, and for a moment could not remember what his wife looked like.

"How many your age have that? Look at me. I haven't been able to have a woman for years now. And children? All my children have forgotten me. And you have money, Senhor Caliban, while we who are old and without must keep dragging around a dead carcass, breathing death over everybody, working till our end . . ." Henriques stirred heavily in the chair, looking, with the costumes draped behind him and the cummerbund girding his middle, like some old, sated regent.

"Yes," he said, and followed Caliban's stare into space. "You are retiring at the right time, senhor, and with dignity. Putting up the signs all over the city shows style. You are saying good-by to

Rio in the proper way, which is only right, since it was here that
you became famous. Rio made you, after all."

"Of course."

"Now once a year during carnival you will perform before the
President at Copacabana Palace Hotel and all of Rio will weep
remembering your greatness. . ."

Caliban restrained him with a gesture and in the silence his
dark skin seemed to grow ashen as if inside some abstract terror
had cramped his heart. "What to do, Henriques," he said, and
shrugged. "I am an old man. Did you see me tonight? The last
show especially? I could hardly move. I forgot lines so that the
jokes didn't make sense. I was all right in the beginning, but once
I gave the knockout punch I was through. That punch took all
my strength. I feel it here," he touched his right shoulder, his chest.
"Oh, I know I could go on working at the Casa Samba for a while
longer, I am an institution here, but I don't love it any more. I don't
feel the crowd. And then that pig Miranda has gotten so lousy."

"Did you have her name put on the signs?"

"To hell with her. No," he shouted, swept suddenly by the
same anger he had felt on stage. He jumped up and began dressing under Henriques' somnolent eye, wonder at the intensity of his
anger, knowing remotely that it reached beyond Miranda to something greater.

"But haven't you told her?"

"I told her. I even told her about the signs. But like you she
didn't believe me. She just laughed. The pig," he cried suddenly,
and the light flickered. "Did you hear her cursing me just now,
and cursing my wife and my unborn child. She has become crazy
this past year. All because I married." Suddenly, facing the door,
he shouted, "It's my business that I married, pig, not yours. And
if I chose to marry a child of twenty-five, it is my business still."

He waited, quivering, as though expecting Miranda to burst
into the room. Then, turning again to Henriques, he said, "You
would not believe it, Henriques, but I still give her everything she
wants even though I married. Last month she saw one of those
fancy circular beds in a magazine from Hollywood and I had one
custom made for her. A while back, she took out all the light fix-
tures and put in chandeliers, even in the kitchen, so that her
place looks like the grand ballroom of the Copacabana Palace
Hotel. I bought the chandeliers for her, of course, as I have bought
nearly everything she has—while she has been saving her money
all these years. And even though I married I still go and spend
part of the evening with her before we come to the club. . . So

she complains I will have nothing to do with her any more. But after all, Henriques, I am an old man and I have a young wife. Besides it was always a little grotesque with her. . ."

"They say it's never good to keep a woman around once you're finished with her."

"I should have kicked her out, yes—and long ago. She was never any good for me or for the act. From the very beginning she tried to take over both of us. And I only included her in the act for effect. She wasn't supposed to do anything more than stand there like a mannequin. But she kept insisting—she would wake me at night begging me to let her do more. And so . . ." He motioned hopelessly and sat down.

"I should have never taken up with her." Then he said softly, "But she was a weakness with me in the beginning." He gave Henriques an oblique, almost apologetic glance. "And what I said just now was not true. She was good for me in the beginning—and we were good together. We were the same, you see. Me, as I am—" and with a gesture he offered Henriques his shrunken body—"and she, so tall, and she was skinny then. They were laughing at her the first time I saw her in a show at the Miramar almost fifteen years ago now. She couldn't dance. She couldn't sing. She hadn't bleached her hair yet and she looked lousy. . . I understood what it was for her being so tall—" His voice dropped, becoming entangled with the memory. "And she was good for the act in the beginning. She had imagination and the comic touch. She was the one who thought up the prize-fighter routine, which is still the most famous. But then something went wrong with her, Henriques, and she began doing everything wrong. I've been carrying her for years now. Perhaps I would have had another five, ten years left, if not for her. She has become a bane. She has used me till I'm dry, the pig!"

"But what of her now?"

Caliban, dressed in an expensive mohair suit with a white handkerchief embroidered with a red *C* in the breast pocket, patent-leather shoes with built-up heels and diamond cuff links glinting in turn with the many rings he wore, turned sharply toward the door as if to rush from the room and the question. "What of her? That's not my worry. The day those signs go up is the day I finish with her, the parasite. Let her spend some of the money she sits on. She has talked for years about doing her own act. Now she'll have a chance to do it."

"But does she have the talent for that?"

"No, and she knows it. Do you think she would have stayed with me all this time if she had, Henriques? Not Miranda."

"Well, she will find someone to keep her. She is like Rio. There will always be somebody to admire her." Henriques heaved up from the chair, and, as his unwieldy bulk filled the small room, the dusk whirred up like frightened birds and settled further away. He began picking up Caliban's clothes.

"Yes," Caliban said thoughtfully, "she will find somebody to use, the bitch. For a while anyway." He hurried to the door, eager to escape the room which had suddenly become crowded with the image of Miranda and hot from his anger. As he opened it, he sensed the vague, illusory form of his fear rush past him like a draft and lead him through the clutter backstage, out the back door and across the denuded yard to the entrance, where the neon lights pulsed the name CASA SAMBA into the night and a large sign at the door announced the nightly appearance of O Grande Caliban.

The club was closing; the last of the crowd clustered under the awning while the doorman called up the taxis. Beyond the radius of neon lights the night itself was a vast awning under which the city slept, exhausted from its nightly revelry, its few remaining lights like dull reflections of the stars. Its mountains, like so many dark breasts thrusting into the sky, gave height and prominence and solidity to the night.

The Casa Samba had been built on the sloping street leading to the *Pão de Açúcar* and as Caliban walked toward his car he was aware, as if for the first time, of the mountain's high, solid cone, black against the lesser blackness of the sky, benevolent, rising protectively over the sleeping city. He could make out the cable line of the aerial railway looped in a slender thread between *Pão de Açúcar* and its satellite, Mount Urca. What had been for years just another detail in the familiar frieze that was Rio was suddenly separate and distinct, restored. . . He paused beside his car, hoping (but unaware of the hope) that a part of himself which he had long since ceased to see might emerge into consciousness as the mountain had emerged, thinking (and he was aware of this) that there might be a wind the day after tomorrow when the signs announcing his retirement went up, a wind strong enough to tear them down before they could be read and whip them out to sea. He was half smiling, his worn eyelids closing with pleasure at the thought, when a taxi with a group of Americans from the night club stopped and one of them called to him in English, "Say, do you speak English?"

He turned, annoyed. The man's voice, the harsh, unmelodic, almost gutteral English he spoke, his pale face floating in the darkness seemed to snatch his pleasure, to declare that there would be no wind the day after tomorrow and the signs would remain.

As the taxi's headlights singled him out, he felt as if he had been caught on stage without the armor of his scarlet shirt and loose trunks—suddenly defenseless, shorter than his five feet, insignificant. He quickly assumed his martial pose.

"I speak some little English," he said stiffly.

"Well, then maybe you can explain to our driver here—" and the driver protested in Portuguese to Caliban that he had understood them and could speak English—"that we want to go someplace else, not back to the hotel, but to another night club. Are there any that stay open all night? Do you understand what I'm saying? Some place where we can dance."

Without answering, Caliban turned and told the driver where to take them. Then he said in English, "He will take you to a place."

"Thanks. Say, aren't you the comedian from the club? What's your name again?"

He wanted to fling the full title—O Grande Caliban—in the man's face and walk away, but he could not even say Caliban. For some reason he felt suddenly divested of that title and its distinction, no longer entitled to use it.

The man was whispering to the others in the car. "What was his name again? You know, the old guy telling the jokes. With the blonde."

"The name is Heitor Guimares," Caliban said suddenly.

"No, I mean your stage name."

"Hey, wait, I remember," someone in the car called. "It was from Shakespeare. Caliban . . ."

"Heitor Baptista Guimares," he cried, his voice loud and severe, addressed not only to them but to the mountain and the night. Turning, he walked to his car.

He did not drive away but remained perched like a small, ruffled bird on the cushions he used to raise the driver's seat, his rings winking angrily in the dimness as he watched the taillights of the taxi define the slope as it sped down, trying to order his breathing, which had suddenly become a conscious and complex act. The taillights vanished and with them the momentary annoyance he had felt with the tourists. He was alone then, with only the vague form of his anxiety (and he had never felt such loneliness) and the unfamiliar name echoing in his mind.

"Heitor Guimares," he said slowly. "Heitor Guimares." But although he repeated it until his tongue was heavy, it had no reality. It was the name of a stranger who had lived at another time.

By the time Caliban reached the modern house of glass walls and stone he had built in a suburb near Corcovado, the mountain of Christ, a thin, opalescent dawn had nudged aside the darkness, and, as he walked hesitantly across the patio, through the living room, down the hall to the bedrooms, the sound of his raised heels on the tiles was like the failing pulse of the dying night.

He paused at the opened door of the master bedroom. He could not hear his wife's breathing but he could see it in the small, steady flame of the candle before the Madonna in the niche near the bed. In the faint light he made out her stomach, like a low hill on the wide plain of the bed, and the dark outline of her face framed by the pillows. He did not have to see that face to know its mildness and repose. The first time he had met her on the tour last year which had taken him through the small town in Minas Gerais where he had been born (she was the granddaughter of a distant cousin of his and it had been easy to arrange the marriage), he had almost, instinctively, crossed himself. She had looked like a Madonna painted black. He had wanted to confess to her as to a priest, seeing her that first time. He would have confessed now if he could have named his fear—whispering to her while she slept. And she would have, blindly in her sleep, curved her body to receive him, nesting him within the warm hollow of her back as if he were the child she bore. He hesitated though, feeling, oddly, that he was no longer entitled to her comfort, just as he was no longer entitled to use the name Caliban.

He closed the door and went to the small room at the end of the hall which he used as a den and stretched out on the cot there without undressing. As always when he was troubled, he slept quickly and his dream was that he was caught in a mine shaft without a lantern to light his way.

As quickly, light rushed at him from one end of the shaft and he awoke to the afternoon sun which had invaded the room. Like a reveler the sunlight did a sprightly dance on the framed photographs on the walls (they were all of Caliban, one with the President of Brazil during the carnival of 1946 and another with Carmen Miranda the year before she died), on the mementoes and awards on top of the desk; it leaped across the floor and landed in the arms of his wife as she opened the door.

had already been to Mass, yet a thin haze from her long sleep

She did not enter the room but stood, like a petitioner, in the doorway, holding a cup of coffee as though it was an offering. She filmed her eyes; her body, Caliban knew, would still be warm and pliant from the bed. He felt neither pleasure nor passion at the thought, though—and as if she understood this and blamed herself, she bowed her head.

"Caliban . . ." she said finally, and hesitated. Then: "You have slept in all your clothes and in your rings."

"It's nothing," he said, and sat up, waving her off as she started forward to help him. "I was tired last night, that's all."

His body felt strange: sore as though he had been beaten while he slept, constricted by the clothes which seemed to have shrunk overnight. The taste of the name he had spoken aloud in the car was still in his mouth. "Let me have the coffee," he said.

The coffee was the color and texture of his sleep and he drank it quickly, wishing that it was a potion which would bring on that sleep again. "Is there a wind today?"

"Only at the top of the road, near the church." And she quickly added, "But I wore a coat."

His thought had been of the signs, not of her, and, ashamed suddenly, he said in the paternal, indulgent tone he used with her, "Tell me, Clara, how would you like to live somewhere else for a while? Somewhere in Minas again perhaps . . ."

She could not disguise her reluctance. "Back to Minas? But what of your work?"

"You let me worry about that, little Clara."

"And this house?"

"Sell it and build a bigger one there."

"Yes, of course. But then Rio is nice too. I mean there is carnival here and . . ."

"We will come down for carnival each year."

"Of course. Then there is the child. It would be nice if it were born in Rio. Perhaps after the child we could return to Minas . . ."

"No, I don't want a child of mine to be born in Rio and be called a *Carioca*."

"Yes, Caliban."

"Say Heitor," he said sharply, startling her.

"Heitor?" She frowned.

"Don't you know my real name?"

"Of course."

"Well, then, you can begin using it."

She would have asked why (he could see the question stir within the haze), but she was not bold enough.

For the first time her timidity annoyed him and he leaped up, his movement so abrupt that she drew back. "Tell me," he said, appealing to her suddenly, "did your mother ever speak about me? Or your grandmother? Did they ever talk about me as a young man? About Heitor?"

"Of course."

"What did they say I was like?"

She was silent for so long he repeated the question, his voice high and urgent. "What did they say?"

"I know they used to talk about how big a success you were . . ." she said hesitantly.

"As a young man, I said. Before I came to Rio. I was different then . . ."

"I know they used to talk, but I can't remember all that they said. I only know that when you were famous they always looked for your name in the papers."

He sat down on the edge of the cot, showing his disgust with her by a limp wave and feeling unreasonably that she had failed him. It was as if he had married her hoping that she would bring, like a dowry, the stories and memories of him as a young man, as Heitor, only to discover that he had been cheated.

"Heitor Guimares . . . Senhora Guimares," she was murmuring, touching herself and smiling abstractly.

"What are you laughing about? You don't like the name?"

"No, it's just that until I get used to it I will keep looking for someone else when I say it because I'm so used to you being Caliban."

It was not clear whether he hurled the cup at her or at the floor, but it missed her and, as it broke on the tiles, the sunlight scuttled from the room and the spilled coffee spread in a dark stain between them. "And who will you be looking for?" His shout was strident with the same abstract rage of the night before. "Who? Tell me. Some boy your age perhaps? Some tall, handsome boy, eh, some *Carioca* who will dance with you in the streets during carnival and jounce you on my bed behind my back? Is he the one you will be looking for?"

She said nothing. She had uttered a muted cry when the cup broke, but now, as he leaped up again, she calmly placed her hands over her swollen stomach, protecting it from the violence of his movement and, as he shouted, her fat child's fingers spread wider, deflecting the sound.

"Tell me!" he charged her. "Who is this person you will be looking for when you call my name?"

She remained as silent and resigned as the Virgin in their bedroom, her head bent in submission, her hands guarding the stomach.

Her silence was a defense he could not shake and as he stood there, menacing her with his shouts, he felt his anger rebound from the thick, invisible wall of silence which shielded her and flail him. He was the victim of his own rage, and bruised, beaten, he rushed from the room, from her, his heels clattering like small hoofs on the tile.

"Caliban!" He heard her cry over the sound of the motor as he started the car, and then a snatch of words as he drove off: "You have not changed your clothes."

He realized this when he was some distance from the house and had calmed a little. And the feel of the stale, sodden clothes recalled the time when he had first come to Rio and had had to wear secondhand clothes that were invariably too large for him and shiny from long wear and smelling always of the former owners. That had been the time, of course, when he had been only Heitor Guimares and people calling him by that name had not looked for anyone else, nor had he felt strange saying it. He tried to restore those years in his mind, but the memories were without form or coherence. They filtered down at random, blown like dust through his mind, and as he reached out to snatch them—desperate suddenly to recapture that time and that self—they eluded his fingers.

One memory paused though: he saw a street, the Rua Gloria, and the restaurant where he had worked until he had won the contest at the Teatro Municipal. The pattern of the tile floor over which he had swung the mop three times a day, the tables—slabs of cheap white marble upon which he had placed the food—were suddenly clear. He had left a part of himself there. Suddenly he brought his foot down on the accelerator, standing up and gripping the steering wheel to give himself leverage, and the big car bounded forward, bearing him to the city and the Rua Gloria.

As the car swept down the mountain roads, the sea appeared, vast and benign, mirroring the sky's paleness and breaking the sun's image into fragments, then the bays—sure, graceful curves, forming an arabesque design with the hills between—and finally the city itself—white, opulent, languorous under the sun's caress, taking its afternoon rest now in preparation for the night.

The Rua Gloria was in the old section of Rio and Caliban found it easily, recognizing the house on the corner with its Moorish-style balcony and checker-pane windows. The house was a ruin but somehow it promised that he would find the restaurant at the other end of the street. Parking the car, he started down, eager suddenly. Instinctively, as if the years had not passed, his legs made the slight adjustment to the sloping street and his feet sought out the old holes in the pavement; halfway down he passed the boys' school and his head turned automatically, expecting the boys in the yard to wave and shout, "*Ohlá*, Senhor Heitor, when are you going to stop growing?"

There were boys in the yard now, playing soccer in the eddying dust, and they looked no different from those he had known. But they did not wave, and, although they shouted and rushed out the gate when he passed, it was only because he was a stranger. They pointed to his mohair suit, his shoes with the raised heels, his rings dancing in the sunlight, whispering among themselves. And then one of them cried, "O Grande Caliban," and, with that abruptness which Caliban had perfected, dropped to a fighter's crouch. The others took up his cry and the name O Grande Caliban rose in a piercing chorale.

They trailed him, trumpeting the name, a scuffing retinue in their school uniforms. Caliban stiffened each time they tossed his name into the air like a football, but he welcomed them. They were a solid wall between him and the apprehensiveness which trailed him. Because of them he was certain that he would find the restaurant intact, like the setting of a play which had not been dismantled.

And it was there, but unrecognizable save for the glazed tiles in the entrance way which were all broken now and the stone doorsill in which the old groove had been worn deeper. Where the awning had been, a huge sign said BEBE COCA-COLA and below that, on the modern glass front, was the new name of the restaurant: O RESTAURANTE GRANDE CALIBAN.

The boys crowded behind him, pressing him inside, and he saw that the tile floor whose every imperfection he could have traced in the dark had been covered in bright linoleum; chrome chairs and tables had replaced the marble tables and wire-back chairs, while booths covered in simulated leather lined one wall. The air smelled of stale coffee and as Caliban, jarred by the sight of faded newspaper photographs of himself crowding the walls and a garish oil painting of him in the scarlet shirt hanging over the bar, placed his hand on a table to steady himself, a fly there stirred its wings but did not move.

The only occupant was a man—the waiter or owner perhaps —half-asleep at the bar, his stout haunches overlapping the stool. He stirred into wakefulness now with the same blind, stubborn movement as the fly. He was a *sarará* with an abundance of sandy hair curling out of the sweat-shirt he wore, fair skin pitted from smallpox and small, agate-colored eyes set within morose features. He turned, querulous with sleep, and missing Caliban, who was, after all, no taller than most of the boys, he shouted, "Get out of here, you little bandits, before you let in the flies."

"We come with Caliban," they hurled at him, "O Grande Caliban."

The man started suspiciously and peered, his head lowered as though he was about to charge, through the fog of sleep. As he spotted Caliban his agate-colored eyes glittered like one of Caliban's rings, and an awed smile groped its way around his mouth. "Senhor Caliban . . .?" he whispered, and slipped from the stool into a bow so fluid and perfect it looked rehearsed.

"Senhor Caliban, it is a great honor . . ." With a proud wave he presented Caliban with the large portrait over the bar, the photographs, the chrome chairs and the linoleum. "Please . . ." He motioned him to a booth, then to a table.

Caliban would have turned and left if the boys had not been behind him, barring his way. He wanted to escape, for the restaurant had profaned his past with chrome and simulated leather, and the portrait, the faded photographs, his name on the window had effaced the Heitor Guimares who had wielded the mop over the tiles.

"Who put up those pictures?" he asked sharply.

The man's smile faltered and he said, puzzled, "I found them here when I bought the place, Senhor Caliban, all except the portrait. I did that. I am something of a painter—an artist like yourself, Senhor Caliban. I did it in your honor . . ." He gave the supple bow again.

"Who owned the place before you?"

"A man named DaCruz. He had many debts so I got it cheap . . ."

"Did he put them up?"

"No, I think it was his great-uncle, old Nacimento, the one, Senhor Caliban, who must have owned the restaurant when you worked here. Perhaps you've forgotten him?"

"Yes, I had forgotten," Caliban said, and paused, trying to summon Nacimento's face from the blurred assortment of faces in his mind. "Is he still alive?"

"He was the last time I heard, Senhor Caliban, but he is very sick because of course he is so old. And he has nothing now, I hear, and lives in the *favelas*."

"Which one?"

"The one above Copacabana . . . Senhor Caliban, a *café Sinho* perhaps?"

But Caliban had already turned and with an abrupt wave scattered the boys out of his way.

"A *café Sinho*, at least!" The man shouted from the doorway over the heads of the boys, but Caliban, his small back slanted forward, was already rushing up the street, his patent-leather shoes flashing in the sunlight.

Later, as Caliban climbed the first slope leading to the *favela*, his shoes became covered with red dust and clay. He could see just above him the beginning of the slums—a vast, squalid rookery for the poor of Rio clinging to the hill above Copacabana, a nest of shacks built with the refuse of the city: the discarded crates and boxes, bits of galvanized iron and tin, old worm-eaten boards and shingles—and all of this piled in confused, listing tiers along the hillside, the wood bleached gray by the sun. The *favela* was another city above Rio which boldly tapped its electricity from below—so that at night the hills were strewn with lights—and repulsed the government's efforts to remove it. It was an affront—for that squalor rising above Rio implied that Rio herself was only a pretense; it was a threat—for it seemed that at any moment the *favela* would collapse and hurtle down, burying the city below.

Caliban had long ago ceased to see the *favelas*. He would glance up at the hills occasionally to watch them shift miraculously as the shadows moving across then shifted, but his eye passed quickly over the ugliness there: it was too much a reminder of what he had known. Now the *favela* claimed his eye. It seemed to rush down at him, bringing with it a sure and violent death—and he remembered the stories of strangers who had ventured into the *favelas* and had either disappeared or been found garroted the next day at the foot of the hill.

In pursuing the old man, it was as if, suddenly, he was pursuing his own death. And because he was exhausted, the thought of that death was almost pleasurable. He imagined the thronged cathedral, the crowds standing a thousand deep outside, the city hung in crape; he heard the priest intoning his name—and at the thought that perhaps no one would recognize the name Heitor Guimares, he stumbled and nearly fell.

The children of the *favela* appeared, slipping quietly down amid the scrub which lined the path, some of them balancing gallon tins of water on their heads or smaller children on their hips. They seemed born of the dust which covered them, like small, tough plants sprung from the worn soil, and their flat, incurious eyes seemed to mirror the defeated lives they had yet to live.

They watched him climb without comment, recognizing that he was a stranger from the city below who brought with him the trappings of that world: the flashing rings and stylish clothes. Their empty stares seemed to push him up the hill toward some final discovery.

Caliban could not look at them, and said, his eyes averted, "*Ohlá*, can any of you tell me where to find Nacimento, the old man?"

Their answer was a stolid silence and he called down the line, addressing each one in turn: "Do you know him? Which is his house? Do you know who I'm talking about?" Finally he cried, his voice strained thin by the dust and his exertion, "Do you know him; he is an old friend!"

"His house is the one there," a boy said finally, pointing. "The one beside the tree without a head."

Caliban saw the tree, a dead palm without its headdress of fronds, starting out of the ground like a derisive finger, and then the house beside it, a makeshift of old boards and tin and dried fronds. It looked untenanted: Nacimento might have died and left the house as a monument. Caliban turned to the children, the fear dropping like a weight inside him.

"He's there," the boy said. "He doesn't like the sun."

And suddenly Caliban remembered Nacimento sending him to roll down the restaurant awning against the sun each afternoon. The warped door he pushed open now seemed to declare the age of the man inside and, as he entered the room, shutting out the glare behind him, it was as if the night was in hiding there, waiting for the sun to set before it rushed out and, charging down the hill, lay siege to the city.

"Nacimento . . ." he called softly. He could not see the old man but he heard his breathing—a thin *râle* like the fluting of an instrument Nacimento played to ease his loneliness. Presently Caliban made out a table because of a white cup there, then a cot whose legs had been painted white and finally the dark form of the old man.

He was seated before the boarded-up window, facing it as though it was open, and he was watching the sun arching down the sky or the children waiting around the dead palm for Caliban to emerge.

"Nacimento," Caliban said, and knew that the old man was blind. "Senhor Nacimento."

"Is there someone?" the old man asked uncertainly, as though he could no longer distinguish between those voices which probably filled his fantasies sitting there alone and those that were real. He did not turn from the window.

"Yes, it is Heitor Guimares."

"Who is the person?" The old man said formally, turning now.

"Heitor."

"Heitor?"

"Yes, from the restaurant years ago. You remember. He . . . I used to be the waiter . . ."

"Heitor . . ." the old man said slowly, as though searching for the face to which the name belonged.

Hopeful, Caliban drew closer. He could see Nacimento's eyes now, two yellow smears in the dimness which reflected nothing and the face wincing, it seemed, in unrelieved pain.

"Yes, Heitor," Caliban said coaxingly. "You used to call me Little Heitor from Minas. You remember . . ."

"I know no Heitor," the old man said sorrowfully, and then, starting apprehensively, he cried, "Is the door closed? The sun ruins everything."

Caliban's voice rose, tremulous and insistent. "But of course you remember. After all, every day you used to tell me the same thing—to close the door, to roll down the awning against the sun. It was I—Heitor Guimares—who would sometimes tell a few jokes at night to keep the customers drinking. But then, you must remember because it was you, after all, who made me enter the amateur contest at the Teatro Municipal. You even went with me that night and gave me a shirt to wear with ruffles down the front like a movie star. The Teatro Municipal!" he shouted as the old man shook his head confusedly. "We wept on each other's shoulder when they told me I had won and put me in the regular show with the name of Caliban . . ."

"O Grande Caliban," the old man said severely.

"Yes, but I was Heitor Guimares when I worked for you, not Caliban."

"O Grande Caliban. He was the best they ever had at the Teatro Municipal. I told him he would win and he was the best . . ."

"But I was Heitor then!"

"I know no Heitor," Nacimento cried piteously, and turned to the boarded-up window, reaching up as though he would open it and call for help. "I know no Heitor. . . ."

Caliban believed him. It was no use. The old man, he understood, going suddenly limp, had retained only a few things: his fear of the sun, the name O Grande Caliban, a moment of success in a crowded theater in which he had shared. That was all. The rest had been stripped away in preparation for his death which, in a way, had already begun. Caliban smelled its stench in the room suddenly and wanted to flee as he had fled the restaurant earlier. Groping toward the door, he jarred against the table and the cup there fell and broke. The old man whimpered at the sound and Caliban remembered his wife's muted outcry that morning over the other cup he had broken. The day seemed to be closing in on him, squeezing his life from him, and his panic was like a stitch

421

in his side as he rushed out, forgetting to close the door behind him.

The night might have escaped through the open door and followed him down the hill, for as he sat in his car, crumpled with exhaustion, knowing that his search had been futile and he could do nothing now but go to Miranda as he did each evening at this time, he saw the first of the dusk surge across the hill in a dark, purposeful wave, drowning out the *favela*, and then charge down the slopes, deepening into night as it came.

The city, in quick defense, turned on her lights, and as Caliban drove out of the tunnel onto the road which followed the wide arc of Copacabana Bay he saw the lights go on in the apartment buildings and hotels piled like white angular cliffs against the black hills. Seen from a distance those lighted windows resembled very large, fine diamonds, an iridescent amber now in the last of the sunlight, which would turn to a fiery yellow once the darkness settled. Rio—still warm from the sun, murmurous with the cadence of the sea, bejeweled with lights—was readying herself for the nightly carousal, waiting for the wind to summon her lovers.

Caliban had been one of her lovers, but as he drove through her midst, he felt her indifference to his confusion, to his sense of a loss which remained nameless; moreover, he suspected that she had even been indifferent to his success. "After all Rio has made you," Henriques had said, but he had not added that she would quickly choose another jester to her court once he was gone. Caliban hated the city suddenly—and as that hate became unbearable he shifted its weight onto Miranda. He accused her. Hadn't Henriques said that she and Rio were the same? He brought his foot down on the accelerator and the car leaped forward like a startled horse, leaving black streaks on the road.

Oddly enough, Miranda's apartment, in a new building at the end of Copacabana, reflected in the city. The great squares of black and white tile in the foyer suggested not only the stark white buildings reared against the dark hills and the sidewalks of Copacabana —a painstaking mosaic of small black and white stones, but the faces of the *Cariocas* themselves—endless combinations of black and white. The green rug in the living room could have been a swatch cut from one of the hills, while the other furnishings there —elaborate period pieces of an ivory finish, marble tables cluttered with figurines, sofas of pale silk and down, white drapes and gilt-edged mirrors—repeated the opulence, self-indulgence, the lavish whiteness of the city. And the chandeliers with their fiery crystal spears, which rustled like frosted leaves as Caliban slammed the door, caught the brilliance of Rio at night.

For the first time Caliban was aware of how the room expressed the city, and of himself, reflected in one of the mirrors, in relation to it. He was like a house pet, a tiny dog, who lent the room an amusing touch but had no real place there. The pale walls and ivory furniture, the abundance of white throughout stripped him of importance, denied him all significance. He felt like whimpering as the old man, Nacimento, had whimpered when the cup broke—and he must have unknowingly, for Miranda suddenly called from the adjoining bedroom, "What in the hell are you muttering to yourself about out there?"

He turned and through the half-opened door saw her enthroned amid a tumble of pink satin cushions on the circular bed he had bought her, while her maid massaged her feet in a basin of scented water—the girl's black hands wavering out of shape under the water. Miranda had already dressed her hair for the night club —the stiff froth of blond curls piled high above her white brow— and applied her make-up (she had spent the afternoon at it, Caliban knew), but her body beneath the sheer pink dressing gown was still bare, the tops of the breasts a darker pink than the gown. Knowing how slack those breasts had become, Caliban felt repelled, weary and then angry again; he understood suddenly that her refusal ever to leave him and marry, to have children and use those ample breasts, was, simply, her desire to remain the child herself—willful, dependent, indulged—and that she had used him to this end, just as she would use someone else now that she had exhausted him.

As always when he was truly angry, he became calm, and in that calm he could always feel his nerves, the muscles of his abrupt little arms and legs, his heart, quietly marshaling their force for the inevitable outburst. He came and stood in the doorway, very still, the only exterior signs of his anger a tightness around his mouth, a slight tension to his wide nose and a chill light within his even gaze.

Without looking up from polishing her nails, Miranda said querulously, "You come in late slamming my doors and then you stand outside talking to yourself. Where have you been all day anyway? People have been calling here looking for you after they called your house and that stupid child you married said she didn't know where you had gone."

She glanced up, still sullen and truculent from their quarrel the night before—and stiffened. Her maid felt her foot go taut and turned, puzzled.

"Go home, Luiz," he said quietly.

Miranda screamed, the sound jarring the bottle of nail polish from her hand and it spilled, staining the pink covers red. "No, Luiz . . ." She reached toward the girl. "Wait, Luiz . . ."

"Go home, Luiz," he repeated.

The girl stood up then as though jerked to her feet and, holding the basin of water, looked from him to Miranda for a single distraught moment and then broke for the door, the water sloshing on the rug. As she passed him, Caliban said gently, "Good night, Luiz," and closed the door behind her.

"*Luiz!*"

Caliban came and sat across the bed from her and deliberately placed his trouser leg with the red dust and clay from the *favela* against the pink coverlet.

Miranda stared at the leg, her gray eyes dull with hysteria and disbelief, at the nail polish streaked like fresh blood on the bedclothes and her hands, at the trail of water the maid had left on the rug and then across to the closed door. Her skin blanched with terror and her scream convulsed the air again, higher this time, so that the chandelier over her bed swayed anxiously. And still screaming, cursing incoherently, she frantically began drawing up the sheet around her.

"Tell me," Caliban said evenly, "do you know a Heitor Guimares?"

She did not hear him at first and he waited until her scream broke off and then repeated in the same quiet tone, "I asked you if you know somebody named Heitor Guimares?"

"Who?" The word was uttered at the same high pitch as her scream.

"Heitor Guimares."

"Heitor who . . . ? Guimares. No. Who is that? I don't know anybody by that name. Guimares . . . ?" Wary, suspicious, she said after a pause, "Why do you ask?" and then emboldened by his silence, shouted, "What is this? Why do you come asking me about someone I don't know. Who's this Heitor Guimares anyway? Why do you come in here looking as if you slept in the sewers and muttering to yourself, scaring me, scaring my maid, slamming my doors and ruining my bed with your dirt. Oh, God, what's wrong now? It's going to be hell tonight. You'll do everything wrong in the show and blame me. You're old!" she screamed, and started up in the bed. "And losing your mind. You should retire. Go back to Minas, peasant . . . And that little bitch, she's fired. I won't pay her a cent for ruining the rug. Everything ruined . . ." she said tragically, and paused, looking tearfully down at the spilled nail polish on her hands, quiet for the moment, and then her head snapped up. "Who is this Heitor Guimares now? I lie here alone all day, all night, alone, always alone, and then you come in here accusing me of someone I don't know. Bastard! Suppose I did know someone by that name. It would be my business. You don't own me. I'm not your scared little mamita. Heitor Guimares! Who is he? Somebody has been feeding you lies."

"I am Heitor Guimares."

She stared at him, the rest of what she had to say lying dead on her lips and the wildness still in her eyes. Then her bewilderment collapsed into a laugh that was as shrill, in relief, as her scream had been. The sheet she was holding around her dropped and her arm shot out, stiff with scorn. "You? No, senhor, you are Caliban. O Grande Caliban!" And leaping from the bed, her great breasts swinging, she dropped to his familiar fighter's crouch, her fists cocked menacingly and her smile confirming what the others —his wife that morning, the boys on the Rua Gloria chanting behind him, the man in the restaurant that had been made into a shrine, and, finally, the old man, Nacimento—had all insisted was true, and what he, and certainly Miranda, had really known all along: simply, that Caliban had become his only reality and anything else he might have been was lost. The image Miranda had created for him was all he had now and once that was taken—as it would be tomorrow when the signs announcing his retirement went up— he would be left without a self.

Miranda did not see him pick up the small boudoir chair, for her head was lowered over her fists and she was doing the little shuffling fighter's dance he had made famous. But as the chair cut the air above her, her head snapped up, her hand started up and she watched its flight with the mocking smile her shock and stupefaction had fixed on her face. She tried to move but could not. It was too late anyway; the chair smashed into the low-hanging chandelier and brought it down in a roar of shattered crystal onto the bed—and in the light from the small lamps along the walls the bed seemed to explode in a thick, mushrooming cloud of pink dust.

Caliban's destruction of the apartment was swift and complete. It was as if the illusion of strength he had created on stage for so long had been finally given to him. While Miranda stood transfixed, a dazed horror spreading like a patina over her face (and she was never to lose that expression), he hauled down drapes and curtains, overturned furniture, scattered drawers and their frivolous contents across the floor, broke the figurines against the white walls, smashed the mirrors and his reflection there—and then, with a jagged piece of glass, slashed open the silk sofas and chairs so that the down drifted up over the wreckage like small kites. Finally, wielding a heavy curtain rod as if it were a lance, he climbed onto a marble table and swung repeatedly at the large chandelier in the living room, sending the glass pendants winging over the room. With each blow he felt the confusion and despair congested within him fall away, leaving an emptiness which, he knew, would remain with him until he died. He wanted to sleep suddenly, beside his wife, in the room with the Madonna.

A glass spear struck Miranda, who had staggered, weeping and impotent, to the door, and she shrieked. Her outcry was the sound of the trumpet the night before, a high, whinnying note that reached beyond all sound into a kind of silence. The scream broke her paralysis and she rushed at him with a powerful animal grace, the gown flaring open around her bare body, and reaching up caught the rod.

He let it go, but from his high place he leaned down and struck her with his small fist on her head, and the hair cascaded down like a curtain over her stunned face.

He was at the elevator, the automatic door sliding open in front of him, when he heard her frightened, tearful voice calling him down the hall. "Caliban! Caliban! Where are you going? The show! Are you crazy—what about the show tonight? Oh, Mary, full of grace, look what the bastard's done. The place! He's killed me inside. Oh, God, where is he going? Crazy bastard, come back here. What did I do? Was it me, Caliban? Caliban, *meu negrinho,* was it me . . . ?"

ERNEST
J.
GAINES
1933-

Ernest J. Gaines was born on a planta-
tion near Oscar, Louisiana. When he was fifteen, his family moved
to Vallejo, California. After two years in the army, 1953–1955, he
attended San Francisco State College, graduating in 1957. He won
a Wallace Stegner Fellowship in Creative Writing in 1958, for a
year of study at Stanford University. The following year, he received
the Joseph Henry Jackson Literary Award for creative writing. He
completed his first novel, *Barren Summer*, in 1963. Although some
of his stories were beginning to appear in *Negro Digest* and elsewhere by that time, no collection of them appeared before *Bloodline*
(1968). His first-published novel was *Catherine Carmier* (1964).
His second, *Of Love and Dust* (1967), was brought out while he
was at work in San Francisco on *Bloodline*.

Gaines believes that Richard Wright "had to get his material
out of the American soil, not out of a European library." He himself seems intent upon exhuming from his native Louisiana soil—
to which he hopes to return from San Francisco—what Henry
James might call the "stuff of consciousness" for a novel of mag-
nitude. Gaines, who thinks that the artist is the only free man left
in the world, has so far been concerned in his fiction (usually
about rural Louisianians) with individuals determined, often hero-
ically, either to maintain their codes of conduct among debasing
or confusing forces, or to ride out the storm of consequences attending their decisions to change with the times.

In "The Sky Is Gray," which first appeared in *Negro Digest* in August 1963, Gaines unforgettably emphasizes the code of independence and pride so quietly dramatized before the concluding line, "You a man." The eight-year-old boy's pathetic killing of the redbirds, his sacrificial toothache, and his love for his mother are rehearsals for the kind of manhood apparently viewed by the author, within and beyond the story, as requisite to meaningful social change. The realistically balanced forces of Negro nonviolent militance and white humaneness add the warmth of controversial prophecy to the atmospheric cold of the story.

The Sky Is Gray

GO'N BE COMING in a few minutes. Coming 'round that bend down there full speed. And I'm go'n get out my hankercher and I'm go'n wave it down, and us go'n get on it and go.

I keep on looking for it, but Mama don't look that way no more. She looking down the road where us jest come from. It's a long old road, and far's you can see you don't see nothing but gravel. You got dry weeds on both sides, and you got trees on both sides, and fences on both sides, too. And you got cows in the pastures and they standing close together. And when us was coming out yer to catch the bus I seen the smoke coming out o' the cow's nose.

I look at my mama and I know what she thinking. I been with Mama so much, jest me and her, I know what she thinking all the time. Right now it's home—Auntie and them. She thinking if they got 'nough wood—if she left 'nough there to keep 'em warm till us get back. She thinking if it go'n rain and if any of 'em go'n have to go out in the rain. She thinking 'bout the hog—if he go'n get out, and if Ty and Val be able to get him back in. She always worry like that when she leave the house. She don't worry too much if she leave me there with the smaller ones 'cause she know I'm go'n look after 'em and look after Auntie and everything else. I'm the oldest and she say I'm the man.

I look at my mama and I love my mama. She wearing that black coat and that black hat and she looking sad. I love my mama and I want put my arm 'round her and tell her. But I'm not s'pose to do that. She say that's weakness and that's cry-baby stuff, and she don't want no cry-baby 'round her. She don't want you to be scared neither. 'Cause Ty scared of ghosts and she always whipping him. I'm scared of the dark, too. But I make 'tend I ain't. I make 'tend I ain't 'cause I'm the oldest, and I got to set a good sample for the rest. I can't ever be scared and I can't ever cry. And that's the reason I didn't never say nothing 'bout my teef. It been hurting me and hurting me close to a month now. But I didn't say it. I didn't say it 'cause I didn't want act like no cry-baby, and 'cause I know us didn't have 'nough money to have it pulled. But, Lord, it been hurting me. And look like it won't start till at night when you trying to get little sleep. Then soon's you shet your eyes—umm-umm, Lord, Look like it go right down to your heart string.

"Hurting, hanh?" Ty'd say.

I'd shake my head, but I wouldn't open my mouth for nothing. You open your mouth and let that wind in, and it almost kill you.

I'd just lay there and listen to 'em snore. Ty, there, right 'side me, and Auntie and Val over by the fireplace. Val younger 'an me and Ty, and he sleep with Auntie. Mama sleep 'round the other side with Louis and Walker.

I'd just lay there and listen to 'em, and listen to that wind out there, and listen to that fire in the fireplace. Sometime it'd stop long enough to let me get little rest. Sometime it just hurt, hurt, hurt. Lord, have mercy.

II

Auntie knowed it was hurting me. I didn't tell nobody but Ty, 'cause us buddies and he ain't go'n tell nobody. But some kind o' way Auntie found out. When she asked me, I told her no, nothing was wrong. But she knowed it all the time. She told me to mash up a piece o' aspirin and wrap it in some cotton and jugg it down in that hole. I did it, but it didn't do no good. It stopped for a little while, and started right back again. She wanted to tell Mama, but I told her Uh-uh. 'Cause I knowed it didn't have no money, and it jest was go'n make her mad again. So she told Monsieur Bayonne, and Monsieur Bayonne came to the house and told me to kneel down 'side him on the fireplace. He put his finger in his mouth and made the Sign of the Cross on my jaw. The tip of Monsieur Bayonne finger is some hard, 'cause he always playing on that guitar. If us sit outside at night us can always hear Monsieur Bayonne playing on his guitar. Sometime us leave him out there playing on the guitar.

He made the Sign of the Cross over and over on my jaw, but that didn't do no good. Even when he prayed and told me to pray some, too, that teef still hurt.

"How you feeling?" he say.

"Same," I say.

He kept on praying and making the Sign of the Cross and I kept on praying, too.

"Still hurting?" he say.

"Yes, sir."

Monsieur Bayonne mashed harder and harder on my jaw. He mashed so hard he almost pushed me on Ty. But then he stopped.

"What kind o' prayers you praying, boy?" he say.

"Baptist," I say.

"Well, I'll be—no wonder that teef still killing him. I'm going one way and he going the other. Boy, don't you know any Catholic prayers?"

"Hail Mary," I say.

"Then you better start saying it."

"Yes, sir."

He started mashing again, and I could hear him praying at the same time. And, sure 'nough, afterwhile it stopped.

Me and Ty went outside where Monsieur Bayonne two hounds was, and us started playing with 'em. "Let's go hunting," Ty say. "All right," I say; and us went on back in the pasture. Soon the hounds got on a trail, and me and Ty followed 'em all cross the pasture and then back in the woods, too. And then they cornered this little old rabbit and killed him, and me and Ty made 'em get back, and us picked up the rabbit and started on back home. But it had started hurting me again. It was hurting me plenty now, but I wouldn't tell Monsieur Bayonne. That night I didn't sleep a bit, and first thing in the morning Auntie told me go back and let Monsieur Bayonne pray over me some more. Monsieur Bayonne was in his kitchen making coffee when I got there. Soon's he seen me, he knowed what was wrong.

"All right, kneel down there 'side that stove," he say. "And this time pray Catholic. I don't know nothing 'bout Baptist, and don't want know nothing 'bout him."

III

Last night Mama say: "Tomorrow us going to town."

"It ain't hurting me no more," I say. "I can eat anything on it."

"Tomorrow us going to town," she say.

And after she finished eating, she got up and went to bed. She always go to bed early now. 'Fore Daddy went in the Army, she used to stay up late. All o' us sitting out on the gallery or 'round the fire. But now, look like soon's she finish eating she go to bed.

This morning when I woke up, her and Auntie was standing 'fore the fireplace. She say: " 'Nough to get there and back. Dollar and a half to have it pulled. Twenty-five for me to go, twenty-five for him. Twenty-five for me to come back, twenty-five for him. Fifty cents left. Guess I get a little piece o' salt meat with that."

"Sure can use a piece," Auntie say. "White beans and no salt meat ain't white beans."

"I do the best I can," Mama say.

They was quiet after that, and I made 'tend I was still sleep.

"James, hit the floor," Auntie say.

I still made 'tend I was sleep. I didn't want 'em to know I was listening.

"All right," Auntie say, shaking me by the shoulder. "Come on. Today's the day."

I pushed the cover down to get out, and Ty grabbed it and pulled it back.

"You, too, Ty," Auntie say.

"I ain't getting no teef pulled," Ty say.

"Don't mean it ain't time to get up," Auntie say. "Hit it, Ty."

Ty got up grumbling.

"James, you hurry up and get in your clothes and eat your food," Auntie say. "What time y'all coming back?" she say to Mama.

"That 'leven o'clock bus," Mama say. "Got to get back in that field this evening."

"Get a move on you, James," Auntie say.

I went in the kitchen and washed my face, then I ate my breakfast. I was having bread and syrup. The bread was warm and hard and tasted good. And I tried to make it last a long time.

Ty came back there, grumbling and mad at me.

"Got to get up," he say. "I ain't having no teef pulled. What I got to be getting up for."

Ty poured some syrup in his pan and got a piece of bread. He didn't wash his hands, neither his face, and I could see that white stuff in his eyes.

"You the one getting a teef pulled," he say. "What I got to get up for. I bet you if I was getting a teef pulled, you wouldn't be getting up. Shucks; syrup again. I'm getting tired of this old syrup. Syrup, syrup, syrup. I want me some bacon sometime."

"Go out in the field and work and you can have bacon," Auntie say. She stood in the middle door looking at Ty. "You better be glad you got syrup. Some people ain't got that—hard's time is."

"Shucks," Ty say. "How can I be strong."

"I don't know too much 'bout your strength," Auntie say; "but I know where you go'n be hot, you keep that grumbling up. James, get a move on you; your mama waiting."

I ate my last piece of bread and went in the front room. Mama was standing 'fore the fireplace warming her hands. I put on my coat and my cap, and us left the house.

IV

I look down there again, but it still ain't coming. I almost say, "It ain't coming, yet," but I keep my mouth shet. 'Cause that's something else she don't like. She don't like for you to say something just for nothing. She can see it ain't coming, I can see it ain't coming, so why say it ain't coming. I don't say it, and I turn and look at the river that's back o' us. It so cold the smoke just raising up from the water. I see a bunch of pull-doos not too far out—jest on the other side the lilies. I'm wondering if you can eat pull-doos. I ain't too sure, 'cause I ain't never ate none. But I done ate owls and black birds, and I done ate red birds, too. I didn't want kill the red birds, but she made me kill 'em. They had two of 'em back there. One in my trap, one in Ty trap. Me and Ty was go'n play with 'em and let 'em go. But she made me kill 'em 'cause us needed the food.

"I can't," I say. "I can't."

"Here," she say. "Take it."

"I can't," I say. "I can't. I can't kill him, Mama. Please."

"Here," she say. "Take this fork, James."

"Please, Mama, I can't kill him," I say.

I could tell she was go'n hit me. And I jecked back, but I didn't jeck back soon enough.

"Take it," she say.

I took it and reached in for him, but he kept hopping to the back.

"I can't, Mama," I say. The water just kept running down my face. "I can't."

"Get him out o' there," she say.

I reached in for him and he kept hopping to the back. Then I reached in farther, and he pecked me on the hand.

"I can't Mama," I say.

She slapped me again.

I reached in again, but he kept hopping out my way. Then he hopped to one side, and I reached there. The fork got him on the leg and I heard his leg pop. I pulled my hand out 'cause I had hurt him.

"Give it here," she say, and jecked the fork out my hand.

She reached and got the little bird right in the neck. I heard the fork go in his neck, and I heard it go in the ground. She brought him out and helt him right in front o' me.

"That's one," she say. She shook him off and gived me the fork. "Get the other one."

"I can't, Mama. I do anything. But I can't do that."

She went to the corner o' the fence and broke the biggest switch over there. I knelt 'side the trap crying.

"Get him out o' there," she say.

"I can't, Mama."

She started hitting me cross the back. I went down on the ground crying.

"Get him," she say.

"Octavia," Auntie say.

'Cause she had come out o' the house and she was standing by the tree looking at us.

"Get him out o' there," Mama say.

"Octavia," Auntie say; "explain to him. Explain to him. Jest don't beat him. Explain to him."

But she hit me and hit me and hit me.

I'm still young. I ain't no more'an eight. But I know now. I know why I had to. (They was so little, though. They was so little. I 'member how I picked the feathers off 'em and cleaned 'em and helt 'em over the fire. Then us all ate 'em. Ain't had but little bitty piece, but us all had little bitty piece, and ever'body jest looked at me, 'cause they was so proud.) S'pose she had to go away? That's why I had to do it. S'pose she had to go away like Daddy went away? Then who was go'n look after us? They had to be somebody left to carry on. I didn't know it then, but I know it now. Auntie and Monsieur Bayonne talked to me and made me see.

V

Time I see it, I get out my hankercher and start waving. It still 'way down there, but I keep waving anyhow. Then it come closer and stop and me and Mama get on. Mama tell me go sit in the back while she pay. I do like she say, and the people look at me. When I pass the little sign that say White and Colored, I start looking for a seat. I jest see one of 'em back there, but I don't take it, 'cause I want my mama to sit down herself. She come in the back and sit down, and I lean on the seat. They got seats in the front, but I know I can't sit there, 'cause I have to sit back o' the sign. Anyhow, I don't want sit there if my mama go'n sit back here.

They got a lady sitting 'side my mama and she look at me and grin little bit. I grin back, but I don't open my mouth, 'cause the wind'll get in and make that teef hurt. The lady take out a pack o' gum and reach me a slice, but I shake my head. She reach Mama a slice, and Mama shake her head. The lady jest can't understand why a little boy'll turn down gum, and she reached me a slice again. This time I point to my jaw. The lady understand and grin little bit, and I grin little bit, but I don't open my mouth, though.

They got a girl sitting 'cross from me. She got on a red overcoat, and her hair plaited in one big plait. First, I make 'tend I don't even see her. But then I start looking at her little bit. She make 'tend she don't see me neither, but I catch her looking that way. She got a cold, and ever' now and then she hist that little hankercher to her nose. She ought to blow it, but she don't. Must think she too much a lady or something.

Ever' time she hist that little hankercher, the lady 'side her say something in her yer. She shake her head and lay her hands in her lap again. Then I catch her kind o' looking where I'm at. I grin at her. But think she'll grin back? No. She turn up her little old nose like I got some snot on my face or something. Well, I show her both o' us can turn us head. I turn mine, too, and look out at the river.

The river is gray. The sky is gray. They have pull-doos on the water. The water is wavey, and the pull-doos go up and down. The bus go 'round a turn, and you got plenty trees hiding the river. Then the bus go 'round another turn, and I can see the river again.

I look to the front where all the white people sitting. Then I look at that little old gal again. I don't look right at her, 'cause I don't want all them people to know I love her. I jest look at her little bit, like I'm looking out that window over there. But she know I'm looking that way, and she kind o' look at me, too. The lady sitting 'side her catch her this time, and she lean over and say something in her yer.

"I don't love him nothing," that little old gal say out loud.

Ever'body back there yer her mouth, and all of 'em look at us and laugh.

"I don't love you, neither," I say. "So you don't have to turn up your nose, Miss."

"You the one looking," she say.

"I wasn't looking at you," I say. "I was looking out that window, there."

"Out that window, my foot," she say. "I seen you. Ever' time I turn 'round you look at me."

"You must o' been looking yourself if you seen me all them times," I say.

"Shucks," she say. "I got me all kind o' boyfriends."

"I got girlfriends, too," I say.

"Well, I just don't want you to get your hopes up," she say.

I don't say no more to that little old gal, 'cause I don't want have to bust her in the mouth. I lean on the seat where Mama sitting, and I don't even look that way no more. When us get to Bayonne, she jugg her little old tongue out at me. I make 'tend I'm go'n hit her, and she duck down side her mama. And all the people laugh at us again.

VI

Me and Mama get off and start walking in town. Bayonne is a little bitty town. Baton Rouge is a hundred times bigger 'an Bayonne. I went to Baton Rouge once—me, Ty, Mama, and Daddy. But that was 'way back yonder—'fore he went in the Army. I wonder when us go'n see him again. I wonder when. Look like he ain't ever coming home. . . . Even the pavement all cracked in Bayonne. Got grass shooting right out the sidewalk. Got weeds in the ditch, too; jest like they got home.

It some cold in Bayonne. Look like it colder 'an it is home. The wind blow in my face, and I feel that stuff running down my nose. I sniff. Mama say use that hankercher. I blow my nose and put it back.

Us pass a school and I see them white children playing in the yard. Big old red school, and them children jest running and playing. Then us pass a café, and I see a bunch of 'em in there eating. I wish I was in there 'cause I'm cold. Mama tell me keep my eyes in front where they blonks.

Us pass stores that got dummies, and us pass another café, and then us pass a shoe shop, and that baldhead man in there fixing on a shoe. I look at him and I butt into that white lady, and Mama jeck me in front and tell me stay there.

Us come to the courthouse, and I see the flag waving there. This one yer ain't like the one us got at school. This one yer ain't got but a handful of stars. One at school got a big pile of stars—one for ever' state. Us pass it and us turn and there it is—the dentist office. Me and Mama go in, and they got people sitting ever' where you look. They even got a little boy in there younger 'an me.

Me and Mama sit on that bench, and a white lady come in there and ask me what my name. Mama tell her, and the white lady go back. Then I yer somebody hollering in there. And soon's that little boy hear him hollering, he start hollering, too. His mama pat him and pat him, trying to make him hush up, but he ain't thinking 'bout her.

The man that was hollering in there come out holding his jaw.

"Got it, hanh?" another man say.

The man shake his head.

"Man, I thought they was killing you in there," the other man say. "Hollering like a pig under a gate."

The man don't say nothing. He jest head for the door, and the other man follow him.

"John Lee," the white lady say. "John Lee Williams."

The little boy jugg his head down in his mama lap and holler more now. His mama tell him go with the nurse, but he ain't thinking 'bout her. His mama tell him again, but he don't even yer. His mama pick him up and take him in there, and even when the white lady shet the door I can still hear him hollering.

"I often wonder why the Lord let a child like that suffer," a lady say to my mama. The lady's sitting right in front o' us on another bench. She got on a white dress and a black sweater. She must be a nurse or something herself, I reckoned.

"Not us to question," a man say.

"Sometimes I don't know if we shouldn't," the lady say.

"I know definitely we shouldn't," the man say. The man look like a preacher. He big and fat and he got on a black suit. He got a gold chain, too.

"Why?" the lady say.

"Why anything?" the preacher say.

"Yes," the lady say. "Why anything?"

"Not us to question," the preacher say.

The lady look at the preacher a little while and look at Mama again.

"And look like it's the poor who do most the suffering," she say. "I don't understand it."

"Best not to even try," the preacher say. "He works in mysterious ways. Wonders to perform."

Right then Little John Lee bust out hollering, and ever'body turn they head.

"He's not a good dentist," the lady say. "Dr. Robillard is much better. But more expensive. That's why most of the colored people come here. The white people go to Dr. Robillard. Y'all from Bayonne?"

"Down the river," my mama say. And that's all she go'n say, 'cause she don't talk much. But the lady keep on looking at her, and so she say: "Near Morgan."

"I see," the lady say.

VII

"That's the trouble with the black people in this country today," somebody else say. This one yer sitting on the same side me and Mama sitting, and he kind o'sitting in front of that preacher. He look like a teacher or somebody that go to college. He got on a suit, and he got a book that he been reading. "We don't question is exactly the trouble," he say. "We should question and question and question. Question everything."

The preacher jest look at him a long time. He done put a toothpick or something in his mouth, and he jest keep turning it and turning it. You can see he don't like that boy with that book.

"Maybe you can explain what you mean," he say.

"I said what I meant," the boy say. "Question everything. Every stripe, every star, every word spoken. Everything."

"It 'pears to me this young lady and I was talking 'bout God, young man," the preacher say.

"Question Him, too," the boy say.

"Wait," the preacher say. "Wait now."

"You heard me right," the boy say. "His existence as well as everything else. Everything."

The preacher jest look cross the room at the boy. You can see he getting madder and madder. But mad or no mad, the boy ain't thinking 'bout him. He look at the preacher jest's hard's the preacher look at him.

"Is this what they coming to?" the preacher say. "Is this what we educating them for?"

"You're not educating me," the boy say. "I wash dishes at night to go to school in the day. So even the words you spoke need questioning."

The preacher jest look at him and shake his head.

"When I come in this room and seen you there with your book, I said to myself, There's an intelligent man. How wrong a person can be."

"Show me one reason to believe in the existence of a God," the boy say.

"My heart tell me," the preacher say.

"My heart tells me," the boy say. "My heart tells me. Sure, my heart tells me. And as long as you listen to what your heart tells you, you will have only what the white man gives you and nothing more. Me, I don't listen to my heart. The purpose of the heart is to pump blood throughout the body, and nothing else."

"Who's your paw, boy?" the preacher say.

"Why?"

"Who is he?"

"He's dead."

"And your mom?"

"She's in Charity Hospital with pneumonia. Half killed herself working for nothing."

"And 'cause he's dead and she sick, you mad at the world?"

"I'm not mad at the world. I'm questioning the world. I'm questioning it with cold logic, sir. What do words like Freedom, Liberty, God, White, Colored mean? I want to know. That's why *you* are sending us to school, to read and to ask questions. And because we ask these questions, you call us mad. No, sir, it is not us who are mad."

"You keep saying 'us'?"

" 'Us' . . . why not? I'm not alone."

The preacher jest shake his head. Then he look at ever'body in the room—ever'body. Some of the people look down at the floor, keep from looking at him. I kind o' look 'way myself, but soon's I know he done turn his head, I look that way again.

"I'm sorry for you," he say.

"Why?" the boy say. "Why not be sorry for yourself? Why are you so much better off than I am? Why aren't you sorry for these other people in here? Why not be sorry for the lady who had to drag her child into the dentist office? Why not be sorry for the lady sitting on that bench over there? Be sorry for them. Not for me. Some way or other I'm going to make it."

"No, I'm sorry for you," the preacher say.

"Of course. Of course," the boy say, shaking his head. "You're sorry for me because I rock that pillar you're leaning on."

"You can't ever rock the pillar I'm leaning on, young man. It's stronger than anything man can ever do."

"You believe in God because a man told you to believe in God. A white man told you to believe in God. And why? To keep you ignorant, so he can keep you under his feet."

"So now, we the ignorant?"

"Yes," the boy say. "Yes." And he open his book again.

The preacher jest look at him there. The boy done forgot all about him. Ever'body else make 'tend they done forgot 'bout the squabble, too.

Then I see that preacher getting up real slow. Preacher a great big old man, and he got to brace hisself to get up. He come 'cross the room where the boy is. He jest stand there looking at him, but the boy don't raise his head.

"Stand up, boy," preacher say.

The boy look up at him, then he shet his book real slow and stand up. Preacher jest draw back and hit him in the face. The boy fall 'gainst the wall, but he straighten hisself up and look right back at that preacher.

"You forgot the other cheek," he say.

The preacher hit him again on the other side. But this time the boy don't fall.

"That hasn't changed a thing," he say.

The preacher jest look at the boy. The preacher breathing real hard like he jest run up a hill. The boy sit down and open his book again.

"I feel sorry for you," the preacher say. "I never felt so sorry for a man before."

The boy make 'tend he don't even hear that preacher. He keep on reading his book. The preacher go back and get his hat off the chair.

"Excuse me," he say to us. "I'll come back some other time. Y'all, please excuse me."

And he look at the boy and go out the room. The boy hist his hand up to his mouth one time, to wipe 'way some blood. All the rest o' the time he keep on reading.

VIII

The lady and her little boy come out the dentist, and the nurse call somebody else in. Then little bit later they come out, and the nurse call another name. But fast's she call somebody in there, somebody else come in the place where we at, and the room stay full.

The people coming in now, all of 'em wearing big coats. One of 'em say something 'bout sleeting, and another one say he hope not. Another one say he think it ain't nothing but rain. 'Cause, he say, rain can get awful cold this time o' year.

All 'cross the room they talking. Some of 'em talking to people right by 'em, some of 'em talking to people clare 'cross the room, some of 'em talking to anybody'll listen. It's a little bitty room, no bigger 'an us kitchen, and I can see ever'body in there. The little old room 's full of smoke, 'cause you got two old men smoking pipes. I think I feel my teef thumping me some, and I hold my breath and wait. I wait and wait, but it don't thump me no more. Thank God for that.

I feel like going to sleep, and I lean back 'gainst the wall. But I'm scared to go to sleep: Scared 'cause the nurse might call my name and I won't hear her. And Mama might go to sleep, too, and she be mad if neither us heard the nurse.

I look up at Mama. I love my mama. I love my mama. And when cotton come I'm go'n get her a newer coat. And I ain't go'n get a black one neither. I think I'm go'n get her a red one.

"They got some books over there," I say. "Want read one of 'em?"

Mama look at the books, but she don't answer me.

"You got yourself a little man there," the lady say.

Mama don't say nothing to the lady, but she must 'a' grin a little bit, 'cause I seen the lady grinning back. The lady look at me a little while, like she feeling sorry for me.

"You sure got that preacher out here in a hurry," she say to that other boy.

The boy look up at her and look in his book again. When I grow up I want be jest like him. I want clothes like that and I want keep a book with me, too.

"You really don't believe in God?" the lady say.

"No," he say.

"But why?" the lady say.

"Because the wind is pink," he say.

"What?" the lady say.

The boy don't answer her no more. He jest read in his book.

"Talking 'bout the wind is pink," that old lady say. She sitting on the same bench with the boy, and she trying to look in his face. The boy make 'tend the old lady ain't even there. He jest keep reading. "Wind is pink," she say again. "Eh, Lord, what children go'n be saying next?"

The lady 'cross from us bust out laughing.

"That's a good one," she say. "The wind is pink. Yes, sir, that's a good one."

"Don't you believe the wind is pink?" the boy say. He keep his head down in the book.

"Course I believe it, Honey," the lady say. "Course I do." She look at us and wink her eye. "And what color is grass, Honey?"

"Grass? Grass is black."

She bust out laughing again. The boy look at her.

"Don't you believe grass is black?" he say.

The lady quit laughing and look at him. Ever'body else look at him now. The place quiet, quiet.

"Grass is green, Honey," the lady say. "It was green yesterday, it's green today, and it's go'n be green tomorrow."

"How do you know it's green?"

"I know because I know."

"You don't know it's green. You believe it's green because someone told you it was green. If someone had told you it was black you'd believe it was black."

"It's green," the lady say. "I know green when I see green."

"Prove it's green."

"Surely, now," the lady say. "Don't tell me it's coming to that?"

"It's coming to just that," the boy say. "Words mean nothing. One means no more than the other."

"That's what it all coming to?" that old lady say. That old lady got on a turban and she got on two sweaters. She got a green sweater under a black sweater. I can see the green sweater 'cause some of the buttons on the other sweater missing.

"Yes, ma'am," the boy say. "Words mean nothing. Action is the only thing. Doing. That's the only thing."

"Other words, you want the Lord to come down here and show Hisself to you?" she say.

"Exactly, ma'am."

"You don't mean that, I'm sure?"

"I do, ma'am."

"Done, Jesus," the old lady say, shaking her head.

"I didn't go 'long with that preacher at first," the other lady say; "but now—I don't know. When a person say the grass is black, he's either a lunatic or something wrong."

"Prove to me that it's green."

"It's green because the people say it's green."

"Those same people say we're citizens of the United States."

"I think I'm a citizen."

"Citizens have certain rights. Name me one right that you have. One right, granted by the Constitution, that you can exercise in Bayonne."

The lady don't answer him. She jest look at him like she don't know what he talking 'bout. I know I don't.

"Things changing," she say.

"Things are changing because some black men have begun to follow their brains instead of their hearts."

"You trying to say these people don't believe in God?"

"I'm sure some of them do. Maybe most of them do. But they don't believe that God is going to touch these white people's hearts and change them tomorrow. Things change through action. By no other way."

Ever'body sit quiet and look at the boy. Nobody say a thing. Then the lady 'cross from me and Mama jest shake her head.

"Let's hope that not all your generation feel the same way you do," she say.

"Think what you please, it doesn't matter," the boy say. "But it will be men who listen to their heads and not their hearts who will see that your children have a better chance than you had."

"Let's hope they ain't all like you, though," the old lady say. "Done forgot the heart absolutely."

"Yes, ma'am, I hope they aren't all like me," the boy say. "Unfortunately I was born too late to believe in your God. Let's hope that the ones who come after will have your faith—if not in your God, then in something else, something definitely that they can lean on. I haven't anything. For me, the wind is pink; the grass is black."

IX

The nurse come in the room where us all sitting and waiting and say the doctor won't take no more patients till one o'clock this evening. My mama jump up off the bench and go up to the white lady.

"Nurse, I have to go back in the field this evening," she say.

"The doctor is treating his last patient now," the nurse say. "One o'clock this evening."

"Can I at least speak to the doctor?" my mama say.

"I'm his nurse," the lady say.

"My little boy sick," my mama say. "Right now his teef almost killing him."

The nurse look at me. She trying to make up her mind if to let me come in. I look at her real pitiful. The teef ain't hurting me a tall, but Mama say it is, so I make 'tend for her sake.

"This evening," the nurse say, and go back in the office.

"Don't feel 'jected, Honey," the lady say to Mama. "I been 'round 'em a long time—they take you when they want to. If you was white, that's something else; but you the wrong shade."

Mama don't say nothing to the lady, and me and her go outside and stand 'gainst the wall. It's cold out there. I can feel that wind going through my coat. Some of the other people come out of the room and go up the street. Me and Mama stand there a little while and start to walking. I don't know where us going. When us come to the other street us jest stand there.

"You don't have to make water, do you?" Mama say.

"No, ma'am," I say.

Us go up the street. Walking real slow. I can tell Mama don't know where she going. When us come to a store us stand there and look at the dummies. I look at a little boy with a brown overcoat. He got on brown shoes, too. I look at my old shoes and look at his'n again. You wait till summer, I say.

Me and Mama walk away. Us come up to another store and us stop and look at them dummies, too. Then us go again. Us pass a café where the white people in there eating. Mama tell me keep my eyes in front where they blonks, but I can't help from seeing them people eat. My stomach start to growling 'cause I'm hungry. When I see people eating, I get hungry; when I see a coat, I get cold.

A man whistle at my mama when us go by a filling station. She make 'tend she don't even see him. I look back and I feel like hitting him in the mouth. If I was bigger, I say. If I was bigger, you see.

Us keep on going. I'm getting colder and colder, but I don't say nothing. I feel that stuff running down my nose and I sniff.

"That rag," she say.

I git it out and wipe my nose. I'm getting cold all over now— my face, my hands, my feet, ever'thing. Us pass another little café, but this'n for white people, too, and us can't go in there neither. So us jest walk. I'm so cold now, I'm 'bout ready to say it. If I knowed where us was going, I wouldn't be so cold, but I don't know where us going. Us go, us go, us go. Us walk clean out o' Bayonne. Then us cross the street and us come back. Same thing I seen when I got off the bus. Same old trees, same old walk, same old weeds, same old cracked pave—same old ever'thing.

I sniff again.

"That rag," she say.

I wipe my nose real fast and jugg that hankercher back in my pocket 'fore my hand get too cold. I raise my head and I can see David hardware store. When us come up to it, us go in. I don't know why, but I'm glad.

It warm in there. It so warm in there you don't want ever leave. I look for the heater, and I see it over by them ba'ls. Three white men standing 'round the heater talking in Creole. One of 'em come to see what Mama want.

"Got any ax handle?" she say.

Me, Mama, and the white man start to the back, but Mama stop me when us come to the heater. Her and the white man go on. I hold my hand over the heater and look at 'em. They go all the way in the back, and I see the white man point to the ax handle 'gainst the wall. Mama take one of 'em and shake it like she trying to figure how much it weigh. Then she rub her hand over it from one end to the other. She turn it over and look at the other side, then she shake it again, and shake her head and put it back. She get another one and she do it jest like she did the first one, then she shake her head. Then she get a brown one and do it that, too. But she don't like this one neither. Then she get another one, but 'fore she shake it or anything, she look at me. Look like she trying to say something to me, but I don't know what it is. All I know is

I done got warm now and I'm feeling right smart better. Mama shake this ax handle jest like she done the others, and shake her head and say something to the white man. The white man jest look at his pile of ax handle, and when Mama pass by him to come to the front, the white man jest scratch his head and follow her. She tell me come on, and us go on out and start walking again.

Us walk and walk, and no time at all I'm cold again. Look like I'm colder now 'cause I can still remember how good it was back there. My stomach growl and I suck it in to keep Mama from yering it. She walking right 'side me, and it growl so loud you can yer it a mile. But Mama don't say a word.

X

When us come up to the courthouse, I look at the clock. It got quarter to twelve. Mean us got another hour and a quarter to be out yer in the cold. Us go and stand side a building. Something hit my cap and I look up at the sky. Sleet falling.

I look at Mama standing there. I want stand close 'side her, but she don't like that. She say that's cry-baby stuff. She say you got to stand for yourself, by yourself.

"Let's go back to that office," she say.

Us cross the street. When us get to the dentist I try to open the door, but I can't. Mama push me on the side and she twist the knob. But she can't open it neither. She twist it some more, harder, but she can't open it. She turn 'way from the door. I look at her, but I don't move and I don't say nothing. I done seen her like this before and I'm scared.

"You hungry?" she say. She say it like she mad at me, like I'm the one cause of ever'thing.

"No, ma'am," I say.

"You want eat and walk back, or you rather don't eat and ride?"

"I ain't hungry," I say.

I ain't jest hungry, but I'm cold, too. I'm so hungry and I'm so cold I want cry. And look like I'm getting colder and colder. My feet done got numb. I try to work my toes, but I can't. Look like I'm go'n die. Look like I'm go'n stand right here and freeze to death. I think about home. I think about Val and Auntie and Ty and Louis and Walker. It 'bout twelve o'clock and I know they eating dinner. I can hear Ty making jokes. That's Ty. Always trying to make some kind o' joke. I wish I was right there listening to him. Give anything in the world if I was home 'round the fire.

445

"Come on," Mama say.

Us start walking again. My feet so numb I can't hardly feel 'em. Us turn the corner and go back up the street. The clock start hitting for twelve.

The sleet's coming down plenty now. They hit the pave and bounce like rice. Oh, Lord; oh, Lord, I pray. Don't let me die. Don't let me die. Don't let me die, Lord.

XI

Now I know where us going. Us going back o' town where the colored people eat. I don't care if I don't eat. I been hungry before. I can stand it. But I can't stand the cold.

I can see us go'n have a long walk. It 'bout a mile down there. But I don't mind. I know when I get there I'm go'n warm myself. I think I can hold out. My hands numb in my pockets and my feet numb, too, but if I keep moving I can hold out. Jest don't stop no more, that's all.

The sky's gray. The sleet keep falling. Falling like rain now—plenty, plenty. You can hear it hitting the pave. You can see it bouncing. Sometimes it bounce two times 'fore it settle.

Us keep going. Us don't say nothing. Us jest keep going, keep going.

I wonder what Mama thinking. I hope she ain't mad with me. When summer come I'm go'n pick plenty cotton and get her a coat. I'm go'n get her a red one.

I hope they make it summer all the time. I be glad if it was summer all the time—but it ain't. Us got to have winter, too. Lord, I hate the winter. I guess ever'body hate the winter.

I don't sniff this time. I get out my hankercher and wipe my nose. My hand so cold I can hardly hold the hankercher.

I think us getting close, but us ain't there yet. I wonder where ever'body is. Can't see nobody but us. Look like us the only two people moving 'round today. Must be too cold for the rest of the people to move 'round.

I can hear my teefes. I hope they don't knock together too hard and make that bad one hurt. Lord, that's all I need, for that bad one to start off.

I hear a church bell somewhere. But today ain't Sunday. They must be ringing for a funeral or something.

I wonder what they doing at home. They must be eating. Monsieur Bayonne might be there with his guitar. One day Ty played with Monsieur Bayonne guitar and broke one o' the string.

Monsieur Bayonne got some mad with Ty. He say Ty ain't go'n never 'mount to nothing. Ty can go jest like him when he ain't there. Ty can make ever'body laugh mocking Monsieur Bayonne.

I used to like to be with Mama and Daddy. Us used to be happy. But they took him in the Army. Now, nobody happy no more. . . . I be glad when he come back.

Monsieur Bayonne say it wasn't fair for 'em to take Daddy and give Mama nothing and give us nothing. Auntie say, Shhh, Etienne. Don't let 'em yer you talk like that. Monsieur Bayonne say, It's God truth. What they giving his children? They have to walk three and a half mile to school hot or cold. That's anything to give for a paw? She's got to work in the field rain or shine jest to make ends meet. That's anything to give for a husband? Auntie say, Shhh, Etienne, shhh. Yes, you right, Monsieur Bayonne say. Best don't say it in front of 'em now. But one day they go'n find out. One day. Yes, s'pose so, Auntie say. Then what, Rose Mary? Monsieur Bayonne say. I don't know, Etienne, Auntie say. All us can do is us job, and leave ever'thing else in His hand. . . .

Us getting closer, now. Us getting closer. I can see the railroad tracks.

Us cross the tracks, and now I see the café. Jest to get in there, I say. Jest to get in there. Already I'm starting to feel little better.

XII

Us go in. Ahh, it good. I look for the heater; there 'gainst the wall. One of them little brown ones. I jest stand there and hold my hand over it. I can't open my hands too wide 'cause they almost froze.

Mama standing right 'side me. She done unbuttoned her coat. Smoke rise out the coat, and the coat smell like a wet dog.

I move to the side so Mama can have more room. She open out her hands and rub 'em together. I rub mine together, too, 'cause this keeps 'em from hurting. If you let 'em warm too fast, they hurt you sure. But if you let 'em warm jest little bit at a time, and you keep rubbing 'em, they be all right ever' time.

They got jest two more people in the café. A lady back o' the counter, and a man on this side the counter. They been watching us ever since us come in.

Mama get out the hankercher and count the money. Both o' us know how much money she got there. Three dollars. No, she ain't got three dollars. 'Cause she had to pay us way up here. She ain't got but two dollars and a half left. Dollar and a half to get my teef pulled, and fifty cents for us to go back on, and fifty cents worse o' salt meat.

She stir the money 'round with her finger. Most o' the money is change 'cause I can hear it rubbing together. She stir it and stir it. Then she look at the door. It still sleeting. I can yer it hitting 'gainst the wall like rice.

"I ain't hungry, Mama," I say.

"Got to pay 'em something for they heat," she say.

She take a quarter out the hankercher and tie the hankercher up again. She look over her shoulder at the people, but she still don't move. I hope she don't spend the money. I don't want her spend it on me. I'm hungry, I'm almost starving I'm so hungry, but I don't want her spending the money on me.

She flip the quarter over like she thinking. She must be thinking 'bout us walking back home. Lord, I sure don't want walk home. If I thought it done any good to say something, I say it. But my mama make up her own mind.

She turn way from the heater right fast, like she better hurry up and do it 'fore she change her mind. I turn to look at her go to the counter. The man and the lady look at her, too. She tell the lady something and the lady walk away. The man keep on looking at her. Her back turn to the man, and Mama don't even know he standing there.

The lady put some cakes and a glass o' milk on the counter. Then she pour up a cup o' coffee and set it side the other stuff. Mama pay her for the things and come back where I'm at. She tell me sit down at that table 'gainst the wall.

The milk and the cakes for me. The coffee for my mama. I eat slow, and I look at her. She looking outside at the sleet. She looking real sad. I say to myself, I'm go'n make all this up one day. You see, one day, I'm go'n make all this up. I want to say it now. I want to tell how I feel right now. But Mama don't like for us to talk like that.

"I can't eat all this," I say.

They got just three little cakes there. And I'm so hungry right now, the Lord know I can eat a hundred times three. But I want her to have one.

She don't even look my way. She know I'm hungry. She know I want it. I let it stay there a while, then I get it and eat it. I eat jest on my front teefes, 'cause if it tech that back teef I know what'll happen. Thank God it ain't hurt me a tall today.

After I finish eating I see the man go to the juke box. He drop a nickel in it, then he jest stand there looking at the record. Mama tell me keep my eyes in front where they blonks. I turn my head like she say, but then I yer the man coming towards us.

"Dance, Pretty?" he say.

Mama get up to dance with him. But 'fore you know it, she done grabbed the little man and done throwed him 'side the wall. He hit the wall so hard he stop the juke box from playing.

"Some pimp," the lady back o' the counter say. "Some pimp."

The little man jump off the floor and start towards my mama. 'Fore you know it, Mama done sprung open her knife and she waiting for him.

"Come on," she say. "Come on. I'll cut you from your neighbo to your throat. Come on."

I go up to the little man to hit him, but Mama make me come and stand 'side her. The little man look at me and Mama and go back to the counter.

"Some pimp," the lady back o' the counter say. "Some pimp." She start laughing and pointing at the little man. "Yes, sir, you a pimp, all right. Yes, sir."

XIII

"Fasten that coat. Let's go," Mama say.

"You don't have to leave," the lady say.

Mama don't answer the lady, and us right out in the cold again. I'm warm right now—my hands, my yers, my feet—but I know this ain't go'n last too long. It done sleet so much now you got ice ever'where.

Us cross the railroad tracks, and soon's us do, I get cold. That wind go through this little old coat like it ain't nothing. I got a shirt and a sweater under it, but that wind don't pay 'em no mind. I look up and I can see us got a long way to go. I wonder if us go'n make it 'fore I get too cold.

Us cross over to walk on the sidewalk. They got jest one sidewalk back here. It's over there.

After us go jest a little piece, I smell bread cooking. I look, then I see a baker shop. When us get closer, I can smell it more better. I shet my eyes and make 'tend I'm eating. But I keep 'em shet too long and I butt up 'gainst a telephone post. Mama grab me and see if I'm hurt. I ain't bleeding or nothing and she turn me loose.

I can feel I'm getting colder and colder, and I look up to see how far us still got to go. Uptown is 'way up yonder. A half mile,

I reckoned. I try to think of something. They say think and you won't get cold. I think of that poem, *Annabel Lee*. I ain't been to school in so long—this bad weather—I reckoned they done passed *Annabel Lee*. But passed it or not, I'm sure Miss Walker go'n make me recite it when I get there. That woman don't never forget nothing. I ain't never seen nobody like that.

I'm still getting cold. *Annabel Lee* or no *Annabel Lee*, I'm still getting cold. But I can see us getting closer. Us getting there gradually.

Soon's us turn the corner, I see a little old white lady up in front o' us. She the only lady on the street. She all in black and she got a long black rag over her head.

"Stop," she say.

Me and Mama stop and look at her. She must be crazy to be out in all this sleet. Ain't got but a few other people out there, and all of 'em men.

"Yall done ate?" she say.

"Jest finished," Mama say.

"Yall must be cold then?" she say.

"Us headed for the dentist," Mama say. "Us'll warm up when us get there."

"What dentist?" the old lady say. "Mr. Bassett?"

"Yes, ma'am," Mama say.

"Come on in," the old lady say. "I'll telephone him and tell him yall coming."

Me and Mama follow the old lady in the store. It's a little bitty store, and it don't have much in there. The old lady take off her head piece and fold it up.

"Helena?" somebody call from the back.

"Yes, Alnest?" the old lady say.

"Did you see them?"

"They're here. Standing beside me."

"Good. Now you can stay inside."

The old lady look at Mama. Mama waiting to hear what she brought us in here for. I'm waiting for that, too.

"I saw yall each time you went by," she say. "I came out to catch you, but you were gone."

"Us went back o' town," Mama say.

"Did you eat?"

"Yes, ma'am."

The old lady look at Mama a long time, like she thinking Mama might be jest saying that. Mama look right back at her. The old lady look at me to see what I got to say. I don't say nothing. I sure ain't going 'gainst my mama.

"There's food in the kitchen," she say to Mama. "I've been keeping it warm."

Mama turn right around and start for the door.

"Just a minute," the old lady say. Mama stop. "The boy'll have to work for it. It isn't free."

"Us don't take no handout," Mama say.

"I'm not handing out anything," the old lady say. "I need my garbage moved to the front. Ernest has a bad cold and can't go out there."

"James'll move it for you," Mama say.

"Not unless you eat," the old lady say. "I'm old, but I have my pride, too, you know."

Mama can see she ain't go'n beat this old lady down, so she jest shake her head.

"All right," the old lady say. "Come into the kitchen."

She lead the way with that rag in her hand. The kitchen is a little bitty thing, too. The table and the stove jest about fill it up. They got a little room to the side. Somebody in there laying cross the bed. Must be the person she was talking with: Alnest or Ernest —I forget what she call him.

"Sit down," the old lady say to Mama. "Not you," she say to me. "You have to move the cans."

"Helena?" somebody say in the other room.

"Yes, Alnest?" the old lady say.

"Are you going out there again?"

"I must show the boy where the garbage is," the old lady say.

"Keep that shawl over your head," the old man say.

"You don't have to remind me. Come boy," the old lady say.

Us go out in the yard. Little old back yard ain't no bigger 'an the store or the kitchen. But it can sleet here jest like it can sleet in any big back yard. And 'fore you know it I'm trembling.

"There," the old lady say, pointing to the cans. I pick up one of the cans. The can so light I put it back down to look inside o' it.

"Here," the old lady say. "Leave that cap alone."

I look at her in the door. She got that black rag wrapped 'round her shoulders, and she pointing one of her fingers at me.

"Pick it up and carry it to the front," she say. I go by her with the can. I'm sure the thing 's empty. She could 'a' carried the thing by herself, I'm sure. "Set it on the sidewalk by the door and come back for the other one," she say.

I go and come back, Mama look at me when I pass her. I get the other can and take it to the front. It don't feel no heavier 'an the other one. I tell myself to look inside and see just what I been hauling. First, I look up and down the street. Nobody coming. Then I look over my shoulder. Little old lady done slipped there jest 's quiet 's mouse, watching me. Look like she knowed I was go'n try that.

"Ehh, Lord," she say. "Children, children. Come in here, boy, and go wash your hands."

I follow her into the kitchen, and she point, and I go to the bathroom. When I come out, the old lady done dished up the food. Rice, gravy, meat, and she even got some lettuce and tomato in a saucer. She even got a glass o' milk and a piece o' cake there, too. It look so good. I almost start eating 'fore I say my blessing.

"Helena?" the old man say.

"Yes, Alnest?" she say.

"Are they eating?"

"Yes," she say.

"Good," he say. "Now you'll stay inside."

The old lady go in there where he is and I can hear 'em talking. I look at Mama. She eating slow like she thinking. I wonder what 's the matter now. I reckoned she think 'bout home.

The old lady come back in the kitchen.

"I talked to Dr. Bassett's nurse," she say. "Dr. Bassett will take you as soon as you get there."

"Thank you, ma'am," Mama say.

"Perfectly all right," the old lady say. "Which one is it?"

Mama nod towards me. The old lady look at me real sad. I look sad, too.

"You're not afraid, are you?" she say.

"No'm," I say.

"That's a good boy," the old lady say. "Nothing to be afraid of."

When me and Mama get through eating, us thank the old lady again.

"Helena, are they leaving?" the old man say.

"Yes, Alnest."

"Tell them I say good-by."

"They can hear you, Alnest."

"Good-by both mother and son," the old man say. "And may God be with you."

Me and Mama tell the old man good-by, and us follow the old lady in the front. Mama open the door to go out, but she stop and come back in the store.

"You sell salt meat?" she say.

"Yes."

"Give me two bits worse."

"That isn't very much salt meat," the old lady say.

"That'll all I have," Mama say.

The old lady go back o' the counter and cut a big piece off the chunk. Then she wrap it and put it in a paper bag.

"Two bits," she say.

"That look like awful lot of meat for a quarter," Mama say.

"Two bits," the old lady say. "I've been selling salt meat behind this counter twenty-five years. I think I know what I'm doing."

"You got a scale there," Mama say.

"What?" the old lady say.

"Weigh it," Mama say.

"What?" the old lady say. "Are you telling me how to run my business?"

"Thanks very much for the food," Mama say.

"Just a minute," the old lady say.

"James," Mama say to me. I move towards the door.

"Just one minute, I said," the old lady say.

Me and Mama stop again and look at her. The old lady take the meat out the bag and unwrap it and cut 'bout half o' it off. Then she wrap it up again and jugg it back in the bag and give it to Mama. Mama lay the quarter on the counter.

"Your kindness will never be forgotten," she say. "James," she say to me.

Us go out, and the old lady come to the door to look at us. After us go a little piece I look back, and she still there watching us.

The sleet's coming down heavy, heavy now, and I turn up my collar to keep my neck warm. My mama tell me turn it right back down.

"You not a bum," she say. "You a man."

WILLIAM MELVIN KELLEY

1937-

William Melvin Kelley, born in New York City, was educated at the Fieldston School and at Harvard University, where he studied creative writing under Archibald MacLeish and John Hawkes. After receiving the Dana Reed Prize in 1960 for his writing at Harvard, as well as fellowships to the New York Writers Conference and the Bread Loaf Writers Conference in Vermont and a grant from the John Hay Whitney Foundation, he won the Richard and Hinda Rosenthal Foundation Award of the National Institute of Arts and Letters for his first novel, *A Different Drummer* (1962). During much of 1964, he and his wife lived in Rome. After their return to New York, Kelley served as author-in-residence at the State University College at Geneseo and published stories and articles in *Esquire, Mademoiselle, Saturday Evening Post,* and *Negro Digest.*

Kelley's first story, "Spring Planting," had appeared in *Accent* in 1959. Before 1962, his fiction and essays also appeared in the short-lived *The Urbanite,* the *Harvard Advocate,* and *The New York Times Sunday Magazine.* After finishing *A Different Drummer,* which shows his sensitivity to irony and horror, along with his myth-making faculty and his tentative faith in historical justice, Kelley stated that he intended to write about "the plight of Negroes, *as individual human beings,* in America." In *Dancers on the Shore* (1964), the best of his sixteen stories, notably "Cry for Me," "The

Only Man on Liberty Street," and "The Life You Save," accomplish that intention.

In his second novel, *A Drop of Patience* (1965), in which blind Ludlow's jazz is his sole exuberance, and his fated distrust of people his sole motivation, Kelley's loaded dice roll hard, perhaps to win freedom from sentimentality in his future prose. Satire, not sentimentality, and bitter fantasy, rather than anger, control the surrealistically conceived novel, *Dem* (1967).

Negro Digest's 1968 poll of Negro writers shows Kelley totaling more votes than James Baldwin and LeRoi Jones in three categories of "important" or "most promising" writers. Kelley's pronouncements are racially even-tempered: in 1962 he said, "Each lone Negro must find something in himself that he feels is worthy of respect . . ."; in 1965, he updated himself with "The Negro writer must use his art . . . to help repair the damage done to the soul of the Negro in the past three centuries."

In "Cry for Me," which re-forms and rehearses Kelley's main themes and moods, his imagination is mythic, as in *A Different Drummer;* centrally tragic, as in *A Drop of Patience;* and tuned to paradox, as in *Dem.* Black Bedlow's art is as pure as truth; his thronging listeners' inability to applaud, as they gratefully absorb the pain of his meaning, betokens Kelley's belief in human integrity. The author's arresting use of field-hand imagery and elliptical folk diction, crossed with an urban boy's whims as Greenwich Village guide and narrator, adds humor and tension to this story of mankind's longing for affectional ties.

Cry for Me

THIS IS ABOUT my Uncle Wallace, who most of you know by his last name—Bedlow—because that's all they ever put on his records. I only got one of his albums myself. It has a picture of him on it, sitting, holding his two guitars, wearing his white dinner jacket, his mouth wide open and his eyes squinted shut. The name of the album is: *Bedlow—Big Voice Crying in the Wilderness* and I got it in particular because it has the only two songs he sang that I really like: *Cotton Field Blues* and *John Henry.* Besides that, I don't much like folk songs or folk singers. But I liked Uncle Wallace all right.

I guess I should tell you about the first time I met Uncle Wallace; this was even before he was folk singing, or maybe before any of us *knew* it. We just knew he was a relative, my old man's brother, come North from the South.

That was in June of 1957. We went to Pennsylvania Station to meet him. He sent us a telegram; there wasn't enough time for him to write a letter because, he told us later, he only decided to come two days before he showed up.

So we went to the station, and the loud-speaker called out his train from down South. A *whole* bunch of colored people got off the train, all looking like somebody been keeping it a secret from them they been free for a hundred years, all bulgy-eyed and confused, carrying suitcases and shopping bags and boxes and little kids.

My old man was craning his neck, looking to find Uncle Wallace. None of us would-a recognized him because when my old man come North twenty years ago he didn't bring but one picture of Uncle Wallace and that was of him when he was about seven. But my old man been back South once and saw Uncle Wallace a man. He would recognize him all right.

But I heard my old man say to my mother, "Don't see him yet."

And then we did see him; we could not-a missed him because he come rumbling out the crowd—the size of a black Grant's Tomb with a white dinner jacket draped over it (he had the jacket even then, having won it in some kind-a contest driving piles, or cutting wood)—and punched my old man square in the chops so he flew back about twenty feet, knocking over this little redcap, and springing all the locks on the four suitcases he was carrying, scattering clothes in all directions like a flock of pigeons in Central Park you tossed a rock at.

My old man is about six-five and two-fifty and works in heavy construction and I ain't never seen anyone hit him, let alone knock him off his feet, and I thought sure he'd go nuts and get mad, but he didn't; he started to laugh, and Uncle Wallace stood over him and said: "How you doing, Little Brother? I see you ain't been keeping up your strength. Use to have more trouble with you when I was six." And he reached out his hand to my old man, who got up, and even though he was on his feet still looked like he was lying down because Uncle Wallace was at least a head taller.

My old man said, "Never could beat you, Wallace. Pa's the only man could." And I remember figuring how to be able to do that, my Grandpa Mance Bedlow must-a been close to eight feet tall and made of some kind of fireproof metal.

Then my old man turned to us and said: "I'd like you to meet my family. This is my wife, Irene." He pointed at my mother. "And this is Mance; we call him Little Brother." He pointed at my brother. "And this is my first-born, Carlyle junior." And he pointed at me and I reached up my hand to Uncle Wallace before I realized he'd probably crush it. He took it, but didn't crush it at all, just squeezed it a little and smiled, looking down at me out tiny, red eyes in his black-moon face.

So we took Uncle Wallace home to the Bronx.

My old man got him a job with the same construction company he worked for, and the foreman, he'd send them both up on the girders and give them enough work for eight men and they'd get it done, and then they'd come home and Uncle Wallace'd watch television until one and then go to sleep. He never seen it before and it knocked him out.

He hadn't seen anything of New York but our house and the building he and my old man was practically putting up single-handed. That's why one Friday night, my old man said: "Carlyle, why don't you take old Wallace downtown and show him the city?"

I really didn't want to go; I mean, that's *nowhere*, getting stuck with a man could be your father, but I went.

First I took him to Harlem near where we used to live and we said hello to some of my old friends who was standing in front of a bar, watching the girls swishing by in dresses where you could see everything, either because the dresses was so tight over what they should-a been covering, or because there wasn't no dress covering the other parts. I guess Uncle Wallace liked that pretty much because everybody was colored and where we live in the Bronx, everybody is Italian. So in Harlem, he must-a felt at home.

Then we went to Times Square. I don't think he liked that too much, too big and noisy for him, him being right out of a cotton field. I was about to take him home, but then I said: "Hey, Uncle Wallace, you ever seen a queer?"

He looked down at me. "What's that, Carlyle?"

I was about to laugh because I figured maybe he ain't seen a queer, but I would-a thought *everybody* knew what they was. But then I decided just to explain—I knew how strong he was, but hadn't been knowing him long enough to know how fast he got mad. So I just told him what a queer was.

He looked down at me blank and sort of stupid. "No stuff?"

"I wouldn't lie to you, Uncle Wallace." I took him by the arm. "Come on, I'll show you some queers."

That's why we went to Greenwich Village.

It was comical to see him looking at his first queer, who was as queer as a giraffe sitting on a bird's nest. Uncle Wallace just gaped like he seen a farmer hitch a chipmunk to a plow, then turned to me. "Well, I'll be lynched, Carlyle!"

After that we walked around past the handbag and sandal shops and the coffee houses and dug the queers and some girls in sort of black underwear, and then all of a sudden, he wasn't with me no more. I turned all the way around, a little scared because if he would-a got his-self lost, I'd never see him again. He was halfway back up the block, his head way above everybody else's like he was standing on a box, and a look on his face like he been knocked up side his head with a cast-iron Cadillac. I ran back up to him, but by the time I got to where he been standing, he was most down some steps leading into a cellar coffee shop called *The Lantern*. I called to him but he must-a not heard me over the singing that was coming from inside. He was already at the door and a cross-eyed little blond girl was telling him to put a dollar in the basket she was tending. So I followed him down, paid my dollar, and caught up to him. "Hey, Uncle Wallace, what's the matter?"

He put his hand on my shoulder, grabbing it tight so I could hear the bones shift around. "Hush, boy." And then he turned to this little lit-up stage and there was this scrawny yellow Negro sitting on a stool playing the guitar and singing some folk song. He was wearing a green shirt open to his belly button, and a pair of tight black pants. What a queer!

The song he was singing was all about how life is tough—he

looked like the toughest day he ever spent was when his boy friend didn't serve him breakfast in bed—and how when you're picking cotton, the sun seems to be as big as the whole sky. The last line was about how he'd pick all the cotton in the world and not plant no more and wouldn't have to work again and how he'd finally win out over the sun. When he finished, everybody snapped their fingers, which is what they do in the Village instead of clap.

Then he said: "And now, ladies and gentlemen, this next piece is another from the collection of Francis Mazer, a song he found during his 1948 trip through the South. A blues called *Wasn't That a Man*." He struck a chord and started to sing: something about a Negro who swum a flooded, raging river with his two sons and his wife tied on his back. He sang it very fast so all the words ran together.

Uncle Wallace listened through one chorus, his eyes narrowing all the time until they about disappeared, and then he was moving, like a black battleship, and I grabbed his coat so he wouldn't make a fool of his-self in front of all them white folks, but then I just let him go. It was his business if he wanted to act like a nigger, and I couldn't stop him anyway. So I just stood there watching him walk in the dark between the little tables and looming out in the spotlight, burying the yellow Negro in his shadow.

Uncle Wallace reached out and put his hand around the neck of the guitar and the notes choked off. His hand must-a gone around the neck about three times.

The yellow Negro looked up at him, sort of shook. "I beg your pardon?"

"Brother, you better start begging somebody's pardon for what you doing to that song. You sings it all wrong."

Then a bald man in a shirt with the points of the collar all twisted and bent come up and patted Uncle Wallace on the back, hard. "Come on, buddy. Let's move out."

Uncle Wallace about-faced and looked way down at him. "Brother, next time you come up behind me and touch me, you'll find yourself peeping at me out of that guitar."

The bald man took a step back. Uncle Wallace looked at the yellow Negro again. "Now, look-a-here, colored brother, you can't sing my songs that way. You sing them like I made them up or don't sing them at all. And if you *do* sing them your way, then you may just never sing again, ever." He was still holding the neck of the guitar.

"Your songs? You didn't write these songs," the yellow Negro said. "They grew up out of the Rural Southern Negro Culture."

"Go on, nigger! They grew up out-a me. That song you was

just singing now, about the man and the river, I wrote that song about my very own Daddy."

A couple people in the audience started to sit up and listen. But that little yellow flit of a Negro didn't believe it. "I tell you, these songs were collected in 1948 by Francis Mazer, and there's no telling how long they've been sung. I heard the original tapes myself."

Uncle Wallace's eyes went blank for a second. Then he said: "What's this Francis Mazer look like? He a little old gray-haired man with a game leg?"

That stopped the yellow Negro for a while. "Yessss." He held onto the word like he didn't want to let it out.

"Sure enough, I remember him. He was a mighty sweet old gentleman, told me all he wanted to do was put my songs on a little strip of plastic. I asked him if he meant to write *all* my songs on that small space. He said I got him wrong, that the machine he had with him would make a record of them. And I said for him to go on. I was playing a dance and the folks was happy and I sang from Friday night until the next afternoon, and that little gentleman stood by just putting them spools in his machine and smiling. And when I got done he give me thirty dollars, U.S. currency, and I went out and bought me some new strings and a plow too." Uncle Wallace stopped and shook his head. "Mighty sweet old gentleman. And you say his name was Mazer?"

"This has gone far enough!" The yellow Negro was real ticked off now, sort of cross like a chick. "Arthur, get him out of here." He was talking to the bald man.

Uncle Wallace looked at the bald man too, sort of menacing. Then he looked at the yellow Negro. "I don't want you singing my songs *at all*." Then he just walked away, out of the lights and it was like the sun come up on the yellow Negro all at once.

But the bald man wouldn't let it stop there and said: "Hey, you, mister, wait!" He was talking to Uncle Wallace, who didn't stop because (he told me later) he never in his life got called *Mister* by no white man, so he thought the bald man was talking to someone else.

The bald man run after him and was about to put his hand on his shoulder, but remembered what Uncle Wallace said before and hot-footed it around in front of him and started to talk, backing up. "I'm Arthur Friedlander. I own this place. If you're what you say you are, then I'd like you to sing some songs."

That stopped Uncle Wallace, who told me once he'd sing for anybody, even a president of a White Citizen's Council, if he got asked. So he came to a halt like a coal truck at a sudden red light and looked down on Mister Friedlander and said: "You want me to sing?"

And Mister Friedlander said: "If you can. Sure, go on."

"But I ain't brung my guitars."

"He'll let you use his. Go on." He reached out sort of timid, like at a real mean dog, and took Uncle Wallace's arm and started to lead him back to the lights.

The yellow Negro, he didn't really want to give up his guitar, but I guess he figured Mister Friedlander would fire him if he didn't, so he left it resting against the stool and stormed off the stage.

Uncle Wallace and Mister Friedlander went up there and Uncle Wallace picked up the guitar and ran his fingers over the strings. It looked like he was holding a ukulele.

Mister Friedlander looked at the audience and said: *"The Lantern* takes pleasure in presenting a new folk singer." He realized he didn't know Uncle Wallace's name and turned around.

"Bedlow," Uncle Wallace said, sort-a shy.

"Bedlow," said Mister Friedlander to the audience.

A couple people giggled and a couple others snapped their fingers, but they was joking. Uncle Wallace whacked the guitar again, and all of a sudden music come out of it. I was surprised because way down deep I thought sure Uncle Wallace was just a fool. He didn't play right off, though, just hit it a couple times and started to talk:

"That song the other fellow was playing, I wrote that when my Daddy died, for his funeral. That was 1947. It's all about how when I was a boy we had a flood down home and where we was living got filled up with water. There was only one safe, high spot in that country—an island in mid-river. But none of us could swim but my Daddy, so he tied me and my brother on his back and my Mama, she hung on and he swum the whole parcel of us over. So everybody remembered that and when he was taken I made a song about it to sing over his trench . . ." He hit another chord, but still didn't sing yet, just stopped.

"Say," he said, "anybody got another guitar?"

Some folks started mumbling about him being a fake and stalling and a couple of them laughed. I was thinking maybe they was right.

A white boy with a beard come up with a guitar case and opened it and reached over a guitar to Uncle Wallace and so now he had two guitars. I thought he didn't like the yellow Negro's guitar, but he started to get them in the same tune—hitting one and then the other. And when he judged they was all right, he put one on his left knee, with his left hand around the neck like anybody would hold a guitar, and then put the other one on his right knee and grabbed the neck of that one with his right hand. His arms was way out and he looked like he was about to fly away. Then he clamped his fingers down on the strings of them both so hard and so fast they both sounded, not just a little noise, but a loud chord like an organ in church, or two men playing guitars. Then he started to stamp his feet and clamp his fingers and you could hear the blues get going and then he was singing . . .

Well, not really, because the most you could say about his voice was that it was on key, and it was sure loud! It wasn't deep and hollow, or high and sweet. It didn't even sound like singing. In fact, I don't think anybody ever heard him sing or really listened to him. It wasn't a voice you heard or listened to; it was a voice you swallowed, because it always seemed to upset your stomach. I heard him sing lots of times and it was always the same: not hearing anything, but feeling kind of sick, like you been drinking a gallon of wine, and the wine was fighting you inside, grabbing at your belly and twisting it around so you wanted to yell out, but didn't because you was scared the wine might take offense and tear you to pieces. And when he stopped and the grabbing stopped, you'd feel all weak and terrible, like maybe you would feel if you gotten a date with a girl you thought might give you some tail and you been thinking about it all day in school and then you went out with her and when you took her home, her folks was out, and so she took you inside and you *did* get some tail and now that it was all over, you wished she'd run inside and not given you anything because then it wouldn't be all over now and you'd still have it to look forward to. But pretty soon he'd start singing again and everything would be like it was before, feeling sick, and wishing you was *still* sick when you didn't feel sick no more.

So that's the way it was that Friday in the Village; that's the way it always was. And the people was always the same. When he got through grabbing at them, no one snapped their fingers; no one ordered anything. The cooks come out the kitchen and the waitresses sat down with the customers. People come down the steps and paid their money and managed to get into a seat before he reached out and caught them, and when the seats was all gone— because nobody left—people kept coming until they was standing and sitting in the aisles, packed right to the doors, and even on the stage with him, nobody moving or making a sound, just getting sick in the stomach and hating it and loving it all at the same time.

So Uncle Wallace sang right until Saturday morning at four. And then we went home and I slept all day.

That was how we found out what Uncle Wallace was, or did. But for a while after he sang that Friday, he didn't sing no more. It was like before: Uncle Wallace going to work, him and my old man building their building, coming home, and Uncle Wallace gassing himself on TV until one, then going to sleep.

But then the phone call came from Mister Friedlander and I answered it. He sounded real tired and said: "Hello? Is this the Bedlow residence? Do you have someone living with you or know of someone named Bedlow who sings folk songs?"

And when I answered the questions Yes, there was a silence and then I could hear sobbing on the other end of the line and through all the sobbing, him saying, "Thank God; Thank God," for about five minutes.

So at first I was about to hang up because I heard of guys calling up and cursing at women and all that mess, but then he said: "Who am I talking to?" I told him. "You were with that man who sang in my place four weeks ago? *The Lantern*? I'm Arthur Friedlander." So I said Hello, because I remembered him. He asked me what Uncle Wallace was to me and I told him.

"Carlyle," he said, "I've been trying to find your uncle for three weeks. I called Bedfords and Bradfords for the first two. It's like this, kid, every night a hundred people come into the place and ask for him and I have to say he isn't here and they get so mad they go away. He's ruining me! Where's your uncle now?"

I told him Uncle Wallace was at work.

"Listen, kid, there's a five in it for you if you can get him down here tonight by seven-thirty. And tell him I'll pay him thirty —no, make that fifty a week."

I said I could only *try* like I figured it might be hard to get Uncle Wallace to sing. Mister Friedlander give me his number and told me to call him back when I had an answer and hung up.

When Uncle Wallace come home, I said: "That man you sang for a month ago?—he wants you to come again . . . for money." I didn't have to add the money part because I could tell by his face, he was ready to go.

So I called Mister Friedlander and told him we was coming. I said that to get Uncle Wallace to sing, which he hadn't wanted to do, I had to say Mister Friedlander was paying him seventy-five dollars a week.

Mister Friedlander didn't even seem surprised. He just said, "But you got him to come?"

"Yes, sir," I said.

"Good boy! I'm giving you ten dollars instead of five." Which is what I figured he'd do if I told him I had trouble.

When we turned the corner into *The Lantern*'s block there was a riot going on, with a hundred people, maybe even a thousand there, not all Village people either. A whole bunch of them was in suits, and fur coats, and jewels. Man, if I been a pickpocket I could-a retired on what I could-a got there that night. And there was cops in their green cars with flashing lights going off and on, and on horses. Folks was pushing each other into the gutter and throwing punches. I looked up at Uncle Wallace and said: "Hey, we better split. We ain't got nothing to do with this, and you know how cops pick on colored folks."

"But I promised the man I'd sing, Carlyle," he said. But I could tell it wasn't that: he just wanted to sing, promise or no promise.

So we tried to sneak around behind all the rioting to get into *The Lantern*. And we most made it, but someone said: "Is that him?"

And someone answered: "Got to be."

I poked Uncle Wallace and said: "Now we really better get out-a here. These white folks think you done something."

"What?" he asked.

"I don't know, but we better get out-a here, *now*." And I grabbed his arm and started to pull him away, out-a there. I could tell he didn't want to go; he wanted to sing, but I figured I had to keep him out-a jail if I could.

Then someone started to yell at us to stop and I turned around to see how big they was and if there was more than we could handle, because either Uncle Wallace could flatten them or we could outrun them. But it was Mister Friedlander, chugging up the stairs, yelling.

We stopped.

He got to us and said, "What's wrong?"

"They think Uncle Wallace did something. He didn't do nothing. We just got here. We don't know nothing about this riot."

"Come inside. I'll explain," Mister Friedlander said. So we went down the stairs and inside, and he locked the door.

The place was jammed! There was more people there than that first Friday night.

Mister Friedlander said: "After you called, I put a sign in the window saying: *Bedlow here tonight*. Those people, they're here to see him. That's what the riot is." Then he asked me if I read that

New York Sunday paper which weighs so much and ain't got no funnies. I told him No.

"Well, that Friday night your Uncle Wallace was here, there was a guy here from that paper. And the next Sunday he wrote an article—wait, I'll show you." So he ran behind the counter and come out with this page of a newspaper that he got magnified around forty times and pasted on cardboard. At the top of the page was this title: *Big Voice Crying in the Wilderness.*

The article under it was about Uncle Wallace. It told all about that other Friday night and said that Uncle Wallace was a voice speaking for all the colored folks and that to hear him was to understand the pain of discrimination and segregation and all that kind of stuff, which seemed like a lot of B-S to me because I didn't understand Uncle Wallace hardly myself; I didn't understand why he sang folk songs when he could sing rock-and-roll or jazz. So how the hell could he be *my* voice or the voice of anybody like me? But that's what this writer said anyway.

When I looked up from the story I must-a been frowning, or maybe looked like I didn't get it, because Mister Friedlander grabbed me by the shoulders and shook me. "Don't you see? Your uncle is the hottest thing to hit New York since the Chicago Fire. He's a fad!"

And all the time he was telling me this, Uncle Wallace was standing by the window looking out at the people, not realizing this was all about him. That was when I started to dig something about him I never had before, and when I started to really like him and decided I'd have to look after him, even though he was old enough and big enough and smart enough to look after his-self: Uncle Wallace was innocent. To him you didn't sing for money, or for people even, but because you wanted to. And I guess the most important thing was that he wasn't some guy singing about love who never loved, or hard work who never worked hard, because he done all that, loved women and picked cotton and plowed and chopped trees. And even though he was in show business, he wasn't at all like anybody else in it. He was more real somehow.

Anyway, I could say he was better that night than he was before, but that wouldn't be really honest because I didn't dig his music so I don't know if he was better or not. I think the people liked him better, but I can't be sure of *that* either because when he finished, they was in so much pain, they never snapped their fingers for him, just sat staring, sad and hurting like before.

After he sung three sets and was sitting back in the kitchen drinking gin and fruit juice, this man come in with Mister Friedlander. "Bedlow, this is A. V. Berger. He wants to speak to you a minute."

This Mister Berger was five feet tall—tops—but weighed close to three hundred pounds, with black hair, straight and greasy. He was wearing a black wool suit—this was in midsummer now— with a vest and a scarf, which was black wool too. And the English this man spoke was fantabulous! I can only *try* to copy it. He hemmed and hawed a lot too so it sounded like:

"Mister Bedlow, (hem) I'm a concert producer. And (hem) I have been watching you perform. It seems quite likely that (hem) I can use you in a concert (hem) I'm staging at Carnegie Hall." He stopped there. I could see he was looking for Uncle Wallace to jump in the air and clap his hands. I knew what Carnegie Hall was, but I bet Uncle Wallace didn't. Mister Berger thought Uncle Wallace was playing it cagey.

"Mister Bedlow, (hem) I'm prepared to offer you a good price to appear in the show."

"What's it to be? A dance?" Uncle Wallace said. "Sure, I'll play for a dance. That's what I done down home."

"No, Mister Bedlow. You (hem) misunderstand. This will be a concert."

"Like what?" He turned to me. "Like what, Carlyle?"

"A concert, Uncle Wallace. That's when a whole lot of folk come and just sit and listen to you sing."

"You mean just like here?"

"No, Uncle Wallace. It's like a church." I was thinking about how the seats was arranged, but he didn't get me.

"But I don't sing church music, Carlyle. My songs is too dirty for church. They never let me sing in no church." He looked back at Mister Berger. "What kind-a church you running mister, that they sing my kind-a songs in there?"

"(hem) I don't run a church, Mister Bedlow." Mister Berger looked sort-a bleak and confused.

"No, Uncle Wallace, it ain't in no church," I said. "It's in a big hall and they want you to sing for a couple thousand people."

"No stuff?"

"Yeah, sure," I said.

"That's (hem) right," said Mister Berger.

"Go on, Bedlow," chimed in Mister Friedlander.

So he did.

But that concert wasn't until October and Mister Berger asked him to appear in early July, so there was a lot of time in between, when Uncle Wallace was making all his records.

And there was that damn movie. It was about this plantation

family and all their problems in the Civil War. It wasn't really such a bad movie, but Uncle Wallace made it worse. I mean, he was the best thing in it, but after he was on the screen you couldn't look at the movie no more.

The movie would be going on all right and then would come Uncle Wallace's scene. He be sitting on this log in raggedy clothes and they *even* had a bandana around his head. You know how they make movies about colored people in Hollywood; the slaves act like slavery was the best God-damn thing ever happened to them and all they did all day was sit around on logs and sing and love Old Master, instead of breaking their asses in his cotton field and waiting for the chance to run away or slit Old Master's throat wide open. But that wasn't the worst. Dig this! They made him sing *John Henry*. But it didn't matter. They didn't know Uncle Wallace. He started playing and singing, and when he got through, you had the feeling old John Henry wasn't no idiot after all. I mean, I heard some guy sing that song once and I said to myself: what an idiot this John Henry must-a been, killing his-self to beat a machine when he could-a joined a union, like my old man's, and made twice the money and kept the machine out.

But when Uncle Wallace sang *John Henry* you didn't feel that way. You felt like old John Henry was trapped and he had to do what he did, like when a fellow says your Mama screws for syphilitic blind men, you got to hit him; you don't think about it; it don't even matter if he joking or not, you just got to hit him even if he beats all hell out-a you. Well, that's what Uncle Wallace did to you.

So when them white folks come back on the screen with their dumb problems, and started kissing it up, you could see they was cardboard; you could see they was acting, and you got up and left out of there because you had to see real people again, and even when you got out in the street you sort-a felt like the people *out there* wasn't real neither, so what you did was go back in and stand in the lobby until the next showing, when Uncle Wallace come on again for his two minutes and you'd go in and see him. Then you'd walk out again to the lobby. There was always a whole lot of folks out there, waiting like you and not looking at you because you was as cardboardy to them as they was to you, and you'd wait for his two minutes again, and like that all day until you got too hungry to see.

After he made the movie he come back East and it was October and it was time for the concert at Carnegie Hall. And I guess you know what happened at the concert, but I'll tell it again and also some things I felt about it.

Mister Berger had-a told Uncle Wallace to play it cool and

save his best until last, which meant that Uncle Wallace was to come out and sing a couple songs with only one guitar and then—bingo!—lay the two guitars on them. So they fixed me up in a tux and when the time come, I paraded out and give him the other guitar.

Uncle Wallace was tuning the second guitar when a voice come whispering up from the dark in the front row. "Hey, nigger, you the same one, ain't you."

Uncle Wallace squinted down, and there in the front row with all them rich white folks was this dark little Negro. There was a woman with him and a whole bunch of little kids, all shabby-looking, all their eyes shining like a row of white marbles.

"The same as what?" Uncle Wallace said.

And the voice come back. "The same fellow what played at a East Willson café in 1948."

"Yeah, I played there that year."

"There was that one night in particular, when a cripple white man was taping you, and we all danced until the next day."

"Sure, it was!" Uncle Wallace snapped his fingers. "I remember you. You was with a *pretty* girl."

"You right, man. Here she is; my wife." He turned to the woman. "Honey, get up and meet Mister Bedlow." She did, and Uncle Wallace leaned over the edge of the stage and shook her hand. "Say, you know, I bought these big money seats because I wanted my kids to see you up close. Them is them." He pointed at the row of kids. "The oldest one, he's Bedlow. I named him after you because me and the wife wasn't getting on so good until that night." It was like they was all alone in that great big place, just those two down-home Negroes talking over old times. "And them others is Booker, Carver, Robeson, Robinson, and Bunche."

"Man, you do me proud. Pleased to meet you all. Say, you want to come up here and sit with me?"

"Now, you do *me* proud." So they all come up on stage like a row of ducks.

Then Uncle Wallace started to play and the littlest kid, that was Bunche—he was about three—he sat there for about one minute and then I saw him jump on his feet and start to do these wild little steps, just his feet moving like little pistons. Then the man got up and asked his wife to dance, and the next thing I knew, everybody was dancing—even me; I danced right out on stage—and all the rich white folks was on their feet in the aisles and their wives was hugging strangers, black and white, and taking off their jewelry and tossing it in the air and all the poor people was ignoring the jewelry, was dancing instead, and you could see everybody laughing like crazy and having the best old time ever. Colored folks was teaching white folks to dance, and white folks was dancing with colored folks, and all the seats was empty and people was coming on stage to dance. Then the other singers backstage come out and started to back up Uncle Wallace and we was all dancing, all of us, and over all the noise and laughing you could hear Uncle Wallace with his two guitars. You could hear him over the whole thing.

Then the air changed; you could feel it. It wasn't just air any more, it started to get sweet-tasting to breathe, like perfume, and the people started to run down the aisles toward the stage, and everybody on the stage started to dance in toward Uncle Wallace, and everybody, *everybody* in the whole place was sobbing and crying and tears was pouring down their cheeks and smearing their make-up and making their eyes red and big. I could hear Uncle Wallace singing louder than ever. The people was rushing toward him. They was all crying and smiling too like people busting into a trance in church and it seemed like everybody in the place was on stage, trying to get near enough to touch him, grab his hand and shake it and hug him and kiss him even. And then the singing stopped.

I pushed my way through the crowd up to his chair. The first thing I seen was his two guitars all tore up and smashed and the strings busted. Uncle Wallace was sitting in his chair, slumped over, his face in his lap. And this was real strange; he looked like an old, punctured black balloon, deflated and all. There wasn't a mark on him, but he was dead all right.

Mister Berger called in a whole bunch of doctors, but they just stood around shaking their heads. They couldn't figure out how he'd died. One of them said, "There isn't nothing wrong with him, except he's dead."

Now I know this'll sound lame to you, but I don't think anything killed him except maybe at that second, he'd done everything that he ever wanted to do; he'd taken all them people, and sung to them, and made them forget who they was, and what they come from, and remember only that they was people. So he'd seen all he wanted to see and there was no use going on with it. I mean, he'd made it. He got over.

It's kind of like that girl I was telling you about—the one who'd promised you some tail, and when you got it, you was sorry, because then you'd still have it to look forward to? Well, I think it's like that: getting tail and coming out of her house and there ain't nothing but pussycats and garbage cans in the street, and it's lonely and late and you wished you hadn't done it, but then you shrug and say to yourself: "Hell, man, you did, and that's it." And there ain't nothing to do but leave, because it's finished. But then there's something else. You're walking along and all at once you smile, and maybe even laugh, and you say: "Man, that was some *good* tail!" And it's a nice memory to walk home with.

MELVIN
B.
TOLSON
1900-1966

Melvin B. Tolson was born in Moberly, Missouri, and was educated at Fisk and Lincoln Universities prior to receiving his M.A. at Columbia. Before his final semesters at Tuskegee Institute, he taught for decades both at Wiley College in Texas and at Langston University in Oklahoma, known for his debating and drama club work, his political activities (including four terms as mayor of Langston), and his vivid poetry readings. He has received fellowships, awards, and prizes for his poetry; in addition he was commissioned Poet Laureate of Liberia in 1947, to write his verse drama, *Libretto for the Republic of Liberia*, published in 1953.

Tolson's poems have been published in *Atlantic Monthly*, *Poetry*, and *The Prairie Schooner*, as well as in such anthologies as *The Negro Caravan*, *The Poetry of the Negro: 1746–1949*, *Soon, One Morning*, *American Negro Poetry*, and *Kaleidoscope*. Less known are his early plays: *The Moses of Beale Street* (a collaboration), *Southern Front*, and dramatizations of the novels *Black No More* (by George Schuyler) and *Fire in the Flint* (by Walter White).

Tolson's poetic evolution moves from the erudition and lyricism of *Rendezvous with America* (1944), through the modernist complexities of the *Libretto*, to the brilliant versatilities of *Harlem Gallery* (1965). The befuddling scholarly allusions in *Harlem Gallery*, balanced by picturesque realities and nuances from urban

471

Negro life, have won enthusiastic support from Karl Shapiro, Theodore Roethke, Robert Frost, John Ciardi, Stanley Hyman, and others. Allen Tate's now-famous complimentary preface to the *Libretto* (marred by his objection that Negro subject matter imposes "provincial mediocrity") is enhanced by Shapiro's praise of Tolson as a great poet who truly "writes and thinks in Negro," but who is almost unknown because of racism in the poetic Establishment.

The immediate future of Tolson's reputation may depend largely upon the rise of Negro critics and upon the attitude taken by them and by Negro poets toward the new "Black Aesthetic." One Negro poet and editor, Dudley Randall, points out that Tolson is admired but little imitated. Another Negro poet, also a critic, Sarah Webster Fabio of Merritt College in California, argues that Tolson cultivated a "vast, bizarre, pseudo-literary diction," not significantly Negro, to meet the criteria of the Establishment—while many of his fellow Negro poets were abandoning Pound and Eliot for a creed closer to the needs of their race.

Yet, Tolson's contribution to the Negro tradition in American poetry, merging high-blown intellectualism with "ham hocks, ribs, and jowls" straight from Harlem, is secure. The startling waywardness of the poet's genius is suggested in an excerpt from the "Nu" section of the epic narrative, *Harlem Gallery*, in which Hideho Heights, the Lenox Avenue bard, regales the Zulu Club Wits with enough folk and anecdotal substance to carry them through his esoteric leaps of thought. Tolson's down-home exuberance, his "Bitchville, Lousyana" rancor, his burnished vulgarities, his allusiveness and obscurity—all are present.

from Harlem Gallery

. . .

The night John Henry is born an ax
of lightning splits the sky,
and a hammer of thunder pounds the earth,
and the eagles and panthers cry!

. . .

Wafer Waite—
an ex-peon from the Brazos Bottoms,
who was in the M.-K.-T. station
when a dipping funnel
canyoned the Cotton Market Capital—
leaps to his feet and shouts,
"Didn't John Henry's Ma and Pa
get no warning?"

Hideho,
with the tolerance of Diogenes
naked in the market place on a frosty morning,
replies:
"Brother,
the tornado alarm became
tongue-tied."

. . .

John Henry—he says to his Ma and Pa:
"Get a gallon of barleycorn.
I want to start right, like a he-man child,
the night that I am born!"

. . .

The Zulu Club patrons whoop and stomp,
clap thighs and backs and knees:
the poet and the audience one,
each gears itself to please.

Says: "I want some ham hocks, ribs, and jowls,
a pot of cabbage and greens;
some hoecakes, jam, and buttermilk,
a platter of pork and beans!"

Reprinted from *Harlem Gallery* (New York: Twayne Publishers, Inc., 1965), pp. 81–85.

John Henry's Ma—she wrings her hands,
and his Pa—he scratches his head.
John Henry—he curses in giraffe-tall words,
flops over, and kicks down the bed.

He's burning mad, like a bear on fire—
so he tears to the riverside.
As he stoops to drink, Old Man River gets scared
and runs upstream to hide!

Some say he was born in Georgia—O Lord!
Some say in Alabam.
But it's writ on the rock at the Big Bend Tunnel:
"Lousyana was my home. So scram!"

. . .

The Zulu Club Wits
(dusky vestiges of the University Wits)
screech like a fanfare of hunting horns
when Hideho flourishes his hip-pocket bottle.

High as the ace of trumps,
an egghead says, " 'The artist is a strange bird,' Lenin says."
Dipping in every direction like a quaquaversal,
the M. C. guffaws: "Hideho, that swig would make
a squirrel spit in the eye of a bulldog!"

Bedlam beggars
at a poet's feast in a people's dusk of dawn counterpoint
protest and pride
in honky-tonk rhythms
hot as an ache in a cold hand warmed.
The creative impulse in the Zulu Club
leaps from Hideho's lips to Frog Legs' fingers,
like the electric fire from the clouds
that blued the gap between
Franklin's key and his Leyden jar.
A Creole co-ed from Basin Street by way of
Morningside Heights
—circumspect as a lady in waiting—
brushes my shattered cocktail glass into a tray.
Am I a Basilidian anchoret rapt in secret studies?
O spiritual, work-song, ragtime, blues, jazz—
consorts of
the march, quadrille, polka, and waltz!

Witness to a miracle
—I muse—
the birth of a blues,
the flesh
made André Gide's
musique nègre!

.   .   .

I was born in Bitchville, Lousyana.
A son of Ham, I had to scram!
I was born in Bitchville, Lousyana;
so I ain't worth a T.B. damn!

.   .   .

My boon crony,
Vincent Aveline, sports editor
of the *Harlem Gazette*,
anchors himself at my table.
"What a night!" he groans. "*What* a night!"
. . . I wonder . . .
Was he stewed or not
when he sneaked Hideho's
Skid Row Ballads
from my walk-up apartment?
Then the You advises the I,
Every bookworm is a potential thief.

.   .   .

Ma taught me to pray. Pa taught me to grin.
It pays, Black Boy; oh, it pays!
So I pray to God and grin at the Whites
in seventy-seven different ways!

I came to Lenox Avenue.
Poor Boy Blue! Poor Boy Blue!
I came to Lenox Avenue,
but I find up here a Bitchville, too!

.   .   .

Like an explorer
on the deck of the *Albatross*,
ex-professor of philosophy, Joshua Nitze,
sounds the wet unknown;
then, in humor, he refreshes the Zulu Club Wits
with an anecdote on integration,

from the Athens of the Cumberland:
"A black stevedore bulked his butt
in a high-hat restaurant
not far from the bronze equestrian statue
of Andrew Jackson.
The ofay waitress hi-fied,
'What can I do for you, Mister?'
Imagine, if you can, Harlem nitwits,
a black man mistered by a white dame
in the Bible Belt of the pale phallus and the chalk clitoris!
The South quaked.
Gabriel hadn't high-Ced his horn,
nor the Africans invaded from Mars.
It was only the end-man's bones of Jeff Davis
rattling the *Dies Irae*
in the Hollywood Cemetery!
The Negro dock hand said,
'Ma'am, a platter of chitterlings.'
The ofay waitress smiled a blond dolichocephalic smile,
'That's not on the menu, Mister.'
Then the stevedore sneered:
'Night and day, Ma'am,
I've been telling Black Folks
you White Folks ain't ready for integration!' "

ARNA
BONTEMPS
1902-

Arna Bontemps, born in Alexandria, Louisiana, and reared in California, graduated from Pacific Union College in 1923 and left the following year for Harlem, exchanging his former ambition to become a doctor for the thrills of a "new Negro" writer. In New York in the 1920's, he won several poetry prizes and taught in private schools. In the 1930's, he wrote the novel that denoted the end of the Harlem craze, *God Sends Sunday*, wrote short stories and two more novels and two children's books, and taught school in Alabama and Chicago. In the 1940's, after studying at Columbia and the University of Chicago, he began his long tenure as Head Librarian at Fisk University (1943–1965), edited his first anthology of Negro poetry (and collaborated on another with Langston Hughes), began a series of biographical and historical books, wrote a musical based on his first novel, and worked with W. C. Handy on that famous musician's autobiography.

Besides continuing his book reviews, scholarly essays, and lectures, since 1950 Bontemps has published biographies of Frederick Douglass and of other Negroes, has written historical volumes alone and with Jack Conroy, has collaborated anew with Hughes on a book of folklore, and has edited a volume of poetry by Negroes and published a collection of his own. In 1965, Bontemps became Director of University Relations at Fisk; in 1968, he completed the editing of a volume of children's poetry while teaching at the Chicago Circle campus of the University of Illinois.

Since what he has called his "golden" years in the Harlem of house rent parties, pig knuckles, and bathtub gin, Bontemps has earned Rosenwald and Guggenheim fellowships, the Jane Addams Children's Book Award, and other honors. His forty-five years of writing, teaching, and encouraging Negro writers have left him one of today's most widely acquainted and informed Negro literary men.

Bontemps' main poems, stories, and essays are traceable in every important anthology of Negro writings since 1925. His most significant individually written books are *Black Thunder* (1936, a historical novel), *Story of the Negro* (1958, a history), *One Hundred Years of Negro Freedom* (1961, a biography), and *Personals* (1963, poems). His principal edited volumes are those done with Hughes—*The Poetry of the Negro* (1949) and *The Book of Negro Folklore* (1958)—and his own *American Negro Poetry* (1963).

Bontemps' poems, written mostly during the 1920's, are generally meditative, lyrical, and often stately in rhythm; their racial substance is characteristically historical and sometimes prophetic. Among his early poems, "Southern Mansion" (anthologized in *The Book of American Negro Poetry*, 1931) typically fuses the poet's sensory delicacy with his racial vision of cosmic retribution; and "Miracles" (anthologized in *Golden Slippers*, 1941) unites nature, man, and God in a contemplative lyric that is both religious and warmly secular. "Reconnaissance" (printed in *American Negro Poetry*), the best example of Bontemps' renewed occasional production after a lapse of many years, pictures a momentary island of beauty and peace in the midst of war.

Southern Mansion

Poplars are standing there still as death
And ghosts of dead men
Meet their ladies walking
Two by two beneath the shade
And standing on the marble steps.

There is a sound of music echoing
Through the open door
And in the field there is
Another sound tinkling in the cotton:
Chains of bondmen dragging on the ground.

The years go back with an iron clank,
A hand is on the gate,
A dry leaf trembles on the wall.
Ghosts are walking.
They have broken roses down
And poplars stand there still as death.

Miracles

Doubt no longer miracles,
this spring day makes it plain
a man may crumble into dust
and straightway live again.

A jug of water in the sun
will easy turn to wine
if love is stopping at the well
and love's brown arms entwine.

"Southern Mansion," reprinted from *American Negro Poetry*, ed. Arna Bontemps (New York: Hill and Wang, 1963).

"Miracles," reprinted from *Golden Slippers* (New York: Harper and Brothers, 1941).

And you who think Him only man,
I tell you faithfully
that I have seen Christ clothed in rain
walking on the sea.

Reconnaissance

After the cloud embankments,
The lamentation of wind,
And the starry descent into time,
We came to the flashing waters and shaded our eyes
From the glare.

Alone with the shore and the harbor,
The stems of the cocoanut trees,
The fronds of silence and hushed music,
We cried for the new revelation
And waited for miracles to rise.

Where elements touch and merge,
Where shadows swoon like outcasts on the sand
And the tired moment waits, its courage gone—
There were we

In latitudes where storms are born.

Reprinted from *American Negro Poetry*, ed. Arna Bontemps (New York: Hill and Wang, 1963).

ROBERT E. HAYDEN

1913-

Robert Earl Hayden, born in Detroit, Michigan, graduated from Wayne State University and received an M.A. from the University of Michigan; after teaching English at the latter from 1944 to 1946, he began his tenure at Fisk University, where he is now Professor of English. He is married and has a daughter. His other activity has included supervising research in local Negro history and folklore under the Federal Writers' Project, writing music and drama criticism for the *Michigan Chronicle*, editing poetry in The Counterpoise Series (which he also published) and in *World Order*, the magazine of the Baha'i World Faith to which he belongs, and giving lectures and readings at such colleges as Oberlin, Brooklyn, and Peabody. Among his various honors are Hopwood awards for poetry in 1938 and 1942, Rosenwald and other fellowships in creative writing in 1946 and 1947, a Ford Foundation fellowship for 1954–1955 travel and writing in Mexico, and the Grand Prize for Poetry at the First World Festival of Negro Arts held in Dakar, Senegal, in 1965.

Hayden, whose early works include radio scripts and a play (*Go Down Moses*, about the Underground Railroad), has had poems published in many journals—among them *Poetry, Atlantic Monthly, Phylon,* and *Midwest Journal*—as well as in anthologies. Collections of his own verse are *Heart-Shape in the Dust* (1940), the collaborative *The Lion and the Archer* (1948), the prizewinning *A Ballad of Remembrance* (1962), and *Selected Poems* (1966).

A self-critical, original craftsman with an imagination both passionate and detached, Hayden authentically records his direct observations as well as his responses to the history and folklore of his race. Although he rejects the label "Negro poet," such early pieces as "Gabriel" combine with others like "Letter from the South" to reveal deep sensitivity to racial oppression. The three poems selected for this anthology adequately suggest Hayden's range. "The Diver," which opens his *Selected Poems,* is an excellent example of his functional form, his vivid and learned and economical phraseology, and his apt allusiveness (to Keats in this instance). "Frederick Douglass," found in *The Poetry of the Negro* (1949), is Hayden's flowing, majestic tribute to a man whose heroism ideally complements the poet's aesthetic criteria. "Runagate Runagate," providing a study of Hayden's frequent revisions, from 1949 in this case to 1964, the year of its revision for Rosey E. Pool's *I Am the New Negro,* dramatically shows the picturesque dread and excitement in which Harriet Tubman's leveled pistol and "keep on going now or die" became a legendary principle for escaping slaves.

The Diver

Sank through easeful
azure. Flower
creatures flashed and
shimmered there—
lost images
fadingly remembered.
Swiftly descended
into canyon of cold
nightgreen emptiness.
Freefalling, weightless
as in dreams of
wingless flight,
plunged through infra-
space and came to
the dead ship,
carcass that swarmed with
voracious life.
Angelfish, their
lively blue and
yellow prised from
darkness by the
flashlight's beam,
thronged her portholes.
Moss of bryozoans
blurred, obscured her
metal. Snappers,
gold groupers explored her,
fearless of bubbling
manfish. I entered
the wreck, awed by her silence,
feeling more keenly
the iron cold.
With flashlight probing
fogs of water
saw the sad slow
dance of gilded
chairs, the ectoplasmic
swirl of garments,

drowned instruments
of buoyancy,
drunken shoes. Then
livid gesturings,
eldritch hide and
seek of laughing
faces. I yearned to
find those hidden
ones, to fling aside
the mask and call to them,
yield to rapturous
whisperings, have
done with self and
every dinning
vain complexity.
Yet in languid
frenzy strove, as
one freezing fights off
sleep desiring sleep;
strove against the
cancelling arms that
suddenly surrounded
me, fled the numbing
kisses that I craved.
Reflex of life-wish?
Respirator's brittle
belling? Swam from
the ship somehow;
somehow began the
measured rise.

Frederick Douglass

When it is finally ours, this freedom, this liberty, this beautiful
and terrible thing, needful to man as air,
usable as earth; when it belongs at last to our children,
when it is truly instinct, brain matter, diastole, systole,
reflex action; when it is finally won; when it is more
than the gaudy mumbo jumbo of politicians:
this man, this Douglass, this former slave, this Negro
beaten to his knees, exiled, visioning a world
where none is lonely, none hunted, alien,
this man, superb in love and logic, this man
shall be remembered. Oh, not with statues' rhetoric,
not with legends and poems and wreaths of bronze alone,
but with the lives grown out of his life, the lives
fleshing his dream of the beautiful, needful thing.

Runagate Runagate

I.

Runs falls rises stumbles on from darkness into darkness
and the darkness thicketed with shapes of terror
and the hunters pursuing and the hounds pursuing
and the night cold and the night long and the river
to cross and the jack-muh-lanterns beckoning beckoning
and blackness ahead and when shall I reach that somewhere
morning and keep on going and never turn back and keep on going

      Runagate
          Runagate
             Runagate

Many thousands rise and go
many thousands crossing over

> O mythic North
> O star-shaped yonder Bible city

Some go weeping and some rejoicing
some in coffins and some in carriages
some in silks and some in shackles

> Rise and go or fare you well

No more auction block for me
no more driver's lash for me

> If you see my Pompey, 30 yrs of age,
> new breeches, plain stockings, negro shoes;
> if you see my Anna, likely young mulatto
> branded E on the right cheek, R on the left,
> catch them if you can and notify subscriber.
> Catch them if you can, but it won't be easy.
> They'll dart underground when you try to catch them,
> plunge into quicksand, whirlpools, mazes,
> turn into scorpions when you try to catch them.

And before I'll be a slave
I'll be buried in my grave

> North star and bonanza gold
> I'm bound for the freedom, freedom-bound
> and oh Susyanna don't you cry for me

> Runagate

> Runagate

II.

Rises from their anguish and their power,

> Harriet Tubman,

> woman of earth, whipscarred,
> a summoning, a shining

> Mean to be free

And this was the way of it, brethren brethren,
way we journeyed from Can't to Can.
Moon so bright and no place to hide,
the cry up and the patterollers riding,
hound dogs belling in bladed air.
And fear starts a-murbling, Never make it,
we'll never make it. *Hush that now,*
and she's turned upon us, levelled pistol
glinting in the moonlight:
Dead folks can't jaybird-talk, she says;
you keep on going now or die, she says.

Wanted   Harriet Tubman   alias The General
alias Moses   Stealer of Slaves

In league with Garrison   Alcott   Emerson
Garrett   Douglass   Thoreau   John Brown

Armed and known to be Dangerous

Wanted   Reward   Dead or Alive

Tell me, Ezekiel, oh tell me do you see
mailed Jehovah coming to deliver me?

Hoot-owl calling in the ghosted air,
five times calling to the hants in the air.
Shadow of a face in the scary leaves,
shadow of a voice in the talking leaves:

Come ride-a my train

Oh that train, ghost-story train
through swamp and savanna movering movering,
over trestles of dew, through caves of the wish,
Midnight Special on a sabre track movering movering,
first stop Mercy and the last Hallelujah.

Come ride-a my train

Mean mean mean to be free.

DUDLEY RANDALL
1914-

Born in Washington, D.C., Dudley Randall earned his B.A. at Wayne University in 1949 and his M.A. in library science at the University of Michigan in 1951. While studying for an M.A. in humanities at Wayne State, he continues as a reference librarian in the Wayne County (Michigan) Federated Library System. Earlier he did foundry and post-office work, and was a librarian at Lincoln (Missouri) University and at Morgan State College. During World War II, he served with a Signal Corps unit in the South Pacific. He and his wife, who have a married daughter, live in Detroit.

Randall's short stories, articles, and book reviews have appeared in *Midwest Journal, Negro Digest, Negro History Bulletin,* and other journals. His Broadside Press, established in 1965, has issued a number of attractively designed broadsides of poems by well-known Negro poets. His translations of Russian, French, and Latin poetry have occasionally appeared. His work as editor and publisher, begun with Margaret Burroughs in their anthology, *For Malcolm: Poems on the Life and the Death of Malcolm X* (1967), has expanded with his production in 1968 of volumes of poetry by Don L. Lee, Etheridge Knight, and James A. Emanuel.

His own poems, a few of which have been set to music, have been printed in *Beloit Poetry Journal, Wayne Review, Umbra, Free Lance,* and other periodicals that have used his prose. Some of the anthologies containing his poems are *Beyond the Blues* (1962),

American Negro Poetry (1963), *New Negro Poets: U.S.A.* (1964), and *Kaleidoscope* (1967). *Poem Counterpoem* (1966) combines ten of Randall's poems with ten by Margaret Danner, but *Cities Burning* (1968), another volume printed by Broadside Press, is comprised solely of poems by Randall.

Randall's poetry, which won the Tompkins Award in 1962 and 1966, and which he reads in public, is usually meditative, rhythmical, formally designed. His racial material tends to be somber, historical, and morally urgent, although tempered with sympathy and occasional humor. "The Southern Road," apparently from the middle 1940's, grim through classical allusions to Hades, and mixing love, hatred, beauty, and bestiality, is Randall's best expression of ancestral and racial devotion, conveyed almost hypnotically in the refrain. "Booker T. and W. E. B.," which appeared in *Midwest Journal* (Winter 1952–53), is witty poetizing of the still unresolved Washington-DuBois controversy. In "Perspectives," anthologized in *American Negro Poetry*, Randall expertly guides the flow of meaning through conventional form, treating a theme also found in his short stories. "To the Mercy Killers," printed in *Negro Digest* in September 1966, has the universal appeal of unflagging courage, the will to live, expressed with terse vigor. It squares with Randall's aesthetic creed: that a writer "must serve only the truth as he sees it."

The Southern Road

There the black river, boundary to hell.
And here the iron bridge, the ancient car,
And grim conductor, who with surly yell
Forbids white soldiers where the black ones are.
And I re-live the enforced avatar
Of desperate journey to a dark abode
Made by my sires before another war;
And I set forth upon the southern road.

To a land where shadowed songs like flowers swell
And where the earth is scarlet as a scar
Friezed by the bleeding lash that fell (O fell)
Upon my fathers' flesh. O far, far, far
And deep my blood has drenched it. None can bar
My birthright to the loveliness bestowed
Upon this country haughty as a star.
And I set forth upon the southern road.

This darkness and these mountains loom a spell
Of peak-roofed town where yearning steeples soar
And the holy holy chanting of a bell
Shakes human incense on the throbbing air
Where bonfires blaze and quivering bodies char.
Whose is the hair that crisped, and fiercely glowed?
I know it; and my entrails melt like tar
And I set forth upon the southern road.

O fertile hillsides where my fathers are,
From which my griefs like troubled streams have flowed,
I have to love you, though they sweep me far.
And I set forth upon the southern road.

Reprinted from *Poem Counterpoem* (Detroit: Broadside Press, 1966).

Booker T. and W. E. B.*

"It seems to me," said Booker T.,
"It shows a mighty lot of cheek
To study chemistry and Greek
When Mister Charlie needs a hand
To hoe the cotton on his land,
And when Miss Ann looks for a cook,
Why stick your nose inside a book?"

"I don't agree," said W.E.B.,
"If I should have the drive to seek
Knowledge of chemistry or Greek,
I'll do it. Charles and Miss can look
Another place for hand or cook.
Some men rejoice in skill of hand,
And some in cultivating land,
But there are others who maintain
The right to cultivate the brain."

"It seems to me," said Booker T.,
"That all you folks have missed the boat
Who shout about the right to vote,
And spend vain days and sleepless nights
In uproar over civil rights.
Just keep your mouths shut, do not grouse,
But work, and save, and buy a house."

"I don't agree," said W. E. B.,
"For what can property avail
If dignity and justice fail.
Unless you help to make the laws,
They'll steal your house with trumped-up clause.
A rope's as tight, a fire as hot,
No matter how much cash you've got.
Speak soft, and try your little plan,
But as for me, I'll be a man."

Reprinted from *Kaleidoscope* (New York: Harcourt, Brace & World, Inc., 1967); first appeared in *Midwest Journal* (Winter 1952–53).
 * Booker T. Washington (1856–1915) and Dr. William Edward Burghardt DuBois (1868–1963).

"It seems to me," said Booker T.—

"I don't agree,"
Said W. E. B.

Perspectives

Futile to chide the stinging shower
Or prosecute the thorn
Or set a curse upon the hour
In which my love was born.

All's done, all's vanished, like a sail
That's dwindled down the bay.
Even the mountains vast and tall
The sea dissolves away.

To The Mercy Killers

If ever mercy move you murder me,
I pray you, gentle killers, let me live.
Never conspire with death to set me free,
But let me know such life as pain can give.
Even though I be a clot, an aching clench,
A stub, a stump, a butt, a scab, a knob,
A roaring pain, a putrefying stench,
Still let me live so long as life shall throb.
Even though I be such traitor to myself
As beg to die, do not accomplice me.
Even though I seem not human, a mute shelf
Of glucose, bottled blood, machinery
To swell the lung and pump the heart—even so,
Do not put out my life. Let me still glow.

"Perspectives," reprinted from *American Negro Poetry*, ed. Arna Bontemps (New York: Hill and Wang, 1963).

"To The Mercy Killers," reprinted from *Negro Digest* (September 1966).

MARGARET A. WALKER

1915-

Margaret Abigail Walker, born in Birmingham, Alabama, the daughter of a Methodist minister, was educated there and in Mississippi and Louisiana before earning advanced degrees at Northwestern (B.A., 1935) and Iowa State (M.A., 1940). After serving as a social worker, newspaper reporter, magazine editor, and teacher of English at Livingstone College in North Carolina and at West Virginia State College, she settled in her present teaching post at Jackson State College in Mississippi.

Sudden prominence enveloped Margaret Walker in 1942 when her first book of poetry, *For My People*, appeared as a result of her winning the Yale University Younger Poets competition. Although a Rosenwald Fellowship for creative writing followed in 1944, over twenty years of relative silence ensued—decades filled, however, with the preoccupations of a wife (she is Mrs. Alexander in private life) and mother of two boys and two girls, augmented by teaching duties. In 1966, with the aid of a Houghton Mifflin Fellowship and after much research in the history of the Civil War, she published her long novel, *Jubilee*.

Her novel, important largely for its indication that imaginative reconstruction of the Civil War decade could be a unique province of Negro writers, and her intermittent poems and articles of the last twenty-five years (such as her work in *Beyond the Angry Black*) leave Margaret Walker's reputation still anchored in her poetic efforts of the depression and early World War II years. Her collisions with unanticipated prejudice during her college years and her memories of personal anguish in the South toughen and racially kindle that verse. She forthrightly pictures Ku Klux Klan-style violence, delta-folk poverty, "slum scabs on city faces," shameful betrayals of her people who "have been believers"; and she exhorts, "Let a bloody peace be written in the sky."

Yet she is lyrically attuned to "sugar sands and islands of fern" in Africa and to golden grain and purple fruit in the Mississippi valleys. Her bardic touch is light when she treats folk heroes; and the literal witchery in "Molly Means," excerpted here from the ballads in the second section of *For My People*, is enhanced by the poet's onomatopoeic conception of the action. The typical verse paragraphs of the title poem, which appeared in *Poetry* in 1937, swirl with enough nostalgia, disillusion, sympathetic understanding, and national challenge both to explain and to serve artfully her people's needs.

For My People

For my people everywhere singing their slave songs repeatedly:
their dirges and their ditties and their blues and jubilees,
praying their prayers nightly to an unknown god, bending their knees humbly to an unseen power;

For my people lending their strength to the years: to the gone
years and the now years and the maybe years, washing
ironing cooking scrubbing sewing mending hoeing plow-
ing digging planting pruning patching dragging along
never gaining never reaping never knowing and never
understanding;

For my playmates in the clay and dust and sand of Alabama
backyards playing baptizing and preaching, and doctor
and jail and soldier and school and mama and cooking
and playhouse and concert and store and Miss Choomby
and hair and company;

For the cramped bewildered years we went to school to learn
to know the reasons why and the answers to and the
people who and the places where and the days when, in
memory of the bitter hours when we discovered we were
black and poor and small and different and nobody wondered and nobody understood;

For the boys and girls who grew in spite of these things to
be Man and Woman, to laugh and dance and sing and
play and drink their wine and religion and success, to
marry their playmates and bear children and then die of
consumption and anemia and lynching;

For my people thronging 47th Street in Chicago and Lenox
Avenue in New York and Rampart Street in New Orleans,
lost disinherited dispossessed and HAPPY people filling
the cabarets and taverns and other people's pockets needing bread and shoes and milk and land and money and
Something—Something all our own;

For my people walking blindly, spreading joy, losing time
being lazy, sleeping when hungry, shouting when burdened, drinking when hopeless, tied and shackled and
tangled among ourselves by the unseen creatures who
tower over us omnisciently and laugh;

For my people blundering and groping and floundering in the dark of churches and schools and clubs and societies, associations and councils and committees and conventions, distressed and disturbed and deceived and devoured by money-hungry glory-craving leeches, preyed on by facile force of state and fad and novelty by false prophet and holy believer;

For my people standing staring trying to fashion a better way from confusion from hypocrisy and misunderstanding, trying to fashion a world that will hold all the people all the faces all the adams and eves and their countless generations;

Let a new earth rise. Let another world be born. Let a bloody peace be written in the sky. Let a second generation full of courage issue forth, let a people loving freedom come to growth, let a beauty full of healing and a strength of final clenching be the pulsing in our spirits and our blood. Let the martial songs be written, let the dirges disappear. Let a race of men now rise and take control!

Molly Means

Old Molly Means was a hag and a witch;
Chile of the devil, the dark, and sitch.
Her heavy hair hung thick in ropes
And her blazing eyes was black as pitch.
Imp at three and wench at 'leben
She counted her husbands to the number seben.
O Molly, Molly, Molly Means
There goes the ghost of Molly Means.

Some say she was born with a veil on her face
So she could look through unnatchal space
Through the future and through the past
And charm a body or an evil place
And every man could well despise
The evil look in her coal black eyes.
Old Molly, Molly, Molly Means
Dark is the ghost of Molly Means.

And when the tale begun to spread
Of evil and of holy dread:
Her black-hand arts and her evil powers
How she cast her spells and called the dead,
The younguns was afraid at night
And the farmers feared their crops would blight.
    Old Molly, Molly, Molly Means
    Cold is the ghost of Molly Means.

Then one dark day she put a spell
On a young gal-bride just come to dwell
In the lane just down from Molly's shack
And when her husband come riding back
His wife was barking like a dog
And on all fours like a common hog.
    O Molly, Molly, Molly Means
    Where is the ghost of Molly Means?

The neighbors come and they went away
And said she'd die before break of day
But her husband held her in his arms
And swore he'd break the wicked charms,
He'd search all up and down the land
And turn the spell on Molly's hand.
    O Molly, Molly, Molly Means
    Sharp is the ghost of Molly Means.

So he rode all day and he rode all night
And at the dawn he come in sight
Of a man who said he could move the spell
And cause the awful thing to dwell
On Molly Means, to bark and bleed
Till she died at the hands of her evil deed.
    Old Molly, Molly, Molly Means
    This is the ghost of Molly Means.

Sometimes at night through the shadowy trees
She rides along on a winter breeze.
You can hear her holler and whine and cry.
Her voice is thin and her moan is high,
And her cackling laugh or her barking cold
Bring terror to the young and old.
    O Molly, Molly, Molly Means
    Lean is the ghost of Molly Means.

GWENDOLYN BROOKS

1917-

Born in Topeka, Kansas, but taken a month later to Chicago, where she has always lived, Gwendolyn Brooks finished Englewood High School in 1934 and Wilson Junior College in 1936. Before her marriage to Henry L. Blakely in 1939, she did newspaper, magazine, and general office work. Their son and daughter were born in 1940 and 1951, respectively. Throughout the years—the poet always considering herself a housewife and mother first, a writer only in her spare time—Gwendolyn Brooks has continued her poetry readings (ranging in setting from the Detroit English Club to the Library of Congress). In her creative writing classes (recently concurrent at three Illinois colleges: Elmhurst, Columbia, and Northeastern State), she has often personally awarded cash prizes to the best of her young charges. In the fall of 1967, she began full-time duties at Chicago Teachers College, North.

Living with parents and a brother all interested in music and art, Gwendolyn Brooks wrote poems at seven and published one at thirteen. Many were printed by the *Chicago Defender*. Further encouraged by teachers and aided by later instruction under Inez Cunningham Stark at the Southside Community Art Center, she won four first prizes in poetry between 1943 and 1945 at Midwestern Writers Conferences at Northwestern University, where samples of her work, already appearing in *Poetry*, were requested by publishers.

Critical praise of *A Street in Bronzeville* (1945) was followed by honors and awards: selection by *Mademoiselle* in 1945 as one of "Ten Women of the Year," and in 1946 a thousand-dollar award from the American Academy of Arts and Letters and a Guggenheim Fellowship—the latter renewed in 1947. For *Annie Allen* (1949), the author received *Poetry's* Eunice Tietjens Memorial Award, capped in 1950 by the Pulitzer Prize. By then her work had appeared in *Harper's, Yale Review, Saturday Review of Literature, Negro Story, Common Ground,* and other magazines, as well as in the anthologies *Cross-Section* (1945) and *The Poetry of the Negro* (1949). Her novel, *Maud Martha* (1953), using poetic, realistic vignettes to trace the aborted dreams in the youth and womanhood of a fat little colored girl, was followed by her children's book, *Bronzeville Boys and Girls* (1956), and two more volumes of poems, *The Bean Eaters* (1960) and *Selected Poems* (1963). Since then, stories and poems have appeared in magazines and in the anthologies *Soon, One Morning* and *Beyond the Angry Black.*

Her best poetry, much of it written in her twenties in a small second-floor apartment at 623 East 63rd Street in Chicago, has "the concentration, the crush" which she declares important in her effort "to vivify the universal fact" wearing contemporary clothing. The four poems reprinted here—all but "The Egg Boiler" appearing in *Annie Allen*—show Gwendolyn Brooks at her best. Only line-by-line commentary on the three numbered, untitled poems, two of them sonnets, from "The Womanhood" section of that volume can fully reveal her artfulness and humanity. The Petrarchan sonnet beginning with "First fight. Then fiddle," for example, is a compact, masterfully ordered fusion of the images and meanings of violin music with precisely related allusions to thuggee, the ritualized kind of murder offered to the goddess Kali in nineteenth-century India. In "The Egg Boiler," a sonnet briefly echoing Keats and Frost, the poet places literary beauty and truth above utilitarian fact.

Gwendolyn Brooks, looking down from her corner window on Chicago's South Side, or shopping among its crowded markets, has obeyed her own advice for writers: "live richly with eyes open, and heart, too." Her poems illuminating ghetto life, in the words of poet Conrad Kent Rivers, are almost "too sad and delicate for the ears of white America." They are marked, adds William Barrow, "by a simple beauty that is almost unbearable."

I

THE CHILDREN OF THE POOR

1

People who have no children can be hard:
Attain a mail of ice and insolence:
Need not pause in the fire, and in no sense
Hesitate in the hurricane to guard.
And when wide world is bitten and bewarred
They perish purely, waving their spirits hence
Without a trace of grace or of offense
To laugh or fail, diffident, wonder-starred.
While through a throttling dark we others hear
The little lifting helplessness, the queer
Whimper-whine; whose unridiculous
Lost softness softly makes a trap for us.
And makes a curse. And makes a sugar of
The malocclusions, the inconditions of love.

4

First fight. Then fiddle. Ply the slipping string
With feathery sorcery; muzzle the note
With hurting love; the music that they wrote
Bewitch, bewilder. Qualify to sing
Threadwise. Devise no salt, no hempen thing
For the dear instrument to bear. Devote
The bow to silks and honey. Be remote
A while from malice and from murdering.
But first to arms, to armor. Carry hate
In front of you and harmony behind.
Be deaf to music and to beauty blind.
Win war. Rise bloody, maybe not too late
For having first to civilize a space
Wherein to play your violin with grace.

II

Life for my child is simple, and is good.
He knows his wish. Yes, but that is not all.
Because I know mine too.
And we both want joy of undeep and unabiding things,
Like kicking over a chair or throwing blocks out of a window
Or tipping over an icebox pan
Or snatching down curtains or fingering an electric outlet
Or a journey or a friend or an illegal kiss.
No. There is more to it than that.
It is that he has never been afraid.
Rather, he reaches out and lo the chair falls with a beautiful crash,
And the blocks fall, down on the people's heads,
And the water comes slooshing sloppily out across the floor.
And so forth.
Not that success, for him, is sure, infallible.
But never has he been afraid to reach.
His lesions are legion.
But reaching is his rule.

The Egg Boiler

Being you, you cut your poetry from wood.
The boiling of an egg is heavy art.
You come upon it as an artist should,
With rich-eyed passion, and with straining heart.
We fools, we cut our poems out of air,
Night color, wind soprano, and such stuff.
And sometimes weightlessness is much to bear.
You mock it, though, you name it Not Enough.
The egg, spooned gently to the avid pan,
And left the strict three minutes, or the four,
Is your Enough and art for any man.
We fools give courteous ear—then cut some more,
Shaping a gorgeous Nothingness from cloud.
You watch us, eat your egg, and laugh aloud.

JAMES A. EMANUEL

1921-

James A. Emanuel, born and reared in Alliance, Nebraska, attended Howard (B.A., 1950), Northwestern (M.A., 1953), and Columbia (Ph.D., 1962). As a teen-ager, he worked on ranches and farms in Nebraska, ran elevators in Colorado and Iowa, managed a Civilian Conservation Corps canteen in Kansas, and was a baling machine operator and weighmaster in Illinois. At twenty, he came to Washington, D.C., to become Confidential Secretary to General Benjamin O. Davis, Sr., the Assistant Inspector General of the U.S. Army, then did wartime duty in the South Pacific, mostly with the 93rd Infantry Division. A supervisory job in the civil service in Chicago, where he married in 1950, preceded a 1954–56 teaching post in a YWCA secretarial school in Harlem. His career at the City College of the City University of New York, where he is now an assistant professor teaching literature, began in 1957. In 1968, he accepted an invitation from the University of Grenoble in France to spend a year there as Visiting Professor of American Literature.

Emanuel's poetry was first published in college periodicals and in *Ebony Rhythm* (1948). In 1958, his work began to appear in *Phylon, Negro Digest, Midwest Quarterly, The New York Times, Freedomways,* and other periodicals. Some of his work, which he has been reading publicly since 1964, has been anthologized in *Sixes and Sevens* (1962, London), in *La Poésie Négro Américaine* (1966, Paris), and in several collections and textbooks in America.

His first volume is entitled *The Treehouse and Other Poems* (1968). He has also published a critical study, *Langston Hughes* (1967), as well as literary essays and book reviews, and has received fellowships from the John Hay Whitney Foundation and the Eugene F. Saxton Memorial Trust.

The four poems printed here (all but "A Pause for a Fine Phrase" published between 1963 and 1965 in *The New York Times*) represent some of Emanuel's main themes. "A Clown at Ten" is one of about a dozen poems inspired by his son James. "Emmett Till" suggests the absorption of an atrocious murder into a body of racial legend. Based on Emanuel's high-school days, "After the Record Is Broken" explores the possibilities of human effort. In "A Pause for a Fine Phrase," appearing in *Phylon* in 1963, the poet aims to re-create both the reflection and the exhilaration induced by superb language.

A Clown at Ten

We should have guessed—
When he pounced home in a flailing dance,
Clucking like a hen possessed,
Elbows flapping in a sidelong prance,
Grinning grimly,
Mocking primly
A saucy schoolmate's slur—
The deepdown bite of her.

We should have known
His pull-ups on the closet pole,
His swimming in the kitchen zone,
His pugilistic body roll
On the church pew
And museum queue
Were ways to storm the pass
For the smallest in his class.

Each noon he licked his silly grin
And ate beyond our discipline.
We called him fool
And fed him shame,
This little giant
With our name.

Emmett Till

I hear a whistling
Through the water.
Little Emmett
Won't be still.
He keeps floating
Round the darkness,
Edging through
The silent chill.

Tell me, please,
That bedtime story
Of the fairy
River Boy
Who swims forever,
Deep in treasures,
Necklaced in
A coral toy.

After the Record Is Broken

My mind slips back to lesser men,
Their how, their when.
Champions then:
Big Stilley, with his bandaged hands,
Broke through the Sidney line, the stands
Hysterical, profuse the rival bands.
Poor Ackerman, his spikes undone,
His strap awry, gave way to none,
Not even pride. The mile he won.

Now higher, faster, farther. Stars crossed
Recede, and legends twinkle out, far lost,
Far discus-spun and javelin-tossed,
Nor raise again that pull and sweat,
That dig and burn, that crouch-get-set
Aglimmer in old trophies yet.
Now smoother, softer, trimmed for speed,
The champion seems a better breed,
His victory a showroom deed.

Oh, what have we to do with men
Like champions, but cry again
How high, how fast, how far? What then?
Remember men when records fall.
Unclap your hands, draw close your shawl:
The lesser men have done it all.

A Pause for a Fine Phrase

I meditate right off the page.
Quick memory and pleasing rage
And soothing slide of conscious mind
Move to the brink, and there I find
A meaning more than what you meant
Gleaming in a corner bent
Right out of flooring that you laid
For stud and joist you never made.
The corner turns and comes to me,
Then something fits, and I am free
To lift my finger off the line
That you have made completely mine.

From *Phylon*, XXIV, No. 2 (Summer 1963), 196; corrected by the author.

MARI
EVANS
19—

Mari Evans, born and reared in Toledo, Ohio, attended the University of Toledo. Now a divorcée living with two sons in Indianapolis, Indiana, she has worked in civil service and has been at different times a musician, choir director, church organist, and director of adult program promotion at the Indianapolis Fall Creek Parkway YMCA. Since 1964 she has been associate editor of an industrial magazine, and recently she has supervised publications at the Atterbury Job Corps Center.

Mari Evans' poetry has become known in the 1960's to readers of *Phylon, Negro Digest,* and *Dialog.* It has been anthologized by Rosey Pool (*Beyond the Blues* and *Ik Ben de Nieuwe Neger*), Arna Bontemps, Langston Hughes, Walter Lowenfels (*Poets of Today*), Dudley Randall and Margaret Burroughs (*For Malcolm*), and Janheinz Jahn (*Schwarzer Orpheus*). It also has been used in a few radio, television, and Broadway productions, and in the 1963 Aldeburgh Poetry Festival in England. Her first small volume, *Where Is All the Music?* (1968), selectively presents her achievement.

Usually spare in form, restrained or whimsical in tone, and characterized by few punctuation marks, capital letters, or rhyming words, Mari Evans' poetry blends modernity of style with traditional and racial matter. "The Alarm Clock," which appeared in *Negro Digest* in January 1966, with perfect racial cadence turns

* Date withheld at poet's request.

a moment of dreamy lunch counter dalliance into a jarring reminder of enveloping prejudice. ". . . And the Old Women Gathered," found in *New Negro Poets: U.S.A.*, strikingly employs a simile to multiply the image of the Negro matriarch who has endured everything without losing her inner song of resolute hopefulness. The humor of "When in Rome," printed in *American Negro Poetry,* springs from ironically contrasted speakers: the well-meaning lady of the house and her hungry—and therefore surly—maid; its domestic action, the offering of sardines and cottage cheese to satisfy a craving for "soul food" meat and black-eyed peas, is played in the shadow of national drama. That same drama intensifies the resentment in one of the poet's latest works, "Black jam for dr. negro," a surly, thumping poem, tense with repression and desperate readiness.

The Alarm Clock

Alarm clock
sure sound
loud
this mornin' . . .
remind me of the time
I sat down
in a drug store
with my
mind
away far off . . .
until the girl
and she was small
it seems to me
with yellow hair
a hangin'
smiled up and said
"I'm sorry but
we don't serve
you people
here"
and I woke up
quick
like I did this mornin'
when the
alarm
went off . . .
It don't do
to wake up
quick . . .

Reprinted from *Negro Digest* (January 1966).

. . . And the Old Women Gathered

(THE GOSPEL SINGERS)

and the old women gathered
and sang His praises
standing
resolutely together
like supply sergeants who
have seen
everything
and are still
Regular Army: It
was fierce and
not melodic and
although we ran
the sound of it
stayed in our ears . . .

When in Rome

Marrie dear
the box is full . . .
take
whatever you like
to eat . . .

    (an egg
    or soup
    . . . there ain't no meat.)

there's endive there
and
cottage cheese . . .

    (whew! if I had some
    black-eyed peas . . .)

there's sardines
on the shelves
and such . . .
but
don't
get my anchovies . . .
they cost
too much!

    (me get the
    anchovies indeed!
    what she think, she got—
    a bird to feed?)

there's plenty in there
to fill you up . . .

    (yes'm. just the
    sight's
    enough!

    Hope I lives till I get
    home
    I'm tired of eatin'
    what they eats in Rome . . .)

". . . And the Old Women Gathered" reprinted from *Kaleidoscope*, ed. Robert Hayden; formerly in *New Negro Poets, U.S.A.*, ed. Langston Hughes (Bloomington: Indiana University Press, 1964).

"When in Rome" reprinted from *American Negro Poetry*, ed. Arna Bontemps (New York: Hill and Wang, 1963).

Black jam for dr. negro

Pullin me in off the corner to wash my face an
cut my afro turn
my collar
down
when that aint my
thang I
walk heels first
nose round an tilted
up
my ancient
eyes
see your thang
baby
an it aint
shit
your thang
puts my eyes out baby
turns my seeking fingers
    into splintering fists
messes up my head
an I scream you out
your thang
is whats wrong
    an you keep
    pilin it on rubbin it
    in
    smoothly
    doin it
    to death

what you sweatin
baby your
        guts
puked an rotten
waitin
to be defended

LEROI
JONES
1934 -
LeRoi Jones, born and reared in New-
ark, New Jersey—his father being a postal supervisor and his
mother a social worker—graduated from Barringer High. Interested in religion, he went to Rutgers University for a year; but,
feeling like an outsider, transferred to Howard. After graduating
in 1954 as an English major, he took advanced courses at Columbia
and the New School for Social Research. During his more than two
years serving the Strategic Air Command, in which he became a
sergeant, he determined to become an author, although his efforts
in writing dated back to his seventh-grade comic strip, "The Crime
Wave," in Central Avenue School, and to his science fiction produced for his high-school magazine. With a background of extensive military travel in Africa, the Middle East, and Europe, Jones
was in New York teaching poetry and writing at the New School
in the late 1950's to support his wife and two children. By 1964,
he was also a lecturer in theater arts at Columbia and was settled
in a fourth-floor walk-up apartment in Greenwich Village.

Although Jones considers himself primarily a poet, his plays
and essays have added hectic controversy to the arts. His plays,
beginning in 1959 with "Revolt of the Moonflowers," lost in manuscript, include brief works like *Baptism, The 8th Ditch, Home on
the Range,* and *Arm Yrself or Harm Yrself.* His shocking plays of
1964, *The Dutchman* (his first professionally produced play and
winner of the 1964 off-Broadway Obie Award), *The Slave,* and

513

The Toilet (written in six hours), are the soft-spoken author's most disturbing contributions to the stage. His 1960–1965 social essays, chronicling his evolving thought, appear in *Home* (1966); later significant pieces have been printed by *Negro Digest* and *Evergreen Review*.

Other less controversial authorship—and some strife-ridden activity—represents Jones's involvements. A writer on jazz for *Downbeat, Metronome, Jazz,* and *Jazz Review,* his knowledge in this area has been recorded in *Blues People: Negro Music in White America* (1963) and in *Black Music* (1967). There is some illumination of Jones's own character in his semiautobiographical novel, *The System of Dante's Hell* (1965); his sixteen stories in *Tales* (1967) throw similar light on the "angry young man" of the black ghetto. Jones's editorial work—on the magazines *Yugen, Kulchur,* and *The Floating Bear;* on the staffs of Corinth Books, Jihad Productions, and Totem Press; and as compiler of *The Moderns* (1963) —adds substance to his contributions. His increasingly direct support of racial art is evidenced in his establishment of the Black Arts Repertory Theater in Harlem, and in his later association with the Spirit House Movers and Players, a similar enterprise in Newark.

Much of Jones's poetry, found often in *The Nation, Poetry, Harper's, Negro Digest,* and many other periodicals, and widely anthologized, seems almost homicidal to some, certainly vitriolic to others, but also delicate and gentle to still others. Collected in *Preface to a Twenty Volume Suicide Note* (1961), *The Dead Lecturer* (1964), and the mimeographed *Black Art* (1966), it is savored in the three poems reprinted here. "Preface to a Twenty Volume Suicide Note," existentialist in its rejection of the meaning of life, ends with excellent use of dramatic irony. *Negro Digest,* in September 1965, published "A Poem for Black Hearts," a tribute to Malcolm X made breathless through punctuation and mounting emotion and lengthening line, a poem as darkly sincere as its brooding author. "Jitterbugs," printed the following April by the same magazine, expresses a more inward brooding, but with a more universal significance made ironic by the title, itself multiple commentary from a poet who uniquely "cant go anywhere without awareness of the hurt."

Preface to a Twenty Volume Suicide Note

Lately, I've become accustomed to the way
The ground opens up and envelops me
Each time I go out to walk the dog.
Or the broad edged silly music the wind
Makes when I run for a bus—

Things have come to that.

And now, each night I count the stars,
And each night I get the same number.
And when they will not come to be counted
I count the holes they leave.

Nobody sings anymore.

And then last night, I tiptoed up
To my daughter's room and heard her
Talking to someone, and when I opened
The door, there was no one there . . .
Only she on her knees,
Peeking into her own clasped hands.

A Poem for Black Hearts

For Malcolm's eyes, when they broke
the face of some dumb white man. For
Malcolm's hands raised to bless us
all black and strong in his image
of ourselves, for Malcolm's words
fire darts, the victor's tireless
thrusts, words hung above the world
change as it may, he said it, and
for this he was killed, for saying,
and feeling, and being/ change, all
collected hot in his heart, For Malcolm's
heart, raising us above our filthy cities,

for his stride, and his beat, and his address
to the grey monsters of the world, For Malcolm's
pleas for your dignity, black men, for your life,
black men, for the filling of your minds
with righteousness, For all of him dead and
gone and vanished from us, and all of him which
clings to our speech black god of our time.
For all of him, and all of yourself, look up,
black man, quit stuttering and shuffling, look up,
black man, quit whining and stooping, for all of him,
For Great Malcolm a prince of the earth, let nothing in us rest
until we avenge ourselves for his death, stupid animals
that killed him, let us never breathe a pure breath if
we fail, and white men call us faggots till the end of
the earth.

Jitterbugs

The imperfection of the world
is a burden, if you know it, think
about it, at all. Look up in the sky
wishing you were free, placed so terribly
in time, mind out among new stars, working
propositions, and not this planet where you
cant go anywhere without awareness of the hurt
the white man has put on the people. Any people. You
cant escape, there's no where to go. They have made
this star unsafe, and this age, primitive, though yr mind
is somewhere else, your ass aint.

ARTHUR P. DAVIS

1904-   Arthur Paul Davis, born in Hampton, Virginia, secured his three degrees at Columbia, which awarded him his Ph.D. in 1942. A college professor for all of his adult life, Davis taught at North Carolina College (1927–1928), and at Virginia Union (1929–1944) before beginning his long tenure at Howard University, where he has been teaching literature since 1944.

Davis's first influential literary achievement was his coediting *The Negro Caravan* (1941) with Sterling A. Brown and Ulysses Lee. After completing his doctoral dissertation on Isaac Watts in 1942, he published *Isaac Watts: His Life and Works* (1943). His scholarly essays have appeared frequently in *Phylon*, although additional articles and narratives of the 1940's can be traced in *Common Ground*. Davis's interest in Negro authors, expressed in his first articles and book reviews (such as those in *Opportunity* in the early 1930's), predominates in his more recent publications. His critical analyses of works by Phillis Wheatley, Langston Hughes, and Countee Cullen are perceptive and historically important in the tradition of literary scholarship by and about Negroes.

"Trends in Negro American Literature (1940–65)," an updated elaboration of Davis's "Integration and Race Literature" (in *Phylon* in 1956), appeared in Howard University's student magazine, *The Promethean*, in May 1967. It is interesting for its hopeful theme of the relationship between militant writing and the "mainstream" of American literature. Davis's perspective of almost half a century of Negro themes—"lynching-passing" in the twenties and thirties, "protest and problems" in the forties, the Integration Movement in the fifties, backsliding into the Black Revolt of the sixties —is patent oversimplification. In the light of the white racism documented in 1968 by the President's National Advisory Commission on Civil Disorders, his faith seems anachronistic. But in his implicit thesis that Negro authors thrive or fade according to their ability to dramatize the truths of their times, he offers the only comfort that a writer of integrity could wish for.

Trends in Negro American Literature (1940–65)

THE COURSE OF Negro American literature has been high-lighted by a series of social and political crises over the Negro's position in America. The Abolition Movement, the Civil War, Recon-struction, and the riot-lynching periods both before and after World War I have all radically influenced Negro writing. Each crisis has brought in new themes, new motivations, new character-types, new viewpoints; and as each crisis has passed, the Negro writer has tended to drop most of the special attitudes which the crisis pro-duced and to move toward the so-called mainstream of American literature.

Between, roughly, 1940 and 1965, two new crises occurred: the Integration Movement (which was climaxed by the 1954 Su-preme Court Decision) and the Civil Rights Revolution (which is still with us and which began to take on its present day character-istics around 1960). Each of these movements has affected Negro writing. Twenty-five years is obviously a short time in which to show literary changes resulting from *one* movement, to say nothing of two, but we live in stirring and fast-moving times. For example, within a single decade a supposedly well-established program of non-violence and passive resistance has given way to a new and militant nationalist movement that makes the work of Martin Luther King seem almost gradualistic. Riots have taken the place of "marches," and the objectives of Negroes have shifted from inte-gration to goals entirely alien to anything the black middle class envisioned. These changes have been incredibly swift and phe-nomenal, but Negro literature during the period in question has reflected them to a greater extent than is commonly realized.

Let us examine the Integration Movement first. Forces of in-tegration had been at work long before 1954, but it is convenient to date the movement from that year. And, of course, the official stamp given it by the Supreme Court accelerated the social changes already in progress. After 1954 the ferment of integration seemed to go to work immediately—not only in the public schools, but in the armed forces, in Southern state universities, and in several other areas as well. A few institutions and localities and segments of the nation naturally held out, and are still holding out, but even

Reprinted from *The Promethean* (*Howard University Art and Literary Magazine*), May 1967, with the permission of the author. An earlier version appeared in *Phylon*.

the harshest critics of American democracy had to admit that substantial progress towards integration had been made, that the nation had committed itself officially and spiritually to that ideal. And though the commitment was largely theoretical or at best token, it changed the racial climate of America.

This change of climate, however, inadvertently dealt the Negro writer of the fifties a crushing blow. Up to that decade, our literature had been predominantly a protest literature. Ironical though it may seem, we had capitalized on oppression (in a literary sense, of course). Although one may deplore and condemn the cause, there is great creative motivation in a movement which brings all members of a group together and cements them in a common bond. And that is just what segregation did for the Negro especially during the twenties and thirties when full segregation was not only practiced in the South but tacitly condoned by the whole nation. As long as there was this common enemy, we had a common purpose and a strong urge to transform into artistic terms our deep-rooted feelings of bitterness and scorn. When the enemy capitulated, he shattered our most fruitful literary tradition. The possibility of imminent integration tended to destroy during the fifties the protest element in Negro writing.

And one must always keep in mind the paradox involved. We did not have actual integration anywhere. There was surface and token integration in many areas, but the everyday pattern of life for the overwhelming majority was unchanged. But we did have— and this is of the utmost importance—the spiritual commitment and climate out of which full integration could develop. The Negro literary artist recognized and acknowledged that climate; he accepted it in good faith; and he resolved to work with it at all costs. In the meantime, he had to live between two worlds, and that for any artist is a disturbing experience. For the Negro writers of the fifties, especially those in their middle years, it became almost a tragic experience because it meant giving up a tradition in which they had done their apprentice and journeyman work, giving it up when they were prepared to make use of that tradition as master craftsmen.

Another disturbing factor which must be considered here is that this change of climate came about rather suddenly. Perhaps it would be more exact to say that the full awareness came suddenly because there were signs of its approach all during the forties, and Negro writers from time to time showed that they recognized these signs. But the full awareness did not come until the fifties, and it came with some degree of abruptness. For example, all through World War II, all through the forties, most Negro writers were still grinding out protest and problem novels, many of them influenced by *Native Son* (1940). The list of these works is impressive: Attaway's *Blood on the Forge* (1941), Offord's *The White Face* (1943), Himes' *If He Hollers* (1945), Petry's *The Street* (1946), Kaye's *Taffy* (1950), and there were others—practically all of them naturalistic novels with the same message of protest against America's treatment of its black minority.

The poets wrote in a similar view. Walker's *For My People* (1942), Hughes' *Freedom's Plow* (1943), Brooks' *A Street in Bronzeville* (1945), and Dodson's *Powerful Long Ladder* (1946) all had strong protest elements; all dealt in part with the Negro's fight against segregation and discrimination at home and in the armed services.

Noting the dates of these works—both fiction and poetry—one realizes that, roughly speaking, up to 1950 the protest tradition was in full bloom, and that most of our best writers were still using it. Then came this awareness of a radical change in the nation's climate and with it the realization that the old protest themes had to be abandoned. The new climate tended to *date* the problem works of the forties as definitely as time had dated the New Negro "lynching-passing" literature of the twenties and thirties. In other words, protest writing had become the first casualty of the new racial climate.

Faced with the loss of his oldest and most cherished tradition, the Negro writer was forced to seek fresh ways to use his material. First of all, he attempted to find new themes within the racial framework. Retaining the Negro character and background, he shifted his emphasis from the protest aspect of Negro living and placed it on the problems and conflicts within the group itself. For example, Chester Himes pursuing this course in *Third Generation*, explores school life in the Deep South. His main conflict in this work is not concerned with interracial protest but with discord within a Negro family caused by color differences and other problems. The whole racial tone of this novel is quite different from that of *If He Hollers,* a typical protest work. One came out in 1945, the other in 1953. The two books are a good index to the changes which took place in the years separating them.

In like manner, Owen Dodson and Gwendolyn Brooks in their novels, *Boy at the Window* (1951) and *Maud Martha* (1953), respectively, show this tendency to find new themes within the racial framework. Both publications are "little novels," giving intimate and subtle vignettes of middle class living. Their main stress is on life within the group, not on conflict with outside forces. Taking a different approach, William Demby in *Beetlecreek* (1950), completely reversed the protest pattern by showing the black man's inhumanity to his white brother. In *The Outsider* (1953), Richard Wright took an even more subtle approach. He used a Negro main character, but by adroitly and persistently minimizing that character's racial importance, he succeeded in divorcing him from any real association with the traditional protest alignment. And Langston Hughes in *Sweet Flypaper of Life* (1955), though using all Negro characters, does not touch on the matter of inter-racial protest. All of these authors, it seems to me, show their awareness of the new climate by either playing down or avoiding entirely the traditional protest approach.

Another group of writers (and there is some overlapping here) showed their awareness by avoiding the Negro character. Among them are William Gardner Smith (*Anger at Innocence*), Ann Petry (*Country Place*), Richard Wright (*Savage Holiday*), and Willard Motley (*Knock on Any Door*). None of these works has Negro main characters. With the exception of *Knock on Any Door*, each was a "second" novel, following a work written in the forties which had Negro characters and background, and which was written in the protest vein. In each case, the first work was popular, and yet each of these novelists elected to avoid the theme which gave him his initial success.

So far I have spoken only of the novelists, but Negro poets also sensed the change of climate in America and reacted to it. Incidentally, several of our outstanding protest poets of the thirties and forties simply dropped out of the picture as poets. I cannot say, of course, that the new climate alone silenced them, but I do feel that it was a contributing cause. It is hard for a mature writer to slough off a tradition in which he has worked during all of his formative years. Acquiring a new approach in any field of art is a very serious and trying experience. One must also remember that the protest tradition was no mere surface fad with the Negro writer. It was part of his self-respect, part of his philosophy of life, part of his inner being. It was almost a religious experience with those of us who came up through the dark days of the twenties and thirties. When a tradition so deeply ingrained is abandoned, it tends to leave a spiritual numbness—a kind of void not easily filled with new interests or motivations. Several of our ablest poets—and novelists too, for that matter—did not try to fill that void.

A few of the poets, however, met the challenge of the new climate, among them the late M. B. Tolson and Gwendolyn Brooks. A comparison of the early and later works of these poets will show a tendency in the later works either to avoid protest themes entirely or to approach them more subtly and obliquely. Compare, for example, Tolson's *Rendezvous with America* (1944) with *A Libretto for the Republic of Liberia* (1953). The thumping rhythms of the protest verse in the former work gave way in the latter to a new technique, one that was influenced largely by Hart Crane. With this new work, Tolson successfully turned his back on the tradition in which he came to maturity. Concerning the work, Allen Tate felt that: "For the first time . . . a Negro poet has assimilated completely the full poetic language of his time and, by implication, the language of the Anglo-American poetic tradition." Two works of Gwendolyn Brooks also show a change in attitude. There is far more racial protest in *A Street in Bronzeville* (1945) than in her Pulitzer Prize-winning *Annie Allen* (1949). Moreover, the few pieces in the latter work which concern the "problem" are different in approach and technique from those in her first work.

Summing up then, I believe we can say that the Integration Movement influenced Negro writing in the following ways: it forced the black creative artist to play down his most cherished tradition; it sent him in search of new themes; it made him abandon, at least on occasion, the Negro character and background; and it possibly helped to silence a few of the older writers then living. But before the Integration Movement could come to full fruition, it was cut off by the Civil Rights Revolution, particularly the black nationalist elements in the revolution. I speak here, of course, of the literary tendencies of both movements. The main thrust, the principal tenets of black nationalism, in their very essence, negate the paramount aim of the integrationist writer which is to lose himself in the American literary mainstream.

During the 1925 New Negro Renaissance, there was an embryonic black nationalist movement, founded and led by Marcus Garvey. Though short-lived and abortive, it, nevertheless, influenced to some degree the works of Hughes, Cullen, McKay, and other New Negro poets. But Garveyism never achieved the popularity or possessed the civil and "spiritual" strength that the present day black nationalist program has. The influence of this movement goes far beyond the obvious and sensational evidences of it seen in the press or on the T.V. For better or worse, the ideas of black nationalism have influenced the thinking of far more Negroes than one would expect, and this influence has brought to recent Negro writing new themes and a new attitude on the part of the black author.

Perhaps the most important of these new attitudes is the repudiation of American middle class culture and all of the things —the good, on occasion, along with the bad—for which that culture stands. This repudiation may take various forms, and it appears in the poetry (that of LeRoi Jones, for example) as well as in the novels. One form of this attack concerns the Negro woman. She is accused of "emasculating" her husbands and lovers by insisting that they conform to middle class standards. This theme is found in Chester Himes' *Third Generation* (also in other recent works by him), and there is a strain of it in Kelley's *A Drop of Patience* (1965). In Fair's *Hog Butcher* (1966), the author not only attacks the Negro middle class in his story, but in the "Prologue to Part II," he steps into the work, after the manner of Fielding, and delivers a scathing lecture on the subject. The most striking statement of the repudiation of America's white middle class comes from Baldwin's "Letter to My Nephew" in *The Fire Next Time* (1963): "There is no reason for you to try to become like white people and there is no basis whatever for their impertinent assumption that *they* must accept *you*. The really terrible thing, old buddy, is that *you* must accept *them*. And I mean that very seriously. You must accept them and accept them with love. For these innocent people have no other hope."

The influence of the Black Revolt is also seen in the revival of the moribund protest theme in Negro writing. In some cases, the protest novel has returned practically unchanged in the matter of technique and point of view. Frank London Brown's *Trumbull Park* (1958) and Richard Wright's *The Long Dream* (1958) are very similar in spirit to the protest works of the forties. It is curious to note that Wright, after taking a sort of vacation from the protest tradition in *The Outsider* and *Savage Holiday*, comes back to it in *The Long Dream*. Though he deals with discrimination in the Army and though he moves his scene finally from America to Australia, Killens in *And Then We Heard the Thunder* (1963) is still using the old protest tradition. (This, of course, is no reflection on the quality of the novel.) And William Gardner Smith is doing the same thing although in *Stone Face* (1963) he deals primarily with French prejudice against Algerians. There are, however, two recent works in this neo-protest tradition which show freshness and originality. One of them is Kelley's *A Different Drummer* (1962). Making use of fantasy, symbol, and other modern devices and techniques, Kelley gives us not only a new, bitter, and effective type of protest novel, but also a new type of Negro character as well. Ronald Fair's *Many Thousands Gone* (1966) is equally as fresh in its approach and equally as effective. Through a morbidly exaggerated description of life in a mythical Southern locality, Fair tells us symbolically many things about the race situation in America today. He calls his work "An American Fable."

From the twenties on down to the present, the jazz musician

has been popular with black writers, but he has never before received the kind and the amount of attention now given him. In these days of black nationalism and "negritude," the jazz musician has acquired a new significance. He has become for many Negro writers a symbol of the spontaneous creative impulse of the race; he represents black "original genius," something that is not indebted in any way to middle class culture. As depicted in recent works, the Negro jazz musician is often crude, sexy, uninhibited, uneducated, yet wise with a folk wisdom far superior to that which comes from schools and books. We find variants of this character in John A. Williams' *Night Song* (1961), in Kelley's *A Drop of Patience* (1965), and though the character is not fully developed, in Rufus in Baldwin's *Another Country*. On occasion these characters are based on the actual lives of famous jazz musicians.

Black Revolt literature takes an interesting and by no means simple attitude towards whites—an attitude which ranges from pity and contempt to the kind of sadistic love-hatred found in *Another Country*. In several of these novels, the black man-white woman love affair is portrayed. We find this not only in Baldwin's work, but also in *A Drop of Patience*, in *And Then We Heard the Thunder*, and in *Night Song* (a very complex analysis of guilt-laden frustration on the part of the man). LeRoi Jones' *The Dutchman*, whatever else it may be saying, also comments on this theme. To see the new type of white woman and the new role she is playing in these affairs, one should compare a novel like Himes' *If He Hollers* with, let us say, *Night Song*. It is ironic that the white woman should figure as largely as she does in the literature of the Black Revolt.

A minor theme of Black Revolt literature deals with the Negro slum boy, usually depicted as the victim of our indifferent middle class society. Three excellent and intriguing studies of the ghetto kid are found in the following works: Kennedy's *The Pecking Order* (1953), Mayfield's *The Long Night* (1958), and Fair's *Hog Butcher* (1966). In delineating the "culturally deprived" boy, the authors naturally give a lot of space and attention to police brutality, relief, bad housing for Negroes, corrupt and prejudiced city officials, and all of the other evils that the present day militant protest groups attack.

Summing up again—these, then, are the trends I find in the literature of the Black Revolt: a repudiation of American middle class values; a revival of interest in protest writing; the glorification of the black jazz musician; a "mixed" attitude towards whites, particularly white women; and a tendency to depict through the ghetto kid the evils of the inner city. In the works of the period which I have read, I have found two or three highly competent productions but none of the caliber and scope of *Invisible Man,* the finest fruit of the Integration Movement. Perhaps it is far too soon to expect that kind of synthesis.

What about the future? Where will these tendencies lead? When America grants full equality to the Negro (as it will), several of these current attitudes and themes will be dropped. The Negro American writer will do then what he has always done after each crisis in the past—continue on his trek to the mainstream of American literature.

PHILIP BUTCHER

1918-

Charles Philip Butcher, born in Washington, D.C., acquired his advanced education there at Howard University (A.B., 1942; M.A., 1947) and at Columbia, where he received his Ph.D. in 1956. After spending the years 1943–46 in the U.S. Army and the following year or so at Howard, he was aided by fellowships from the General Education Board, 1948–49, and from the John Hay Whitney Foundation, 1951–52. Starting his college teaching career in 1947 as an instructor in English at Morgan State College in Baltimore, Butcher gained full professorial rank there in 1959 and has remained on the faculty since then.

During the same year that he became a college teacher, he began a two-year term as Literary Editor of *Opportunity*. His essays then commenced to appear in that journal; and by 1949, *Phylon* began to publish additional essays and an occasional poem. Butcher's later scholarly articles and book reviews are available in *Journal of Negro History, CLA Journal, Shakespeare Quarterly,* and other periodicals, including the newly established *American Literary Realism, 1870–1910,* to whose first number (Fall 1967) he contributed an essay on George Washington Cable. Cable, upon whom Butcher completed his dissertation at Columbia, was the subject of his books, *George W. Cable: The Northampton Years* (1959)— which made use of materials previously unknown to scholars—and *George W. Cable,* Volume 24 of Twayne's United States Authors Series (1962).

"Emerson and the South," which was published in *Phylon* in 1956, represents the able scholarship produced by many Negroes in the academic community. Augmenting Butcher's published evaluations of both Negro and white authors (Claude McKay, for example, as well as Robert Burns), this essay on the Sage of Concord adequately chronicles the development of Emerson's main ideas about Southern character and customs.

Emerson and the South

RALPH WALDO EMERSON'S importance in American culture rests largely upon his genius as a speculative thinker, an essayist, and an influence upon significant native writers of his own and later times. He was a man noted for personal integrity, humanitarian sympathy, persistent curiosity, and broad intellectual interests. Students of pure philosophy sometimes lament his conversion to the cause of the abolitionists on the ground that preoccupation with the evils of slavery interfered with his achievement as a thinker even while it contributed to his development as a man. That conversion began before he was twenty; his journal for 1822 records his conviction that slavery was a moral wrong and that Southerners who defended it did so with an ingenious sophistry rather than reason, for their vested interest in the institution naturally prejudiced them in its favor. This view, which resulted from soul searching and careful analysis of what information and misinformation was available to him, he seems to have held to all his life. Gradually his opinion of the South's "peculiar institution" hardened into the mold fashioned by the abolitionists and, as slavery became a national issue and one cause for the Civil War, his antipathy for slavery came to include the whole region which practiced it.

He gave expression to his long interest in the South in a letter he wrote on March 12, 1822 to John B. Hill, an acquaintance who was teaching at Garrison Forest Academy near Baltimore.

> What kind of people are the Southerners in your vicinity? Have they legs & eyes? Do they walk & eat? You know our idea of an accomplished Southerner—to wit—as ignorant as a bear, as irascible & nettled as any porcupine, as polite as a troubadour, & a very John Randolph in character & address.[1]

He evidently sent a similar inquiry a month later to Mellish Irving Motte, a Harvard classmate from Charleston, South Carolina, requesting details on Southern education.[2] His interest in Southern culture may have resulted in part from his admiration for another

Reprinted from *Phylon*, XVII (1956), 179–185.

[1] Ralph L. Rusk, ed., *The Letters of Ralph Waldo Emerson* (New York, 1939), I, 107.

[2] *Ibid.*, I, 108–109.

Charleston classmate, John G. K. Gourdin, who was his roommate during his junior year.[3]

When ill health forced young Emerson to go South in 1827, he was able to satisfy his curiosity in some degree at first hand. From St. Augustine, Florida, he wrote to his brother William on January 29:

It is a queer place, this city of St. Augustine. There are eleven or twelve hundred people, and these are invalids, public officers, Spaniards, or rather Minorcans. What is done here? Nothing. It was reported one morning that a man was at work in the public square & all our family turned out to see him. What is grown here? Oranges—on which no cultivation seems to be bestowed beyond the sluggish attention of one or two negroes to each grove of 5 or 6 hundred trees. The Americans live on their offices. The Spaniards keep billiard tables, or, if not, they send their negroes to the mud to bring oysters, or to the shore to bring fish, & the rest of the time fiddle, masque, & dance. The Catholic clergyman lately represented at a masquerade the character of a drunken sailor with laughable fidelity.[4]

A few days later he wrote his younger brother Charles more about what he considered to be the laziness of the residents of this outpost of civilization. "Whosoever is in St. Augustine resembles what may also be seen in St. Augustine, — the barnacles on a ledge of rocks which the tide has deserted. . . ."[5]

In the journal he kept during his stay in the old Florida town which had been in American control only half a dozen years, the young Unitarian minister recorded his experiences with the local Bible Society.

The treasurer of this institution is Marshall of the district & by a somewhat unfortunate arrangement had appointed a special meeting of the Society & a Slave Auction at the same time & place, one being in the Government house & the other in the adjoining yard. One ear therefore heard the glad tidings of great joy whilst the other was regaled with 'going gentlemen, going!' And almost without changing our position we might aid in sending the Scriptures into Africa or bid for 'four children without the mother' who had been kidnapped therefrom. . . . There is something wonderfully piquant in the manners of the place, theological or civil. A Mr. Jerry, a Methodist minister, preached here two Sundays ago, who confined himself in the afternoon to some pretty intelligible strictures upon the character of a President

[3] Ralph L. Rusk, *The Life of Ralph Waldo Emerson* (New York, 1949), p. 76.
[4] Rusk, *The Letters of Ralph Waldo Emerson*, I, 189.
[5] James Elliot Cabot, *A Memoir of Ralph Waldo Emerson* (Boston, 1887), I. 122.

of the Bible Soc. who swears. The gentleman alluded to was present. And it really exceeded all power of face to be grave during the divine's very plain analysis of the motives which probably actuated the individual in seeking the office which he holds.[6]

Emerson attended a meeting of the Bible Society on March 1. He wrote in his journal:

I found here a gentleman from N. Carolina who gave me some accounts of the monstrous absurdities of the Methodists at their Camp Meetings in that state. He related an instance of several of these fanatics jumping about on all fours, imitating the barking of dogs & surrounding a tree in which they pretended they had 'treed Jesus.'[7]

Emerson did not neglect to praise the wonders of the climate which did much to restore his health. He left St. Augustine in the congenial company of Achille Murat, nephew of Napoleon and son of the cavalry officer who was later Marshal of France and King of Naples. Murat was a Charleston resident and the husband of an American woman who was distantly related to George Washington.[8] Emerson admired the Frenchman's learning but not his atheism or his adopted city. On May 3, he wrote to Samuel Ripley:

I think I had scolded in an earlier letter to you about the wretched aspect of Charleston. I liked the town no better at our second interview. But I began to doubt whether I was not deceived by the juvenile error of thinking all that was unaccustomed to be precisely in that degree *wrong;* & I so bigoted a Yankee as not to be honest to the beauty of Southern municipal architecture. But when I got to Baltimore, my judgment sat firm in his seat again, for I found fine houses streets churches abounding in a place where I am yet more a stranger than in Charleston. It is a fine city & in general & in particular looks like Boston.[9]

Emerson called himself a "bigoted Yankee" again when he wrote to William a month later, and perhaps not altogether without justification. Clearly his admiration for Baltimore resulted from what resemblance he saw to his beloved Boston, not from its distinctive characteristics.

[6] "Ralph Waldo Emerson's Little Journal at St. Augustine, January, February, March, 1827," *The Florida Historical Quarterly,* XVIII (October, 1939), 88. In the same issue, pp. 75–83, see Mrs. Henry L. Richmond's "Ralph Waldo Emerson in Florida."
[7] *Ibid.,* p. 91.
[8] Rusk, *The Life of Ralph Waldo Emerson,* p. 121.
[9] Rusk, *The Letters of Ralph Waldo Emerson,* I, 196.

His attitude toward Charleston was not entirely disparaging. He noted:

. . . no man has travelled in the United States from the North to the South without observing the change and amelioration of manners. In this city (Charleston), it is most observable, the use of the conventions of address among the lowest classes, which are coarsely neglected by the labouring classes at the North. Two negroes recognize each other in the street, though both in rags, and both, it may be, balancing a burden on their heads, with the same graduated advances of salutation that well-bred men who are strangers to each other would use in Boston. They do not part before they have shaken hands and bid good-bye with an inclination of the head. There is a grace and perfection too about these courtesies which could not be imitated by a Northern labourer where he designed to be extremely civil. Indeed I have never seen an awkward Carolinian.[10]

Emerson cherished kindly feelings toward some Southerners —men like Robert Woodward Barnwell whom he knew and respected—and his regard for these friends of his youth did not abate over the years.[11] But as his abolitionist sentiments became more pronounced in the 1840's, his censure of the South and his generalizations about its people became more severe. In his lecture on New England in 1843 he said:

The Southerner lives for the moment; relies on himself and conquers by personal address. He is wholly there in that thing which is now to be done. The Northerner lives for the year, and does not rely on himself, but on the whole apparatus of means he is wont to employ. . . . The Southerner is haughty, wilful, generous, unscrupulous; will have his way and has it. The Northerner must think the thing over, and his conscience and his common sense throw a thousand obstacles between himself and his wishes which perplex his decision and unsettle his behavior. The Northerner always has the advantage at the end of ten years, and the Southerner always has the advantage to-day.[12]

He was less dispassionate two years later when he wrote in his journal that unruly South Carolina excluded

. . . every gentleman, every man of honour, every man of humanity, every freedom from its territory. Is that a country in which I wish to walk where I am assured beforehand that I shall not meet a great man?

[10] E. W. Emerson and W. E. Forbes, eds., *The Journals of Ralph Waldo Emerson* (Boston, 1909–1914), II, 141–142.
[11] Rusk, *The Life of Ralph Waldo Emerson*, p. 429.
[12] Cabot, *op. cit.*, II, 594–595.

that all the men are cotton gins? where a great man cannot live, where the people are degraded, for they go with padlocked lips, and with seared conscience?[13]

Emerson's 1844 address, "Emancipation in the British West Indies," criticized Northern statesmen for permitting themselves to be dominated by a Southern minority. He disagreed with John Brown's confidence in the superiority of the Northerner as a fighting man, for he felt that the slave states were able to prevail over the nation as a whole because the Southerner was a fighter and the Northerner was not.[14] This perverted virtue was perhaps one of the "good and plausible things" which the transcendentalist acknowledged might be said for the South ten years later when he made his address repudiating the Fugitive Slave Law.[15] But by this time Emerson held that the moral evil to which the section was committed made such "good and plausible things" of little consequence, and he did not elaborate on them.

For him the purpose of the Civil War was to bring an end to slavery, not to preserve a union which countenanced slavery anywhere within its borders. As early as 1856, outraged when Preston Brooks of South Carolina assaulted Charles Sumner in the Senate, he wrote in his journal, "Suppose we propose a Northern Union."[16] The rough draft of his letter to Oliver Wendell Holmes, written in March, 1856, rejects the idea of any kind of union with slavery.[17] Yet he knew that institution was not the only cause of the War, for he saw that there were other serious economic and political differences between the two sections and he sometimes thought of it as a war of manners.[18] He regarded it as a necessary evil and one which might bring unexpected benefits. For one thing, it might force Southerners to abandon what he considered an inexcusable laziness.

I think they have never . . . appeared to such advantage. They have waked to energy, to self-help, to economy, to valor, to self-knowledge and progress. They have put forth for the first time their sleepy, half-palsied limbs, and as soon as the blood begins to tingle and flow, it will creep with new life into the moribund extremes of the system and the 'white trash' will say, 'We, too, are men.'[19]

[13] Emerson and Forbes, *op. cit.*, VII, 21.
[14] Cabot, *loc. cit.*
[15] Brooks Atkinson, ed., *The Complete Essays and other Writings of Ralph Waldo Emerson* (New York, 1940), p. 865.
[16] Emerson and Forbes, *op. cit.*, IX, 47.
[17] Rusk, *The Letters of Ralph Waldo Emerson*, V, 17–18.
[18] Rusk, *The Life of Ralph Waldo Emerson*, p. 412.
[19] Cabot, *op. cit.*, II, 602–603.

Emerson was at the height of his powers during the war years and he spent much of his energy in support of the Northern cause. He greeted emancipation, "an event worth the dreadful war,"[20] with elation, and in his "Boston Hymn" he scornfully rejected his earlier opinion that the planters should be reimbursed for their slaves.

> Pay ransom to the owner
> And fill the bag to the brim.
> Who is the owner? The slave is owner,
> And ever was. Pay him.

Once Emerson had felt that as much as he hated slavery his own responsibility was "to quite other slaves than those negroes, to wit, imprisoned spirits, imprisoned thoughts . . . which, important to the republic of man, have no other watchman, or lover, or defender, but I."[21] When the war was over he resumed the congenial role of speculative thinker, but he did not lose interest in the issues of the conflict and continued to be critical of the South. He considered General Grant's terms too lenient and the reconstruction policy too generous; he was distressed about public apathy toward the rights of the freedmen. But he turned away from political controversy and applied his flagging powers to lectures and readings which were, by about 1870, mere echoes of his earlier work, echoes so disorganized and delivered in such faint tones that his audiences in New England and the West sometimes applauded what they did not quite hear or understand. In January of 1872 he ventured as far South as Baltimore where he gave a series of readings at Peabody Institute.[22] Walt Whitman, who came over from Washington to hear him, was disappointed that his comments showed no advance in his thinking and had no relevance to the immediate problems of the day. Whitman delivered to Emerson an invitation to visit with Charles Sumner in Washington. When Professor John M. Langston called on Sumner on the morning of January 6 and found Emerson at breakfast with him, he persuaded the transcendentalist to promise to visit Howard University.[23] On

---

[20] Atkinson, *op. cit.*, p. 887.

[21] Emerson and Forbes, *op. cit.*, VIII, 316.

[22] Rusk, *The Letters of Ralph Waldo Emerson*, VI, 193n gives the series as "Imagination and Poetry," Jan. 2; "Resources and Inspiration," Jan. 4; "Homes and Hospitality," Jan. 9; and "Art and Nature," Jan. 11.

[23] *Ibid.*, 194–196, and John Mercer Langston, *From the Virginia Plantation to the National Capitol* (Hartford, Conn., 1894), pp. 301–302. Langston was dean of the Law Department. Like Emerson, he was a staunch supporter of Sumner, who was then sponsoring legislation designed to guarantee the civil rights of the freedmen.

arriving at the institution the next day, Emerson was embarrassed to find that he was expected to address the students. His impromptu remarks on what books to read had no special pertinence to the times or his audience.[24]

Four years later, his powers far gone, Emerson returned to the South for the last time. The invitation to deliver the commencement address at the University of Virginia was evidence of some healing of sectional wounds, for to the South Emerson was a Yankee abolitionist philosopher. When the large audience found it could not hear the oration it became inattentive. A few determined students crowded close to the platform, but the noise grew as the bulk of the audience gave up the attempt to make out the faint words of the speaker. Disappointed by his performance, Emerson was content that the main purpose of the expedition, to extend to the South the hand of fellowship, had been achieved.[25] But his willingness to reconcile sectional differences represented no change in his principles.

Emerson did not form hasty judgments, and although age dimmed his faculties it did not alter his convictions. In the twilight existence of his last years, when rumors circulated that the transcendental sage had reverted to orthodoxy, he authorized his son to state that he had not joined any church or repudiated any of the views he had published since leaving the ministry. In the course of his career Emerson endorsed women's rights, protested to President Van Buren about what he considered to be mistreatment of the Cherokee Indians, and denounced his government when the Fugitive Slave Law was enacted. An altruist who believed that all men have equal rights because they are identical in nature, Emerson summed up in his war-time essay, "Civilization," his disapproval of a section of the country which was alien to his philosophy.

But if there be a country where knowledge cannot be diffused without perils of mob-law and statute-law; where speech is not free; where the post-office is violated, mail-bags opened, and letters tampered with; where public debts and private debts outside of the State are repudiated; where liberty is attacked in the primary institution of social life; where the position of the white woman is injuriously affected by the outlawry of the black woman; where the arts, such as they have, are all imported, having no indigenous life; where the laborer is not secured in the earnings of his own hands; where suffrage is not free or equal;

[24] A long report of the speech appeared in the New York *Tribune*, January 11, 1872 and in the Boston *Daily Evening Telegraph*, January 22, 1872.

[25] Rusk, *The Life of Ralph Waldo Emerson*, pp. 496–498. See also Hubert H. Hoeltje, "Emerson in Virginia," *The New England Quarterly*, V (October, 1932), 753–768.

—that country is, in all these respects, not civil but barbarious; and no advantages of soil, climate or coast can resist these suicidal mischiefs.[26]

For Emerson, as for any liberal speculative thinker, "the highest proof of civility is that the whole public action of the State is directed in securing the greatest good of the greatest number."[27]

Emerson's strictures cannot be discounted as merely the petty objections of a complacent, provincial New Englander who disparaged whatever manners and morals differed from his own. He was primarily an idealist, not a partisan social critic; his concern was principles rather than people. His attitude toward the South was the result of his observation that it, more than any other section of the nation, fell short of the ideal.

[26] *Society and Solitude* (Boston, 1904), pp. 33–34. See also pp. 351–352.
[27] *Ibid.*, p. 34.

NATHAN A. SCOTT JR.

1925–

Nathan Alexander Scott, Jr., the son of a Cleveland lawyer, received his advanced education at the University of Michigan (A.B., 1944), Union Theological Seminary in New York (B.D., 1946), and Columbia (Ph.D., 1949). The father of two children after his marriage in 1946, Scott was an Episcopal priest before becoming, in 1955, a professor of theology and literature at the University of Chicago, where he is now Chairman of the Theology and Literature Field of the Divinity School. He is Canon Theologian of the Cathedral of St. James, Chicago, and a Fellow of Indiana University's School of Letters. He has also served as Coeditor of the *Journal of Religion* and as Literary Editor of *Christian Scholar*.

Scott's constant additional labors as a writer have resulted in publications impressive in number, variety, and quality. Since 1951, his typically long essays in *Religion in Life, Journal of Religion, Review of Metaphysics,* and *Christian Century,* as well as in the more literary *Saturday Review, The Kenyon Review, The Chicago Review, The London Magazine,* and other journals have revealed a probing, versatile intelligence. His earliest essays—"T. S. Eliot's *The Cocktail Party*," "Relation of Theology to Literary Criticism," and "Poetry, Religion, and the Modern Mind," for example —show his diversity. Others published in the 1950's on Richard Wright, Edna St. Vincent Millay, William Faulkner, and Robert

Penn Warren; on Jacques Maritain; and on "Christian poetics" and Catholic novelists further demonstrate his range.

At least ten recent anthologies contain long literary essays by Scott, among them *Literature and Belief* (1958), *Symbolism in Religion and Literature* (1960), *The Search for Identity* (1964), *Comedy: Meaning and Form* (1965), and *Conflicting Images of Man* (1966). Scott, in turn, has himself edited anthologies: *The Tragic Vision and the Christian Faith* in 1957, two in 1964 (*The Climate of Faith in Modern Literature* and *The New Orpheus: Essays Toward a Christian Poetic*), three in 1965 (*Man in the Modern Theatre, Four Ways of Modern Poetry,* and *Forms of Extremity in the Modern Novel*), and one in 1968 (*Adversity and Grace: Studies in Recent American Literature*).

Indefatigable in his declared efforts "to search out and explore those areas of interrelationship in the modern period that unite the literary and the religious imagination," Scott has written seven books entirely his own: *Rehearsals of Discomposure: Alienation and Reconciliation in Modern Literature*—on Kafka, Lawrence, Silone, and Eliot (1952), *Modern Literature and the Religious Frontier* (1958), *Albert Camus* (1962), *Reinhold Niebuhr* (1963), *Samuel Beckett* (1965), *The Broken Center: Studies in the Theological Horizon of Modern Literature* (1966), and *Craters of the Spirit: Studies in the Modern Novel* (1968). In addition to his teaching, research, and writing, Scott occasionally gives lectures. In December 1966, for example, at Marymount College in New York, his lecture on avant-garde art included detailed comment on writers, painters, electronic composers, and film directors.

Scott's dedication to humanistic learning, the acumen and grace of style with which he has so abundantly expressed his literary reflections, merit solid respect. He is a remarkable example of the "invisible men" of American letters: those critics relatively unknown as Negroes who have brilliantly recorded their love of literature. The following, Chapter Seven of *The Broken Center* (which appeared in 1964 as an essay, slightly different in form, in *The Search for Identity*), speaks eloquently for itself. "Society and the Self in Recent American Literature" awakens the reader to the presence of a critical genius among us.

Society and the Self in Recent American Literature

—FOR RALPH ELLISON

IN ROMANO GUARDINI'S famous little book, *The Spirit of the Liturgy*, there is a chapter in which we are asked to think of the Church's liturgy as a kind of play, as a kind of sacred game. Mngr. Guardini is, of course, aware that this is a perspective that will be offensive to those grave and earnest rationalists in the Church for whom every aspect of its life must have a moral purpose: they will be quick to suppose that to view the liturgy in this way is to reduce it to a mere theatrical trifle, and they will therefore want to insist that the Church's liturgical actions are channels of grace and serve the indispensable purpose of the soul's renewal and edification. But, in his sprightly wisdom, Mngr. Guardini denies that the liturgy is informed by "the austere guidance of the sense of purpose." The prayers, the gestures, the garments, the colors, the holy vessels, the complicated arrangements of the calendar are all, he asserts, simply "incomprehensible when . . . measured by the objective standard of strict suitability for a purpose." For the liturgy, in quite the same way as a child's play, has no purpose. "The child, when it plays, does not aim at anything. It has no purpose. It does not want to do anything but to exercise its youthful powers, [to] pour forth its life in an aimless series of movements, words and actions," "all of which is purposeless, but full of meaning nevertheless. . . . That is what play means; it is life, pouring itself forth without an aim." And, similarly, the liturgy "speaks measuredly and melodiously," "employs formal, rhythmic gestures," "is clothed in colours and garments foreign to everyday life," "is carried out in places and at hours which have been coordinated and systematised. . . . It is in the highest sense the life of a child, in which everything is picture, melody and song." It is a pouring forth of "the sacred, God-given life of the soul": it is a kind of holy play in which the soul, with utter abandon, learns how "to waste time for the sake of God."[1]

The liturgy, in short,—and Mngr. Guardini is aware of the

Reprinted from *The Broken Center* (New Haven: Yale University Press, 1966). Originally in *The Search for Identity: Essays on the American Character*, ed. Roger L. Shinn (New York, 1964). Used with permission of the copyright holder and original publisher, the Institute for Religious and Social Studies.

[1] Romano Guardini, *The Spirit of the Liturgy*, trans. Ada Lane (New York, Sheed and Ward, 1937), pp. 92, 95–96, 98–99, 101–102, 104, 106.

implication here—is a form of art. For whenever the human spirit, in a deep and radical way, apprehends through the configuration of things and events a threshold beyond which is a Something More, the taproot and fecund abyss of everything that has reality —whenever the human spirit is granted such a moment of contact with the unplumbed Mystery from which everything is sprung— its most primitive impulse, in Jonathan Edwards' phrase, is simply to "consent to Being." This consent expresses itself at once in terms of reverence and homage and in terms of the kind of play that we call art: indeed, in their most primitive—that is, in their purest and most essential—forms, the religious and the artistic as modes of response to the fullness of reality, though distinguishable from each other, are virtually inseparable. For it is what Paul Tillich calls the shock of being that forms the matrix out of which both are born—in, as it were, the same moment, each participating immanently in the dynamism of the other.

Rudolf Otto is, of course, the great phenomenologist in modern tradition of this primitive experience of "shock" or "stupor" before the plenteous Mystery of Being, and, though he was primarily interested in its distinctively religious consequences, he was by no means unalive to the fact that it is also this same shock that calls forth and energizes the artistic impulse. He was also aware that primitive art was motivated by fear of the unknown forces of nature, the desire to placate hostile powers, and the desire to arrest the flux of existence by creating images of stability and rest. But he believed, as I also am persuaded, that "the change to the motive of *expression* must have been from the outset far too vividly stimulated not to [have occurred] . . . at a very early date."[2] And when one looks, say, at Paleolithic rock engravings of the Aurignacian period or at the rock-paintings of the Bushmen, one cannot help but feel that what these works express fundamentally is a kind of dance performed by the imagination, not for any purpose at all but only as a spirited utterance of consent to Being-itself.

Now it is this most primitive aspect of art—which has never been completely lost—that has doubtless led many theorists to interpret art as being essentially a form of play: this notion has cropped up in the thought of such otherwise divergent figures as Plato and Aristotle, Schiller and Hegel, Freud and Santayana, and it seems to have commended itself again and again as a fundamental hypothesis about the nature of art. The latest echoing of it

[2] Rudolf Otto, *The Idea of the Holy*, trans. John W. Harvey (New York, Oxford University Press, 1943), p. 68.

that I can recall occurs, not very surprisingly, in an essay by Karl Barth on Mozart, in the course of which this distinguished Swiss theologian wants in various ways to say that the most remarkable gift that Mozart has to offer us is the strangely exciting and wonderful kind of "childlike play" that is in his music.[3] And I speak of not being surprised that Dr. Barth should take this view of Mozart, for his is a way of relating Christianity to culture which, on the side of faith, is not prepared to brook any competition at all from culture so far as the definition of man's nature and destiny is concerned; and thus, on the basis of his very radical kind of Protestantism, it only becomes possible to enfranchise art under the firmament of Christian value when it is accepted merely as a form of play.

This is a conception of art to which art itself conforms in some fashion—for as long as Being is in view. For, when it is born out of an easy commerce between the artist's imagination and the mysterious depths of reality, and when it lives under "the sunlit regime of the Logos,"[4] then it is easy and unstrained: then it is all melody and song—and play—even when the song speaks of what is most profoundly tragic in life. And this may be at least a part of what Baudelaire had in mind when he said, "Great poetry is essentially *stupid,* it *believes,* and that is what makes its glory and its force."[5] For when art enjoys the kind of security that proceeds from a basic sense of the ontological simplicity of the world, it is relieved of any necessity to develop metaphysical aspirations. But when it loses any certitude of an irrefragable connection between man and the inner life of the world, when the deep Mystery of Being can no longer be known through affective union and connaturality, then art undergoes a *crise de conscience:* it suffers the wound that is inflicted by a time of dearth, when the light of heaven has gone into eclipse and the sun is lost. And, in the muddle that ensues, art loses its primitive innocence; it can then no longer afford to be "stupid," for, in order to survive at all, it must now take the great hazardous step into that chilly, inclement region of its period's deepest perplexity—there, as Hölderlin says, to "name" the gods all over again. In this region, where "the absence of God moves about . . . with the intimacy of a presence,"[6] art ceases, in any central and decisive sense, to be an affair of

---

[3] Karl Barth, "Wolfgang Amadeus Mozart," in *Religion and Culture: Essays in Honor of Paul Tillich,* ed. Walter Leibrecht (New York, Harper, 1959), p. 66.

[4] Maritain, *Creative Intuition,* p. 231.

[5] Charles Baudelaire, *Œuvres posthumes* (Paris, Mercure de France, 1908), p. 167.

[6] Hopper, "Naming of the Gods," p. 158.

play, for here, as Eliot says in "East Coker" and "Burnt Norton," the poet is desperately

> Trying to learn to use words, and every attempt
> Is a wholly new start, and a different kind of failure. . . .
>   And so each venture
> Is a new beginning, a raid on the inarticulate

and always:

> Words strain,
> Crack and sometimes break, under the burden,
> Under the tension.

This is, of course, the precarious region that the artist in our time inhabits—the region, that is, where, being wounded by our transgressions and bruised by our chastisement, he seeks to make his work a glass of vision through which new orders of meaning and hope may be discerned. It was perhaps inevitable that the artists of the word should play the leading part in this; and, among their various forms, it is undoubtedly the novel that has been the most effective agent of the modern imagination. Indeed, the regularity with which the prognosticators of the literary life annually debate whether or not the novel may be dying or already dead is perhaps itself a testimony to our anxiousness about the health of that form of art which seems more fully to comprehend the variousness and complexity of human experience than any other. "Being a novelist," said D. H. Lawrence, "I consider myself superior to the saint, the scientist, the philosopher and the poet. The novel is the one bright book of life." And insofar as Lawrence speaks for the modern novelist generally, as indeed he very considerably does, it must be said that his is a claim that we have been prepared, particularly on the American scene, more readily to grant than similar claims coming from artists working in the other great established forms of art.

American drama, it is generally agreed, continues, as it has over a long period, to be in a seriously bad way. If Tennessee Williams ever succeeds in outgrowing the frivolousness and vulgarity that have disfigured so much of his work, there is reason to suppose that the creator of *The Glass Menagerie* and *Streetcar* might well become a major presence in the modern theatre; and Thornton Wilder, in going his own quite special way, has achieved an honorable, if minor, dignity among the best playwrights of our time. But, among our living contemporaries, there is no one else whom one would dare to propose as belonging to the company of Pirandello and Brecht and Sartre and Beckett;[7] and, among non-living contemporaries, there is only the uncertain case of O'Neill. Our poetry is, of course, another matter, and one about which a national pride is permissible. For, among the great magisterial figures of our period, we can lay claim to Eliot and Pound; nor can we forget in this galaxy Robert Frost and Hart Crane, E. E. Cummings and Marianne Moore and William Carlos Williams, and many others; and, in the current generation of Robert Lowell, there is a vigor nowhere surpassed on the contemporary scene. Frost is, of course, the only poet who has played any large role in the life of our culture, for the broad commonalty of the American people—but he has generally been admired for reasons bearing only a very slight relation to his actual achievement. So, when one thinks of the kind of quasi-scriptural eminence that belongs to such works as *The Great Gatsby* and *The Sun Also Rises* and *The Sound and the Fury*, it is difficult to resist the conclusion that in America the novel has exerted a kind of pressure on thought and sensibility more decisive than that which could be claimed by any other department of our literature.

The high prestige of the novel in American cultural life is, in part, a consequence of the impoverishment of our theatre and, in part, of the speciality of idiom and reference that has made our poetry something whose vigor was not readily perceptible in the national forum. But, more positively considered, it is doubtless in far larger part a consequence of our having supposed that the very spaciousness of the form permitted it to render a unique justice to the breadth and diversity of the land and its multi-faceted life. For a people by whom "experience" has been held in such high regard as it has amongst ourselves, the tendency of the novel in all its classic expressions to obliterate the distinction between art and experience has surely been a great point in its favor in the American climate. It has appeared to be a form of art that has a special tolerance of the rough, ragged contingency and the viscous untidiness of historical existence. And where the deepest national feeling is, as Heidegger would say, that of having been "thrown" into history, it was perhaps inevitable that those artists using what Lawrence called the book of life should win something like a bardic status. So to press forward an inquiry into the testimony that is being made by American fiction at the present time is to negotiate

[7] The one highly gifted newcomer is Edward Albee, but, despite the rich promise of his initial work, his career is perhaps only just beginning.

a transaction which ought to yield evidence of a very crucial sort.

The terrain of recent American fiction is, however, one on which it is difficult to descry signs and landmarks that give an easy sense of orientation. But in the response that was made to one fairly recent event we may find at least a suggestion of what is distinctive about our literary dispensation of the last ten or fifteen years. I have in mind the gasp of resentful astonishment that was heard in 1962 when the news was released over our radio and television networks that John Steinbeck had been awarded the Nobel Prize. I have no doubt but that Arthur Mizener's guess comes close to the truth, that "the time had [simply] come around for some American to receive the award, and among Europeans Steinbeck turned out to be, for one or another reason, the most widely read American author, just as Sinclair Lewis was when he received the . . . Prize in 1930."[8] I do not, however, have any desire to offer an affront to Mr. Steinbeck, and the appropriateness of the award is not the issue with which I am presently concerned. Although if Mr. Mizener is right in thinking that 1962 was the American year, it does seem more than a little strange (if the award is intended to have any real cultural meaning) that, at a time when both Robert Frost and William Carlos Williams were still alive and neither had been offered this garland, it should have gone to Mr. Steinbeck. What I want chiefly to remark, however, is my having been persuaded at the time that the amazement that was so generally expressed sprang not out of a sense of incommensurateness between the *éclat* of the Prize and the real importance of Mr. Steinbeck's achievement as an artist, but sprang rather out of a simple disbelief that the embattled social humanism that animated *The Grapes of Wrath* and *In Dubious Battle* could, as an attitude toward the world, be adjudged by anyone today as worthy of a large and handsome honor.

Now it is just such a disbelief that comprises a sort of phenomenon, a sort of tendency, in American cultural life today, most especially in our literature where it begins to be apparent that the ruling principle is a profound lack of faith in the possibility of the great, gross reality of society ever becoming anything with which the self might do any kind of significant business. Indeed, Norman Mailer—whose work presents a central example of our recent fiction—tells us that, since we are fated to live in an age which surrounds us on every side with death and destruction, "the only life-giving answer is to accept the terms of death, to live with death

---

[8] Arthur Mizener, "Does a Moral Vision of the Thirties Deserve a Nobel Prize?" *The New York Times Book Review* (December 9, 1962), p. 45.

as immediate danger, to divorce oneself from society, to exist without roots, to set out on that uncharted journey into the rebellious imperatives of the self."[9] And it is the resolute intention to enfranchise precisely these imperatives that appears now to have been the governing motive behind our most characteristic literature of the last fifteen years. For, when we all feel the sense of impotence that we often do today before the events of our collective life, and when, therefore, the social and political order—particularly in its international aspect—is felt only as a source of gratuitous oppression and unmanageable danger, then those whose nerves are most exposed will perform a motion of recoil; and, given the disorder in the State and the unavailability of the Church except to a minority, their retreat will be into the self. Their literary spokesman will discover his task to be largely one of defining the self in relation to "the massive brute social fact . . . that surrounds and threatens to overwhelm it," and surely in some such way as this it has come to be the case that, "for the advanced writer of our time, the self is his supreme, even sole, referent."[10] To him the action that promises to have the most deeply renovating effect on human life is an action of entrenchment behind a barricade whose purpose is to afford protection against whatever may threaten to undo the self. "Keep your hands off my soul," says a character in James Purdy's *Malcolm* (1959). And a similar demand, as R. W. B. Lewis has also noticed,[11] is expressed in many American books of the last few years: it is the whole burden of the embittered deliverance that is hurled at the world by the nameless protagonist of Ralph Ellison's *Invisible Man*: it is the essential core of what Salinger's Holden Caulfield has to say to us in *The Catcher in the Rye*: it is the requirement of the hero of John Knowles' *A Separate Peace*, and also, in a way, of Cass Kinsolving in William Styron's *Set This House on Fire*, and of that engaging gentleman whose adventures Saul Bellow chronicles in *Herzog*. "Keep your hands off my soul": it is with this simple and radical demand that the world is faced by the most representative figures in American literature of the present time.

The whole style of mind and art of which I take James Purdy's *Malcolm* as a convenient example has of course had to suffer the exactions necessitated by its special bias. And ever since critics such as John Aldridge and Malcolm Cowley initiated discussion

[9] Mailer, *Advertisements for Myself* (New York, New American Library, 1960), p. 304.

[10] Diana Trilling, "Norman Mailer," *Encounter, 19* (November 1962), 46.

[11] R. W. B. Lewis, "American Letters: A Projection," *The Yale Review, 51* (1962), 222.

at the end of the forties, of our postwar fiction, they, and others, have increasingly noticed how large an area of experience our novelists are prompted to neglect by this preoccupation with the sovereign reality of the self. Already in 1954, Mr. Cowley, for example, was observing that the scene of the new fiction

is seldom one of the centers where policy decisions are made; it is never Capitol Hill or the Pentagon or the board-room of any corporation or political London or Paris. . . . Preferring to deal with private lives, the new fiction is likely to have a remote and peripheral scene, for example . . . a lonely ranch in Colorado, a village in East Texas, a small town in Georgia, various plantation houses in Louisiana and Mississippi (all rotting into the dark loam), a country house in Maine . . . an abandoned summer hotel, two beach resorts full of homosexuals, several freshwater colleges.

And, in a similar way, Mr. Cowley also commented on the defining quality of the characters in this literature—which he specified as one of disaffiliation. The characters are, he said,

distinguished by their lack of a functional relationship with American life. They don't sow or reap, build, mine, process, promote or sell, repair, heal, plead, administer, or legislate. . . . One widely observed feature of present-day America is that the lives of most individuals are defined by their relations with an interlocking series of institutions— for example, government bureaus, churches, schools and universities, the armed services, labor unions, chambers of commerce, farm bureaus . . . and, for most of us, that center of our daily activities, the office. But characters in the new fiction are exceptional persons who keep away from offices . . . and are generally as unattached as Daniel Boone. . . . The characters likely to be treated at length are students of both sexes, young artists and writers, gentlemen on their travels, divorced or widowed mothers, gay boys, neurotic bitches . . . old women on their deathbeds, and preternaturally wise little girls.[12]

At the time Mr. Cowley wrote these lines, as at the present time, exceptions here and there could be cited as examples that refuse to fit his generalization. These are not, however, exceptions that are to be drawn from the sleek entertainments-for-the-millions that are produced by the Cameron Hawleys and Herman Wouks and Sloan Wilsons and Allen Drurys; for these journeymen, to be sure, use a "public" scene and handle characters affiliated with the centers of power and decision in our society, but they are writers

---

[12] Malcolm Cowley, *The Literary Situation* (New York, Viking Press, 1954), pp. 45–47.

whose unconcern with anything beyond the old stockpot of hack-neyed experience and comment disqualifies them from considera-tion as serious artists. The exceptions—those writers who do not create "a tidy room in Bedlam"—are rather to be found in such artists as the Ralph Ellison of *Invisible Man*, the Bernard Malamud of *The Assistant*, the Frederick Buechner of *The Return of Ansel Gibbs*, the James Baldwin of *Another Country*, the Bellow of *Augie March*—for these are all writers whose focus is on the self, but on the self at that point of juncture where it encounters a significant social reality.

And in one other particular it may also be necessary to com-plicate somewhat Mr. Cowley's perspective. For many of those writers whose work exhibits the extreme specialty of material that he complains of do yet manage, however obliquely, to handle that material in such a way as to situate the problem of selfhood within a larger compass. One thinks, for example, of Saul Bellow's *Hen-derson the Rain King*, whose American millionaire protagonist is so dedicated to the inner necessities of his personal being that a voice within him is constantly crying, "I want, I want, I want." And this solitary proficient in self-realization, fleeing all attach-ments and loyalties, goes off to Africa, a place more remote even than any of those which Mr. Cowley enumerates in his list: yet in the African wilderness he discovers the need that we have for some great encounter with reality to "wake the spirit's sleep," and it is apparent that this is a redemptive principle in the light of which he is prepared to make a very radical kind of judgment on the somnolence that pervades his native land. Or one thinks, say, of that holy fool, Haze Motes, the young preacher of the Church Without Christ in Flannery O'Connor's *Wise Blood*, who proclaims the gospel of "no truth behind all truths." This self-ordained back-woods evangelist of an hysterical nihilism lives in darkness: yet, amidst this darkness, he is a "pinpoint of light," whose grotesque extremism of speech and behavior provides a deeply ironical meas-ure of what is really heretical in the smug Philistinism represented by both the conventional heretics and the conventional believers. One also feels a similarly tough and serious realism in quite a dif-ferent kind of book, in William Styron's brilliant novel of 1960, *Set This House on Fire*, which, through its torrid story of lust and violence and despair in an Italian village on the Mediterranean coast, seems to move toward some large metaphor on the nature of man's dispeace and how his house, afire "with agues and palsies . . . with fevers . . . and heavy apprehensions," may be put in order.

But though such observations as these may be made by way

of partially extenuating Mr. Cowley's case, the main thrust of his charge remains essentially sound. For when one thinks of such representative works of the last few years as Truman Capote's *Other Voices, Other Rooms* (1948), Carson McCullers' *The Ballad of the Sad Cafe* (1951), Jean Stafford's *The Catherine Wheel* (1952), Howard Nemerov's *Federigo, Or, The Power of Love* (1954), James Purdy's *Malcolm* (1959), John Updike's *Rabbit, Run* (1960), and J. D. Salinger's *Franny and Zooey* (1961), then it does become apparent that, despite their technical brilliance and moral seriousness, they are all, in one way or another, committed to the registration of the tremors of the self's experience of its own inwardness in an adverse world. And this is a bias, as Mr. Cowley has contended, that deeply inhibits the penetration of the great Bedlam of history that literature risks when it is in full possession of its proper health and courage.

Now it may well be just this confinement to the narrow enclave of the self that makes for the peculiar irony represented by recent American fiction—namely, the irony that a literature committed above all else to the self has yet only very rarely produced any memorable characters. Salinger's Holden Caulfield and Bellow's Augie March, to be sure, have become a part of the furniture of our imaginations—but of how many other characters in American fiction of the postwar period could this be said? Hardly, I suspect, could we make such a claim with respect to any others, with possibly one or two exceptions.

Of course, even for me to remark this fact as a fact of impoverishment is to risk having my bit of testimony utterly discounted as representing an impossibly old-fashioned kind of literary primitivism. For, as I will be told by numerous bright young men teaching literature in the universities, what matters in a novel, what really matters, is "organic development of a thematic structure of images," and the complex subtlety with which "ironies" and "tensions" are held in a poised and delicate balance. This is the dreary patois in which fiction has come to be talked about in our time, and the dominant perspective is one that encourages the supposition that so primitive a quantity as character is of no consequence. For many years, for example, it has been fashionable to patronize the late A. C. Bradley as an example of such a preoccupation with character, in his case the characters of Shakespearean tragedy,[13] as inordinately moves quite beyond the limits of all decorum. And in the very title that he gave to an essay in the early nineteen-thirties—"How Many Children Had Lady Macbeth?"[14]—

---

[13] See A. C. Bradley, *Shakespearean Tragedy* (New York, Macmillan, 1904).
[14] See L. C. Knights, *Explorations* (New York, George W. Stewart, 1947).

the English critic L. C. Knights has helped a whole generation to make Bradley and his style of criticism (despite its genuine greatness) the object of a deadly joking.

But, in this regard, we have long been engaged in a very great self-deception—as when, for example, we insist upon talking about *Bleak House* or *Germinal* or *The Portrait of a Lady* or *The Sound and Fury* exclusively in the terms of "controlling metaphor" and "thematic structure" and "symbolic action." For surely (merely to remark so elementary a fact is embarrassing) one of the great reasons for any adult mind's consenting to devote a large measure of time to reading novels (or any other form of mimetic literature) is our insatiable craving for large images of human engagement in the life of the world, and for images that have the power of increasing our own capacity for life. Nor does the Flaubert who said, *"Madame Bovary, c'est moi,"* stand as the norm of the kind of novelist into whose hands we want to put ourselves. For, when we are simple and honest, we will admit that we are most deeply drawn not to the artist whose personages are merely elements of his own personality but, rather, to him whose characters are a part of Nature and who therefore "make us feel that 'there is a world elsewhere' "[15]—that is, the world of which we are living members— and who show us something of how the human spirit goes about surviving in that world. It is a misfortune that the criticism of our own period takes so slight an interest in character, for, though Aristotle was right to remind us in the *Poetics* that character is only a means to an end, it is surely an indispensable means for effecting in us that liberating exhilaration which it is the peculiar glory of literature to accomplish when it consents to take a serious and steady interest in a Hester Prynne, an Ahab, a Huck Finn, a Jay Gatsby.

There is, I repeat, a notable irony in the fact that a literature so devoted to the self as the novel has been in America over the last two decades should be populated by so many pale and bloodless ghosts and should so generally have failed to produce any sizeable group of memorable characters—rich and full-bodied in their conduct and aspiration and eccentricity. Yet it may be that this failure is the consequence that should have been expected of the kind of retreat from the public sector that has also been a notable feature of this literature. For the self achieves definition only as it pits itself against the hard, recalcitrant stuff of social and political reality: it wins its real identity only through this kind of testing: and a fiction that is not deeply informed by knowledge of this truth

[15] John Bayley, *The Characters of Love: A Study in the Literature of Personality* (New York, Basic Books, 1960), p. 280.

is not likely to realize any profound and comprehensive images of human life.

However, the advantage that is gained when fiction finds its ballast in a solid substratum of social reality is nicely illustrated by the literature that is being produced by those young Englishmen who are exactly contemporaneous with the generation of Salinger and Buechner and Purdy and Updike. What is perhaps most immediately noticeable in the novels of this younger generation across the Atlantic is, as Irving Howe remarks, their "quick apprehension and notation of contemporary life."[16] English life since World War II has, of course, in many ways been sharply abraded by the entrance into the national polity of a new corps bent on finding "room at the top," the tribe of working-class and lower middle-class boys who were smart and who managed to win scholarships at red-brick universities and who now, having been divorced from their plebeian backgrounds, are pressing their noses against the glass and peeking in at the Establishment—and not merely peeking in but curtly demanding admittance. But these "dissentients," as Kenneth Allsop calls them, though they sullenly, and angrily, clamor for a larger slice of the pie, are also to be distinguished by the kind of dual vision that their alienated position affords. And theirs is of course often a most painful alienation: "they feel a mixture of guilt about renegading from their hereditary background and contempt for the oafish orthodoxy of their families," which means that "they are strangers to their own sort": yet, at the same time, "they are acutely conscious of lacking the arrogant composure of the ruling-class line."[17] And thus, in bringing the promise of "the top" near enough to "the new men" to arouse "great expectations" while yet holding it far enough away to frustrate ambition and desire, the Welfare State has created a knotty social scene, and one which gives the unassimilated a privileged perspective on the whole gamut of contemporary English life. This is the ruling perspective in much of the literature produced by the ablest younger novelists in England since the early fifties, and one's general impression is that the force and cogency of this literature are in large part the consequence of a responsiveness to social and political actuality that is notably lacking in recent American literature.

Nor is it at all unlikely that just here we have the chief explanation of how it has come about that there is such energy and liveliness in many of the chief personages of recent English fiction: the three young men at the center of William Cooper's *Scenes from*

---

[16] Irving Howe, "Mass Society and Post-Modern Fiction," *Partisan Review*, 26 (1959), 434.

[17] Kenneth Allsop, *The Angry Decade* (London, Peter Owen, 1958), Ch. 1, p. 19.

Provincial Life,[18] the Jim Dixon of Kingsley Amis' *Lucky Jim*, the Jake Donaghue of Iris Murdoch's *Under the Net*, the Joe Lampton of John Braine's *Room at the Top*, and the Arthur Seaton of Alan Sillitoe's *Saturday Night and Sunday Morning*, to mention only a few, are the tough, assertive, tangy figures they are because they know how things look and feel, how they are organized and what they cost, and the insolent nerve it takes to get one's proper share. In short, they live *in* the human polity, they are creatures of history, and, in them, the mettle of the self has been tried and proven in the matrix of a dynamic culture: so, as images of what is stout and vital in man, even under the pressure of partly adverse conditions, they bear the stamp of authenticity, of truth to contemporary actuality.

It may also be this same openness to the larger scene of contemporary life that gives this literature its vital roughness of grain and keeps it from achieving the kind of taut fragility of poetic form that such American books as William Goyen's *The House of Breath* and Frederick Buechner's *A Long Day's Dying* and Saul Bellow's *Seize the Day* have helped to establish as a dominant mode of our fiction. And when I speak of our fiction taking on the form of poetry, I do not mean that its movement has been in the direction of the kind of oddity that T. S. Eliot chose to praise back in the thirties when he prepared an Introduction to Djuna Barnes' *Nightwood*. On the contrary, there is very little indication of any considerable interest among the most serious American novelists today in what used to be called poetic prose. Though the rhetorical extravagances of James and Faulkner and Penn Warren seem occasionally to have had their influence, the language of this fiction is generally an unpretentious and soberly efficient instrument of exposition and narration. Its poetic character is rather an affair not so much of verbal inventiveness and audacity as of cunningly shaped analogical conceits in dramatic form, of highly selfconscious adaptations of traditional myth and ritual, of crankily nihilistic forms of joking and horseplay, of rigorous concision and stylization in the development of plot and action and character, and of a stringent exclusion of all those great masses of extraneous matter that give to the fiction of a Stendhal or a George Eliot or a Faulkner its special weight and density. One hesitates bluntly to denominate all this as simply a stratagem of evasion, as a kind of dandyism whose uncalculated purpose is to retreat from the inclement weather of our time. Indeed, as Albert Guerard suggested in one

---

[18] Mr. Cooper is somewhat older than "the angry young men," but his work belongs to their whole ethos. *Scenes from Provincial Life* (1950) was indeed the immediate forerunner of *Lucky Jim* (1954).

of the first attempts to characterize the postwar period in American fiction, it is possible for style to be "an answer to surrounding ambiguity." For, in a period when the course of history seems unalterable by the individual voice, when men are by way of being overwhelmed by the sheer gratuitousness of events, and when human life everywhere has taken on an eschatological cast, it may be "an act of resistance" for the novelist to submit "some small chosen area" to a great deal of control, since in this way at least he can "express his small human identity, the free play of his mind,"[19] and thus in effect express a kind of denial that History or Events or Civilization is all. But what needs also to be said is that, even so, this is a testimony whose muteness of style forfeits much of the masculine force and assertiveness and rhetorical power that the novel, in its most vigorous moments, has taught us to regard as a part of its peculiar genius.

In his brilliant and justly famous essay of 1948, "Art and Fortune," Lionel Trilling ventured the prediction that the novelist of the coming years would tend to forego "consciously literary," "elaborately styled" types of artistic form, and would do so in order to reclaim something of the "headlong, profuse, often careless quality of the novel" with "its bold and immediate grasp on life." "For the modern highly trained literary sensibility, form suggests completeness and the ends tucked in; resolution is seen only as all contradictions equated, and although form thus understood has its manifest charm," Mr. Trilling foresaw the novelist coming to recognize that such a notion of form "will not adequately serve the modern experience."[20] But things have, of course, not gone as Mr. Trilling predicted, and a critic of his sophistication has in all likelihood not been surprised by this fact, since his original statement was doubtless less a prediction than a recommendation of the course by which the novelist might best guarantee the future health of his form.

Yet, at our present remove of a little more than fifteen years from Mr. Trilling's prophecy, though it has not been generally fulfilled in the intervening period, it remains a good course to pin one's faith on, for the renewal of American fiction. And I am not at all convinced that the realization of this course will be furthered —indeed, I rather suspect that it will be hindered—by our granting R. W. B. Lewis the point he has made, that the ambience of the new American novelists is an irredeemably *post*-Christian dispensation.[21] Among those who like to bandy about the *recherché* catch-

---

[19] Albert J. Guerard, "The Ivory Tower and the Dust Bowl," in *New World Writing.* 3 (New York, New American Library, 1953), 348.

[20] Trilling, *The Liberal Imagination*, pp. 278, 272–73.

[21] Lewis, "American Letters," p. 224.

words of the moment, there is surely far too much loose talk these days about ours having become a post-Christian world: it is a piece of verbiage that, in a curious way, has suddenly become very modish and pleasurable, but its relevance to religious and cultural actuality is something extremely difficult to specify with precision. And though a thinker of Mr. Lewis's brilliance is not given to loose talk, it is just his customary acuteness that makes us expect him to exert a more critical pressure on the literary imagination in America at the present time.

When one recalls the disintegrated world of Norman Mailer's *Barbary Shore,* John Clellon Holmes' *Go,* Edward Loomis' *The Charcoal Horse,* William Styron's *Set This House on Fire,* and John Updike's *Rabbit, Run*—when one recalls such books as these, in which "the rebellious imperative of the self" is the single and sovereign principle, there can, of course, be no question but that our younger novelists are prepared, many of them, to settle for allegiances which, if not post-Christian, are at least far removed from the full Christian sense of reality in any of its classic versions. But what needs to be noticed is that this alienation from anything resembling the traditional Christian soulscape has carried a very great cost. St. Teresa says, "I require of you only to look." Only to *look.* And this has traditionally been the genius of Incarnational faith when it has been in full possession of its sacramental vision —to empower men to *face,* without flinching, the arduous welter of nature and historical existence, since, frail though the flesh may be, it was proven by the Incarnation to be stout enough for the tabernacling of that than which nothing is more ultimate—namely, God Himself. But when such a faith is in abeyance, when nature and history, and the flesh and the world have lost the profound import that such a faith gives them, then, should the weathers of the historical climate seem inclement or menacing, it will be difficult to avoid such a conclusion as that which is reached by Philip Roth, the gifted young author of *Goodby, Columbus* and *Letting Go,* who has said in *Commentary* that the novelist cannot "make credible much of American reality" today since "it stupefies, it sickens, it infuriates, and finally it is even a kind of embarrassment to one's own meager imagination." In other words, without something at least analogous to the sacramental vision of reality that is created for Christianity by its doctrine of Creation and of the Incarnation—without something at least analogous to this—the likelihood is that, when faced by entangled and unpromising circumstances of life, the writer may be able to manage nothing better than a querulous retreat into the privacies of the isolate self: the kind of querulousness that is expressed by James Baldwin when he says that "there is no structure in American life today and there are no human beings," or that John Cheever, the author of *The Wapshot Chronicle*, expresses when he complains that "life in the United States . . . is hell."

But querulousness is a most unfruitful basis for literature, and most especially for the novel: so I suggest that we had better not be in too much of a hurry to agree with the new generation in American letters when it is inclined to assign itself to some not-so-brave new world that is believed to be "post-Christian." Nothing, of course, could be more futile than the kind of debate that sometimes goes on amongst churchmen as to how, in programmatic terms, the literary imagination in our time may be "rebaptized": for such a work is a work for the Holy Spirit, and the Spirit bloweth where it listeth. But, strange and unmanageable as its workings may sometimes be, at least we can pray for rain.

JULIAN MAYFIELD

1928-

Julian Mayfield, born in Greer, South Carolina, was reared there and in Washington, D.C., where his family migrated when he was ten. After finishing high school, he enlisted in the army, served in the Pacific area, then returned to study at Lincoln University in Pennsylvania. He worked as dishwasher, taxi driver, shipping clerk, house painter, radio announcer, and newspaperman before he could pursue his chosen career. In Africa and Europe, as well as at home, Mayfield has become known as a novelist, essayist, and editor. His theatrical work has consisted of reviewing; writing, producing, and directing plays for presentation in Harlem and off-Broadway; and acting (he created the feature role of the son Absalom in the Broadway play, *Lost in the Stars*). The husband of a physician and the father of two boys, Mayfield recently returned to America after several years in Africa and Europe. He has been collaborating on a book on Ghana, and has been working on a fourth novel while engaged as a teaching fellow at Cornell University.

In addition to editorial and critical work on the staffs of the *Puerto Rico World Journal* and the *African Review* in Accra, Mayfield has published such typical political essays as "Challenge to Negro Leadership" (in *Commentary*) and "Love Affair with the United States" (in *The New Republic*), as well as articles in *The Nation* and other periodicals. His novels (*The Hit*, 1957; *The Long Night*, 1958; and *The Grand Parade*, 1961), which have been variously translated into French, German, Czech, and Japanese, develop his most urgent perceptions of the difficulties, and solaces too, of his race in America, usually combining the humor and anguish common to both the Harlem of his first novel and the fictional Gainesboro of his third.

"Into the Mainstream and Oblivion," published next to Arthur P. Davis's contrasting essay, "Integration and Race Literature," in the American Society of African Culture's booklet entitled *The American Negro Writer and His Roots* (1960), anticipates a decade of insistence by American black men that the varied preciousness of their group identity be publicly recognized and turned into racial profit. The literary equivalent of this demand is not closely argued by Mayfield; but his antiwar theme is prophetically joined to other demurrals on behalf of the Negro writer who "sings the national anthem *sotto voce* and has trouble reconciling the 'dream' to the reality he knows."

Into the Mainstream and Oblivion

RECENTLY AN AFRICAN STUDENT, long resident in this country, confessed to a group of his intimates that he did not trust the American Negro. "What will you do," he asked them, "in the unlikely event that the United States becomes involved in a colonial war in Africa?" The immediate answer was: "Man, we will shoot you down like dogs." The remark prompted general laughter, but, on reflection, it is not amusing.

The visiting student had sensed what his friends already took for granted: that the contemporary American Negro is faced with a most perplexing dilemma. He does not know who he is or where his loyalties belong. Moreover, he has every right to his confusion for he exists on a moving plateau that is rapidly shifting away from the candid oppression of the past toward—what? The future of the American Negro is most often depicted as an increasingly accelerated absorption into the mainstream of American life where, presumably, he will find happiness as a first-class citizen. This is perhaps the rosy view, but it already has validity insofar as it represents the attitude and aspiration of a majority of Negroes, especially those who are called leaders.

Unfortunately—and one cannot see how it could have been otherwise—the Negro writer has been unable to escape this confusion. The AMSAC writers' conference demonstrated that the Negro writer is having trouble squaring his art and his sense of reality with the American dream. He, too, finds himself wondering who he is, an American or what? And if finally the scholars convince him that he is indeed an American, he asks if this condition must be the extent of his vision. He is all too aware that in recent years a myth that was once accepted without question has shown signs of being discredited. This myth implied that if one could become a real American, he had achieved the best that world could offer.

The conference panel on social protest was especially interesting in regard to the advisability of the Negro's embracing the white American's literary values in exchange for those of his own that he now finds outmoded. Many of the speakers felt that social protest as we have known it, had outlived its usefulness. They

Reprinted from *The American Negro Writer and His Roots* (New York: American Society of African Culture, 1960), pp. 29–34.

knew, of course, that racial injustice still flourishes in our national life, but they felt that the moral climate has been established for the eventual breakdown of racism, and that they need not therefore employ their literary tools to attack it in the same old way, that is to say, directly and violently. To this participant it seemed that the younger writer was seeking a new way of defining himself. Grudgingly he admitted that his work in the past may have suffered artistically because of his preoccupation with the problem of being a Negro in the United States. Yet he seemed reluctant to leap head first into the nation's literary mainstream (a word that was heard repeatedly throughout the conference).

In this I believe the writers were being wiser than most of our church, civic, and political leaders, who are pushing with singular concentration toward one objective: integration. This is to be applauded and actively encouraged so long as integration is interpreted to mean the attainment of full citizenship rights in such areas as voting, housing, education, employment, and the like. But if, as the writers have reason to suspect, integration means completely identifying the Negro with the American image—that great-power face that the world knows and the Negro knows better —then the writer must not be judged too harshly for balking at the prospect.

Perhaps some of them had seen a recent film called *The Defiant Ones*, which attracted world-wide attention because of its graphic, symbolic depiction of American Negro-white relations. In the film a black convict and a white convict are chained to one another in a desperate bid for freedom. Each hates the other intensely, but both soon realize that if they are to find freedom they must cooperate for their mutual good. By the time their actual chains are removed, they have come to believe that they are bound together in a larger way—that their fates, their destinies, are intertwined—so much so that in the end, most remarkably (and, one hopes, not prophetically) the Negro foregoes his chance for freedom because his white comrade is too weak to escape.

The symbolism is obvious and, to one observer at least, disturbing in its implications. For it is not uncommon to hear nowadays that the American Negro and the white are forever bound together and must, perforce, pursue a common destiny. On the face of it this approach seems soundly based on common sense. Throughout his long, cruel history in this land, the Negro has been the most avid seeker of the American dream—most avid because for him its realization was often a matter of life and death. If he could but grasp the dream, he could walk in dignity without fear of the abuse heaped on him by a scornful white majority. So fervid has been his pursuit of the dream that in every war and regardless of the nature of the war, his leaders have offered up his sons, the strength of any race, saying, "Take our youth—take our youth and they will prove their worth as Americans."

But the dream has proved elusive, and there is reason to believe that for the Negro it never had a chance of realization. Now, because of a combination of international and domestic pressures, a social climate is being created wherein, at least in theory, he may win the trappings of freedom that other citizens already take for granted. One may suggest that during this period of transition the Negro would do well to consider if the best use of these trappings will be to align himself totally to the objectives of the dominant sections of the American nation. Just as an insurance company will not issue a policy without determining the life expectancy of the buyer, neither should the Negro—in this case the buyer—accept the policy before he determines if the company is solvent. If the dream he has chased for three centuries is now dying even for white Americans, he would be wise to consider alternative objectives. The urgency of our times demands a deeper and more critical approach from Negro leadership. This new approach is suggested by the Negro mother who, having lost one of her sons in the Korean adventures, was heard to remark: "I don't care if the army is integrated; next time I want to know what kind of war my boy is being taken to."

In the same sense the Negro writer is being gently nudged toward a rather vague thing called "the mainstream of American literature." This trend also would seem to be based on common sense. But before plunging into it he owes it to the future of his art to analyze the contents of the American mainstream to determine the full significance of his commitment to it. He may decide that, though the music is sweet, he would rather play in another orchestra. Or, to place himself in the position of the black convict in *The Defiant Ones*, he may decide that he need not necessarily share the fate of his white companion who, after all, proffers the hand of friendship a little late. The Negro writer may conclude that his best salvation lies in escaping the narrow national orbit—artistic, cultural and political—and soaring into the space of more universal experience.

What are the principal characteristics of the mainstream of American literature? To this observer they are apathy and either a reluctance or a fear of writing about anything that matters. William Barrett in *The New York Times* (May 10, 1959) asserts that power, vitality and energy have been abundant in recent American writing, but concedes that "the writers have lacked a center somewhere, they have been without great and central themes."

The phenomenon of our era is the seeming lack of concern shown by American creative writers for the great questions facing the peoples of the world. The most important of these, and the most obvious, is the madness of war. There are other great issues that challenge us, but the American writer has turned his back on them. He deals with the foibles of suburban living, the junior executive, dope addiction, homosexuality, incest and divorce.

I am not suggesting that anyone (least of all the present writer) should sit down with the grand purpose of writing a novel against war. But I do mean to imply that writers of the mainstream, reflecting the attitude of the American people generally, seem determined not to become involved in any of the genuine fury, turmoil, and passion of life; and it is only such involvement that makes life worth living. Where, for instance, is the humor that once characterized our national literature, and what has happened to the American's ability, indeed his proclivity, to laugh at himself? A stultifying respectability hangs over the land, and that is always a sign of decline, for it inhibits the flowering of new ideas that lead to progress and cultural regeneration. In short, the literary mainstream seems to be running dangerously shallow.

It would be pleasant to report that Negro writers have been unaffected by the current literary atmosphere, but it would not be candid. If the AMSAC conference demonstrated any one thing, it was that Negro writers generally are uncertain about the path they should explore in seeking to illuminate the life of man. I say "generally," for the individual writer charts his own course and follows or changes it at will. But it is interesting that there was evident so little unity of approach. One would have thought that Negro writers, representing a tragic and unique experience in our national history, would be bound together by a dominant theme in their work. But if this is the case, it was not obvious at the conference, and such a theme is difficult to detect in recent novels and plays.

The advantage of the Negro writer, the factor that may keep his work above the vacuity of the American mainstream, is that for him the façade of the American way of life is always transparent. He sings the national anthem *sotto voce* and has trouble reconciling the "dream" to the reality he knows. If he feels American at all, it is only when he is on foreign soil and, peculiarly enough, often finds himself defending that which he hated at home. He walks the streets of his nation an alien, and yet he feels no bond to the continent of his ancestors. He is indeed the man without a country. And yet this very detachment may give him the insight of the stranger in the house, placing him in a better position to illuminate contemporary American life as few writers of the mainstream can. This alienation should serve also to make him more sensitive to philosophical and artistic influences that originate beyond our national cultural boundaries.

Finally, if the situation I have described is real, a tragic future is indicated for the American Negro people. Unlike most of the colored peoples of the earth, he has no land and cannot realistically aspire to supremacy in the environment that has been his home for three centuries. In his most optimistic moods—and this period is one of them—the best he can hope for is submersion in what is euphemistically called the American melting pot. Despite the vigorous efforts of Negro leaders and the international pressures on the United States, it seems unlikely that this submersion will occur to any large degree within the foreseeable future. The likelihood is that the Negro people will continue for several decades to occupy, to a diminishing degree, the position of the unwanted child who, having been brought for a visit, must remain for the rest of his life. This is a hard conclusion to draw, but if it has validity, it is better recognized than ignored.

BIBLIOGRAPHY

BIBLIOGRAPHY

The Study of Negro Literature in America

The professional study of Negro literature in America has scarcely begun. Authoritative editions of works now unavailable need to be reprinted; reliable biographies and comprehensive, annotated bibliographies should be prepared; memoirs, letters, and documents of cultural interest need to be edited and published.

In the preparation of *Dark Symphony: Negro Literature in America*, the authors have investigated a vast body of scholarship concerned with Negro culture; indeed another volume would be necessary to suggest the full scope of this growing field. The following information can only be selective, but it will orient the reader and permit him to pursue his interests in Negro literature.

Repositories

In addition to those listed here, other important holdings, too numerous and extensive to describe, may be found at the following institutions: Hampton Institute; Hall Branch of the Chicago Public Library; Library of Congress; The Historical Society of Pennsylvania; Bucknell Library of Crozier Theological Seminary; The New York Public Library (main branch); The New York Historical Society; The Western Reserve Historical Society; and Oberlin College.

ATLANTA UNIVERSITY (Atlanta, Georgia)*

The Trevor-Arnett Library has a Negro Collection with about 17,000 items, about 4,000 of which are manuscript items. The Countee Cullen Memorial Collection, established in 1942, has about 1,300 manuscripts. The Slaughter Collection, purchased in 1946, has about 1,000 manuscripts.

BOSTON PUBLIC LIBRARY (Boston, Massachusetts)*

Because of gifts of the libraries of William Lloyd Garrison, Wendell Phillips, and Benjamin Pierce Hunt, the library has much manuscript material on the abolitionist movement, extending to England, the Continent, and the West Indies.

BOSTON UNIVERSITY (Boston, Massachusetts)*

The library has the papers of outstanding contemporary Negroes, including the Reverend Martin Luther King; P. D. East; Allen Knight Chalmers (clergyman); John Oliver Killens; Tey Richard Kennedy; Frank Yerby; General Manning Force (with Gov. Humphrey of Mississippi during the Civil War).

The library has been promised the papers of the following men and women: James Farmer, Thurgood Marshall, Sammy Davis, Jr., Leontyne Price.

COLUMBIA UNIVERSITY (New York, N.Y.)

Columbia University's Alexander Gumby Collection, in Special Collections Reading Room, 654 Butler Library. This Collection has

---

* For data on starred repositories, the authors are indebted to Lorenzo J. Green's articles in the March and October 1967 numbers of *Negro History Bulletin*.

clippings and miscellaneous items mounted in scrapbooks arranged in subject groupings.

FISK UNIVERSITY (Nashville, Tennessee)

One of the strongest repositories for the study of the Negro in the South, the library has a Negroana Collection.

HOWARD UNIVERSITY (Washington, D.C.)

The Moorland Foundation has over 10,000 items, including valuable Tappan, Grimké, and Joel Spingarn papers.

The Arthur B. Spingarn Collection of Negro Authors has over 5,000 items, including books, pamphlets, magazines, newspapers, and ephemeral pieces (programs, announcements, circulars, etc.). With the addition of the Spingarn Collection, Howard's Negro Collection contains more than 30,000 items.

HENRY E. HUNTINGTON LIBRARY AND ART GALLERY

(San Marino, California)
The library has many manuscripts, especially concerning the antebellum period, 1800–1860.

THE ARTHUR SCHOMBURG COLLECTION OF NEGRO LITERATURE AND HISTORY (a branch of the New York Public Library, at 135th Street and Lenox Avenue, New York)

"This is a reference and research library devoted to Negro life and history and is considered one of the most important centers in the world for the study of the Negro. International in scope, it covers every phase of Negro activity, wherever Negroes have lived, and its materials range from early rarities to current happenings and from Mississippi to Timbuctoo. The nucleus of the collection is the private library assembled by Arthur A. Schomburg, a Puerto Rican of African descent. In 1926, the Carnegie Corporation of New York purchased Schomburg's collection from him and presented it to the New York Public Library. Today its materials have been expanded and it serves as a major resource to those seeking documentation about the Negro, his past, and present activities." (This description is taken from the Schomburg Collection brochure.)

The Library has large holdings (more than 11,000 books,

3,000 manuscripts, and 2,000 prints) for the Negro in the West Indies and Africa as well as the United States.

WILBERFORCE UNIVERSITY (Wilberforce, Ohio)*

The library has different holdings, such as the papers of Levi Jenkins Coppin, Clarence Harvey Mills, Bishop Daniel A. Payne, Reverdy Cassius Ransom. More important to literary researchers may be the papers of William Sanders Scarborough (936 items, including typescripts, manuscripts, and letters).

YALE UNIVERSITY (New Haven, Connecticut)

The James Weldon Johnson Memorial Collection of Negro Arts and Letters, established on January 7, 1950, owes its importance to materials left by Carl Van Vechten. Included in the Collection are manuscripts, typescripts, letters, photographs, and autographed copies of works of American Negroes of the 1920's, 1930's, and 1940's.

Yale University also has the Ulrich B. Phillips library.

Magazines

CLA JOURNAL (of The College Language Association). Morgan State College, Baltimore, Maryland 21212.

THE CRISIS. National Association for the Advancement of Colored People, 1790 Broadway, New York, New York 10019.

EBONY. 1820 South Michigan Avenue, Chicago, Illinois 60616.

FREEDOMWAYS, A Quarterly Review of the Negro Freedom Movement. 799 Broadway, New York, New York 10003.

THE JOURNAL OF NEGRO EDUCATION. Howard University, Washington, D.C. 20001.

THE JOURNAL OF NEGRO HISTORY. The Association for the Study of Negro Life and History, 1538 Ninth Street, N.W., Washington, D.C. 20001.

NEGRO DIGEST. 1820 South Michigan Avenue, Chicago, Illinois 60616.

NEGRO HISTORY BULLETIN. 1538 Ninth Street, N.W., Washington, D.C. 20001.

OPPORTUNITY, JOURNAL OF NEGRO LIFE. 1923–1949. National Urban League, 1133 Broadway, New York or 14 East 48th Street, New York, New York 10017.

PHYLON. The Atlanta University Review of Race and Culture. Atlanta University, 223 Chestnut Street, S.W., Atlanta, Georgia 30314.

Reference Works

BARDOLPH, RICHARD. "Essay on Authorities" in *The Negro Vanguard*. New York: Rinehart, Inc., 1959. Vintage Books reprint, 1961.

Bibliographic Survey: The Negro in Print. Washington, D.C.: The Negro Bibliographic and Research Center, Inc., Volumes I–III, 1965–1968.

MILLER, ELIZABETH W. (compiler for The American Academy of Arts and Sciences). *The Negro in America: A Bibliography*. Cambridge, Mass.: Harvard University Press, 1966.

The Negro in the United States: A List of Significant Books, 9th ed. revised. New York: New York Public Library, 1965.

PORTER, DOROTHY B. *North American Negro Poets: A Bibliographical Check List of Their Writings (1760–1944)*. Hattiesburg, Miss.: The Book Farm, 1945. Reprinted, New York: Burt Franklin, 1963.

WELSCH, ERWIN K. *The Negro in the United States: A Research Guide*. Bloomington: Indiana University Press, 1965.

WHITEMAN, MAXWELL. *A Century of Fiction by American Negroes, 1853–1952*. Philadelphia: Saifer, 1955.

Background Works

BOND, FREDERICK W. *The Negro and the Drama.* Washington, D.C.: Associated Publishers, 1940.

BONE, ROBERT A. *The Negro Novel in America.* New Haven: Yale University Press, 1958. Revised edition, 1966.

BRAITHWAITE, WILLIAM S. "The Negro in Literature," *Crisis,* XXVIII (September, 1924), 204–10.

BRAWLEY, BENJAMIN. "The Negro in Fiction," *Dial,* LX (May 11, 1916), 445–50.

———. *The Negro Genius.* New York: Dodd, Mead & Co., 1937.

———. *The Negro in Literature and Art.* New York: Duffield and Company, 1929.

———. *A Short History of the American Negro.* New York: The Macmillan Co., 1931.

———. *A Social History of the American Negro.* New York: The Macmillan Co., 1921.

BUTCHER, MARGARET JUST. *The Negro in American Culture* (based on materials left by Alain Locke). New York: Alfred A. Knopf, Inc., 1956.

CHARTERS, SAMUEL B. *The Country Blues.* New York: Holt, Rinehart and Winston, 1959.

DOVER, CEDRIC. *American Negro Art.* 2nd ed. Greenwich, Conn.: New York Graphic Society, 1962.

DREER, HERMAN. *American Literature by Negro Authors.* New York: The Macmillan Co., 1950.

FRANKLIN, JOHN HOPE. *From Slavery to Freedom: A History of American Negroes.* 3rd ed., rev. and enl. New York: Alfred Knopf, Inc., 1967.

FRAZIER, E. FRANKLIN. *Black Bourgeoisie.* Glencoe, Ill.: The Free Press, 1957. Collier paperback, 1962.

———. *The Negro Church in America.* New York: Schocken Books, 1964.

———. *The Negro Family in the United States.* Chicago: The University of Chicago Press, 1939.

———. *The Negro in the United States*. Rev. ed. New York: The Macmillan Co., 1957.

GLICKSBERG, CHARLES. "The Alienation of Negro Literature," *Phylon*, XI (First Quarter, 1950), 49–58.

———. "Bias, Fiction, and the Negro," *Phylon*, XIII (Second Quarter, 1952), 127–35.

———. "The Furies in Negro Fiction," *Western Review*, XIII (Winter, 1949), 107–114.

———. "The God of Fiction," *Colorado Quarterly*, VII (Autumn, 1958), 207–220.

———. "Negro Fiction in America," *South Atlantic Quarterly*, XLV (October, 1946), 477–88.

GLOSTER, HUGH M. *Negro Voices in American Fiction*. Chapel Hill: The University of North Carolina Press, 1948. Reprinted in 1965.

HUGHES, CARL MILTON. *The Negro Novelist*. New York: Citadel, 1953.

ISAACS, EDITH. *The Negro in the American Theatre*. New York: Theatre Arts Books, 1947.

JOHNSON, CHARLES S. *The Negro in American Civilization*. New York: Henry Holt and Co., 1930.

LASH, JOHN S. "The American Negro in American Literature," *Journal of Negro Education*, XV (Fall, 1946), 722–30.

LITTLEJOHN, DAVID. *Black on White: A Critical Survey of Writing by American Negroes*. New York: Grossman, 1966.

LOGAN, RAYFORD W. *The Negro in American Life and Thought: The Nadir, 1877–1901*. New York: Dial Press, 1954. 2nd edition: *The Betrayal of the Negro: From Rutherford B. Hayes to Woodrow Wilson*. New York: Collier Books, 1965.

———. *The Negro in the United States*. Princeton: D. Van Nostrand Company, Inc., 1957.

LOGGINS, VERNON. *The Negro Author: His Development in America to 1900*. New York: Columbia University Press, 1931. Reprinted: Port Washington, New York: Kennikat Press, 1964.

MAYS, BENJAMIN. *The Negro's God, as Reflected in His Literature*. Boston: Chapman and Grimes, 1938.

MEIER, AUGUST. *Negro Thought in America, 1880–1915.* Ann Arbor: University of Michigan Press, 1963.

MYRDAL, GUNNAR. *An American Dilemma.* Rev. ed. New York: Harper and Row, 1962.

NELSON, JOHN H. *The Negro Character in American Literature.* Lawrence, Kansas: University of Kansas Press, 1926.

REDDING, J. SAUNDERS. "American Negro Literature," *American Scholar*, XVIII (Spring, 1949), 137–48.

———. *The Lonesome Road: The Story of the Negro's Part in America.* Garden City: Doubleday, 1958.

———. *On Being Negro in America.* Indianapolis: The Bobbs-Merrill Co., Inc., 1951.

———. "The Negro Writer and His Relationship to His Roots," *The American Negro Writer and His Roots.* New York: American Society of African Culture, 1960. Pp. 1–8.

———. *They Came in Chains.* Philadelphia: J. P. Lippincott, 1950.

———. *To Make a Poet Black.* Chapel Hill: The University of North Carolina Press, 1939.

STAMPP, KENNETH M. *The Peculiar Institution.* New York: Alfred Knopf, Inc., 1956. Vintage Books reprint, V253 [n.d.].

WATKINS, SYLVESTER C., ed. *Anthology of American Negro Literature.* New York: The Modern Library, 1944.

WOODSON, CARTER GODWIN and CHARLES H. WESLEY. *The Negro in Our History.* 10th rev. ed. Washington, D.C.: The Associated Publishers, 1962.

Early Literature

GENERAL

DAMON, S. FOSTER. "The Negro in Early American Songsters," *Papers of the Bibliographical Society of America*, XXVIII (1934), 132–63.

GAINES, FRANCIS PENDELTON. *The Southern Plantation.* New York: The Columbia University Press, 1924.

GROSS, THEODORE L. "The Negro in the Literature of the Reconstruction," *Phylon*, XXII (First Quarter, 1961), 5–14. Reprinted in *Images of the Negro in American Literature*, ed. Seymour L. Gross and John Edward Hardy. Chicago: The University of Chicago Press, pp. 71–84.

GREENE, LORENZO J. *The Negro in Colonial New England, 1620–1776.* New York: Columbia University Press, 1942.

MC DOWELL, TREMAINE. "The Negro in the Southern Novel Prior to 1850," *Journal of English and Germanic Philology*, XXV (October, 1926), 455–73. Reprinted in *Images of the Negro in American Literature*, pp. 54–70.

NICHOLS, CHARLES H., JR. "Slave Narratives and the Plantation Legend," *Phylon*, X (Third Quarter, 1949), 201–10.

PATTERSON, CECIL L. "A Different Drum: The Image of the Negro in the Nineteenth Century Songster," *CLA Journal*, VIII (September, 1964), 44–50.

SIMMS, H. H. "A Critical Analysis of Abolition Literature, 1830–1840," *Journal of Southern History*, VI (August, 1940), 368–82.

WILSON, EDMUND. *Patriotic Gore.* New York: Oxford University Press, 1962.

ZANGER, JULES. "The 'Tragic Octoroon' in Pre-Civil War Fiction," *American Quarterly*, XVIII (Spring, 1966), 63–70.

INDIVIDUAL AUTHORS

FREDERICK DOUGLASS

PRIMARY SOURCES*

Narrative of the Life of Frederick Douglass. Edited by Benjamin Quarles, from the 1845 *Narrative*. Cambridge: Belknap Press, 1960.

Life and Times of Frederick Douglass. Rev. & enl. from *My Bondage and My Freedom* (1855). Boston: DeWolfe, Fiske, and Co., 1892. New York: Pathway Press, 1941. New York: Collier Books, 1962.

SECONDARY SOURCES

APTHEKER, HERBERT. "DuBois on Douglass: 1895," *Journal of Negro History*, XLIX (October, 1964), 264–68.

* The works of the individual authors are listed chronologically.

BENNETT, LERONE, JR. "Frederick Douglass: Father of the Protest Movement," *Ebony*, XVIII (September, 1963), 50–52.

BOROMÉ, JOSEPH A. "Some Additional Light on Frederick Douglass," *Journal of Negro History*, XXXVIII (April, 1953), 216–24.

CHESNUTT, CHARLES W. *Frederick Douglass*. Boston: Small, Maynard and Co., 1899.

FONER, PHILIP S. *Frederick Douglass*. New York: Citadel Press, 1964.

GRAHAM, SHIRLEY. *There Was Once a Slave: The Heroic Story of Frederick Douglass*. New York: Julian Messner, Inc., 1947.

QUARLES, BENJAMIN. *Frederick Douglass*. Washington: The Associated Publishers, Inc., 1948.

————. "Frederick Douglass: American Fighter for Freedom," *UNESCO Courier*, XV (February, 1962), 12–14.

SHEPPERSON, G. "Frederick Douglass and Scotland," *Journal of Negro History*, XXXVIII (July, 1953), 307–21.

CHARLES W. CHESNUTT

PRIMARY SOURCES

The Conjure Woman. Boston: Houghton, Mifflin and Co., 1899.

The Wife of His Youth and Other Stories of the Color Line. Boston: Houghton, Mifflin and Co., 1899.

The House Behind the Cedars. Boston: Houghton, Mifflin and Co., 1900.

The Marrow of Tradition. Boston: Houghton, Mifflin and Co., 1901.

The Colonel's Dream. New York: Doubleday, Page and Co., 1905.

SECONDARY SOURCES

AMES, RUSSELL. "Social Realism in Charles Chesnutt," *Phylon*, XIV (June, 1953), 199–206.

CHESNUTT, HELEN M. *Charles Waddell Chesnutt: Pioneer of the Color Line*. Chapel Hill: University of North Carolina Press, 1952.

GLOSTER, HUGH M. "Charles W. Chesnutt: Pioneer in the Fiction of Negro Life," *Phylon*, II (First Quarter, 1941), 57–66.

HUGLEY, G. "Charles Waddell Chesnutt," *Negro History Bulletin,* XIX (December, 1955), 54–55.

SILLEN, SAMUEL. "Charles W. Chesnutt: A Pioneer Negro Novelist," *Masses and Mainstream,* VI (February, 1953), 8–14.

SMITH, ROBERT A. "A Note on the Folktales of Charles Chesnutt," *CLA Journal,* V (March, 1962), 229–32.

PAUL LAURENCE DUNBAR

PRIMARY SOURCES

The Strength of Gideon and Other Stories. New York: Dodd, Mead, and Co., 1900.

The Sport of the Gods. New York: Dodd, Mead, and Co., 1902.

In Old Plantation Days. New York: Dodd, Mead, and Co., 1903.

The Heart of Happy Hollow. New York: Dodd, Mead, and Co., 1904.

The Complete Poems of Paul Laurence Dunbar. New York: Dodd, Mead, and Co., 1940.

SECONDARY SOURCES

ARNOLD, EDWARD F. "Some Personal Reminiscences of Paul Laurence Dunbar," *Journal of Negro History,* XVII (October, 1932), 400–408.

BRAWLEY, BENJAMIN. *Paul Laurence Dunbar: Poet of His People.* Chapel Hill: University of North Carolina Press, 1936.

BURCH, CHARLES E. "The Plantation Negro in Dunbar's Poetry," *Southern Workman,* L (October, 1921), 469–73.

BUTCHER, PHILIP. "Mutual Appreciation: Dunbar and Cable," *CLA Journal,* I (March, 1958), 101–2.

CUNNINGHAM, VIRGINIA. *Paul Laurence Dunbar and His Song.* New York: Dodd, Mead, and Co., 1947.

DANIEL, T. W. "Paul Laurence Dunbar and the Democratic Ideal," *Negro History Bulletin,* VI (June, 1943), 206–8.

DUNBAR, ALICE M. *et al. Paul Laurence Dunbar: Poet Laureate of the Negro Race.* Philadelphia: A.M.E. Church Review, 1914.

LAWSON, VICTOR. *Dunbar Critically Examined.* Washington: The Associated Publishers, Inc., 1941.

TURNER, DARWIN. "Paul Laurence Dunbar: The Rejected Symbol," *Journal of Negro History,* LII (January, 1967), 1–13.

W. E. B. DUBOIS

PRIMARY SOURCES

The Philadelphia Negro: A Social Study. Philadelphia: University of Pennsylvania Press, 1899. New York: B. Blom, 1967. New York: Schocken Books, Inc., 1967.

The Souls of Black Folk: Essays and Sketches. Chicago: A. C. McClurg and Co., 1903. New York: Fawcett World Library, 1961.

The Quest of the Silver Fleece. Chicago: A. C. McClurg and Co., 1911.

Darkwater: The Twentieth Century Completion of Uncle Tom's Cabin. Washington: A. Jenkins Co., 1920. New York: Harcourt, Brace and Howe (with subtitle *Voices from Within the Veil*), 1930.

Dark Princess. New York: Harcourt, Brace and Co., 1928.

Black Reconstruction in America, 1860–1880. New York: Harcourt, Brace and Co., 1935.

Black Folk, Then and Now: An Essay in the History and Sociology of the Negro Race. New York: Henry Holt and Co., 1939.

Dusk of Dawn: An Essay Toward an Autobiography of a Race Concept. New York: Harcourt, Brace and Co., 1940. New York: Schocken Books, Inc., 1968.

The Black Flame—A Trilogy: The Ordeal of Mansart, Mansart Builds a School, and *Worlds of Color.* New York: Mainstream Publishers, 1957, 1959, 1961.

The Autobiography of W. E. B. DuBois: A Soliloquy on Viewing My Life from the Last Decade of Its First Century. Edited by Herbert Aptheker. New York: International Publishers Co., 1968.

SECONDARY SOURCES

APTHEKER, HERBERT. "Some Unpublished Writings of W. E. B. DuBois," *Freedomways,* V, No. 1 (Winter, 1965), 103–28. [W. E. B. DuBois Memorial Issue, hereafter called *FDMI.*]

BOND, HORACE MANN *et al.* "The Legacy of W. E. B. DuBois," *FDMI,* 16–40.

BRODERICK, FRANCIS L. *W. E. B. DuBois, Negro Leader in a Time of Crisis.* Stanford: Stanford University Press, 1959.

CHAFFEE, M. L. "William E. B. DuBois' Concept of the Racial Problem in the United States," *Journal of Negro History,* XLI (July, 1956), 241–58.

DUBERMAN, M. "DuBois as Prophet," *New Republic,* CLVIII (March 23, 1968), 36–39.

FINKELSTEIN, SIDNEY. "W. E. B. DuBois' Trilogy: A Literary Triumph," *Mainstream,* XIV (1961), 6–17.

HANSBERRY, WILLIAM LEE. "W. E. B. DuBois' Influence on African History," *FDMI,* 73–87.

HOLMES, EUGENE C. "W. E. B. DuBois—Philosopher," *FDMI,* 41–46.

HOWE, IRVING. "Remarkable Man, Ambiguous Legacy," *Harper's Magazine,* CCXXXVI (March, 1968), 143–49.

KAISER, ERNEST. "A Selected Bibliography of the Published Writings of W. E. B. DuBois," *FDMI,* 207–213.

KING, MARTIN LUTHER, JR. "Honoring Dr. DuBois," *Freedomways,* VIII, No. 2 (Spring, 1968), 104–111.

MOORE, RICHARD B. "DuBois and Pan Africa," *FDMI,* 166–87.

RUDWICK, ELLIOTT M. *W. E. B. DuBois: A Study in Minority Group Leadership.* Philadelphia: University of Pennsylvania Press, 1961.

———. "W. E. B. DuBois in the Role of *Crisis* Editor," *Journal of Negro History,* XLIII (July, 1958), 214–40.

ROWAN, CARL T. "Heart of a Passionate Dilemma." *Saturday Review,* XLII (August 1, 1959), 20–21.

"Selected Poems of W. E. B. DuBois," *FDMI,* 88–102.

THORPE, E. E. "W. E. B. DuBois and Booker T. Washington," *Negro History Bulletin,* XX (November, 1956), 39–42.

WESLEY, CHARLES H. "W. E. B. DuBois, The Historian," *FDMI,* 59–72.

The Negro Awakening

GENERAL

BRAWLEY, BENJAMIN. "The Negro Literary Renaissance," *Southern Workman,* LVI (April, 1927), 177–84.

BRONZ, STEPHEN H. *Roots of Negro Racial Consciousness. The 1920's: Three Harlem Renaissance Authors.* New York: Libra Publishers, Inc., 1964. (James Weldon Johnson; Countee Cullen; Claude McKay.)

CALVERTON, V. F. "The Advance of Negro Literature," *Opportunity,* IV (February, 1926), 54–55.

————. "The Negro's New Belligerent Attitude," *Current History,* XXX (September, 1929), 1081–88.

————. "The New Negro," *Current History,* XXIII (February, 1926), 694–98.

JACKSON, AUGUST V. "The Renascence of Negro Literature 1922 to 1929." Unpublished Master's Thesis. Atlanta, Georgia, Atlanta University, June, 1936.

LOCKE, ALAIN L. *The New Negro; An Interpretation* (Editor and Contributor). New York: A. & C. Boni, 1925.

MORRIS, LLOYD. "The Negro 'Renaissance,'" *Southern Workman,* LIX (February, 1930), 82–86.

VAN DOREN, CARL. "Negro Renaissance," *Century,* CXI (March, 1926), 635–37.

INDIVIDUAL AUTHORS

JAMES WELDON JOHNSON

The Autobiography of an Ex-Coloured Man. New York: Sherman, French and Co., 1912. Reprinted (with intro. by Carl Van Vechten). New York: Alfred A. Knopf, Inc., 1927. New York: Hill and Wang, Inc. (American Century Series), 1960.

Fifty Years and Other Poems. Boston: The Cornhill Company, 1917.

Self-determining Haiti. New York: The Latin, 1920.

Ed. *The Book of American Negro Poetry.* New York: Harcourt, Brace and Co., 1922. Revised edition, 1931.

"The Larger Success [Commencement Address, Hampton Institute, June, 1923]," Hampton, Virginia, 1923.

Ed. (with J. Rosamond Johnson) *The Books of American Negro Spirituals.* New York: Viking, 1940. Contains *The Book of American Negro Spirituals* (1925) and *The Second Book of Negro Spirituals* (1926).

God's Trombones, seven Negro sermons in verse. New York: The Viking Press, 1927.

"The Practice of Lynching," *The Century Magazine,* CXV, No. 1 (November, 1927), 65–70.

"The Dilemma of the Negro Author," *American Mercury,* XV, No. 60 (December, 1928), 477–81.

"Race Prejudice and the Negro Artist," *Harper's,* CLVII (November, 1928), 769–76.

Black Manhattan. New York: Alfred A. Knopf Co., 1930.

Along This Way. New York: The Viking Press, 1933.

Negro Americans, What Now? New York: The Viking Press, 1934.

St. Peter Relates an Incident. New York: The Viking Press, 1935.

ALAIN L. LOCKE

For a complete bibliography of Locke's works see Robert E. Martin, "Bibliography of the Writings of Alain Leroy Locke," *The New Negro Thirty Years Afterwards.* Papers Contributed to the Sixteenth Annual Spring Conference of the Social Sciences, April 20, 21, and 22, 1955. Washington, D. C.: Howard University Press, 1955, pp. 89–96.

Ed. *The New Negro; An Interpretation.* New York: A. & C. Boni, 1925.

Ed. *Plays of Negro Life; A Source-book of Native American Drama.* New York: Harper and Bros., 1927.

"The Negro in American Culture," in *Anthology of American Negro Literature,* ed. V. F. Calverton. New York: Modern Library Series, 1929, pp. 248–66.

"American Negro as Artist," *American Magazine of Art,* XXIII (September, 1931), 210–220.

The Negro in America. Chicago: American Library Association, 1933. (Reading with a purpose, No. 68.)

The Negro and His Music. Washington, D.C.; Associates in Negro Folk Education, 1936. No. 2 in the Bronze Booklet series.

"The Negro's Contribution to American Culture," *Journal of Negro Education,* VIII (July, 1939), 521–29.

The Negro in Art; A Pictorial Record of the Negro Artist and of the Negro Theme in Art. Washington, D.C.: Associates in Negro Folk Education, 1940.

"Of Native Sons: Real and Otherwise," *Opportunity,* XIX (January and February, 1941), 4–9, 48–52.

"Reason and Race, a Review of the Literature of the Negro for 1946," *Phylon,* VIII (First Quarter, 1947), 17–27. (See also First Quarter issues of *Phylon,* 1948–1953, for Locke's review of Negro literature in the previous year.)

"Self-Criticism: The Third Dimension in Culture," *Phylon,* XI (Fourth Quarter, 1950), 391–94.

"The Negro in American Literature," *New World Writing,* a Mentor Book. New York: New American Library, April, 1952, pp. 18–33.

CLAUDE MC KAY

PRIMARY SOURCES

Constab Ballads. London: Watts and Company, 1912.

Songs from Jamaica. London: Augener, Ltd., 1912.

Songs of Jamaica. Kingston, Jamaica: Aston W. Gardner & Co.

Spring in New Hampshire, and other poems. London: Grant Richard, 1920.

Harlem Shadows. New York: Harcourt, Brace & Co., 1922.

Home to Harlem. New York: Harper & Bros., 1928.

Banjo, a story without a plot. New York: Harper & Bros., 1929.

Gingertown. New York: Harper & Bros., 1932.

Banana Bottom. New York: Harper & Bros., 1933.

A Long Way from Home. New York: Lee, Furman, Inc., 1937.

Harlem: Negro Metropolis. New York: E. P. Dutton & Co., Inc., 1940.

"Boyhood in Jamaica," *Phylon*, XIII (Second Quarter, 1952), 134–45.

Selected Poems. New York: Bookman Associates, 1953.

SECONDARY SOURCES

BARTON, REBECCA C. "A Long Way from Home: Claude McKay," *Witnesses for Freedom.* New York: Harper & Bros., 1948.

BUTCHER, PHILIP. "Claude McKay—'If We Must Die,'" *Opportunity*, XXVI (Fall, 1948), 127.

COOPER, WAYNE. "Claude McKay and the New Negro of the 1920's," *Phylon*, XXV (Third Quarter, 1964), 297–306.

JACKSON, BLYDEN. "The Essential McKay," *Phylon*, XIV (Second Quarter, 1953), 216–17.

SMITH, ROBERT A. "Claude McKay: An Essay in Criticism," *Phylon*, IX (Third Quarter, 1948), 270–73.

JEAN TOOMER

PRIMARY SOURCES

Cane. New York: Boni and Liveright, 1923.

"Winter on Earth," *The Second American Caravan, A Yearbook of American Literature*, ed. Alfred Kreymborg *et al.* New York: Macaulay, 1928, pp. 694–715.

"Race Problems and Modern Society," *Problems of Civilization.* New York: D. Van Nostrand, 1929.

"York Beach," *The New American Caravan*, ed. Alfred Kreymborg. New York: Macaulay, 1929, pp. 12–83.

Essentials. Definitions and aphorisms. Private edition. Chicago: Lakeside Press, 1931.

The Flavor of Man. Philadelphia: Young Friends Movement of the Philadelphia Yearly meetings, 1949.

SECONDARY SOURCES

BONTEMPS, ARNA. "The Harlem Renaissance," *Saturday Review of Literature*, XXX (March 22, 1947), 12–13, 44.

———. "The Negro Renaissance: Jean Toomer and the Harlem Writers of the 1920's," in *Anger, and Beyond, The Negro Writer in the United States*, ed. Herbert Hill (New York: Harper & Row, 1966).

DUBOIS, W. E. B. and ALAIN LOCKE. "The Younger Literary Movement," *Crisis*, XXVII (February, 1924), 161–63.

HOLMES, EUGENE. "Jean Toomer, Apostle of Beauty," *Opportunity*, III (August, 1925), 252–54, 260.

MUNSON, GORHAM. "The Significance of Jean Toomer," *Opportunity*, III (September, 1925), 262–63.

ROSENFELD, PAUL. "Jean Toomer," *Men Seen.* New York: Dial Press, 1925.

TURNER, DARWIN T. "And Another Passing," *Negro American Literature Forum*, I, No. 1 (Fall, 1967) [unnumbered pages], 3–4.

RUDOLPH FISHER

"The City of Refuge," *Atlantic Monthly*, CXXXV (February, 1925), 178–87.

"Ringtail," *Atlantic Monthly*, CXXXV (May, 1925), 652–60.

"High Yaller," *Crisis*, 30, No. 6 (October-November, 1925), 281–86.

"The Promised Land," *Atlantic Monthly*, CXXXIX (January, 1927), 37–45.

"The Backslider," *McClure's Magazine* (August, 1927).

"Blades of Steel," *Atlantic Monthly*, CXL (August, 1927), 183–92.

"Fire By Night," *McClure's Magazine* (December, 1927).

"The Shadow of White," *Survey Graphic* (December, 1927).

"The Caucasian Invades Harlem," *American Mercury*, XI (August, 1927), 393–98.

The Walls of Jericho. New York: Alfred A. Knopf, Inc., 1928.

"Common Meter," *Negro News Syndicate* (February, 1930).

"Dust," *Opportunity*, IX (February, 1931), 46–47.

The Conjure Man Dies. New York: Covici, Friede, 1932.

"Ezekiel," *Junior Red Cross News* (March, 1932).
"Ezekiel Learns," *Junior Red Cross News* (February, 1933).
"Guardian of the Law," *Opportunity*, XI (March, 1933), 82–85.
"Miss Cynthie," *Story* (June, 1933).
"South Lingers On," *Survey Graphic*, VI (March, 1925), 644.
"John Archer's Nose," *Metropolitan Magazine* (January, 1935).

ERIC WALROND

Tropic Death. New York: Boni and Liveright, 1926.
"Englishman What Now?" *The Daily Gleaner*, Saturday, June 1, 1935.

STERLING BROWN

Southern Road. New York: Harcourt, Brace and Co., 1932.
"Negro Character as Seen by White Authors," *Journal of Negro Education*, II (January, 1933), 179–203.
The Negro in American Fiction. Washington, D.C.: The Associates in Negro Folk Education, 1937.
Negro Poetry and Drama. Washington, D.C.: The Associates in Negro Folk Education, 1937.
"The American Race Problem as Reflected in American Literature," *Journal of Negro Education*, VIII (July, 1939), 275–90.
"The Negro Author and His Publisher," *The Quarterly Review of Higher Education Among Negroes*, IX (July, 1941), 140–46.
"The Negro Author and His Publisher," *Negro Quarterly*, I (1945), 7–20.
Introductions, *The Negro Caravan.* Edited with Arthur P. Davis and Ulysses Lee. New York: The Dryden Press, 1941.
"Negro Folk Expression," *Phylon*, XI (Fourth Quarter, 1950), 318–27.
"The Blues," *Phylon*, XIII (Fourth Quarter, 1952), 286–92.
"Negro Folk Expression: Spirituals, Seculars, Ballads and Songs," *Phylon*, XIV (First Quarter, 1953), 50–60.
"The New Negro in Literature (1925–1955)," *The New Negro Thirty Years Afterwards.* Washington, D.C.: Howard University Press, 1955, pp. 57–72.
"A Century of Negro Portraiture in American Literature," *Massachusetts Review*, VII (Winter, 1966), 73–96.

COUNTEE CULLEN

PRIMARY SOURCES

Color. New York: Harper & Bros., 1925.
Ballad of the Brown Girl. New York: Harper & Bros., 1927.
Ed. *Caroling Dusk.* New York: Harper & Bros., 1927.
Copper Sun. New York: Harper & Bros., 1927.
The Black Christ and Other Poems. New York: Harper & Bros., 1929.
One Way to Heaven. New York: Harper & Bros., 1932.
The Medea and Other Poems. New York: Harper & Bros., 1935.
The Lost Zoo. New York: Harper & Bros., 1940.
My Nine Lives and How I Lost Them. New York: Harper & Bros., 1942.
On These I Stand. New York: Harper and Row, 1947.

SECONDARY SOURCES

DAVIS, ARTHUR P. "The Alien-and-Exile Theme in Countee Cullen's Racial Poems," *Phylon*, XIV (Fourth Quarter, 1953), 390–400.
DINGER, HELEN. "A Study of Countee Cullen, with Emphasis on his Poetical Works." Unpublished Master's Thesis, Columbia University, 1953.
FERGUSON, BLANCHE. *Countee Cullen and the Negro Renaissance.* New York: Dodd and Mead, 1966.
PERRY, MARGARET. "A Bio-Bibliography of Countee P. Cullen." Unpublished Master's Thesis, Catholic University of America, 1959.
REIMHERR, BEULAH. "Countee Cullen: A Biographical and Critical Study." Unpublished Master's Thesis, University of Maryland, 1960.
ROBB, IZETTA W. "From the Darker Side," *Opportunity*, IV (December, 1926), 381–82.
SMITH, ROBERT. "The Poetry of Countee Cullen," *Phylon*, XI (Third Quarter, 1950), 216–21.
WEBSTER, HARVEY. "A Difficult Career," *Poetry*, LXX (July, 1947), 222–25.
WOODRUFF, BERTRAM. "The Poetic Philosophy of Countee Cullen," *Phylon*, I (Third Quarter, 1940), 213–23.

Major Authors

LANGSTON HUGHES

PRIMARY SOURCES

"The Negro Artist and the Racial Mountain," *The Nation*, CXXII (June 23, 1926), 692–94.

The Weary Blues. New York: Alfred A. Knopf, 1926.

The Ways of White Folks. New York: Alfred A. Knopf, 1934.

The Big Sea. New York: Alfred A. Knopf, 1940. New York: Hill and Wang, 1963.

Shakespeare in Harlem. New York: Alfred A. Knopf, 1942.

"My Adventures as a Social Poet," *Phylon*, VIII (Fall, 1947), 205–212.

New York Post interviews. By Mary Harrington (April 10, 1947), Martha MacGregor (September 15, 1957), Ted Poston (November 24, 1957, and June 17, 1962).

Montage of a Dream Deferred. New York: Henry Holt, 1951.

I Wonder As I Wander. New York: Rinehart, 1956. New York: Hill and Wang, 1964.

The Langston Hughes Reader. New York: George Braziller, 1958.

Selected Poems of Langston Hughes. New York: Alfred A. Knopf, 1959.

Tambourines to Glory. New York: John Day, 1959.

"Viewpoint" Series interview. By Dana F. Kennedy [script from broadcast tape available]. New York: Division of Radio and Television, National Council of the Protestant Episcopal Church, December 10, 1960.

Ask Your Mama. New York: Alfred A. Knopf, 1961.

The Best of Simple. New York: Hill and Wang, 1961.

"Simple" columns. *Chicago Defender*, 1943–1965; *New York Post*, 1962–1965.

Five Plays by Langston Hughes. Edited by Webster Smalley. Bloomington: Indiana University Press, 1963.

Something in Common and Other Stories. New York: Hill and Wang, 1963.

The Panther and the Lash. New York: Alfred A. Knopf, 1967.

SECONDARY SOURCES

DAVIS, ARTHUR P. "The Harlem of Langston Hughes' Poetry," *Phylon*, XIII (Winter, 1952), 276–83.

————. "Jesse B. Semple: Negro American," *Phylon*, XV (Spring, 1954), 21–28.

————. "The Tragic Mulatto Theme in Six Works of Langston Hughes," *Phylon*, XVI (Winter, 1955), 195–204.

DICKINSON, DONALD C. *A Bio-Bibliography of Langston Hughes: 1902–1967*. Hamden, Connecticut: Archon Books, 1967.

EMANUEL, JAMES A. *Langston Hughes*. Volume 123, Twayne's United States Authors Series. New York: Twayne Publishers, 1967.

————. *The Short Stories of Langston Hughes*. Unpublished Ph.D. dissertation, Columbia University, 1962.

PRESLEY, JAMES. "The American Dream of Langston Hughes," *Southwest Review*, XLVIII (Autumn, 1963), 380–86.

QUINOT, RAYMOND. *Langston Hughes, ou L'Étoile Noire*. Bruxelles: Editions C.E.L.F., 1964.

SMALLEY, WEBSTER. Introduction, *Five Plays by Langston Hughes*. Bloomington: Indiana University Press, 1963.

Special Langston Hughes Number. *CLA Journal*, XI, No. 4 (June, 1968).

Special Supplement on Langston Hughes. *Freedomways*, VIII, No. 2 (Spring, 1968).

RICHARD WRIGHT

For a complete bibliography of Wright's works see Michel Fabre and Edward Margolies, "Richard Wright (1908–1960)," *Bulletin of Bibliography*, XXIV (1965), 131–33, 137. Reprinted in Constance Webb, *Richard Wright, A Biography*. New York: G. P. Putnam's Sons, 1968, pp. 423–29.

PRIMARY SOURCES

"Blueprint for Negro Writing," *New Challenge*, II (Fall, 1937), 53–65.

Uncle Tom's Children: Four Nouvellas. New York: Harper & Bros., 1938.

Native Son. New York: Harper & Bros., 1940.

"How 'Bigger' Was Born," *Saturday Review*, XXII (June 1, 1940), 17–20.

Uncle Tom's Children: Five Long Stories. New York: Harper & Bros., 1940.

12 Million Voices: A Folk History of the Negro in the United States. New York: The Viking Press, 1941.

Native Son, the Biography of a Young American. A Play in Ten Scenes. By Paul Green and Richard Wright. New York: Harper & Bros., 1941.

"I Tried To Be a Communist," *Atlantic Monthly,* CLXXXIV (August, 1944), 61–70; (September, 1944), 48–56. Included in Richard H. S. Crossman, ed., *The God That Failed.* New York: Harper & Bros., 1949.

Black Boy; a Record of Childhood and Youth. New York: Harper & Bros., 1945.

"How Jim Crow Feels," *True Magazine,* November, 1946. Reprinted in *Negro Digest,* V (January, 1947), 44–53.

The Outsider. New York: Harper & Bros., 1953.

Savage Holiday. New York, Avon, 1954.

Black Power; a Record of Reactions in a Land of Pathos. New York: Harper & Bros., 1954.

The Color Curtain; a Report on the Bandung Conference. Cleveland and New York: Bobson Books, Ltd., 1956.

White Man, Listen! Garden City, New York: Doubleday, 1957.

Pagan Spain. New York: Harper & Bros., 1957.

The Long Dream. Garden City, New York: Doubleday, 1958.

Eight Men. Cleveland and New York: Avon, 1961.

Lawd Today. New York: Walker and Company, 1963.

"Five Episodes" (from an unfinished novel), in *Soon, One Morning,* ed. Herbert Hill (New York: Random House, 1963, pp. 140–64).

SECONDARY SOURCES

BALDWIN, JAMES. "Many Thousands Gone," *Notes of a Native Son.* Boston: Beacon Press, 1955, pp. 24–46.

———. "Alas Poor Richard (i. Eight Men; ii. The Exile; iii. Alas, Poor Richard)," *Nobody Knows My Name.* New York: The Dial Press, 1961, pp. 181–215.

BRYER, JACKSON. "Richard Wright: A Selected Checklist of Criticism," *Wisconsin Studies in Contemporary Literature,* I (Fall, 1960), 22–33.

BURGUM, EDWIN BERRY. "The Promise of Democracy in Richard Wright's *Native Son," The Novel and the World's Dilemma.* New York: Oxford University Press, 1947.

COHN, DAVID L. "The Negro Novel: Richard Wright," *Atlantic Monthly,* CLXV (May, 1940), 659–61.

DAVIS, ARTHUR P. *"The Outsider* as a Novel of Race," *Midwest Journal,* VII (1955–56), 320–26.

ELLISON, RALPH. "Richard Wright's Blues," *Shadow and Act.* New York: Random House, 1964.

EMBREE, EDWIN. "Native Son," *Thirteen Against the Odds.* New York: The Viking Press, 1944, pp. 25–46.

FABRE, MICHEL and MARGOLIES, EDWARD. "Richard Wright (1908–1960)," *Bulletin of Bibliography,* XXIV (1965), 131–33, 137.

GLICKSBERG, CHARLES I. "Existentialism in *The Outsider,*" *Four Quarters,* VII (January, 1958), 17–26.

GLOSTER, HUGH M. "Richard Wright: Interpreter of Racial and Economic Maladjustments," *Opportunity,* XIX (December, 1941), 361–65.

KNOX, GEORGE. "The Negro Novelist's Sensibility and the Outsider Theme," *Western Humanities Review,* XI (Spring, 1957), 137–48.

LEWIS, T. "The Saga of Bigger Thomas," *Catholic World,* CLIII (May, 1941), 201–206.

RASCOE, BURTON. "Negro Novel and White Reviewers: Richard Wright's *Native Son,*" *American Mercury,* L (May, 1940), 113–117.

SCOTT, NATHAN A., JR. "Search for Beliefs: The Fiction of Richard Wright," *University of Kansas City Review,* XXIII (1956), 19–24.

———. "The Dark and Haunted Tower of Richard Wright," *Graduate Comment,* VII (July, 1964), 93–99.

SILLEN, SAMUEL. "The Meaning of Bigger Thomas," *New Masses,* XXXV (April, 1960), 13–21.

SLOCHOWER, HARRY. *No Voice Is Wholly Lost.* New York: Creative Age Press, 1945, pp. 87–92.

WEBB, CONSTANCE. *Richard Wright, A Biography.* New York: G. P. Putnam's Sons, 1968.

WHITE, RALPH K. "Black Boy: A Valuable Analysis," *Journal of Abnormal and Social Psychology,* XLII (October, 1947), 440–61.

WIDMER, KINGSLEY. "The Existential Darkness: Richard Wright's *The Outsider,*" *Wisconsin Studies in Contemporary Literature,* I (Fall, 1960), 13–21.

RALPH ELLISON

PRIMARY SOURCES

"Slick Gonna Learn," *Direction* (September, 1939), pp. 10–16.

"Afternoon," *American Writing,* ed. Hans Otto Storm & others, pp. 28–37. Reprinted in *Negro Story* (March-April, 1945).

"Mister Toussan," *The New Masses,* XLI (November 4, 1941), 19, 20.

"That I Had the Wings," *Common Ground,* III (Summer, 1943), 30–37.

"Flying Home," *Cross Section,* ed. Edwin Seaver. New York: L. B. Fischer, 1944, pp. 469–85.

"In A Strange Country," *Tomorrow,* III (July, 1944), 41–44.

"King of the Bingo Game," *Tomorrow,* IV (November, 1944), 29–33.

Invisible Man. New York: Random House, 1952.

"Did You Ever Dream Lucky?" *New World Writing #5.* New York: The New American Library of World Literature, Inc., 1954, pp. 134–45.

"A Coupla Scalped Indians," *New World Writing #9.* New York: The New American Library of World Literature, Inc., 1956, pp. 225–36.

"And Hickman Arrives," *The Noble Savage* I, 1956.

Shadow and Act. New York: Random House, 1964.

SECONDARY SOURCES

BAUMBACH, JONATHAN. "Nightmare of a Native Son: Ellison's *Invisible Man,*" *Criticism,* VI (1963), 48–65. Reprinted in *The Landscape of Nightmare.* New York: New York University Press, 1965.

BONE, ROBERT. "Ralph Ellison and the Uses of Imagination," *Tri-Quarterly,* Number Six (1966), 39–54. Reprinted in *Anger, and Beyond,* ed. Herbert Hill (New York: Harper & Row, 1966).

GLICKSBERG, CHARLES I. "The Symbolism of Vision," *Southwest Review,* XXXIX (1954), 259–65.

HASSAN, IHAB. *Radical Innocence: Studies in the Contemporary American Novel.* Princeton: Princeton University Press, 1961. Reprinted by Harper & Row Publishers, pp. 168–78.

HOROWITZ, FLOYD ROSS. "The Enigma of Ellison's Intellectual Man," *CLA Journal,* VII (December, 1963), 126–32.

———. "Ralph Ellison's Modern Version of Brer Bear and Brer Rabbit in *Invisible Man,*" *MidContinent American Studies Journal,* IV, ii (1963), 21–27.

KLEIN, MARCUS. "Ralph Ellison," in *After Alienation: American Novels in Mid-Century.* New York: The World Publishing Company (Meridian Books), 1962, pp. 71–146.

ROVIT, EARL. "Ralph Ellison and the American Comic Tradition," *Wisconsin Studies in Contemporary Literature,* I (Fall, 1960), 34–42.

WARREN, ROBERT PENN. "The Unity of Experience," *Commentary*, XXXIX (May, 1965), 91–96.

JAMES BALDWIN

PRIMARY SOURCES

Go Tell It on the Mountain. New York: Alfred A. Knopf, Inc., 1953.

Notes of a Native Son. Boston: Beacon Press, 1955.

Giovanni's Room. New York: Dial Press, 1956.

Nobody Knows My Name: More Notes of a Native Son. New York: Dial Press, 1961.

Another Country. New York: Dial Press, 1962.

The Fire Next Time. New York: Dial Press, 1963.

Nothing Personal. Photos by Richard Avedon and text by James Baldwin. New York: Atheneum, 1964.

Blues for Mister Charlie. New York: Dial Press, 1964.

Going to Meet the Man. New York: Dial Press, 1965.

Tell Me How Long The Train's Been Gone. New York: Dial Press, 1968.

SECONDARY SOURCES

BONE, ROBERT A. "The Novels of James Baldwin," *Tri-Quarterly* (Winter, 1965), 3–20.

BONOSKY, PHILIP. "The Negro Writer and Commitment," *Mainstream*, XV (1962), 16–22.

CHARNEY, MAURICE. "James Baldwin's Quarrel with Richard Wright," *American Quarterly*, XV (Spring, 1963), 65–75.

COLES, ROBERT. "Baldwin's Burden," *Partisan Review*, XXXI (Summer, 1964), 409–16.

COX, C. B., and JONES, A. R. "After the Tranquilized Fifties: Notes on Sylvia Plath and James Baldwin," *Critical Quarterly*, VI (Summer, 1964), 107–22.

FEATHERSTONE, J. "Blues for Mr. Charlie," *New Republic*, CLIII (November 27, 1965), 34–36.

FINN, JAMES. "The Identity of James Baldwin," *Commonweal*, LXXVII (October 26, 1962), 113–116, 365–66.

GROSS, THEODORE L. "The World of James Baldwin," *Critique*, VII (Winter, 1964–1965), 139–49.

HAGOPIAN, JOHN V. "James Baldwin: The Black and the Red-White-and-Blue," *CLA Journal*, VII (1963), 133–40.

JACOBSON, DAN. "James Baldwin as Spokesman," *Commentary*, XXXII (December, 1961), 497–502.

KENT, GEORGE. "Baldwin and the Problem of Being," *CLA Journal*, VII (March, 1964), 202–214.

KLEIN, MARCUS. "James Baldwin: A Question of Identity," *After Alienation: American Novels in Mid-Century*. New York: The World Publishing Company (Meridian Books), 1962, pp. 147–195.

LASH, JOHN S. "Baldwin Beside Himself: A Study in Modern Phallicism," *CLA Journal*, VIII (December, 1964), 132–40.

LEVIN, DAVID. "Baldwin's Autobiographical Essays: The Problem of Negro Identity," *Massachusetts Review*, V (Winter, 1964), 239–47.

MAC INNES, COLIN. "Dark Angel: The Writings of James Baldwin," *Encounter*, XXI, ii (August, 1963), 22–33.

MORRISON, ALLAN. "The Angriest Young Man," *Ebony*, XVI (October, 1961), 23–30.

O'DANIEL, THERMAN B. "James Baldwin: An Interpretive Study," *CLA Journal*, VII (September, 1963), 37–47.

PODHORETZ, NORMAN. "In Defense of James Baldwin," *Doings and Undoings*. New York: Farrar, Straus and Co., 1964, pp. 244–50.

ROTH, PHILLIP. "Channel X: Two Plays on the Race Conflict," *New York Review of Books*, II (May 28, 1964), 10–13.

SPENDER, STEPHEN. "James Baldwin: Voice of a Revolution," *Partisan Review*, XXX (Summer, 1963), 256–60.

Contemporary Literature

GENERAL

The American Negro Writer and His Roots, Selected Papers from The First Conference of Negro Writers. New York: American Society of African Culture, 1960.

ECHERUO, M. J. C. "American Negro Poetry," *Phylon*, XXIV, No. 1 (Spring, 1963), 62–68.

ESSIEN-UDOM, ESSIEN U. *Black Nationalism: A Search for an Identity in America*. Chicago: University of Chicago Press, 1962.

FORD, NICK AARON. "Battle of the Books: A Critical Survey of Significant Books by and About Negroes Published in 1960," *Phylon*, XXII (Second Quarter, 1961). 119–34.

FORD, NICK AARON. *The Contemporary Negro Novel.* Boston: Meador Publishing Co., 1936.

————. "The Fire Next Time? A Critical Survey of Belles Lettres by and about Negroes Published in 1963," *Phylon,* XXV (Second Quarter, 1964), 123–34.

————. "Four Popular Negro Novelists," *Phylon,* XV (First Quarter, 1954), 29–39.

HILL, HERBERT, ed. *Anger, and Beyond: The Negro Writer in the United States.* New York: Harper & Row, Publishers, 1966.

————, ed. *Soon, One Morning: New Writing by American Negroes 1940–1962.* New York: Alfred A. Knopf, 1963.

LEHAN, RICHARD. "Existentialism in Recent American Fiction: The Demonic Quest," *Texas Studies in Literature and Language,* I (Summer, 1959), 181–202.

LINCOLN, C. ERIC. *The Black Muslims in America.* Boston: Beacon Press, 1961.

MAUND, ALFRED. "The Negro Novelist and the Contemporary Scene," *Chicago Jewish Forum,* XIII (Fall, 1954), 28–34.

The New Negro Thirty Years Afterwards. Washington, D.C.: Howard University Press, 1955.

"The Negro in Literature: The Current Scene," *Phylon,* XI (Fourth Quarter, 1950). (The entire journal.)

INDIVIDUAL AUTHORS

ALBERT MURRAY

"Something Different, Something More," *Anger, and Beyond,* ed. Herbert Hill (New York: Harper and Row, 1966).

"The Illusive Black Image," Review of *The Crisis of the Negro Intellectual, From the Ashes, Black Power,* and *The Burden of Race* in *Book Week, Chicago Sun-Times,* November 26, 1967.

Review of *The Confessions of Nat Turner* in *The New Leader,* L, No. 24 (December 4, 1967), 18–21.

JOHN A. WILLIAMS

PRIMARY SOURCES

Night Song. New York: Farrar, Straus and Cudahy, 1961.

Sissie. New York: Farrar, Straus and Cudahy, 1963.

"Negro Literature Today," *Ebony*, XVIII (September, 1963), 73–76.

"This Is My Country Too," *Holiday*, XXXVI (August, 1964), 30–33; (September), 58–59; (October), 4; and "This Is My Country Too: A Pessimistic Postscript" in *Holiday*, XLI (June, 1967), 8.

This Is My Country Too. New York: New American Library, 1965.

"Open Letter to an African," *Negro Digest*, XIV, No. 11 (September, 1965), 22, 28–35.

"Black Man in Europe," *Holiday*, XLI (January, 1967), 8.

"Race, War and Politics," *Negro Digest*, XVI, No. 10 (August, 1967), 4–9, 36–47.

The Man Who Cried I Am. Boston: Little, Brown, and Co., 1967.

"U. S. a Nice Place to Visit," *Saturday Review*, LI (January 27, 1968), 30–31.

SECONDARY SOURCES

LEONARD, JOHN. "Author at Bay," *New York Times Book Review*, October 29, 1967, p. 66.

"Black Writers' Views on Literary Lions and Values," Symposium in *Negro Digest*, XVII, No. 3 (January, 1968), 10–48, 81–89. Hereafter called "Black Writers' Views."

PAULE MARSHALL

PRIMARY SOURCES

Brown Girl, Brownstones. New York: Random House, 1959.

Soul Clap Hands and Sing. New York: Atheneum Publishers, 1961.

"Reena," *Harper's Magazine*, CCXXV (October, 1962), 154–63.

SECONDARY SOURCE

SEREBNICK, J. "New Creative Writers," *Library Journal*, XXCIV (June 1, 1959), 1870.

ERNEST J. GAINES

PRIMARY SOURCES

Catherine Carmier. New York: Atheneum Publishers, 1964.
Of Love and Dust. New York: Dial Press, 1967.

Bloodline. New York: Dial Press, 1968.
"Black Writers' Views."

SECONDARY SOURCE

Contemporary Authors. Volumes 11–12 (1965).

WILLIAM MELVIN KELLEY

PRIMARY SOURCES

A Different Drummer. New York: Doubleday and Co., 1962.
"If You're Woke You Dig It," *New York Times Magazine*, May
20, 1962, p. 45.
"Ivy League Negro," *Esquire*, LX (August, 1963), 54–56.
Dancers on the Shore. New York: Doubleday and Co., 1964.
"American in Rome," *Mademoiselle*, LX (March, 1965), 202.
A Drop of Patience. New York: Doubleday and Co., 1965.
"On Racism, Exploitation, and the White Liberal," *Negro
Digest*, XVI, No. 3 (January, 1967), 5–12.
Dem. New York: Doubleday and Co., 1967.
"On Africa in the United States," *Negro Digest*, XVII, No. 7
(May, 1968), 10–15.

SECONDARY SOURCES

"Black Writers' Views."
LOTTMAN, HERBERT, "The Action Is Everywhere the Black
Man Goes," *The New York Times Book Review* (April 21,
1968), pp. 6–7, 48–49.
RANDALL, DUDLEY. "On the Conference Beat," *Negro Digest*,
XVI, No. 5 (March, 1967), 89–93.
SEREBNICK, J. "New Creative Writers," *Library Journal*, XXCIV
(October 1, 1959), 3015.
"Talent's 'New Wave' " [on Kelley, James Earl Jones, and Alvin
Ailey]. *Negro Digest*, XI, No. 12 (October, 1962), 43–47.

MELVIN B. TOLSON

PRIMARY SOURCES

Rendezvous with America. New York: Dodd, Mead and Co.,
1944.
Libretto for the Republic of Liberia. New York: Twayne Publishers, 1953.

"Claude McKay's Art," *Poetry*, XXCIII (February, 1954), 287–90.

Harlem Gallery. New York: Twayne Publishers, 1965.

SECONDARY SOURCES

FABIO, SARAH WEBSTER. "Who Speaks Negro?" *Negro Digest*, XVI, No. 2 (December, 1966), 54–58.

RANDALL, DUDLEY. "Melvin B. Tolson: Portrait of a Poet as Raconteur," *Negro Digest*, XV, No. 3 (January, 1966), 54–57.

SHAPIRO, KARL. "Melvin B. Tolson, Poet," *Book Week, New York Herald Tribune*, January 10, 1965. Reprinted in *Negro Digest*, XIV, No. 7 (May, 1965), 75–77.

TATE, ALLEN. "Preface to *Libretto for the Republic of Liberia*," *Poetry*, LXXVI (July, 1950), 216–18.

THOMPSON, D. G., "Tolson's Gallery Brings Poetry Home," *Negro History Bulletin*, XXIX (December, 1965), 69–70.

ARNA BONTEMPS

PRIMARY SOURCES

God Sends Sunday. New York: Harcourt, Brace and Co., 1931.

Black Thunder. New York: The MacMillan Co., 1936.

Sad-Faced Boy. Boston: Houghton Mifflin Co., 1937.

We Have Tomorrow. Boston: Houghton Mifflin Co., 1945.

"The Harlem Renaissance," *Saturday Review of Literature*, XXX (March 22, 1947), 12–13, 44.

"Negro Poets, Then and Now," *Phylon*, XI (Fourth Quarter, 1950), 355–60.

Chariot in the Sky. Chicago: John C. Winston Co., 1951.

"Chesnutt Papers Go to Fisk," *Library Journal*, LXXVII (August, 1952), 1288.

Introduction, *The Book of Negro Folklore*. Edited with Langston Hughes. New York: Dodd, Mead and Co., 1958.

Story of the Negro. New York: Alfred A. Knopf, Inc., 1958.

One Hundred Years of Negro Freedom. New York: Dodd, Mead and Co., 1961.

"The New Black Renaissance," *Negro Digest*, XIII, No. 1 (November, 1961), 52–58.

"Negro Awakening: What Librarians Can Do," *Library Journal*, XXCVIII (September 1, 1963), 2997–2999.

Personals. London: Paul Breman, Ltd., 1963.

Introduction, *American Negro Poetry*. New York: Hill and Wang, 1963.

"Why I Returned," *Harper's Magazine*, CCXXX (April, 1965), 176–82.

"Lonesome Boy Theme," *Horn Book*, XLII (December, 1966), 672–80.

"The Negro Renaissance: Jean Toomer and the Harlem Writers of the 1920's," in *Anger, and Beyond: The Negro Writer in the United States*, ed. Herbert Hill (New York: Harper & Row, 1966).

SECONDARY SOURCE

Contemporary Authors. Volume 1 (1962).

ROBERT E. HAYDEN

PRIMARY SOURCES

Heart-Shape in the Dust. Detroit: Falcon Press, 1940.

The Lion and the Archer. With Myron O'Higgins. Nashville: Hemphill Press, 1948.

Figure of Time. Nashville: Hemphill Press, 1955.

A Ballad of Remembrance. London: Paul Breman, Ltd., 1962.

Selected Poems. New York: October House, Inc., 1966.

"Black Writers' Views."

SECONDARY SOURCES

GALLER, D. "Three Recent Volumes," *Poetry*, CX (July, 1967), 268.

Negro History Bulletin, XXI (October, 1957), 15. Biographical sketch, portrait.

POOL, ROSEY E. "Robert Hayden: Poet Laureate," *Negro Digest*, XV, No. 8 (June, 1966), 39–43.

DUDLEY RANDALL

"White Poet, Black Critic," *Negro Digest*, XIV, No. 4 (February, 1965), 46–48.

"*Ubi Sunt* and *Hic Sum*," *Negro Digest*, XIV, No. 11 (September, 1965), 73–76.

"Melvin B. Tolson: Portrait of a Poet as Raconteur," *Negro Digest*, XV, No. 3 (January, 1966), 54–57.

"A Report on the Black Arts Convention," *Negro Digest*, XV, No. 10 (August, 1966), 54–58.

"Black Power, Its Meaning and Measure: A Symposium," *Negro Digest*, XVI, No. 1 (November, 1966), 20–36, 81–96.

Poem Counterpoem. With Margaret Danner. Detroit: Broadside Press, 1966.

"On the Conference Beat," *Negro Digest*, XVI, No. 5 (March 1967), 89–93.

"The Second Annual Black Arts Convention," *Negro Digest*, XVII, No. 1 (November, 1967), 42–48.

"Black Writers' Views."

Cities Burning. Detroit: Broadside Press, 1968.

MARGARET A. WALKER

PRIMARY SOURCES

For My People. New Haven: Yale University Press, 1942.

"New Poets," *Phylon*, XI (1950), 345–54.

"Nausea of Sartre," *Yale Review*, XLII, No. 2 (December, 1952), 251–61.

Jubilee. Boston: Houghton Mifflin Co., 1966.

"Soul-Searching in Tennessee," *Saturday Review*, L (January 7, 1967), 35.

"Black Writers' Views."

SECONDARY SOURCE

Current Biography (1943).

GWENDOLYN BROOKS

PRIMARY SOURCES

A Street in Bronzeville. New York: Harper and Bros., 1945.

Annie Allen. New York: Harper and Bros., 1949.

"They Call It Bronzeville," *Holiday*, X (October, 1951), 60–64.

Maud Martha. New York: Harper and Bros., 1953.

Bronzeville Boys and Girls. New York: Harper and Bros., 1956.

The Bean Eaters. New York: Harper and Bros., 1960.

Selected Poems. New York: Harper and Bros., 1963.

"Langston Hughes," *The Nation*, CCV (July 3, 1967), 7.

We Asked Gwendolyn Brooks. Booklet on interview by Paul M. Angle. Chicago: Illinois Bell Telephone Co. [1967].

SECONDARY SOURCES

"Black Writers' Views."

BROWN, FRANK LONDON. "Chicago's Great Lady of Poetry," *Negro Digest*, XI, No. 2 (December, 1961), 53–57.

Contemporary Authors, Volume 1 (1962).

CROCKETT, J. "An Essay on Gwendolyn Brooks," *Negro History Bulletin*, XIX (November, 1955), 37–39.

Current Biography (1950).

CUTLER, B. "Long Reach, Strong Speech," *Poetry*, CIII (March, 1964), 388–89.

DAVIS, ARTHUR P. "The Black and Tan Motif in the Poetry of Gwendolyn Brooks," *CLA Journal*, VI (December, 1962), 90–97.

———. "Gwendolyn Brooks: A Poet of the Unheroic," *CLA Journal*, VII (December, 1963), 114–25.

EMANUEL, JAMES A. "A Note on the Future of Negro Poetry," *Negro American Literature Forum*, I, No. 1 (Fall, 1967), [unnumbered] 2–3.

KUNITZ, STANLEY. "Bronze by Gold," *Poetry*, LXXVI (April, 1950), 52–56.

ROLLINS, CHARLEMAE. *Famous American Negro Poets*. New York: Dodd, Mead and Co., 1965.

Twentieth Century Authors, First Supplement (1955).

JAMES A. EMANUEL

PRIMARY SOURCES

"Emersonian Virtue: A Definition," *American Speech*, XXXVI, No. 2 (May, 1961), 117–22.

"Langston Hughes' First Short Story: 'Mary Winosky,'" *Phylon*, XXII, No. 3 (Fall, 1961), 267–72.

"The Invisible Men of American Literature," *Books Abroad*, XXXVII, No. 4 (Autumn, 1963), 391–94.

Langston Hughes. Volume 123, Twayne's United States Authors Series. New York: Twayne Publishers, 1967.

"'Bodies in the Moonlight': A Critical Analysis," *Readers & Writers*, I, No. 5 (November-January, 1968), 38–39, 42.

"Black Writers' Views."

"The Literary Experiments of Langston Hughes," *CLA Journal*, XI, No. 4 (June, 1968).

SECONDARY SOURCES

Contemporary Authors, Volumes 21–22 (1968).

Directory of American Scholars, Fifth Edition (1968).
Who's Who in the East, Twelfth Edition (1968).

MARI EVANS

Where Is All the Music. London: Paul Breman, Ltd., 1968.
"I'm with You," *Negro Digest*, XVII, No. 7 (May, 1968), 31–36, 77–80.

LEROI JONES

PRIMARY SOURCES

Preface to a Twenty Volume Suicide Note. New York: Totem Press-Corinth Books, 1961.
Blues People: Negro Music in White America. New York: William Morrow and Co., 1963.
"Harlem Considered: A Symposium," *Negro Digest*, XIII, No. 11 (September, 1964), 16–26. Reprinted from *New York Herald Tribune.*
"What Does Non-Violence Mean?" *Negro Digest*, XIII, No. 12 (October, 1964), 4–19. Reprinted from *Midstream.*
The Dead Lecturer. New York: Grove Press, 1964.
Dutchman and The Slave. New York: Apollo Editions, Inc., 1964.
Black Art. Newark: Jihad Productions, 1966. Mimeographed.
Home: Social Essays. New York: William Morrow and Co., 1966.
"Slave Ship: A Historical Pageant," *Negro Digest*, XVI, No. 6 (April, 1967), 62–74.
Tales. New York: Grove Press, 1967.
Black Music. New York: William Morrcw and Co., 1967.

SECONDARY SOURCES

"Black Writers' Views."
Commentary on *Dutchman: Partisan Review*, XXXI (Summer, 1964), 389–94. *Hudson Review*, XVII (Autumn, 1964), 424.
Commentary on *The Slave* and *The Toilet: The Nation*, CC (January 4, 1965), 16–17. *Saturday Review*, XLVIII (January 9, 1965), 46. *The New Republic*, CLII (January 23, 1965), 32–33.
DENNISON, GEORGE. "The Demagogy of LeRoi Jones," *Commentary*, XXXIX (February, 1965), 67–70.

GOTTLIEB, SAUL (interview). "They Think You're an Airplane and You're Really a Bird!" *Evergreen Review No. 50*, XI (December, 1967), 50–53, 96–97.

LEVERTOV, DENISE. "Poets of the Given Ground," *The Nation*, CXCIII (October 14, 1961), 251–52.

MAJOR, CLARENCE. "The Poetry of LeRoi Jones," *Negro Digest*, XIV, No. 5 (March, 1965), 54–56.

"New Script in Newark," *Time*, XCI (April 26, 1968), 18–19.

ROTH, PHILLIP. "Channel X: Two Plays on the Race Conflict," *New York Review of Books*, II (May 28, 1964), 10–13.

SMITH, R. H. "Jersey Justice and LeRoi Jones," *Publishers' Weekly*, CXCIII (January 15, 1968), 66.

ARTHUR P. DAVIS

PRIMARY SOURCES

Introductions, *The Negro Caravan*. Edited with Sterling A. Brown and Ulysses Lee. New York: The Dryden Press, 1941.

Issac Watts: His Life and Works. New York: The Dryden Press, 1943.

"The Harlem of Langston Hughes' Poetry," *Phylon*, XIII (Winter, 1952), 276–83.

"Personal Elements in the Poetry of Phillis Wheatley," *Phylon*, XIV (Summer, 1953), 191–98.

"The Alien-and-Exile Theme in Countee Cullen's Racial Poems," *Phylon*, XIV (Winter, 1953), 390–400.

"Jesse B. Semple: Negro American," *Phylon*, XV (Spring, 1954), 21–28.

"The Tragic Mulatto Theme in Six Works of Langston Hughes," *Phylon*, XVI (Winter, 1955), 195–204.

"*The Outsider* as a Novel of Race," *Midwest Journal*, VII (1955-56), 320–26.

"I Go to Whittier School," *Phylon*, XXI (Summer, 1960), 155–66.

"The Black and Tan Motif in the Poetry of Gwendolyn Brooks," *CLA Journal*, VI (December, 1962), 90–97.

"Gwendolyn Brooks: A Poet of the Unheroic," *CLA Journal*, VII (1963), 114–25.

SECONDARY SOURCE

Directory of American Scholars, Volume II, Fourth Edition (1964).

PHILIP BUTCHER

PRIMARY SOURCES

"Robert Burns and the Democratic Spirit," *Phylon*, X, No. 3 (Third Quarter, 1949), 265–72.

"George W. Cable and Negro Education," *Journal of Negro History*, XXXIV (April, 1949), 119–34.

George W. Cable: The Northampton Years. New York: Columbia University Press, 1959.

"The Younger Novelists and the Urban Negro," *CLA Journal*, IV (March, 1961), 196–203.

George W. Cable. Volume 24, Twayne's United States Authors Series. New York: Twayne Publishers, 1962.

"Mark Twain Sells Roxy down the River," *CLA Journal*, VIII (March, 1965), 225–33.

SECONDARY SOURCE

Directory of American Scholars, Volume II, Fourth Edition (1964).

NATHAN A. SCOTT, JR.

PRIMARY SOURCES

Rehearsals of Discomposure: Alienation and Reconciliation in Modern Literature. New York: Columbia University Press, 1952.

"Search for Beliefs: The Fiction of Richard Wright," *University of Kansas City Review*, XXIII (1956), 19–24.

Modern Literature and the Religious Frontier. New York: Harper and Bros., 1958.

Albert Camus. New York: Hillary House Publishers, 1962.

Reinhold Niebuhr. Minneapolis: University of Minnesota Press, 1963.

"The Dark and Haunted Tower of Richard Wright," *Graduate Comment*, VII (July, 1964), 93–99.

Samuel Beckett. New York: Hillary House Publishers, 1965.

The Broken Center: Studies in the Theological Horizon of Modern Literature. New Haven: Yale University Press, 1966.

"Judgment Marked by a Cellar: The American Negro Writer and the Dialectic of Despair," *University of Denver Quarterly*, II, No. 2 (Summer, 1967), 5–35.

Craters of the Spirit: Studies in the Modern Novel. Washington: Corpus Books, 1968.

SECONDARY SOURCE

Contemporary Authors, Volumes 9–10 (1964).

JULIAN MAYFIELD

PRIMARY SOURCES

The Hit. New York: Vanguard Press, 1957.
The Long Night. New York: Vanguard Press, 1958.
The Grand Parade. New York: Vanguard Press, 1961.
"Challenge to Negro Leadership," *Commentary*, XXXI (April, 1961), 297–305.

SECONDARY SOURCES

"Black Writers' Views."
Contemporary Authors, Volumes 13–14 (1965).

INDEX

This index deals solely with the introductory material contributed by the editors of this book.